ADVANCE PRAISE FOR **Dreaming Kurdistan**

"Carol Prunhuber has written a fast-paced, stirring account of Iran's treacherous assassination, in July 1989, of the charismatic Iranian Kurdish leader Abdul Rahman Ghassemlou in Vienna while he was trying to negotiate peace. Her investigative journalism reveals all we know of this tragic event and is highly recommended reading."

MICHAEL GUNTER, Professor of Political Science,
Tennessee Technological University

"Carol Prunhuber's invaluable firsthand evaluation of Abdul Rahman Ghassemlou makes clear why he was the preeminent Kurdish leader of his era. Carol Prunhuber, who knew Ghassemlou in Kurdistan and in Paris, faithfully honored his request that she write his biography, which today illustrates his prescience about the Kurds' fate—and why the ayatollahs assassinated him in 1989."

JONATHAN RANDAL, former *Washington Post* correspondent and
author of *After Such Knowledge What Forgiveness? My Encounters with Kurdistan*

"Carol Prunhuber, with links to the Kurdish world since the early 1980s, knew Dr. Ghassemlou and spent time in the mountains with his guerrillas. Her biography is an impassioned, meticulously documented investigation that vividly evokes the enthralling life and final days of this incomparable Kurdish leader. This book, which reads like a novel, is indispensable for all those who are concerned about Iran or intrigued by the Kurds."

KENDAL NEZAN, President, Kurdish Institute of Paris

Dreaming Kurdistan

This book is part of the Peter Lang Regional Studies list.
Every volume is peer reviewed and meets
the highest quality standards for content and production.

PETER LANG
New York • Bern • Berlin
Brussels • Vienna • Oxford • Warsaw

Carol Prunhuber

Dreaming Kurdistan

The Life and Death of Kurdish Leader Abdul Rahman Ghassemlou

PETER LANG

New York • Bern • Berlin
Brussels • Vienna • Oxford • Warsaw

Library of Congress Cataloging-in-Publication Data

Names: Prunhuber, Carol, author.
Title: Dreaming Kurdistan: The Life and Death of Kurdish Leader
Abdul Rahman Ghassemlou / Carol Prunhuber.
Description: New York, NY: Peter Lang, 2019.
Includes bibliographical references and index.
Identifiers: LCCN 2019006814 | ISBN 978-1-4331-6784-3 (paperback: alk. paper)
ISBN 978-1-4331-6893-2 (ebook pdf) | ISBN 978-1-4331-6894-9 (epub)
ISBN 978-1-4331-6895-6 (mobi)
Subjects: LCSH: Ghassemlou, Abdul Rahman.
Hizb-i Dimukrati-i Kurdistan-i Iran.
Kurds—Iran—Biography.
Politicians—Iran—Biography.
Kurds—Iran—Politics and government—20th century.
Iran—Politics and government—20th century.
Classification: LCC DS316.9.G49 P78 2019 | DDC 324.255/083092 [B]—dc23
LC record available at https://lccn.loc.gov/2019006814
DOI 10.3726/b15588

Bibliographic information published by **Die Deutsche Nationalbibliothek**.
Die Deutsche Nationalbibliothek lists this publication in the "Deutsche
Nationalbibliografie"; detailed bibliographic data are available
on the Internet at http://dnb.d-nb.de/.

Kurdistan; map courtesy Kurdish Institute of Paris

CONTENTS

Photographs are to be found between Part III and Part IV.

PROLOGUE

It was in Paris, in 1983, that I first met Abdul Rahman Ghassemlou. We were introduced at the Kurdish Institute, where I was attending an art exhibition with Kurdish filmmaker Yilmaz Güney and his wife, Fatosh, from Turkey.

I had met Güney at the Cannes Film Festival in 1982. That year he had won the Palme d'Or, the Golden Palm award, and the publicity that followed brought worldwide attention to the plight of the Kurdish nation. As a Venezuelan journalist, my limited impression of the Kurds was that they were fierce warriors who lived in unknown and distant mountains somewhere in the Middle East. Yilmaz Güney taught me about the free-spirited Kurdish people, opening my eyes to the oppression they had endured for centuries. Their situation touched me deeply and I began to write articles on the Kurds for Venezuelan newspapers and magazines.

One year later in Paris, I found myself standing face-to-face with this sophisticated, charming, and charismatic Middle Eastern leader of millions of Kurds in Iran. Ghassemlou spoke nine languages with ease. He began reciting Sufi poets like Hafiz and Rumi in Farsi and then seamlessly rendered them in French. I was struck by his knowledge of Western art and culture. To the assembled group, he described his life in the mountains alongside his people. That evening Ghassemlou was the center of attention with his powerful presence, broad smile, and refined sense of humor.

After our meeting in Paris, Ghassemlou invited me to come to Kurdistan. Two years later, I arrived there alongside the French Gamma TV crew to film the Kurdish conflict in Iran. The seed for this book was planted at that time.

Once I saw the Kurdish people up close and the promise that Ghassemlou presented to this war-torn land, the Kurds began to occupy an endearing place in my being. When I showed him a eulogy I had written for Güney after his death, Ghassemlou turned to me and said: "When I die, I would like you to write a book, telling the story of my life and the Kurdish cause."

❧

Thanks to the towering mountains they call home, the Kurdish people have survived persecution for centuries. This stateless nation, with its people numbering approximately thirty million[1] or more, is a territory that spans nearly five hundred thousand square kilometers. Their homeland stretches across five countries: Turkey, Iran, Iraq, Syria, and Armenia.

A view long held in Kurdish culture is that their lineage descends from the guardians of the sacred fire that burned in Zoroaster's temple. The Kurds trace their origins to ancient Mesopotamia, a conviction that finds support from Sumerian textual evidence.[2] They are not Arabic, but belong to the Indo-European family. They are not of Semitic origin, nor related to the Turks who came from Central Asia. Their language belongs to the Iranian branch of Indo-European and is, for some specialists, a derivation of Avestan, the ancient language through which Zoroaster transmitted his teachings.

The legend that the Kurdish epic, the *Sheref Nameh* ("Splendors of the Kurdish Nation"),[3] recounts was written in Farsi toward the end of the sixteenth century. It describes the origin of these fearless, freedom-loving mountain people.

The tyrant Zohak, fifth king of a mythological Iranian dynasty, terrorized the populace under his rule. In turn, he suffered a dreadful affliction: two serpents sprang from his shoulders and were fed daily with the brains of two children. To avoid extermination, the subjugated citizens decided to dupe the tyrant by mixing the brain of a boy with the brain of a lamb and offering half of this mixture to each serpent. In this way, every day one young person survived and escaped to the mountains, where they perpetuated the Kurdish people. This myth in some way set the tone for the survival of the Kurds for hundreds of years to come.

Moving from mythic to historical times: in the seventh century C.E. Arab armies, energized by Muhammad's unifying message, exploded out of Arabia into the sprawling empires and hinterlands of the Middle East. In a resistance that was more sociocultural than religious, Kurdish tribes managed to hold off the Arabs for nearly one hundred years before yielding to the inevitable.[4] "All methods were used to coax the Kurds and convert them to Islam," reports Kendal Nezan, president of the Kurdish Institute of Paris—"even, for example, the matrimonial strategy: the mother of the last Omayyad caliph, Marwan Hakim, was Kurdish."[5]

After their century of fierce opposition, the Kurds accepted Islam without thereby being "Arabized";[6] the majority converted to Sunni Islam. But there would be no peace for the Kurds. The medieval and modern eras would see a series of incursions that would subject their lands to centuries of life under foreign rule: Seljuk Turks, Mongols, Persian Safavids, and the Ottoman Empire.[7]

Half a millennium later, in 1187 c.e., the Kurds stepped into the spotlight of history when Saladin—a Kurdish warrior, and the great hero of the Crusades—wrested Jerusalem from the Franks, ending nearly ninety years of Western control.[8] Saladin emerged from his successful challenge to the Western champion, Richard the Lionheart, to assume leadership of the Muslim world. The lineage he founded, the Ayyubid dynasty (1169–1250), would carry his authority forward for nearly a century, embracing not only Kurdistan but Syria, Egypt, and even Yemen.

By the end of the thirteenth century, however, the Kurdish homelands were invaded once more, this time by Mongols and Turks intent upon control of the treasured commercial routes—especially those for silks and spices. In the sixteenth century, the Kurdish lands became a tempting target in the game of empires between Persians and Ottomans. Persia's Safavid shah, having imposed Shi'a Islam in his domain, moved vigorously outward. But the Ottomans, alarmed at the Persian expansion, pushed back; to secure their Iranian border and leave themselves free to pursue their own military ambitions against the Arabs, they invited Kurdish feudal lords to an alliance. This alliance would be not only military, but also religious: Sunni Kurds and Ottomans, allied against Shi'ite Safavids.

Caught between the two superpowers of the day, the Kurds, with their patchwork of fiefdoms, chiefdoms, and small kingdoms, had no chance of survival as a free people. The choice they faced was stark, but clear: the clear and present danger of Persian annexation, or accepting Ottoman suzerainty with its promise of an essentially autonomous self-rule.[9]

"This particular status," observes Kendal Nezan, "was to assure Kurdistan about three centuries of peace," and would function "without any major hitch" until the outset of the eighteenth century. Those centuries of peace witnessed a flowering of Kurdish creativity in literature, music, and culture; it was this golden era that saw the composition of the epic *Sheref Nameh* in 1596.[10]

When, moving forward into the modern era, both the Ottomans and the Persians began to consolidate as states, this political shift provoked a chain reaction in the Kurds; they saw that their own sovereignty was threatened.[11] In 1638 the shah of Persia and the Ottoman sultan signed an agreement that legalized the first division of Kurdistan between their empires. Since that day,

Kurdistan has been an object of plunder. The Kurds today have become the most populated nation in the world without an indigenous state.

The Kurdish question is similar to that confronting modern-day Palestinians and Armenians; for each of these peoples, the challenges today took shape with the fall of the Ottoman Empire when, at the end of World War I, the victors divided the Middle East among themselves. The Treaty of Sèvres, in 1920, promised the Kurds an autonomous regime, but the Treaty of Lausanne, in 1923, deprived them of it.

Since then the Kurds have remained the targeted interest both of regional ruling regimes and of world powers. The reason for this is simple: beneath the arid soil of their mountains lies an ocean of oil. Because of this twenty-first-century goldmine, no one has been ready or willing to concede nationhood to the Kurds, nor the usufruct of their resources. In Kurdistan too are enormous reserves of water that, in the near future, will surely prove to be of greater value even than oil for the region and the world.

Over the centuries, multiple forces, circumstances, and competing interests have dragged the Kurds into internal strife. Even today they continue to be divided. They have been in conflict among themselves in an endless round of internecine feud. This seemingly permanent state of division, combined with their tribal traditions and fierce independence, has brought particularly ruthless repression from the governments of countries where they live.

Consider the experience of the Kurds in Turkey. At the beginning of the twentieth century, Turkish nationalist leaders deported 700,000 Kurds from their home region. Again in Turkey between 1925 and 1939, the Kurds were once more forced to leave their land. This systematic dispersion of the Kurdish population was interrupted by World War I. Since then, Ankara has denied the Kurds' cultural identity, considering them to be "Mountain Turks." For forty-nine years of the existence of the Turkish Republic, the Kurds have been under a state of emergency. It was only in 2003 that martial law was lifted in Turkish Kurdistan.[12] In 2008, the Turkish parliament at last authorized national radio and television channels to broadcast programs in Kurdish, twenty-four hours a day; however, the content is limited to news, music, and offerings about traditional culture. In 2012, schools were allowed to teach Kurdish language as an optional course. Kurds in Turkey are free to speak their native tongue. Despite these openings, however, the Kurds are still not recognized as a minority in Turkey with full cultural expression, rights, or political autonomy. And even with this loosening of official strictures on Kurdish culture since 1991, the release of imprisoned Kurdish political activists, and other minimal cultural reforms, violence and discrimination against them has not completely ceased.

Since 2014 the Turkish government's alleged relations with the Islamic State (ISIS) and the blind eye it has turned toward the movement of ISIS jihadists back and forth across its border[13] have provoked mounting anger among its Kurdish population and put at risk a dialogue with the PKK, the Kurdistan Workers' Party, begun in 2013. A fragile ceasefire brokered between Turkey and the PKK was terminated in July 2015, and as of 2018 Turkey has been making incursions against Kurdish enclaves in Syria.

In Iraq as well, the Kurds have undergone tremendous tribulation. Saddam Hussein's regime destroyed more than two thousand villages and deported their inhabitants to the lowlands.[14] In 1988 Hussein rained down vengeance on the Kurdish rebellion by attacking the village of Halabja with toxic gas, causing the death of five thousand people. In the wake of the Gulf War of 1991, the Iraqi army marched on Kurdistan, provoking one of the largest population exoduses in contemporary history.

With the support of the Allied U.S.-British air force, in 1991 the United States created a safe haven as a no-fly zone that protected the Kurds in Iraq from attacks by the Iraqi regime. Soon after, United Nations Security Council resolution 688 condemned "the repression of the Iraqi civilian population . . . in Kurdish populated areas" and demanded an end to this policy.[15] In 1992, the Iraqi Kurds, by popular vote, created the Kurdistan Regional Government with an elected parliament. Yet the two main Kurdish parties—the Kurdistan Democratic Party (KDP) led by Masoud Barzani and the Patriotic Union of Kurdistan (PUK) headed by Jalal Talabani—battled each other in what amounted to a civil war from 1994 to 1998, when the United States facilitated a ceasefire. Since then the parties have shared governance of the Kurdistan Region. With peace, and a growing prosperity from oil-sale revenues granted by Iraq after 1995, the Kurdistan Region saw an unprecedented cultural and democratic flourishing with the growth of universities, an efficient political administration, and institutions that could assure a stable economy.

The twenty-first century has brought Kurds both further political presence in Iraq and increasing recognition on the international scene. The primary Kurdish parties supported the coalition led by the United States against Saddam Hussein and the Iraq invasion of 2003. In 2005 a new constitution was adopted in Iraq; elections were held, and Jalal Talabani became president, while Masoud Barzani was elected president of the Kurdistan Regional Government (KRG).

The Kurdistan Regional Government, despite tension due to political and economic disagreements with the central government in Baghdad, developed in relative tranquility compared with the rest of present-day Iraq until the summer of 2014, when ISIS, the Islamic State, took over Mosul and other key cities. Thousands fled as the forces of ISIS killed, raped, and tortured innocent civilians, and continued their advance toward Baghdad and other territories in western Iraq. Kurdish *peshmerga* (literally those "who walk in front of death," voluntary military forces) took control of the oil-producing city of Kirkuk, which Iraqi Kurds considered their capital.

The KRG dispatched peshmerga to northern Syria and Iraq to fight against ISIS, with limited support from U.S.-led coalition airstrikes. The Islamic Republic of Iran also provided weapons and training to the Kurdish forces as well as funding, training, and military advisors to the Iraqi military offensive against ISIS.

The Kurdish peshmerga have been known for their bravery and ferocity in battle. After an initial setback in the battle with ISIS in Iraq, Kurdish peshmerga forced ISIS to retreat from strategic areas and managed to recover lost ground even without the heavy weaponry and ongoing supply of ammunition they requested from the West. In both Iraq and Syria Kurdish peshmerga, with their fighting spirit, became the frontline defense against ISIS advance. Women, too, served in the peshmerga and played a major role in combat, particularly in Syria. The advance of ISIS thrust Iraqi Kurdistan into the limelight of history and the international community, earning their bravery international recognition, especially during the defense of Kobane, a Kurdish town in Syria bordering Turkey.[16]

Since 2014, in Syria, Kurdish homegrown defense forces, the People's Protection Units (YPG), have held back ISIS incursions from the Rojava region and maintained control of the majority of cities inhabited by the Kurds. Turkey, which regards the YPG as part of the PKK, has been set on destroying the possibility of Kurds' having an autonomous region in Syria. In 2018, with the Kurds embroiled in the fierce battle with Isis, Turkish forces allied with Syrian rebels—Sunni Arabs—overran the Syrian border to occupy the Afrin Kurdish Canton, forcing the displacement of hundreds of thousands. Though supported by the U.S. for their fight against ISIS, at this writing Kurds in Rojava, east of the Euphrates, are potential targets of a full-fledged attack by Turkish forces.[17]

☙

In Iran, throughout the twentieth century and into the twenty-first, the position of the Kurds has been particularly precarious. For a single shining moment in 1946, during the sociopolitical reshuffling in the postwar Middle East, Iranian Kurdistan carved out a national self-identity and political self-rule as an autonomous state, a democratic republic centered on the city of Mahabad. The achievement, however, was brief; without effective international alliances, the fledgling republic collapsed in the face of Iranian force. The tragic experience of the Democratic Republic of Kurdistan became emblematic, through most of the rest of the twentieth century, for the continuing fate of Kurdish nationalists. The preeminent Iraqi Kurdish war hero General Mustafa Barzani once characterized the Kurds as "the orphans of the universe."

This is an appropriate description for a people who have neither a national state nor, until relatively recently, a politically powerful organization in their diaspora. Unlike displaced Armenians or Jews, the Kurds have lacked a lobby abroad. Yet they remain loyal to their cause and their origins. The Kurds *are* Kurds, and they live in Kurdistan. As Ghassemlou had said, more than once, their only friends are the mountains.

In the case of the Kurds of Iran, they live in the only country in the Middle East besides Egypt that constitutes a true state. At the time when Europe was a patchwork of tribes in conflict with and at times in subjugation to the encroachments of the Roman Empire, Persia was already Persia. Iran and Egypt are the only states, from Morocco to India, that do not owe their borders to the postcolonial division of territory: their roots go back to antiquity. Composed today of a Shi'ite majority and many national minorities—Arabs, Turkmen, Baluchis, Kurds, Assyrians, and Azeris—and religions that include Sunni Muslims, Zoroastrians, Christians, Baha'is, and Jews, Iran has long existed as a geopolitical entity.

Iranian history essentially consists of innumerable compromises between the Persians and the Azeri Turks. It is around this balance that the central power is constructed and, aside from a few exceptions, has always governed by coercion. The Persian obsession is to keep the minorities pulled together into the centralized state. When the central power in Iran is weakened, a centrifugal force makes itself felt and the minorities feel tempted to flee from the center.

Ghassemlou reflected much on this unending problem. He recognized that there existed a Kurdish irredentism in the countries where they live; even in the face of long-standing intentions to drown their cultural identity, their language and lifeways are very much alive. And yet despite their centuries of resistance, it is only in the twentieth century that the Kurds as a people have begun to develop a national consciousness. Today it is natural to have a Kurdish demand for independence, for the realization of a national Kurdish project.

An independent Kurdistan, reflected Ghassemlou, would be a state without access to the sea. Yet at the same time, it would be a state rich in oil and, even more importantly, in possession of immense sources of water.

Water is the most critical environmental concern in the Middle East. The future wars in that region will be for water. Without oil, its people are poor; without water, they cannot survive. And the great reserves of water are in Kurdistan.[18]

Ghassemlou was the first Kurdish leader to elaborate a theory that rests upon a recognition of the geopolitical components that conspire against the creation of a Kurdish state, and that is why he accepted as realistic this more feasible plan: to renounce the immediate drive for independent statehood and choose the path of regional autonomy.

His breadth of vision was recognized beyond his borders. In the eyes, and the words, of Dr. Bernard Kouchner, former French minister of foreign affairs: "He was the only Kurd with an international perspective."[19]

☙

In the last half century, the Kurdish world has seen two great political leaders: Mustafa Barzani in Iraq during the sixties and seventies, and in Iran, Abdul Rahman Ghassemlou in the eighties.

Barzani ended his life in exile in the United States. Ghassemlou, after a decade of resistance to the theocratic regime of Ayatollah[20] Khomeini, was brutally murdered by envoys of the Islamic Republic of Iran[21] in July 1989, in Vienna—where he had traveled to engage in peace negotiations with that very regime. His wise humanitarian leadership had promised a luminous future for the country; his death was devastating for the prospect of lasting autonomy in Iranian Kurdistan.

Dreaming Kurdistan: The Life and Death of Kurdish Leader Abdul Rahman Ghassemlou is the book Ghassemlou asked me to write—a journalistic testimony that has ended by depicting the real events surrounding his murder, reconstructed through political documents and speeches, police reports, taped material, testimonies, letters, and interviews. The current revised and much-expanded edition brings in further evidence that has come to light, together with additional statements and perspectives from those who have known Ghassemlou and witnessed the history through which he moved. These materials, taken together, offer a broadened testimony to the events that formed both the life and death of Abdul Rahman Ghassemlou. The interviews included in this expanded edition incorporate conversations with more than sixty individuals who played—and continue to play—important roles in Iran and Iraq today.

His own untimely and brutal assassination, of course, was not the theme of the book Ghassemlou had envisioned. But in the retelling, fate was to weave a more intricate web. I had started out intending to bring to life the story of a relatively unknown international leader; instead I found myself investigating and writing his death.

Thirty years have passed since Ghassemlou's assassination, and the reality of the Kurds has shifted dramatically. Though the Kurds in Iraq have attained an autonomous government and maintain ongoing relations with the Iranian regime, the Kurds in Iran still suffer persecution and discrimination. While several international human-rights organizations persevere in bringing to light the plight of the Iranian Kurds, the international press has focused upon the unfolding developments in Iraqi Kurdistan, and now in Syria. Ghassemlou's story reminds us that the basic human cause he championed was that of the Kurds of Iran.

Because of their international implications, Iran's political maneuvering and concerns about its nuclear program occupy center stage today. Yet, hidden in the wings, the day-to-day struggle of the Kurdish nation persists. It is my wish that this book will serve to rekindle the resolute voice of Abdul Rahman Ghassemlou—who spoke for millions of Kurdish people in their determination to reclaim their right to freedom and dignity within the Islamic Republic of Iran.

His demise was the price paid by Ghassemlou in his fight for recognition of the identity of the Kurdish people, and for their inherent rights as a nation. Through his life and death, we better understand the volatile politics of this vital region of the Middle East, and the historical currents that have influenced it to this day.

One thing is very certain: throughout his life, Abdul Rahman Ghassem-lou never limited himself to being simply an Iranian party chief. He lived as a farsighted leader and, above all, as a Kurd who held a dream for his homeland and an overarching love for his people. In the end, he gave up his life while reaching for that dream. His unwavering spirit and light live on in the hearts and rugged mountains of a nation called Kurdistan.

Notes

1. There is no official census on the Kurdish population; Kurds themselves maintain the number around 40 million.
2. Research indicates cultural links dating back to the Medes as well as Zoroastrians. See Maria T. O'Shea, *Trapped Between the Map and Reality: Geography and Perceptions of Kurdistan* (New York and London: Routledge, 2004), 23.
3. Kendal Nezan, "A Brief Survey of the History of the Kurds," Kurdish Institute of Paris, http://www.institutkurde.org/en/institute/who_are_the_kurds.php (accessed January 18, 2015).
4. Ibid.
5. Ibid.
6. Ibid.
7. See Kurdish History Timeline, http://www.infoplease.com/spot/kurds3.html#7#ixzz3PEFv-JvJJ (accessed January 30, 2015).
8. Saladin, Ṣalāḥ al-Dīn Yūsuf ibn Ayyūb ("Righteousness of the Faith, Joseph, Son of Job"), 1137–1193, ruling from Damascus as the Muslim sultan of Egypt, Syria, Yemen, and Palestine, has always been regarded in the West as the most famous of Muslim heroes. "Saladin," *Encyclopædia Britannica*, updated November 11, 2014; http://www.britannica.com/EBchecked/topic/518809/Saladin (accessed January 30, 2015).
9. Nezan, "A Brief Survey."
10. Ibid.
11. Among the Kurds were some who were able to see these developments not merely as threat but as inspiration. "In 1675," notes Kendal Nezan, "more than a century before the French Revolution, which spreads the idea of the nation and the state-nation in the West, the poet Khani, in his epic in verse 'Mem-o-Zin,' calls the Kurds to unite and create their own unified state. [But] he'll scarcely be listened to by either the aristocracy or the population." Not until the nineteenth century would any movement toward a unified Kurdistan emerge, when first stirrings would arise in response to Ottoman interference. Even into the twentieth century "Kurdish society approached the First World War divided, decapitated, without a collective plan for its future." The Anglo-French Sykes-Picot agreement of 1915 foreshadowed the partition of the Kurdish lands that would take place following World War I. Nezan, "A Brief Survey."

12. *Quelle Turquie pour quelle Europe?* Dossier published by the Comité international pour la libération des députés Kurdes emprisonnés en Turquie, with the collaboration of the Institut Kurde de Paris and the Fondation France-Libertés (Paris: December 1995).

13. Tim Arango and Eric Schmitt, "A Path to ISIS, Through a Porous Turkish Border," *New York Times*, March 9, 2015, http://www.nytimes.com/2015/03/10/world/europe/despite-crackdown-path-to-join-isis-often-winds-through-porous-turkish-border.html?_r=. The article goes on to cite Western officials' perception of "a degree of ambivalence among Turkish officials who do not see the Islamic State as a primary enemy." U.S. director of national intelligence James R. Clapper, Jr., speaking before Congress, stated bluntly his perception that "the Turks . . . are more concerned with opposing Kurdish autonomy within Syria than in fighting the Islamic State." Ibid.

14. Population estimates from Human Rights Watch, http://www.hrw.org/reports/1993/iraqanfal/ANFALINT.htm, and Agence France Press, cited by Institute Kurde de Paris, http://www.institutkurde.org/info/depeches/anfal-un-genocide-de-saddam-hussein-contre-les-kurdes-861.html.

15. See Michael Gunter, "The Kurdish Question in Perspective," *World Affairs*, Vol. 166, No. 4, Spring 2004, 202.

16. This development has been noted in news coverage. See Zana Gulmohamad, "Report: Iraqi Kurdistan's rise on the international scene amid the expansion of the Islamic State," Your Middle East, November 30, 2014, http://www.yourmiddleeast.com/culture/report-iraqi-kurdistans-rise-on-the-international-scene-amid-the-expansion-of-the-islamic-state_28218 (accessed March 20, 2015). See also Nick Robins-Early, "The Role of the Kurds in the Fight against ISIS," The World Post (a partnership of Huffington Post and the Berggruen Institute), October 11, 2014, http://www.huffingtonpost.com/2014/10/11/kurds-iraq-syria_n_5960428.html?; Mariam Karouny, "Islamic State under pressure as Kurds seize Syrian town," Reuters, UK Edition, February 27, 2015, http://uk.reuters.com/article/2015/02/27/uk-mideast-crisis-syria-kurds-idUKKBN0LV1NM20150227; Fazel Hawramy, "Kurdish peshmerga, IS reach stalemate," Al-Monitor, the Pulse of the Middle East, February 6, 2015, http://www.al-monitor.com/pulse/originals/2015/02/iraq-kurdistan-peshmerga-wait-islamic-state.html#; and Dexter Filkins, "The Fight of Their Lives," *The New Yorker*, September 29, 2014, http://www.newyorker.com/magazine/2014/09/29/fight-lives (accessed March 20, 2015).

17. "Turkey primed to start offensive against US-backed Kurds in Syria," *The Guardian*, December 12, 2018, https://www.theguardian.com/world/2018/dec/12/turkey-primed-to-start-offensive-against-us-backed-kurds-in-syria (accessed December 27, 2018). Reuters news service has carried an ongoing series of dispatches on the emerging situation for the Kurds in Syria; see Ellen Francis, "Let Down by U.S., Syrian Leaders Look to Russia and Assad," https://www.reuters.com/article/us-mideast-crisis-syria-kurds/let-down-by-u-s-syrian-kurdish-leaders-look-to-russia-and-assad-idUSKCN1OQ18E?fbclid=IwAR2pcxLYQa1FdoM6JV3ZL3ulYzcwf39Y-ASZE5UZX5roK5gBTjajvA-tA7Y (accessed December 27, 2018).

18. For the most part, the Kurdish regions have abundant water. Only some areas in Iraq and Syria—those that border the desert—lack water, not only for agriculture but even for basic personal needs. The headwaters of massive rivers arise in the mountains of Kurdistan: the

Aras, whose course of 920 kilometers flows into the Caspian Sea; the Tigris, 1,850 kilo-
meters, which joins the Euphrates, Western Asia's longest river, with 2,800 kilometers.
Additionally, a vast swath of Kurdistan is situated between two extensive lakes: Van and
Urmia, with surface areas of 3,765 and 6,000 square kilometers, respectively.

19. Dr. Bernard Kouchner, interview with the author, Paris, 1991.

20. *Ayatollah*: the highest position in the Shi'ite religious hierarchy. The title, which means
"sign of God," is gained "by general acknowledgment of a mullah's scholarship and piety
rather than by appointment or election." Robin Wright, *In the Name of God: The Khomeini
Decade* (New York: Simon and Schuster, 1989).

21. The Islamic Republic of Iran was established by Ayatollah Khomeini in 1979 after the
overthrow of the Shah of Iran.

PART I

THE CRIME

· 1 ·

MEETING IN VIENNA

Ề

Soothsayer: Beware the ides of March. . . .
Caesar: The ides of March are come.
Soothsayer: Aye, Caesar, but not gone.
—William Shakespeare, *Julius Caesar*

Vienna, Thursday, July 13, 1989. The day he was murdered, Abdul Rahman Ghassemlou woke up and was in a lively mood. As always, he shaved while listening to the radio. He showered and leisurely dressed himself.

It was summer and Vienna was flooded with light. Ghassemlou was staying with friends, Azad and Charlotte. He walked into the living room, where his friends were already up. He inquired about Abdullah, his assistant, who had been ill the day before with a stomachache and severe intestinal upset. Ghassemlou did not usually adopt a paternalistic attitude toward his assistant, but on that morning, he was worried about his young friend. Perhaps because of the age difference between them, Ghassemlou, then fifty-eight years old, felt a certain affection and tenderness for his thirty-seven-year-old comrade. Their friendship and political activities bonded them. Abdullah Ghaderi-Azar represented the Democratic Party of Iranian Kurdistan (PDKI)[1] in Europe— and Ghassemlou was its secretary-general.

Charlotte had already prepared breakfast by the time the guests got up. The dark-haired, blue-eyed Viennese woman and her husband, Azad, worshiped their soft-mannered and gracious guest, who would appear as often and as suddenly as he would disappear from their lives. One day Ghassemlou would be in Kurdistan, and three days later he might call from Paris or Stockholm. When he was in Vienna, they never knew what political or diplomatic activities he was there to carry out.

He had spent several weeks with them in December and January. But neither Charlotte nor any of the other members of the small Kurdish community in Vienna knew that he was then in the midst of secret negotiations with envoys of the Islamic Republic regime. While Ghassemlou had told a few intimate friends, it was important to keep that information from the party at large because, as Ghassemlou often said, with a twinkle in his eye, the Kurds could never keep a secret. Among the Kurds themselves there was a saying, "If a word is leaked from even one mouth it is leaked to a city." The survival of an underground organization requires a clandestine structure and ways of doing things. Given the intense security surrounding the meetings, the situation required that Ghassemlou keep information to a very trusted few.

Azad and Charlotte had shared their house with Ghassemlou during those frigid winter weeks, but his presence was never a burden. Apart from the devotion they felt for him, Ghassemlou was fun and a real talker—and women used to perceive him as a *charmeur*. Within the party apparatus and while leading a war, on the other hand, he could be quite firm.

Staying with his friends, Ghassemlou would retire to his room at midnight, reading and listening to the radio before going to sleep. Every morning, he woke up sharp at eight. Ghassemlou was a tremendously vigorous and agile man. He was a tireless walker—not unusual for a guerrilla leader who had spent a good part of his life amid the precipitous mountains of Kurdistan.

Life there was not easy. At the beginning of his party's retreat to the mountains, those at the hidden headquarters lived in tents; concrete block housing would not be built until the mid-1980s. When the cold weather came and the snow fell, neither the waterproof tents nor the rugs that covered the earthen floors prevented the damp from leaking through. Ghassemlou would spend hours sitting on the floor in the Kurdish way; because of this, he had developed pain in his knees and sciatica that sometimes made movement difficult. Overall, however, he was a healthy man, as his recent medical exams in Paris had shown. His wife Hélène remembered that a doctor had told him once that his robust health was that of a man from the mountains.

❧

That July morning they all ate breakfast together. As always Ghassemlou drank tea and then a cup of coffee. He spoke with his friends and sat down to read an array of international newspapers.

Charlotte was cleaning the kitchen when Ghassemlou got up to show her an article in the *International Herald Tribune*. It analyzed the situation in Iran in the aftermath of Khomeini's recent death and stated clearly that the man who was taking over was the *hojatoleslam* Akbar Hashemi Rafsanjani.[2]

"The article," Charlotte later recalled, "said that Rafsanjani was going to open up to Europe and the Western countries and that Iran's government would be more stable and less fundamentalist. This piece confirmed Dr. Ghassemlou's privately held view about the future direction of Iran."[3]

Ghassemlou was happy and proposed they go out and have a special lunch. As Charlotte was on vacation and Azad was available for whatever Ghassemlou wanted, they accepted. But Abdullah was still feeling indisposed and ominous feelings of dread were troubling him. He agreed to come along, but he only wanted yoghurt.

They all climbed into the couple's car, a blue Renault 12, and drove toward the hills of Wienerwald, an area of forests and vineyards. Half an hour later, they arrived at a restaurant from which you could see the entire city of Vienna. It was noon—a bit early if you consider that the Viennese usually have lunch at 12:30.

Ghassemlou ordered aperitifs for everyone, but Charlotte did not want one. "Impossible!" he said. "Today you must drink with us."

They had some Camparis and ordered lunch. Ghassemlou ordered Tafelspitz, a typical Viennese dish with stewed beef, root vegetables, and roasted potatoes, along with a smooth mix of horseradish and white bread and salad.

"Since we are eating dark meat, we will have red wine," he said, asking Charlotte to choose. They bought a bottle of Zweigelt. "The wine is good. You have chosen well," he smiled.

Ghassemlou was animated. Everything seemed splendid, especially the majestic view of Vienna. Then he confided that the day before, Wednesday, he had met with an old friend—the former president of Algeria, Ahmed Ben Bella—and he was pleased about their meeting. "We will invite him to a dinner," Ghassemlou said to his friends, "and I'll think about a date."[4]

During coffee, Azad was contemplating a conversation he'd had two days before, on July 11, with Ghassemlou, Abdullah, and two other PDKI members, Fatah and Mostafa.[5] Ghassemlou had spoken about potential negotiations with the regime. Azad was not against the idea, he'd said, but he was not optimistic that they would succeed. He was convinced that the Iranians would never accept an autonomous Kurdistan. If the most conservative sector of the Shi'ite clerics had not tolerated the "dangerous liberal" Ayatollah Montazeri, who had been Khomeini's disciple and designated successor, how would they possibly accept Ghassemlou?[6]

As Azad was speaking, Ghassemlou sat pensively, smoking a cigarette.

"We have to take precautions. Perhaps they have plans," Ghassemlou
answered gravely.

❧

They left the restaurant at 1:30 p.m. Ghassemlou was in excellent spirits and
on the way back he stopped at a shop near the restaurant. Every time he traveled, he always made a point of bringing offerings to his hosts or those he was
visiting. "He was always very keen about bringing flowers, gifts, or good wine
when we visited friends of the party and Kurdish people in Paris and elsewhere
in Europe," remembered his assistant in Paris, Kawe Madani. "He also brought
small gifts back to Kurdistan from Europe. Usually, I bought flowers and wines
when we visited someone and he used to joke and say 'You are always buying
expensive bouquets and wines, you are going to ruin us!'"[7]

That day he purchased a scarf. Was it for the wife of Ted Kennedy, or
Senator Pell's wife—both of whom he was scheduled to meet the next week
in Washington?[8] Or was it for Hélène, his ex-wife, from whom he had been
divorced for some years earlier and with whom he continued to maintain a
close friendship?[9] When he'd visited Hélène in Paris before coming to Vienna,
he had asked her to accompany him to the United States.

Ghassemlou was extremely enthusiastic about his upcoming U.S. trip.
Throughout his life, he had been denied entry to America. The State Department had put him on a blacklist that included those regarded as Communists
and Third World revolutionaries. It was ironic that he was still on that list;
Ghassemlou had long been one of the few men who represented moderation
in an explosive Middle East.

The truth was that politically, he was closer to the Social Democrats than
to the Communists. American authorities had created many obstacles to his
making this trip. But now, finally, a group of Democrats in the U.S. Senate
had been able to procure him an entry visa to visit the country.

In a PDKI central committee plenum session, Ghassemlou once shared an
anecdote about meeting April Glaspie, the American ambassador at the U.S.
embassy in Baghdad. After shaking her hand and exchanging some niceties,
he told her that he'd been battling American domination throughout his life.
But had he known that the United States had such a beautiful ambassador,
he commented humorously, he'd never have resisted American imperialism.[10]

The ambassador clearly took this with humor, as it was intended. April
Glaspie would recall with warmth the circumstances of her meeting with
Ghassemlou in 1988, when she arrived in Iraq as the first American woman

ambassador to the Middle East. "I met Dr. Qassemlou in Baghdad at a time when the Kurds were, as so often, under serious attack. . . . He came to my home, calmly threading his way through Saddam's obtrusive watchers, and we talked," she wrote journalist Jonathan Randal.[11]

"Like so many before me," she continued, "I discovered a consummate diplomat, not merely a clever political tactician, but a man with an extraordinary ability to carry on his life's work despite the inevitable and never-ending challenges he faced, not the least of which were created by some who had recently announced themselves his allies."

What struck her above all else, she told Randal, was the trust Ghassemlou inspired. "Trust, based on undoubted honesty, is the sine qua non without which no diplomat can ever succeed," she wrote. "Who could recall this fine gentleman without a smile. Somehow he was able to push aside however briefly the vast difficulties he was facing every day. Burdened as he was with the well-being—the fate—of his besieged people, he was always a delightful companion, and the best-dressed revolutionary I ever met." Ghassemlou had immense charm, she said; even the way he smoked was memorable: "Ah, those Davidoff cigarettes."[12] ("Very expensive Davidoff cigarettes," she added.)[13]

The United States finally issued Ghassemlou a visa in 1988. About the lifting of his blacklist, which had been in force since his years living and teaching in Communist Czechoslovakia, Randal asked himself, "Did April Glaspie intervene with the State Department to bring about this change of heart? Or was it part of a general loosening of a rigid ban on anyone, even a Third World exile who had taken refuge behind the now visibly crumbling Iron Curtain?"[14]

Anticipation of his upcoming American trip contributed to Ghassemlou's present high spirits. Even though Kurdistan was in a delicate situation with the ceasefire between Iraq and Iran that summer, Ghassemlou continued envisioning new possibilities for his country.

America opening its doors to Ghassemlou was one new, promising sign. And now Hojatoleslam Hashemi Rafsanjani, at the cusp of his political power in Iran, had also invited him to negotiate with his emissaries over the issue of autonomy for Kurdistan and the legalization of his party. This was the reason he had secretly come to Vienna.

Ghassemlou's former wife, Hélène Krulich, however—tall, slender, with a stately bearing, penetrating gaze, and a quick, sharp intellect—did not agree with him about the upcoming trip to Vienna. Born in Czechoslovakia, she had shared her life with him, and continued to do so even after he left for the mountains to head his partisan forces, the peshmerga, against the Islamic clerics in Iran. The evening before he left for Vienna, they had argued in her small Parisian apartment. She did not believe in the good intentions of the Iranians—nor that the clerics were interested in granting the Kurds autonomy.

Ghassemlou was convinced that the death of Khomeini had weakened the regime's rigidity. In his view Khomeini's death had created an opening within the regime for pragmatic resolution of the dire situation in Iran following the war with Iraq: "Among his [Khomeini's] successors," Ghassemlou had said in an interview prior to his trip to Vienna, "there will certainly be realists who wish to find a solution to the problems that the country is facing, including [the problem of] Kurdistan."[15] Chief among these successors, and a self-proclaimed pragmatist, was Rafsanjani.[16] Ghassemlou's conviction was strengthened by the article he would show Charlotte on Thursday, July 13.

The day before he left for Vienna Ghassemlou spent with Hélène working on his English skills and a translation of the speech he would give in the U.S. in August. When they had finished their work Ghassemlou told her he was going to Vienna to meet with envoys from the regime. This was the moment, Ghassemlou believed, to sit down and negotiate with the Iranians.

"I knew about his failed winter negotiations and I was upset [with his decision]," Hélène would later explain. "He said the *mullahs* wanted to end the war in Kurdistan, and that to do so they needed him. Therefore, they would not harm the only person who could help them carry out their plan.

"I still couldn't believe he was serious. I reminded him how Simko [the iconic Kurdish leader of the early twentieth century] had lost his head when he went to negotiate with the Shah's envoys. I told him it was exactly the time the mullahs needed to get rid of him."[17]

She confronted Ghassemlou. "Listen," she told him. "Should you disappear, what will happen to your party? So far, you have no successor."[18]

For the time being," Ghassemlou replied, "there is Sadeq Sharafkandi and in three or four years there will be others."[19]

"He accused me of dramatizing," Hélène would write, "of exaggerating and of being over-sensitive."[20]

In the heat of their discussion Ghassemlou insisted, "Khomeini has died! Rafsanjani needs me!"

"The only thing Rafsanjani needs is *your head!*" she retorted.[21]

❧

On the following day, July 11, a Tuesday, he left for Vienna. When he said good-bye to Hélène, neither of them seriously imagined that this would be their final adieu.

Two days later, on Thursday afternoon, while negotiating with Iranian envoys, Abdul Rahman Ghassemlou would be shot with three bullets and killed in a tranquil Viennese apartment.

Also murdered would be Abdullah Ghaderi-Azar, whose gut feelings would warn him of the danger the day before. There would also be a third man, Fadil Rasul, an exiled Kurd from Iraq, who had been the intermediary between the Kurds and the Iranians.

Rasul, it would be stated later by one of his brothers, had received a personal letter from Rafsanjani encouraging him to contact Ghassemlou and invite him to begin negotiations with the Iranian regime. Rasul, young and naïve, unknowingly would lead to his death the most influential Kurdish leader of his time, the preeminent political head of the Iranian opposition. For his part in this, however innocent, he too would pay with his own life.

The murder would take place in the vacant apartment of Renata Faistauer at 5 Linke Bahngasse. The apartment would be unoccupied; Renata spent the better part of her year in Cairo. And Renata, as everyone in the Kurdish community knew, was Rasul's lover.

Notes

1. The original name of the party was the Democratic Party of Kurdistan, KDP. The word *Iran* was added in parentheses in 1973, during the party's Third Congress, and then it became the Democratic Party of Kurdistan (Iran). During the Fourth Congress, in early 1980, the parenthesis was lifted and the official name became the Democratic Party of Iranian Kurdistan, KDPI, also known by the French acronym PDKI. For clarity, except where specifically noting the party's transition from one self-reference to the next, we will use the French acronym PDKI throughout, since it has been more widely recognized and for the last ten years has been used by the party itself as its own designation. This also distinguishes it clearly from the Kurdistan Democratic Party (KDP) in Iraqi Kurdistan, which was established one year after the PDKI.

2. In the Islamic Republic of Iran it is understood that the Supreme Leader is a Grand Ayatollah, *ayatollah al-uzma* ("Great Sign of God," also written as *ayatollah uzma*). Next in eminence is the *ayatollah* (literally, "Sign of God"), and below that the *hojatoleslam*, the "proof of Islam" (or authority on Islam). Akbar Hashemi Rafsanjani, president or speaker

of the Majlis (Iranian parliament) throughout the 1980s, became the president of Iran in 1989. On his way up the ladder of power, Rafsanjani would be the second cleric charged with responsibility for oversight of the *pasdaran*, the Revolutionary Guards, established by Khomeini's decree in May 1979. See Shaul Bakhash, *The Reign of the Ayatollahs: Iran and the Islamic Revolution* (New York: Basic Books, Inc., 1984), 63.

Like most members of the religious hierarchy, Rafsanjani wore a white turban; the exclusive privilege of wearing a black turban was reserved for Imam Khomeini and other clerics who claimed descent from the Prophet. For more on the hierarchy of clerical titles see *Encyclopædia Iranica*, http://www.iranicaonline.org/articles/ayatallah, http://www.iranicaonline.org/articles/hojjat-al-eslam; for more on the concept, doctrine, and attributes of the imam, see http://www.iranicaonline.org/articles/shiite-doctrine.

3. "Charlotte," interview with Gabriel Fernández, Vienna, 1990. Further descriptions of events in this chapter, except where otherwise specified, are from this interview. ("Charlotte" is a pseudonym; to protect the identity of members of the Kurdish community in Vienna closely associated with Ghassemlou, pseudonyms are used throughout.)

The Kurds called Ghassemlou "Doctor" out of respect and to emphasize that he had actually completed a doctorate from the University of Economics in Prague. Abdullah, as well as Talabani and many others, referred to him as "Dr. Ghassemlou." Hélène and some friends simply called him "Rahman." Other close friends called him "ARG," from his initials.

4. "Azad," personal communication to the author, June 21, 2016. For purposes of privacy and security, "Azad," like "Charlotte," is a pseudonym.

5. "Fatah" and "Mostafa" are also pseudonyms used for security purposes.

6. In the 1950s, Hussein Ali Montazeri was one of Khomeini's disciples in Qom and one of the ideologues of the Islamic Republic. Montazeri closely followed Khomeini's career, declaration of war against the Shah, and exile. During the Shah's rule he headed a subversive network of clerics in the mosques, set up by Khomeini to rouse anti-Shah sentiment; for this, he was imprisoned by the Shah's regime in 1974. Once freed in 1978, he played a fundamental role in the popularization and impact of Imam Khomeini's preaching.

Designated Khomeini's successor in 1985, Montazeri fell out with Khomeini in 1988–1989 over human-rights abuses—including the execution of several thousand political prisoners—and government corruption. While firmly Islamist in supporting a theocratic model for governance, he saw the ideal role for the clergy as advisory, not as absolutist.

In 1989, reviewing the past ten years of the Islamist state, Montazeri concluded in a public statement that the people had not gained anything with the revolution. This earned him Khomeini's censure as a "dangerous liberal." Stripped of his status as successor to Khomeini, he was subsequently put under house arrest for criticizing the authority of the new Supreme Leader, Ali Hosseini Khamenei.

His house arrest ended in 2003, likely thanks to government fears of widespread public backlash should he die in custody. After his passing on December 19, 2009, his funeral turned into a protest against the Iranian regime. One year later, the regime had his tombstone removed. See "Iran releases dissident cleric," BBC *World Edition*, January 30, 2003, http://news.bbc.co.uk/2/hi/middle_east/2707513.stm; Baqer Moin, "Grand Ayatollah Hossein Ali Montazeri: Dissident Iranian cleric who became a hero to the reform movement challenging last June's election results," *The Guardian*, December 20, 2009, https://www.theguardian.com/theguardian/2009/dec/20/grand-ayatollah-hossein-ali-montazeri-obituary (accessed December 15, 2019). See also Gerhard Konzelman, *La espada de Ala: El avance de los chiitas* [The sword of Allah: The ascent of the Shi'ites] (Madrid: Editorial Planeta, 1990).

7. Kawe Madani, interview with the author, February 26, 2016. Madani, who worked closely with Ghassemlou in Paris, was responsible for the administration of the Paris office of the PDKI from 1981 until 1988.

8. Ghassemlou was scheduled to travel to the U.S.A. on July 19. He was planning on taking a short trip to Prague before returning to Paris to prepare for his trip to America.

9. Hélène Krulich, *Une Européenne au pays des Kurdes* (Paris: Éditions Karthala, 2011), 244. Throughout this chapter, statements from Hélène Krulich are taken from this written narrative or from a series of interviews she gave to the author and Gabriel Fernández in 1990–1991, and from personal communications to the author since that time.

10. Ebrahim Salehrad Lajani, PDKI central committee member and director of the Spi-Seng ("White Stone") region of Iranian Kurdistan in 1989, personal communication to the author, July 2010.

11. April Glaspie, e-mail to Jonathan Randal, quoted in Randal's presentation at "Hommage à Abdul Rahman Ghassemlou" on the twenty-fifth anniversary of his murder, French National Assembly, Paris, June 21, 2014.

12. Ibid.

13. April Glaspie, personal communication to the author, July 23, 2009.

14. Jonathan Randal, presentation at "Hommage à Abdul Rahman Ghassemlou," French National Assembly, June 21, 2014.

15. José Garçon and François Sergent, "Un Kurde victime d'un piège Iranien," *Libération*, July 18, 1989.

16. Rafsanjani, as a close ally of Khomeini, became Iran's fourth president after the Ayatollah's death. His main goals were the reconstruction of the country and social and economic reform. Considered a pragmatist, he brought some socioeconomic liberalization to the country. See "Hojjatoleslam Akbar Hashemi Rafsanjani," Global Security, http://www.globalsecurity.org/military/world/iran/rafsanjani.htm (accessed April 3, 2013). For more, also see Anoushivaran Ehteshami and Mahjoob Zweiri, *Iran and the Rise of Its Neoconservatives: The Politics of Tehran's Silent Revolution* (London: I. B. Tauris, 2007), 1–20.

17. Hélène Krulich, personal communication to the author, March 3, 2016.

18. Hélène Krulich-Ghassemlou, *Love Against All Reason: A European Woman Involved in the Kurdish Fight for Freedom in Iran* (Vienna: Lit Verlag, 2017), 237.

19. Ibid., 238.

20. Hélène Krulich, personal communication to the author, March 3, 2016.

21. Hélène Krulich, interviews with the author and Gabriel Fernández, 1990–1991.

· 2 ·

A FEARLESS MAN

⋄

So much time has passed,
so little remains—don't slacken now!
—Sufi saying

Tuesday, July 11. Ghassemlou and Abdullah arrived in Vienna on Tuesday; Azad, Fatah, and Mostafa were waiting for them at the airport. These three Kurds were old friends. Fatah was a former peshmerga. He represented the party in Austria. Mostafa was an expert in mineralogy and one of the most educated members of the party. Both had known Azad since they were children. All three were married to Austrian women.

Ghassemlou informed them that he would only stay in Vienna for a few days and that the following Wednesday, July 19, he would be traveling from Paris to the United States.

"We asked him what he was going to do in the United States. He replied that he was going to meet politicians, give interviews to the press, and perhaps meet some people from the government. He was extremely happy about this trip. He was even checking a newspaper in English to see what the weather was like in the United States and grumbling about the heat there—it was almost forty degrees centigrade," Charlotte recalled.[1]

Ghassemlou and Abdullah settled into Azad and Charlotte's apartment. Ghassemlou told his hosts that no one except the closest people should know he was in Vienna. After that, he called Rasul, and they arranged to meet in a café the following morning.

Wednesday, July 12. Azad parked his car and went into the café, where he found Ghassemlou, Abdullah, and Rasul. They seemed to be chatting about banal things. Rasul soon bid them farewell and left.

They had an uneventful lunch. Back at Azad's, Ghassemlou took a nap and at three in the afternoon Azad took them to Rasul's apartment on Wasagasse. Rasul was waiting for them, along with a special guest, Ahmed Ben Bella.

What followed was a cordial meeting between two notable politicians—Ahmed Ben Bella, the historical leader of the Algerian revolution against the French, and Abdul Rahman Ghassemlou, leader of the Kurdish resistance against the Islamic Republic of Iran.

These two men, while both revolutionaries, embodied divergent stances vis-à-vis the Iranian regime. The Kurdish leader, a democrat, was heading an armed resistance to the Islamists; Ben Bella, for his part, maintained relations with Tehran from his own exile in Switzerland, as did Rasul.

Here in the Austrian capital, each had a different agenda. Ben Bella had come to participate in a meeting with the editorial board of a global Islamic intellectual magazine. Ghassemlou was there to negotiate with the Iranians over Kurdish autonomy.

❧

These negotiations were something Ghassemlou sought for reasons both personally close to heart and political. Politically he believed that reaching some agreement with the regime in Tehran would end the bloodshed in Kurdistan. Agreement was all the more urgent because the recent end of the Iran-Iraq war would deprive the Kurds of their leverage with the regime in Baghdad. Moreover, serious consideration had to be given to the fact that both regimes were turning against the Kurds in their respective countries.

Additionally, Ghassemlou was facing internal problems within his party. According to his former party colleague Abdullah Hassanzadeh, a group that had left the party in March 1988 had issued a statement justifying themselves with "untrue things" and "accusations" against Ghassemlou "that were far from the truth and fairness."[2] The shock of this schism—five hundred party members left with the split—may have added fuel to Ghassemlou's urgency to negotiate.[3]

And at the same time, he was feeling the burden of his age, and the burden of the war he was waging. He shared some of this with Hélène. They spoke "about aging and wanting to retire from his post," she recalled. "His tasks were multiple, and he must have been tired, but his morale was never down. He loved to be happy and loved to be taken as such."[4] Ghassemlou was a master of maintaining optimism—not only his own inner state but, as well, a positive face, the demonstration of strength, to encourage his people and his peshmerga. But the struggle was going on and on; and both his experience and his political analysis, above all, may have intensified his apprehension that he was racing against time. In December 1988, I remember him visibly tired, even dispirited. "Age comes upon me," he had written to me earlier that year, "and I feel more vulnerable."[5]

In his letter, I could sense that he was feeling more and more solitary in the mountains—and was acutely aware of the passage of time. He was increasingly convinced that he had a limited time to complete his life's project. His words seemed to reflect a certain sorrow brought on by the transient nature of life. Somehow he knew he would not see his dream fulfilled. Was this another element in his urgency to sit down to serious negotiations with the Iranian government? One thing was certain: he badly needed a triumph after so many years of fighting and adversity.

In the view of his party colleague Abdullah Hassanzadeh, Ghassemlou had as a goal to do the best for all the Kurdish people. Iraq had become a haven for the exiled Kurdish resistance movements from Iran, Turkey, and Syria, since Saddam Hussein's government had uneasy relations with all three. But it was becoming clear that asylum in Iraq could hardly be relied upon, and that the party was facing a new phase of amplified challenge in their struggle for Kurdish autonomy. The strategy Ghassemlou proposed, accepted by the party during its central committee plenum in 1987, was to move party headquarters from Gawrade, deep inside Iraq, to a strategic location in the no-man's-land along the Iran-Iraq border, in the remote Qandil mountains, away from Baghdad's military control, as a secure base of operations from which to embark on a program of guerilla resistance.[6]

"A year before his murder, in 1988, when the war between Iran and Iraq ended, there had been an agreement between the Iraqi and Iranian governments to crush the Kurdish rebellions in both countries," Ghassemlou's colleague Hassanzadeh explained.[7]

"Dr. Ghassemlou was aware of this, and he wanted to reach a minimal agreement so the Iranian as well as the Iraqi Kurds could have security. . . . He was concerned that the same scenario as in 1975 would be repeated." He feared a replay of the Algiers Accord, which by resolving the differences between Iran and Iraq had stripped the Kurds of all foreign support.

According to Ghassemlou's long-time friend Iraqi Kurdish intellectual and academic Ezzedin Mustafa Rasul, "He was also tired and fed up with his relations with the Iraqi government."[8]

At the outset of the Iran-Iraq war, the Iraqi government permitted all groups in opposition to the Islamic Republic to settle along its border with Iran and the PDKI established its headquarters there. PDKI members entered and left Kurdistan via Baghdad. The relationship with Saddam Hussein's regime was not easy, however. The Iraqis continually pressured the party to participate in military operations and share intelligence with them. But the PDKI had forbidden its members this kind of cooperation under penalty of expulsion from the party. "No members, cadres, or even leadership members were allowed contact with Saddam's regime, except for those designated by Dr. Ghassemlou himself. He was very serious about this issue."[9]

PDKI's military head Hassan Ibrahimi, known as Hassan Shiwasali, confirmed Ghassemlou's feeling on the need for timely discussions with the Iranian government.[10] In a plenary session of the PDKI in March 1989, the central committee had approved Ghassemlou's suggestion of continued negotiations with the regime. The committee had stipulated, however, that only after all the details had been finalized with the regime by delegated PDKI negotiators should Ghassemlou join the talks, for a signing of the agreement with high-ranking Iranian officials.[11]

Shiwasali opposed entirely the proposal to negotiate at all. A few days later, at Shiwasali's home and in the presence of others, Ghassemlou said, "Despite the opposition of some"—he was clearly referring to Shiwasali—"I am off to Europe." Shiwasali, agitated, reiterated to Ghassemlou his stance and the reasons for his opposition. He could not trust in the negotiations because he couldn't trust the regime itself.

Ghassemlou found this position entirely understandable—Shiwasali had, after all, been the target of a failed assassination attempt on December 7, 1987. "Your opposition comes from a different perspective," Ghassemlou told him, "and mostly because you have bitter experiences with the Islamic Republic; 'He who is bitten by a snake fears a lizard.'"

Still, Ghassemlou went on to outline why he thought negotiations were necessary and why, this time, they would lead somewhere. "The Islamic Republic has lost the war and has experienced a burdensome situation. The mullahs are too smart not to recognize the likelihood of danger. That is why they are trying to find more influences [establish more contacts] in Iran, in Kurdistan as well as in the rest of the world. . . . The Kurdish armed struggle against the Islamic Republic is a big obstacle for the regime. They want to solve it. At present they are feeling vulnerable; they pretend they are in a position of power and are now willing to solve the Kurdish issue."

PDKI's network of alliances also needed a change of direction. "You also know that the only channel between our party and the outside world is Iraq," Ghassemlou went on. "However, from the very beginning we have built our relations in such a way that if they [Baghdad] help us without any conditions, then it is okay; otherwise, we will not accept the possibility of an opportunity or help based on any condition. In all my meetings and whenever given the opportunity I have reminded the Ba'ath authorities of this position. That is why they have offered us the minimum of help. But we are satisfied with our standing."

One major impetus forcing negotiations, Ghassemlou told Shiwasali, was Saddam Hussein's brutality against the Kurds in Iraq. In the face of the outbreak of Saddam's genocidal Operation Anfal,[12] PDKI's maintaining relations with the Iraqi regime was now undermining the party's credibility.[13]

Bernard Kouchner, a physician, a personal friend of Ghassemlou's, and the French secretary of state for humanitarian action, had met with Ghassemlou and Abdullah on Sunday, July 9, in Paris. Kouchner had invited them for dinner at his house, where along with journalist friends they had met K., a member of the DGSE, the French intelligence service, who specialized in the Palestinian situation.

Kouchner said later that Ghassemlou looked worn out. "There was a genuine fatigue in his bearing; or perhaps he was just getting old."[14] Perhaps it was fallout from a decade of resistance and the ensuing loss of life. "It's a hard struggle," Ghassemlou confided to him; "so many of us are dead."[15]

They spoke about the duplicity of the Iranians and how difficult it was to trust them. But Ghassemlou refused to change his mind.

"We spoke at length with Rahman before dinner," Kouchner recalled. "He said he was going to Vienna, and even mentioned it a second time later in the evening. I said: 'Why are you going? Don't go. Don't trust them. What are you expecting from them?'

"Rahman took it all with humor. He was excited. 'Stay with us,' I said. But he wanted to go to Vienna, no matter what, against all advice. He wanted to get his people out of the mountains. He sensed that he was losing time and that, given the divisions in his party, he could stay [locked into interminable struggle] in Kurdistan for years."

During the last ten years of his life, Abdul Rahman Ghassemlou led a paradoxical life: though he was a sociable person, always laughing and enjoying the company of others, at a deeper level he led a solitary existence. "Oddly, he could feel very lonely in spite of being surrounded by so many people in the mountains," recalled a close associate.[16]

Kouchner believed that the marital separation had deeply distressed him, though Ghassemlou never spoke about it. One of Ghassemlou's comrades shared a similar impression, that in the Kurdish hinterlands, the divorce had affected him deeply and contributed to a sense of solitude. The divorce had occurred in 1981. "Hélène had asked for a divorce," he said. "Ghassemlou had relied on Hélène for decades. I believe that emotionally, he felt more lonely after the divorce. After all, they had been married for many years and they had endured hardship and clandestine life with two kids."[17]

Hélène saw it otherwise: "His divorce did not cause him downheartedness. Our divorce was agreed on about seven years before and was validated three years after. Enough time to get used to it, especially occupied by difficult tasks and problems he had to think about, resolve or fulfill."[18] And the tasks and problems were indeed difficult enough: the years of turmoil, the weight of the deaths of hundreds of fallen comrades, the knife-edge survival of his people, the uncertain prospects for a viable solution.

The loss of so many friends and colleagues through the years of war was a special burden that he bore as a leader. Sharafkandi would later speak about how often Ghassemlou visited the tombs of fallen peshmerga to pay his respects—and of Ghassemlou's encouragement to the Kurdish freedom fighters that the best way to honor their comrades' sacrifice was to "continue in their path": "We either win," he said, "or die, and join the caravan of martyrs."[19]

Far from the circle of family, friends, and ease, occupied with challenges, strategies, and the Kurds' precarious existence, Ghassemlou's life in the mountains certainly carried its own special form of isolation. With male friends and comrades, Ghassemlou was guarded about his feelings, never speaking about them; with Hélène and other women friends, he sometimes let down his guard and revealed the concerns behind the humor and confidence others saw in him.

Though he was sparing in expressing his innermost feelings, Ghassemlou did at times communicate awareness of the ever-present risk to his life. One week before his trip to Vienna, he met with a friend for dinner in Paris. "A man like me always has to protect himself and be alert," he told her. "Death is stalking everywhere."[20] In retrospect, she said later, the intensity and weight of his words made it clear he was always on the alert, always wary.

And always aware of time. Like Martin Luther King, Jr., who in the months leading up to his death seemed driven by a sense that the time left to him would not be long,[21] Ghassemlou seemed impelled by a deep urgency. Time was urging him on.

☙

Wednesday afternoon, July 12. The venue for the negotiations was the apartment at 5 Linke Bahngasse made available by Fadil Rasul. Before the negotiation sessions began, theoretically neither of the parties knew the location or the layout of the building.

In separate trips that afternoon, Rasul picked up and delivered both Dr. Ghassemlou and the Iranian delegation to this venue. The first day of negotiations made no substantial headway, and the parties agreed to meet again the next day.[22]

Despite the apparent lack of progress that day, to Ghassemlou, the first set of conversations seemed to have gone well.

Wednesday, 7:15 p.m., Museum Café. After the meeting with the Iranians, Ghassemlou, Abdullah, and Rasul went for a drink. Before setting out for the negotiations that afternoon, Ghassemlou had told Azad that Rasul would bring them back home, but Azad did not want Rasul to know where he lived. So when Rasul had asked for directions, Azad lied: "My wife and I will be on our way out to meet a friend, so it's better that I come downtown to meet you," he said. Azad asked Rasul to drop Ghassemlou and Abdullah at the café, and went with Charlotte to pick them up.

When they arrived, Rasul had already left. Ghassemlou was drinking a beer. Charlotte recalled: "They invited us to have a drink, but Azad was restless; he thought that place was dangerous. I remember this very well. Azad told Dr. Ghassemlou they had to leave soon."

"No," he answered. "Have something to drink."

"I had a mineral water," Charlotte recounted, "and Azad ordered a beer. When we finished, we drove to Mostafa and Hildegaard's apartment."[23]

Ghassemlou was extremely happy. He and Mostafa planned to get a car on Friday and travel to Prague, where he had good friends from his youth that he wanted to see before embarking for America.

Abdullah, too, seemed to be feeling more cheerful, Azad later recalled, perhaps "because nothing he feared had actually transpired. And Ghassemlou was not afraid because he didn't think anything would happen."[24]

It was typical that Ghassemlou would disregard his security, in spite of all the perils he had weathered in his life. Or perhaps precisely because of the constant presence of danger as an unvarying background, he was not particularly prudent and took few precautions. His friends chided him constantly about this. In fact, it was a miracle he had survived this long.

"He never had a sense of danger," Hélène scolded. "In Kurdistan, people often came to see me and asked me to convince him to be careful."[25] He did not listen to the warnings of his collaborators, she would write. "In Europe he would ignore rules of security. His bodyguards and himself were unarmed; he would disappear and leave everybody anxious, waiting for him to reappear. . . . His bodyguards were afraid for his life."[26]

Ghassemlou's attitude, however, was something she could understand. "To live under constant surveillance is suffocating. . . . [he] became tired of the unrelenting responsibility and did all to retain his independence."[27]

An aphorism from Maria Callas that Ghassemlou copied into his journal expressed the ever-present polarity with which he lived: "I could have been happy, but I chose independence. In general, one's happiness depends on others and that is the beginning of the end."[28]

Ghassemlou's attitude may have embodied a sort of fatalism. Given the history of the assassination of Kurdish leaders, like Simko in 1930 by the Iranian state during "negotiations," his father had warned him more than once about the Persians. "The Kurds have always had bad luck," said Ghassemlou's colleague Abdullah Hassanzadeh, "and I believe this is what overshadowed Dr. Ghassemlou's mind. He was always repeating a saying his father had." "If you see an *ajam*,"[29] Ghassemlou used to say, "you either kill him or run, because he will kill you."[30] But despite all his erudition, Hélène said later, Ghassemlou's analysis of the depth of Iranian treachery—and his appreciation of the danger it posed him—had not gone far enough. And in practice, she added, "he also ignored his father's warning to beware of ajams even though he repeated it whenever an occasion presented itself."[31]

In Paris, just days before his death, Ghassemlou confided to his good friends Bernard Kouchner and Michel Bonnot that he was traveling to Vienna to resume secret negotiations with the Iranians.

Bonnot had been offering his medical expertise for years to the PDKI in the mountains. "The first time I saw Ghassemlou in Paris," Bonnot remembered, "was a few years before. We went to eat in Saint-Germain. We never knew where he lived. He took precautions then, but that was ten years ago. Little by little he had become more lax about this."[32]

In 1988, when Ghassemlou had visited both his doctor friends at the Ministry of Humanitarian Aid in Paris, his friends inquired about police protection for him.

"He came several times," said Bonnot, "and the fifth time, we didn't ask for any reinforcement. We told him once, 'You should have protection; you need bodyguards. If not, we will ask permission for one of your peshmerga to be armed.' Still, he always opposed having a personal bodyguard. He wanted to be able to walk freely through the streets of Paris."

"Be careful in Vienna," his friends warned him again now.

"But I'm going there to speak about peace," he replied. And then he changed the subject.

Everyone else sensed the danger. Jalal Talabani, an Iraqi Kurdish leader and an old friend, warned him, "Be careful. They are demons."[33]

Talabani had good cause to know about the Iranians, and about security measures. Six months earlier, in December–January, Talabani had served as an intermediary during the initial set of negotiations between Ghassemlou and the Islamic regime. On that occasion, Ghassemlou had gone to the meeting under the protection of Talabani's armed guards.[34] But now he was going without any precaution at all, totally trusting—as if he were attending an ordinary business meeting.

Ghassemlou was wearing a light summer suit and a white shirt with a tie. He was carrying only his passport, cigarettes, some cash, and a briefcase containing a tape recorder and cassettes.

He seemed utterly convinced that Rafsanjani needed him.

Wednesday night, Azad's apartment. After the first contact with his enemies for this new round of negotiations, Ghassemlou felt satisfied. He had also enjoyed his meeting with Ben Bella. "Kak Doctor"[35]—the endearing and respectful term the Kurds used to refer to Ghassemlou—"spoke so much in Arabic with Ben Bella that my head was about to explode," laughed Abdullah.[36]

But the others did not share Ghassemlou's enthusiasm. For a number of reasons, many of the Kurds who knew Rasul, especially the expatriate Kurds in Vienna, did not trust him. For some of them, it was Rasul's relations with the Iranian regime that marked him as unreliable; for others, the reasons for distrust seemed more personal. That night after dinner, Azad tried once more to convince Ghassemlou to be careful of Rasul. It was useless. Ghassemlou would not accept his input. After a long conversation, he ended the discussion and returned to his room.

Azad became anguished and appealed to Abdullah, recounting dubious incidents in his experience with Rasul. Abdullah seemed shaken, but he refused to accept Azad's arguments. "Abdullah just laughed and didn`t want to argue," Azad recalled later. "He said the decision was in Ghassemlou's hands, and he could not do anything against it."[37]

"I don't know Rasul," said Abdullah. "But Dr. Ghassemlou knows him."

Azad did not realize, that night, that Abdullah too might have had reservations about this meeting. But Abdullah had an unshakable sense of discipline and loyalty.[38]

In Michel Bonnot's estimation, Abdullah was also a romantic. They had met in Kurdistan when Abdullah was the director of a hospital constructed in the mountains with the support of Aide Médical International. They had become extremely close from the common concerns of their daily life together as well as the shared danger of the unending bombings by the Iranian air force.

"He was my son's godfather," Bonnot remembered. "Ghassemlou was a politician, and I admired him. But Abdullah was my peer and friend. We saw each other often. Abdullah continued to be a romantic. He did not want to have a girlfriend because he was a combatant, and he could die."

In serving as Ghassemlou's bodyguard, Abdullah took on a difficult task, made all the more difficult by Ghassemlou's persistent flouting of the rules of security and his constant disappearances. Yet Abdullah never wavered in his mission to protect him. He knew he would be with him until the end. "Don't forget," he said to Hélène, "the day the doctor is assassinated, I will be by his side."[39]

Notes

1. Charlotte, interview with Gabriel Fernández, Vienna, 1990.
2. Abdullah Hassanzadeh, *Niw Sede Xebat* [Half a century of struggle: A retrospect of struggle and activity of the Democratic Party of Iranian Kurdistan] [in Kurdish], Vol. 1 (Gawrade: Press Commission of the Kurdistan Democratic Party of Iran, August 1995), 168–69; translation Salah Piroty.
3. Kawe Madani, interview with the author, February 26, 2016.
4. Hélène Krulich, personal communication to the author, March 3, 2016.
5. Abdul Rahman Ghassemlou, letter to the author, February 1988.
6. Jafar Hamedi, former member of the PDKI central committee and head of the party secretariat office, now a lecturer at the Norwegian University of Life Sciences, has provided details on what transpired at the PDKI plenum in 1988. Jafar Hamedi, interview conducted by PDKI party member Salah Piroty, May 21, 2016; translation Salah Piroty.
7. Abdullah Hassanzadeh, interview with the author, Koya Sanjak, Iraqi Kurdistan, July 2009. Hassanzadeh became secretary-general of the PDKI in 1995 at the Tenth Congress, three years after Ghassemlou's successor Sadegh Sharafkandi was murdered in Berlin with three other Kurdish collaborators. Hassanzadeh was succeeded by Mustafa Hijri, who has served as secretary-general of the party since 2006. See the PDKI website, http://pdki.org/english/a-brief-biography-of-mustafa-hijri/.

8. Ezzedin Mustafa Rasul, interview with the author, Koya Sanjak, Iraqi Kurdistan, July 2009. Rasul was a member of the Communist Party of Iraq, and Fadil Rasul's cousin.

9. Jafar Hamedi, personal communication to Salah Piroty, February 21, 2019.

10. Hassan (Ibrahimi) Shiwasali, e-mail correspondence with Salah Piroty, May 21, 2016; translation Salah Piroty. The account of the dialogue with Ghassemlou that follows is as stated from Shiwasali's memories. Shiwasali, then military commander in the Sardasht region and a former member of the PDKI leadership, is currently an honorary member of the PDKI central committee.

11. Mustafa Hijri, *Nisko u Dabiran* [Resilience in the face of decline and division] [in Kurdish] (Kurdistan: Sardam Publishing, 2015), 19–20; translation Esmail Ebrahimi.

12. Operation Anfal, led by Ali Hassan al-Majid or "Chemical Ali," was a genocidal campaign against the Kurds in Iraq which included the destruction of villages, mass deportation, executions, and chemical attacks. In 1988, the Iraqi air force attacked Kurdish civilians in Iraqi Kurdistan, launching mustard gas over the city of Halabja. It is estimated that about five thousand people died. Iraq was condemned in international forums, while the United States abstained from comment; America regarded Iraq as a friendly force that could control the rising threat of Iran. In 1991, encouraged by the victorious multinational Coalition Forces' pushing back Iraq's invasion of Kuwait, the Iraqi Kurds in the north and the Shi'ites in the south rebelled against Saddam Hussein. But Baghdad's troops prevailed; they crushed the Shi'ite revolt and provoked a massive Kurdish exodus toward the Turkish and Iranian borders. Thousands of Kurds perished. Hundreds of thousands were left in refugee camps that were actually concentration camps. The world watched and was horrified when the Kurds were abandoned by the broad U.S.-led Coalition of the Gulf War and left to fend for themselves. (The Coalition had drawn forces from a broad international spectrum of thirty-four countries: Argentina, Australia, Bahrain, Bangladesh, Belgium, Canada, Denmark, Egypt, France, Greece, Italy, Kuwait, Morocco, the Netherlands, New Zealand, Niger, Norway, Oman, Pakistan, Portugal, Qatar, South Korea, Saudi Arabia, Senegal, Sierra Leone, Singapore, Spain, Syria, the United Arab Emirates, the United Kingdom, and the U.S. itself.)

    For more information see Human Rights Watch, http://www.hrw.org/reports/1993/iraqanfal/ (accessed April 3, 2013). See also Human Rights Watch, *Iraq's Crime of Genocide: The Anfal Campaign against the Kurds* (New Haven, CT: Yale University Press, 1995), and *Teaching about Genocide: Issues, Approaches, and Resources*, edited by Samuel Totten, Case Study 8: "The 1988 Anfal Operations in Iraqi Kurdistan" by Michiel Leezenberg (New Haven, CT: Yale University Press, 2004), 181–92.

13. Hassan [Ibrahimi] Shiwasali, July 17, 2011, audio file posted at http://arkiv.peshmergekan. eu/Deng/kak_mela_hassan/mela_hasam_qasmlu_danishtn_20110717_.mp3?fbclid= IwAR0YulYSIfzDIWHSD9iYZdXMFmP0WdafW50w_FUnH-te6zjeeSof5m8hfG0. Translations by Salah Piroty and Sharif Behruz.

14. Bernard Kouchner, M.D., interview with the author, Paris, 1991. In 2007, Kouchner left the French Socialist Party to become President Nicolas Sarkozy's minister of foreign affairs.

15. Tribute by Bernard Kouchner at Ghassemlou's funeral, published in *Abdul Rahman Ghassemlou: A Man of Peace and Dialogue* (PDKI publication, 1989), 40.

16. Personal communication to the author from a former colleague of Ghassemlou's, February 2016.

17. Ibid.

18. Hélène Krulich, personal communication to the author, March 3, 2016.

19. Said Sharafkandi, speech given after Ghassemlou's assassination, at Martyrs' Cemetery, PDKI headquarters, Qandil mountains, Iraqi Kurdistan, July 16, 1989; see https://www.youtube.com/watch?v=1ZuTIuiqC_Q, posted July 15, 2014.

20. "Z," conversation with the author, Paris, 2009. For security reasons, Z prefers not to be identified.

21. Coretta Scott King, *My Life, My Love, My Legacy* (New York: Henry Holt and Company, 2017), 160.

22. IHRDC, Iran Human Rights Documentation Center, *No Safe Haven: Iran's Global Assassination Campaign* (New Haven, CT: May 2008), 4.4 Dr. Abdol-Rahman Ghassemlou, in https://iranhrdc.org/no-safe-haven-irans-global-assassination-campaign/ (accessed January 19, 2019). Information for this report was taken principally from Peter Pilz, *Eskorte nach Teheran: Der Österreichische Rechtsstaat und die Kurdenmorde* [Escort to Tehran: The Austrian constitutional state and the murders of the Kurds] (Vienna: Ibera & Molden, 1997). As a member of government, Pilz had access to many documents that the IHRDC had yet to acquire.

23. Charlotte, interview with Gabriel Fernández.

24. Azad, interviews with Gabriel Fernández, Vienna, 1990–1991. Further statements from Azad in this chapter are from these interviews.

25. Hélène Krulich, interview with Gabriel Fernández and the author, Paris, 1990.

26. Hélène Krulich-Ghassemlou, *Love Against All Reason: A European Woman Involved in the Kurdish Fight for Freedom in Iran* (Vienna: Lit Verlag, 2017), 233.

27. Ibid., 233

28. Ibid., 233

29. *Ajam* refers to a non-Kurd. Theoretically this could mean either a Turk or a Persian, but is used mostly for Azeri Turks, who have been at odds with the Kurds in Iran for centuries. Ghassemlou gave different renderings of this saying of his father's; sometimes he phrased it as "Run, because they can dupe and kill you." When speaking with Westerners, Ghassemlou would use the specific term *Persians* to make his meaning clear.

30. Abdullah Hassanzadeh, interview with the author, Koya Sanjak, Iraqi Kurdistan, July 2009.

31. Hélène Krulich, personal communication to the author, March 3, 2016.

32. Michel Bonnot, interview with the author, 1991. Further statements from Bonnot are from this interview.

33. Jalal Talabani, interview with the author, Paris, 1991. Talabani, then leader of the PUK, the Patriotic Union of Kurdistan, would go on to become president of Iraq in 2005.

34. According to Mustafa Hijri, Ghassemlou had advised party officials that Jalal Talabani had placed some of his friends, armed with pistols, behind the door of the meeting room and in another strategic location near the meeting place. Hijri, *Resilience in the Face of Decline and Division*, 11, translation Chiman Moradi and Esmail Ebrahimi.

35. *Kak*, an honorific with shades of meaning from "sir" to "brother," is a common expression in Kurdistan used in addressing an older brother or any esteemed or respected man.

36. Azad, interview with Gabriel Fernandez, 1990–1991.

37. Azad, personal communication to the author, June 21, 2016.

38. Abdullah Ghaderi-Azar was born in 1951 in Naghadeh in Iranian Kurdistan. He came from a modest family, one of many children. He went to school in Naghadeh and then earned a technical diploma from his high school in Urmia. He did two years of military service as a teacher in the towns of the Alamut district in the Ghazvin region before going on to study at the Institute of Arts in Tehran. When he finished his studies four years later, he worked as a teacher in the high schools of the town where he was born.

   After the revolutionary events of 1978 he joined the PDKI, where he was politically active until the end of his life; he was underground until the Shah fell, and afterward "he took on many responsibilities with an exceptional talent" in the region of Naghadeh.

   During the party's Seventh Congress, he was elected a member of the central committee. The party's political bureau then named him representative in Europe in 1985, where he served until his death. "All those who knew him," says his biography, "people from around the world, always highlighted his modesty, calmness, and capacity to listen, qualities worthy of a true intellectual man." *Bulletin de liaison et d'information*, Institut Kurde de Paris, July–August 1989.

39. Hélène Krulich, *Une Européenne au pays des Kurdes* (Paris: Éditions Karthala, 2011), 250.

· 3 ·

THE INTERMEDIARY

৵

The Kurds of Vienna did not trust Rasul. They had been avoiding him for a long time—despite every effort the young man made to befriend them.

Rasul's political history was complex: as a Maoist militant, he had been exiled from Iraq for years in Lebanon. There he worked with the PLO, the Palestinian Liberation Organization. He finally ended up in Austria, where a large contingent of his numerous family lived. He held Austrian citizenship.

At university he had met Susanne Rockenschaub, who came from an aristocratic family. She was the daughter of a well-known university professor from the Social Democratic Party of Austria. When Rasul met her, she was participating in the Trotskyist movement. They married, but had no children.

Rasul's influence over her was particularly strong. When he abandoned Marxism and turned toward the Islamic faith, Susanne, who was a medical doctor at the time, followed him in this path. Delicate and cultivated, fluent in several languages, this Viennese woman became a Muslim during their courtship. Following her ideological conversion, she pursued a natural and authentic passion for the Islamic Revolution.

Azad was alarmed to discover this political affinity in 1981, when Rasul and Susanne were his guests in Iranian Kurdistan. To his dismay, he discovered Rasul speaking on the phone from his house with friends in Tehran, Iranian government functionaries.

The topic of discussion between Rasul and his friends was Tehran's war against the Kurds. Azad overhead Rasul saying he was convinced the war was going to end. Among other scraps of the conversation he was able to overhear was Rasul mentioning that he knew Banisadr well—Abolhassan Banisadr, then president of the Islamic Republic and a protégé of Imam Khomeini—and that he wanted to translate a book Banisadr had written.[1]

During their 1981 visit, Azad, Suzanne, and Rasul had traveled with a group of friends by car through the north of Iran. The whole time they were on the road, Rasul was restless. Azad's efforts to calm him were fruitless.

"Don't worry, all this area is in the hands of the Kurds," Azad would tell him.

"I'm afraid . . . There could be Iraqi agents here," Rasul said.

Azad became suspicious of Rasul. Once back in Vienna, they distanced themselves from each other. When Azad found out that Rasul had contacts with the Iranian embassy, they never crossed paths again—until Ghassemlou's visit to Vienna for the meetings.

Mostafa did not trust him either. When Mostafa settled in Vienna as the new representative of the PDKI, Rasul made unsuccessful attempts at contact with him. The Kurds did not want to see him. That is why in the summer of 1989 when Ghassemlou came to the Austrian capital and Rasul seemed so close to him there was alarm among the Kurds.

How had the connection come about between Ghassemlou and this suspect young man?

ॐ

When Ghassemlou and Ahmed Ben Bella met at Rasul's apartment in Vienna on Wednesday, July 12, to speak about the upcoming negotiations with the Iranians, what neither of them knew was that Ben Bella had been originally proposed—by Rasul—as the organizer of the sessions.

According to information pieced together from a number of sources, Rasul had been contacted by Iranian emissaries at the beginning of July 1989 with a request to organize a meeting with Ghassemlou in Vienna. At first, Rasul refused; "If I accept," he said to a family member, "the Iraqis will never forgive me." Instead, Rasul suggested the meeting be facilitated by "an important personality" like former Algerian president Ahmed Ben Bella.[2]

Details here become scanty, and what bits of information have surfaced are muddied and obscure. One source has it that a principal Iranian emissary had given Rasul a definitive "No" to a request for Ben Bella's participation in the meetings.[3] A witness who was present remembers the head of the Iranian negotiating team saying "Vehemently no" to Rasul.[4] At the time, the witness did not know what was under discussion; it was only in hindsight that he connected the dots. Despite this vehement "No," apparently, Rasul told Ben Bella that "it was possible there might be a meeting [of Iran] with the Kurds."[5]

Sometime still early in July, Rasul had traveled to Paris to convey word to Ghassemlou that Hashemi Rafsanjani desired to resume negotiations once again. Khomeini had just died in June, and Rafsanjani, a political higher-up in Iran, was ascending unstoppably toward the presidency.

Nobody knows for sure, but rumors have it that Rasul told Ghassemlou that he'd received a letter from Rafsanjani asking his help to set up a meeting in Vienna. On this matter, Rasul had maintained silence; no one was privy to the content of such a letter, or the circumstances of the conversation between the young man and Ghassemlou. To this day, no one can confirm the existence of this letter. Yet days after the crime, mention of this purported presidential missive was being made by members of Rasul's family in Vienna.

All that is known as a fact, after all the dust of the details has settled, is that at the beginning of July, Rasul had through some means been contacted by Iranian emissaries with a request to organize the Vienna meeting with Ghassemlou.

The other fact now pieced together is that the Iranian delegation was led by Mohammad Jafari Sahrarudi, Iranian intelligence agent, and included Hadji Mostafawi,[6] who worked for the Ministry of Information, and Amir Mansur Buzorguian, an alleged bodyguard—and an agent of the Iranian secret police.

Notes

1. Azad, interviews with Gabriel Fernández, Vienna, 1990–1991. The book in question may have been Abolhassan Banisadr and Jean-Charles Deniau, Le Complot des ayatollahs [The conspiracy of the ayatollahs] (Paris: Éditions la Découverte, 1989).
2. Marc Kravetz, "Téhéran-Vienne: Récit d'un crime," Libération, August 7, 1989.
3. Ibid. Another source adds the following details: "Both the Iranians and Ben Bella accepted the proposal, and on the eve of the July talks Qassemlou [Ghassemlou], Rassoul [Rasul] and the Algerian [Ben Bella] met in Vienna to discuss the arrangements. Because of the Iranian demand that the encounter should be kept totally secret, neither Talabani nor Qassemlou's closest collaborators in the KDP of Iran knew of the arrangements. The Kurds even bowed to the Iranians' demand that Ben Bella should not be allowed to attend the talks in person." John Bulloch and Harvey Morris, No Friends but the Mountains: The Tragic History of the Kurds (New York: Oxford University Press, 1992), 193.
4. The head of the negotiating team was Mohammad Jafari Sahrarudi, an agent for Iranian intelligence. He was a former commander of the Revolutionary Guards' Ramazan Brigade in Kermanshah, in charge of missions inside Iraq. He was also the deputy head of Iran's

National Security Council and one of the commanders of the Quds Force, and responsible for terrorism and assassinations in Iraq.

5. Kravetz, "Récit d'un crime."
6. Hadji Mostafawi also used the aliases Adjavi and Layevardi. According to Austrian parliamentarian Peter Pilz in *Eskorte nach Teheran*, n232, his real name was Mostafa Ajoudi and he was in fact the Iranian governor of the Province of Kurdistan. Cited in IHRDC, Iran Human Rights Documentation Center, *No Safe Haven: Iran's Global Assassination Campaign* (New Haven, CT: May 2008), 4.4. Dr. Abdol-Rahman Ghassemlou.

· 4 ·

THE MURDERERS

෨

Abdul Rahman Ghassemlou was killed by three bullets, shot at close range by two pistols with silencers.

Abdullah received eleven gunshot wounds; Rasul received five. A bullet to the head finished off each of the three men.

Ghassemlou died instantly. He did not even have time to react. Judging from this, he must have been the first target. According to a report by Austrian parliamentarian Peter Pilz, the initial crime-scene impression was that Ghassemlou and Rasul were caught by surprise and killed in a seated position.[1]

Other readings of the evidence, however, reportedly indicate that both Fadil Rasul and Abdullah Ghaderi-Azar resisted the murderers. The positions in which their bodies were found suggest that they struggled with the attackers.[2] Medical forensics discovered traces of skin under their nails.[3] The sheer number of wounds Abdullah sustained, in particular, strongly suggests an active resistance. In Abdullah's clothing they also found traces of blood from Mohammad Jafari Sahrarudi, one of the Iranian envoys.

The Austrian police found the living room in chaotic disarray, as shown by the photos taken during the first days of the investigation.

The police found sixteen shells in the room. In the course of the investigation, a total of fifteen bullets would eventually be recovered: six in the bodies of the victims, and nine more elsewhere in the room at the crime scene. Autopsy by forensic physicians would determine, however, that the three victims sustained a total of nineteen wounds.

Thursday, July 13, afternoon. After a short nap, Ghassemlou and Abdullah visited the Ministry of Internal Affairs, where Azad dropped them off. Ghassemlou had an appointment with Dr. Matzka, a ministry official who was considered a friend of the Kurds. Ghassemlou wanted to thank him for having helped obtain his visa.

Ghassemlou had entered Austria with his Iranian passport, which he typically used.[4] His passport was authentically Iranian, albeit falsified—an official document, but the name and photo had been tampered with. It had been ten years since the Iranian authorities had last issued him one.

At the ministry, Dr. Matzka was not in. So Ghassemlou tried to see Chancellor Franz Vranitzky. Ghassemlou was told that he would have to wait. He lingered for a while. But he could not stay longer; he put down his card and some documents from his party, and left.

At 4:00 p.m. that afternoon, Ghassemlou was scheduled to meet with fifteen members of the PDKI at Fatah's house. None of these party members had any idea that Ghassemlou's purpose in Vienna was to meet with the Iranians. Since he had been delayed at the ministry, Ghassemlou asked Azad to call and tell the group that he would meet them after 7:00 p.m.

"Let's go to the Hilton," he told Azad.

Azad started up his Renault 12. He arrived at the Ring and headed toward the bus terminal near the Hilton, the passenger terminus for the shuttle to the airport. He did not know where Ghassemlou was going; he wondered if he was going to meet Ben Bella.

When they arrived at the Vienna Hilton, Ghassemlou and Abdullah got out of the car.

"Come and pick us up at seven fifteen—or better yet, seven thirty," he told Azad. Ghassemlou always made a point of being punctual and precise about time.

Azad dropped them off and drove to Fatah's house, where the fifteen party members were waiting for Ghassemlou; they had news from Kurdistan. Before going in, following Ghassemlou's instructions, he scouted around the neighborhood for a shop to buy chocolate and flowers for Maria Theresia, Fatah's wife. When Azad walked into the apartment with the flowers it was full of people.

Thursday, July 13, 7:15 p.m. Azad returned to the air terminal in front of the Hilton. There was no one there; he decided to walk around. He returned at 7:30, but Ghassemlou and Abdullah still had not appeared. He sat and waited in the car.

At 8:00, he became worried and got out of his car, locked the door, and found a phone booth. He called Fatah, who was the representative of the party in Vienna, and also a good friend.

From the phone booth, Azad could see the intersection with Linke Bahngasse, about a hundred meters from the international hotel. Down that street there was tremendous confusion—a lot of movement, blinking lights, police-men. "Something has happened," he realized.

Fatah answered the phone.

"There are tons of policemen in the street," Azad told him. "Our friends have not come back, and they should have returned already."

"Wait there. I'm coming with Mostafa," answered Fatah.

Fatah and Mostafa arrived a few minutes later to find that the street had been closed off. They stopped beside other onlookers from a point where they could see the front of number 5 in the Linke Bahngasse. It was then that Mostafa recognized the building.

"It's Renata's apartment," Fatah said.

Then, instinctively, Azad knew: "Everything is over. The negotia-tions . . . that's where the negotiations were happening. Now the police are there . . . Our friends are dead."

The Kurds moved toward the building. A policeman on guard informed them that three men had been murdered, and another was wounded. Azad hoped against hope that the injured person would be one of his friends.

"Are these the victims?" asked Fatah, giving the policeman the names of their friends.

An officer approached and showed them a piece of paper. It was Abdul-lah's identification card. "Do you know this man?"

"Yes," they answered. The policeman sensed that they were not simply curious bystanders and asked them to follow him.

They climbed the stairs to the fifth floor.

Fatah was right; it was the apartment of Renata Faistauer, Fadil Rasul's Austrian lover. On the dark brown apartment door there was a makeshift sign that read: *I ♥ KURDISTAN.*

They went in. It was very quiet. Tensely and solemnly, the police ordered the three Kurds not to touch anything and to keep their hands by their sides. Separated, they went in one by one to the small living room. Though there was not much light, they could see the room was a shambles. The three bodies sprawled on the floor were covered with blood.

Azad recognized Ghassemlou and Abdullah, he said later, but not Rasul. Ghassemlou was reclining with his back against the sofa, without his jacket, with his tie and his white shirt soaked in blood. In the midst of the scene of carnage and chaos his expression was strangely serene, like the face of a Bud-dha. Abdullah was lying on his back, in the center of the room; the third man was near the door, lying on his stomach.

By the reckoning of the forensic investigators, the deaths all occurred at 7:20 p.m. According to the police, the murderers took the victims' documents before they fled. They took Ghaderi-Azar's briefcase but somehow forgot his identification card. The police confirmed that none of the victims were armed.

When Mostafa and Fatah went out into the street it was already dark. It was 8:30. The police took them to the police station and interrogated them. The investigation was being conducted by the police and the antiterrorist group known as Cobra II.

The Kurds were now suspects and had to undergo a paraffin test to check if they had fired any guns. The results were negative.

The three men were devastated. For years, they had lived through the tragedy of their country, the repression of Kurdistan, the Shah's dictatorship, the Islamic regime's persecution, the endless exile. Two of them had been peshmerga, had fought in the mountains and seen their companions die. But they had never suffered a loss like the one that night. They were terrified and overwrought.

Azad, whose family had close contacts with the Ghassemlous and who had known Abdullah since childhood, was shattered. It was a moment he would never forget. "I´m a doctor," he said, many years later. "I have seen many dead—even murdered—bodies in my life. But I have never been so hard hit . . . because those were my friends."[5]

Only at midnight were they finally allowed to call their families.

"We're at the police," said Fatah tersely. "But we're all right."

Back at home, their apartment was full of people who did not understand what was happening. The phone was ringing nonstop. Confusing accounts about the crime were already circulating in the city and other European capitals. There were calls from Vienna, Paris, cities in Germany. Like everyone else, Maria Theresia was in a state of shock. "Please do not call anymore. We need to keep this phone line open," she asked everyone who called.

Uncertainty reigned, and the atmosphere was laden with tears and feelings of dread until the three men arrived home. At 6:00 in the morning, the exhausted Kurds, their friends and loved ones, took leave of one another and went home.

❧

The details of the crime are still unresolved to this day. The murder scene can only be reconstructed by deduction.[6]

Abdul Rahman Ghassemlou and Abdullah Ghaderi-Azar were seen alive for the last time when they got out of Azad's car at 5:00 p.m. at the air terminal. Because it was late, it is probable that they did not stop at the Hilton, but decided to walk to their meeting.

The Vienna Hilton is an enormous structure. The bus terminal and public restrooms are located near the lobby area. Close by is a vast open space with boutiques and souvenir shops. There are also at least five places where the Kurds could have met someone—the Café am Park, the Kleine Konditorei, the Klimt Bar, the Terminal Pub, and the Rotisserie Prinz Eugen.

It's possible that Ghassemlou and Abdullah crossed through the lobby, and went out the rear entrance to the Landstrasser Hauptstrasse, a wide street lined with an array of shops. A hundred meters down is the intersection with the Linke Bahngasse. Walking, you can reach number 5 Linke Bahngasse in five minutes. The front of the building is gray and light green, with thirty-eight large windows and five floors; the building houses middle-class flats. In front, across the street, is a rail line that dives underground at that point. Further afield are a park and the small Beethoven Platz.

Ghassemlou and Abdullah must have entered the building around 5:00 p.m. The first shot was fired sometime between 7:00 and 7:20 p.m. The only proof of this timetable is a set of tapes which apparently recorded the conversations that were interrupted when two pistols, an Italian Beretta and a Spanish Llama, emptied their clips into the three Kurds.

Only three people can tell us what happened: Mohammad Jafari Sahrarudi and Amir Mansur Buzorguian, Iranian emissaries who were taken into custody and questioned by the police; and Hadji Mostafawi, who disappeared without a trace.

The first, Sahrarudi, was the head of the Iranian delegation that met with Ghassemlou, a high-ranking officer of the Ministry of Intelligence, a specialist in Kurdish affairs and the Iranian regime's point person for contact with Iraqi Kurdish groups.[7] As commander and adjunct chief of the 15th Division of the Islamic Revolutionary Guard Corps (IRGC)—the Sepah Pasdaran[8]—Sahrarudi was a man well trusted by Rafsanjani.

Mostafawi, for his part, worked under the orders of Mohammed Mohammadi Reyshahri, the minister of information (intelligence and security)—one of the hawks of the regime. Mostafawi was in charge of the secret service for the province of West Azerbaijan in Kurdistan.[9]

As Iranian negotiators, both were in the room when the crime was committed.

The third Iranian was Amir Mansur Buzorguian, who presented himself as Sahrarudi's bodyguard, and who held an Iranian diplomatic passport.[10] His real name was Haj Ghafour Darjazi,[11] and he was a member of the Sepah-i Quds—the "Jerusalem Force"—an elite force of the Army of the Revolutionary Guards, in charge of special operations outside of Iran.

Only three people can tell us what happened, and their stories have gaps and inconsistencies.

At the end of the negotiation session, Sahrarudi later told investigators, two or three assailants had thrown open the door and entered the room. He was injured, he said, before he could get a good look at the men, and once injured feigned death, to fool the attackers.

Where was the bodyguard during all this?

Sahrarudi claimed that Buzorguian was in the bathroom at the time of the shootings.[12]

But Buzorguian declared to the police that he was coming back from eating a quick meal at a McDonald's, and he saw nothing. The police and the Kurds find it incomprehensible that a bodyguard should leave his post to grab a snack at a distant fast-food emporium, leaving unattended the man he was supposedly protecting.

The essential fact is that on that afternoon, two gunmen fired a Beretta and a Llama at Abdul Rahman Ghassemlou, Abdullah Ghaderi-Azar, and Fadil Rasul. Judging from the number of shells recovered from the bodies and the site, each weapon was fired eight times. Yet the victims sustained nineteen wounds, Sahrarudi receiving multiple wounds from one bullet. Early reportage on the incident suggested that neither the number of bullets nor the number of shells coincided with the number of times ballistic tests reportedly determined that these weapons had been fired.

Perhaps due to poor aim on the part of the gunmen, or perhaps in the mêlée when the shooting erupted, Sahrarudi was in the line of fire. One of the bullets hit the *pasdar*'s hand. It ricocheted from his arm, penetrated his neck, and lodged in his mouth. Fortunately for him, these wounds, though dramatic, were not lethal.

Had it not been for this single unfortunate bullet, the murderers would have fled without leaving a trace. Nobody but Rasul knew where the negotiations were taking place. Only Susanne, Rasul's wife, knew the identities of the Iranian envoys. It would have taken the police hours—or perhaps days—to find the bodies. It would have been a perfect crime.

But Sahrarudi's arm and face were bleeding profusely. In a panic, this trained Revolutionary Guard, accustomed to facing death and the suffering of others, staggered from the room at about 7:20 p.m. and rang a neighbor's doorbell, crying "Help! Police! Help!" Alerted, the neighbors immediately called the police, who arrived at the scene at 7:37 p.m. Sahrarudi, meanwhile, made his way down five flights of stairs to the ground floor, where one report says that he continued calling for help.[13]

Sahrarudi remained in the street until the police arrived.

Buzorguian, according to his own testimony, arrived at that moment and tried to help the wounded man. Sahrarudi was trying to be calm; he handed Buzorguian a package, which Buzorguian slipped into his jacket. Next, the bodyguard ran to a phone booth, made a call, and came back.

A police car arrived and pulled up in front of them. The officers assisted the bleeding man, who spoke to them in English. One of the policemen called for reinforcements.

Sahrarudi was taken to the Kaiser Franz Josef Hospital. He was admitted to the throat and nose section and sent into surgery. Buzorguian was taken to the police headquarters in Schottenring.[14] There agents confiscated the package that Sahrarudi had given him. It contained some documents and US$9,000.

Throughout the night, the police interrogated Buzorguian. He declared and repeated that he was a simple bodyguard, who at the time of the shooting was coming back from McDonald's. He said that Sahrarudi and Mostafawi were part of a delegation sent by the Iranian government to negotiate with the Kurds and that he had been in the apartment almost to the end of the talks that afternoon. Then he decided to go and eat something. He reiterated that he did not know anything else.

The Austrian government was alarmed. Oswald Kessler, chief of the national security police force, the Staatspolizei, arrived immediately. Without knowing at this stage the depth of the drama, he mobilized the best investigators from the Vienna police. After the first moments, he realized this was a political crime. He was overheard saying, "We've got dead Kurds and surviving Iranians. The matter is clear. The rest will be politics."[15]

Later he delegated agents to comb the city and begin questioning possible suspects.

By 9:00 p.m. that night, the police were only aware of the following elements:

- Three bodies in the apartment owned by Renata Faistauer, who was away in Cairo;

- Three Kurds, friends of the victims, who were given a paraffin test and detained for hours;
- An Iranian with a diplomatic passport, wounded by a bullet, now under surgery;
- A fellow countryman with a packet of documents (their content was never disclosed) and US$9,000, who said he was the bodyguard of the wounded Iranian;
- An alleged third Iranian who had disappeared, by name Hadji Mosta-fawi, whom nobody knew.

Hours later the police discovered, over three kilometers from the apartment in a trashcan near the Pilgramgasse U-bahn station on Linke Wienzeli, a packet containing a brown bloodstained windbreaker, a key and a bill of sale[16] for a Suzuki GSX500E red motorcycle,[17] and three weapons. These were a submachine Beretta and two handguns with silencers, with their serial numbers and brand names scratched out. Experts in ballistics later concluded that the two handguns were the ones that had fired the bullets whose shells were found at the crime location.

The police confirmed that the door to the apartment had not been forced open. Security for the door to the building lobby downstairs included an intercom system and three security locks. But in the entrance to the building they found a piece of adhesive tape blocking the latch, leaving the outer door unlocked.

Within hours following the crime, the news hit the worldwide press from New Delhi to Madrid: An Iranian Kurdish leader named Abdul Rahman Ghassemlou had been murdered in a Western European capital. The identity of the murderers was unknown. Total confusion raged unabated for two days, as the Iranian regime engaged in a campaign of disinformation designed to blame Iraq for the murder.

"The day after his murder," recalled one colleague, "Dr. Said [Sadegh Sharafkandi][18] called me and told me Dr. Ghassemlou had been murdered. I thought immediately it was Iraq [that had ordered his assassination] because recently Dr. Ghassemlou had given a decidedly critical interview to an Arab magazine about Halabja.[19] But Said told me that Dr. Ghassemlou had been in dialogue with the Iranians, and then I knew it was them."[20]

The Iranian embassy in Vienna declared that the murders had been the act of enemies of Iran and that the Kurds had been negotiating to guarantee the return of Ghassemlou to Iran, to pursue talks on the Kurdish question with Iranian authorities.

Radio Tehran announced that Ghassemlou, leader of the PDKI, "was about to change sides and abandon his alliance with Iraq and make an agreement with Iran."[21]

IRNA, the Iranian news agency, issued a press release from the embassy declaring, "In the last months, due to the changes that have taken place in Iraqi Kurdistan, some groups of Iranian Kurds who had collaborated with the Iraqi government have expressed their wish to change their former stance and negotiate with the Islamic Republic through some Iraqi Kurds that had good relations with the Islamic Republic."

Echoing these news pieces, on Saturday, July 15, the Agence France-Presse reported that Iraq "was probably behind the murder."[22] Rasul's wife Susanne denounced Baghdad as the source of the assassination.

Iran and Iraq volleyed mutual accusations at one another. Relations between Baghdad and Tehran continued to deteriorate. In Tehran, Rafsanjani, president of the Majlis (parliament), sent his chief of staff to convey his condolences to Jalal Talabani, the Iraqi Kurdish leader who, as friend of the Islamists and personal friend of Ghassemlou, had served as intermediary during Ghassemlou's earlier negotiations with Tehran in December 1988–January 1989.

Rafsanjani's chief of staff accused the Mujahedin-e Khalq (MEK),[23] a leftist Iranian Islamic group, and told Talabani that he did not discard the possibility that a "hostile Iranian faction" was the instigator of this assassination. Talabani told me later that he had accepted this version of events; the idea that a clique of hard-liners within the regime had wanted to subvert any softening toward the Kurds was not that hard to believe, in a milieu where different factions were jockeying for power.[24]

Nonetheless, on Monday, July 17, the PDKI declared in Paris: "The responsibility of this murder lies with the regime of the Islamic Republic."

Two days later in the Vienna airport, after having met with officials of the Austrian police, Hélène Krulich reconfirmed this by accusing "representatives of the Iranian regime"[25] of this crime.

Meanwhile, mere hours after the tragedy, the Iranian ambassador in Vienna demanded to see Sahrarudi in the hospital. To an official of the Austrian Ministry of Foreign Affairs, he ominously pronounced the Iranian people "very sensitive" and warned that "the Iranian authorities could not guarantee the security of the Austrian embassy in Tehran if anything happened to Mr. Sahrarudi."[26]

Sahrarudi had surgery that very day, Thursday, so the police were not able to interrogate him until Saturday. The police kept his testimony a secret, but the weekly magazine Profil revealed it.

Repeating the storyline given by Sahrarudi, the pasdaran's ostensibly intrepid security chief, Profil reported: As the meeting with the Kurds was coming to an end, one or two people, he could not be precise, burst into the room. One was wearing a light cap. One of the intruders shot Sahrarudi and the others. Sahrarudi was wounded and therefore not able to see much more. Mostafawi, he said, had left the room before the assault.

Once he saw he was wounded, Sahrarudi said, he ran to the corridor, where he found Buzorguian and Mostafawi. His declarations contradict those of his bodyguard, which state he was not there because he had gone to McDonald's. The fact is, however, that nobody remembered seeing Buzorguian at McDonald's. No one recognized him.[27]

Sahrarudi did not clarify how the supposed assailants entered the apartment. He insisted that they had fired from the doorway. But analysis of the shooting, at least by some reports, determined that the assassins could not have fired at the Kurds from the entrance to the apartment. Instead, the shots had come from the side of the room *opposite* the door, and from assailants who were in a seated position. The trajectory of the bullets indicated that they had been fired from the direction occupied by the Iranian delegation: discarded shell casings were found not near the doorway, but where the Iranian negotiators had been sitting.[28] A senior Austrian government official told *Time* magazine: "Buzorguian and Sahrarudi told us someone had forced their way into the room and opened fire. They lied. By all appearances, the murderers were inside the room at the time of the crime."[29]

The Viennese government gave way to the Iranian pressure.[30] Buzorguian, who had been detained for questioning, was let go. He immediately took refuge in the Iranian embassy, a solid building in the Jauresgasse, one street over and seven hundred meters from the Linke Bahngasse murder site. It is a residential neighborhood; across the street from the Iranian embassy stand the Soviet embassy and the Russian Orthodox church.

Buzorguian had a reserved seat on the Iran Air flight for Tehran that Saturday, July 15. The police were worried. The plane was leaving at 7:00 p.m. and the bodyguard was free of all charges.

The police had a judge order arrest warrants for Buzorguian and Mostafawi,[31] on minor charges of failure to assist a wounded person—namely, and ironically, Sahrarudi. These warrants for a minor charge in Austrian law[32] were merely a legitimizing pretext for holding the suspects. The warrants were ready at 5:50 p.m., and with them, Buzorguian's flight was thwarted.

However, Iranian authorities refused to allow Buzorguian to appear without a guarantee that he would return to the Iranian embassy and remain within its walls. In order to gain Buzorguian's consent to be questioned again,

the Austrian minister of justice, Egmont Foregger, agreed to lift Buzorguian's arrest warrant temporarily for his audience with the judge. To the judge,
Buzorguian repeated that he was part of a delegation that had come to negotiate with the Iranian Kurds. He said that he was not there when the shooting
happened. He'd been hungry and had gone to get something to eat.

Buzorguian was allowed to return to the Iranian embassy. He was never
seen again.

Iran intensified the tone of its accusations against Vienna. The following Wednesday, July 19, irritated by the warrants of arrest against Buzorguian
and Mostafawi, Tehran warned the Viennese government about its "illogical
behavior." Iran's minister of foreign affairs denounced the "ambiguity" of the
Austrian "politics" in the crime investigation.

"The gesture of the Austrian government can only be the consequence of
one of two things," the Iranian ministry asserted: "one being pressure exerted
by certain political currents of that country that have tight ties with the enemies of Iran, or secondly, the incompetence of the police and the forces of
security who were incapable of uncovering the authors of this crime."[33]

A diplomatic war began between Vienna and Tehran. Alois Mock,
Austrian minister of foreign affairs, declared on July 21 to the Viennese daily
Die Presse that Iran was "probably" behind the crime. "The Iranian reaction is
disgusting," he declared, referring to the embassy's demand to annul the arrest
warrants. He added that Iran "apparently set a trap" for the Kurdish leaders—
having them come to Vienna to negotiate an eventual return to Iran.

Sahrarudi was more fortunate than Buzorguian. Wounded on July 13,
interrogated on the fifteenth and identified as the owner of the mysterious red
Suzuki, he left the hospital on July 19 and was freed of any charge on Friday
the twenty-first, eight days following the crime.

The haste with which Sahrarudi's hospital sojourn was processed was
anything but medically or administratively typical. Though medical staff
considered Sahrarudi's wound serious, requiring at least twenty-four days of
hospitalization, he was released in just over one week. Had he remained in
hospital, the police would have had over two weeks longer for their inquiry
with Sahrarudi in medical safekeeping.[34]

The police asked the investigating judge, Michael Danek, to issue a warrant
for Sahrarudi. Judge Danek, however, preferred to question Sahrarudi himself
before issuing a warrant. Such procedure was routine in those days; Sahrarudi
insisted he would speak with Danek only if a representative of the Iranian
embassy was present.[35] The judge visited the wounded Iranian in the hospital

on July 20 and Sahrarudi denied, against all evidence, having bought the motor-cycle. He insisted that he was not in Vienna on the day of the sale, January 10. He said that he had left the country on the fourth of January and had come back on the fourteenth. Strangely, the stamps in his passport confirmed this.

The role of the motorcycle, oddly enough, was never publicly clarified and to this day remains obscure. One theory is that the Suzuki could have been used by Mostafawi to flee the scene of the crime, although, French journal-ist Marc Kravetz reported, "he was later identified as the passenger of a taxi which he hired to take him to Vienna airport before diverting to the Iranian embassy."[36]

The police, however, continued to believe that the testimony of the sales-man of the Suzuki was both valid and essential. Conveyed to the hospital, the salesman reconfirmed the identity of the convalescent Sahrarudi as the purchaser of the motorcycle. The police asked again that an arrest warrant be issued against the Iranian. But the judge again did not deem it necessary and gave Sahrarudi back his diplomatic passport and the US$9,000. Now a free man, Sahrarudi returned to the embassy.

There, a medical team sent by Tehran took care of him. On Saturday, July 22, at 7:00 p.m., under their care and under the protection of the Austrian police, who helped him board the plane, Sahrarudi flew via Iran Air back to his country. A group of Iranian diplomats who had arrived in Vienna the pre-vious day accompanied him.

Judge Michael Danek and state attorney Sepp-Dieter Fasching had deter-mined that letting Sahrarudi go was a reasonable thing to do. They had noth-ing against him.

On July 27, however, Austrian minister of internal affairs Franz Löschnak pronounced himself in favor of an order of extradition. The law, he said, should prevail over affairs of state.[37] In Iran, the regime responded through its news agency IRNA: "Vienna has given herself to a suspicious political game and to a campaign of propaganda instead of searching for the criminals."[38]

∾

Two weeks after the crime, on Thursday, July 27, the bodies of Abdul Rahman Ghassemlou and Abdullah Ghaderi-Azar were laid to rest in Paris. Fadil Rasul was buried in Iraq. Through incomprehensible decisions on the part of the judge, the only witnesses had disappeared and the Viennese police had been left empty-handed. Sahrarudi had left for Iran. Buzorguian was protected by the diplomatic immunity of the embassy, and Mostafawi had vanished. An elusive fourth man, Mohamed Magaby, never more than an insubstantial rumor, had mysteriously dropped from sight.

In Vienna, hundreds of Kurds and Austrian sympathizers demonstrated in front of the Ministry of Foreign Affairs, where a delegation was received with kindness. They were reminded that the Austrian judicial power was independent from the ministry. But the pressure of the Iranian government on Austria continued. Though Austrian officials had assured the Kurdish delegation that Austria would not be intimidated, the Austrian business attaché in Tehran received threats.[39]

Both the crime and its investigation clouded Austrian politics. The minister of internal affairs, Franz Löschnak, accused the minister of foreign affairs, Alois Mock, of having sacrificed the fight against terrorism to the interests of state.[40]

Perhaps to maintain appearances, Iran demanded that the Austrians find Mostafawi, a supposed victim of the events. But nobody knew Mostafawi in Austria, and Tehran never sent his photo or description to Vienna. Meanwhile, according to Talabani, Mostafawi was freely walking the streets of Tehran.

On Saturday, July 28, the Kurds demonstrated once more, this time at the Vienna airport. The weekly Iran Air flight to Tehran left with an Iranian passenger protected by the police. According to his Iranian passport, this mysterious fourth man—a redheaded man with a sharp face—was Mohamed Magaby.[41] The demonstrators recognized him; they had seen him with Sahrarudi, Mostafawi, and Buzorguian during the days prior to the murder. Magaby too had been questioned by the police and then released and allowed to return to Iran.

There are many aspects to the crime that remain unclear; contradictions, unanswered questions. Until the Austrian government releases the results of the police investigation, the interrogations, and any other materials, forensic or otherwise, questions and doubts will go unanswered.

At the end of the day, however, the central facts can be summarized very succinctly: The crime investigation had found no results. And the presumed murderers had escaped justice.

Notes

1. IHRDC, Iran Human Rights Documentation Center, *No Safe Haven: Iran's Global Assassination Campaign* (New Haven, CT: May 2008), 4.4 Dr. Abdol-Rahman Ghassemlou, citing Peter Pilz, *Eskorte nach Teheran*.

2. Ibid., quoting Pilz, *Eskorte nach Teheran*.

3. Marc Kravetz, "Téhéran-Vienne: Récit d'un crime," *Libération*, August 7, 1989.

4. Ghassemlou also had an Iraqi passport, which he used at times as well—an interesting detail that shows how he operated. In 1987 I was surprised to see him traveling to Spain with an Iraqi passport. When I asked him about it he told me that the party had people who could get them Iranian passports, but depending on where he was going, he used one or the other. Abdul Rahman Ghassemlou, personal communication to the author, Madrid, 1987.

5. Azad, personal communication to the author, June 21, 2016.

6. The outline that follows, except where otherwise noted, is from the contemporaneous account by French journalist Marc Kravetz, "Récit d'un crime."

7. John Bulloch and Harvey Morris, *No Friends but the Mountains: The Tragic History of the Kurds* (New York: Oxford University Press, 1992), 192.

8. The Islamic Revolutionary Guard Corps (*Sepah-e Pasdaran-e Enghelab-e Eslami*) is a para-military force created by Khomeini upon his return to Iran from exile in Paris in February 1979. *Sepah* designates a militant organized group or army. Its members were known as *pasdaran*—"guardian, protector" in Farsi. They were responsible for internal security, totally loyal to the Ayatollah and under his direct orders. Khomeini ordered his followers to "form an army under the name *Sepah-e Enghelab* made up of responsible people who believed in the revolution in order to protect the bloody achievements of the revolution." IHRDC, *Haunted Memories: The Islamic Republic's Executions of Kurds in 1979* (New Haven, CT: 2011), 3. After the February 1979 Islamic Revolution, https://iranhrdc.org/haunted-memories-the-islamic-republics-executions-of-kurds-in-1979/ (accessed September 23, 2018).

9. *Bulletin de liaison et d'information*, Institut Kurde de Paris, July–August 1989.

10. Bulloch and Morris, *No Friends but the Mountains*, 192.

11. Lutz Bucklitsch, "July 13, 1989—Vienna assassination of Iranian politicians: Mohamed Ahmadinejad suspected," in https://fluechtlingshilfeiranev2010.wordpress.com/2012/01/28/13-juli-1989-wiener-attentat-auf-iranischen-kurden-politiker-ver-dachtigt-mohamed-ahmadinejad/ (accessed December 23, 2018); and INU staff, "Rouhani and the assassination of Iranian Kurdish leader in Vienna in 1989," Iran News Update, March 28, 2016 (accessed December 23, 2018).

12. IHRDC, *No Safe Haven*, 4.4 Dr. Abdol-Rahman Ghassemlou. As a source for this detail, the IHRDC report cites *"Angeklagt"* [Suspect], *News*, September 17, 1997 (accessed January 19, 2019).

13. IHRDC, *No Safe Haven*, 4.4 Dr. Abdol-Rahman Ghassemlou (accessed January 19, 2019).

14. According to Peter Heindl of the Austrian Ministry of the Interior, Sahrarudi was given a paraffin test which was negative; but it is not clear where or when the test was administered. This is another in an endless series of fragmentary details that isn't clearly attested. Kravetz, "Récit d'un crime."

15. "Dr. Ghassemlou, Twenty Years after the Assassination in Vienna: A Tale about the Power of Cowardice and the Weakness of Media Power," presentation by Austrian journalist Sissy Danninger during the international symposium "Hommage à Abdul Rahman Ghassemlou," Paris, July 17, 2009. Published online at http://www.kurdmedia.com/article.aspx?id=15870.

16. This document led the police to a salesman who identified Sahrarudi as having purchased the motorcycle. Seemingly just to compound confusion, Sahrarudi had used the pseudonym "Mostafa Mostafavi" for the transaction (IHRDC, *No Safe Haven*, 4.4. Dr. Abdol-Rahman Ghassemlou). At the same time, again according to Peter Pilz, the man known in Vienna as Hadji Mostafawi was using his true name, Mostafa Ajoudi, as a pseudonym (Ibid., n232).

17. The role of the motorcycle remains obscure. Early reports say that at one point that evening, Buzorguian was seen leaving the building on a motorcycle, only to return later on foot; IHRDC, *No Safe Haven*, 4.4 Dr Abdol-Rahman Ghassemlou, citing *Eskorte nach Teheran* (accessed January 19, 2019).

18. Dr. Said: Sadegh Sharafkandi, a member of the PDKI political bureau, became secretary-general of the party after Ghassemlou's murder. Like many members of the party who needed to maintain public anonymity to protect their families living in Iran, he was known by a pseudonym—in his case, "Dr. Said."

19. Halabja: the Iraqi Kurdish village decimated by a poison-gas attack ordered by Saddam Hussein in 1988. Five thousand innocent men, women, and children lost their lives in this chemical bombing.

20. Abdullah Hassanzadeh, interview with the author, Koya Sanjak, Iraqi Kurdistan, July 2009.

21. Kravetz, "Récit d'un crime."

22. Agence France-Presse, Paris, July 15, 1989.

23. MEK, with a mix of Islam and Marxism, had a big following among students and progressive groups. Ervand Abrahamian, *Radical Islam: The Iranian Mojahedin*, 186–224, as quoted in Ray Takeyh, *Guardians of the Revolution: Iran and the World in the Age of the Ayatollahs* (New York: Oxford University Press, 2009), 23.

24. Jalal Talabani, interview with the author, Paris, 1991. French journalist Marc Kravetz, reporting at the time of the crime and its aftermath, soon came to the conclusion that it was Jafari Sahrarudi, as one of Rafsanjani's men, who probably planned the negotiation in which Hadji Mostafawi would be the assassin with the help of Buzorguian and a fourth man, Mohamed Magaby, also known as Mazafar. Kravetz, "Récit d'un crime."

    Two years later, Talabani stated that he had been deceived: "I was given information that led me to that conclusion. They told me the murder had been done by the Mujahedin and the Iraqis and perhaps by the Iranian hard-liners who did not want the negotiations to be successful." Jalal Talabani, interview with the author, Paris, 1991.

25. Agence France-Presse, Vienna, July 19, 1989.

26. Kravetz, "Récit d'un crime."

27. Ibid.

28. IHRDC, *No Safe Haven*, 4.4 Dr Abdol-Rahman Ghassemlou, citing *Eskorte nach Teheran* (accessed January 19, 2019). Here again, details are unclear or, in part, conflicting. According to journalist Marc Kravetz, there were actually two axes of gunfire: one from the chair where it was said that Sahrarudi was sitting, and one from the door as well; Kravetz, "Récit d'un crime." Every scrap of information that emerges, even now, over twenty years later, seems to generate at least as many questions as it settles.

29. Thomas Sancton, Nomi Morris, Elaine Shannon, and Kenneth R. Timmerman, "The Tehran Connection," *Time* magazine, March 21, 1994, http://www.time.com/time/magazine/article/0,9171,980361,00.html#ixzz2QBiQeiPu (accessed April 2, 2013).

30. Noghrehkar Shirazi, the Islamic Republic's ambassador in Vienna, put tremendous effort into the release and return of Sahrarudi and Buzorguian. IHRDC, *No Safe Haven*, 4.4 Dr Abdol-Rahman Ghassemlou, citing *Eskorte nach Teheran* (accessed January 19, 2019).

31. Austrian police reportedly had photographs showing Mostafawi in the Iranian embassy. Jonathan Randal, *The Washington Post*, August 2, 1989.

32. Four months later, in November 1989, "the Austrian state prosecutor issued arrest warrants for Sahraroudi, Bozorgian and Moustafavi. Police made a show of cordoning off the Iranian embassy in Vienna on the theory that Bozorgian might still be holed up there, but the cordon was quietly withdrawn a few weeks later. In January 1992, Austrian authorities sent a 16-page inquiry to Tehran, seeking information on the case. The Iranians have never replied, but that has not stopped Austria from maintaining cordial diplomatic relations and signing commercial contracts with the mullahs." Sancton et al., "The Tehran Connection."

33. Agence France-Presse, Tehran, July 19, 1989.

34. Hasan Ayoubzadeh, personal communication to the author, May 3, 2015. Ayoubzadeh, an attorney, was a member of the PDKI's editorial board and the PDKI radio until the end of 1988, when he left the party.

35. Much later, an Austrian judicial reform replaced the investigating judge in his role with a prosecutor attorney. Sissy Danninger, personal communication, April 4, 2013.

36. Bulloch and Morris, *No Friends but the Mountains*, 195.

37. Kravetz, "Récit d'un crime."

38. Ibid.

39. "From a well-informed source, we know that the Austrian Ministry of Foreign Affairs was bombarded with telegrams from Tehran, threatening to kidnap Austrian nationals as well as employ other forms of terrorism." *Bulletin de liaison et d'information*, Institut Kurde de Paris, July–August 1989.

40. Kravetz, "Récit d'un crime."

41. According to French journalist Marc Kravetz, Mohamed Magaby, also known as Mozafar, was the fourth man involved in the murder—or perhaps the driver of the motorcycle. Kravetz, "Récit d'un crime." He had been interrogated by the police and held for forty-eight hours before being put on the flight to Tehran. Bulloch and Morris, *No Friends but the Mountains*, 196.

PART II

GOD'S REVOLUTION

· 1 ·

MOFSED-E-FILARZ

ə

One thousand friends are not enough;
one enemy is too much.

—Kurdish proverb

It was ten years before, on the evening of August 18, 1979, that Khomeini had condemned Abdul Rahman Ghassemlou to death. Six months had passed since the victory over the old regime, and power was in the hands of the elderly cleric with almost no opposition. But in the northwestern cities and rural areas of Kurdistan, blood was flowing without mercy. The Ayatollah's revolutionary fury was engulfing the Kurds.

That August evening in 1979, Ghassemlou was waiting in a friend's house in Mahabad[1] for his party's decision about whether or not he should attend the sessions of the Constitutional Council of Experts,[2] also known as the Assembly of Experts for the Constitution, in Tehran. He had been elected a member of the council just a few days earlier by a substantial popular vote.

Not only had he obtained a clear majority of the vote, but he was also one of the only two secularists elected to that body, created to draft the constitution for the new Islamic Republic. And in contrast even with his fellow secularist, Ghassemlou was the only elected representative who did not want an Islamic republic. Clerics and other religious fundamentalists occupied the majority of the seats. And while Ghassemlou was poring through the pages of the Qur'an searching for a scriptural explanation to the Ayatollah's intolerance, his own party's central committee decided that he should not attend.[3]

At 8:00 p.m., he put down the book to listen to the news on television. Khomeini appeared on the screen. He was inaugurating the sessions of the Assembly of Experts for the Constitution.

The assembly, or council, was formed by venerable members of the *ulama*, religious legal scholars whose specialty was exegesis of the Qur'an and Islamic law; their grave faces and turbaned heads appeared, row upon row, in the scanning eye of the television cameras. They were regarded as wise men, honed by the silence of prayer, some hardened by prison and exile, and it was their time to rule. Accustomed to the subtle power that a cleric has over the faithful, these men were now consumed by political ambition. They were going to install the kingdom of Allah on earth.

What Ghassemlou remembered of that evening, looking back, was Khomeini speaking to the assembly in a soft, monotonous voice, like a whisper, the tone he used in his moments of fury. Just days before in Kurdistan, despite their smaller showing of men and arms, Kurds had repelled attacks by Iranian forces attempting to reoccupy cities that had been under de facto Kurdish control since the beginning of the revolution. In a village near the city of Paveh, Kurds had enacted a nonviolent sit-in in defense of their existing autonomy, demanding "local control over security and governance."[4] Iranian forces attacked the demonstrators and clashes ensued between Kurds and the IRGC, the Revolutionary Guards.[5] On August 16, after fierce combat with government forces, Kurds had taken back control in Paveh. They had defeated the forces of the central power, and Khomeini felt defied.

On that day Khomeini, enraged, had threatened the officers of the army with dire punishment for their ignominious defeat and declared himself commander-in-chief of the armed forces. He was ready to personally lead operations against the rebels. Who dared to defy the Islamic power, and the wielder of that power? Who dared to defy him who had brought down a formidable regime and sought to bring the true faith back to the Islamic world?

Now, this evening, looking out at the silent ulama, he said, "The Kurdistan Democratic Party is a subversive group, a corrupt group. We cannot allow them to continue to act as they wish."[6]

With no acknowledgment of the fact of the Iranian attack on a peaceful demonstration that had sparked the Kurdish defense, he went on: "They accuse us of committing actions like those actions *they* did yesterday and a few days ago. . . .

"They create such anarchy, and they blame others," Khomeini continued. "They are subversives, saboteurs. . . . They are just a handful of traitors and hypocrites."

Without raising his voice, his eyes sweeping the room, he said in a steely tone: "And Ezzedin and Ghassemlou—who is not here among you—are corrupt."

No one moved. But the contained fury of the cleric concentrated in his dark eyes fixed intently on the assembly.

The next words Ghassemlou remembered hearing—though they do not appear in any transcript of the speech or media report—shocked him to the core: "If that *mofsed-e-filarz* had come today, I would have had him executed."

Mofsed-e-filarz—corrupter of the earth![7] Terrible words in the mouth of an imam, the highest religious leader. The very label with which the Ayatollah had branded Ghassemlou and Ezzedin—*corrupt*—carried the threat of death. In Ghassemlou's mind, he had just been excommunicated in front of the whole world. He had been exiled from the world of the just. From now on, he was sure, he would be a fugitive exposed to the saintly fury of any faithful believer.

The party was cursed, and Khomeini had expelled Ghassemlou from the Assembly of Experts.[8]

Sitting in front of the television in Mahabad, Ghassemlou was convinced he was listening to his death sentence. The Shah's secret police had mal-treated him, sent him into exile and stripped him of his passport. Even France had forced him to leave the country under pressure from the Shah. The Iraqi regime had expelled him. The Czechoslovakian Communists had expelled him from Prague. But until now, no one had sentenced him to death. That night, Khomeini became his mortal enemy.

The phone began to ring off the hook. People were calling from cities all across the country. Sadegh Sharafkandi called from Tehran, where he was working clandestinely for the party. Everyone in PDKI leadership was advising Ghassemlou not to come to Tehran.

His friend Jalal Talabani was among those who said they had warned him. "I told him not to go to Tehran," Talabani recalled. "I was coming back from Montazeri's house.[9] There people were talking a lot, and they were comment-ing upon what we had just seen. They didn't know who I was. When I returned to Sardasht I ran into Hassan Restegar,[10] and I told him to go to Mahabad and warn Dr. Ghassemlou not to travel to Tehran. I sent him a letter, and when he got it, he decided not to go. 'I saved your life,' I used to joke with him."[11]

There remains some mystery here: if no transcript documents the mor-tal threat Ghassemlou—and, apparently, the many friends who called him—remembered so vividly, where did the alarm signal come from?

The statements from Khomeini that Ghassemlou recalled hearing that evening may in fact have been made—though made the previous evening, and not in front of cameras in a public setting. In June 1989, speaking with journalist Enayat Fani for a documentary a month before his assassination,

Ghassemlou would share a slightly different narrative of the sequence of events. "When I was elected as the only nonreligious member of the Assembly of Experts, the night before I was to go to Tehran [the night before the opening of the assembly], Khomeini called together all the members of the assembly and spoke against me. He denounced me as the Enemy of God, and you know that the penalty for this in their system is execution. And so I did not go to Tehran."[12] Ghassemlou may well have heard the details of this denunciation from associates who attended that meeting, or who had spoken directly with individuals who had been present.

It is also worth noting, however, that Ghassemlou's honed ability to read between the lines—or, in this case, to *hear* between the lines—would have alerted him to the meaning embedded in Khomeini's statement in the public broadcast. In labeling Ghassemlou as corrupt, the Ayatollah, without saying so explicitly, had characterized Ghassemlou as culpable of actions punishable by death. To Ghassemlou, and likely to other concerned listeners, the intention would have been clear.

There were reasons why the Ayatollah wanted Ghassemlou's death. Ghassemlou was no longer the unknown politician who had visited Khomeini in Neauphle-le-Château a year before, when they were both living as exiles in France. Now Ghassemlou was the leader of a party whose influence was growing, and he had received a significant fraction of votes in Kurdistan for a seat on the Assembly of Experts. He had thousands of peshmerga ready for armed resistance; and much of Iranian Kurdistan, prior to the party's retreat to the mountains in 1983, remained under PDKI control. Above all, Ghassemlou was determined to procure autonomy for Kurdistan from the central power and promote democracy for Iran at large—an autonomy that Khomeini had never agreed to grant. Nor did Khomeini endorse democracy, which he condemned as a Western phenomenon and antithetical to the theocratic state he wanted.

They were two incompatible beings: Ruhollah Musavi Khomeini, a self-righteous fundamentalist Islamic cleric; and Abdul Rahman Ghassemlou, an economist, a secular intellectual with strong democratic and socialist inclinations who genuinely wished to gain self-determination for Iranian Kurds and promote democratic principles in Iran. The Kurd was a man who loved life, with a profound interest in literature and philosophy, a refined taste for good wine and the company of people in a diversity of social settings, charming to all, especially with women. In contrast, Khomeini had been a fundamentalist clergyman, dedicated to theology for nearly six decades. And he extolled martyrdom publicly as a revolutionary virtue to advance the cause of Islam.

Physically vigorous and with a fine sense of humor, Ghassemlou had studied in postwar Paris and at the University of Prague during the Stalin era. He had unconditionally supported the proletarian revolution during his student years—yet in the end he'd become disillusioned by Soviet brutality.

Khomeini, born at the beginning of the twentieth century, was poor in health. He had written abstruse works on theology. He was a purist who would wake up, according to strict Muslim rule, before dawn for his prayers, and then have a short nap until breakfast. He would eat bread and honey and fruit juice at 11:00 a.m., and rice and roasted meat at midday. The only other things he ate were mashed potatoes, steamed vegetables, and yoghurt. He ate with a spoon; he never used a fork or a knife. He never drank alcohol or smoked. And they say he rarely spoke on the telephone. He would lie down for a short nap after lunch and then, after an evening of study, prayer, and a walk to the mosque, not go to bed until after midnight.[13]

With all their differences, Ghassemlou and Khomeini shared a history. Ghassemlou, toward the end of 1978, was a forty-eight-year-old intellectual and the secretary-general of the Democratic Party of Iranian Kurdistan, a once-decimated party whose resurgence was drawing thousands of new members. He was known in some Parisian circles but not in Iran. His exile had begun twenty years before, when during the 1950s the PDKI was almost annihilated by the Shah's army and the SAVAK,[14] the Shah's dreaded secret police; most of the surviving party leaders had fled to Iraq and then many moved on to exile in Europe.[15] Still, the party had a certain prestige inherited from the short-lived era of the Republic of Kurdistan, proclaimed by Qazi Mohammad, the first leader of PDKI, in 1946.

Ghassemlou was conscious of the impending fall of the Shah and decided to visit Khomeini before returning to Iran. Since Khomeini's arrival in France in October 1978, the small house of the émigré cleric in Neauphle-le-Château, a few kilometers to the west of Paris, had become a center for political exiles and their conspiracy against the Shah.

Ghassemlou was one of the many who came to visit him in the enormous reception tent erected in front of Khomeini's house in Neauphle-le-Château, where Iranian visitors to the Imam might total hundreds per day.[16] When Khomeini was informed by one of his aides that Ghassemlou wanted to meet him, the Imam[17] exclaimed, "Who allowed him in? I have nothing to discuss with that man."[18] Ghassemlou returned again a few days later, with the same result.

Everything separated them except the fact that they were both political exiles and that both opposed Reza Pahlavi's regime.

"I knew him as a religious Shi'ite leader, and I had read his books," Ghassemlou later said of Khomeini. "He did not want to meet alone with me. I listened to him and already understood what he wanted to do. I knew he was a reactionary and that his political proposal was medieval for Iran. But I never imagined that he could be so bloodthirsty."[19]

Even so, Ghassemlou gave Khomeini his support, as everyone did. Ibrahim Auyyar, an Iraqi Communist, remembered that in 1978 Ghassemlou signed documents endorsing Khomeini. When Auyyar asked Ghassemlou why he was doing this, Ghassemlou replied, "Khomeini has sworn that he will not give up the fight before he overthrows the Shah." Auyyar recalled, "So many people had photos of the Imam, and we knew who he was. But Ghassemlou insisted that Khomeini's oath was genuine. He felt that lending him support was not a mistake. The opposition needed a symbol."[20]

While the journalists and the crowds swarming before the Ayatollah's house did not notice Ghassemlou, the Western press was watching every gesture that Khomeini made. So were the interested agents of the intelligence services.

The European Left and the progressive movement, particularly in France, had converted the Ayatollah into a mythic revolutionary of the Third World. Toward the end of the seventies, a certain sector of the European Left adored Ayatollah Khomeini. The cleric had ignored the fads of what he considered the corrupted and superficial West. Within days of his arrival in France, he was being lionized in the French media with imagery evocative of Mahatma Gandhi, depicting him as "a deeply religious man who abstained from worldly things," a model of modesty in contrast to the Shah's extravagance.[21] In the American and British spheres of influence, the Western press had consistently presented the Shah as a friend and modernizer; but with France's shifting international political alignments, Khomeini was now gaining support in the West against "the dictator."[22]

Support came from many directions; visitors to Khomeini's compound outside Paris included "like-minded revolutionaries" from among the PLO and a representative of Qaddafi's regime in Libya. The thousands of Iranians who visited Khomeini[23] over his four-month stay in France contributed donations totaling more than 20 million pounds, including significant amounts in untraceable cash.[24] Allegations of the Ayatollah's receipt of financial support from sources as diverse as the PLO, Iranian-American students, the Iranian bazaar, and even the CIA abound to this day: "Khomeini," according to the general consensus, "was tendered arms and money in support of the revolution."[25]

While support from Iranian and Middle Eastern sources seemed only to be expected, France's special attitude of accommodation toward Khomeini was more mystifying. The French *gendarmerie* had granted permits to Khomeini's bodyguards for weapons, including a pair of machine guns.[26] The local post office put at his disposal two telex lines, six phone lines, and an audio recording studio. Thousands of tapes of Khomeini's vitriolic daily interviews and fulminations against the Shah were immediately dispatched to Tehran, inciting Iranians to revolt. The Shah's close palace circle was stupefied at the French government's permissiveness, appalled that France was "allowing the exiled cleric to incite a rebellion, contrary to the international rules governing political refugees."[27]

France's wooing of Khomeini may have had roots in its own historical hegemonic strivings as well as economic self-interest. In the wake of the 1967 Six-Day War, while Britain and America backed Israel, de Gaulle had cultivated Arab countries. Beyond "boosting trade ties with oil-rich nations," the larger intent seems to have been "extending French influence in an area which had been dominated by the 'Anglo-Saxons.' . . . The belief that diplomacy can work wonders without the threat of force, and a perennial reluctance to follow the Anglo-Saxons' lead, [were] probably as strong as any perceived economic interest" as a motivating force.[28] And now, whether sparked by French intelligence or by the French Foreign Ministry, the conviction was growing of Khomeini's significance as Iran's future leader.[29] The French were convinced that once in power Khomeini "would offer them a golden opportunity in Iran."[30]

Finally, broader support was garnered in response to Khomeini's brilliant exploitation of the media through a duplicitous appeal to cherished Western ideologies. In his more than one hundred interviews and broadcasts,[31] Khomeini had given "assurances that under him Iran would be a free society, and he hinted at democracy, equality and rights, even for women, though naturally qualified in accordance with Islam."[32]

Khomeini was masterful in manipulating and deceiving Westerners by not revealing his "radical views on social and legal issues" and telling them what they wanted to hear. In interview after interview with the international press, he presented himself as a moderate man who wanted to end the Shah's "tyranny and corruption,"[33] but who had no desire to pursue personal power for himself.[34]

A recitation of Khomeini's statements to the press reads like a litany. To *The Guardian*, he said: "I don't want to have the power or the government in my hand; I am not interested in personal power" (Paris, November 16, 1978). In an interview for Austrian TV, he said, "I don't want to be the leader of the Islamic Republic. . . . I only guide the people in selecting the system" (Paris, November 16, 1978). To *Le Journal*, he said: "Personally, I can't accept any special role or responsibility" (Paris, November 28, 1978). To *Le Monde*: "I will not become a president nor accept any other leadership role. Just like before, I limit my activities only to guiding and directing the people" (Paris, January 9, 1979). And to Reuters, for international distribution: "In Islamic Iran the clergy themselves will not govern, but only observe and support the government's leaders. The government of the country at all levels will be observed, evaluated, and publicly criticized" (Paris, October 26, 1978).

In this, Khomeini was using "all the traditional techniques of Shi'ite leadership," above all employing *khod'eh*, "tricking one's enemy into a misjudgment of one's true position"—and its closely parallel practice, *taqiyya*, "concealment"—not by telling direct lies, but by voicing, or even barely implying, half-truths.[35]

One telling example is related by French journalist Paul Balta, whom Khomeini invited to cover his stay in France. A concern voiced in the media on which Khomeini had repeatedly issued statements reassuring to Western sensibilities had been the status of women. On this question, Khomeini had told German reporters: "These words that you have heard regarding women in the future Islamic government are all hostile propaganda. In the Islamic Republic women have complete freedom, in their education, in everything that they do, just as men are free in everything" (Paris, November 12, 1978). To the *Guardian*, he had repeated, "Women are free in the Islamic Republic in the selection of their activities and their future and their clothing" (Paris, November 6, 1978).[36] Now, in a January 1979 interview for *Le Monde* in France, Balta asked Khomeini about his vision for the role of women in Iran once he'd accomplished his revolution. The Ayatollah responded, "Our women fight like lions. They deserve our admiration. In the Islamic state they will have the status they deserve."

Mere weeks later, back in Qom, Khomeini "proclaimed compulsory wearing" of the *chador*. Balta, astonished, asked Khomeini about the chador and the Ayatollah replied, "I told you they deserve our admiration. It is always the case, but I added as in the Islamic state, they will have the status that they deserve."[37]

About such disingenuous statements, Banisadr quoted Khomeini as saying: "In Paris, I found it opportune to say what I said. In Iran, I find it opportune to deny it, and I deny it."[38] Some years later, Khomeini acknowledged that he had used khod'eh "in order to trick 'the enemies of Islam.'"[39] He'd done this by qualifying every assurance with phrases such as "in accordance with Islam" or "on the basis of the Qur'an."[40]

"Iran's future," one commentator summed up, "was depicted by almost every faction as one of democratic development and pluralistic politics. Khomeini actively encouraged such illusions in accordance with another Shi'ite tactic—that of *tanfih*, which means taking the sting out of one's potential rivals or enemies. The tactic of *taqieh*—which means misleading everyone about one's true beliefs in a hostile environment—was also used by Khomeini and his adjutants *inside* Iran."[41] The truth is that Khomeini deceived Iranians and foreigners alike by his skillful use of time-honored techniques, honed through bitter centuries of Shi'ite experience in the politics of survival.[42] But in modern times, Khomeini and his successors have used it to advance the hegemonic plans of the Islamic Republic in the Middle East.

&

Despised initially because of his clerical stance, Khomeini was destined to change Iranian history. He was a man of God and was beginning to concern the primary world powers. Until now ignored by a Eurocentric vision that blinded Westerners to an understanding of the Muslim universe, Khomeini was steadily becoming a more prominent personality.

Khomeini had lived for many years in silence—first in his exile in Iraq and now in the suburbs of Paris. Now his voice could be heard all over the world.

The revolution of 1979 caught the West by surprise—but not the Ayatollah himself.

Notes

1. Mahabad, while not the administrative capital of Iranian Kurdistan, was and is the symbolic center of its political life.
2. *Majles-e Khebregan-e Rahbari* or *Majles-e Khobregan*, sometimes translated as "Constitutional Council of Experts," is also translated as "Assembly of Experts for the Constitution." Both designations are encountered in the media, "Assembly of Experts" somewhat more commonly.

3. According to Abdullah Hassanzadeh, a long-time former member of PDKI leadership and a Ghassemlou confidant, Ghassemlou wanted to attend the sessions. Because he had been legitimately elected, he reasoned, the Iranian authorities would not dare to take any action against him. The party's political bureau believed it was too dangerous, however, and dissuaded Ghassemlou from attending. Abdullah Hassanzadeh, interview with the author, Koya Sanjak, Iraqi Kurdistan, July 2009.

4. IHRDC, *Haunted Memories: The Islamic Republic's Executions of Kurds in 1979* (New Haven, CT: 2011), https://iranhrdc.org/english/publications/reports/3508-haunted-memories-the-islamic-republics-executions-of-kurds-in-1979.html, 4. Executions and Battles Continue, https://iranhrdc.org/haunted-memories-the-islamic-republics-executions-of-kurds-in-1979/ (accessed January 6, 2019).

5. The IRGC, Islamic Revolutionary Guard Corps, was responsible to local revolutionary committees to protect the country's Islamic revolution; see "Chronology," *Middle East Journal*, September 1979, 357, and IHRDC, *Haunted Memories*, 3. After the February Islamic Revolution (accessed January 6, 2019). The new Islamic constitution would provide that in addition to a regular military force responsible for the defense of Iran's borders and internal security, a separate force comprised of Revolutionary Guards, pasdaran, would take charge of protecting the Islamic system. BBC, update October 9, 2009, http://news.bbc.co.uk/2/hi/middle_east/7064353.stm (accessed November 5, 2012). See also Shaul Bakhash, *The Reign of the Ayatollahs: Iran and the Islamic Revolution* (New York: Basic Books, Inc., 1984), 63.

6. Khomeini's address to the representatives of the Assembly of Experts at the city of Qom on Saturday, August 18, 1979 (28 Merdad, 1358 in the Muslim calendar), as reported in the Iranian daily *Kayhan* on August 19, 1979. Translation Salah Piroty.

7. *Mofsed fel-arz*, colloquial Arabic; *mofsed-e-filarz*, Farsi; *mufsid fil-ard*, classical Arabic, literally, "corrupter of the earth," an offense or status deemed punishable by death.

   After the revolution the regime had adjusted the civil code. *Mofsed fel-arz*, the spreading of corruption or corrupting conditions, expanded to embrace actions ranging from drug dealing or sexual offenses to atheism or divergence from the revolutionary regime. This offense was and continues to be used by the Islamic regime to incarcerate and execute activists and political opposition.

   For *mofsed fel-arz* as applied to the treatment of minorities like the Baha'i community in Iran, see Iran Press Watch, http://www.iranpresswatch.org/post/2737: "While the term previously referred to traditional Islamic ideas relating to sin, Ayatollah Khomeini transformed it into a tool to be wielded by the Islamic state against its perceived enemies." Iran Press Watch, citing Reza Afshari, *Human Rights in Iran: The Abuse of Cultural Relativism* (Philadelphia: University of Pennsylvania Press, 2001), 33.

8. This episode was one that Ghassemlou would recall with all his dramatic capacity—not devoid of humor—when speaking of his tumultuous past. In his last years, Ghassemlou would reminisce about many of his memories to friends, especially the journalist Jonathan Randal, this author, and members of his party.

9. Montazeri, once Khomeini's designated successor, fell out with Khomeini in 1989 over human-rights abuses and government corruption. He would be subjected to house arrest from 1997 to 2003, and released only for government fear of public outrage. His funeral,

following his death in December 2009, became the occasion for demonstrations against the Iranian regime.

10. Hassan Restegar, an influential member within the PDKI, left the party in March 1988, following the PDKI's Eighth Congress (January 18, 1988) and political disagreements with Ghassemlou and the majority within the party. He collaborated in founding the splinter group KDPI–RL, the Kurdistan Democratic Party of Iran–Revolutionary Leadership, established March 21. Almost five hundred members left the PDKI to join the new party. Nearly a decade later, on January 8, 1997, the KDPI–RL would rejoin the PDKI. Restegar would leave once again in December 2006 when the party would split once more.

11. Jalal Talabani, interview with the author, Paris, 1991. This was the sequence of events as Talabani recalled them.

12. Abdul Rahman Ghassemlou, interview by Enayat Fani, June 1989; translation Beyan Farshi and Esmail Ebrahimi. Part of this interview was used in BBC Channel 4 TV's documentary "Iran: the Other Story." An extended version of the interview was broadcast on BBC Persian TV in July 2014; See YouTube, "Abdul-Rahman Ghassemlou, BBC Persian," posted July 16, 2014, https://www.youtube.com/watch?v=SGsfvkcMn8U; (accessed February 20, 2017).

13. See "A Day in the Life of Imam Khomeini," YouTube, http://www.youtube.com/watch?v=Aai5Wwm7idQ, uploaded December 9, 2009 (accessed July 10, 2013).

14. For further details on SAVAK, its development and activities, see Part Two, Chapter II, "Shah *Raft*! Shah *Raft*!"

15. See Martin van Bruinessen, "Major Kurdish Organizations in Iran," *MERIP Reports* 141, Vol. 16 (July/August 1986).

16. Amir Taheri, *The Spirit of Allah: Khomeini and the Islamic Revolution* (Bethesda, MD: Adler & Adler, 1986), 228. Taheri's statement that visitors totaled as much as one thousand per day may reflect overestimated reports.

17. When Khomeini returned to Iran he was greeted as "the Imam." In Arabic the term *imam* means a leader or prayer leader. In Shi'ite Iran the title was reserved for the twelve infallible leaders of the early Shi'a. By encouraging its use, Khomeini's supporters exploited popular religious feelings and implied that Khomeini was the long-awaited Hidden Imam. Baqer Moin, *Khomeini: Life of the Ayatollah* (New York: Thomas Dunne Books, 2000), 201.

18. Hélène Krulich, *Une Européenne au pays des Kurdes* (Paris: Éditions Karthala, 2011), 209.

19. Abdul Rahman Ghassemlou, interview with Jonathan Randal, Paris, 1986. Unless otherwise cited, further statements from Ghassemlou in this chapter are from this interview.

20. Ibrahim Auyyar, interview with the author, Paris, 1991.

21. Mike Evans, *Jimmy Carter: The Liberal Left and World Chaos* (Phoenix, AZ: Time Worthy Books, 2009), 226. The Ayatollah attracted favorable reviews in the American press as well; Taheri notes, "Andrew Young, then U.S. ambassador to the United Nations and a close friend and adviser of President Carter, described Khomeini as a 'twentieth-century saint.'" Taheri, *The Spirit of Allah*, 229.

22. Evans, *Jimmy Carter*, 232.

23. Taheri, *The Spirit of Allah*, 228, reports a total of one hundred thousand visitors.

24. David Pryce-Jones, *Betrayal: France, the Arabs, and the Jews* (New York: Encounter Books, 2006), 125.

25. Evans, *Jimmy Carter*, 232. Pryce-Jones adds that the Palestinians in particular provided arms. Pryce-Jones, *Betrayal*, 126.

26. Pryce-Jones, *Betrayal*, 125–26.

27. Ibid., 126, citing Fereydoun Hoveyda, brother of the Shah's prime minister Amir Abbas Hoveyda.

28. See Henri Astier, "Iraq—the French Connection," *Decision Makers and Diplomacy*, BBC, February 23, 1998, http://news.bbc.co.uk/2/hi/events/crisis_in_the_gulf/decision_makers_and_diplomacy/58568.stm (accessed July 10, 2013).

29. Pryce-Jones, *Betrayal*, 124.

30. Taheri, *The Spirit of Allah*, 228.

31. Ibid.

32. Pryce-Jones, *Betrayal*, 125; see also Iran Heritage, http://www.iran-heritage.org/interest-groups/government-article2.htm. Taheri adds that Khomeini also "went out of his way to reassure the Iranian middle class that the fall of the Shah would not change the country's social and economic system and that every 'rightful privilege' would be retained. He also allayed the West's fear that an 'Islamic' government might threaten the flow of oil and trade in the Persian Gulf." Taheri, *The Spirit of Allah*, 228.

33. Ibid.

34. *The Guardian*, Paris, November 16, 1978; Austrian television interview, Paris, November 16, 1978; *Le Journal*, Paris, November 28, 1978; *Le Monde*, Paris, January 9, 1979; Reuters, Paris, October 26, 1978.

35. Taheri, *The Spirit of Allah*, 229.

36. The Iranian: Khomeini before and after revolution: Dr Jalal Matini, "Democracy? I meant theocracy—the most truthful individual in recent history," August 5, 2003, http://iranian.com/Opinion/2003/August/Khomeini/.

37. Evans, *Jimmy Carter*, 227–28; Paul Balta, "La république islamique," *Le monde de Clio*, http://www.clio.fr/BIBLIOTHEQUE/la_republique_islamique_diran.asp (accessed July 25, 2013).

38. Pryce-Jones, *Betrayal*, 127.

39. Taheri, *The Spirit of Allah*, 229.

40. Ibid., 229, 230.

41. Ibid., 230; emphasis added.

42. Taheri, *The Spirit of Allah*, 228–31, gives an expanded discussion of the use of tactics by Khomeini and his supporters. Extended commentary and speculations on Khomeini's rise and sources of support in France are further detailed by Paul Balta, Amir Taheri, and David Pryce-Jones. In a review of Pryce-Jones' *Betrayal* in *Literary Review*, Daniel Johnson sums up: ". . . it was the French who enabled Ayatollah Khomeini to launch his Islamic revolution from a suburb of Paris." Daniel Johnson, "J'Accuse," *Literary Review*, http://www.literaryreview.co.uk/johnson_12_06.html (accessed July 29, 2013).

· 2 ·

SHAH *RAFT*! SHAH *RAFT*!

❧

In the face of the adverse political conditions, in 1978 the heads of the PDKI met in Iraqi Kurdistan to discuss the pros and cons of their return to Iran from exile. The move was dangerous and not advisable. The regime and SAVAK,[1] the secret police, were prowling like caged beasts.

Ghassemlou had summoned Sadegh Sharafkandi,[2] his PDKI colleague "Dr. Said," to Paris to study the situation. He thought Iran was entering a revolutionary stage and that all members and leaders of the party should return. Ghassemlou asked Sharafkandi: if he, Ghassemlou, were to return in a clandestine way, would they be able to work together for the party and be effective?

"I was worried about his personal security," Sharafkandi recalled. "I told him anybody else could return, but he could not."[3]

Nevertheless, Ghassemlou told Sharafkandi that if he returned, he would reenter the country under the alias of Jamil Sharifi, and he would inform Sharafkandi if he decided to do so.

The majority of the party's central committee did not concur with his determination to return. But without letting anyone know, Ghassemlou and other friends did come back.

Ghassemlou left Paris for his homeland on August 31, 1978.[4] He first went to Baghdad to resolve political issues.[5] There the party's central committee decided to create a new central committee called Zagros which would have full authority. The members of Zagros were to work in different parts of the country and Ghassemlou was designated to Tehran.[6]

By November the Zagros committee was preparing to return but the Iraqi government thwarted their plans; no one would be allowed to cross the Iraqi borders back into Iran.[7]

Nonetheless, the Zagros group came up with a plan. To trick the Iraqis, Ghassemlou would be the last person to leave, while the others would wait eight to nine days before departure.[8]

Ghassemlou entered Iran clandestinely on November 17, 1978, through Sune in the southern region of the Pishdar District of Iraqi Kurdistan.[9] He reached Mahabad the next night.[10] In the streets, filled with smoke and burning tires, there was an eerie and chaotic atmosphere. As throughout the rest of the country, in the cities of Kurdistan demonstrators were staging protests against the Shah.[11] And the crumbling of the Shah's administration, already underway, seemed to be opening a way for the reactivation of the party.[12]

Sharafkandi, who was a professor at the University of Tehran and not suspected by the SAVAK, had found out through some friends that Ghassemlou was back in Kurdistan. After five weeks in Mahabad, Ghassemlou's presence had become known; he had to hide.

"The SAVAK was very active," Sharafkandi recalled. "I traveled to Mahabad, brought Dr. Ghassemlou to Tehran, and hid him in my house. Nobody knew where he was. The SAVAK was looking for him in Mahabad. He was safe with me."[13]

Sharafkandi had known of him by reputation in the fifties when Ghassemlou was responsible for the underground party. They met for the first time in Paris in 1973, the year the party had reconstructed itself, celebrated its Third Congress, and written its program. Ghassemlou had gone to see Sharafkandi and given him documents that explained the principles of the PDKI. When Sharafkandi asked for time to study them, Ghassemlou responded that this was not necessary if he was in agreement with their main thrust. Once at work together inside the party, they could discuss the details. As a result of this encounter, Sharafkandi immediately became affiliated with the party.

They became friends and spent a lot of time together in Paris. In 1976, Sharafkandi returned to Tehran. The two men maintained ongoing contact between their respective cities through codes and underground communication.

Sharafkandi later shared: "It was nice working with Dr. Ghassemlou because you were always learning. But it was also hard because he demanded a lot. He worked hard, and he asked the same of his friends. He was a democrat and remained so until his murder. Even though we were good friends, we had heated discussions at every meeting. But afterward [after every debate], we forgot politics."

Back in Iran in 1978, Ghassemlou found that the party was much debilitated. Many of its members were in prison or in exile, and a considerable number had been executed. This tattered remnant, essentially the sole organ of political opposition in the region, banned as a party and operating clandestinely,[14] could muster scarcely one hundred and fifty militants. But by February 1979, the PDKI would have more than fifty thousand members.

First in Tehran, and then in Mahabad, Ghassemlou covertly began to organize the party, creating secret committees and political cells. It was necessary to set the ideological and practical foundation of the organization, reorient and retrain its cadres, multiply its militants, and incorporate young people. The Kurds had to prepare for the change of regime that was clearly approaching.

Ghassemlou met with his friend Jalal Talabani, leader of the Iraqi Kurdish PUK, who had been active in both Iraqi and Iranian Kurdistan. Very soon in the area that came to be known as the Valley of the Parties,[15] the mountainous region along the Iran-Iraq border that sheltered a number of leftist groups, Ghassemlou put forth a common program which ensured cooperation between the two Kurdish parties in Iran and Iraq. They agreed to help one another, but to never interfere in each other's affairs.[16]

The situation was different vis-à-vis the Democratic Party of Kurdistan in Iraq (also known as the KDP, not to be confused with Ghassemlou's PDKI) of General Mustafa Barzani. After the Algiers Accord of 1975 that had settled border disputes between Iran and Iraq, several hundred thousand of Barzani's followers had sought refuge in Iran. "Most were in heavily guarded camps, without jobs, living on near starvation rations and continually threatened with forcible return to Iraq or dispersion to remote areas of Iran"; Barzani himself was virtually under house arrest and cut off from his followers.[17] Soon after the Iranian revolution, Barzani's sons Masoud and Idris, the new leaders of the Iraqi KDP, established an alliance with Iran's new Islamic regime; Iran would become the rear base for the peshmerga of Barzani's KDP. According to journalist Chris Kutschera, the agreement concluded in May 1979 with Iranian minister of defense Mustafa Chamran achieved "immediate improvement of conditions for the Iraqi Kurdish refugees in Iran and especially financial aid and restitution of weapons confiscated by the Shah's army when [Barzani's] peshmerga had taken refuge in Iran after the debacle in 1975. In exchange for Iranian support, Barzani's KDP committed to 'clean' the Kurdish Iraqi movement of its leftist elements and to participate in policing operations against the Iranian PDK, Ghassemlou's PDKI."[18] The deterioration of relations between the Iranian and Iraqi Kurdish parties would play out later during ongoing confrontations between the PDKI and Iran's central government.[19]

☙

Reentering the Iranian arena, Ghassemlou was an unknown. He had been absent for twenty-one years. Despite his leadership position as the secretary-general of Iran's resurgent nationalist Kurdish party, his name meant little in the turbulent Iran to which he was returning.

Azad, as one of the young men who joined the movement, remembered that people knew Ghassemlou's brother, who was a physician and resembled him closely, but they did not know Abdul Rahman. Azad had heard his name and one day decided to go meet him.

"I had a critical attitude toward the PDKI," he recalled. "I did not believe in it because it had not been in the country. It was a paralyzed party."[20]

Until then, Azad had been politically active with the Communists from the Tudeh Party without being a member of it. The young Kurd was wondering what the place of his people would be in an Iranian Communist party.[21] The Tudeh was a hard-line small Communist party, typical of the times of Stalin: clinging to orthodoxy, loyal to Moscow, closed to local reality, heroic, sectarian, completely alien to nationalist aspirations, and foreign to Kurdish ideals.

Like the majority of young people, Azad had suffered the rigors of repression. He despised those who were now returning from Europe or the United States for their lack of knowledge about the realities of Iran.

In his first meeting with Ghassemlou, Azad expounded his Marxist-Leninist viewpoints in an impetuous way, filled with the intolerance of youth. Ghassemlou listened in silence, without interrupting him. Then Ghassemlou spoke, in simple words, as he always did, but his words showed a superior understanding. "Little by little," Azad said, "he convinced me."

Despite the years of absence, his European intellectual orientation, and the fact that he did not know how to put on a turban, Ghassemlou was profoundly Kurdish. He knew how to talk to people and how to convince them. He impressed them by the simplicity of his manner, his directness, and his knowledge. Young people, locked in by their dogmatism and schooled by the Tudeh, were dazzled by Ghassemlou. His message was clear: he favored an independent Kurdish party that asserted as essential the rights of the Kurdish people.

&

By Christmas Day 1978, while Khomeini was the center of the revolution in France and Ghassemlou was at work in Kurdistan reorganizing the party, the Shah was already a lame duck. The popular revolution was out in the streets, overwhelming a regime supported now only by the army, the SAVAK, and the Americans. The regime was being challenged by all sectors of society: the students, the powerful business interests of the *bazaaris*,[22] the clerics, elements of the middle class, and the ethnic minorities, including the Kurds.

While the radical Left was supporting armed conflict with the Shah's regime, from France Khomeini was opposing it and instead, as an alternative strategy, calling upon the Shah's soldiers to desert. "Leave in small numbers, singly or in twos and threes," he urged them. "You are the soldiers of God. Take your weapons with you, for they are God's weapons."[23]

In January 1979, antiaircraft battalions from the region of Mashhad deserted with all their weapons. Khomeini was inciting the tumult of the crowds, strikes, and all forms of protest, but not a confrontation with the military.

"Do not attack the army physically, in the breast, but through their heart," he said. "You must appeal to the soldiers' hearts even if they fire on you and kill you. Let them kill five thousand, ten thousand, twenty thousand; they are our brothers and we will welcome them. We will prove that blood is more powerful than the sword."[24]

Khomeini was appealing to the purist Shi'ite tradition. "It is sometimes said that the hero is the essence of history. But those who say it are wrong. It is the martyr who is the essence of history, the motivating spirit of history. So bare your breasts to the army, for the Shah is going to make use of the army and the army is going to obey him. . . . Your blood, and the love which you show them as you are dying, will convince them."[25]

On January 6, 1979, the Shah made a move to contain the wave of countrywide rebellion by appointing a moderate liberal opposition leader, Shapour Bakhtiar,[26] as prime minister, and prepared to abandon the country. Ghassemlou and his party received this news with a certain relief: a new freedom was being restored in the country. Ghassemlou's response, remembered a party colleague, was cogent: "The end of the tunnel is still unknown," said Ghassemlou, "so it is better to support Shapour Bakhtiar. His government can be supported. If he is not there [in office], we don't know who will replace him. At least we know him. And the revolution continues to deepen."[27]

"It's not that we were pro-*Bakhtiar*, per se," Ghassemlou later explained; "what we were *for* was the opposition. If we could have maintained that situation [the continued existence of a moderate liberal government] for several months, we and other organizations could have consolidated ourselves and Khomeini would not have seized power."[28]

Ghassemlou was convinced that with Khomeini, Iran would go from a dictatorship to a medieval regime. He had taken the Ayatollah very seriously; he had read Khomeini's books and tried to understand him. He was convinced that Khomeini would be a step backward. But the majority of Iranian leftist intellectuals, he thought, had not even read Khomeini's writings and did not understand who he was. Yet at the beginning Ghassemlou, like the majority of Iranians, supported Khomeini—for he symbolized the resistance against the Shah.

Ghassemlou used to say that Khomeini was intelligent, but you could not expect democratic gains from him. "Dr. Ghassemlou listened to all his [Khomeini's] discourses, even two or three times, with attention," said Sharafkandi. "For us, it was something amusing. We made fun of Khomeini because he was an ayatollah who spoke nonsense. But Kak Doctor would say: 'You have to listen to him to understand what's behind his words.' He considered Khomeini a politician." And what defines a politician is the concern for power.

Ghassemlou knew that Khomeini's power resided in the mosques. Throughout the country, a network of over a hundred thousand Shi'ite clerics formed a web linked to the landlords of the peasant areas, and to the powerful bazaar that contributed to the mosques' finances, as well as controlling commerce and a good part of the national economy.

Perhaps because of his understanding of Khomeini's unspoken intention to institute a medieval theocracy, Ghassemlou disapproved of the role that the Islamic clerics, the mullahs, were playing in the political life of Iran. Yet, even in a nation with eighty thousand mosques, Ghassemlou believed the clerics could still be prevented from gaining full control if all Iranian moderates could work together in a democratic manner.

Bakhtiar, for his part, even while an opposition leader, a liberal, and a nationalist, was not a friend of the Kurds. Very soon he made what Ghassemlou considered "chauvinist declarations" against the Kurds. "We were not then the party that we became afterward," Ghassemlou said later. "We got in contact with him and advised him not to keep making anti-Kurd declarations. We were ready to support him in maintaining democracy. Some individual members of the party's political bureau who later went over to the Tudeh accused me of being a partisan of Bakhtiar."[29]

Educated in France, as a young man Bakhtiar had been a leftist. While still a student, he supported the Republicans during the Spanish Civil War, then joined the French army and collaborated with the anti-Nazi resistance. Back in Iran after completing his studies, he was a supporter of the nationalist Mohammed Mossadegh[30] and served in his government, in regional offices of the Ministry of Labor. Following the CIA-supported coup[31] that restored the Shah to power in 1953, Bakhtiar's continued campaign for the restoration of democratic rights, his criticism of the Shah, and his prominence as a liberal in the National Front coalition earned him five years in prison.

But in the face of the rising tide of revolutionary fervor, the intolerance of the Shah's regime toward all forms of opposition could not be maintained. Recognition of the immediate need for some form of rapprochement with the Shah's adversaries could not be avoided. The inclusion in the government of moderate liberals like Bakhtiar and the National Front may have appeared as the only feasible option, a potentially manageable conciliation to avert impending disaster.

When the National Front, the coalition of which Bakhtiar's Iran Party was a member, refused the monarch's invitation to participate in a government of unity, the Shah offered the position of prime minister to Bakhtiar. On the Shah's part it seemed a last-minute gesture of concession to the forces of mounting opposition. Bakhtiar, anxious to avert the destruction he foresaw in the event of extremist revolution, accepted the appointment. The cost of his acceptance was high: expulsion from his own party.

Washington hastened to declare its willingness to support Bakhtiar. But it was too little, too late. Bakhtiar would find himself beset from all directions. The National Front accused him of having committed "treason to our cause." And Khomeini, from Paris, declared that to obey Bakhtiar would be "obeying Satan."[32]

☙

Contradiction defined and debilitated the government of Shapour Bakhtiar. The American ambassador, William H. Sullivan, compared him to a fig leaf,[33] insufficient to the task, his administration insubstantial, liable to fall at any moment. Bakhtiar's program, always that of a moderate, attempted to steer a course of democratization while honoring rising Islamist claims. In his presentation before the Majlis on January 11, 1979, Bakhtiar made public a plan of seventeen points, which included the dissolution of the SAVAK, the gradual elimination of martial law, punishment of human-rights violators, liberation and payment of compensation to political prisoners, and—as a specific concession of his own to the Islamists—a larger role for religious leaders in the drafting of legislation. He promised better relations with the Arab world and support for the Palestinians. Bakhtiar also pledged that Iran would not sell oil either to Israel or to South Africa.

His hope was to humanize an inhuman regime that, until then, had kept the Left, the clerics, the bazaar, the students, and the laborers of the country firmly pushed to the fringes of any political decision making.

҈

At 2:30 p.m. on January 16, 1979, a light blue Boeing took off from the Tehran airport. It carried two luxury-class passengers—the fifty-nine-year-old Shah, Mohammad Reza Pahlavi, and his wife Farah.

They were leaving for a long exile. For the Shah, it was déjà vu, the repeat of an experience that he had known twenty-five years before. Once again, the monarch was fleeing the country, banished by the fury of the people. *Shah raft!* was announced on Radio Tehran—"The Shah has gone!" *Shah raft! Shah raft!*

Allahu akbar! shouted the people. *Allahu akbar!*

The Shah has gone! God is great! The Shah's regime, even with the weight of twenty-five hundred years of autocratic and despotic tradition, could not stand in the face of the overwhelming power of massing revolutionary fervor. It was out of a nationalistic fervor that Iranian revolutionaries who walked the streets of the cities were seizing the weapons of soldiers and police. And it was a deep-seated religious fervor, coupled with wrenching economic and social dislocations, that impelled the masses of the population to join the uprising.

҈

Ghassemlou lived days of anguish, recalled Azad. He did not want Bakhtiar to fail; he did not want to go back to a clandestine existence. He believed that Bakhtiar's government would concede to some of the demands of the PDKI. If not, Ghassemlou's people would have to abandon the cities and take refuge in the mountains.

Despite his charisma and political intuition, Ghassemlou lost much energy in small internal disputes within the party. "There is nothing harder than organizing the Kurds," he used to repeat. This was an arduous task that would fall upon his shoulders for the next ten years.

Ghassemlou could see further than others, but he was alone. In the eager anticipation of Khomeini's arrival the country was awash in enthusiasm for the Ayatollah.

Toward the end of January 1979, a friend took Ghassemlou to a meeting. Everyone there was a leftist, educated in Europe or the United States. They called themselves Marxists.

"They did not know who I was," Ghassemlou recalled: "all they were talking about was the reception they would give Khomeini."

It was Ghassemlou's habit to listen to others and try to show them his point of view in a gentle way. He would not insist on imposing his opinion. Since Ghassemlou was not saying anything, one of the members of the meeting asked him: "Are you coming to the airport to welcome the Ayatollah?"

"No," he answered. "And I regret that you are going. If you, the intellectuals, go to welcome him, what will the simple people feel compelled to do?"

"They looked at me, as we say in Persian, like a wise man observing a madman," Ghassemlou remembered. "But in truth, they were the madmen."[34]

While young leftists may have looked askance at Ghassemlou as an overintellectual interloper and a latecomer to the dance of opposition on the ground in Iran, Ghassemlou's instincts were sure and his vision was clear when it came to Khomeini. Years later, a then-young member of his extended family recalled: "I was a student in Tehran and was a leftist and did not always agree with Dr. Ghassemlou, and at times I was aggressive defending my point of view. We thought Khomeini would return to Qom after the revolution and continue there as a spiritual leader. But Ghassemlou understood early on who Khomeini was."[35]

٨

Khomeini arrived at the Tehran airport February 1, 1979, on an Air France flight. The self-proclaimed "servant of the people" had come home from exile to serve the nation.[36] Millions of zealous people were waiting for him. "The soul of Hussein is coming back!" "The doors of Paradise have been opened again!" "Now is the hour of martyrdom!" they shouted.[37]

Inside the terminal, Khomeini briefly addressed the huge crowd. "This is just the first step," he announced, in the battle to overthrow the remaining structures of the Shah's regime. And he issued a warning to Bakhtiar as well: "If you do not surrender to the nation, the nation will put you in your place."[38]

Crowds lined the route of the Imam's journey to the Behesht-e Zahra cemetery, forty-three kilometers from the center of Tehran, to pay homage to victims of the Shah's dictatorship. So thick was the press of people at the cemetery that a security helicopter was enlisted to take him to section 17 of the grounds, where martyrs from recent uprisings were interred. Khomeini, the saint of Qom, was returning, acclaimed by the multitude as a demigod.

Ghassemlou was a witness to this reception, and afterward he left for the north, for Kurdistan.

❧

The revolution had arrived. And with it, the moment for moderation was swept away.

Confronted with the shock of Khomeini's return and his immediate and peremptory demand for an Islamic republic, Bakhtiar made desperate efforts to hold the line. In an interview with Radio Tehran, he called for unity: "[This] 'Islamic Republic' is an unknown for me," he said; "Iran has one government. More than this is intolerable, either for me or for you or for any other Iranian. . . . As a Muslim, I had not heard that jihad refers to one Muslim against other Muslims." His declarations veered from a plea for peaceful dialogue to a threat to meet violence with violence: "Those fermenting a civil war will be put in front of the firing squad. . . . I will compromise neither with the Shah nor with Khomeini. . . . I shall reply to Molotov cocktails by Molotov cocktails." On the one hand, he insisted on the legitimacy of his standing as prime minister—"I will not give permission to Ayatollah Khomeini to form an interim government"—and on the other, he pledged to placate Islamist concerns: "I will implement all of Ayatollah Khomeini's views in law." Finally, he said: "An Islamic government limited to Qom is permissible, and we shall then have a Vatican too."[39]

On February 5, before the assembled international media at his first-ever press conference in the country, Khomeini publicly designated as prime minister Mehdi Bazargan, seventy-one years old, a respected politician known for his honesty and dour demeanor.[40] Flanked by Khomeini and the Ayatollah's close collaborator Rafsanjani,[41] Bazargan modestly demurred: "With this frail body, my shortcomings and my defects, . . . I should have not accepted this position and such responsibility."[42] But the Imam's word had the force of divine command: "I hereby pronounce Bazargan as the ruler," Khomeini proclaimed, "and since I have appointed him, he must be obeyed. The nation must obey him. . . . Revolt against God's government is a revolt against God. Revolt against God is blasphemy."[43] The Ayatollah exhorted Iranians to show their support for the Islamic Republic and Bazargan's government through the media and "peaceful demonstrations."[44]

Shapour Bakhtiar, as the prime minister designated by the Shah, remained formally in office, but his government was impotent. Bakhtiar did not accept the declaration of an alternative government or the designation of an alternative prime minister: "The Iranian nation and Iranian state are indivisible entities: one country, one government, one constitution, or nothing else. We will tolerate this thing"—what he dismissed as "the joke of anyone forming their own government"—as long as it remained at the level of words only, "but if they take actions in this regard, we shall reply with our own actions." He went on to declare, "If blood is spilled and if aggression is committed against the people, I will expose the aggressors without regard to their name or position right here [in parliament]." His final pronouncement: "I shall remain . . . the legitimate prime minister of this country until future free elections are held. . . . Whoever enjoys a majority, shall then govern."[45]

So for a few days in Iran that February, there were two prime ministers: one designated by the Shah and the other by Khomeini. And Bazargan, invested by the highest revolutionary authority, waited in his home for the Bakhtiar government to fall.

આ

Mehdi Bazargan was one of the few men the cleric trusted. Ironically, his early life and political trajectory shared many parallels with that of Bakhtiar. He had been educated at the École Centrale, the most prestigious educational institution in France, which accepted only students with high academic standing. Once a colleague of Mossadegh and a member of the Iranian National Front in the fifties, he had gone on to found the Freedom Movement of Iran, an Islamic party. He was an engineer; though he later described himself as a "weak donkey,"[46] he was a brave man. In 1961, Bazargan had vigorously defended himself before a political tribunal by speaking out against both the Shah and his father, Reza Shah Pahlavi. This won him the respect of many of his fellow citizens. He was simultaneously a nationalist and a faithful observer of Shi'ite religious practices, such as not shaving one's beard. He was bent on demonstrating that science and religion were not opposed.

Khomeini knew Bazargan was loyal. His loyalty had been tested just three months before. In November 1978, Bazargan was incarcerated in the Qasr, one of the SAVAK's prisons, when he received a visit from General Nasser

Moghadam,[47] head of the feared secret police. "I bring you a message from the Shah," Moghadam told him. "His Majesty is ready to reign and not to rule . . . like the Queen of England! He is prepared to accept the role of constitutional monarch, because now that the great visions he had for his country have been brought to nothing, he is willing to let the Iranian people have their way. If a constitutional monarchy is what they want, then they can have it. Why do you not cooperate with him?"[48]

The SAVAK freed him. Bazargan became the link between Hojatoleslam Hashemi Rafsanjani and the Americans, who were trying in vain to avert the catastrophic fall of the monarchy. To the Americans Iran was a fabulous client that produced oil and bought everything else in enormous quantities. The Shah's ambitions—to turn his country into the fifth major world power by the end of the twentieth century—had fit well with the analysis and aims of U.S. Secretary of State Henry Kissinger. Kissinger saw a guarantee for global balance in the existence of an assemblage of intermediate powers, and the United States regarded with benevolence the fact that the Shah was buying arms without limit.[49]

The Iranian army, with 700,000 men, stood unconditionally by the Shah, while Rafsanjani was supporting the training of the pro-Khomeini Revolutionary Guards that were being formed in the mosques. "We faced the prospect," Bazargan later recounted, "of a civil war and a massacre on an unprecedented scale."[50]

Alarmed at the ominous prospect of civil war, Bazargan traveled to Paris in October 1978. In the French capital, Bazargan confided his fears to Khomeini, who remained unmoved.

"You must not compromise," said the Imam. "The ferment is at its peak. This is the best guarantee for victory."[51] He dismissed Bazargan's fears of catastrophe with a telling comment: "If now you start talking about law and order the Revolution will lose everything. The people's enthusiasm will evaporate; they will go back to their homes and you will lose your army of supporters."

Bazargan had doubts. Could Khomeini guarantee a victory over the Iranian army, the United States, and the Europeans?

"I have confidence in God," the Imam answered.

"We have always worked under your leadership, and we will continue to do so," said Bazargan, "but I must confess that I am worried."[52]

๛

Within a week of Khomeini's return to Iran, by February 8, 1979, millions of Iranians were demonstrating in Tehran, and in cities and villages in the provinces, in support of the Ayatollah and Bazargan's government. The personnel of eleven ministries and several other government agencies declared their allegiance to Bazargan.

Bakhtiar, weighed down by the pressure of massive demonstrations and total disempowerment, declared his willingness "to cooperate with supporters of Ayatollah Khomeini."[53] Army units had been joining the demonstrators; the army was collapsing. Military officers reported to General Abbas Gharabaghi,[54] chief of staff of the Iranian armed forces, that they were now generals without an army.[55] Gharabaghi himself would, soon enough, turn his back on Bakhtiar and declare that the armed forces would not interfere in politics.[56]

Meanwhile in the provinces, bloody clashes were occurring between the demonstrators and remnants of the army. These clashes extended to Kurdistan, where, as early as February 1, the Kurds took over an army garrison near the city of Sardasht, seizing ammunition and supplies.[57] As the uprising continued throughout the country, Khomeini thanked the Iranian nation for their support of the interim government: "The armed forces must return to the people, just as many people and many groups have returned, and we have welcomed them with open arms."[58]

The majority of the junior officers in the armed forces had joined the revolution.[59] Morale was also low among rank-and-file enlisted men, who were deserting from their posts. Gharabaghi met with Bazargan and declared that he would support a revolutionary Islamic republic.[60] Bazargan began negotiating with high-ranking army officers.

Ironically, it would be a conflict within the armed forces that would trigger the final spark that ignited the full force of revolution.[61]

છ

On February 9, an evening curfew was initiated.[62] Following the evening news, a program featuring scenes of Ayatollah Khomeini from his time in France to his arrival in Tehran and his pilgrimage to Behest-e Zahra cemetery was broadcast by order of the Bakhtiar government as a reconciliatory gesture toward the forces of revolution.

Soon after the broadcast began, an incident erupted between officers and enlistee technicians at an air-force barracks in east Tehran. Units of the "Immortals," the Imperial Guard, were called in to restore order. News of the fighting reached the streets, and the curfew was effectively broken.[63] Convinced the enlisted men were being massacred, people swarmed into the streets. "Units of revolutionary guerillas, People's Feda'iyan and Mojahedin-e Khalq, rushed to the scene to support the [air force] technicians and the fighting quickly spread to the rest of Tehran," reported journalist Baqer Moin.[64] Arsenals were raided. Crowds of civilians were now armed. Heavily armed Guard forces fired against the crowds; dozens were killed and wounded.

Tehran had become a war zone.

The next day, February 10, Khomeini condemned the aggression of the Guards and urged the populace to ignore the curfew ordered by Tehran's military governor: "The communiqué of the military authorities is against the principles of Islam, and the people should not pay any attention to it." He reviled the "inhumane aggression" of the Imperial Guard as "fratricide." He had not ordered a "holy Jihad," he said; he wanted to keep the peace and proceed "in accordance with the law and the wishes of the people." But "I cannot tolerate such barbarism," he declared, and warned of consequences "if these acts of fratricide are not stopped, and the Guard units do not return to their barracks and the army commanders do not step in to stop such aggressions." And finally, he said, "the responsibility will be with those committing the aggression and those transgressing."[65]

On February 11, army units from the provinces converged in Tehran and fired upon the people in the streets. Hundreds were killed and thousands wounded. The revolution was in full spate, and the government of Bakhtiar would be swept away like a dry leaf.

Army officers asked Khomeini for permission to forsake their oath to defend the Shah and the imperial regime so they could join the Islamic movement. "Those who have taken such an oath," Khomeini replied, "should act contrary to it."[66]

The Shah's generals were impotent as soldiers and officers alike deserted the ranks. Some generals were murdered by their own officers, others summarily tried by self-appointed tribunals and executed; some committed suicide with their own weapons, or just disappeared. General Gharabaghi beseeched Bazargan "to send someone to take over the army from him,"[67] and appoint a head of the army. But the truth was that the army had already dissolved.

The Shah's regime was now no more than a formality, and it crumbled. Leftist revolutionaries attacked military bases, seized weapons, took over public buildings, and freed political prisoners.[68]

As the last vestige of military force was wrested from the moribund regime into the hands of the revolutionaries, "the voice of Jamshid Adili [a well-known media figure] came on the air: '*In sedaaye enghelaab-e mardom-e Iran ast*'—'This is the voice of the Revolution of the Iranian people.' He repeated the line, almost in tears. The Revolution had toppled the monarchy."[69]

❧

Mehdi Bazargan was a reasonable man who believed in the rule of law and respect for human rights and who thought he should lead his government step by step. This prudence benefited the fundamentalists, by buying time and gradually breaking down opposition to their political agenda for sweeping change. The Islamists were satisfied with the first step: a revolution in the political arena.

But seventy-five-year-old Bazargan did not understand the hopes of the minority. For him, the Kurds, who in the past had declared an independent Democratic Republic of Kurdistan, were dangerous separatists.

In revolutionary Iran, there were deep divisions between the multiplicity of factions that had opposed the Shah. There were moderates like both Bakhtiar and Bazargan, who had spent formative years in Europe and assimilated Western intellectual views on democratization and the value of modern national development. There were those who, like Ghassemlou, had traveled back and forth between developing theory and networks in exile and practical organizing on home ground. There were leaders who had remained free and active, and those who had spent years in prison or in exile nursing their dreams. "There was conflict between the mullahs and the intellectuals, and between the insiders and the outsiders," Egyptian journalist Mohamed Hassanein Heikal[70] summed up: "There was a rivalry between those who had remained all the time in Iran, facing the tortures of SAVAK and the bullets of the army, and those who had organized the revolution abroad and returned in triumph with the Imam."[71]

In their isolation from on-the-ground developments in their homeland, those returning from abroad with the Ayatollah had not realized that under the Shah, Iranian society had undergone momentous change. There had been no significant political and social reforms, but there had been a meaningful change of mentality. Women in urban settings, the middle class, and students were no longer the same.

Nor were the Kurds. The Iranian PDK—it was not yet known as the PDKI, but as PDK (Iran)—did not aspire for independence, but for autonomy and self-governance within Iran's geographical borders. The party did not pursue revolution, because they had adopted what Ghassemlou would come to characterize as a democratic socialist model. Their platform did not idealize violence, and rejected terrorism as a matter of principle—but it did demand democracy.

However, in Iran the fundamentalists and the old men were ruling.

Notes

1. SAVAK, *Sazman-e Ettela'at va Amniat-e Keshvar*, Organization of Intelligence and National Security, was Reza Shah's secret police and intelligence service between 1957 and 1979, created with support from the CIA and British intelligence services and trained with the expertise of instructors from Israel's Mossad. Iran's "most hated and feared institution," with unlimited powers, it "monitored, persecuted, arrested, tortured and executed the Shah's political opponents." See World: "SAVAK: Like CIA," *Time* magazine (February 19, 1979), http://www.time.com/time/subscriber/article/0,33009,912364,00. html (accessed June 18, 2013).

    Established to mop up remnants of the outlawed Iranian Communist party Tudeh, SAVAK soon added intelligence gathering and "neutralizing" dissidents to its portfolio. Within Iran its eyes were everywhere, as agents and a host of paid informants surveilled every aspect of life that had any even potentially political impact: journalists, writers, the academy, labor unions. Outside the country, activities included keeping tabs on Iranian students abroad for any signs of opposition to the Shah. *Library of Congress Country Studies*, http://lcweb2.loc.gov/cgi-bin/query/r?frd/cstdy:@field(DOCID+ir0187 (accessed June 18, 2013).

    SAVAK was replaced by SAVAMA, *Sazman-e Ettela'at va Amniat-e Melli-e Iran*. The Ministry of Intelligence and National Security of Iran is known today as VEVAK (*Vezarat-e Ettela'at va Amniyat-e Keshvar*). According to sociologist Charles Kurzman, SAVAK was never dismantled but rather changed its name and leadership and continued on with the same codes of operation, and a relatively unchanged "staff." Charles Kurzman, *The Unthinkable Revolution in Iran* (Cambridge, MA: Harvard University Press, 2004). For further writings and analysis from Kurzman, see http://kurzman.unc.edu/.

2. For Sadegh Sharafkandi see Kurdistan Media, http://www.kurdistanmedia.com/farsi/index.php?besh=dreje&id=138 (accessed November 13, 2013); link and translation Salah Piroty.

3. Sadegh Sharafkandi, interview with Bernard Granjon, PDKI general headquarters in Kurdistan, Iran-Iraq border, 1991. Further statements from Sharafkandi in this chapter are from this interview.

4. Hélène Krulich, *Une Européenne au pays des Kurdes* (Paris: Éditions Karthala, 2011), 210.

5. Hoshmand Ali Mahmud Shekhani, *Abdul Rehman Ghassemlu: His Life and Role in the Kurdish Liberation Movement* [in Kurdish] (Erbil, Iraq: Shahab Publisher, 2007), 133–34, http://www.pertwk.com/ktebxane/; translation by Sharif Behruz.

6. Abdullah Hassanzadeh, *Niw Sede Xebat* [Half a century of struggle: A retrospect of struggle and activity of the Democratic Party of Iranian Kurdistan] [in Kurdish], Vol. 1 (Gawrade: Press Commission of the Kurdistan Democratic Party of Iran, August 1995), 120, translation Salah Piroty. "Amir Ghazi was sent to Kermanshah, Hashem Karimi to Sanandaj, Saeed Rasoul Dehghan to Piranshar and Naghadeh, Hassan Shiwasali to Urmia and Abdulla Hassanzadeh to Mahabad, Salim Babanzadeh who wasn't a Zagros committee member, was sent to Bukan and later, when Hamadamin Seraji returned he was sent to Saqqez." 120.

7. Ibid., 111.

8. Ibid., 112.

9. Ibid.

10. Kawe Bahrami, *Dr Qasimlû: Rêberêkî Modêrn u Şorşgêrêkî Dêmukrat* [Dr. Ghassemlou, modern leader and revolutionary democrat] [in Kurdish] (Koya Sanjak, Iraq: PDKI Publishers, 2003), 35–36.

11. Chris Kutschera, *Le défi kurde ou le rêve fou de l'indépendance* [The Kurdish defiance, or the mad dream of independence] (Paris: Bayard Éditions, 1997), 157.

12. Ibid., 179. See also Martin Van Bruinessen, "Major Kurdish Organizations in Iran," *Middle East Report* 141 (July/August 1986).

13. Sharafkandi also shared this account with French journalist Chris Kutschera in an interview in Paris, August 4, 1992; see Kutschera, *Le défi kurde*, 158. For his reportage Kutschera also conducted a number of interviews with Ghassemlou between 1973 and 1976 in France and Iraq.

14. Ali Ezzatyar, *The Last Mufti of Iranian Kurdistan: Ethnic and Religious Implications in the Greater Middle East* (New York: Palgrave McMillan, 2016), 120. Ezzatyar, an attorney and U.S. diplomat, has served with the Foreign Service and USAID and maintains a voice in public dialogue through print and broadcast media. See Pacific Council on International Policy, https://www.pacificcouncil.org/about/network/profile/ali-ezzatyar.

15. The PUK, together with the Iraqi Communist Party, the Socialist Party of Kurdistan, and a number of Iranian parties, had formerly been based in Nawzeng, the "Valley of the Parties," some distance to the north. But they were driven out in 1983, when the Iranian army attacked and the Iraqis moved in to retake the area. The Jafati valley housed contingents of the Iranian KDP and Komala parties, in addition to the PUK. Martin Van Bruinessen, *Agha, Shaikh and State: The Social and Political Structures of Kurdistan* (London and New Jersey: Zed Books, 1992), 39.

    Human Rights Watch confirmed that parties that had taken refuge in the area included the PUK, the Iraqi Communist Party, the Socialist Party of Kurdistan, a number of Iranian parties, PDKI, and Komala. Human Rights Watch, http://www.hrw.org/reports/1993/iraqanfal/ANFAL3.htm (accessed June 19, 2013).

16. Krulich, *Une Européenne*, 210. According to Jafar Hamidi a former member of PDKI leadership, this was formalized in 1982 when Ghassemlou sent a delegation to the PUK and signed an agreement with them. PDKI member Salah Piroty, personal communication, August 14, 2016.

17. David A. Korn, "The Last Years of Mustafa Barzani," *Middle East Quarterly* (June 1994), http://www.meforum.org/220/the-last-years-of-mustafa-barzani (accessed October 10, 2009).

18. Kutschera, *Le défi kurde*, 47. In protracted hostilities with Saddam Hussein's Iraq and long-standing contention with Iranian Kurds, the Shah's regime had supported Barzani's Iraqi Kurdish party, with the demand that they keep the PDKI in check. In 1968, Barzani killed or handed over to the Shah's forces more than forty PDKI members (David McDowall, *A Modern History of the Kurds* (London, New York: I. B. Tauris, 2007), 253. While Iran later discontinued direct aid to Barzani, his Iraqi Kurds were still offered refuge in Iran. In the same way, Khomeini's regime would now offer Barzani's sons support in exchange for continued action against the PDKI. Kutschera, *Le défi kurde*, 153.

19. A series of three serious incidents between August and September 1979, in Mahabad, Oshnavieh, and Paveh, would exemplify the disunity among the Kurds promoted by political alignment with the Iraqi/Iranian regimes. One instance cited by Kutschera: During combat in Paveh, vice-minister of defense Mustafa Chamran, supervising the operations from a nearby village, would narrowly escape capture by the PDKI. It would be the intervention of Idris Barzani's Iraqi Kurdish guerrillas that would save him, cutting off the supply of munitions to the PDKI units that had encircled him. "This," Kutschera remarked, was "one of the not-glorious chapters of the history of division among the Kurds." Kutschera, *Le défi kurde*, 171. In a second incident, on September 7 in Oshnavieh, Barzani's men would fire upon Iranian Kurds who were participating in a demonstration organized by Ghassemlou's PDKI. This incident would provoke a schism in Barzani's KDP; Ibid., 177. In the wake of these incidents, Ghassemlou's stated opinion of Idris Barzani was that Barzani had acted on behalf of Khomeini's agenda.

20. Azad, interview with Gabriel Fernández, Vienna, 1991. Further statements from Azad in this chapter are from this interview.

21. As the traditional Communist party of Iran, Tudeh was historically loyal not only to Moscow's orthodoxy, but to its interests in Persia as well.

22. The *bazaar*, or marketplace, is a political, economic, and social force in Iran. It has always been central to the Iranian economy. The Shah sought to undermine it in his quest for modernization. Despite the Shah's hostility, the bazaar flourished under his rule, and maintained its autonomy to such an extent that it played an important role in the Islamic revolution. For a full discussion of the bazaar as an entity, its socioeconomic functions, and its roles vis-à-vis the Iranian regime, see "Bāzār 'market (place),'" http://www.iranicaonline.org/articles/bazar-index, and "Socioeconomic and Political Role of the Bāzār," http://www.iranicaonline.org/articles/bazar-iii.

23. Mohamed Heikal, *Iran: The Untold Story* (New York: Pantheon Books, 1982), 144.

24. Ibid., 145–46.

25. Ibid., 146. Shi'a Islam is the predominant sect in Iran. Shi'a sprang from the hostility between Ali, the fourth caliph and son-in-law of the Prophet, and the Umayyad caliphate (661–750 c.e.). After Ali's death, the Shi'a, Ali's party, demanded the restoration of power to his family. From this stems the Shi'ite concept of legitimacy, the divine right of the sacred family to rule. With time, the Shi'ites turned the figure of the leader or imam ("exemplary leader") into a metaphysical being, a manifestation of God. The truth hidden

in the Qur'an's revelation could be known only through the imam. Only the imam was infallible.

Shi'ites developed a doctrine of esoteric knowledge. Orthodox Shi'ites recognized a lineage of Twelve Imams, the last of whom had disappeared in the ninth century. Since then, the *mujtahid*—the divine men of Shi'a Islam, religious scholars qualified as authoritative interpreters of the religious law—have been empowered to interpret both law and doctrine under the guidance of the imam. According to the fundamental principle of *imami*, "imamology," Shi'ites emphasize an idealism that contrasts with the pragmatism of the Sunnis. While Sunnis recognize the consensus of the community as a source for decision and knowledge, Shi'ites believe that knowledge that derives from fallible sources is useless, and that the only infallible knowledge comes from the imam.

Parallel to this doctrine Shi'a Islam, in the wake of its first defeats and persecutions, developed the principle of taqiyya, concealment of faith in the midst of a hostile environment. From the spiritual point of view, the biggest difference between Shi'ites and Sunnis is the Shi'ite introduction into Islam of *passion*—the ideal of the sufferings of a martyr.

The violent death of Hussein, son of Ali (680 c.e.), at the hands of Umayyad forces is celebrated with prayers, theatrical plays, and processions in which those who participate strike themselves with chains and sharp instruments, wounding their bodies. Shi'a Islam extols martyrdom and death.

For further history and analysis, see *Encyclopædia Iranica*, http://www.iranicaonline.org/articles/shiite-doctrine; *Encyclopædia Britannica*, http://www.britannica.com/EBchecked/topic/540503/Shiite (accessed May 19, 2013).

26. Shapour Bakhtiar had been a leader of the resistance against military rule and the despotism of the Shah's regime. Between 1964 and 1977 this moderate nationalist had called for the restoration of democratic rights within a constitutional monarchy. He was imprisoned for opposing the Shah. At the end of 1978, as the Shah's regime was falling, Bakhtiar, as a well-known politician of the opposition, was invited to become part of a government of national unity. As a concession to the forces of opposition, the Shah named him prime minister. But the window of opportunity for moderation had closed. With the return of Khomeini and the unleashing of the full flood of the Islamic revolution, Bakhtiar's government would fall on February 11, 1979. He would escape to France in April 1979, ultimately to be assassinated on August 7, 1991, in Paris.

27. Aziz Mameli, interview with the author, Paris, July 21, 2015. In 1979 Mameli, an attorney, was acting as an assistant to Ghassemlou in Mahabad. Ghassemlou, Mameli reported, "came one night and stayed with us in Saqqez. This was, I remember, two days before Bakhtiar had come to power. Ghassemlou made a statement on behalf of the PDKI. . . . In this [single] statement, he indicated everything"—pointing out the forces that were in play and the direction that developments would take. Further statements from Mameli in the chapters that follow are taken from this interview.

28. Abdul Rahman Ghassemlou, interview with Jonathan Randal, Paris, 1986. Unless otherwise cited, further statements from Ghassemlou in this chapter are from this interview.

29. Ibid.

30. Mohammed Mossadegh, democratically elected prime minister, had nationalized oil at the beginning of the 1950s. His popularity decreased as his standoff with the British over

the sale of Iranian oil weakened Iran's economy. He was overthrown by the coup d'état of 1953 organized by the CIA and British intelligence with the support of the Shah's circle and the clergy. See Ray Takeyh, "What Really Happened in Iran: The CIA, the Ouster of Mosaddeq, and the Restoration of the Shah," *Foreign Affairs*, July/August 2014, https://www.foreignaffairs.com/articles/middle-east/2014-06-16/what-really-happened-iran.

31. Recently declassified documents posted in August 2013 on the National Security Archives of George Washington University "amount to 'the CIA's first formal acknowledgement that the agency helped to plan and execute the coup.'" See Kimberly Dozier, "Documents detail CIA's role in 1953 coup in Iran," *US News and World Report*, August 20, 2013, http://www.usnews.com/news/politics/articles/2013/08/20/documents-detail-cias-role-in-1953-coup-in-iran (accessed August 21, 2013). For a more recent perspective on the role of the CIA in the coup, see also Ray Takeyh, "What Really Happened in Iran." The version of events that lays full responsibility for the coup on the CIA, in Takeyh's view, "has also been promoted by Iran's theocratic leaders, who have exploited it to stoke anti-Americanism and to obscure the fact that the clergy itself played a major role in toppling Mosaddeq."

    Had not it been for ayatollahs Kashani and Behbahani ordering the mob, explains CIA Iran specialist Edward Shirley, the coup d'état would not have succeeded. Edward Shirley, *Know Thine Enemy: A Spy's Journey into Revolutionary Iran* (Boulder, Colorado: Westview Press, 1999), 77.

32. Heikal, *Iran: The Untold Story*, 173.

33. Ibid., 169.

34. Abdul Rahman Ghassemlou, interview with Jonathan Randal, Paris, 1986.

35. Member of Ghassemlou's family, personal communication, to the author March 2, 2013.

36. Muhammad Sahimi, "The Ten Days That Changed Iran," PBS *Frontline*, February 3, 2010, http://www.pbs.org/wgbh/pages/frontline/tehranbureau/2010/02/fajr-10-days-that-changed-iran.html#ixzz2WcruV6QC (accessed June 18, 2013).

37. Heikal, *Iran: The Untold Story*, 177.

38. Shapour Bakhtiar, interview with Radio Tehran, as quoted by Sahimi, "The Ten Days That Changed Iran," http://www.pbs.org/wgbh/pages/frontline/tehranbureau/2010/02/fajr-10-days-that-changed-iran.html#ixzz2SNJcKhSk (accessed May 5, 2013).

39. Shapour Bakhtiar, interview with Radio Tehran, in Sahimi, "The Ten Days That Changed Iran."

40. Baqer Moin, *Khomeini: Life of the Ayatollah* (New York: Thomas Dunne Books, 2000), 205; also see World: "Yankee, We've Come to Do You In," *Time* magazine, February 26, 1979, http://www.time.com/time/magazine/article/0,9171,920156,00.html (accessed May 15, 2013).

41. On his way up the ladder of power, Hojatoleslam Akbar Hasheni Rafsanjani would be the second cleric charged with responsibility for oversight of the pasdaran, the Revolutionary Guards, established by Khomeini's decree in May 1979. See Shaul Bakhash, *The Reign of the Ayatollahs: Iran and the Islamic Revolution* (New York: Basic Books, Inc., 1984), 63.

42. Moin, *Khomeini*, 204.

43. Ibid.

44. Sahimi, "The Ten Days That Changed Iran."

45. Shapour Bakhtiar, address to Iranian parliament, quoted by Sahimi, "The Ten Days That Changed Iran."

46. World: "Yankee," *Time* magazine, February 26, 1979.

47. Lieutenant General Nasser Moghadam (1921–1979) was the fourth and final chief of SAVAK, serving from June 6, 1978 to February 12, 1979. He succeeded General Nematollah Nassiri, who had been arrested by the Shah's order in 1978. He would be executed by order of Ayatollah Khomeini on April 11, 1979. Moghadam has been described as bringing a "liberalizing attitude" to his directorship of the dreaded agency; 'Abbās Mīlānī, *Eminent Persians: The Men and Women who Made Modern Iran, 1941–1979*, Volume 1 (Syracuse, NY: Syracuse University Press, 2008), 290.

Moghadam's son also attested passionately to his father's moderation, extolling the "dignity, honesty, modesty and intelligence" with which he treated others and characterizing him as liberal and pro-Western. See cached material from http://www.zoominfo.com/CachedPage/?archive_id=0&page_id=55549670&page_url=//www.nadermoghadam.com/generalmoghadam.htm&page_last_updated=2000-11-15T16:16:10&firstName=C.&lastName=Savak (accessed August 11, 2013).

48. Heikal, *Iran: The Untold Story*, 162.

49. Fernando Mas, "La revolución iraní," *Historia universal del siglo XX* (Madrid: Historia 16, 1979). After the Shah's downfall, Spanish journalist Mas notes, arms dealers would find themselves holding undelivered Iranian orders valued at more than $20 billion; ibid.

50. Heikal, 168–69.

51. Ibid. The dialogue between Bazargan and Khomeini is recounted.

52. Bazargan was worried enough to write, after his October 1978 meeting with Khomeini, that he was "'astonished and frightened' by Khomeini's lack of interest in the view of others, his unawareness of the immense problems Iran faced, his calm certainty of victory, his confidence that the path would be smooth once the Shah was overthrown." Bakhash, *The Reign of the Ayatollahs*, 51.

53. BBC news, February 7, 1979, posted by Payman Arabshahi, "Memory Lane: Looking back at the road to revolution," *The Iranian*, updated February 11, 2001, http://iranian.com/History/Feb98/Revolution/ (accessed May 4, 2013).

54. General Abbas Gharabaghi was appointed on January 7, 1979, to support the Shah until he left Iran, and to support the government of Bakhtiar. After the confrontation in the streets of Tehran and throughout the provinces, on February 11 he and twenty-two senior military leaders would withdraw their support from Bakhtiar and declare the "army's neutrality" in order to prevent more bloodshed. Report by *The Guardian*, February 12, 1979, http://www.guardian.co.uk/world/1979/feb/12/iran.lizthurgood, posted on by Arabshahi, "Memory Lane."

55. Heikal, *Iran: The Untold Story*, 177–78.

56. General Gharabaghi, speaking in graduation ceremonies at the Iranian officer's college, which were reportedly conducted under heavy security and without a single photo or mention of the Shah. Arabshahi, "Memory Lane," *The Iranian*.

57. Kutschera, *Le défi kurde*, 164.

58. Ayatollah Khomeini, February 8, 1979, reported by Sahimi, "The Ten Days That Changed Iran."

59. Heikal, *Iran: The Untold Story*, 178.
60. *The Guardian*, February 12, 1979, http://www.guardian.co.uk/world/1979/feb/12/iran.
    lizthurgood.
61. Moin, *Khomeini*, 205.
62. The description of events that follows is recounted by Sahimi, "The Ten Days That
    Changed Iran."
63. Ibid.
64. Moin, *Khomeini*, 205.
65. Sahimi, "The Ten Days That Changed Iran."
66. Ibid.
67. Heikal, *Iran: The Untold Story*, 179.
68. For additional details, see Moin: "Guerrilla units attacked the barracks of the Immortals,
    and took over American military buildings, the Evin prison, the television and radio sta-
    tion and numerous government offices. By next morning the Supreme Council of the
    Armed Forces had decided that nothing more could be done and at 1.15 pm Tehran broad-
    cast the following statement: '[Armed forces leadership] decided unanimously to declare
    itself neutral in the current political disputes and ordered military personnel to return to
    base.'" Moin, *Khomeini*, 205.
69. Sahimi, "The Ten Days That Changed Iran."
70. For more on Heikal see *Encyclopædia Britannica*, http://www.britannica.com/EBchecked/
    topic/259606/Muhammad-Hassanein-Heikal.
71. Heikal, *Iran: The Untold Story*, 182.

· 3 ·

KURDISTAN OR *GHABRESTAN*!

ও

The Kurds have always been key players in the mosaic population of Iran. Throughout the modern era, any weakening of the central power has always encouraged independent movements. Dominated by the Persians, the country could not be governed without agreement by the Azeris, who comprised nearly one third of the population and who played significant roles in the national economy, military, and administration. Kurdistan itself was home to a significant Azeri population.[1] Any rebellion by Azerbaijan against the central power would critically wound Iran.[2]

The Azeri middle and lower-middle classes had allied themselves with the Shah. Historically, their relationship with the Kurds in some respects had come to assume the appearance of a zero-sum game. They would not fuel the surge of a serious nationalist movement. The challenge to the central power arose from other minorities: Kurds, Arabs of Khuzestan, Turkmen, and Baluchistanis—and especially the Kurds.

On the eve of the revolution, the Kurds constituted an estimated 17 percent of Iran's population and occupied 7 percent of the country's territory. Their resistance to the old regime had been long and turbulent; protests and demonstrations had flared again and again across Kurdistan during the autumn of 1978, fanned by every new wave of rumored unrest in the capital and in cities across Iran.[3] Now, about the time that Khomeini reinstalled himself in Qom and while the beleaguered Bazargan was struggling to restore order in the office relinquished by Bakhtiar, the Kurds began to pose a problem to the new regime. "Iranian Kurdistan," notes former U.S. diplomat Ali Ezzatyar, "was the only major region in Iran that did not see mass showings of support for the Ayatollah."[4] And Kurdistan's revivified party, PDKI, held no trust toward the prospect of an Islamic government or for Khomeini's declarations.[5]

Revolution had opened the doors to popular demonstrations. In the city of Mahabad, Komala[6] and the Feda'iyan[7] (the Organization of the Iranian People's Guerrillas) had a large presence and were making that presence felt in the streets. For the PDKI, the focus was the local garrison, held by the Shah's army; the regiment there included Kurdish soldiers and officers.[8]

On February 12, while in Tehran the Shah's forces were unraveling before the onslaught of revolution in the streets, in Mahabad the army's tanks positioned before the gendarmerie opened fire on the civilian population, killing dozens.[9] But before that month would end, the gendarmerie would fall into the hands of the Kurds—and so would the army garrison. While the PDKI itself would take no part in any action against the garrison, the party would find itself involved in the dynamics of the times. This situation, Ghassemlou would later recall, would become "one of the most delicate I have experienced."[10]

঑

On February 17,[11] in preparation for meetings to be held February 18–19, amidst enormous tension a government delegation headed by Dariush Foruhar arrived in Mahabad.[12] The proliferation of incidents in Kurdistan had roused Bazargan to send Foruhar, deputy secretary-general of the National Front and president of the Mellat-e Iran, the Nation of Iran Party, to deal with troubles there.[13] With his party's long alliance with the nationalism of Mossadegh and the National Front and its history of liberal support for secular democracy and the separation of religion and state in Iran, Foruhar likely seemed a natural emissary to approach the Kurds. Now minister of labor in the new government, Foruhar also had a potentially advantageous diplomatic standing: he was the brother-in-law of General Ehsanullah Pezeshkpour, commander of the Mahabad garrison. He had come to negotiate with Sheikh Ezzedin Hosseini, a Sunni cleric and a rising political leader in Kurdistan.

Sheikh Ezzedin was one of the most progressive clerics in Iran, and a vivid contrast to Shi'ite clerics who were comfortably subsidized by the bazaar.[14] With his white turban, black-framed glasses, unkempt gray beard, and worn-out Kurdish clothes, Sheikh Ezzedin lived off meager earnings from the classes in Arabic he taught in the Qur'an school of Mahabad.[15] He owned no land and would accept no monetary gifts from his admirers.[16]

Born in 1922 in Baneh, Iranian Kurdistan, to a prominent spiritual family, he was a *sayyid*, a descendant of the Prophet. As a religious scholar in

Kurdistan, a *sheikh*, since 1969 he had been the imam of Friday prayer in Mahabad; as a Kurd, he had become progressively more concerned about Kurdish rights, which increasingly he addressed without religious rhetoric.[17] In 1978, Sheikh Ezzedin was elected chairman of the council of Mahabad. Alongside thousands of Kurds he participated actively in the massive demonstrations against the Shah.[18]

Cultivated, refined, and a publicly recognized nationalist, Sheikh Ezzedin asked Ghassemlou to accompany him to meet the government delegates. Though the cleric was politically committed to the leftists who considered Ghassemlou to be a nationalist bourgeois, this was his way of honoring Ghassemlou.

Ghassemlou and Sheikh Ezzedin got along extremely well. There was no rivalry between them; on the contrary, they shared a genuine mutual empathy. Ghassemlou used to joke with Sheikh Ezzedin by telling him that he should limit his role to the religious aspects of life.

"I studied Marxism for twenty-five years and taught it to students, but I don't talk about Marxism," Ghassemlou would say to Sheikh Ezzedin. "Yet you are a mullah, and you speak about Marxism! You should be content with your religious role, which is very important, while I cannot attend to that."

"Of course what *you* want to do is look after the temporal affairs of this world, while I take care of the affairs of the other world," Sheikh Ezzedin would answer mischievously.

On February 18, Sheikh Ezzedin and Ghassemlou met with the Iranian delegation preliminary to a plenary gathering set for that evening. Both they and the Iranian government representatives then attended the evening assembly, where a small panel of Kurds was to be chosen to meet and negotiate with the Tehran delegation. Representatives from cities across Iranian Kurdistan had come to Mahabad to meet the government deputation and the Kurdish negotiation team.[19]

There were about fifty people at that meeting, Ghassemlou recalled. "Even though I had been out of the country for twenty-one years and did not know the majority of the people there, I spoke up. A young man interrupted me and told me that I had no right to speak on behalf of the Kurds because my party was nonexistent. Yet thanks to Sheikh Ezzedin's support, I was one of the five Kurds chosen."[20]

Sheikh Ezzedin and Abdul Rahman Ghassemlou were two of the five appointed to hold talks with the government delegation, in what would be Ghassemlou's first formal public role.[21] Though the meetings took place in a "congenial atmosphere,"[22] the negotiation with the envoys from Tehran was not an easy one. Q. M., a witness who was present and who now lives in exile outside Iran, thought "the Iranian delegation represented a weak government; and on the Kurdish side, it was clear that Ghassemlou was the leader."[23] But the delegation had no good news for the people of Kurdistan, nor did it have any authority to make decisions.[24]

The Kurds presented an eight-point proposal.[25] It outlined their right to administer the local affairs of the provinces of Kurdistan through an autonomous government, to be stated clearly in the constitution, and to defend their traditions, culture, and language. National defense, foreign relations, and Iranian economic and long-term monetary planning would be in the hands of the central government. The Iranian delegation and the Kurds together signed the eight-point agreement.

Two significant issues raised during the talks were the understanding that the geographical limits of Kurdistan would be chosen "according to historic and geographic factors and the decision of the majority of people living in those areas," and the Kurdish "demand that the Mahabad garrison be placed under the control of the 'revolutionary council' of Mahabad."[26] Throughout the negotiations Foruhar explained to the Kurdish representatives that the demands for self-determination would need to be discussed when the new Iranian constitutional assembly was created. In response, Ghassemlou emphasized, "It is important not only for us to have Kurdish schools and economic development, but most importantly, the Kurdish people must feel they govern themselves."[27]

At the negotiation session that evening, an Iranian officer approached Ghassemlou. "I've been looking for you for months," he told him.

It was General Ehsanullah Pezeshkpour, commander of the Mahabad garrison. Ghassemlou reacted with surprise: "Are you searching for me so you can arrest me?"

"No, of course not," replied the general. "I've heard about you and wanted to meet you . . . The people from Komala had told me not to talk to you because you are a symbol of the Shah's reactionary stance."[28]

But later that very night, through an unexpected series of events, General Pezeshkpour would be removed from his garrison command by the visiting Tehran delegation. And by the next morning, in the void left by his removal and through an equally unanticipated series of responses by Kurdish officers stationed there, the garrison would surrender to a Kurdish takeover without a single shot being fired by the peshmerga.

The events of those crucial twenty-four hours were confusing to those on the ground and in retrospect have lost none of their complexity. But some picture can be pieced together from reports from Kurdish officers as well as from Ghassemlou himself, who was on the scene.

൭

One account we have, from a Kurdish officer in the Shah's military, is that of Colonel Iraj Ghaderi.[29] Ghaderi, whose personal history and rise through the military exemplified the collective experience of the Kurds in the latter half of the twentieth century, was born in a village near Piranshar. His family were Sunni Muslim landowners who joined Mahabad's Democratic Republic of Kurdistan in 1946. His father and uncle were imprisoned for their participation.

When the Shah later ordered an amnesty and it now became possible to do so, Ghaderi and many young men like him were sent by their families to military school. Military life offered prestige and power. Ghaderi knew his country well and became the commander of a battalion in Mahabad.

When the Shah's regime began to crumble, Ghaderi contacted some members of the PDKI and secretly joined the party. It was a risky move because he felt he was under surveillance by the SAVAK and military intelligence. Kurdish officers were a minority, and they were suspect. In general, the government did not send them to posts in Kurdistan, where, if ordered to repress the population, they might very well refuse. Ghaderi attested that those who were posted to Kurdistan were non-Kurdish officers, police, or *jash*[30]—traitorous Kurdish collaborators.

Despite the fact that some Kurdish officers had access to key posts in the Iranian army, discrimination against Kurds within the armed forces was extensive. In the garrisons and camps, Ghaderi recalls, there were heated "discussions between the Kurdish and non-Kurdish officers, especially with the Turks and Persians. This was also happening among the soldiers. There were ethnic and religious differences. In the army, they [the Kurds] were visible because of their names: Sunnis often chose names like Omar or Osman and Shi'ites used to insult them for this. Some soldiers and officers had to change their names. Shi'ites do not tolerate Sunnis."

Within the army, the idea of creating a Kurdish nationalist movement caught fire. According to Ghaderi, his own nationalist sentiment grew and strengthened with his contact with the freedom fighters among the Barzani

Kurds[31] while he was stationed on the Iraq border. Ghaderi and other officers discussed the prospects for their own rebellion in Iranian Kurdistan. But it was not easy. "We were controlled by the Department of Military Intelligence," he recalled. "They were following us; we were under constant surveillance."

When the Shah fell, and the Kurds discovered the intelligence files on themselves in Mahabad, they were able to verify firsthand the extent to which they had indeed been under surveillance.

⁂

The night of February 18, after the large general gathering, a group of Mahabad youth accosted General Pezeshkpour on the street and literally stripped him of his stars.[32] They accused him of killing forty-eight young inhabitants of Mahabad. In the face of the accusations and complaints against the general, Foruhar and his delegation ordered Pezeshkpour to pack up and return to Tehran with them for reassignment to another post. This sudden loss of their commandant lowered the morale of officers at the garrison—both those residually loyal to the old order and those committed to the new regime.[33]

The removal of General Pezeshkpour left a void that needed to be filled. The next morning, February 19, at 11:00 a.m., through a quick-thinking, opportune series of actions by the Kurdish garrison officers, the base yielded without a struggle.

While the enlisted men stationed at the garrison were primarily Persians[34] and Turks, Ghaderi's impression was that regardless of ethnicity, virtually all the rank and file were "against the Shah."[35] According to Ghaderi, the takeover process was very straightforward: "The non-Kurdish officers were detained, and we asked the soldiers to leave and drop their weapons." This request apparently met with no opposition from the enlisted men, who seemed eager to leave: "They thought the region was a very insecure place," Ghaderi said. "And besides, they were in a hurry to join Khomeini's forces in Tehran."

⁂

At 2:00 p.m. that afternoon, Ghassemlou was in a meeting at the PDKI office.

From the far end of the room Ghassemlou saw a friend gesturing, hurrying toward him through the crowd. "You have to come immediately," his friend exclaimed. "If you don't, we will lose the garrison. The soldiers have rebelled and someone has wounded the general."

Ghassemlou followed his friend without a word. To his surprise, at the garrison the soldiers cheered him like a hero.

"Can we leave?" they asked Ghassemlou.

"Of course you can go," he answered with immense relief.

Without hesitating, Ghassemlou gathered all the officers and said, "This is a revolution. We have nothing against you. We have to protect the garrison, and we need your help."

The cooperation of the officers was vital. Just as critical was the pressing need for a clear chain of command, and a commanding officer. And newly arrived in Mahabad was a candidate for this post: Colonel Habibullah Abbasi,[36] a Kurdish officer who had fled the Shah's army in Tehran when the first stages of the Iranian revolution erupted there, and who had just appeared in Mahabad.

"Colonel Habibullah Abbasi is here with us," Ghassemlou told the garrison officers. "Inform Mahabad radio and television and tell them Colonel Abbasi is the new commander of the garrison."[37]

There was a serious situation here that needed urgent resolution. Ghassemlou recognized that the takeover was not good timing, given that the Kurds were in active negotiation with the government delegation.[38] But the materiel they were able to appropriate was important. In the garrison that day, Ghassemlou and his men would discover, there were stockpiled three thousand weapons, including mortars, missiles, and eighteen tanks.[39] In Iran, every political group was armed, or scavenging for arms, and the PDKI could not be left behind. If the local population found out the garrison was undefended, Ghassemlou feared, they would come running, searching for weapons. Without systematic organization of available armaments, the Kurds were not at all ready to carry forward the revolution to secure their rights; only five members of his own party had weapons. Ghassemlou needed a group of men who would protect the garrison.

Ghassemlou found twelve trustworthy men. He turned over to them the weapons abandoned by the soldiers and entrusted them with the custody of the garrison. He also issued an order that no one be allowed to enter the army base.

These men formed the seed that was to expand into a military force during the coming months—a force that came to be comprised of twelve thousand valiant peshmerga. The PDKI would first create an armed group in Sardasht, and later in Piranshar and Oshnavieh. Within a few months, the party would have thousands of armed combatants.[40]

Yet to arrive at that point the PDKI had to navigate enormous challenges. Ghassemlou described the trials and tasks of expansion in a series of wide-ranging interviews with French journalist Chris Kutschera. "From one day to the next," Ghassemlou said, "a clandestine party which had as a goal one member for every one thousand inhabitants—about five thousand members for all of Iranian Kurdistan—had to take over the administration of a vast territory, about one fifth the size of France." In the process, Kutschera said, the "PDKI had a problem with recruitment, not for lack of candidates—on the contrary, but for an excess of adherents": "Today," Ghassemlou told him, "everyone wants to be a member of the party. They say: I've been a member of the party for twenty years! And if you challenge them, they get mad. . . . They don't know that you have to know the program of the party, its directives, [you have to] make a contribution, be active politically. . . ."[41]

Recruitment, organization, discipline, and training were all vital. The absence of military training, Ghassemlou told Kutschera, created the biggest problems: "Many youth have taken a rifle without any training. And they don't know how to use modern weapons," the new weapons taken from the Mahabad and Sardasht arsenals.

"We have five thousand peshmerga. It's too much; we need twenty-five hundred this year and five thousand next year,"[42] Ghassemlou explained. What the party needed was time: time to plan, time to train, time to sort out and systematize. But time was moving, and moving fast.

&

What took place at Mahabad was, in an important sense, neither local nor Kurdish. Essentially, the takeover and disarming of the Mahabad garrison occurred in the name of the Iranian revolution and of throwing off what was left of the monarchist regime. The incident that stripped General Pezeshkpour of his stars was the spark that ignited the spontaneous series of events that led to the garrison's surrender.[43] We have no clear account of the general's encounter with his assailants, which took place outside the garrison. It seems clear, however, that nothing about the takeover itself was planned in advance. Incredibly, the only injury that took place—at the very outset, during the disorderly street incident with Mahabad youths—was that sustained by General Pezeshkpour himself.

Eleven days later, on March 2, 1979, the Kurdistan Democratic Party (Iran) would officially announce in Mahabad that it had resumed its political activities. Thirty-two years of clandestine activity had ended. And soon all eyes would be on Kurdistan and on the PDKI, its renascent party.

❧

The garrison takeover of February 19 was initially welcomed by Bazargan's provisional government. In every region across Iran where garrisons were still under control by army contingents loyal to the monarchy, takeovers were springing up as the Shah's army fled or melted away. However, when the new government learned that a Kurdish officer had been put in charge of the Mahabad garrison, their mistrust of the Kurds flared up in an angry response. "While no major party . . . publicly denounced the new revolutionary government's platform at this early juncture," Ezzatyar points out, Kurdistan would come to be perceived across Iran "as the first region to splinter from the revolution's general direction."[44]

Looking back at these events in an interview with Persian journalist Enayat Fani a decade after the revolution, Ghassemlou would recall: "You know after the fall of the Shah's regime, Iranians entered the military bases and took control of these bases. [But] when we, Kurds, did the same in Kurdistan, especially in Mahabad and Sanandaj—which, by the way, occurred without violence and bloodshed—the new Islamic regime fought against us."[45]

In this, the ferocity of the war against the Kurds may have been intensified by the stirrings of oncoming confrontation between Iraq and Iran; the presence of Kurdish militant activity in the region continually impeded army reinforcements from reaching additional outposts near the Iraqi border.[46] The garrison at Mahabad was a vital center in Kurdistan, and the government in Tehran was not willing to lose control of it.

The takeover put Foruhar, as the regime's delegated negotiator, in a difficult position. It is entirely possible that one reason the regime had taken the initiative to send a delegation to negotiate at all was to forestall the takeover of military bases during the unrest in Kurdistan. It is also likely, given the intransigence of Khomeini and the regime, that negotiations were meant to gain time, that there was never really any intention to accept Kurdish demands. In hindsight it seems clear that strategic stonewalling, not compromise, was the regime's objective. Any concession to Kurdish petitions for local self-rule were treated as demands for secession. This can be seen clearly when,

on February 20, Bazargan's deputy prime minister, Ebrahim Yazdi, would pronounce, "We do not approve of the independence of Kurdistan in any way. It
is the policy of the state not to allow the secession of any part and territory
of Iran's land and such an event will be forestalled with unfettered power."[47]

In light of this, Foruhar's championing of a plan for Kurdish self-determination within the Islamic Republic,[48] embodied in the eight-point agreement
his delegation had signed with the Kurds, was dead from the start. When
Foruhar presented his report to Tehran, even while making it quite clear that
the Kurds' demands were for cultural and administrative autonomy while
rejecting any idea of secession, the government responded that it could not
make any decisions before the creation of a constituent assembly.[49] In Foruhar's express estimation, "After fifty years of having their demands repressed
the Kurds have the right to some type of autonomy."[50] But his promise to the
Kurds would be swept aside.

❧

Foruhar's report was never made public. His assurances to the Kurds were
ignored by the government, which warned that an independent Kurdistan
was "out of the question."[51] An independent Kurdistan was never a stated
demand of the eight-point agreement; it was the *idée fixe* of the Islamists that
any demands for self-rule were tantamount to secession.

To ward off the imagined threat, Tehran intensified its efforts to exac-
erbate differences between Kurdish groups, fomenting conflicts among the
Kurds themselves. Where disputes existed, Khomeini backed the claims of
Shi'ites, and of other groups whose leaders had pronounced themselves in
favor of the Islamic republic and in support of the Ayatollah.

In addition to buying time with negotiations, the regime was ready to
use force as needed. Iranian offensives to regain territory from the Kurds also
served to distract discussions from real issues and from Kurdish demands to
negotiate resolution of emerging problems. The outcome would be a series
of violent clashes between Iranian forces and Kurdish resistance that would
end with carnage in Sanandaj, the administrative capital of Kurdistan, five
hundred kilometers west of Tehran and nearly four hundred kilometers south
of Mahabad.

On the eighteenth of March, during Nowruz, the New Year celebrated by
Kurds and Iranians, fierce fighting would break out between Kurdish rebels
and government forces[52] when Kurdish peshmerga launched an attempt on

the army base there. Sanandaj, nestled among high mountains, would become a battleground. Emotions would run so high that even Sheikh Ezzedin's attempts to broker mediation would fail.[53]

Sanandaj had, since early in the revolution, been under peshmerga command. From the Kurds' perspective they had a right to maintain control of their towns and cities. From the perspective of the regime, however, the Kurds' insistence on self-governance was the source of the conflict. Since the very beginning of hostilities, the underlying root of contention had always been the issue of local control; and when the Kurds would not give in, the regime responded fiercely. To regain control of the area and ensure that major strategic centers like the garrison would not fall into Kurdish hands, Khomeini had appointed Sheikh Hassan Kermani as administrator of the city's garrison. Kermani, a Shi'ite Persian cleric, formed a Shi'ite committee—one among many of the revolutionary *komitehs* set up across Iran to maintain security and law enforcement, buttressing the new order at the local level following the revolution. In the interests of effective local control, the committee—supervised by Shi'ite Persian cleric Mullah Ali Safdari with assistance from a local Shi'ite Kurdish cleric as well—was supported fully by Tehran. Regime support included supplying arms and ammunition.[54]

At this juncture, other sets of forces came into forceful play at Sanandaj. The first emerged at the hands of Sunni Kurdish cleric Ahmad Moftizadeh, "the wise man of God"[55]—leader of the Friday prayer at the Jameh mosque, the most popular Sunni religious leader in Sanandaj, and a prominent political as well as religious figure in the city—who formed a parallel committee.[56] While a proponent of Kurdish cultural rights, Moftizadeh strongly believed in the need for a governance based in Islam, and sought to "articulate his belief in greater rights for Kurdistan through the prism of religion." His hope, notes Ali Ezzatyar, was to see Iran "adopt an Islamic system in line with his interpretations of the shura system advocated for in the Quran."[57] As a form of decision making, *shura*—"consultation," specifically consultation with members of a community whose welfare would be affected by a decision—was intended to ensure appropriate action for all concerned.[58] This form of governance, Moftizadeh believed, "would ultimately bring decentralization and autonomy to the Kurdish region and Iran's Sunnis."[59] Given Moftizadeh's Qur'anic orientation and apparent alignment as "an early supporter of the Islamic revolutionary government," Tehran appeared to be promoting him as a counter to the growing influence of Sheikh Ezzedin.[60]

The second set of forces was arising powerfully as a wave of popular enthusiasm in the wake of the takeover of the garrison at Mahabad. While Moftizadeh's vision of a sociopolitical order based in Islam was classically Sunni,
aligned with tradition to which Kurdish society was accustomed, a new and
secular vision was sweeping the region. "The difference between prior decades
and the year 1979," notes Ezzatyar, "when Kurdish nationalism had matured
significantly, was that now there were galvanized segments of society that took
issue with Islamic symbolism."[61] The events at Mahabad—bypassing negotiation with the direct action of taking the garrison—set the example for a new
direction that was certainly galvanizing to the growing tensions at Sanandaj.
While Moftizadeh's leadership, standing, and popularity remained strong at
Sanandaj, he would find himself increasingly "at odds with the greater Kurdish
region."[62]

Here in Sanandaj at this point, both Shi'a and Sunni committees had
received government recognition and answered to government oversight. The
city seemed calm, and on March 16, feeling secure in the city's support, Moftizadeh traveled to Saqqez.[63] Moftizadeh's Sunni committee, acting on their
officially legitimized status, now lobbied the regime for arms. On March 17,
Moftizadeh wrote to the Kurdish garrison commander, asking for weapons and
ammunition to bolster the city's security. The commander responded that this
decision was the prerogative of Mullah Safdari, who headed the earlier-formed
Shi'a committee. This despite the fact that Khomeini had by now expressed
recognition of Moftizadeh as "the legitimate representative of the Kurdish
people" for purposes of negotiation with the regime.[64]

Amid the chaos of the early months of the revolution, the perception was
growing widespread across Kurdistan that the new regime was backing Shi'a
and non-Kurdish groups by granting them arms, while denying such protection to native Kurds. Agitation grew with the suspicion that Kurdish rights
would be further curtailed by the revolutionary government.[65]

The rebuff to Moftizadeh's request for arms fueled rising anxiety and anger.
Mounting tensions would give way to outright armed clashes. A number of
groups that would coalesce around the Marxist party Komala would strike
at the local gendarmerie and at the garrison. Their determined attempt on
the garrison would fail; the regime would respond fiercely, shelling residential
neighborhoods and killing hundreds.

What follows includes eyewitness testimony from Babasheikh Nasseri,
who at that time in 1979 was a spokesperson for political affairs with the
PDKI's Sherifzadeh force in Sanandaj.[66] On March 18, in protest over the

lack of official response to their request for arms, Moftizadeh's supporters initiated a sit-in in front of the Jameh mosque. Safdari, Nasseri reports, warned the protesters that their demonstration would lend support to "counterrevolutionaries and rioters." His response angered people, who were already on edge from rumors that the government was planning not only to confiscate the armaments kept at the garrison and remove them from Kurdistan altogether, but even to seize the wheat from the city's silos. In reaction to Safdari's warnings Moftizadeh's supporters, with support from the Feda'iyan, accosted the Shi'ite committee; in the ensuing violence, some were killed and others injured.

During this critical time, leadership from among Komala and Feda'iyan, together with city notables, had formed a city council.[67] This interim council, through its speaker Sediq Kemanger, released a series of six broadcasts on radio and television. The first day, which saw the clash between the rival committees, announcements began by encouraging the takeover of the garrison base. Failing that effort, broadcasts fell back to urging people to defend themselves. And they would end with the final fallback, an appeal for a ceasefire.

In Moftizadeh's absence from the city, his supporters, along with members of Feda'iyan and Komala, emboldened by reports of the recent garrison takeover at Mahabad, launched an assault on the Sanandaj garrison, the command of the 28th Division.[68] Urged on by city councilman Sediq Kemanger's broadcasts, the protesters gathered before the Jameh mosque moved against the military garrison.[69] Reports were that the garrison and its commander, Colonel Mashalla Safari, were captured and the gendarmerie barracks looted. The city hall, radio, and TV stations were seized.

Sanandaj's second garrison, the Gendarmarie Regiment, was also attacked.[70] Reports of the takeover, like the attempt itself, however, were premature. Despite Komala's growing popularity, Sanandaj lacked Mahabad's history of rebellion, and its garrison was both stronger and more loyal than that in Mahabad.[71] The military response was vicious: tanks, heavy shelling, and mortars were launched upon the crowd. The battalion taskforce opened fire on those who were storming the doors of the gendarmerie.

The situation was out of hand. The battle between the regime's forces and residents of Sanandaj, reinforced by newly arrived peshmerga sent by the PDKI, went on for days, redoubling when army helicopters fired upon the population. Over these days of fighting, 205 people were killed and four hundred were injured.[72] Among the 141 rebels captured was Abdullah Mohtadi, one of the founders of Komala. The takeover attempt had failed.

In the aftermath, the *Washington Post* summed up on March 19, 1979: "It seems established that the fighting in Sanandaj started after both the local Revolutionary Committee and the military refused requests to distribute arms and ammunition to the local Kurds to defend themselves against the large Iranian minority in the town. . . .

"More fundamentally, however, there seems to have been growing unrest in the region since Khomeini issued a statement dubbing a moderate Kurdish leader, Ahmad Moftizadeh, as the 'Kurds' sole religious and political leader.'

"This was an obvious attempt to undercut the much stronger autonomy demands voiced in Kurdistan by a leading religious figure, Sheik Sayed Ezzedin Husseini, elected after the Islamic revolution by left-of-center Kurds as the spokesman for their demands."[73]

On his return to the city, Moftizadeh called Komala to task for their actions—destructive not only in themselves, but damaging to any progress in "securing further rights in Kurdistan."[74] PDKI member Abdullah Hassanzadeh, too, was critical of the actions, and saw them in part as politically motivated. "It needs to be mentioned," Hassanzadeh notes, "that a few small and less experienced organizations had an effect on the situation. For these organizations, challenging the PDKI was of primary concern. Their fantasy was that since the PDKI had seized the garrison in Mahabad, then to keep a balance of power, they too should seize the significant garrison in Sanandaj— unaware of the fact that seizing such a military garrison with an unorganized and unplanned force, without a detailed military plan as well as without cooperation from enemy ranks, would not be that easy.

"Three days after the war had started, I think, the PDKI dispatched a force of 150 peshmerga, including a few trucks of food and clothing as assistance from the people to Sanandaj. With the arrival of the peshmerga, those organizations, instead of being happy, got worried and started to grumble. The PDKI was acting opportunistically, they claimed, and now that the garrison, as a result of their efforts, was close to surrender, the party was trying to show itself a partner to the victory and the seizing of the garrison. That was why they did not offer any help to the PDKI's forces, and as much as they could they wouldn't let the peshmerga near the front of the fighting."[75]

From Tehran, Khomeini's response was true to form, manipulating the narrative to lay blame for conflict on the Kurds. "A group of people has created chaos in our dear Kurdistan and does not wish the Muslims to live in peace," he declared during a broadcast on March 20, 1979. "This group is acting contrary to Islamic principles." He demanded hostilities cease and cautioned that "any attack on the army and *gendarmerie* post is rejected by us. We have no dispute with our Sunni brothers. We are all members of a single Koran. If anyone attacks them, he is not part of the Muslim people, (but)[76] is an agent of the foreigners."[77]

The aftermath of the debacle at Sanandaj, which came to be christened "Bloody Nowruz," was inevitably deeper polarization: "few Kurds who supported Khomeini before the Revolution remained supporters of his new regime."[78]

❧

On March 23, Ayatollah Mahmud Taleghani, a respected religious leader from Tehran, arrived with a governmental delegation.[79] The fighting came to a halt, though sporadic fire could still be heard.

Taleghani's liberal views were well-known. He had fought for civil and political rights under the monarchy, and lived through many years of imprisonment during which he also endured torture. He was admired by all Iranians. He arrived with three of Khomeini's trusted men: Hashemi Rafsanjani, a close collaborator; Ayatollah Mohamed Hossein Beheshti, leader of the Islamic Republican Party;[80] and Abolhassan Banisadr, an advisor to Bazargan and a future president of Iran.

The three men sat before a Kurdish delegation,[81] led by Sheikh Ezzedin Hosseini,[82] and listened for three hours to their complaints and demands. The scene was fraught with tension. That morning, the conflict had claimed more victims, and low-flying Phantom fighter jets over Sanandaj had further stirred the population. So loud was the roaring of the jets in the sky that the meeting itself and those negotiating were deeply disturbed. If what the Kurds had suffered under the Shah, they were still suffering under Khomeini, what had the revolution accomplished?

One of the tense moments during the session arose in an interchange between Taleghani and Kemanger, witnessed by PDKI member Hassan Khaliqi, who was present.[83] The government delegation had come to the meeting with a subsidiary agenda of bringing Sediq Kemanger and other Kurdish leaders to "Islamic justice." Moftizadeh, too, played a tape of one of Kermanger's broadcasts urging the populace to defend themselves. Not aware that Kemanger was present, Taleghani asked, "Who sent this message? Who is this Sediq Kemanger—so that I can execute him right away?"

Kemanger shouted, "I am Sediq Kemanger." He came forward and played the entire series of tapes from his six broadcasts, including his plea for a cease-fire, and in turn harshly criticized Moftizadeh and questioned his role in the unfolding of events: "When the war erupted in Sanandaj it was Moftizadeh's fault," he said to Taleghani and the Iranian delegation. "He is the agitator, you shouldn't support him. We didn't want the war to happen," Kemanger concluded, while Moftizadeh kept silent.

Taken aback, Taleghani tried to calm the situation: "Calm down, my son. I am sick. May God protect you."[84]

In the face of this unexpected public challenge, said Khaliqi, the delegation was "forced to negotiate with the Kurds and accepted their demands on organizing their own councils." However, as would become the rule in all negotiations between the Kurds and the regime, these negotiated agreements were never implemented.

Reflecting later on the issues then facing the Kurds, Sheikh Ezzedin would tell an interviewer, "The demand for autonomy goes back well before the revolution. The Kurds played an important role in the revolution, and they participated because they thought that under the new regime their rights would be respected. They believed that negotiation would solve the problems that arose."[85] Here and now in Sanandaj, an angry Sheikh Ezzedin exclaimed to the delegation: "What is the difference between the crown and the turban? The essence of the state has not changed; the crown [of the Shah] is gone and it is replaced by the turban [of the Ayatollah]."[86]

While people were trying to gather the dead, two thousand peshmerga who occupied the streets were challenging the fighter planes, brandishing their weapons at the sky and shouting: "We want an autonomous Kurdistan and a democratic Iran! We do not fear death! *Kurdistan ya Ghabrestan!* Kurdistan or the graveyard!"[87]

The two sides reached an initial agreement,[88] signed on March 24, 1979.[89] Taleghani agreed to the release of prisoners and guaranteed the Kurds a certain degree of autonomy, with the condition that they refrain from any assault or takeover attempt on army garrisons and that the peshmerga evacuate any occupied buildings.[90] An interim committee would be set up to administer the city pending local elections.[91] One sticking point was the Kurdish demand that the regime's armed forces, including Khomeini's elite pasdaran, the Revolutionary Guards, be removed from the area and that security and policing be performed by the Kurds themselves. Though Taleghani accepted that the Kurds had the right to create their own future, he would not budge regarding the presence of the army in Sanandaj.

"If I ordered General Gharani [the commander-in-chief] to recall his soldiers, could you govern your own country?" he asked the crowd. His question was rhetorical, and he answered it himself: "No, I don't think so."

To which the crowd shouted: "Yes, we are adults!"

When it was Beheshti's turn to speak he asked for "time to fix the problem," and requested that the Kurds "do nothing which may widen the gap between us."[92]

More than one hundred Kurdish prisoners were released and, reciprocally, "installations captured by [Kurdish] guerrillas, including the airport, local radio and the Army administration offices" were to be "handed back to their original authorities."[93]

In return, the Kurds agreed to support the abolition of the monarchy and a referendum on the new constitution. For now, at least, the violence in Sanandaj was over, and the citizens could begin to pick up the pieces and rebuild their lives.

❧

Taleghani, in whom a lifelong passion for Qur'anic exegesis coexisted with a commitment to economic and social justice, was the voice of an expansive vision and the "advocate of moderation within the Iranian theocracy."[94] This moderation was truly confined within the frame of Islam. When asked, for example, "whether the new Islamic Republic of Iran would have a true democratic system based on majority rule. 'Of course,' Taleghani insisted. Asked what he would do if a majority of the new Parliament passed a law legalizing abortion, for instance, he replied: 'We would dissolve it and send it home!'"[95]

At the same time, he could meet the Kurds' demands on the ground of their shared concerns. "Autonomy is the same thing that we want," he said, "[that] each individual is autonomous and that the Islamic order is free. . . . What person is able to deny cultural freedom, the destiny, and the language of the people of Kurdistan . . . ?"[96] He saw clearly the larger context, in terms that echoed the rallying cry of the PDKI's party program: "If Kurdistan becomes autonomous then Iran becomes democratic."[97]

Taleghani opened the doors for the Kurds to participate in the formulation of the new national constitution—which, it was agreed, would include a guarantee that ethnic minorities would gain their cultural freedom, along with the right to teach their own language in schools, and that the administration of regional affairs, both local government and economy, would be managed by elected Kurdish representatives. The Kurds were also to benefit from the development of natural resources in their provinces to help grow their economy. The central government agreed not to utilize army troops to eradicate internal rebellions. The newly formed Islamic Revolutionary Guard Corps, which had not yet shown its cruel and repressive character, would handle national internal security.

This was a markedly magnanimous gesture from a man who had just arrived from Tehran. It was a gesture of goodwill, delicately brokered among scenes of carnage and urgency, a fragile truce.[98] How long would it hold out its promise?

Notes

1. "Iranian Kurdistan is home to Azeris, especially in Western Azerbaijan, where they represent 35 percent of the population," Kutschera writes. "Mahabad, historic capital of Iranian Kurdistan, [and cities like] Sardasht, Bokan, and Ouchnu [Oshnavieh] are Kurdish; other cities like Urmieh, Miandoab, Naghadeh, Shahpour, Khoi, and Maku [multiethnic cities] are surrounded by Kurdish villages. The Kurds in the city of Sanandaj are mainly Sunni, but the Kurds of Kermanshah are majority Shi'ite; the population of Elam is totally Shi'ite." Chris Kutschera, *Le défi kurde ou le rêve fou de l'indépendance* [The Kurdish defiance, or the mad dream of independence] (Paris: Bayard Éditions, 1997).

2. The Azeris had their own disaffections with Persian domination within Iran and had created their own republic after World War II. For an Azeri perspective, see Alireza Asgharzadeh, *Iran and the Challenge of Diversity: Islamic Fundamentalism, Aryanist Racism, and Democratic Struggles* (London and New York: Palgrave MacMillan US, 2007), http://www.palgrave.com/us/book/9781403980809#otherversion=9780230604889.

3. Ali Ezzatyar, *The Last Mufti of Iranian Kurdistan: Ethnic and Religious Implications in the Greater Middle East* (New York: Palgrave McMillan, 2016), 123.

4. Ibid., 129.

5. Ibid.

6. Komala, from *komele*, "society." As Komalay Shoreshgeri Zahmatkeshani Kurdistani Iran (Organization of Revolutionary Toilers of Iranian Kurdistan; see citation at Federation of American Scientists, http://www.fas.org/irp/world/para/komala.htm), Komala appeared in public in 1978. Influenced by the Chinese revolution, Komala aimed to form cadres which would then go back to the industrial and agricultural centers of Kurdistan and thereby educate and influence the Kurdish populace. Many of its founders came from notable families. Komala considered Kurdish nationalism provincial and narrow-minded and equally denounced Tudeh's "Soviet revisionism." Nationalism was definitely not their goal; their objective was decentralization. David McDowall, *A Modern History of the Kurds* (London, New York: I. B. Tauris, 2004), 265.

While Komala emerged publicly as late as 1978, Ezzatyar notes that Komala "or a predecessor party likely existed in some form as early as the late 1960s"; its secretary-general Abdullah Mohtadi, a founding member, claimed that its first formative meeting took place in 1969. Ezzatyar, *The Last Mufti of Iranian Kurdistan*, 58, n55. Its platform could be characterized as Marxist socialism with a concern for Kurdistan's autonomy; Ibid., 147. "During the early stages of the revolution, Komala referred to itself by the Persian name of Jam'iateh Zahmat Keshan (The Hard Workers)"; however, "it was not active or a known quantity until the revolution was well under way." Ibid., 116.

7. *Fedā'īyān*, loosely translated as "guerillas," literally "those who sacrifice themselves." The Sazman-e Cherikhayeh Feda'iyan-e Khalq-e Iran, a leftist national party, was formed by two main groups of the armed movement against the Shah in the 1960s. The party split after the Iranian revolution into a majority and a minority. The majority faction no longer believed in armed struggle and, with the Tudeh Party of Iran, sided with the Islamist regime. The minority, with members as well as offices in a number of cities of Iranian Kurdistan, remained militant.

8. At the very outset of the revolution, Kurdish rebels had taken over the garrison near the city of Sardasht, on February 1, 1979, commandeering in the process an important stock of supplies and ammunition. Kutschera, *Le défi kurde*, 164.

9. "However, on that day, as I remember," one party member recalled, "dozens of people were killed by the Shah's military—among them my cousin, who was shot and killed by a tank positioned in the middle of the gate of the Mahabad garrison, firing indiscriminately. When I talked to my brother, who was a peshmerga at the time, he confirmed that so many people of Mahabad were killed on that day." PDKI member Salah Piroty, personal communication, April 19, 2017.

10. Abdul Rahman Ghassemlou, interview with Jonathan Randal, Paris, 1986. Unless otherwise cited, further statements from Ghassemlou in this chapter are from this interview.

11. Hamid Gohary, *Xorhelatyi Kurdistan le de Salan da 1356–1366* [Eastern Kurdistan during the decade 1978–1988], Vol. 1 [in Kurdish] (Erbil, Iraq: Rojhelat Publisher, 2011), 103; translation Sharif Behruz.

12. In 1977, Dariush Foruhar had emerged as one of the leaders of the National Front, which represented the educated middle class. Michael Axworthy, *Revolutionary Iran: A History of the Islamic Republic* (New York: Oxford University Press, 2013), 99. Foruhar would later become a leading opposition politician in Iran. He would be brutally murdered in 1998 in his home in Tehran, along with his wife: one in a series of high-profile assassinations of dissidents best known as "chain murders." See the blog by his daughter Parastu Foruhar, http://www.parastou-forouhar.de/english/Documents-Parwaneh-and-Dariush-Forouhar.html (accessed May 10, 2013).

13. Kutschera, *Le défi kurde*, 164.

14. In Iran today, as from the very inception of Muslim society, the giving of alms remains one of the five essential pillars of Islam. "Like traditional *bazaaris*, all the corporate *bazaaris* give alms," reported an American observer and geopolitical analyst. Even in modern times, when "the fruit seller . . . goes over his books with a computer rather than a scratch pad," every merchant, "[a]s a devout Muslim, gives a generous portion of his proceeds to the needy." Robert D. Kaplan, "A Bazaari's World," *The Atlantic*, March 1, 1996, http://www.

theatlantic.com/magazine/archive/1996/03/a-bazaaris-world/304827/?single_page=true (accessed August 26, 2013).

15. *Le Monde*, March 30, 1979.

16. McDowall, *A Modern History of the Kurds*, 282 n32.

17. Ezzatyar, *The Last Mufti of Iranian Kurdistan*, 122.

18. Ahmad Eskandari, "Obituary, Sheikh Ezzedin Hosseini (1922–2011)," in *Wiener Jahrbuch für Kurdische Studien* (Vienna: Wiener Verlag, 2013), http://www.wvfs.at/index.php?link=single_title&titleID=6.

19. Gohary, *Eastern Kurdistan*, 104–05. The Kurdish delegation also included Ghani Bulurian, a former member of the Tudeh and a well-known Kurdish activist imprisoned during the Shah's regime. Bulurian and Foruhar knew each other well, having been prison mates under the Shah. Also members of the Kurdish delegation were Saleh Mukhtari and a representative from Komala. Kutschera, *Le défi kurde*, 164.

20. Abdul Rahman Ghassemlou, interview with Jonathan Randal, Paris, 1986.

21. Kutschera, *Le défi kurde*, 164.

22. Ibid.

23. Q. M., interview with the author, undisclosed location, 1991. Q. M. is the pseudonym used, for security reasons, by an exiled Iranian Kurdish political leader.

24. Abdul Rahman Ghassemlou, *Cil Sal Xebat le Penawi Azadi* [Forty years of struggle for the sake of freedom], Vol. 1 in *Kurtemêjûy Hizbî Dêmukratî Kurdistanî Eran* [A concise history of the Democratic Party of Iranian Kurdistan] [in Kurdish] (Erbil, Iraq: PDKI Publishing House, 2002), 300; translation Sharif Behruz.

25. Specifically, the eight-point plan demanded: "1) Official recognition of Kurdish autonomy and reference to it in the new Iranian Constitution. 2) The autonomous Kurdish region to include the four provinces of Ilam, Kermanshah, Kurdistan, and West Azerbaijan. 3) The election of a Kurdish assembly by secret ballot. The council to select a local government to administer economic, social, cultural, and internal security affairs for the Kurdish region. 4) Kurdish to be considered an official language in schools and official correspondence; Persian to be taught in the Kurdish elementary schools after the fourth grade. 5) The allocation of a portion of the [national] budget to develop the region. 6) Kurdish representatives to be given important positions in the central government. 7) The central government to have control over the army, foreign policy, national [countrywide] economy, and long-term economic planning. 8) The guarantee of freedom of the press, of expression, and of political and religious organization." Edmund Ghareeb, *The Kurdish Question in Iraq* (Syracuse, NY: Syracuse University Press, 1981), 15–16.

26. Kutschera, *Le défi kurde*, 164–65.

27. Jonathan C. Randal, "Kurds' Autonomy Cries Rekindle Ethnic Flashpoint in Iran," *Washington Post*, March 2, 1979, in the Aadel Collection of IHRDC. https://iranhrdc.org/?s=Jonathan+C.+Randal (accessed Jsnusry 14, 2019).

28. Abdul Rahman Ghassemlou, interview with Jonathan Randal, Paris, 1986.

29. Iraj Ghaderi, interview with the author, PDKI general headquarters in Kurdistan on the Iran-Iraq border, 1985. Further statements from Ghaderi are from this interview.

30. *Jash*, literally "jackass," was a popular derogatory term for those regarded as traitors, in this case Kurds who collaborated with the regime.

31. As one of the most prominent among the Kurdish tribes, the Barzani Kurds had waged a decades-long struggle for autonomy in Iraq along the border areas. At the dawn of the Iranian revolution the Barzani insurgence was led by Mulla Mustafa al-Barzani, who had joined the effort as a young man in 1931. Active on both sides of the border, he served as commander of the Kurdish army for the Democratic Republic of Kurdistan. At the fall of the republic in 1946, he took refuge in the Soviet Union, where he carried on the effort to gain support for the Kurdish freedom movement. Following his return to Kurdistan in 1958, he continued to advance the Kurdish cause against the Iraqi regime to the time of his death (from cancer, while seeking medical treatment in the U.S.) in March of 1979. McDowall, *A Modern History of the Kurds*, passim; Quil Lawrence, *Invisible Nation: How the Kurds' Quest for Statehood Is Shaping Iraq and the Middle East* (New York: Walker & Co., 2008), 15.

32. Gohary, *Eastern Kurdistan*, 114.

33. Abdullah Hassanzadeh, *Niw Sede Xebat* [Half a century of struggle], Part 2, Vol. 3 in *A Concise History of the Democratic Party of Iranian Kurdistan* [in Kurdish] (n.p.: PDKI Publishing House, 2002), 299; translation Sharif Behruz.

34. Persians are one of the Iranian ethnicities, so called for the language they speak, Fars. The traditional name *Persia* was used by the West as the official designation for Iran until 1935. *Iran*, "the land of the Aryans," is the modern-day designation and is used officially in a political context. However, both names are used interchangeably to this day. Over 70 percent of the population speaks some kind of Indo-European language or dialect; the other 30 percent speak Turkic and Semitic languages (Arabic). By official census, 53 percent of Iranians speak Persian, 18 percent speak Azeri and other Turkic dialects, and 10 percent speak Kurdish. CIA *World Factbook*, https://www.cia.gov/library/publications/the-world-factbook/geos/ir.html (accessed March 18, 2013); *Encyclopædia Britannica* (accessed March 18, 2013).

35. Iraj Ghaderi, interview with the author, 1985.

36. Colonel Habibullah Abbasi, as a major in the Iranian army under the Shah, was in military service in Tehran when revolution broke out there in the streets; he fled the city, the chaos, and his army post altogether. Veteran party member Jalil Gadani, also in Tehran at the outbreak of the agitation there, brought him back to Mahabad just two days prior to the garrison takeover.

37. Hamid Gohary, *Eastern Kurdistan*, 122.

38. Ghassemlou and the party had not promoted such a takeover, not just of the garrison in Mahabad but of posts throughout the region, because they felt it would not be well received. The Mahabad garrison takeover was an internal affair, and the PDKI stepped in at a critical moment to manage the post's transition.

39. Ghassemlou told journalist Chris Kutschera that there were "more than three thousand rifles and many heavy weapons: RPG-7, machine guns, 81mm and 105mm, TOW missiles, and a dozen tanks. We had to pay a fortune to the truck drivers to transport this equipment to a secure place." Kutschera, *Le défi kurde*, 165.

40. Q. M., interview with the author, 1991.

41. Kutschera, *Le défi kurde*, 179; from an interview with Ghassemlou in October 1979 in Iranian Kurdistan.

42. Ibid., 180.

43. Gohary, *Eastern Kurdistan*, 123.

44. Ezzatyar, *The Last Mufti of Iranian Kurdistan*, 128–29.

45. Abdul Rahman Ghassemlou, interview with Enayat Fani, June 1989; translation Beyan Farshi and Esmail Ebrahimi. Part of this interview was used in Channel 4 TV's documentary "Iran: The Other Story." An extended version of the interview was broadcast on BBC Persian TV in July 2014; see YouTube, "Abdul-Rahman Ghassemlou, BBC Persian," posted July 16, 2014, https://www.youtube.com/watch?v=SGsfvkcMn8U; (accessed February 20, 2017).

46. Ghareeb, *The Kurdish Question*, 15.

47. Said Shamsaddini, lecture at British Parliament, London, July 2008, quoting from the Iranian journal *Ayandegan*.

48. Denise Natali, *The Kurds and the State: Evolving National Identity in Iraq, Turkey and Iran* (Syracuse, NY: Syracuse University Press, 2005), 142.

49. *Le Monde*, March 23, 1979.

50. Denise Natali, *The Kurds and the State*, 142, quoting from the Iranian journals *Kayhan* (1979) and *Ayandegan* (1979).

51. *The Guardian*, February 21, 1979.

52. As reported by Associated Press, "Kurdish rebels tighten hold on Iranian city," *The Baltimore Sun*, March 22, 1979; Kutschera, *Le défi kurde*, 166.

53. See Fred Halliday, "Interview with Shaik Izzedin Husseini: A Dictatorship under the Name of Islam," *Middle East Reports*, No. 113 (March–April 1983), 9.

54. Babasheikh Nasseri, interview with Salah Piroty, March–April 2016; translation Salah Piroty. Nasseri, later a commander for the PDKI's peshmerga in Sanandaj, witnessed these events.

55. Ezzatyar, *The Last Mufti of Iranian Kurdistan*, 121.

56. As well as leading Friday prayer at the Jameh mosque, Moftizadeh was the founder of the Mektebe Qur'an, the Qur'an school, in Sanandaj. "He was approached during the first serious bout of fighting in Sanandaj in March 1979," McDowall noted, "almost certainly to undermine the popular Mahabdmulla Izz al Din Hussayni, who had become a focus for Kurdish resistance. Although Muftizadeh had associated with Kurdish activists, he was widely seen as a reactionary." McDowall, *A Modern History of the Kurds*, 267.

57. Ezzatyar, *The Last Mufti of Iranian Kurdistan*, 128.

58. The concept of shura as intrinsic to governance is based in verse 38 of Sura 42 of the Qur'an, *Al-Shura*. In verse 159 of Sura 3, Muhammad himself is enjoined to consult with believers. See Lamya Hamad, "Shura: Islamic Approach to Decision-Making," at Why Islam?, http://www.whyislam.org/social-values-in-islam/social-ties/shura-islamic-approach-to-decision-making/.

59. Ezzatyar, *The Last Mufti of Iranian Kurdistan*, 128.

60. McDowall, *A Modern History of the Kurds*, 267.

61. Ezzatyar, *The Last Mufti of Iranian Kurdistan*, 125.

62. Ibid., 128.

63. Ibid., 130.

64. Ibid., 129–30.

65. Ibid., 131.

66. Babasheikh Nasseri, interview with Salah Piroty; translation Salah Piroty, April 20, 2016. Nasseri, the appointee for political affairs of the PDKI's Sherifzadeh force or battalion in

1979, later became a commander for the party's peshmerga forces during the war in Sanandaj, which would break out a year later, in April 1980.

67. Leaders and local notables who came together to form the council included Sediq Kemanger and Mozefer Mohammedi, from Komala; Behrouz Suleimani, from Feda'iyan; Shaib Zekeryai, well-known for having been a political prisoner under the Shah; and Dr. Khosrawi Khosrawi, a close associate of Moftizadeh.

68. Gohary, *Eastern Kurdistan*, 136.

69. Associated Press, "Kurdish rebels tighten hold on Iranian city," *The Baltimore Sun*, March 22, 1979; Kutschera, *Le défi kurde*, 166.

70. Gohary, *Eastern Kurdistan*, 136.

71. Ezzatyar, *The Last Mufti of Iranian Kurdistan*, 130–31.

72. Babasheikh Nasseri, interviews with Salah Piroty, April 20, 2016; translation Salah Piroty. IHRDC, *Haunted Memories: The Islamic Republic's Executions of Kurds in 1979* (New Haven, CT: 2011), 3. After the February 1979 Islamic Revolution, also reports 200 fatalities and "many more" wounded. https://iranhrdc.org/english/publications/reports/3508-haunted-memories-the-islamic-republics-executions-of-kurds-in-1979.html.

73. Ronald Koven, "Troubles Erupt in Iran's Border Areas: Disorders in Border Regions Challenges Iran's New Rulers," *Washington Post*, March 19, 1979, https://www.washingtonpost.com/archive/politics/1979/03/20/troubles-erupt-in-irans-border-areas/8e36b188-e49f-4c6b-9728-30cb6ff35b2e/?utm_term=.3af0dd19e13b. The "stronger autonomy demands" issued jointly by Ghassemlou and Sheikh Ezzedin had included "demands that the authorities in Tehran did not feel they could accept. These included the enlargement of the Kurdistan region to include all Kurdish-speaking areas in Iran, a specified share of the national revenue for expenditure in the province, and complete autonomy in provincial administration." See "The Iran Primer: Timeline of Military and Security Events," United States Institute of Peace, http://iranprimer.usip.org/resource/timeline-military-and-security-events.

74. Ezzatyar, *The Last Mufti of Iranian Kurdistan*, 132.

75. Abdullah Hassanzadeh, *Niw Sede Xebat* [Half a century of struggle: A retrospect of struggle and activity of the Democratic Party of Iranian Kurdistan] [in Kurdish], Vol. 1 (Gawrade: Press Commission of the Kurdistan Democratic Party of Iran, August 1995), 140–42; translation Salah Piroty.

76. Parenthesis in the original.

77. Ghareeb, *The Kurdish Question*, 17, quoting broadcast by Khomeini on Radio Tehran, FBIS (U.S. Foreign Broadcast Information Service), March 20, 1979.

78. IHRDC, *Haunted Memories*, 3. After the February 1979 Islamic Revolution, quoting interview with Rauf Kaabi, a former member of the Feda'iyan-e Khalq (the People's Feda'iyan, Sazman-e Cherikhayeh Feda'iyan-e Khalq); (accessed January 3, 2019).

79. Babasheikh Nasseri, interview with Salah Piroty.

80. The Islamic Republican Party brought together all those who unconditionally accepted Khomeini's leadership: "From the beginning of the revolution until its dissolution in 1987, it played a vital role as Khomeini's task force, the vehicle through which opponents, or even undesirable allies, were outmaneuvered and the supremacy of the clergy in government was ensured." Baqer Moin, *Khomeini: Life of the Ayatollah* (New York: Thomas Dunne Books, 2000), 210–11.

81. The Kurdish delegation included PDKI member Abdullah Hassanzadeh and prominent activist Ghani Bulurian. There were five government delegates and a few other notable personalities including Sediq Kemanger. Gohary, *Eastern Kurdistan*, 138.

82. *Le Monde*, March 24, 1991.

83. Hassan Khaliqi, interviews with Salah Piroty, March 2 and April 7, 2017. Khaliqi, a former philosophy professor at University of Tabriz, had joined PDKI in the early days of the Iranian revolution. As a member of the PDKI central committee, he headed the social commission and was director of the political-military academy for some years. He is currently the head of the Kurdish Institute of Stockholm. His published work includes *Islam and Democracy* and *Kurdish Sociology*.

84. Hassan Khaliqi, interviews with Salah Piroty, March 2 and April 7, 2017.

85. Fred Halliday, "Interview with Shaik Izzedin Husseini: A Dictatorship under the Name of Islam," *Middle East Reports*, No. 113 (March–April 1983), 9.

86. Eskandari, "Obituary, Sheikh Ezzedin Hosseini."

87. *Ghabrestan*, literally, "graveyard." The popular slogan meant, essentially, "Liberty or death," "A free Kurdistan or death," "We shall die for Kurdistan and be buried here." Kutschera's source is Jean Gueyras, "Les Kurdes affirment leur volonté d'autonomie en présence de l'Ayatollah Taleghani," *Le Monde*, March 24, 1979.

88. The agreement also stipulated the appointment of a Kurd as governor-general of Kurdistan; the participation of Kurds in the drafting of the new Iranian constitution; the Kurds' right to their culture and to the teaching of Kurdish as well as Persian in schools in the Kurdish region; and administration of local government by elected Kurdish representatives. *The Guardian*, March 26, 1979; IHRDC, *Haunted Memories*, 3. After the February 1979 Islamic Revolution; Ezzatyar, *The Last Mufti of Iranian Kurdistan*, 133–34.

89. Nader Entessar, "The Kurds in Post-Revolutionary Iran and Iraq," *Third World Review* Vol. 6, No. 4 (October 1984), 926–27.

90. *The Guardian*, March 26, 1979; "Chronology," *Middle East Journal*, September 1979, 355–56.

91. Ezzatyar, *The Last Mufti of Iranian Kurdistan*, 134. The election one month later to establish a city administrative council, a permanent body, Ezzatyar notes, "would actually be the first elections in the Islamic Republic's history." Ibid.

92. Dialogue as reported by Kutschera, *Le défi kurde*, 167.

93. Nader Entessar, *Kurdish Politics in the Middle East* (London: Lexington Books, 2010), 41.

94. *Time* magazine, September 24, 1979, obituary of Ayatollah Mahmoud Taleghani in "Milestones," http://content.time.com/time/magazine/article/0,9171,947428,00.html#ixzz2eSMoWmfu (accessed September 11, 2013).

95. Ferdinand Hennerbichler, "Assassination of Abdul Rahman Ghassemlou (1930–1989): New Assessment," in *Wiener Jahrbuch für Kurdische Studien 2013, Schwerpunkt: Transnationalität und kurdische Diaspora in Österreich*, Jahrgang 1/2013 (Vienna: Österreichische Gesellschaft zur Förderung der Kurdologie / Europäisches Zentrum für kurdische Studien, 2013), 291. Hennerbichler interviewed Ghassemlou in Vienna in January 1989 right after the first set of negotiations.

96. Natali, *The Kurds and the State*, 143.

97. Ibid., quoting from the Iranian journals *Kayhan* (1979d) and *Ayandegan* (1979d).

98. Entessar, "The Kurds in Post-Revolutionary Iran and Iraq," 927.

MAHABAD, NATIONALIST CITY

৵

The situation was different in Mahabad. This was a liberated city in which a newfound freedom prevailed. There were no patrols in the streets, nor surveillance at the entrances or exits to the city. Peshmerga maintained order under the PDKI's direction.

Excitement ran high in the bazaars and markets. There, even alcoholic beverages, forbidden in all of Iran by the central government, were sold. The Kurds living in the mountains did not come to the bazaar for consumer goods, but were attracted by the flourishing commerce in weapons, overpriced though they were.

In Mahabad, the party had installed a government that managed the city's affairs. Since it was a secular party, its leaders insisted on separating religion from the state. The city atmosphere was calm and friendly. During Foruhar's stay in the city, Ghassemlou and Foruhar saw each other daily, and the two men had meals with Sheikh Ezzedin Hossein. Foreign journalists arrived every day, and many were surprised to see alcoholic beverages being consumed so openly.

Following its peaceful takeover by Ghassemlou's people, the military garrison was now under the nominal command of a Kurdish chief officer, Parwiz Razmipush, designated by Tehran. But he never came to Mahabad to exercise his duty. In reality, the garrison was controlled by a dozen armed peshmerga under the orders of Hassan Shiwasali, military head of the PDKI.[1]

Mahabad flourished as a nationalistic city while Iran erupted with revolution. The city was celebrating its democracy and had not been affected by the palace conspiracies of Tehran.[2]

Known in the past as Saujbulagh or Savokhbulagh, the city had prospered in the district and province of West Azerbaijan, south of Lake Urmia, a narrow and fertile valley 1302 meters above sea level. Mahabad was a traditional agricultural market hub in a region of vineyards and tobacco fields, and a vital center for wool marketing. In 1979, there were not more than forty thousand people living there.

The Kurds were now reclaiming a power they had not possessed since the times of the Democratic Republic of Kurdistan.[3] The PDKI was reorganizing and strengthening itself day by day and preparing for its first real public gathering under the leadership of Ghassemlou, its secretary-general.

Kendal Nezan, then a nuclear physicist from Turkey and later president of the Kurdish Institute in Paris, visited Mahabad in those days. Arriving from Europe at the Tehran airport, he was surprised to find Ghassemlou waiting for him there with his niece and Sadegh Sharafkandi. "Given the situation," Nezan later recounted, "I imagined he would have had bodyguards. But he was like that, unpretentious and modest. He did not like to flaunt his importance.[4]

"Ghassemlou and Sharafkandi were in Tehran for negotiations. He told us to take advantage [of the freedom] because this situation in Iran was not going to last: 'It will last a few months,' he told me. 'This is the best moment of the revolution. Soon the mullahs will begin to confiscate it.'"

The four went to have dinner. Ghassemlou's niece was driving. After lunch, Ghassemlou told his niece to pay the bill. "In Iran it's not well seen to have a woman pay—and there were three adult men. When the waiter brought the change he put it in front of Rahman and gave him a deadly look. Rahman then explained that this was educational; it was important that men know that women exist. He always fought for the emancipation of women."[5]

It is true that there were not many women at political and social meetings. Nezan thought this was due to the Persian influence in Mahabad, which was extremely conservative. Visiting some friends who had lived in Europe, for instance, here on their home ground he found that he was not able to see their sisters. On the other hand, he added, "in homes where there were only Kurds, everyone ate together, men and women."[6]

Ghassemlou thought that Iran did not have the economic means to launch a military campaign against Kurdistan. He was not expecting a war, and even in light of his comprehensive understanding of the situation, he underestimated Tehran's chaos. He complained that he did not have a credible intermediary with the government: for one negotiation, Tehran might send a mullah who agreed with the Kurds' priorities, and then turn around and send another who did not.

Ghassemlou was not then the undisputed leader of the Kurds, but one among many Kurdish representatives. In Mahabad, the PDKI was one of many political organizations. Each occupied a building with its own peshmerga and displayed its own flag. It was difficult to ascertain the relative importance of any given organization.

The most popular figure was Sheikh Ezzedin. It was only the cadres of the party who knew Ghassemlou. But this was changing. "Thanks to his lucidity and open politics, he was able to communicate in a way that corresponded to the hopes and desires of the population," attested Nezan. "This is how he was able to expand the base of the party, as well as his popularity. Also, for the foreign press and the authorities, he was rapidly emerging as the undisputed leader of the Kurds and their main interlocutor."

For Nezan, this was due to Ghassemlou's strong personality, his capacity for dialogue, and his ability to pursue the perfect argument at the right time.

"He established himself as the ideological leader of the Kurdish nationalist movement while the party was still in an uncertain and precarious phase. During the [large public] meeting [in Mahabad in March] where the PDKI was announcing its political agenda, Ghassemlou addressed large crowds for the first time and emerged as a leader. It is also true that in those days, it was easy to gather the populace. The Kurds were hungry, and they thronged to attend every significant event."

The meeting in question was held under a resplendent sun one morning at the beginning of March, in a football stadium. People began to arrive very early from all corners of Kurdistan. The inhabitants of Mahabad had never seen the city so joyous and enthusiastic. It was like a large celebratory party. The gregarious and passionate Kurds were talking, exchanging opinions, and freely expressing themselves.

Ghassemlou waited at the party's headquarters. Fatah Abdulli, who remembered seeing him that day, recalled that Ghassemlou had changed his European suit for a Kurdish one, which he would wear from now on when he was in Kurdistan.[7]

At 10:00 a.m. on March 2, 1979, Ghassemlou and his colleagues left for the stadium. About twenty peshmerga surrounded him. Ghassemlou got into a Land Rover protected by ten men while the rest surveilled the route toward the stadium. Tens of thousands of people crowded the stadium—an unexpected number in a city the size of Mahabad. This was the PDKI's first political demonstration. Ghassemlou walked in, and as he headed toward the podium, he took the time to speak with everyone who addressed him. "He always made contact," recalled Fatah Abdulli.

The applause stopped only when he asked for silence. He was speaking in public for the first time. For one hour, Ghassemlou read his discourse with a slow and deliberate voice, in a direct manner and with few gestures. His style was decidedly different from Persian speakers, whose eloquence tended to be melodramatic. Propaganda for the party was not an element of his speech. Self-assured and convincing, Ghassemlou transmitted this same confidence to his collaborators.[8]

"It was the first time someone had spoken with clarity and openness about the Kurdish question," Azad remembered. "I began to understand why people loved him so quickly. That day, for the first time the Kurds had a strong sign that their lives could change. He represented national pride."[9]

Under a clear blue sky, Ghassemlou addressed his compatriots. "Maintaining democratic freedoms, ensuring a true democratic rule across the country, is a guarantee to advance the revolution and to gain permissible rights for our people," he proclaimed. "Without a true democratic regime, Kurdish rights won't be fully ensured—and without ensuring Kurdish national rights, a democratic system won't last forever.

"The Kurdish people, like other Iranian ethnics, have the right to be assured officially that the nationwide oppression of the Shah's grim legacy will be eliminated.

"Kurdish representatives should participate in the Constituent Assembly and in drafting a new constitution for Iran, to make sure the Iranian nationalities and the Kurdish people's just rights are to be included in the law.

"Accusing the Kurdish people of separatism is an old song. While we consider this accusation as a conspiracy by enemies of the revolution and totally reject it, we declare that throughout Iranian Kurdistan, there is no separatist political party. People are generally demanding their national rights within Iran."[10]

Ghassemlou announced the political agenda of the PDKI and called on the Tehran government to accept the demands of the Kurds: autonomy for Kurdistan and democracy for Iran. These words became the rallying cry of the party.

This first demonstration launched him in the public eye. Now not only was he known by the Kurds, but also the foreign and Iranian press became fascinated with him. He had embarked on a new stage in his political life. Ghassemlou had become the spokesperson for the Kurdish people, with Iran's central power and the entire world.

After the demonstration, Ghassemlou asked Sheikh Ezzedin Hosseini[11] to accompany him to visit Khomeini in Qom. Ezzedin, as a respected Kurdish Sunni religious leader who held the prestigious post of Friday prayer leader in

Mahabad, was the closest Sunni counterpart to the Imam in Iran. Ghassemlou naturally felt that Ezzedin, as a cleric, could find more common ground for dialogue with Khomeini than he could.

Sheikh Ezzedin refused to accompany him because Komala's leftists opposed the initiative. So Ghassemlou proposed to his party's central committee that he venture to the holy city himself. He argued that this was something that absolutely needed to be done. Everyone was visiting the leader of the revolution. If the Kurds did not go, it could seem suspicious. And with the imminent referendum on the Islamic Republic, a conversation with Khomeini would allow Ghassemlou to assess the Ayatollah's intentions and thus determine the Kurds' best course vis-à-vis the referendum: whether to support it or not.

❧

Two days before the referendum, at the end of March, Ghassemlou traveled to Qom. He had requested a meeting with the Ayatollah. He came with a group of PDKI members. Among them was Jalil Gadani, an old party militant, twice condemned to death by the Shah's regime.[12]

Gadani had more than once served time in prisons. He was detained for the first time when he was a student after a politically compromising letter he had mailed was intercepted. Later, he became politically active with Mossadegh's nationalists. Caught distributing propaganda, he was sent to prison again, this time for seven months. In 1954, accused of being a member of the PDKI, he spent a full year behind bars. He was working with farmers and peasants in 1967 when he was arrested once more. He spent time in prisons in Mahabad, Tehran, and Tabriz. Though condemned to death, he was not executed.

Gadani lived through the harshness of the southern prisons near the Persian Gulf. "There," he recounted, "I suffered physical and psychological torture. The heat was terrible. There were all types of people in jail: intellectuals, peasants, workers. Sometimes we were put together with criminals." He was arrested for the final time in 1969 for having participated in one of the first marches against the Shah. Once more he was condemned to death. "But people's protests stopped the execution."

Gadani was in Tehran when the revolution broke out. He left prison on a Friday in 1979, and his first impression outside was of the people's fear. "At that point, we had not yet gathered around Dr. Ghassemlou. We spoke with people in the mosques and the streets. These groups were all working on their own. I also saw Khomeini when he came back [from exile]. He had offered rights to all the people of Iran, and I was in Tehran when he arrived. I saw him step off the plane. An excited crowd welcomed him. This was the most important reception in the history of Iran."

Years later in the mountains of Kurdistan, speaking about the group's visit with Khomeini on March 28, 1979, to present him with the Kurds' autonomy demands, Gadani explained: "We were five or six.[13] I was there as the one responsible for Tehran; others were responsible for their regions and from the [PDKI] central committee. We were the first political organization that Khomeini received—though in the end, he did not accept our petition."

In Tehran, Ghassemlou stayed at the home of a family member the night before heading for Qom with the delegation. He was very optimistic and hoped the Kurds would be able to open a space for dialogue.[14]

In Qom, the delegation arrived at the house of the leader of the Iranian revolution—a simple two-story dwelling. They entered through a courtyard with a cement-block fountain at its center surrounded by shrubbery, and crossed an alcove lit by a single lightbulb hanging from the ceiling. In this room, countless ministers, ambassadors, politicians, and clerics had awaited their meeting with the Imam. "When we walked in," recalled Ghassemlou, "we found hundreds of children and women in Khomeini's room. Seated on the floor with his legs crossed, the Ayatollah would take a lump of sugar, put it into his mouth, and then he would take it out and give it to one of the boys sitting next to him."[15]

Khomeini was a particularly imposing figure: wide forehead, knitted brow, jet black eyes with thick eyebrows, long beard, and black turban—in the Shi'a tradition, attire permitted only to members of the Prophet's lineage. It was said that his power emanated from God. He was God's voice, the servant of Allah. Always enraged against the evils of the world, he preached intolerance and hatred of Western imperialism and Marxism alike. His mystical appearance was coupled with an iron will. His only weakness seemed to be his penchant for the adulation of the masses.

"I went up to his son Ahmed and told him that we had traveled one thousand kilometers to meet alone with him," Ghassemlou reminisced.

"In five minutes," responded Ahmed.

"Suddenly, everyone left the room. A very small mullah and some members of our central committee stayed by the door to stop people from coming in. No one searched us. It would have been very easy to kill him."[16]

The meeting began in a "relaxed atmosphere."[17] "We were alone with him for one hour," Ghassemlou told American journalist Jonathan Randal. "I explained the situation to him; this included our desire to participate in the referendum . . . as long as our demands were respected."[18]

But, as Ghassemlou recounted later to journalist Chris Kutschera, the delegation's hopes for a clear discussion were met with characteristic deflection by Khomeini's rejoinder: "We are all Muslims, equals before Islam. We must preserve our unity."[19]

When the Kurdish delegates insisted on the need to assure their rights, Khomeini responded, "No problem, you will have roads, schools, hospitals."

"But we want our *political* rights." Ghassemlou was persistent, and shifted his argument with an appeal to the political benefits for Khomeini: "If you make a statement about autonomy, that would be very well seen by Kurds."[20]

But with Khomeini there would be no direct discussion. Evading the question once again, he responded obliquely, and then asked, "Is this not against the unity of Iran?"[21]

When Ghassemlou pressed the Kurds' concerns, as he later described to Jonathan Randal, Khomeini sidestepped the matter completely:[22] "That is not my business," he said with his head bent low. "Go see Bazargan," he said—"without," Ghassemlou added, "even looking at me."

"'That's fine," Ghassemlou replied to the Ayatollah; then asked, "and we would like you to publicly comment about our meeting."

"Ayatollah Taleghani already made a declaration," the Ayatollah muttered, referring to the agreement reached days before, on March 24, after the Sanandaj events. "What more do you want?"

"The Western and Iranian press were waiting outside for us," Ghassemlou remembered, speaking years later to Jonathan Randal. "They suspected that we were clearly in the opposition. I insisted once more: 'So when I leave here, you authorize me to declare that you agree with what Taleghani said?'[23]

"'But I don't know what he said,' he abruptly objected. 'We are all brothers and Muslims.'[24]

"When we insisted upon our objective, he said he was feeling sick and quickly left the room without even looking at us.[25]

"We got up and went outside the house. We saw him on the roof, waving at people. We got into our cars, and before leaving Qom, we decided we would not participate in the referendum."

❧

From Khomeini in Qom the Kurdish delegation traveled to see Bazargan in Tehran, where they presented the prime minister with their demands.

With respect to "autonomy," the prime minister told them, "in principle, we are not against."[26] But confronted with the specific demand for the election of an assembly representing the three Kurdish provinces, he exclaimed: "That is a separatist Kurdistan!" Then he, too, slid away from direct engagement: "Anyway, I am leading a transition government. We will see after the constitution is adopted," he concluded.

Bazargan assured them that the impasse could be solved and announced that he would send three ministers to Kurdistan to look into the details of the agreement.

But the Kurds knew that the government only wanted to buy some time. During a number of press conferences Ghassemlou gave in Tehran, he declared the Kurds would support Bazargan's government as long as it clearly was promoting democracy for Iran and autonomy for Kurdistan.[27]

In Tehran, Ghassemlou once again stayed with his relatives before returning to Kurdistan. His optimism was gone. He told his family how Khomeini had dismissed them with one sentence, and without one look had told them to go see Bazargan. Khomeini's body language and the single sentence he pronounced made it clear there would be no dialogue.

"I know these religious people," Ghassemlou said to his family; "their body language said it all. These people will never dialogue with us. Before, I wasn't sure; but now I am convinced there will be no dialogue."[28]

Indeed, there would not be. When confronted, it would be by his actions, not his evasive words, that Khomeini would make it clear that "in the new Islamic Republic there could be no room for any special treatment or separate system for specific groups with social or religious claims like autonomy for Kurds."[29] The Ayatollah would "confirm the demand of his fraction within the Islamic clergy," the faction already "pushing for autocracy and for the hegemony of religion (autocratic Shia Islam) over politics (democracy) in Iran."[30]

Reflecting ten years later on the frustrations of this time, Ghassemlou would say, "The *akhūnds* [Islamic clerics] claimed they were interested in negotiations, and we accepted. For six months we were negotiating; I personally met with more akhūnds during these six months than I had met in my whole life. Unfortunately, we realized that they never meant to negotiate with us; all they wanted was to gain some time to regain their military strength, and attack us again."[31]

At that early stage in the Islamic Revolution, despite Khomeini's auto-cratic rule, Ghassemlou nevertheless still believed democracy had a chance in Iran. As always, he was constantly gauging what he would come to call "the relationship of forces." By his analysis, "those newly in power had no experience in governance; they were fragmented in various antagonizing frac-tions, depending on split-up armed forces and developing paramilitary groups. Therefore, Ghassemlou thought, they could still be forced to tolerate a dem-ocratic and institutionalized opposition as times went by."[32] And to keep this possibility open, he maintained and strengthened his contacts within govern-ment, religious leadership, and holders of power at the provincial level as well as with members of other opposition groups.[33]

And so on March 29, 1979, the Kurds announced that they would not participate in the referendum planned for March 30–31 because the question, as worded, allowed only the up-or-down vote for a purely Islamic republic: "Are you in favor of replacing the monarchy with an Islamic republic whose constitution will be approved? Yes or no."

At this critical juncture, the Kurds' essential fear seemed ominously well-founded: that "the Islamic state, as envisioned by Ayatollah Khomeini, would result in a Shi'a dictatorship."[34] The Kurds' position toward the referendum had become very pointed: "The slogan 'No referendum, self-determina-tion first' epitomised the Kurdish feelings towards Tehran's latest autonomy scheme."[35]

On the first of April, Ayatollah Khomeini proclaimed the Islamic Repub-lic of Iran,[36] the "first government of God," which would "establish justice and defeat and bury monarchy in the garbage of history."[37]

Still over the horizon was what no one could yet know, but what Ghas-semlou and others could have foreseen: that the new constitution, upon its final approval in December 1979, would essentially give Khomeini "constitu-tional powers unimagined by the shahs."[38]

In Kurdistan, hardly any people voted.

֍

One index of the times can be found in an anecdote related by Ghassemlou. At the March 28 meetings with Khomeini and Bazargan, Ghassemlou had also approached them with a more personal request: he had received an invi-tation from the Palestinian leader Yasser Arafat to visit Lebanon. He needed a passport. The government had issued one to Bulurian, another Kurdish deputy from Mahabad, but would not issue one to him. The only explanation for this discrepancy came with the refusal letter from the passport office: it was an ancient order from the SAVAK, in 1956, that prohibited Ghassemlou from leaving the country.

The SAVAK had been dissolved by the Majlis on February 5, 1979—six days before Bakhtiar's government fell and Khomeini took power. In reality, however, important members of the SAVAK continued to operate under the new Islamist aegis. Long-buried directives would continue to be unearthed, selectively, as needed; a change of regime rarely reaches the police archives.[39]

So while the Shah's feared political police was publicly proscribed and its agents hunted down all over Iran, the Islamic Republic was denying a Kurdish leader a passport based on an order of that very outlawed agency.

ℕ

In April 1979, Ghassemlou began a tour of Kurdistan proclaiming the political program of the PDKI, which was gaining influence. A large public meeting was being organized in the city of Naghadeh, 40 kilometers from Mahabad. While the majority of the city's population and that of its suburbs were Kurds, large numbers of Azeris were present as well.[40] Tension between the two ethnic communities, of long standing, had grown continuously since the revolution.

In his analysis of relations between the Kurds and the Azeri Turks, Iraqi politician and intellectual Nawshirwan Mustafa Amin outlines the origin of conflict between the two nations. Historically, he reports, relations "in the region never attained a normal and peaceful coexistence, but rather took a confrontational form." Conflicts were pervasive and multidimensional: Turkish-speaking Azeri, religiously Shi'ite, regarded Sunnis as "misguided." More to the point, perhaps, was differential ethnic access to resources and power: politically, the regional administrative, financial, and military affairs were all under Azeri control, and the Azeris "enjoyed full support from the central authority and treated the Kurds—who, with the Persians, had settled there thousands of years ago—as peasants."[41]

The Kurds, predominantly Sunni, in turn considered the Shi'ite Azeris "apostates." Linguistically distinct from the newcomer Afshar Turkish tribes settling in northwest Iran, they regarded the Turks as invaders, and pushed back hard against the incoming occupiers of their lands. This long-running conflict reached a state of complexity that took on "political, national, and religious forms that would be reflected in the future relations of both nations economically, socially, culturally, and politically in the region."[42]

The complex and uneasy balance would be tipped by the massing waves of revolution and the agitated expectations it unleashed. With a largely Kurdish population, daily life in almost every town and city of Kurdistan was predominantly Kurdish in color. But in the opening movements of the revolution, as throughout the era of the old regime, significant advantages were firmly in Azeri hands. In garrisons once controlled by the Shah's army, in local revolutionary committees to which weapons taken from those garrisons had now fallen, in committee decisions and deployment of materiel, Azeris remained prime movers and primary beneficiaries. While many Azeris, who were Shi'ites and pro-Khomeini, had received both army support and weapons commandeered by the revolution, the Kurds had not. Insurgence emerging among the Kurds, unleashed in the revolution by rising hopes, could easily appear as a mounting threat to Azeri advantages.

For their part, the Azeris too were demanding autonomy. But Prime Minister Bazargan declared that autonomy would be conceded only after taking into consideration overall national conditions, not the wishes of individual regions. He warned both the Azeri and the Kurdish communities of the dangers of separatism. Reacting to the Kurds' demands, Bazargan said, "They [the Kurds] didn't simply want autonomy; they wanted to be separate from Iran."[43] This despite Kurdish leadership's repeated insistence that the "demand for autonomy held no such implication,"[44] and Ghassemlou's stated perception that "it was reactionaries who shouted about secession. The Kurdish Left wanted a constructive autonomy."[45]

The stage was set. On April 20, twenty-five thousand people congregated at the Naghadeh stadium. Ghassemlou had just begun to speak when shots were heard outside.[46] Immediately Ghassemlou ordered the people to disperse. Unidentified men had opened fire on the PDKI rally, "killing a reported 25 persons and injuring many others."[47]

Ghassemlou's first thought was the safety of the people; for his bodyguard, the first thought was for the safety of their leader. In the panic of that moment, Ghassemlou's party colleague and assistant Aziz Mameli recalled, "We were in the stadium and the first thing we needed to do was to save Ghassemlou. We had to go to get the car in the Turkish neighborhood where we had parked. We left for Mahabad; we barely escaped.

"The war had begun."[48]

Confrontations between Kurds and Azeris were coming to a head. Now, as Azeri bands set out to loot neighboring Kurdish villages, violence escalated, with extensive use of mortars and heavy artillery. There was a heavy toll: in very short order, twelve thousand Kurds were left homeless and at least two hundred died.[49]

Losses mounted when, after two days of fighting, the six hundred troops sent to Naghadeh[50] to intervene sided with the Azeris and indiscriminately fired upon the Kurds.[51] The streets of Naghadeh were strewn with dozens, perhaps hundreds, of corpses. According to Jalil Gadani, there were more than three hundred dead on both sides. "The monarchists and some Shi'ite mullahs," he said, "caused the conflict because they were against peace between the Kurds and the government."[52]

Ghassemlou, recalled his Mahabad assistant Aziz Mameli, had left the safety of Mahabad, returned to the embattled city, and remained in the outskirts of Naghadeh for three days.[53] From the neighboring village of Radeneh, Ghassemlou declared that his party had proof that the incidents had been sparked by "reactionary elements" from Urmia, the capital of West Azerbaijan. One of the agitators, he said, arrested by the PDKI, had confessed that there was a plot to foment confrontation and "to give rise to an uprising of the Shi'ite population of Turkish origin, who belong to the Karapapak tribe, against the Sunni Kurds."[54] In the eyes of PDKI leadership, suspicion fell above all on Mullah Hassani, Urmia's Friday prayer imam; the imam, they believed, had distributed arms to the Karapapak tribe, Azeri Turks, "to prevent the Kurds from claiming Naghadeh as an integral part of Kurdistan."[55]

Ghassemlou would state this suspicion clearly in a press conference in Tehran on May 19: "The incidents of Naghadeh were a plot that still continues. We found out that in Naghadeh, as well as in Urmia, there are some elements that have infiltrated the revolutionary committees. . . . These elements, who in the past worked closely with SAVAK, had the situation under their control. They were under the supervision of Mullah Hassani, the chief of the Urmia committee, before anything [any of these events] ever happened. Mr. Hassani had distributed plenty of weapons among the Turks [Azeris]."[56] "The army [and Islamist militants]," Ghassemlou said, "had ignored the ceasefire and had attacked the Kurdish population with tanks and helicopters. We were fighting against the Turks, and the army joined them."[57]

Later analysts similarly concluded that it was ultranationalist religious Turks loyal to the fundamentalist elements within the new regime that had instigated the infighting;[58] it was they who controlled the revolutionary committees which at this stage of the revolution were running the cities and army divisions. It was the 64th Army Division of Urmia, with sixteen hundred heavy-armed men led by Ayatollah Hassani, Urmia's Friday sermon cleric, that staged the onslaught on Naghadeh.[59]

Sheikh Ezzedin accused paramilitary forces aided by the regular army of committing atrocities against the Kurdish population. He denounced the shelling by eight tanks of Kurdish houses in the city, and the looting of shops by regime forces. City hospitals refused to attend the wounded if they were Kurds.[60]

In Mahabad, during Ghassemlou's absence at the front in Naghadeh, there was agitation and indecision. "During those three days," reported Aziz Mameli,[61] "there were a lot of people who were demanding weapons to fight against the people of [Urmia's imam] Hassani and defend the Kurds of Naghadeh. Mohamad Amin Seradji [a party political bureau member] was there; he would write inefficient communiqués and was incapable of managing the situation. [At the party headquarters] there were so many people in the stairs, surrounding the building. I would tell them: We have no weapons, we don't want the war to continue. [But] we have to fight because Kurds were killed."

Ghassemlou returned to Mahabad. Mameli's memory of the arrival was vivid: "When he saw the crowd, he ordered, 'Out, everyone out.'"

"No one was left. Then he directed us to bring in the members of the PDKI central committee and members of the party's organization in Mahabad; 'In thirty minutes,' he told us, 'we will have a meeting. Those members must be present.'"

"We prepared the office calmly. They came. I then saw his capacity [as a leader]. 'There is a war,' he said. 'We did not want this war. Tell me precisely what we must do: make war, or what?'"

"Each person spoke. Most of them said we had to go to war because people were killed; if we did not resist, we were not defending the principles of the party. The majority thought so."

Ghassemlou, his assistant recalled, established calm, order, and direction. "After everyone spoke, Ghassemlou said, 'We can summarize in four points' (I was amazed: he had organized this meeting, set order, and now was summarizing it in four points without taking notes or writing anything, nothing):

"'One: This government of Bakhtiar is a nationalist government.

"'Two: We will not make war against a government that was established right after the revolution.

"'Three: We will not leave the people in Naghadeh without defense. We will defend them to finish the war, to impose peace.

"'Four: We must do all that's necessary to inform Tehran, the government, of what happened [in Naghadeh]—clarify the situation and explain to them that it was members of SAVAK who infiltrated Naghadeh and initiated [the hostilities]. Hassani (the ayatollah of Urmia, a representative of Khomeini) was a counterrevolutionary. We have to denounce this.'

"His capacity [as a leader] was evident that day. I [couldn't help but] compare how for three days before no one could help me control and keep order—and Ghassemlou, he calmed everyone, clarified [everything], all the time maintaining his position."[62]

ॐ

People were truly desperate. Thousands of refugees were willing to renounce their Iranian citizenship and seek sanctuary in other countries if the government would not compensate them following the devastating destruction.

Meanwhile, hard on the heels of the violence in Naghadeh, terror broke out once more in Sanandaj. Babasheikh Nasseri, as a PDKI official, recalled these dramatic days. "Under the pretext of strengthening the forces along the frontier [for the possibility of war between Iran and Iraq], the government equipped its troops with supplies, sending them from Hamadan to Sanandaj. The army reached the Sanandaj airport on April 16, 1979, without any resistance. The next day, violating the agreement between the garrison commander and the city authorities [elected by the populace], as the army headed into the town, the local population resisted the army. Then the army, intending to take the Qishlakh, Niasar, and Bavaraz routes to the airport, clashed with peshmerga forces. The clashes dragged into the town, which started a war that continued for twenty-four days, until May 14."[63]

In the midst of the chaos in April 1979, at the government's invitation following the eruption of fighting at Sanandaj, Sheikh Ezzedin made a visit to Khomeini. This would be his first meeting with the Ayatollah. During the encounter, he asked Khomeini for autonomy for Kurdistan and an Islamic constitution that was neither Shi'i nor Sunni. As was his wont, Khomeini gave very general responses. Everyone in Iran was oppressed, the Ayatollah said, and now everything would improve.

As Sheikh Ezzedin was leaving, Khomeini took the hem of Ezzedin's cloak and said: "What I am asking from you is the security of Kurdistan." Taking in return the hem of Khomeini's cloak, Ezzedin responded: "What I am asking from you is autonomy for Kurdistan."[64]

Khomeini and Ezzedin would never meet again.[65]

ॐ

Reflecting upon that meeting, Sheikh Ezzedin would later say, "We did our best to solve this problem by political means. But this regime was too reactionary to resolve the difficulties. They are against our nationality and against our religion, since the majority of Iranian Kurds are Sunni Muslims."[66]

Abdul Rahman Ghassemlou had also requested a meeting with Khomeini: "We wanted to tell him," he told journalist Chris Kutschera, "that we had not started the war." So at the beginning of May, Ghassemlou traveled with two companions to Qom[67] to discuss the Naghadeh events with the Ayatollah and request an investigation. This time he and his delegation were searched before being allowed to enter.

"One hour after arriving," Ghassemlou's assistant recalled, "we were shown in to Khomeini. There was a pavilion filled with people, pasdar and ayatollahs. Khomeini was in his office. He came out and welcomed us and then sat on the floor."[68] The atmosphere, Mameli added, was "convivial."

"Ghassemlou began to speak in language appropriate for Khomeini. He began by saying that the Kurdish people had suffered persecution under the Shah and we had participated in the revolution to have public liberties and a democratic regime, to put an end to persecution and dictatorship. Therefore, he said, we were there, first, because of the situation in Naghadeh."

Ghassemlou explained to the Ayatollah that in the incident in Naghadeh the Kurds, far from being the aggressors, had in fact been attacked by Azeris.

"We told Khomeini that there were conspiracies and provocations and that if he did not do anything there would be serious consequences," recalled Ghassemlou.

Witnessing this conversation, Aziz Mameli remembered Ghassemlou telling the Imam: "That war was imposed on us. We came to tell you that there were members of SAVAK in Naghadeh and we ask that you do what's necessary to clean up there." Second, he said, "The Kurdish people need to hear from you the word *khodmokhtari* [autonomy]. We are conscious that the revolution is there [in process], we don't expect [to see you implement] the principle of autonomy or to declare it immediately, but [we ask] you as the guide of the revolution to say you agree with the principle of autonomy."[69]

Once again, true to form in his elliptical fashion, Khomeini began to repeat that in Islam everyone is equal. Then he added, "What separates one from the other is virtue."[70]

Jalil Gadani, present as Ghassemlou's colleague in the conversation, then asked the Ayatollah what he thought of the PDKI program the Kurdish delegation had sent him weeks before. Mameli remembered his saying: "Dear Imam, we came three months ago. I left a [leaflet with the principles] of the PDKI . . . have you read it?"

This time, the Ayatollah's evasive response held a surprising quality of truthfulness. The Ayatollah laughed, Mameli reported—"it was the first time I heard him laugh—and said, 'When you get to my age, you can't even remember what you ate the day before.'"[71]

Nonetheless, Khomeini agreed to send a commission to investigate.

After the meeting with Khomeini, Ghassemlou visited Grand Ayatollah Shariatmadari,[72] who shared with Ayatollah Taleghani an unusual—and uncomfortable—position among Shi'ites: he maintained that clerics should not intervene in the affairs of state. This position was one which generated harsh criticism among the most radical religious elements—and which did not endear him to Khomeini.[73] While viewing religious authority as transcendent to temporal administration, he may have considered, along with traditional "Twelver Shi'ites," that until the return of a truly infallible Imam, the full implementation of Islamic law would be a moot point.[74] When Khomeini's Air France flight had touched down at Tehran in his spectacular return from exile, Shariatmadari had observed with sarcasm that nobody thought that the Hidden Imam, for whom the Shi'ites had been waiting for centuries, would return in an airplane. Khomeini, it had been reported, was not amused by this comment.[75]

"He made us wait a long while," recalled Ghassemlou.[76] "When Shariatmadari arrived, he led us to his private office and gave the order that no one should come in. There were many people waiting outside.

"'Who is Dr. Ghassemlou?' was the first thing Shariatmadari asked me. He did not know it was me.

"'I am Ghassemlou,' I answered.

"'Am I to think that you began the war in Naghadeh?' he asked.

"'No, it was a provocation,' I replied.

"Suddenly, this small man held my hand and pulled me to him. But I did not kiss his hand. I only kiss the hands of the women I love, not his hands. In order that no one present could understand, he spoke to me in Turkish. 'You and I must be united,' he said.

"'I agree; but it all depends on you,' I responded."

ॐ

Ghassemlou's offer to Khomeini to support the new government in Iran, its referendum and opening elections, together with his plea for consideration of the rights of the Kurdish people, had been pointedly ignored. The Kurds, in consequence, would neither participate nor vote in the referendum. "This, I think," Ghassemlou would later reflect, "is one of the reasons that Khomeini hated the Kurds."

Looking back ten years later at this critical turning point, Ghassemlou would spell out three primary reasons for "Khomeini's war against the Kurdish nation":

"First, we were demanding democracy, when he was clearly against democratic values; he believed democracy is a Western system, and he was against the West.

"Second, we wanted autonomy, which was in opposition to Khomeini's so-called Islamic philosophy. He did not believe in [the notion of] nationality and nations' rights, but only in Islamic *umma* [the world community of Muslims].

"Third, the fact that virtually all Kurds are Sunni Muslims, and the regime in Tehran was Shi'ite.

"These three reasons—and also the fact that we were ready to defend our rights and had weapons in our hands and, as it were, were not going to succumb to the central government's pressure—were the rationale for the regime to start two wars . . . [in Sanandaj and Naghadeh]. And then, in August, Khomeini would issue a jihad against the Kurds."[77]

Within a mere matter of hours, Ghassemlou and his people had met with the two most prominent religious men who, while not expressing fundamentally different positions, represented contrasting political approaches among the revolutionary camps: intolerance and dialogue.

But in a precarious political landscape of shifting alliances dominated by radically divergent views on what the Islamic Republic should be and on the role of Islam and the clergy, could dialogue prevail? Could even the proponents of dialogue among the contending factions be trusted? And could Kurdish concerns find a voice in the conversation?

Notes

1. Hassan Ibrahimi, known as Hassan Shiwasali, would survive an assassination attempt on December 7, 1987, when he opened a package bomb delivered to him by a regime collaborator in Iranian Kurdistan. He lost his hands, his sight, and much of his hearing. An honorary member of PDKI's central committee, he currently lives in Sweden. Hélène Krulich, *Une Européenne au pays des Kurdes* (Paris: Éditions Karthala, 2011), 240; and Hassan Shiwasali, interview by e-mail with PDKI member Salah Piroty, July 2012.

2. Mahabad was considered a threat to the regime because it had long been a center of Kurdish nationalism—since before the Soviet occupation during World War II—and continued to be a bastion for Kurdish pride. For expanded discussion on the role of Mahabad see Nader Entessar, *Kurdish Politics in the Middle East* (London: Lexington Books, 2010), William Eagleton, Jr., *The Kurdish Republic of 1946* (London: Oxford University Press, 1963); Archie Roosevelt, Jr., "The Kurdish Republic of Mahabad," *Middle East Journal*, no. 1, July 1947.

3. While officially designated as the Republic of Kurdistan, the republic was sometimes erroneously referred to in the Western press as the Republic of Mahabad.

4. Kendal Nezan, interview with the author, Paris, 1991. Except where otherwise cited, further statements from Nezan are from this interview. Nezan has been director of the Kurdish Institute of Paris since 1983.

5. Kendal Nezan, presentation given during international symposium "Hommage à Abdul Rahman Ghassemlou," Paris, July 17, 2009.

6. Kendal Nezan, interview with the author, Paris, 1991. Further comments from Nezan are taken from this interview.

7. Fatah Abdulli, interview with the author, Paris, 1991. In 1990, Abdulli would become the PDKI representative abroad. Together with Sharafkandi and two colleagues, he would be assassinated in Berlin in 1992, by agents of the Iranian government, in what would become known as the Mykonos murders.

8. Krulich, *Une Européenne*, 77.

9. Azad, interview with Gabriel Fernández, Vienna, 1991.

10. Abdul Rahman Ghassemlou, Mahabad, "A segment of Dr. Ghassemlou's speech announcing the political agenda of the PDKI, March 2, 1979," https://www.youtube.com/watch?v=WytBDIZ1gfQ; posted March 2, 2016, by PDKI member Sharif Behruz.

11. Sheikh Ezzedin Hosseini (1922–2011) was not only a religious leader, but also widely regarded as a Kurdish nationalist. His presence in the negotiations benefited everyone, including the PDKI. Prior to the 1979 revolution, he had led anti-Shah protests and been associated with the 1946 Republic of Kurdistan. "In the early years after the revolution, Sheikh Ezzedin was a principal Kurdish negotiator and enjoyed the support of Komala." He ended his days in Sweden, where he had lived twenty years in exile. IHRDC, *Haunted Memories*, 3. After the February 1979 Islamic Revolution; see also "Hommage à Sheikh Ezzedin Hosseini," Institut Kurde de Paris, http://www.institutkurde.org/activites_culturelles/evenement_287.html.

12. Jalil Gadani, interview with the author, Paris, 1991. Statements from Gadani that follow are from this interview.

13. The PDKI delegation included Ghani Bulurian, Amir Qazi, Mohammed Amine Rowand, Nabi Kadiri, and Ahmed Qazi. Representatives from the extreme left parties, like Sheikh Ezzedin, refused to join them due to pressure from Komala. Chris Kutschera, *Le défi kurde ou le rêve fou de l'indépendance* [The Kurdish defiance, or the mad dream of independence] (Paris: Bayard Éditions, 1997), 325, n15.

14. Personal communication to the author from a member of Ghassemlou's family, February 2013.

15. Abdul Rahman Ghassemlou, interview with Jonathan Randal, Paris, 1986. In narrating the encounter with Khomeini, the description of events is drawn from Randal's interview and from interviews with Ghassemlou conducted by journalist Chris Kutschera as reported in *Le défi kurde*.

16. Abdul Rahman Ghassemlou, interview with Jonathan Randal.

17. Kutschera, *Le défi kurde*, 167, from an interview with Ghassemlou in Iranian Kurdistan in November 1979.

18. Abdul Rahman Ghassemlou, interview with Jonathan Randal.

19. Kutschera, *Le défi kurde*, 167.

20. Ibid.

21. Ibid., from interviews with Ghassemlou in October and November 1979.

22. The rest of the dialogue is as described by Ghassemlou to Jonathan Randal in their 1986 interview in Paris. For more on this encounter see Abdullah Hassanzadeh, *Niw Sede Xebat* [Half a century of struggle: A retrospect of struggle and activity of the Democratic Party of Iranian Kurdistan] [in Kurdish], Vol. 1 (Gawrade: Press Commission of the Kurdistan Democratic Party of Iran, August 1995), 142–44; translation Salah Piroty.

23. In the March 24 agreement ending the carnage in Sanandaj, Taleghani's proposal had "recognized the Kurds in the fundamental laws, protected Kurdish culture, and promised high-level political appointments and Majlis representation for Kurdish leaders." Denise Natali, *The Kurds and the State: Evolving National Identity in Iraq, Turkey and Iran* (Syracuse, NY: Syracuse University Press, 2005), 143.

24. Khomeini would consistently employ the rhetoric of "Muslim unity" to evade, counter, or dismiss pleas for minority rights and representation. At best, he would dismiss such concerns as unnecessary; at worst, he would counter them as outright "anti-Muslim" or "antirevolutionary," and insist that those who raised them were dupes of the Soviets, tools of Western oppression, or "foreignized intellectuals." See Natali, *The Kurds and the State*, 142–43; Shaul Bakhash, *The Reign of the Ayatollahs: Iran and the Islamic Revolution* (New York: Basic Books, Inc., 1984), 78; David Menashri, "Shi'ite Leadership: In the Shadow of Conflicting Ideologies," Iranian Studies, Vol. 13, No. 1/4, *Iranian Revolution in Perspective* (1980), 130.

25. Along with evading issues with glib appeals to "Muslim unity," Khomeini routinely sidestepped difficult conversations by citing frail health. In this case, he employed both strategies. In another account of Khomeini's March 28 meeting with Ghassemlou's six-man Kurdish delegation, the cleric was quoted as saying, "I support Ayatollah Taleghani's decision," first appealing to the notion of "Muslim unity"; "you need to have 'unity of words' and everyone, without any regard for religion or nationality, must live freely and without any oppression in Iran." Then, moving to his alternate evasive tactic: "However,

since I am quite stressed out and need to rest, you need to consult Bazargan on these issues." Hamid Gohary, *Xorhelatyi Kurdistan le de Salan da 1356–1366* [Eastern Kurdistan during the decade 1978–1988], Vol. 1 [in Kurdish] (Erbil, Iraq: Rojhelat Publisher, 2011), 146–47.

Banisadr recalled a similar reaction: "If he [Khomeini] was confronted with an opposing view, his face would become stern, and he would look down. This meant that he was no longer willing to listen or talk, and that the conversation had ended. If one persisted, then Khomeini would either say that he was tired and leave the room, or brusquely say: 'I don't want to hear any more.'" Baqer Moin, *Khomeini: Life of the Ayatollah* (New York: Thomas Dunne Books, 2000), 228.

26. The dialogue with Bazargan is as reported by Kutschera, *Le défi kurde*, 167–68, from interviews with Ghassemlou.

27. Said Shamsaddini, *Nationalism, Political Islam and the Kurdish Question in Iran: Reflections on the Rise and Spread of Political Islam in Iran* (n.p., Germany: VDM Verlag, 2011), 175, quoting from the Iranian journal *Kayhan* no. 10671, March 31, 1979.

28. Personal communication to the author from a member of Ghassemlou's family, February 2013.

29. Ferdinand Hennerbichler, "Assassination of Abdul Rahman Ghassemlou (1930–1989): New Assessment in *Wiener Jahrbuch für Kurdische Studien 2013, Schwerpunkt: Transnationalität und kurdische Diaspora in Österreich, Jahrgang 1/2013* (Vienna: Österreichische Gesellschaft zur Förderung der Kurdologie / Europäisches Zentrum für kurdische Studien, 2013), 291.

30. Ibid.

31. Abdul Rahman Ghassemlou, interview by Enayat Fani, June 1989; translation Beyan Farshi and Esmail Ebrahimi. An extended version of the interview was broadcast on BBC Persian TV in July 2014; See YouTube, "Abdul-Rahman Ghassemlou, BBC Persian," posted July 16, 2014, https://www.youtube.com/watch?v=SGsfvkcMn8U; (accessed February 20, 2017).

32. Hennerbichler, "Assassination of Abdul Rahman Ghassemlou," 291.

33. Ibid.

34. Entessar, *Kurdish Politics*, 38.

35. Entessar, "The Kurds in Post-Revolutionary Iran and Iraq," *Third World Review* Vol. 6, No. 4 (October 1984), 911–33. See openDemocracy, http://www.opendemocracy.net/author/nader-entessar (accessed November 30, 2013). See also Amir Hassanpour, "Hassanpour on Ozoglu, 'Kurdish Notables and the Ottoman State: Evolving Identities, Competing Loyalties, and Shifting Boundaries,'" a review of Hakan Ozoglu, *Kurdish Notables and the Ottoman State: Evolving Identities, Competing Loyalties, and Shifting Boundaries* (Albany: State University of New York Press, 2004), published on H-Turk, September 2007, https://networks.h-net.org/node/11419/reviews/11509/hassanpour-ozoglu-kurdish-notables-and-ottoman-state-evolving.

36. According to some counts, 99 percent of the electorate that took part in the referendum voted approval; see Ervand Abrahamian, *A History of Modern Iran* (Cambridge: Cambridge University Press, 2008), 163. They voted "yes" to an Islamic Republic whose actual form had not been fully defined. When the formal draft for the Islamic constitution would be published on June 14, 1979, with Khomeini's public approval, it would make "no mention

of *Velayat-e-faqih* [Guardianship of the Jurist] and it confined the role of religious jurists to a Guardian Council which could only intervene to declare legislation incompatible with the *shari'a* at the request of specified officials." Moin, *Khomeini*, 217.

37. "Khomeini Proclaims Iran an Islam State After Vote," *Pittsburgh Post-Gazette*, April 2, 1979.

38. Abrahamian, *A History of Modern Iran*, 164–65.

39. "After the revolution," Global Security reported, "Khomeini's revolutionary courts reportedly killed 90% of SAVAK [agents and operatives], with the exception of members who worked in foreign and domestic counterespionage. Key religious leaders, including Majlis speaker Hashemi-Rafsanjani, insisted on recalling former agents to help the regime eliminate domestic opposition. Consequently, some intelligence officers and low-ranking SAVAK and army intelligence officials were asked to return to government service because of their specialized knowledge of the Iranian left. Others had acquired in-depth knowledge of Iraq's Baath Party and proved to be invaluable in helping decision makers." Global Security, http://www.globalsecurity.org/intell/world/iran/vevak-history.htm (accessed November 20, 2012).

40. Describing the multiethnic population of Naghadeh, in Kurdistan's Sindus region between Shino, Piranshar, and Mahabad, as composed of Kurds, Turks, and Gharapapakh [Karapapak] Turks, Gohary adds: "The Turks settled in the district in the late nineteenth century following the Russian-Ottoman war. At the outset of the 1979 Iranian revolution, the Kurds predominated in the city itself and in its surrounding villages." Gohary, *Eastern Kurdistan*, 155; translation Sharif Behruz.

41. Nawshirwan Mustafa Amin, *Kurd û Ajem: Mêjoy Sîasî Kurdekanî Eran* [Kurd and Turk: Political history of Iran's Kurds] [in Kurdish] (Sulaimaniya, Iraq: Roon Publishing House, 2007, third edition); translation Sharif Behruz.

42. Ibid.

43. *Le Monde*, Paris, March 6, 1979, quoted by McDowall, *A Modern History of the Kurds*, 269.

44. McDowall, *A Modern History of the Kurds*, 269.

45. Ibid., again quoting from *Le Monde*.

46. Ghassemlou would describe this event ten years later in a televised interview: "In the city of Naghadeh, during a peaceful meeting of our party, and just as I was starting my speech, bullets were shot, and a three-day-long war resulted in many casualties on both sides." Abdul Rahman Ghassemlou, interview with BBC Persian, June 1989.

47. Associated Press, in *The Victoria* [Texas] *Advocate*, April 23, 1979 (accessed online January 22, 2013).

48. Aziz Mameli, interview with the author, Paris, July 21, 2015.

49. McDowall, *A Modern History of the Kurds*, 270.

50. According to the *New York Times*, witnesses attested that the army sent to the region was mainly composed of Iranian Turks. In "Chronology," *Middle East Journal*, September 1979, 357.

51. According to Reuters, the PDKI declared that "at least 500 persons had been killed in fighting between Kurds and army-backed Azerbaijanis." In *The* [Saskatchewan, Canada] *Star Phoenix*, April 26, 1979 (accessed online January 22, 2013).

52. Jalil Gadani, interview with the author, Paris, 1991. Further statements from Gadani in this chapter are from this interview.

53. Aziz Mameli, interview with the author, Paris, July 21, 2015.

54. Abdul Rahman Ghassemlou, interview with Jonathan Randal, Paris, 1986.

55. Kutschera, *Le défi kurde*, 168. According to contemporary Iranian news reports, "for the Kurdish people, especially in the Western Azerbaijan region, Mullah Hassani was known as a notorious man. As a Friday prayer imam of Urmia, Hassani used his podium to cause ethnic and religious divisions between the Azeris (Shi'i) and the Kurds (Sunni)." *Ayandegan*, May 10, 1979.

56. *Ayandegan*, Tehran, May 10, 1979; translation Salah Piroty.

57. PDKI accusations of tank and helicopter attacks by the army and Islamic militants were reported by the Saskatchewan *Star-Phoenix*, April 26, 1979; by *Le Monde*, April 24, 1979; and by *The Economist*, April 28, 1979.

    Armed local Turks, together with army troops who remained in garrisons that had not been taken over by Kurds, aided in many of the attacks against Kurdish villages and cities. Karim Hussami, *Le Bîreweriyekanim, Bergî Şeşem* [My memoirs], Vol. 6 [in Kurdish] (Stockholm: n.p., 1992), 58–80. According to Hussami, former SAVAK agents such as Maboudi and Morad Qatari commanded the town's Turkish militias and initiated the Turkish onslaught against the Kurdish population in Naghadeh.

58. Also see William Branigin, "Ethnic Feud Divides Warring Turks and Kurds in Iran," *Washington Post*, April 23, 1979, cited by IHRDC at https://iranhrdc.org//?s=William+Branigin (accessed December 27, 2018).

59. Gohary, *Eastern Kurdistan*, 158.

60. *Le Monde*, April 25, 1979.

61. Aziz Mameli, interview with the author, Paris, July 21, 2015.

62. Ibid.

63. Babasheikh Nasseri, "The War for a City," Helwist.com, Kurdish Independent Left Web Publication, April 11, 2015, http://www.helwist.com/Nuseran/BaBa%20shex.Nasry/13%20%204%20%2015%20%20Shery%20Sharik.htm; translation Salah Piroty.

64. Fred Halliday, "Interview with Shaik Izzedin Husseini: A Dictatorship under the Name of Islam," *Middle East Reports*, No. 113 (March–April 1983), 9; Gohary, *Eastern Kurdistan*, 172–73.

65. Entessar, *Kurdish Politics*, 38.

66. Halliday, "A Dictatorship under the Name of Islam," 9.

67. Kutschera, *Le défi kurde*, 168–69. Ghassemlou's dialogue with the Ayatollah is as reported from Kutschera's interviews with Ghassemlou, supplemented where indicated by information from an interview by the author, with Ghassemlou's assistant, Aziz Mameli, in July 2015. The timing of the meeting is confirmed by the May 9 press conference at Tehran's Continental Hotel, reported by the Iranian journal *Ayandegan* on May 10, 1979, in which Ghassemlou mentioned that he had been in Tehran for a week, waiting to meet with government officials.

68. Aziz Mameli, interview with the author, Paris, July 21, 2015.

69. Ibid.

70. As Mameli recalled it, Khomeini said: "What is imposed on us . . . it is the foreigners who wanted to impose on us separation between Sunni and Shi'ites. What characterizes the human being are the virtues." "He said nothing more," Mameli added. "The meeting ended." Ibid.

71. Ibid.

72. Sayyid Mohammad Kazem Shariatmadari was a prominent Shi'a *marj'a* ("source of emulation"), a high authority on religious law, an ayatollah uzma, a "Great Sign of God" in his own right. When Khomeini was arrested by the Shah in 1963, Shariatmadari rescued him from execution by declaring him a Grand Ayatollah; the Iranian constitution pronounced a marj'a immune from execution. While Shariatmadari supported the formation of an Islamic republic, he was firm in his judgment that clerics and religious jurists should not demean themselves and their role by participation in politics and, for many reasons, was especially critical of Khomeini's interpretation of *velayat-e faqih*, "Guardianship of the Jurist"—the ultimate power in government, to be exercised by a religious scholar.

"In sharp contrast to Khomeini, Shariatmadari did not believe that there should be a paramount position for one special jurist to serve as the 'ruling jurist.' . . . In fact, while he recognized fundamental inequalities among religious scholars of differing ranks and learning and spiritual cultivation, Shariatmadari believed that all religious scholars were of an equal rank . . . with respect to temporal political powers." Mehdi Khalaji, "The Iranian Clergy's Silence," *Current Trends in Islamist Ideology* vol. 10, July 12, 2010; Hudson Institute, http://www.currenttrends.org/research/detail/the-iranian-clergys-silence (accessed November 30, 2013).

Within the new Islamic government, Shariatmadari led an Azerbaijani nationalist faction which advocated greater regional autonomy. His request that the constitution be revised to include secularists and opposition parties was denied. David Menashri, "Shi'ite Leadership: In the Shadow of Conflicting Ideologies," *Iranian Studies* 13, no.1/4, Iranian Revolution in Perspective, 126, 134. Shariatmadari stated his position, as reported by *Ettela'at*, May 31, 1979: "I would prefer not to see communist representatives sitting in the Assembly [of Experts to review the constitution] but if . . . they are elected, they must be tolerated." Ibid., 126. "He also demanded that the constitution guarantee autonomy for the ethnic minorities. Most of the centrist political groupings, and the ethnic minorities, as well as some senior ayatollahs, supported Shari'atmadari." Ibid., 135–36.

73. In the view of Baqer Moin, for Khomeini to maintain absolute authority he needed to eliminate Shariatmadari, who not only was one of the leading Shi'ite divines residing in Iran, but had as many followers as the Ayatollah himself. In a meeting arranged by eminent ayatollahs to ease the existing tension between the men, Khomeini arrived with documents and files taken from the imperial archives which, according to Khomeini, showed that Shariatmadari had cooperated with the Shah's regime and had contacts with the U.S. embassy.

In 1982 a plot to assassinate Khomeini would be uncovered. One of the conspirators would confess that "Shariatmadari knew of the coup plan and had given it his blessing. Khomeini's reaction was swift and ruthless. Echoing the worst of the Stalinist show trials, Shariatmadari, whose son was threatened with execution as a co-conspirator, was forced to make a public repentance on television and to plead with Khomeini for forgiveness. He was subsequently 'defrocked'—a happening totally without precedent in Shi'a Islam and deeply shocking. Strictly speaking, it is impossible to defrock a source of emulation since no one appoints him in the first place. He is simply recognized as such by his followers." Moin, *Khomeini*, 252.

Shariatmadari would be placed under house arrest and cut off from his constituency. At his death four years later, he would be buried without any public ceremony. See International Campaign for Human Rights in Iran, "A Brief History of 'House Arrests' and Detentions in 'Safe Houses': What Will be the Fate of Disappeared Leaders?," March 6, 2011, http://www.iranhumanrights.org/2011/03/history-of-house-arrests/ (accessed November 30, 2013).

74. Khalaji, "The Iranian Clergy's Silence."

75. Mohamed Heikal, *Iran: The Untold Story* (New York: Pantheon Books, 1982), 177.

76. The dialogue is as reported by Ghassemlou in his interview with Jonathan Randal in Paris in 1986.

77. Abdul Rahman Ghassemlou, interview with Enayat Fani, June 1989.

· 5 ·

PEASANTS AND *AGHAS*

❧

If we behave like our adversaries,
we are not worth more than they are
and our discourse would lose all credibility.
—Abdul Rahman Ghassemlou

While intrigue consumed the politicians' energy in Tehran and the large cities, violence raged on unabated in Kurdistan. Since autonomy—and, by extension, economic justice—was at the heart of the Kurdish political demand, further conflict had taken birth in defense of land being wrested from the landowners by the peasants.

In the turmoil at the outset of the Iranian revolution, many small farmers seized the opportunity to take control of lands held by the landlords. For the Kurds, and especially for the smallholders and rural workers, regional and cultural autonomy were closely tied to a radical land reform. The question of land reform, which had been featured as a prominent component of the Shah's so-called "White Revolution," had been left unresolved, and now erupted once again.

The Shah's White Revolution, initiated in 1962–1963, was driven by both broad reform goals and strategic political considerations. Its six-point program of modernization and secularization included land reform, women's suffrage and emancipation, universal access to literacy and a modern education, and broadening participation in the judiciary to include non-Muslims.[1] The popular appeal and success of the initiative hinged on the linchpin of land reform. Land redistribution was calculated to win over the peasantry and lower middle class, generating a broad "middling" class to support the Shah's policies.[2] The intent also was to shift power away from the landed gentry, the clerics, mosques, and religious schools, all of which derived both income and influence from their estates and endowments.

The Shah's intention misfired, however. While land reform was indeed popular, the Shah's "commitment to secularization and Westernization was offensive to religious sensibilities; and his dictatorial and arbitrary methods seemed to the ulama to exceed the bounds of what was tolerable."[3] Throughout Iran, widespread anxieties of socioeconomic dislocation, resentment at capitulation to Western intrusion, and the sense of threat to cultural identity fueled a pervasive pushback against both the Shah and secularization. As a general political stance, the clerics came to oppose virtually anything the Shah was advocating, and this meant resisting any land redistribution and, with it, any reform to existing clan or tribal structure.[4] Given the antireligious activism and violent persecution the clerics had suffered under the Shah's father, Khomeini was able to muster wide resistance to the new initiatives as "a reenactment of the Reza Shah experience, a renewed attempt to extend arbitrarily the power of the state and to erode the place of religion in society."[5] Khomeini's appeal to religious traditionalism trumped the appeal of a more secular vision of equitable land redistribution.[6]

The predominant clerical posture toward land reform reflected economic self-interest as well. Many influential clerics themselves owned large pockets of land (this was especially the case outside the borders of Kurdistan, but such enclaves existed within Kurdish areas too), so any plans to reform the system came into direct confrontation with their immediate interests.[7]

Contributing to the failure of the initial efforts at land reform under the Shah was the fact that it was principally the more well-to-do peasants who had gained by redistribution of land during the Shah's modernization efforts;[8] the poorest small farmers and workers on the land had not benefited. The most marginalized of the poor had found their ways to the cities, swelling the ranks of the urban youth who would take the revolution to the streets; those who remained in the rural areas were hungry for land, for improvement of their lives.[9]

"During the Shah's time," Ghassemlou's longtime collaborator Abdullah Hassanzadeh summed up, "land reform was fêted with exaggerated publicity, celebration, and hullabaloo as . . . 'the revolution of the Shah and the nation,' but in fact it was never resolved."[10] Now, following the outbreak of the 1979 revolution, the Kurdish political parties, both PDKI and Komala, sided with the peasants and adopted a policy of land redistribution in the areas where they had leverage.

But in the face of persistent traditional social structures against a landscape of social chaos, implementation of such policies had only spotty success. Lands might be distributed surreptitiously, at night, for instance, and the next day be retaken through traditional gendarmerie who oftentimes sided with the large landowners, mainly to take a stance against the Kurdish political parties. Time-honored methods of influence remained persuasive: "During the period of land distribution," Hassanzadeh noted, "bribe-taking officials saw filling their pockets, rather than solving the issue of the land, as the priority. So everywhere an *agha* or a peasant could offer a better bribe to government officials, it was a guarantee to get better land, [a piece with] a freshwater spring or along a river. As a result, many poor people either did not get any land, or they got so little that they had to sell it or leave it to be a daily wage laborer or go to the brick furnaces."[11]

At local levels, ways could be found to create the appearance of redistribution while keeping it all in the family: landowners might register large pieces of their lands under the names of other family members.[12] And at the national level, even laws enacted by the Islamic Consultative Assembly (Majlis-e Shoraye Eslami, the Iranian parliament) to reform land ownership would simply never be carried out in practice because of the many powerful clerics and influential landowners who would be threatened with loss of their lands.

Throughout the course of the revolution, clerical positions on land reform would shift ground, at times in ways that appeared self-contradictory. The mullahs' stance toward the well-to-do landholders, the aghas, was not invariably affirmative. Everything depended on a specific landowner's or tribal chief's loyalty toward the regime. Those who were loyal and nonthreatening might receive defense and protection; those who were not, might be actively undermined. In the main, the Islamic regime carried on a strategy of arming individual aghas, tribal leaders, and factions and supporting them against the Kurdish political parties—chiefly against the PDKI, which was actively promoting clear land redistribution policies.[13] Many landowning aghas, maintaining their alignment with the socioeconomic status quo, now found ways to gain leverage with the komitehs, the revolutionary committees springing up as local rule in the wake of the revolution,[14] and through these ties received both arms and political reinforcement.

The position of the Kurdish political parties themselves was not monolithic vis-à-vis land reform. Even within the parties, leadership levels harbored a handful of aghas and landowners who could only lose by land redistribution and who would not implement the parties' plans. On a practical level, there were also the common, everyday conciliations and appeasements that arose in the day-to-day reality of "getting along by going along."[15]

The experience of one PDKI member, for instance, may not have been untypical: Rahim Behruz, of the party's Naghadeh committee, was reprimanded as a local party enforcer "when the aghas in our area complained to the PDKI leadership that I was using harsh methods to force them to abandon their lands and leave the peasants alone—the peasants who were now cultivating lands for themselves that they used to cultivate for the aghas.

"I was summoned by Ghassemlou himself about the complaints.

"Ghassemlou acknowledged the shortcomings and problems in enforcing the redistribution plan. But then, on my way out, he tapped me on my shoulder and told me: 'Continue to do your job till every bit of their land is distributed among the peasants . . . And you have my full backing.'"[16]

For many of the landlord class, whose power in the rural areas had not been dislodged either under the Shah or by the onset of the Islamist revolution, "the collapse of the imperial regime was an opportunity to regain land distributed to the peasantry following the White Revolution, or at least to obtain tenant dues for what could not be repossessed."[17]

But now, riding the wave of revolutionary fervor, the peasants were struggling to reclaim the lands that they regarded as their own.

&

In June 1979, swaths of the countryside were in an agitated uprising.[18] The revolutionary committees installed throughout Iran provided support to provisional local government,[19] while the pasdaran,[20] called in to quell disturbances, evicted peasants, destroyed homes and villages, and killed defenseless people. In mid-July, in Marivan, a provincial city of Kurdistan near the Iraqi border, history repeated itself as the pasdaran fired upon the populace.[21]

The PDKI publicly demanded an explanation from Khomeini as to why the revolutionary regime was arming the landowners who had supported the old regime and why the revolutionary committees were rattling against the Kurds.

In an open letter to Khomeini the PDKI stated that "national discrimination"[22] against the Kurds continued in the country. It reproached the government for not selecting Kurdish officials to head up revolutionary committees, even in cities where Kurds constituted the majority of the population, and in fact, it indicted the regime for naming anti-Kurdish officers to oversee Kurdistan. The PDKI repeated its repudiation of allegations of treason against Iran and its people, and repudiated accusations of any separatist agenda. "It would be unreasonable and unjust," they wrote, "if the Kurdish people were suppressed under the banner of separatism while it is only demanding its national rights of self-rule."[23]

The PDKI never received a reply.

❧

In Qom, Egyptian journalist Mohammed Heikal had better luck in getting a clear response from the Ayatollah. During an interview with Khomeini, the Imam told him, chillingly, "The Revolution did not take place to provide people with food."[24]

By this time, Khomeini was an old and extremely frail man. According to Heikal, he was not interested in economic theories—or, apparently, in strategic practicalities. He had survived more than one heart attack and was no longer interested in even studying his country's problems.

"Although all important questions continue to come to him for decision, his reactions are instinctive rather than thought out," wrote Heikal of Khomeini. "He reads no reports. In the early days after his return to Qom, he would complain that every day he received three reports: one from the Foreign Ministry about foreign policy, one about internal affairs, and one on economic matters. He begged the officials in Tehran to stop sending them. 'I never read them,' he confessed."[25]

Khomeini was indifferent to the economy; it comes as no surprise that now, six months after the revolution, it needed urgent measures. The revolutionary process had paralyzed oil export. Hassan Nazih, executive director of NIOC, the National Iranian Oil Company, confessed in February that he could not negotiate with the powerful consortium of fourteen Western companies which had been responsible for the majority of Iran's crude oil exports. The nationalization of foreign corporations, banks, and insurance companies had caused both a decrease in production and a flight of capital. Industrial production had been reduced to half its capacity.

According to the *Tehran Times*, as of the end of summer 1979, one hundred thousand Iranian professionals had left the country. At the same time, around $2 billion had been illegally taken out of Iran.

Of the 250,000 workers and foreign technicians who had worked under the Shah's regime, only ten thousand remained. Corporations such as Bell Helicopter had closed, and no one knew what to do with the fleet of copters they had left behind. In the month of June, the head of Iran's state atomic energy industry had asked "for political, economic, social, humanitarian, and technical reasons" that the government take drastic measures—because the industry lacked the staff to operate the country's nuclear reactors.

The Soviets, while satisfied with the "anti-imperialist character" of the Islamic revolution, noted in *Izvestia,* "One could reasonably doubt that the state theocratic concept would help Iran to become a modern and flourishing country. . . . The provisional government, without authority or willpower, is practically paralyzed. Economic chaos continues. . . ." In the summer of 1979, none of the edgily allied political factions had sufficient power within Iran—or sufficient will, even taken together—to structure effective actions or advance a realistic economic agenda.[26]

Power rested uneasily in two main centers: the Islamic Revolutionary Council (IRC) answerable only to Ayatollah Khomeini, who resided in Qom, one hundred kilometers south of Tehran; and the provisional government of Bazargan. While these both existed by decree of the Ayatollah, their overlapping functions—especially in an unfolding revolutionary setting where every structure was provisional, in the absence of a formal constitutional foundation—locked them into incessant struggle. Bazargan continually complained about the limitation of his government's powers, depending as they did on the sufferance of the Revolutionary Council,[27] and about unending interference from revolutionary tribunals, revolutionary committees, and the pasdaran. In the "fierce struggle for control of the state" that had erupted with the fall of the Shah, it was the forces of Shi'i fundamentalism, led by Khomeini, that triumphed.[28]

Regional governors designated by Tehran were often impotent in the face of conflicts between high officials of the public administration, local clerics, and the spontaneous revolutionary committees. The city of Tabriz alone harbored thirty-four rival committees.

The revolution had decimated the armed forces. In their place had emerged the Islamic Revolutionary Guard Corps, under direct orders of the Imam. The IRGC's mission was to combine the functions of an army, a police force, and the mosque. It would have the power to support liberation movements abroad and spread Iran's Islamic Revolution around the world.[29] Established by Khomeini's decree in May, by summer 1979 the IRGC already had ten thousand permanent pasdaran and an additional hundred thousand in the military reserves.

While in Tehran and Qom factional conflict centered on obtaining the Imam's support, in northwest Iran a civil war was breaking out; there were struggles for possession of land, demonstrations against the central government, and clashes between peshmerga and Iranian security forces. A number of military garrisons and police stations were taken over by the Kurds in West Azerbaijan. The arrival of large contingents of troops, pasdaran, and gendarmerie was received with strong opposition from the population.

In Marivan, the Kurds were demanding that security be maintained by local forces, not by government contingents. To protest the presence of the pasdaran, thousands of residents abandoned the city and moved to tents on a nearby mountain. They would not return, they declared, until the government forces left.

Negotiations failed. Artillery barrages were fired into the surrounding hills where people had sought refuge. Government forces then tried to enter the city, but were met with fierce resistance by contingents of peshmerga in control of the city in its defense and suffered substantial losses. The ensuing battles closed the train lines between Iran and Turkey.

On August 5, the government and Marivan's residents reached an agreement: the city's security would be in the hands of unarmed forces, specifically unarmed soldiers from the local garrison,[30] and the pasdaran would no longer be empowered to arrest individuals.[31] In exchange, the Kurds agreed not to carry arms in the streets.

&

The summer was coming to an end. It had been only months before that the revolution had exploded, in February, when snow covered the mountains of Kurdistan and whitened the endless maze of streets in Tehran. From one season to the next, Iran had transformed radically. The Shah and his American allies had melted away.

As if they had arisen from the shadows, more than one thousand Shi'ite clerics had now taken hold of the reins of power. Like the Rome-centered ecclesiastical establishment of Europe's Middle Ages, the mullahs exerted more and more influence over national life. Politics and religion, state and God, private and public morality became one and the same. The Shah had been replaced not by a liberal democracy, but by an equally absolutist theocracy with its own Inquisition. The Jacobins prevailed.

The mullahs came to monopolize everything from the economy to the army, from justice to public administration. From the big cities to the most remote villages, law was dictated in the mosques, and revolutionary tribunals ensured that these dictates were carried out. Throughout the country, execution squads enforced the new laws without any consideration: death to the monarchists and generals, death to imperialism, homosexuals, and drug addicts, death to blasphemers and adulterers. And now, there was also death to the Kurds.

Revolutionary committees controlled the country—street by street, block by block, house by house. Crowds of fired-up, ragged proletarians, *mostazafin*, "the disinherited," rallied to the mullahs; enthusiastic students drank in the words of the ayatollahs who preached on the campus of Tehran University every Friday or in the sacred cloisters of Qom, Tabriz, Dezful, and Isfahan. The revolution had a wide social base; Iran was being purified after a dark time of sacrilegious aberration. Terror reigned.

❧

It was in this tense climate, reinforced by the events in Kurdistan, that elections for the Assembly of Experts for the Constitution were held on August 3 throughout the country. The Assembly's mission was to draft a new constitution.

The proposed "Assembly of Experts" was a late and even hasty development. Despite Khomeini's consistent refusal to countenance any explicit constitutional reference to the rights of specified minorities, the first formal draft of the Islamic constitution in June 1979 had promised all minorities equal rights.[32] Surprisingly enough—or perhaps as a truly Machiavellian ploy—Khomeini had expressed willingness to allow the draft to go directly to popular referendum. By this time, however, the liberal factions had no trust in the electorate not to be manipulated in such a referendum. "Catastrophically, it was Bazargan and Banisadr who insisted the draft should first be submitted to, and refined by, an elected constitutional assembly. They entirely failed to foresee it would open the floodgates to clerical radicals. On the contrary, it was Ayatollah Hashemi Rafsanjani [himself a cleric] who warned them, 'Who do you think will be elected to a constituent assembly? A fistful of ignorant and fanatic fundamentalists who will do such damage you will regret ever having convened them.' And so it proved to be."[33]

Bazargan's government had organized for the election of a constituent assembly that would consist of three hundred members. But Khomeini and clerical members of the Revolutionary Council, without consulting with Bazargan and his colleagues, decided that a much smaller body—an "Assembly of Experts" with seventy-three members—should be formed to consider the constitution. "The difference was significant," in the estimation of journalist

Baqer Moin. "With fewer candidates standing for membership in the assembly from much larger constituencies, it would be easier to rig the elections—and the likelihood of dissenting voices in the assembly could be reduced to almost nothing."[34]

This, in fact, was reportedly what transpired during the elections. The Islamic Republican Party "orchestrated elections to the Assembly of Experts which the Muslim's People Republican's Party and many of the secularists organizations boycotted in protest," wrote Moin. "Vote-rigging, violence against undesirable candidates and the dissemination of false information were all used to produce an Assembly overwhelmingly dominated by clergy loyal to Khomeini and a handful of laymen who followed the 'Imam line.'"[35]

The election results were contested in Kurdistan; the PDKI, like other opposition groups, simply boycotted the elections.

Even so, and remarkably, Ghassemlou entered the running as a contestant for a seat on the Assembly. It was vital, in his estimation, that the Kurds and their party have serious representation in the constitutional process. Given that the peshmerga effectively controlled much of the region around Mahabad and Paveh, notes Ali Ezzatyar, Ghassemlou's participation was all the more remarkable because "it signified a continued willingness" on the part of the party "to acknowledge sovereignty of the central government over the Kurdish region."[36]

Abdul Rahman Ghassemlou, candidate for the city of Urmia, won by an undisputable majority. Not only had he received an impressive preponderance of the vote; in the ethnically mixed Kurdish/Turkish city, he had even received votes from the mosques, where all the faithful were Azeris. "I had so many votes, they were not able to eliminate me," recalled Ghassemlou. "I occupied the third place in the voting and I received a mandate."[37]

Of the seventy-three candidates elected to the Assembly of Experts, fifty-five were mullahs, four represented religious minorities, and ten were fundamentalist laymen. Among the few Islamist moderates who won seats were Ayatollah Taleghani, Banisadr, and Ezatollah Shahabi, a leading figure in Bazargan's Freedom Movement.[38] The only secularists who did not belong to the Islamic current were Ghassemlou and Moghaddam Maraghi, the leader of a small radical party.

Ghassemlou's message to the authorities was clear: "There is room for all in this country, where everything needs doing or redoing."[39]

Ghassemlou's electoral popularity upset the clerics. He was a man who had been shaped by the purest Stalinist school of thought in his youth[40] and then had turned toward a position he described as democratic socialism. For Islamic orthodox supporters, Marxism and liberalism were equally anathema.[41] In the heady days of revolutionary triumph, Vice Prime Minister Ebrahim Yazdi had condemned Marxism. "We are Muslims," he said, "and hold a monotheist vision of the world. In such a movement, there is no place for creeds that are not Islamic or are anti-Islamic. Marxism is based on dialectic materialism, which fundamentally opposes the Islamic vision, especially in the economic, political, and social areas."

For his part, Khomeini had early on exhorted the faithful to fight, "united and without compassion," against the atheists as they had fought against the Shah. "Liberty without Islam," he fumed, "sovereignty without Islam, makes no sense." As for those sincere (but apparently deluded) Iranians who were demanding a democratic republic, he contended that they should not be listened to, for the republic they proposed was one without Islam, Prophet, or Imam.[42]

Khomeini for months had been preparing the terrain to impose his version of the new constitution. At the end of June, speaking to a delegation of clerics from Mashhad, Khomeini had insisted that deliberations on the draft constitution "take place only within an Islamic framework," and that clerics must exercise authority to prevent the introduction of "non-Islamic principles" into the document.[43] For Khomeini, the constitution of the Islamic Republic meant "the constitution of Islam." "Don't sit back," he urged, "while foreignized intellectuals, who have no faith in Islam, give their views and write the things they write. Pick up your pens and in the mosques, from the altars, in the streets and bazaars, speak of the things that in your view should be included in the constitution."[44]

In the face of Kurdish clerical delegates' concerns at rumors that the constitution—given the predominance of Shi'a Islam among the population of Iran—would be based on Shi'ite doctrine, Khomeini had asked for Sheikh Ezzedin's opinion on this matter. Sheikh Ezzedin had responded, "Since there are various sects and religious beliefs in Iran, it is best if the constitution is not based on one religious belief." Pointing out that the Kurds had suffered much under Reza Shah, he added, "I appeal to you to approve the Kurds' demands for autonomy."[45]

Throughout the deliberations over the constitution as well as the negotiations over an end to the conflict in Kurdistan, this Kurdish appeal would remain an unremitting concern. Proposals and counter-proposals would be promulgated right up to the eve of the final referendum on the constitution, and beyond. It was a problem that would not go away.

෨

As Urmia's delegate to the Assembly, Ghassemlou would have shared constitutional debates with well-versed Shi'ite theologians. He would have
confronted unique figures like Ayatollah Taleghani and Abolhassan Banisadr, Khomeini's advisor, as well as Hossein Ali Montazeri, well respected
by ordinary people and close to the Imam. One of the Assembly's most
formidable characters he would have encountered, a figure of dreaded
force, was Mohammed Hossein Beheshti, leader of the Islamic Republican
Party.

With a salt-and-pepper beard, dark religious robes, black turban, and towering height, Beheshti was such an imposing figure that he stood out in any
crowd. All the journalists were impressed by him. He had a low, cultivated
voice, and his press conferences were the best attended after the Imam's.
He was multilingual, responding in Farsi to local journalists and in German,
English, or French to foreign correspondents. As a result, those who attended
his press conferences in the tumultuous days between 1979 and 1980 were
always left without fully understanding many of the things he had spoken
about. This was one more piece in the general mosaic of confusion that characterized Iranian politics at that time.

During his years in exile from the Shah's regime, in Germany, Beheshti
had worked in silence.[46] His enemies would maliciously say that he had spent
his time amassing a fortune and shamelessly drinking alcohol. At the outset
of the revolution in Iran, with the masses occupying the streets and radical
fundamentalist groups leading the intense and internal war for power, he was
in the most advantageous position: Khomeini trusted him; and he had the
energy the old Imam lacked. The Imam, born at the turn of the twentieth
century, was seventy-nine years old; Beheshti was in his sixties, still vigorous.
Fate had placed him in the direct line of succession, and he was gathering the
reins of power to himself. Not only was he secretary-general of the Islamic
Republican Party, which dominated parliament; he would soon control the
courts as chief of the supreme court of justice.

In an agitated country where revolutionary courts are making law and
purging society of undesirable elements—from monarchists and conspirators
to homosexuals and musicians, adulterers and chess players—the instrument
of justice becomes immensely powerful. This is all the more true if a judicial
process can be completed in a matter of minutes, as used to happen with the
revolutionary courts headed by the bloodthirsty ayatollah Sadegh Khalkhali:

venues from which the condemned person was sent directly to be executed by the firing squad.

Beheshti and Khalkhali, formidable and fearsome; like the Ayatollah himself, they were the face of the new revolutionary order.

&

The voters who turned out in August were fewer than the number who had cast their ballots for the referendum in March. But even without an overwhelming electoral mandate, the Assembly of Experts was an essential organization during those times of revolutionary transition and factional struggle. Over a mere three months, from August 12 to November 11, 1979, the Assembly would create a theocratic republic that would hand over the nation's political power to the clerics. With the Assembly's clerical majority, Iran adopted its unique form of Shi'ism as a state religion. It reaffirmed the establishment of an Islamic republic as provisionally approved during the earlier referendum in March. But unlike the earlier draft in June, the amended constitution included no mention of ethnic minorities, no recognition of Sunnis as equals,[47] and no recognition of Kurdish minority rights "aside from the rights guaranteed to all Iranians."[48] While it continued to recognize three basic branches of government—executive, legislative, and judicial—the revision weakened every one of them by making them answerable to clerical control. Moreover, it added the doctrine of velayat-e faqih, government by a supreme spiritual leader. This was precisely what Ghassemlou and the Kurds had feared.

According to Article 110 of the new constitution, the highest authority in the country would be the velayat-e faqih, the Guardianship of the Jurist, which Khomeini saw as ordained in the Qur'an: "O you believers, obey God, obey the Prophet, and obey those in charge among you."[49] The holder of this office, the Supreme Leader, would be named according to the ideas expressed by Khomeini in his book Hokumat-e Eslami ("Islamic Government").[50] He would have the power to designate or dismiss the high commanders of the armed forces—of which he would become commander-in-chief—as well as members of the judicial authority.

His powers would also authorize him to declare war, and to sign a peace treaty; to approve the candidates for president of the republic, and to dismiss the president by recommendation of the Guardian Council or the Majlis, the parliament; to reduce or annul prison sentences imposed by judicial tribunals, and to designate six clerics as members of the twelve-member Guardian

Council. The Council, in turn, held the power to oversee all legislation as to its compliance with Islam and to veto any legislation in conflict with Islamic principles. Consisting of six *faqihs* (experts in Islamic law) chosen directly by the Supreme Leader and six Islamic jurists chosen by the Majlis "from among the Muslim jurists nominated by the Head of the Judicial power"[51]—who was himself appointed by the Supreme Leader—the Guardian Council solidified clerical control of the state. In short, the velayat-e faqih would embody the legitimacy of the regime and be empowered to intervene, in a direct way or through the Guardian Council, in every aspect of the affairs of state.

Khomeini's ideology had carried the day. Dismissing any concern that the Guardianship of the Jurist—effectively, the "vice-regency of the faqih"— would lead to "bullying and dictatorship," he proclaimed: "The *velayat-e faqih* is not something created by the Assembly of Experts. It is something that God has ordained."[52]

However ordained, the power of the Guardianship of the Jurist would continue to overshadow every aspect of Iranian government. Even today, the Iranian parliament, the Majlis-e Shoraye Eslami, strictly speaking is not a parliament with the right to legislate; it is consultative, and the Guardian Council, an unelected body which is controlled by the Supreme Leader, has the power to review and override the Majlis. In Iran it continues to be the case that there is no popular sovereignty; since the 1989 constitutional reform, which essentially reduced the qualifications for the status of faqih while increasing the powers of the position, the system accords absolute power to the Supreme Leader.[53]

It also continues to be the case that there is no recognition of the rights or the realities of ethnic minorities or subpopulations under the regime; discussion of the concerns of minorities is evaded by the insistence on a theocratic unity. "Sometimes the word minorities is used to refer to people such as Kurds, Lurs, Turks Persians, Baluchis, and such," Khomeini had pronounced in November 1979, in defense of the fact that no mention of ethnic nationalities had been included in the new constitution: "These people should not be called minorities, because this term assumes there is a difference between these brothers. In Islam, such a difference has no place at all. There is no difference between Muslims who speak different languages, for instance, the Arabs or the Persians. It is very probable that such problems have been created by those who do not wish the Muslim countries to be united. . . . They create the issues of nationalism, of pan-Iranism, pan-Turkism, and such –isms which are contrary to Islamic doctrines. Their plan is to destroy Islam and Islamic philosophy."[54]

Sheikh Ezzedin promptly and repeatedly denounced the doctrine of velayat-e faqih as a direct path to an illegitimate absolutism. "Many governments in the past have claimed to act in the name of Islam, but in reality they were not Islamic," he pointed out. "The Safavid and Ottoman governments were cases in point; more recently we have the case of Khomeini in Iran. They are *qeshri*—backward and vulgar—and have ruined Islam and its spirit. What we have is not religious government, but a dictatorship under the name of Islam. They are using the name of religion to oppress the people, and the people know this. In Sunni Islam there is no *imam* as political leader or *na'ib* (deputy) *imam*. The role of the clergy is to be *morshed*, or guide, in knowing God. You will also find some Shi'a clergy who reject Khomeini's concept of the *faqih*. It is not an Islamic regime. . . . Any religious government will end in dictatorship, and religion will become a means of beating, executing and killing in the name of God."[55]

The revolution was fated to become a clerical dictatorship as Ghassemlou, too, had feared. And so it was that he argued that it was imperative that he attend the Assembly of Experts' sessions. By his presence there, he felt, he would be able to oppose this monopolization of power which was bound to once again drown the liberties of the Iranians.

Notes

1. Mohamed Heikal, *Iran: The Untold Story* (New York: Pantheon Books, 1982), 86.
2. Looking back at the trajectory of land reform over the past half-century, some observers have suggested that for the Shah's pursuit of development, the feudal system was a primary obstacle—because central to the process of modernization was the move from a collective-based society to one based on the individual; PDKI member Sharif Behruz, personal communication, April 2015. Behruz—whose father, Rahim Behruz, was a PDKI official charged with enforcement of PDKI land-reform policies in the Naghadeh area—adds his impression that, despite its halting movement as a piecemeal process, in essence "the demise of the feudal system was ultimately a matter of time. Even to this day many tribal families who have long owned large swaths of lands still own them—but owing to the societal transformation over the last century, they can no longer hold the clan or village leadership that once would have been theirs." For an analysis of this period and its policies, see Ervand Abrahamian, *Iran Between Two Revolutions* (Princeton, NJ: Princeton University Press, 1982).
3. Shaul Bakhash, *The Reign of the Ayatollahs: Iran and the Islamic Revolution* (New York: Basic Books, Inc., 1984), 22.
4. Sharif Behruz, personal communication to the author, April 29, 2015.
5. Bakhash, *The Reign of the Ayatollahs*, 22.

6. Ibid.

7. Sharif Behruz, personal communication with the author, April 29, 2015.

8. For more on the Land Reform Act of 1962 and the White Revolution, see Abrahamian, *Iran Between Two Revolutions*, Chapter 9, "The Politics of Uneven Development," 419–49.

9. Ervand Abrahamian, *A History of Modern Iran*, 131–32; and Sussan Siavoshi, *Liberal Nationalism in Iran: The Failure of a Movement* (Boulder, CO: Westview Press, 1990), 28.

10. Abdullah Hassanzadeh, *Niw Sede Xebat* [Half a century of struggle: A retrospect of struggle and activity of the Democratic Party of Iranian Kurdistan] [in Kurdish], Vol. 1 (Gawrade: Press Commission of the Kurdistan Democratic Party of Iran, August 1995), 152–56; translation Salah Piroty.

11. Ibid.

12. Ibid.

13. Sharif Behruz, personal communication to the author, April 2015. Observers at the time noted that "government officials—in particular, the gendarmerie and the revolutionary committees—would rouse landlords to regain their land by distributing guns among them." Hassanzadeh, *Half a Century of Struggle*, Vol. 1, 152–56; translation Sharif Behruz.

14. Already by the end of 1977, local komitehs or revolutionary committees had been created across the country. Organized from the mosques, they were vehicles to mobilize people behind Khomeini. Given arms after the revolution, they took up the task of keeping "order and security" and acting as "the new regime's eyes and ears." Baqer Moin, *Khomeini: Life of the Ayatollah* (New York: Thomas Dunne Books, 2000), 211. The later *Komite-ye Imam* (Imam's Committees) were created upon Khomeini's return to Iran to coordinate his political opposition movement. See Global Security, http://www.globalsecurity.org/military/world/iran/khomeini.htm (accessed January 23, 2014).

15. Sharif Behruz, personal communication to the author, April 29, 2015.

16. Rahim Behruz, interview by his son and PDKI member Sharif Behruz, Ontario, Canada, May 10, 2015.

17. David McDowall, *A Modern History of the Kurds* (London, New York: I. B. Tauris, 2004), 268; see also Hassanzadeh, *Half a Century of Struggle*, Vol. 1, 152–56.

18. As summed up by one analyst, "clashes occurred between forces aligned with the conservative landowning Kurds and peasants who engaged in a series of land seizures in Kurdistan." Nader Entessar, "The Kurds in Post-Revolutionary Iran and Iraq," *Third World Review* Vol. 6, No. 4 (October 1984), 926.

19. McDowall, *A Modern History of the Kurds*, 264.

20. The pasdaran, Iran's Islamic Revolution Guards Corps (IRGC), set up in the immediate aftermath of the 1979 revolution, was now officially responsible for internal security, while the regular army remained responsible for the security of Iran's borders.

21. According to contemporary accounts, the fighting began "after attempts by dispossessed landlords to collect tribute from local farmers who then marched on the local Imam Komiteh to demand 'the expulsion of feudal elements'"; this in turn provoked firing by the pasdaran. *The Guardian*, July 16, 1979.

22. Discrimination against the Kurds in the Islamic Republic would include exclusion from universities and state employment as well as mistreatment of Sunni Kurdish children in

primary schools. IHRDC, *On the Margins: Arrest, Imprisonment and Execution of Kurd-ish Activists in Iran Today* (New Haven, CT: April 2012), in Introduction. See IHRDC. https://iranhrdc.org/on-the-margins-arrest-imprisonment-and-execution-of-kurdish-ac-tivists-in-iran-today/(accessed January 18, 2019).

23. Edmund Ghareeb, *The Kurdish Question in Iraq* (Syracuse, NY: Syracuse University Press, 1981), 18. The letter, published in the secularist Tehran daily *Ayandegan*, was sent on August 5, 1979; Nader Entessar, *Kurdish Politics in the Middle East* (London: Lexington Books, 2010), 42.

24. Heikal, *Iran: The Untold Story*, 185.

25. Ibid.

26. The appointment of Ebrahim Yazdi, deputy prime minister for revolutionary affairs, to "coordinate and reconcile all the forces behind the Revolution, proved to be no more than window-dressing," Heikal reported. "There was only one authority in the country. As Yazdi himself said to me, the Revolution consisted of one man, the Imam, and the millions of followers, with nothing in between." Heikal, *Iran: The Untold Story*, 181.

    "Even in the progress toward a constitution Khomeini bucked the demands of other factions of the revolution. A basic promise of their evolution had been political pluralism and local autonomy. . . . So, when Khomeini returned to Iran and his Revolutionary Com-mittee began to exercise power, the left warned that no single faction should be allowed to monopolize the revolution." Michael M. J. Fischer, *Iran: From Religious Dispute to Revolu-tion* (Cambridge, MA: Harvard University Press, 1980), 220.

27. While the development of a government *structure* was a work in progress as the revolution was consolidated, and while some conflict can be seen as structurally inherent in the transition from "provisional" to constitutionally defined governmental forms, the underlying dynamic was the power struggle that from the beginning was dominated by the fundamentalists. "The fundamentalists first controlled the revolutionary institutions and then created a state within the state to weaken and defeat their rivals." Mohsen M. Milani, *The Making of Iran's Islamic Revolution: From Monarchy to Islamic Republic* (Boulder, CO: Westview Press, 1994), 143. Within this context, "Elite factionalism has been a reality of the IRI's political existence ever since its birth." The struggle between "the Provisional Government faction headed by Mehdi Bazargan against the Revolutionary Council dominated by the IRP and personalities such as Ayatollah Mohammad Hosein Beheshti" was the initial form taken by this tendency, which would continue as an ongoing force in the politics of Iran. Maziar Behrooz, "Factionalism in Iran under Khomeini," *Middle Eastern Studies* Vol. 27, No. 4 (October 1991), 598.

28. Milani, *The Making of Iran's Islamic Revolution*, 142.

29. Exporting the Islamic revolution was one of the regime's main ideological tenets and a goal of Iranian foreign policy. "Indeed, Iran's leaders hold that their country has a special duty to propagate its message throughout the 'oppressed' Muslim world," summed up one analyst. "Iran pursues two objectives. First, it seeks to mobilize the revolutionary fervor of Muslims everywhere to overthrow their respective governments and establish Islamic republics similar to that of Iran. Second, Iran works to restore the unity of the Islamic community—the *ummah*—so as to enable Islam to play its ordained role in history." Haggy Ram, "Exporting Iran's Islamic Revolution: Steering a Path between Pan-Islam and Nationalism," in *Religious Radicalism in the Greater Middle East*, ed. Bruce Maddy-Weitzman and Efraim Inbar (Portland, OR: Frank Cass, 1997), 7.

Though Muslim unity was an avowed pillar of Iranian ideology, the Iranian clerical regime time and again made decisions to protect national integrity based on reasons of state rather than ideology. Ibid., 7.

30. Hamid Gohary, *Xorhelatyi Kurdistan le de Salan da 1356–1366* [Eastern Kurdistan during the decade 1978–1988], Vol. 1 [in Kurdish] (Erbil, Iraq: Rojhelat Publisher, 2011), 205.

31. The truth was that this agreement would not hold. After the residents returned, "the opposition parties never reestablished their bases back in the city for fear of an army attack. . . . Initially, the government ordered troops to be stationed around the city and dispatched unarmed soldiers throughout the city as per the agreement; however, the same unarmed soldiers then arrested many residents." Gohary, *Eastern Kurdistan*, 207–08; translation Sharif Behruz. According to IHRDC, on August 13, "after agreement was reached, the residents began returning to town. One critical point of the agreement was that *pasdaran* did not have the authority to arrest individuals. However, pursuant to Khomeini's *fatwa*, the central government dispatched additional forces to Marivan and began arresting all suspects." IHRDC, *Haunted Memories: The Islamic Republic's Executions of Kurds in 1979* (New Haven, CT: 2011), 3. After the February 1979 Islamic Revolution, 3.3. Mariwan, in https://iranhrdc.org/haunted-memories-the-islamic-republics-executions-of-kurds-in-1979/

32. "Unveiled by Bazargan's government on June 18, 1979, the draft constitution called for the establishment of a strong presidency and a unitary system of government. . . . [M]uch to the satisfaction of the secular parties, including the KDPI, the draft constitution did not give special privileges to the clergy." Entessar, *Kurdish Politics*, 36. Entessar goes on to note, however, that despite the first draft's "democratic dispositions to safeguard the rights of all Iranians," the Kurds' autonomy demands were not addressed to their satisfaction. Together with other "nationalist and secularist groups," the PDKI asked that review and revision of the draft be undertaken by a constitutional assembly of up to five hundred elected members representing a full range of stakeholders. Seeing jeopardy to the specifically Islamist elements of the draft in review by such a diverse group, Khomeini ordered the creation of the Assembly of Experts with just seventy-three members for constitutional review. Pointedly, adds Entessar, "The Kurdish nationalists were not included." Ibid., 117.

33. McDowall, *A Modern History of the Kurds*, 270.

34. Moin, *Khomeini*, 217.

35. Moin, *Khomeini*, 218–19.

36. Ali Ezzatyar, *The Last Mufti of Iranian Kurdistan: Ethnic and Religious Implications in the Greater Middle East* (New York: Palgrave McMillan, 2016), 139.

37. Ghassemlou, interview with Jonathan Randal. According to Kutschera, Ghassemlou received over a third of the votes—113,773 of a total of 325,000 voters. Chris Kutschera, *Le défi kurde ou le rêve fou de l'indépendance* [The Kurdish defiance, or the mad dream of independence] (Paris: Bayard Éditions, 1997), 170–71. Ezzatyar cites Ghassemlou's plurality as 80 percent; Ezzatyar, *The Last Mufti of Iranian Kurdistan*, 139.

38. Moin, *Khomeini*, 218–19.

39. *Abdul Rahman Ghassemlou, a Man of Peace and Dialogue* (Paris: The Democratic Party of Iranian Kurdistan, 1989), 20.

40. Abdul Rahman Ghassemlou, interview with Jonathan Randal, Paris, 1986.

41. Khomeini's pursuit of his anti-Marxism policy went so far as sending a letter to Soviet leader Mikhail Gorbachev, asserting that "the main problem in the Soviet Union was spiritual, not economic nor social" and advising him that "the solution was Islam rather than capitalist-style reform." See http://vaezz.wordpress.com/2010/10/12/islam-marxism-and-revolution-in-iran/ (accessed January 14, 2014). The fall of Marxism, said the Imam, would be due to its avoidance of and enmity toward God—as would the fall of the West. "The Imam always said that we should work on introducing our system as a suitable system in the modern world," recalled Mohammad Javad Larijani, then deputy foreign minister; "his goal was to introduce the Islamic system in lieu of Marxism as a system."

    "When Elaheh Kolai (an ex-minister of parliament) was asked about what she thought regarding the Imam's letter to Gorbachev, she replied: '. . . [T]he Imam talks of the dead end the Soviet Union will face. The truth is that the Imam believed that a society which does not accept God as their creator and as their true sovereign will always fall. According to this theory any society or government which follows an incorrect way of thought, rejects truths and ignores the intrinsic needs of humans, . . . will lead to destruction. Imam Khomeini had a special awareness of political circumstances and this led him in making such a precise prediction.'" See The Ideas of the Imam, "Prediction: the Falling of Communism," http://en.imam-khomeini.ir/en/n3772/The_ideas_of_the_Imam/Imam%E2%80%99s_Prediction/Imam%E2%80%99s_Prediction_on_the_Falling_of_Communism."

42. For Khomeini's speech denouncing the concept of a non-Islamic republic, see YouTube, "Imam Khomeini on a 'non-Islamic Republic' explains concept of 'Freedom' in Iran," http://www.youtube.com/watch?v=DXIJWpde4vM.

43. Bakhash, The Reign of the Ayatollahs, 78, citing Ayandegan, July 9, 1979.

44. Ibid., 78. Khomeini made his wishes very clear to the delegates to the newly elected assembly. "On 10 August," Moin writes, "two days before the Assembly opened, the delegates travelled to Qom to pay their respects to Khomeini, whose address instructed them '. . . to make sure that our constitution is within the framework of the law of shari'a. If any one or all the members negate the shari'a they are not our representatives.'

    "He also made clear his opposition to those who campaigned against the Assembly of Experts. He said those people had 'abused the freedom given to them by the Islamic Republic': 'We will close all parties except the one, or a few which act in a proper manner. . . . We all made mistakes. We thought we were dealing with human beings. It is evident we are not. We are dealing with wild animals. We will not tolerate them anymore.'" Moin, Khomeini, 219.

45. The comments from Sheikh Ezzedin and the Kurdish delegation are recounted by Gohary, Eastern Kurdistan, 172–73. See also Entessar, Kurdish Politics, 38 and 44; and Fred Halliday, "Interview with Shaik Izzedin Husseini: A Dictatorship under the Name of Islam," Middle East Reports, No. 113 (March–April 1983),

46. Since the early 1960s, Beheshti had been involved in activities against the monarchy and was arrested several times by the Shah's secret police, the SAVAK. While in exile in Germany from 1965 to 1970, as head of the Islamic Center in Hamburg he was responsible for the spiritual leadership of religious Iranian students in Germany and Western Europe. In 1969, Beheshti visited Ayatollah Khomeini in Najaf, Iraq, during the Ayatollah's

1965–1978 exile there; see Shahed: The Cultural Website of Martyrdom and Sacrifice, "Biography of Ayatollah Sayed Mohammad Hosseini Beheshti based on dates," http://navideshahed.com/en/index.php?Page=static&UID=49137 (accessed January 23, 2014). There he joined Khomeini's underground movement. Beheshti returned to Iran in 1970; during the 1970s, the center he had reorganized in Hamburg played an important role in mobilizing Iranian students in the West against the Shah, ultimately contributing to the Iranian Revolution. See also Habilian Association, "Ayatollah Dr. Beheshti," http://www.habilian.ir/en/Terror-Victims/ayatollah-dr-beheshti.html (accessed January 23, 2014).

47. "Where the original draft constitution recognized by name the four Sunni law schools, the final draft omitted them while it emphasized the Shi'i nature of the state by requiring that the senior officers of the state, the president and prime minister, must be Shi'i." McDowall, *A Modern History of the Kurds*, 271.

48. Entessar, *Kurdish Politics*, 43.

49. Neil Shevlin, "*Velayat-e Faqih* in the Constitution of Iran: The Implementation of Theocracy," Student Notes, *Journal of Constitutional Law*, University of Pennsylvania Law School, Vol. 1, Issue 2 (1998), https://www.law.upenn.edu/journals/conlaw/articles/volume1/issue2/Shevlin1U.Pa.J.Const.L.358(1998).pdf, 367–72). In Khomeini's view, the imams, and after them the legal scholars, were those delegated by the Prophet to promulgate the law in a system of government that by its nature would be divinely inspired because God has given this government "the same powers that he gave the prophet." Ultimately, in his view, "the power of legislation is confined to God . . . and nobody else has the right to legislate." Ibid.

   It's important to recognize, however, that this doctrine of supreme leadership was not inherently Shi'i. "Not all Shia ulama were persuaded by Khomeini's argument. Some found his line of reasoning and the sources on which it relied weak. Others saw it as a violation of Shia historical tradition and even theology." Vali Nasr, *The Shia Revival* (New York: W. W. Norton & Company, 2007), 125.

50. "Khomeini had carefully chosen the term 'Islamic Government' (hokumat-e eslami) as his revolutionary slogan, and instructed his agents not to discuss his theory of Mandate of the Jurist during the revolutionary mobilization against the Shah." Said Amir Arjomand, *After Khomeini: Iran under his Successors* (Oxford and New York: Oxford University Press, 2009), 26.

51. Iran online, http://www.iranonline.com/iran/iran-info/Government/constitution-6-2.html (accessed February 1, 2014).

52. Khomeini, speaking to a group of clerics on October 22, 1979, as reported by the *International Herald Tribune* on October 24, 1979; Bakhash, *Reign of the Ayatollahs*, 86.

53. Shevlin, "*Velayat-e Faqih* in the Constitution of Iran," 367–72.

54. David Menashri, "Shi'ite Leadership: In the Shadow of Conflicting Ideologies," *Iranian Studies*, Vol. 13, No. 1/4, Iranian Revolution in Perspective (1980), 130, fn49 citing a broadcast from Radio Tehran, December 17, 1979, in BBC/SWB, December 19, 1979.

55. Halliday, "A Dictatorship under the Name of Islam," 9–10. Sheikh Ezzedin would continue to denounce and issue pronouncements against Khomeini's Islamic government proposal and the velayat-e faqih as a vehicle to absolutism which handed all power to one man. Entessar, *Kurdish Politics*, 38.

· 6 ·

THE THREE-MONTH WAR

స

A Kurd will never be the leader of Iran,
but he is the one who dares to fight
Khomeini.

—Abdul Rahman Ghassemlou

Toward the end of the summer of 1979, the peshmerga controlled Kurdistan.
In Tehran, the news reported insurrection in Kurdish areas. The foreign press
was forbidden to travel to the region.

Nevertheless, French journalist Marc Kravetz somehow managed to get
there. "Because my newspaper was not wealthy, I took a bus that left at night,
and since I was sleeping when we passed the control point, they did not realize
I was a foreigner. I arrived at Mahabad, which was under the control of the
Kurds, and was introduced to Ghassemlou."[1]

Kravetz was surprised by the congenial and tranquil atmosphere that
reigned in the Kurdish city, so different from the oppressive and fanatical climate in the capital. In contrast to Tehran, in Mahabad he found that men
were relaxed; and women were not veiled or covered, and would look at him.[2]

The French journalist was extremely impressed with Ghassemlou. "Here I
found a political leader who spoke like a normal person. He analyzed the situation and, given the forces with which he was confronted, he aimed to achieve
some kind of tolerance and a national equilibrium that would permit a strengthening of the Iranian state. Ghassemlou was convinced that autonomy could
be negotiated. Autonomy was already a fact, because the Kurds had created an
autonomous zone. Ghassemlou thought that this was the moment for dialogue."

When Kravetz asked why Ghassemlou was targeted by the regime, he
responded, "I am myself, and I am a Kurd, and that is enough for them."
He talked about the "Kurdish difference," the tradition of hospitality and
tolerance among the Kurds. "Just that," he said, "is intolerable for them. In
Mahabad you will find Jews, Christians, Baha'is, and even atheists, all those

kinds of people who have fled Tehran. We don't have the same concept of Islam as Mr. Khomeini. The Kurds know and empathize with the plight of minorities."[3] Religious and national minorities, he added, would very soon learn that there was no place for differences in the Islamic Republic.

Kravetz believed that Ghassemlou did not underestimate the danger. Ghassemlou was convinced the clerical regime would end up facing enormous difficulties, however, and that once the revolutionary frenzy and the phase of military repression were over, the Islamists would have to negotiate.

Ghassemlou's unique regard for the place and power of negotiation was noted by colleagues and journalists alike. While Ghassemlou expressed optimism when he talked to others, especially people outside party leadership, privately and with close colleagues he was more balanced in his analysis and cautious in his expectations. Dialogue and the process of negotiation was something he saw in a Western sense, as a genuine approach to a workable consensus. Political actors, he believed, on the basis of rational analysis and practical necessity, would realize that reducing politics to a zero-sum game was harmful to everyone, leading only to conflict, and that negotiations would lead to compromise and a win-win situation for all parties.

For these reasons, colleagues noted, he seems to have preferred negotiation as the route to pursue in all situations and with everyone. He seems to have wanted to exhaust all options before responding to coercion and the use of force with resistance and guerilla warfare. Ultimately indeed he did so respond; but he also saw guerilla warfare, as he put it, as "a means to pave the way for negotiations" rather than as a realistic way for the Kurds to prevail over a regime militarily far superior.

He used to say that under the iron grip of the ayatollahs, there could not be democratic progress in Iran or Kurdistan. "But we can't declare a war," he insisted. "Because it is a revolutionary government supported by the population, we must insist on our demands and negotiate right up to the last moment. We must take advantage of every opportunity. Yet we must also prepare ourselves to resist. We must be vigilant and understand that someday we may be under the fire of bombs and a military attack."[4]

On one front, he was organizing the political structure of the party. On a second, he was building the armed resistance of the peshmerga. But always, at the same time, he was trying to reach an agreement with the government.

"Several delegations of the PDKI spoke with Banisadr and other public officials—always trying to avoid a war," recalled Sadegh Sharafkandi. "Dr. Ghassemlou hated war because he knew what it would mean."[5] About this

Ghassemlou said, "War not only destroys lives and buildings. It destroys human beings. But we have no choice. . . . They [the Islamic Republic] are making war; we resist."[6]

He confessed to Hélène that at the beginning of the war he was tormented. "I sent people to war, and I knew that death awaited them. The first victims . . . it was terrible. I could not sleep. Afterwards, you get used to it. That is war."[7]

Ghassemlou lived in a house near what had become the council office of Mahabad. Kravetz was surprised to find no gates there, and to see the degree of trust prevailing among the people. At Ghassemlou's general headquarters, people would come and go with total freedom. Ghassemlou did not take precautions. "He was aware of everything that was going on," said Kravetz. "He reminded me of Arafat in his daily management. But he differed from the Palestinian leader in that he was more precise in his political reasoning. He also did everything. He administered everything."

Geopolitical analyst Gérard Chaliand,[8] who spent time in Kurdistan during those days, remembered that Ghassemlou "was a pedagogue in meetings with the party cadres. He always conducted himself with a caustic spirit and humor. In the morning, he had meetings in the party's offices. It was a large house with a living room that held thirty people." While spacious, the headquarters was very simple: "The living room had enormous sofas," Chaliand noted, "but it was cold because there was no heating."[9]

"Ghassemlou," said Chaliand, "used to go to the battlefront, and toured the region. He visited the families of the fallen peshmerga.

"We went to a large burial for a number of Kurdish families' victims assassinated by the pasdaran in a village near Lake Urmia. There were at least ten to twelve thousand people. Ghassemlou told them that this moment of pain was valuable for everyone because they were all together and this was a way of being a Kurd. Being a Kurd did not imply only that they had the same struggle but that they shared the same victims. With this type of ceremony, he told them, the people would become stronger; it reinforced cohesion and their soul.

"The leafless trees of the cemetery were covered with scraps of multicolored cloth to commemorate the dead. I have never seen cemeteries as impressive as in that region. They genuinely moved you. They had something that is fragile and poetic."

❧

Kurdistan had not suffered difficult times only during the revolution. Now it was also feeling strangled by the Iranian embargo on the region. It was necessary to organize, to administer and impose order. The peshmerga, faced with government troops, made efforts to retrieve more weapons from enemy garrisons. Whenever possible, they avoided direct confrontation; though they were more skilled than the government troops in mountain warfare, they were still guerrillas and not trained military professionals.

In August 1979, Tehran launched a full-scale war against the Kurds.

The town of Paveh, a small town in the province of Kermanshah near the Iraqi border, had been in the hands of the Kurds since the beginning of the revolution. On January 12, amidst the revolutionary upheavals that were sweeping the country, the local population had taken over the police, gendarmerie, and law-enforcement agencies. Now in August, under the pretext of defending the border with Iraq, the regime sent IRGC forces to Paveh, including Iranian Revolutionary Guards commander Abu Sharif; Valiollah Fallahi, chief of the general staff of the armed forces and general commander of ground forces; and then-deputy prime minister Mustafa Chamran.

After having set their base in the center of the city, IRGC forces began a campaign against the PDKI, accusing the party of being anti-religious and anti-Islam. This drew the support of some young supporters of Ahmad Moftizadeh—the prominent local Kurdish political and religious leader who had advocated for an "Islamic Iran with Kurdish autonomy"[10] and initially supported the regime, as had Kurdish Sunni mullahs from the Maktab Qur'an, the Qur'an school. The elected city council, composed mainly of young people, supported the PDKI and gave the responsibility for the security of the city to the party. This was the spark for what would be later known as the war in Paveh.[11]

The regime, in an effort to destabilize PDKI's administration, sent a group of pasdaran known as Mujahidin[12] to cause unrest in Paveh. Demonstrations and strikes began to take place around the city, culminating in a sit-in protest in front of the governor's office.

On August 9, following a quarrel between two young Kurdish men, the pasdaran and those who backed the regime charged that the PDKI was incapable of maintaining order and demanded that government forces take over the city. Endorsing takeover by the central government, regime supporters staged a sit-in. Members of the Qur'an school and a few Sunni Kurdish mullahs began to incite the protestors, seeking to prolong the disturbance, and later accused the PDKI of siding with the agitating protestors. Their goal was to ensure unrest and insecurity in the PDKI-controlled city.

On the same day, in opposition to the demonstrations against the elected Kurdish administration in Paveh, a sit-in with support of the PDKI[13] was organized in Quri Qela, a small town between Paveh and Kermanshah. PDKI members were present to ensure a calm and peaceful protest. This protest expanded into a strike.

"A delegation of trustees and young people asked the Kermanshah state governor and Paveh governor to intercede," recalled Kawe Bahrami, who was part of this delegation.[14]

On August 13, a team under the supervision of the acting state governor and other government officials, among them Haji Akhund, a Persian Shi'ite cleric, visited Quri Qela to hear what the strikers were requesting. Among their requests were the formation of a commission for city and village council elections; establishment of local security forces under the supervision of a city commission for protection; a demand that the pasdaran leave the city, with official recognition that non-Iranian forces residing in the region as political refugees could not and did not have the right, under any circumstances, to interfere in the internal affairs and administration of the area and that the interference of unqualified individuals in regional affairs would not be tolerated; and a demand that a fair court be set up to resolve issues.

After the visit to the strikers, the delegation decided that the strikes had to end in Paveh and Quri Qela, and the strikers too agreed to this.

On the fourteenth of August, however, the civilians rebelled in Paveh. They attacked military garrisons, and in two days of fighting they had taken control of the city.

On August 15 Chamran sent a delegation to the PDKI asking they withdraw from the area. In good faith, the PDKI withdrew. However, that same night Chamran ordered an attack on the peshmerga base in the village of Dorisan, near Paveh. The peshmerga counterattacked, inflicting enormous losses, and forced a retreat.

On the night of the seventeenth of August, an enraged Khomeini stormed out of the religious school of Feyzieh in Qom. It was Friday, the Muslim weekly holy day. On national radio and television he told the country that the revolution was losing an important battle in the northwest provinces. Neither the government nor the army, nor the police, nor the pasdaran, declared Khomeini, had acted as they should have.[15]

To Khomeini, the lack of "revolutionary enthusiasm" on the part of the government was inconceivable. The old cleric was furious. His response was to call for war against all the opposition parties that were participating in "counterrevolutionary" activities.

Khomeini designated himself commander-in-chief of the armed forces, and declared a holy war against the "Kurdish conspirators": "We will take the PDKI leaders to the tribunals and we will judge them. The Kurds are the biggest *kofars* (infidels) and we will respond to their actions with consequences [as they deserve]." And he went further, condemning them as corrupt, subversive, saboteurs, traitors, hypocrites: "You are not democrats," he raged at them, "you are hypocrites—you are dictators who masquerade as a democrat."[16] Like "a poison to the health of the revolution," he thundered, "no trace of them should be left in the country."[17]

The Ayatollah demanded that the armed forces act decisively against the Kurds within the next twenty-four hours. Should they fail to do so, he warned, looking straight into the cameras, those forces would suffer an exemplary punishment. He would "deal with them [the troops] in a revolutionary way."[18]

On Saturday, August 18, Khomeini's *fatwa* against the Kurds was published in the press. Calling for a general mobilization, he assumed direction of the country's affairs, an action which highlighted the magnitude of the crisis. He ordered his general staff to send in the army and police, and with all necessary means—including tanks and cannons—to crush the Kurdish insurrection in Paveh.

The fatwa shocked the Kurdish population. "Khomeini did not issue a fatwa for Jihad (Holy War) against the monarchist government," exclaimed a Kurd from Marivan. "Nor did he issue one during the eight long years his regime fought Saddam's Ba'athist regime. But he issued a fatwa for Jihad against his own Kurdish, Muslim countrymen."[19]

The troops marched north. Ground-force general Valiollah Fallahi and Mustafa Chamran,[20] minister of defense and commander of the pasdaran, marched with them.[21]

Sheikh Ezzedin and Ghassemlou reacted with unease and anger. Review your politics before launching any hasty actions, Ezzedin advised the Imam. Otherwise, they both warned the Ayatollah, Kurdistan will become your very tomb. The struggle of the Kurdish people, they declared, would continue—if need be, for the next fifty years.

In Paveh, the peshmerga awaited the attack. Until now, Tehran's military efforts had been frustrated by the inhospitable terrain. The infantry advanced only with great effort while the Kurdish rebels moved ahead without difficulty.

Peshmerga controlled the gorges that led to the city and blocked the advance of the ground forces. They impeded access by air as well, firing against army helicopters from well-defended positions.

This time the government troops attacked forcefully. With air-force support, pasdaran charged into the city. Paveh, surrounded, was attacked with Phantom F4 fighter jets and helicopters, and with artillery brought in from the base near Kermanshah.

Under the bombs, Ghassemlou ordered his men to retreat into the mountains, and ordered the population evacuated. From their mountain strongholds, even under bombardment with napalm, Kurdish fighters resisted the attacks.[22]

Ghassemlou would try repeatedly to open negotiations with Tehran, to no avail. Months later, in one such attempt during a further attack on Paveh, on February 3, 1980, as reported by the Fars News Agency, Ghassemlou sent the Ayatollah a telegram. "After the Iranian Revolutionary Guards attacked and killed the innocent people in Kamyaran [Province]," he wrote, "right now heavy clashes in the region of Paveh are underway. In these clashes initiated by IRG, helicopters, tanks, and even Phantom fighters have been used; defenseless villages have been bombed, homes destroyed, and many innocent women and children have been massacred.

"I with responsibility and insistency do ask your honor to issue an immediate and serious order to prevent further clashes and to return the IRG to its previous positions in order to end these clashes. And any disregard and delay in making serious decisions to prevent war and fratricide could bring dire consequences."[23]

But the Ayatollah had closed the doors to any dialogue.

Khomeini, not content with ordering the attack on Paveh, also ordered the army to march to Sanandaj, where peace prevailed with no hint of insurrection.

The governor-general of Kurdistan, Mohammed Rashid Shakiba, stated immediately that Tehran's information regarding the situation in Sanandaj was "a total lie. . . . There is no unrest there." Both the town and the garrison were calm, and the commander there had not asked for help. Khomeini, he reported, had not consulted with him before making the decision to march against the city.[24]

Prime Minister Bazargan's view, reported in the international press, was that the Imam had ordered the troops toward Sanandaj not because he had been misinformed, but because he wanted to deliver a harsh lesson. He wanted the ethnic minorities[25] to know firsthand the "uselessness of an insurrection." He also wanted, Bazargan believed, to lift the spirits of the demoralized armed forces[26] and to deprive radical leftist groups of the sanctuary they had found among the Kurds.[27]

In retrospect, Bazargan seemed to have pointed clearly to three long-term, larger goals on Khomeini's part, as historian David Menashri summed up: "To remove the Kurdish threat once and for all; to make all outer minorities understand that rebellion was futile; and to make use of the Kurdish campaign to restore the morale of the armed forces."[28] Khomeini's immediate aim, Menashri added, seemed to have been to assert his authority.[29]

Worth noting in the regime's campaign was the employment of ongoing, systematic demonization of the Kurds in the media. In an interview conducted after the 1979 conflict at Paveh between the Kurds and the forces loyal to Tehran, for instance, Chamran would claim that PDKI forces committed every kind of carnage, even killing the sick in the hospital.[30]

Within a single day of Khomeini's call for mobilization, the rebellion of Paveh was decisively crushed on Sunday, August 19, 1979, by the combined forces of the military, commanded by General Valiollah Fallahi, and the pasdaran.[31] Nearly four hundred people had died. During the next forty-eight hours, Tehran's forces created a reign of terror. Houses were systematically seized and people arrested. Nine alleged PDKI members were condemned to death for "corruption on earth" and "being at war with God and his prophet."[32] The government's firing squads executed twenty-nine people.

Tehran wanted more than to simply suffocate the rebellion; they wanted to eliminate nationalist leaders and the outstanding militants of opposition parties. Repression was indiscriminate and directed against the entire Kurdish population. Once again the old story of a rebellious Kurdistan being crushed by the central power had come into play.

Alongside this story line, there was another: by taking irreversible measures against the Kurdish national struggle, Khomeini had declared the jihad against the Kurdish people. Yet at the same time, this incitement also provided the opportunity for Khomeini and those closest to him to sideline other parties and people within the inner circle such as Bazargan and the army generals. The war against Kurdistan, while aimed specifically against the Kurds, also became a means for the regime to solidify power in the center and within the army command—and for Khomeini to emphasize his dominance.[33]

Clear-minded as ever, Ghassemlou recognized the internecine politics additionally at play in the regime's assault on the Kurds. In a radio message delivered on September 12, 1982, addressing the regime's onslaught against the Kurdish people which had continued unabated since 1979, Ghassem-lou would sum up: "Khomeini's regime—the regime that has conceded defeat on many fronts, inside and outside the country—needs a victory. He thinks by mobilizing a few thousand *Basiji*[34] he can secure this victory in Kurdistan."[35]

In a further public statement, Ghassemlou would charge that regime officials were lying to Khomeini to egg him on to step up violence against the Kurds. "For some time now, regime officials have been touting a huge victory and congratulating each other. They write letters to Imam Khomeini . . . he incites them further to slaughter the people of Kurdistan."[36]

In this slaughter, the behavior of Iranian troops was a direct reflection of the cruelty of revolutionary tribunals imposed by the "hanging judge," Ayatollah Sadegh Khalkhali. In Marc Kravetz's assessment, "the military phase was carried out with the terror provoked by Khalkhali and his assassins, and by the massive use of the air force and helicopters."[37]

Khalkhali had full power in Kurdistan. "He was sent by Khomeini," said Sharafkandi, "to kill people and exert terror." Khalkhali was not merely the creature or creation of Khomeini. Even Banisadr and his advisors defended him. They were laymen and not rigid clerics; but they regarded Ghassemlou as a foreign agent, and for them, this justified every form of repression in Kurdistan. Furthermore, even the moderate laymen within the regime were opposed to Kurdish autonomy. And it was not only against Ghassemlou that such charges were raised; there was a well-established tendency to excuse terror and violence even against "their own" by labeling the offenders as foreign agents.

When Kravetz, interviewing Banisadr's close advisor Ahmed Salamatian, asked him if he believed that Khalkhali's methods respected human rights, Salamatian answered, "For our people, Khalkhali is the rage of God."[38]

"I was the religious magistrate," Khalkhali would later write in his memoirs, "and ordered the execution of five hundred and some criminals and loyalists to the Shah, as well as hundreds of actors in the Kurdistan and Gonbad and Khuzestan incidents and a number of thugs and drug dealers. About these executions, I have no regrets; I am not complaining and my conscience is clear. In fact I believe that I didn't kill enough! Many were deserving of execution whom I didn't manage to catch."[39]

Ghassemlou made an anguished appeal to world leaders to stop what he described as a genocidal act. He denounced the Ayatollah and accused him of pushing Iran toward "a religious medieval dictatorship."

In response to the outcry from international human-rights groups over the executions, Khomeini would reply: "Criminals should not be tried. The trial of a criminal is against human rights. Human rights demand that we should have killed them in the first place when it became known they were criminals. . . . Doesn't the human rights lobby think that criminals must be killed for the sake of human rights, in order to ensure the rights of man and those whom these people killed, tortured and destroyed? Nevertheless we are trying them and we have tried them. Our belief is that criminals should not be tried and must be killed."[40]

The Kurdish population responded by taking to the streets in nine cities; they demanded the immediate release of all prisoners. They threatened to execute one Islamic militant for every Kurd who was executed. The Kurds supported their own nationalist leaders, many of whom would later be arrested.

In the end, government forces took Sanandaj as well as Paveh. The image, on the front page of the *New York Times*, of eleven Kurds falling—blindfolded, dressed in their baggy pants—under the hail of bullets from the pasdaran firing squad shocked the world.

And so it had come to pass that on August 18, during the fateful broadcast of the opening session of the Assembly of Experts, Khomeini publicly stripped Abdul Rahman Ghassemlou of his membership in the Assembly—a virtual excommunication—and utterly outlawed his party.[41] The Imam reproached the government for its passivity. He insisted on the need to impose order in Kurdistan and restore discipline in the armed forces. He went even further; he delineated the ideological direction that the revolution should follow from that point onward and determined that it was necessary, without hesitation, to eliminate the liberal opposition.

The venerable members of the Assembly of Experts for the Constitution listened in reverential silence. They were there to elaborate "a constitution one hundred percent Islamic," in a context where "any other direction would be deemed contrary to the desires of the republic and the people of Iran."[42]

The Imam repented the mistake he had made, he said, when he "did not break the poisoned pens of the corrupt press, or close all the rotten publications that conspired, and for not having judged the heads of these in the courts of Islamic justice. . . . If from the beginning we had prohibited all the political parties that conspired against the revolution, and had hanged all its leaders on public gallows, we wouldn't have the problems we now have."[43]

The Jacobin stage of the revolution was well underway.

❧

On Monday, August 20, thousands of people took to the streets of Tehran in support of Khomeini. The bazaar closed in solidarity with the demonstration against the Kurdish leaders. A multitude of young people accompanied the funeral homage for the pasdaran who were killed in the battle of Paveh, crying, "Death to Ghassemlou! Execute Sheikh Ezzedin!"[44]

That very day, Khomeini ordered Khalkhali to leave for Kermanshah to evaluate the tense situation in the Kurdish region and oversee the administration of justice there—that is, see to the dealings with Kurdish prisoners. Khalkhali traveled with a claim to the Ayatollah's blessing.[45] Following in the wake of the military and the pasdaran during the takeover of Kurdish towns over the next several weeks, Khalkhali "summarily held trials and ordered immediate executions. Both men and boys were condemned to death—within mere days, and at times only hours, following their arrests—without legitimate trials. All these arrests were for alleged anti-revolutionary activities."[46]

In a message August 20 to the Kurdish people, Khomeini said, "Since the victory of the revolution and the announcement of the Islamic Republic, groups that are enemies of Islam, and foreign agents, have been working against the Islamic movement and the Islamic Republic. Some of them even opposed the referendum and boycotted it. Brothers, you yourselves saw that the 'Kurdistan Democratic Party' has a direct affiliation with America and Zionism. . . . You know well that the Democratic Party of Kurdistan is an outlawed party, because the party is supported by USA and Israel and therefore a party of Satan."[47] The Ayatollah exhorted the Kurds to follow their "religious duty": to put a stop to "the conspiracy of traitors and corrupt leaders," and to disclose their hiding places to the army and the government.[48]

Kurdistan responded with the creation of a united front—Hey'ate Khalqe Kurd, the Council of the Kurdish People—formed by Ghassemlou's PDKI, the Kurdish branch of the Feda'iyan of the People, Komala, Ezzedin's followers,[49] and several professional and peasant organizations. They were all aware that a "total war" had been launched.

On the twenty-second of August, in an atmosphere of sorrow throughout Kurdistan, Khomeini showed his magnanimity. He would pardon the Kurds if they "returned to the path of Islam" and gave up their weapons. He promised $70 million for the development of Kurdistan if the rebellion ceased.

It was a ridiculous sum, equivalent to a single day's income from Iran's oil production. But his magnanimity did not extend to Ghassemlou or Sheikh Ezzedin. For them, he offered the wrath of God and the Prophet—and an enormous reward to anyone who brought them to justice.

Between August 22 and August 26, new armed confrontations erupted in Saqqez, north of Sanandaj. Two hundred peshmerga defended the city with the support of the local population. While tanks and heavy artillery attacked, bombers flew straight into the city. The city was demolished. The attacks did not discriminate, and even civilians became legitimate targets.

With mortars, two 106-millimeter cannons, and RPG7 missile launchers, Kurdish resistance held out for two days. When the battle was over, two hundred were dead and five hundred wounded. The pasdaran searched the houses one by one, and brought the male defenders outside and tied them to the railings that lined the windows and doors.

For a few hours, Saqqez was a horror scene, with those men awaiting their fate like lambs in a slaughterhouse. Twenty people were executed that day. They included a teacher from Kermanshah who was bringing medicines and a surgeon from Tehran, Dr. Qasem Rashvand Sardari, who had come to Paveh as a volunteer to treat the wounded.[50] Khalkhali's justification, voiced in a radio interview a few days later, was the claim that Sardari had confessed to being a Communist, to espousing support for the PDKI and for Kurdish separatism, and to "using arms against government forces in Paveh."[51] Khalkhali's most outrageous claim was that the physician had ordered the beheading of pasdaran in the nearby village of Quri Qela.[52]

Newspapers carried a public statement from his medical colleagues from hospitals in Tehran, calling for a government inquiry into the realities of the matter: "Dr. Qasem Rashvand Sardari, born in Tehran, was executed on account of being a Muharib [at war with God]. . . . On Friday, 26/5/1358 [August 17, 1979], he went to Paveh from Tehran to help the injured of the Paveh battle—so any accusation related to his involvement in the unwanted battle of Paveh is unmerited. . . . We urge . . . condemnation of the agents who are in charge of these executions."[53] No record is known of a government reply to their plea.

Executed also that day were nine soldiers accused of being members of the PDKI. And a young man with his leg in a cast, who had fought with the peshmerga, was dragged out of the hospital and shot.[54]

༄

Toward the end of August, nearly every city formerly in the hands of the peshmerga was now controlled by the Islamist power: Sanandaj, Piranshar, Saqqez, and Miandoab. There was left only Mahabad, where Ghassemlou and the PDKI had organized, for the twenty-fifth of August, a meeting representing the minorities of Iran, those experiencing oppression or at risk for similar treatment: the Kurds, Azeris, Baluchis, Luris, and Turkmen. Together these ethnicities represented half of the thirty-six million inhabitants of the country. The purpose of the meeting was to discuss and reach an agreement on their demands that Iran should be restructured as a federation, granting autonomy or self-rule to all regions where non-Persians lived. They also discussed finding a common strategy in the face of "the brutal reaction of Qom."[55]

In an attempt to stop the war, meanwhile, the PDKI with Ghassemlou's assent,[56] had sent a delegation to Tehran with a peace plan. "The government has not asked directly to negotiate," said one delegation member to a large meeting organized by the party, "but through the intermediary of its minister of labor [Dariush Foruhar], we have arrived at a first agreement to send a delegation to Tehran."[57]

On August 27, Mahabad's five-man team traveled to Tehran and proposed the following: an immediate ceasefire; Khalkhali's immediate removal from the Kurdish region; stipulations that the troops cease attacks on Kurdish holdings and that the pasdaran retreat from Kurdish zones; an end to the execution of Kurdish prisoners; and a conference to resolve the issues of Kurdish autonomy through peaceful means.[58] According to the Iranian Association of Political Prisoners, throughout the country fifteen hundred people were waiting to be tried, and a hundred and thirty had already been executed. Among them were many Kurds.

For Ghassemlou, a halt to all combat and the freeing of all Kurdish prisoners were indispensable preconditions to any negotiations, and these were the conditions he tasked the delegation with demanding.[59] The plan seemed well received by the authorities in Tehran, but underwent a series of unlooked-for modifications. An agreement signed by the delegation in Tehran, which Kutschera described as "strange," stipulated that the Iranian army would be allowed to enter Mahabad but then must evacuate; that PDKI militants would be granted amnesty; that the military garrison, relinquished by the army, would become a facility for university education; and that once the city was secured, recruitment of Revolutionary Guards would be done among the local population.[60]

The PDKI denounced the document "the moment the accord was signed," and announced that the people who had negotiated it were not "authentic representatives" of the people.[61] For his part, Khomeini refused to accept it as well, and in any case would not consider any demands acceptable while the Kurds remained in a state of armed resistance.[62] Beheshti, who had acted as a principal to the negotiations on Khomeini's behalf, announced on August 28 that the Ayatollah had decided that neither the Kurds nor other minorities would receive any "specific concession."[63]

The Ayatollah named a cleric, the hojatoleslam Hosseini Kermani, as his special envoy to Kurdistan. He gave Kermani specific orders to crush the Kurds and not negotiate with them. In a follow-up letter with orders to his newly appointed envoy, Khomeini wrote: "The criminal rebels of Kurdistan must be annihilated. If the enemy is not crushed soon, I will personally go to Kurdistan and end the rebellion."[64] Addressing the Kurdish leaders, he concluded: "We will bury you if you do not disappear."[65]

Khomeini soon made good his threat: in retaliation for the losses the Islamist forces had sustained in the face of Kurdish resistance, the military within days would surround Gharna, a suburb of Naghadeh. And on the second of September, government forces would brutally demonstrate what a rebellious Kurdistan could expect.

The villagers there were not initially worried, for there were no peshmerga there to warrant an attack. Nonetheless, first the pasdaran fired, and then armored vehicles and troops entered the village. "The imam of the city, Mullah Mahmud,[66] aware of the pasdarans' intentions, took hold of the Qur'an and marched toward them. The pasdaran responded with a burst of machine-gun fire. Then the pasdaran broke into the houses and fired upon every living being. Old men and children were dragged out of their homes and prodded with rifle butts, lined up against the walls, and shot. Within a few hours, sixty-eight Kurdish people—men, women, and children of all ages—had been executed."[67]

Statements from witnesses to the attack and its aftermath give some sense of the horror. "We found Mullah Mahmud's body in a pit with other people killed by the pasdaran in Gharna," said Omar Karimi, a former resident and witness of the massacre in Gharna; the pasdaran had beheaded the mullah after shooting him. "It was difficult to identify the bodies, because the pasdaran had dumped trash over them after showing them to the people of the area in order to intimidate them. Only their relatives could identify them, the bodies were rotten and worm-eaten. Since we could not find the mullah's head we had to bury him without it."[68]

Under the unceasing pummeling of air and land attacks, the people of Kurdistan had indeed "discovered the real face of the Islamic Republic" and saw themselves facing certain genocide.[69] Now, faced with an attack on Mahabad itself, Ghassemlou said, "We will resist as much as we can, but [from] outside the city. If we cannot stop them, Mahabad will be an open city [undefended]. We will evacuate the combatants. It's the only way to save the population from useless suffering. *They* [the regime forces] have the means to destroy the city, and we do not have the means to defend ourselves. As I have said, our strength lies in the mountains."[70]

Ten thousand peshmerga awaited the offensive, strengthening their positions around Mahabad while the party moved its general headquarters to Sardasht, near the border with Iraq. The army, besieging the city, gave the Kurds an ultimatum, demanding they allow "the peaceful entry" of government forces into the city, in accordance with the "agreement" signed in Tehran. The PDKI refused; they would fight "the battle of destiny" defending Mahabad, they responded, "to the last drop of blood."[71]

The attack began at six in the morning of Monday, September 3, following a siege that had lasted for weeks.[72] The army had tanks, 155-millimeter cannons, and machine guns, supported by air-force fighter bombers and helicopters. During the battle, which lasted over seven hours,[73] the air attacks never ceased.

"Ghassemlou told me that he was leaving Mahabad," recalled Kravetz. "The military front was five or six kilometers distant, but you could feel the imminent attack. Ghassemlou then decided to evacuate, to avoid the slaughter of the population. The city fell; the air force terrorized the people by flying extremely low. The day before the central government's forces entered the city, there was panic and people fled. Of the eighty thousand inhabitants, only one thousand remained."[74]

Before evacuating Mahabad, Ghassemlou called a meeting in the central square. "We will resist. We have the strength to resist this invasion. We must continue fighting until we obtain our demand," he said. The townspeople and the majority of the peshmerga began their retreat. One contingent of peshmerga stayed to protect their flank. At noon, without a single shot being fired by the peshmerga, the tanks entered the deserted city.

That same night, official news reported the "liberation of Mahabad" and in glorious terms described how the courageous soldiers had, in God's name, made the "band of counterrevolutionaries" flee as the people cheered and showered their "liberators" with flowers and rice.[75]

Mahabad was once more under control by the central power. Kravetz was concerned about the consequences of the pasdarans' entering the city, including the treatment he feared he himself might receive at their hands. But he was lucky. The pasdaran commander was Abu Sharif, whom the journalist had met in southern Lebanon in 1967. When the pasdaran troops saw Kravetz with Sharif, they did not bother him.

Three days later, on September 6, the French journalist left in a small bus filled with peasants. He passed through a peshmerga barricade checkpoint and said he wanted to speak with Ghassemlou. The Kurds took him to Ghassemlou in a small village hidden in the mountains, a tiny settlement with no electricity. Kravetz found him happy, directing the operations, even though limited in what he could do. The army was powerful; when the peshmerga went down into the valleys, helicopters attacked them. But fighting on their own ground, the guerillas held the lines; the roads were under the army's control during the day and in the hands of the peshmerga at night.

Ghassemlou had never participated in a war; however, he had studied guerrilla warfare and the conduct of classical wars as well. And according to Sharafkandi, he had gained experience with the Iraqi Kurdish movement, with which he had spent some years.[76] "He knew a lot about the armed movements in Latin America," Sharafkandi said. "He could decide the general direction, but he never got involved in the details of military operations. Still, the peshmerga were convinced that he knew. Even today, it is a PDKI rule that the military leaders do not have the power of decision. It is the political cadres who possess that power. They never stray from the political direction that has been set."[77]

Ghassemlou led the resistance from the mountains in "very hard conditions," recalled Sharafkandi. "The air force bombed the Kurdish cities without pity."

In an interview from the Zagros Mountains, Ghassemlou declared that the revolt would not end and that it would continue as a guerrilla campaign.[78] On October 20, 1979, the peshmerga would regain Mahabad. "After three months," Sharafkandi said, "Ghassemlou returned victorious to Mahabad. The campaign had been a success for him and for the PDKI, who had organized the resistance."

❧

Despite the seemingly straightforward victory in Ghassemlou's return to Mahabad, the broader picture was much less simple. In events as viewed from a distance, two facts emerge more clearly. The first was that, alongside Kurdish armed resistance, independent efforts at negotiation continued to be put forward from both sides. The second was that, even while winning individual battles within the boundaries of Kurdistan, on the broader front of attracting allies from beyond their borders, the Kurdish struggle may have been losing the war for popular and global international support.

Outside the arena of the ground war in Kurdistan, efforts persisted to open avenues of rapprochement. By October 12, negotiations on behalf of the Kurds were underway between Sheikh Ezzedin and Minister of Labor Dariush Foruhar, who had brokered an earlier agreement. While pitched battles continued, and hard-liners clamored to crush the Kurds, Prime Minister Bazargan urged Khomeini to accept the Kurdish proposals that Foruhar was working on.[79] The regime's willingness to negotiate was due only to their losses in the "Three-Month War"; and negotiations, once again, would be accepted only to buy time and prepare for the next offensive.[80]

The offers for negotiation would be accepted, at nearly the same moment that Ghassemlou was reentering Mahabad; and on October 23, a delegation composed of Foruhar and four ministers would be named by Tehran to treat with the Kurds.[81]

On October 29, the minister of the interior, to confirm Tehran's willingness to resume negotiations, announced that all military operations would be interrupted "in order to create a favorable climate for the visiting governmental delegation."[82] A committee headed by Foruhar and two other ministers, dispatched by Bazargan to Kurdistan on November 2, managed through a conciliatory approach to negotiate a ceasefire.[83]

In Kutschera's view, however, the fact was that the PDKI had begun to lose the war against the regime when it evacuated the main cities of Kurdistan. Responding to critiques of the strategy of withdrawal, Ghassemlou stated his view that the Kurdish movement had not suffered military defeat. It was for the purpose of saving lives and infrastructure that the PDKI had decided to retreat voluntarily from the cities and begin a guerrilla warfare.[84]

"We are preparing for a long war," he said, "a guerrilla warfare in all of Iranian Kurdistan, and we will continue until victory, until we reach autonomy within a democratic Iran." This outcome he anticipated with support from the unified front that had been formed with other organizations of democratic opposition.[85]

Analyzing the situation for *Le Monde* in an article on September 5, 1979,[86] French correspondent Eric Rouleau outlined two factors contributing to the

Kurds' ultimate failure in achieving their goals. On the one hand, he believed, the Kurds had been mistaken in their strategy and their grasp of the situation; on the other, Khomeini had demonstrated that he still controlled an effective army. Despite the popular view that the army was politicized, undisciplined, and incapable of playing a police role, it turned out that Khomeini's hold was strong. When he had given the order on August 17 to crush the Kurdish rebellion, his command was obeyed. In less than fifteen days, Khomeini's forces had taken over the Kurdish strongholds.

In Rouleau's view, the Kurds' analysis of the political situation was flawed. Their optimism was "without foundation"—unfounded. They were convinced that Khomeini was isolated; and they were equally convinced that they would receive support from a range of organizations in the opposition, both secular and religious, which, once the regime's offensive had begun, had gone underground.[87] They believed, too, that they could count on Taleghani, who had previously defended ethnic aspirations in Iran; but he dropped them abruptly, accusing the leaders of the PDKI of being "traitors." Persisting in the insurrection, he felt, put Iran at risk of falling under "the camp of imperialism and the counterrevolution."[88] Khomeini's rival Shariatmadari, too, dropped his support of the Kurds. The danger he perceived came from a different direction: in his estimation, prolonging the Kurdish rebellion opened Iran, and its revolution, to the threat of Soviet interference. He accused the USSR of funneling weapons to the Kurdish movement through Poland and Czechoslovakia.

Rouleau saw this universally negative reaction, even from potential allies, as likely due to the mistrust and hostility that the Kurdish movement aroused among Iranian leadership, who saw in Ghassemlou's demand for autonomy the specter of secession. Given the longstanding insistence of every Kurdish population in the region—the Kurds of Iran, Turkey, Iraq, and Syria—on the right to self-determination, the Kurdish proposal for an Iranian federal republic resembled too closely a first step toward the demand for full independence.

Only five years earlier, in 1974, Ghassemlou had criticized Iraqi Kurdish leader General Barzani for his unyielding stance in negotiating with Baghdad. In Ghassemlou's analysis, it would have been preferable for the Iraqi Kurds to accept what Baghdad proposed, even though it was minimal. In Iraq negotiations had stalled over Kirkuk, strategically situated in the oil-rich region to which both Baghdad and the Kurds laid claim. Once the Kurds had autonomy and control over the rest of Iraqi Kurdistan, Ghassemlou believed, they could, at some future point, negotiate over Kirkuk. Now, mirroring Ghassemlou's own criticism, Rouleau asked: If Ghassemlou had accepted the limited agreement to cultural autonomy and administration that Tehran proposed, could he not have "given a precious reprieve" to the Kurds of Iran?—and in the process, created conditions in Iran for the Iraqi Kurds to maintain an operational base against Baghdad?[89]

In retrospect, Rouleau's analysis, too, appears flawed, and his own optimism about the possibility for partial gains without foundation, in his naïveté about the true nature of the regime: a centralized, supremacist command that could not tolerate any form of autonomy or shared power. With its new constitution built on sectarian Shi'ite and anti-democratic foundations, the regime could hardly tolerate any dissent or opposition, let alone Kurdish cultural autonomy.

Beyond Islamist fundamentalism and the surface changes in regime that created the mirage of revolution, a deeper and long-entrenched cultural absolutism remained in play: the drive to Persian cultural and socioeconomic hegemony. The insistence on Persian dominance rendered any demands of minorities for their rights a threat to Persian privilege and preeminence as the supreme ethnic group. This was not confined to the Islamist regime; the Shah had regarded Kurdistan in the same way as imperial Persia's own property. Against Iran's vast landscape, Kurdistan forms an enclave essentially unpopulated by Persians except for government officials posted there, mostly linked with intelligence functions. As it had for the Shah's imperial regime before, the prospect of ethnic national groups' secession from the state remains a profound source of uneasiness for the Islamic Republic, which is always ready to label any movement for political rights as "separatist." "On closer scrutiny," notes political scientist Idris Ahmedi, "one finds that the separatist charge is less motivated by a concern over the territorial disintegration of Iran than serving as a pretext for preserving existing relations of power."[90]

In the end, the Kurdish movement found itself isolated; the army "cleansed" Kurdistan. On September 7, Khalkhali entered Mahabad to convince the population to give up their arms, and prepared an offensive against Sardasht, the last bastion of the Kurdish rebellion.[91]

෴

At this critical moment, events on other fronts intervened in the fate of Kurdistan: a shocking development in Tehran came to the rescue of the Kurds.

On November 4, 1979, a group of students in support of the revolution, protesting the Shah's admission to the United States for medical treatment, stormed the U.S. embassy in Tehran. Occupying the "den of spies," they took sixty-six American hostages.[92]

Bazargan's government was impotent. Once again, as he had in October, Bazargan proffered his resignation; and this time, the Ayatollah accepted it. Khomeini gave his blessing to the takeover. His decision was strategic; it was an opportunity to move Bazargan out of his post as prime minister, thereby "breaking the political stalemate in Iran"[93] between the interim government and the IRC, the Islamic Revolutionary Council. The events of the moment both demonstrated that the real power lay with the IRC[94] and underwrote the legitimacy of the unofficial and powerful parallel government led by Khomeini's radical clerical supporters.

The Iran hostage crisis would last 444 days.

The drama of the unfolding hostage crisis—an action which Ghassemlou condemned both morally and strategically[95]—afforded Khomeini the opportunity to distract the population from the reality of "mounting social and economic problems."[96] He recognized the necessity and seized the opening to make overtures to convince the Kurdish population to support the regime. On November 17, in a speech to the Kurds, he said, "Those who accuse you of conspiring against the Republic are slanderers. I humbly extend my hand and beg you to save our unity; any division can only profit the American imperialism. Will you refuse the modest prayer of a man who is living out his last days?"[97]

In this "conciliatory message to the Kurds" he called them "dear brothers,"[98] conceding that "Bazargan's government had not adequately solved the minorities problem, and promised them support."[99] He ordered a halt to military attacks in Kurdistan and ordered the Revolutionary Guards to "pull back from Kurdish towns." And he sent a committee to meet with a Kurdish delegation headed by Ezzedin Husseini with Ghassemlou as spokesman.[100]

Khomeini's appeal "was received with guarded optimism," said historian David Menashri: "while the Kurds were willing to accept it as a 'formal apology' for the past they demanded tangible evidence of a new policy."[101] But once again Kurds and the regime's representatives did not reach an agreement. And once again, tension mounted. "Montazeri appealed to the Kurds 'to turn their eyes to Islam' and to drop Husayni and Qasemlou, who he claimed, were secretly backing 'Communism, the US and Zionism.'"[102]

Three days later, on November 20, in a massive meeting in Mahabad's Chwar Chira (Four Lights) square, where twenty-two years earlier Qazi Mohammed had proclaimed the Democratic Republic of Kurdistan, Ghassemlou publicly addressed Khomeini's message.

In the crisp mountain air and under a clear blue sky, an excited crowd of one hundred thousand people[103] who had come from every corner of Kurdistan awaited Ghassemlou's response.

"Dear sisters and brothers of Kurdistan! Heroic people of Mahabad!" he began. "We have gathered here today once again to salute the leader of the Islamic Revolution of Iran and tell him that we have heard his message and we say to it, *Labbaik*—we accept, we agree. And we are ready to devote every opportunity to bring an end, as soon as possible, to war and fratricide.[104]

"Of course, in this matter," Ghassemlou continued, "as Imam Khomeini has said, there have been malevolent individuals who did not want to create unity and solidarity, and we ask him that these individuals be punished severely."

These words were no mere conciliatory gesture, as Ghassemlou's restatement of the Kurds' position made clear: "The aim of our struggle has been for democracy in Iran and autonomy for Iranian Kurdistan—and now this is our motto as well."

Nevertheless, he offered an olive branch: "We appreciate the willingness of the Imam, and we only wish that his representatives also manifest willingness."[105]

After the meeting that day, peshmerga and Iranian combatants alike, sworn enemies who until a few days before had been killing each other, were fraternizing in the streets of Mahabad, their rifle barrels adorned with flowers.[106] The city was now under PDKI control, with support from the Kurdish Marxist party, Komala.

In the surrounding mountains, Iranian cannons and tanks still stood ready to intervene. This moment, Ghassemlou believed, was his opportunity to turn "this truce into an armistice."[107] But the government must accept the inclusion of the word *autonomy*—*khodmokhtari*—in the constitutional text. Ghassemlou was convinced he could negotiate from a position of strength.

"It's the moment to negotiate," Ghassemlou told Kutschera. "Khomeini is weak, he's like an old dog, surrounded by a pack of young dogs: when one bites and he turns around, another bites. Also winter is coming, and it's not favorable for the army. The army is demoralized.

"We are not in a hurry, but Khomeini's regime is not eternal: if he is ready to negotiate we must take this opportunity—we don't know who will succeed him. With Khomeini we know where we are heading: if he says yes, it's yes. Whereas others, like Dariush Foruhar, they say one thing and do another.

"Khomeini is stubborn? Perhaps. But he proclaimed the jihad against us; and afterward, when the army suffered a big defeat, in Baneh and Mahabad, he sent a delegation to negotiate with us. . . . But negotiations have not yet begun; we are negotiating the conditions to negotiate. . . ."[108]

The Kurds presented a twenty-six-point plan signed by Sheikh Ezzedin, the PDKI, and Komala. The government responded with a plan "for all the self-governed regions" in Iran.

~

While negotiations persisted, during the month of November Tehran strengthened its military presence in Kurdistan. Once again, hostile incidents multiplied.

At the beginning of the following month, December 2–3, the government held the referendum on the new constitution of the Islamic Republic which "proclaimed Shi'ism the state religion and recognized neither the right to autonomy nor that of self-government."[109] The Kurdish parties' boycott of this referendum meant an almost total abstention from voting in Kurdistan.[110]

Though negotiations continued throughout December, on December 15 an "astonished"[111] Ghassemlou received a four-page government directive entitled "The rights and duties of the self-managed departments of the Islamic Republic of Iran," which proposed a "decentralized administration" for Kurdistan instead of a "true autonomy." In line with the new constitution, this document did not recognize the Kurds either as "a people" or as an "ethnicity."[112]

Ghassemlou was appalled. "Our people will not understand if we accept 'self-management' (khudgardani) after they have shed their blood to attain autonomy (khodmokhtari)," he declared. "They would not understand that we should reduce the Kurdish territory to the rank of a department, to an administrative unit that furthermore is not equipped with an executive council deriving from an assembly elected by universal suffrage."[113]

Ghassemlou "was convinced that the conflict in Kurdistan could bring about the downfall of the regime"; at the same time, he feared that "a more conservative power, even more unfavorable to the Kurds, could take over."[114] "It is not ideology, but the relation of forces that will decide the result of the conflict. . . . I don't exclude an acceptable compromise," he declared.[115] "It's the government that imposed war on us last August, and it is we who have imposed the current ceasefire. We are convinced that war will not resolve any problem: there should be neither victor nor vanquished among people who are brothers."[116]

Upcoming events, however, Kutschera noted, would show that Ghassemlou's "analysis of the relation of forces" was mistaken. Neither Tehran nor Qom made further overtures to the Kurds after the four-page directive, and the government "continued to establish institutions [administrative structures] without considering the Kurds."[117]

For the PDKI, the last straw came when the government decided to leave the pasdaran deployed in Kurdistan.[118] The PDKI announced that it would boycott the first presidential election, to be held the next month, on January 25, 1980.[119]

Qom's response could only be regarded as disingenuous. As a move to induce the Kurds to participate in the election, Khomeini declared that he would "consider asking the authorities to add an amendment 'guaranteeing specific rights for Sunni minorities.'" The Kurds were virtually certain to reject this proposal as inadequate: "They wanted recognition as a distinct ethnic, not religious, group because the Kurdish population contained both Sunni and Shi'a Muslims."[120] The issue was not recognition and rights as Sunni or Shi'a, but as Kurds.

This election would bring Abolhassan Banisadr to the presidency. Like Bazargan before him, Banisadr was not without sympathy to minority concerns and had initially favored some degree of compromise;[121] as president, however, he could not support the Kurds' full-scale proposal for self-rule.[122] He would be willing to accept a series of moderate demands the PDKI would submit to him early in his presidency, but would be unable to win over the Revolutionary Council.[123] Even with a president who "came to office believing he had won a sweeping mandate to 'redress' the revolution and to rescue it from 'a fistful of fascist clerics,'"[124] the cycle of violence and repression in Kurdistan would not be resolved.

That cycle, the relationship between the Kurds and the regime, would continue to alternate between attempts at conciliation and fallback into violence. "During each cycle of talks," Menashri has summed up, initial optimism would fade when, "just before the concluding stage, the Kurds realized that the regime had no intention of honoring its promises." The result once more would be "a new wave of violence."[125] For the regime, insistence on the Kurds' total disarmament was the prerequisite for any negotiation, and in their minds a limited, cultural autonomy would be the best concession the Kurds could expect. But for the Kurds, retaining their arms was their only defense, and the sole leverage they had to force the regime to negotiate. For the Kurds, the "fundamental claim" was for full autonomy—and a refusal to lay down their arms, which would mean relinquishing their only leverage. The bottom lines were irreconcilable. Again and again, the impasse would be reached.[126]

❧

Kravetz and American journalist Jonathan Randal, who was covering events in Tabriz, decided to go to Mahabad. "When we arrived," Randal reported, "Ghassemlou was holding a meeting in his office. We sat at the back of the room. He let us know that he had seen us and that we would have dinner together.

"Later, Ghassemlou appeared with a glass of whisky, so we could also have a drink. It was a way of saying that freedom was for all—freedom to drink or not to drink. We spoke about the negotiations, which to him were key. He knew the regime was arming itself. Yet whenever there was someone willing to negotiate, he always accepted [the opening]. 'There is no other solution but negotiation,' he would often say."[127]

❧

The Kurds speak about this period as the "Three-Month War." But in truth, the war would continue for years. Iranian military forces occupied Kurdistan permanently, and the peshmerga of the PDKI would respond by withdrawing further into the mountains.

Notes

1. Marc Kravetz, journalist for the daily *Libération*, interview with the author, Paris, 1991. Except where otherwise cited, further statements from Kravetz are from this interview.
2. Marc Kravetz, "Épilogue," in Hélène Krulich, *Une Européenne au pays des Kurdes* (Paris: Éditions Karthala, 2011), 262.
3. Ibid., 264.
4. Abdul Rahman Ghassemlou, interview with Marc Kravetz, Mahabad, Iranian Kurdistan, 1991.
5. Sadegh Sharafkandi, interview with Bernard Granjon, PDKI general headquarters in Kurdistan, Iran-Iraq border, 1991.
6. Kravetz, "Épilogue," in Krulich, *Une Européenne*, 266, n165.
7. Krulich, *Une Européenne*, 241.
8. Chaliand, a French geopolitical analyst, is a specialist in strategy.

9. Gérard Chaliand, interview with the author, Paris, 1991.

10. Ali Ezzatyar, *The Last Mufti of Iranian Kurdistan: Ethnic and Religious Implications in the Greater Middle East* (New York: Palgrave McMillan, 2016), 147.

11. Kawe Bahrami, personal communication to PDKI member, Salah Piroty, April 4, 2016.

12. *Mujahidin* or *Mujahedin*, Arabic, those engaged in jihad, the struggle for Islam; the group in question here is not to be confused with the Islamic Marxist party MEK, Mujahedin-e Khalq.

13. Present that day was Sayyed Reza Droudger, a well-known former member of the PDKI central committee, who passed away in Europe in 2016.

14. Kawe Bahrami, personal communication to Salah Piroty, April 4, 2016.

15. "Dustbin of Death Awaits Left, Warns Khomeini," *The Guardian*, August 17, 1979, posted at IHRDC, *The* [Baltimore MD] *Sun*, "Iran troops sweep into Kurdish town," August 19, 1979, and IHRDC, *Haunted Memories: The Islamic Republic's Executions of Kurds in 1979* (New Haven, CT: 2011), 3. After the February 1979 Islamic Revolution, at https://iranhrdc.org/haunted-memories-the-islamic-republics-executions-of-kurds-in-1979/ (accessed January 7, 2019).

16. Chris Kutschera, *Le défi kurde ou le rêve fou de l'indépendance* [The Kurdish defiance, or the mad dream of independence] (Paris: Bayard Éditions, 1997), 172; *Kayhan*, August 19, 1979 (Sunday, 28 Mordad, 1358), 3. "These schemers are non-believers in God. These schemer groups in Kurdistan and in other parts are evil groups," Khomeini raged. "They must be eliminated by force. . . . The army must destroy them. We will take hard grips against them. We will defeat them and all those who are in dialogue with them. . . . Prosecutor must punish all opposing political parties and their leaders. Throw away the hesitation, go defeat the evil." Khomeini, August 17, 1979, posted at The Iranian, http://iranian.com/posts/view/post/21162 (accessed January 30, 2014).

17. David Menashri, *Iran: A Decade of War and Revolution* (New York: Holmes & Meier, 1990), 90.

18. *IRHDC, Haunted Memories*, 3. After the February 1979 Islamic Revolution, https://iranhrdc.org/haunted-memories-the-islamic-republics-executions-of-kurds-in-1979 (accessed January 19, 2019).

19. IHRDC, *Haunted Memories*, 3. After the February 1979 Islamic Revolution, https://iranhrdc.org/haunted-memories-the-islamic-republics-executions-of-kurds-in-1979/. The fatwa was published in *Kayhan* and can be found on PDKI's website at http://pdki.org/english/joint-statement-by-pdki-and-komala-on-khomeinis-declaration-of-jihad-against-the-kurdish-people/ (accessed December 10, 2013). Valiollah Fallahi was chief of the general staff of the armed forces as well as general commander of ground forces; Mustafa Chamran, then deputy prime minister, was later minister of defense.

20. Mustafa Chamran was instrumental in breaking the rebellion in Kurdistan. Nader Entessar, *Kurdish Politics in the Middle East* (London: Lexington Books, 2010), 40. The measure of Chamran's devotion to the ideology of the Islamic Republic and his disengagement from its human consequences can be taken in an incident recounted by Iranian-American journalist Azadeh Moaveni in her book *Lipstick Jihad*. "My uncle," she wrote, "had been roommates at Berkley with Mustafa Chamran, who became one of the leaders in the uprising. They had been friendly in those college days, and when at the dawn of the revolution

my uncle was taken to prison, he contacted his old roommate Chamran. No reply. 'Your type must go,' came a message, through a friend." Azadeh Moaveni, *Lipstick Jihad* (New York: Public Affairs, 2005), 6.

21. IHRDC, *Haunted Memories*, 3. After the February 1979 Islamic Revolution, https://iranhrdc.org/haunted-memories-the-islamic-republics-executions-of-kurds-in-1979 (accessed January 19, 2019).

22. *L'Express*, Paris, October 10, 1979.

23. Akhbar Rooz, http://www.akhbar-rooz.com/article.jsp?essayId=15065 (accessed October 2, 2016); translation Salah Piroty. The post, in Farsi, includes Ghassemlou's interview with *Kayhan* following the Iranian revolution.

24. IHRDC, *Haunted Memories*, 9, n51, citing *Kayhan*, May 7, 1983, https://iranhrdc.org/haunted-memories-the-islamic-republics-executions-of-kurds-in-1979/ (accessed January 19, 2019). Also reported by Associated Press in (Bowling Green, KY) *Daily News*, "Khomeini vows all-out war on rebellious Kurds," August 20, 1979 (accessed January 17, 2014). See also Menashri, *Iran: A Decade of War and Revolution*, 90, citing *International Herald Tribune* (Paris) and *Daily Telegraph* (London), August 1979. Months later, as reported by the media, Mir Hossein Mousavi, who would serve as prime minister October 1981–August 1989, admitted that the campaign had been based on false reports. IHRDC, *Haunted Memories*, 3. After the February 1979 Islamic Revolution, n51 (citing *Kayhan*, May 7. 1983); Menashri, *Iran: A Decade of War and Revolution*, 90, n144, citing *The Guardian*, September 10, 1979, and *Daily Report: Middle East and Africa* (Washington), March 13, 1980.

25. The government was concerned that the Kurds' rebellion and their demand for some form of autonomy would encourage other minorities to do the same. In August, Khomeini sent envoys to Khuzestan and Tabriz to address the demands of the Arab and Azeri minorities respectively. *Ettela'at*, May 15 and August 4, 1979, cited in IHRDC, *Haunted Memories*, 3. After the February 1979 Islamic Revolution, n45, https://iranhrdc.org/haunted-memories-the-islamic-republics-executions-of-kurds-in-1979 (accessed January 19, 2019).

26. How massive the mobilization was against the Kurds was underlined by journalist Dilip Hiro, who pointed out that the capture of the Kurdish centers was achieved "only by deploying a large majority of its 110,000 army troops in Kurdistan. . . . Even then, the rural areas remained under the control of the coalition of Kurdish autonomists, now composed of the KDP, the Fedai, and the Komala." Dilip Hiro, *Iran under the Ayatollahs* (London: Routledge & Kegan Paul, 1985), 130. Hardly a wonder, then, that the army was demoralized.

27. *L'Express*, Paris, October 10, 1979.

28. Menashri, *Iran: A Decade of War and Revolution*, 90.

29. Ibid., 90.

30. See "Martyr Chamran's Interview after the Liberation of Paveh," conducted by Iranian state television, https://www.youtube.com/watch?v=UIj4g1PsqaM (accessed July 14, 2017).

    The ways in which clerics, too, used dissemination of misinformation to galvanize Iranian public opinion against the Kurds can be seen in another video made to glorify the pasdaran against the Kurds. Throughout, Kurds are labeled "antirevolutionary," and Ghassemlou can be seen giving out machine guns to the newly trained peshmerga: "The Commanders—Martyr Mahmoud Kawah," https://www.youtube.com/watch?v=2grYkX-JS8So (accessed July 14, 2017).

31. IHRDC, *Haunted Memories*, 3. After the February 1979 Islamic Revolution, https://iranhrdc.org/haunted-memories-the-islamic-republics-executions-of-kurds-in-1979/ (accessed January 19, 2019)

It is interesting to see how Chamran himself viewed the actions of his forces in Paveh. In a series of interviews on Iranian television, Chamran described his troops' situation after one of their helicopters and a Phantom jet were shot down in the city.

"We were in the lap of these tragedies when the famous invasion began. I gave instructions on how to act in confronting the enemy. This is our last night, I said to my friends, and we, sacrificing ourselves, must open a bloody page in history. I asked them to fight to the end. With the barrage going on from both sides—it did not stop for a second—we had to deal with the situation until morning. We were running out of ammunition and under a tight siege.

"Suddenly, the pasdaran were shouting, "God is great!" Imam Khomeini had issued a pronouncement, they said, and the enemy ran away. . . .

"In the space of another few days, we launched attacks on many places, like the airport, previously taken by the enemy." "Shaheed Dr. Chamran, Part 5: interviews with Shaheed Chamran," uploaded June 24, 2008, https://www.youtube.com/watch?v=sHM-16TRefNo (accessed October 2, 2016).

32. *Ettela'at*, August 21, 1979, cited in IHRDC, *Haunted Memories*, 3. After the February 1979 Islamic Revolution, 3.2 Paveh.

33. Menashri, *Iran: A Decade of War and Revolution*, 90.

34. In 1980 Khomeini ordered the Revolutionary Guards to create a people's militia: the Basij, Sazmane Basij-e Mostaz'afin, literally "Organization for Mobilization of the Oppressed." It was originally created to recruit volunteers to fight the Iran-Iraq war; Global Security, http://www.globalsecurity.org/intell/world/iran/basij.htm. Every Iranian male age sixteen or older had to serve. The group, "which was formed as a civil defence force, but in practice became a grass-roots intelligence organisation, was largely made up of young boys aged between ten and sixteen and, during the war, unemployed old men, some in their eighties." Baqer Moin, *Khomeini: Life of the Ayatollah* (New York: Thomas Dunne Books, 2000), 249. As a paramilitary fundamentalist force subordinated to the IRGC, the Basij has since been used to patrol the streets as moral police and also to crush any protests against the regime.

35. Kawe Bahrami, *Tawgey Heqiqet* [The waterfall of truth] [in Kurdish] (Sulaimaniya, Iraq: n.p., spring 2005). 175.

36. Ibid., 192.

37. Marc Kravetz, *Irano Nox* (Paris: Éditions Grasset), 1982.

38. Ibid., 33.

39. Cited in IHRDC, *Haunted Memories*, 3. After the February 1979 Islamic Revolution, 3. 1 Ayatollah Sadegh Khalkhali.

40. Moin, *Khomeini*, 208–09.

41. See Menashri, *Iran: A Decade of War and Revolution*, 90. Khomeini's fatwa, published Saturday, August 18, in *Kayhan*, a national daily newspaper, included a series of statements from the Ayatollah: "Requests have been made on behalf of different groups in the armed forces and the *Pasdaran* and honorable people," Khomeini said, "for me to order [the forces] to go towards Paveh and end the clashes. I thank them and warn the government,

the armed forces and the Police that, if within 24 hours, a move towards Paveh is not made with canons [sic], tanks, and equipped forces, I consider all responsible.

"As the head of the armed forces," Khomeini continued, "I order the head of the army headquarters to dispatch to the region immediately, fully equipped, and I order all the bases of the military and police to not waste time and not wait for another order and dispatch to Paveh with full equipment. I order the government to immediately provide for the dispatching of the *Pasdaran*. Until further notice, I consider the armed forces responsible for this violent killing, and if they disobey my order, I will deal with them in a revolutionary manner. Repeated messages from the region say that the government and the armed forces are not taking any actions so [I announce] that if a positive action does not take place within the next 24 hours, I will hold the heads of the military and police responsible." *Kayhan*, August 18, 1979, cited in IHRDC, *Haunted Memories*, 3. After the February 1979 Islamic Revolution, 3, https://iranhrdc.org/haunted-memories-the-islamic-republics-executions-of-kurds-in-1979 (accessed January 19, 2019).

42. *Le Monde*, August 22, 1979.

43. Ayatollah Khomeini, in a talk in Qom, July 23, 1979, posted at Iran Heritage, http://www.iran-heritage.org/interestgroups/government-article2.htm (accessed January 28, 2014). See also The Iranian, http://iranian.com/posts/view/post/21162 (accessed January 28, 2014). Details from the talk can be accessed at YouTube: "If from the beginning of defeating the [Shah's] corrupt regime we had acted in a revolutionary manner—had broken all of the pens, had closed all the corrupt magazines and press and brought their corrupt directors to justice, had banned corrupt parties and punished their leaders, had set up gallows for execution and had reaped [killed] the corruptors—then these problems would not have happened. I am asking the Most High God and the beloved nation for forgiveness that we were not a revolutionary people. If we had been, we wouldn't have let these things happen . . . and I repent for the mistake I made. . . ." http://www.youtube.com/watch?v=b-ZVvs61F0X8; translation Salah Piroty (accessed Jan 24, 2014).

44. IHRDC, *Haunted Memories*, 3. After the February 1979 Islamic Revolution, citing n55, https://iranhrdc.org/haunted-memories-the-islamic-republics-executions-of-kurds-in-1979 (accessed January 19, 2019).

"Iran's Leaders Move in to Crush Opposition Press and Parties," *The Guardian*, Aug. 21, 1979, reporting that authorities shut down opposition newspapers and ordered opposition parties to turn in weapons seized during February (accessed April 20, 2017).

45. Ibid., 13; see also Kutschera, *Le défi kurde*, 172.

46. *Ettela'at*, August 20 and 23, 1979, citing n72 and n73 in IHRDC, *Haunted Memories*, 1. Introduction and 3. After the February 1979 Islamic Revolution. https://iranhrdc.org/haunted-memories-the-islamic-republics-executions-of-kurds-in-1979 (accessed January 19, 2019).

47. Ayatollah Khomeini, August 20, 1979, posted on The Iranian, http://iranian.com/posts/view/post/21162 (accessed January 30, 2014). See also Jamaran.ir, citing Khomeini, "The Illegality of the Kurdistan Democratic Party," August 20, 1979, http://www.jamaran.ir/fa/1842/with Imam/scriptures of Imam Khomeini/volume 9/, translation Salah Piroty; and Menashri, *Iran: A Decade of War and Revolution*, 90.

48. Jamaran.ir, "The Illegality of the Kurdistan Democratic Party."

49. Menashri, *Iran: A Decade of War and Revolution*, 139, notes that Ezzedin headed the council, with Ghassemlou acting as its spokesperson.

50. IHRDC, *Haunted Memories*, 3. After the February 1979 Islamic Revolution, citing n74 in https://iranhrdc.org/haunted-memories-the-islamic-republics-executions-of-kurds-in-1979 (accessed January 19, 2019).

51. IHRDC, *Haunted Memories*, 3. After the February 1979 Islamic Revolution, 3.1 Ayatollah Sadegh Khalkhali (accessed January 19, 2019).

52. Ibid.

53. Ibid.

54. *El País*, Madrid, August 26, 1979.

55. *L'Express*, Paris, August 8, 1979.

56. Kutschera, *Le défi kurde*, 173.

57. *L'Express*, Paris, August 9, 1979.

58. Entessar, "The Kurds in Post-Revolutionary Iran and Iraq," *Third World Review* Vol. 6, No.4 (October 1984), 927. Entessar summed up: "The plan's six points included the immediate removal of Sheikh Sadeq Khalkhali from the Kurdish areas (Khalkhali was responsible for condemning several hundred Kurdish nationalists to death), an end to the execution of Kurdish activists, the withdrawal of non-Kurdish *pasdaran* from Kurdistan and their replacement with Kurdish guards, an immediate ceasefire, an end to the bombardment of Kurdish strongholds, and convening of a comprehensive conference to grant the Kurds autonomy within the framework of the Iranian state." Ibid., 927.

59. Kutschera, *Le défi kurde*, 173.

60. Ibid.

61. Ibid.

62. Entessar, "The Kurds in Post-Revolutionary Iran and Iraq," 927.

63. Ibid.

64. As reported in *The Guardian*, August 29, 1979, posted at IHRDC, https://iranhrdc.org/1979-newspapers-about-iranian-kurdistan/ (accessed January 15, 2019).

65. *Le Monde*, August 30, 1979.

66. "Massacre in Gharna," interview with Omar Karimi, Radio Zamaneh (based in the Netherlands), posted September 16, 2010, http://zamaaneh.com/humanrights/2010/09/post_703.html. Link and translation Salah Piroty (accessed January 8, 2012).

67. "Dustbin of Death Awaits Left, Warns Khomeini," *The Guardian*, August 17, 1979, and IHRDC, *Haunted Memories*, 3. After the February 1979 Islamic Revolution, https://iranhrdc.org/haunted-memories-the-islamic-republics-executions-of-kurds-in-1979/ (accessed January 14, 2019).

68. "Massacre in Gharna," interview with Omar Karimi, Radio Zamaneh.

69. "The cities and towns of Kurdistan lived under a constant barrage of bombs. Artillery and bulletproof vehicles repressed the Kurdish movement. Bombers flew over Kurdistan nonstop. The pasdaran, the representatives of the Islamic committees, and the armed hezbollahis harassed the population. There was death and looting. The population had discovered the real face of the Islamic Republic after the bloody events in Sanandaj and Naghadeh, and refused to give up the weapons they had acquired during the fight against the Shah. The resentment against the Kurdish people was such that there was no pity in the

repression taking place. After the events in Naghadeh, in West Azerbaijan, former members of the SAVAK, who had become the advisors of Mullah Hassani and Colonel Sayyad [Shirazi], were preparing the extermination of the Kurdish population in that region." *Actualités du Kurdistan*, no. 34 (Paris: PDKI publication), Septembre–October 1988.

70. Kravetz, " Épilogue," in Krulich, *Une Européenne au pays des Kurdes*, 266.

71. Kutschera, *Le défi kurde*, 174.

72. The Iranian army had essentially forced the Kurds to scatter their forces by simultaneously attacking Bokan, Piranshar, and Mahabad.

73. Estimates differ; Kutschera's sources say that the battle went on for eight hours. Kutschera, *Le défi kurde*, 175.

74. Marc Kravetz, interview with the author, Paris, 1991. There is considerable variation in the estimates of the population of Mahabad; while the Iranian Encyclopedia put the 1979 population at over 196,000, the entry doesn't specify whether the number is for the central city of Mahabad alone or it includes suburbs as well. Estimates by journalists and other observers of the urban population itself have varied from 40,000 to 80,000. With ongoing unrest, turmoil, and outright warfare in the countryside, it is possible that the populations of the rural areas and the city actually underwent continual and significant shifts. See Hamid Gohary, *The Kurdistan Republic* (Erbil: Shahab Publications, April 2011).

75. Kutschera, *Le défi kurde*, 268.

76. Sadegh Sharafkandi, interview with Bernard Granjon, PDKI general headquarters in Kurdistan, Iran-Iraq border, 1991.

77. Ibid.

78. *Le Monde*, October 7–9, 1979.

79. Kutschera, *Le défi kurde*, 181.

80. Abdullah Hassanzadeh, *Niw Sede Xebat* [Half a century of struggle: A retrospect of struggle and activity of the Democratic Party of Iranian Kurdistan] [in Kurdish], Vol. 1, [Gawrade: Press Commission of the Kurdistan Democratic Party of Iran, August 1995], 178; translation Salah Piroty.

81. Ibid.

82. Ibid., 182.

83. Menashri, *Iran: A Decade of War and Revolution*, 139. Foruhar's committee, headed by Foruhar together with Hashem Sabbaghyan and Yadollah Sahabi, would continue its efforts even after the fall of Bazargan's interim government; Ibid.

84. Kutschera, *Le défi kurde*, 177, quoting Ghassemlou's interview with *Libération*, September 9, 1979.

85. Ibid., 177. About the decision to take to the hills and remove the fighting from the cities and populated areas, in a February 1981 interview with Fred Halliday Ghassemlou would reiterate, "We voluntarily withdrew from the larger towns to avoid causing destruction to the economic life of the people." "KDP's Qassemlu: 'The Clergy Have Confiscated the Revolution.'" *Middle East Reports*, No. 98, *Iran Two Years After* (July/August 1981), 18.

86. Éric Rouleau, "L'armée a occupé sans coup férir une des dernières villes contrôlées par les Kurdes. Les faux calculs des rebelles" [With no opposition, the army has occupied one

of the last cities controlled by the Kurds. The miscalculations of the rebels], *Le Monde*, September 5, 1979.

87. The Feda'iyan were able to go underground in the nick of time; the Mujahedin evacuated their general headquarters in Tehran and kept silent. Tudeh continued their activities in a state of semi-legality, supporting what they deemed "legitimate demands" but rejecting the PDKI's actions. Rouleau, "L'armée a occupé sans coup férir."

88. Ibid.

89. Ibid.

90. Idris Ahmedi, "Iran, Diversity, Democracy and Federalism," presentation at the Middle East Institute, Washington DC, March 18, 2010. Idris Ahmedi, PhD, is currently a lecturer in political science at Karlstad University, in Sweden.

91. "After government forces entered Mahabad on September 3 following the three-week siege, the residents sent a telegram to Khomeini begging that Mahabad be spared summary trials and executions. However, on September 6, it was reported that Khalkhali had ordered the execution of 80 Kurds and that he was planning to travel to Mahabad despite Tehran's orders to return to the capital." Liz Thurgood, "Iranian forces pursue retreating Kurds," *The Guardian*, September 6, 1979. The *Guardian* went on to report Khalkhali's arrival in Mahabad on Friday, September 7. Thurgood, "Kurds may wage mountain warfare," *The Guardian*, September 8, 1979.

92. Of the sixty-six original captives, thirteen were released November 19–20, 1979, and one was released July 11, 1980. The remaining fifty-two endured nearly fifteen months until their release January 20, 1981, in the beginning days of Ronald Reagan's presidency. For more on the hostage crisis see Mark Bowden, *Guests of the Ayatollah: The First Battle in America's War with Militant Islam* (New York: Grove Press, 2006).

93. Robin Wright, *In the Name of God: The Khomeini Decade* (New York: Simon and Schuster, 1989), 80.

94. Moin, *Khomeini*, 215.

95. Ghassemlou, interview with Fred Halliday: "All we have done by taking the hostages is to lose a lot of friends: world opinion has been mobilized against us. . . . The KDP condemned the taking of the hostages from the start: what we wanted to see was a real uprooting of the US influence in our country." "KDP's Qassemlu: 'The Clergy Have Confiscated the Revolution' *MERIP Reports* (No. 98), 11:6 (July-August 1981). 17.

96. In the view of Khomeini's grandson and advisor, Sayed Khossein, the embassy seizure also "enabled us to open the way for a strategic alliance between the Islamic movement and secular and leftist formations as well as a tactical alliance with the Soviet Union." James Phillips, "Iran, the U.S., and the Hostages: After 300 Days," The Heritage Foundation, August 29, 1980, http://www.heritage.org/research/reports/1980/08/iran-the-us-and-the-hostages-after-300-days.

97. Kutschera, *Le défi kurde*, 184

98. Menashri, *Iran: A Decade of War and Revolution*, 139.

99. Ibid.

100. Ibid.

101. Ibid., 140.

102. Ibid.

103. Kutschera, *Le défi kurde*, 184.

104. *Ettela'at*, November 20, 1979 (accessed January 21, 2014); translation Salah Piroty.

105. Ibid.

106. Kutschera, *Le défi kurde*, 185. "I was personally present when Dr. Ghassemlou delivered his speech," one PDKI member reported. "After his speech there were some soldiers in the crowd who were happy with the situation, and they brought some flowers to show their goodwill." PDKI member Salah Piroty, personal communication, January 23, 2014.

107. Kutschera, *Le défi kurde*, 185.

108. Ibid.

109. Kutschera, *Le défi kurde*, 188.

110. Ibid.

111. Ibid., citing an article by Rouleau, "La colère des minorités nationales" [The anger of national minorities], *Le Monde*, December 2, 1979. Rouleau was in Mahabad when Ghassemlou received the government directive. Describing Ghassemlou's response, he wrote: "Sitting cross-legged, A. R. Ghassemlou could not believe his eyes as he read the four-page text that he'd just received from Tehran." Ibid., 185.

112. Ibid., 188, 190.

113. Ibid., 190–91, citing Rouleau, "Les négociations sur le Kurdistan iranien" [Negotiations over Iranian Kurdistan], *Le Monde*, December 18, 1979. See also Menashri, *Iran*, 140.

114. Kutschera, *Le défi kurde*, 191.

115. Ibid.

116. Ibid.

117. Ibid.

118. Ibid.

119. As it would, essentially. At the first parliamentary elections in the Islamic republic, held March 14, 1980, participation would be voter participation would be lowest in Kurdistan, at 22.49 percent Ferdinand Hennerbichler, "Assassination of Abdul Rahman Ghassemlou (1930–1989): New Asessment," in *Wiener Jahrbuch für Kurdische Studien 2013, Schwerpunkt: Transnationalität und kurdische Diaspora in Österreich, Jahrgang 1/2013* (Vienna: Österreichische Gesellschaft zur Förderung der Kurdologie / Europäisches Zentrum für kurdische Studien, 2013), 295. Accessed at http://www.kurdologie.at/jahrbuch.html.

120. Entessar, *Kurdish Politics*, 44.

121. Menashri, *Iran*, 140, 200.

122. Ibid., 200.

123. Ibid., 140.

124. Shaul Bakhash, *The Reign of the Ayatollahs: Iran and the Islamic Revolution* (New York: Basic Books, Inc., 1984), 97, citing *Le Monde*, January 20, January 27, January 28, and February 12, 1980; *Kayhan*, February 5, 1989; and *Ettela'at*, February 16, 1980.

125. Menashri, *Iran*, 138–39.

126. Ibid., 139–40.

127. Jonathan Randal, interview with the author, Paris, 1991.

PART III

ORPHANS OF THE UNIVERSE

· 1 ·

KURDISTAN AT WAR

&

The resistance against the Islamic
Republic begins with cutting your beard.
—Abdul Rahman Ghassemlou

In Iranian Kurdistan, thousands had died during the last months of 1979.[1] The war had thrown the entire country into mourning. Yet the Iranian military forces continued their offensive. For most of the next decade, the struggle of the Kurds would unfold within the larger scenario of the Iran-Iraq war. Ghassemlou and his men left Mahabad and headed toward the refuge of the mountains. The PDKI began its long march.

By 1981, its leaders were settling into what came to be known as "the Valley of the Democrats," Dôli Demokrât, in the hinterlands of the Iran-Iraq border, along the banks of a small, nameless river encircled by snow-capped peaks. The PDKI was soon joined by other opposition groups who also set up their headquarters in the hidden valley.[2]

"At the beginning, at the *daftar* [the PDKI general headquarters]," one witness remembered, "we had nothing to eat, nothing to live on. It was a bad situation. But the people slowly adapted and came to help the party to continue the struggle. They gave whatever they had. The party was the people and the people were the party; their sons and daughters were part of the party."[3]

In March 1980, Hélène Krulich arrived at the daftar near Mahabad, in Gök Tapa; "a small village," she remembers it, "with square concrete houses."[4] In her memoirs, she describes Ghassemlou's daily life. He would go to sleep around midnight and wake up at 7:00 a.m. During the day he would meet with his headquarters staff and organize their work, and meet with the party's press and broadcasting team. He often traveled around the area for specific missions that could last a couple of days or longer.[5]

He appeared, Hélène says, to be "happy, content and full of determination, but the responsibility that weighed on his shoulders was immense. It seemed too much for one person; his collaborators made no decision without consulting him, people came to ask him to resolve their problems, his lunch or dinner time was continually interrupted by urgent work, by comings and goings. . . . He had become a solitary leader, accountable for every decision."[6]

"It was a huge task," recalls Hélène, who traveled back and forth to Kurdistan and spent extended time there. "I joined him several times in the mountains, spent months and was active there, but was always sent back to work for them, the party, in Europe."[7] In Kurdistan, the transformations she witnessed were impressive. "The party built schools everywhere and taught people to read and write. They built hospitals, and in 1981, they even had their own prisons in the mountains,"[8] for captured Iranian prisoners of war and for Kurds adjudged guilty of criminal actions. "Jailors were instructed to respect the prisoners, and classes to eliminate illiteracy for both jailors and prisoners were under preparation."[9]

When Hélène returned to Paris in 1980, she "was taken via safe routes, free of military control." It was, she writes, "a journey of desolation."[10] It had taken the Islamic revolution just one year to destroy Kurdistan with bombings, even raining down napalm[11] in certain areas, and shatter its economy. All she saw were ruined factories, broken-down electric power stations, and abandoned farms.

Despite the destruction, between 1979 and 1983, the structures put in place by the PDKI continued to ensure mandatory education in Kurdish for both boys and girls. Radio and press went on operating in Kurdish as well, and the training prison guards had received to treat inmates with respect remained in force.

But along with the physical devastation, an embargo imposed by the regime on the liberated territories in Kurdistan was impacting the population. So at the same time that he was learning the art of war, Ghassemlou began to put in place an economy and a social and political order parallel to that of the state.[12]

One witness to this development in Kurdistan was Hasan Ayoubzadeh, who had served as an official in the legal system during the Pahlavi regime before joining Ghassemlou's reorganization efforts. "I was living in Bokan," he said; "I did not know Ghassemlou. But I had read his book *Kurdistan and the Kurds*.[13]

"About six months after the revolution—this was following Khomeini's referendum to establish an Islamic regime—I received a letter from Ghassemlou inviting me to visit him in Parastan, a village in the Gewirkan District near the Zimziran Mountains.

"[When I arrived,] there were many people there: young, old, even teenagers—listening to Ghassemlou make a presentation. . . . He spoke about emergent situations in Iran, especially in Kurdistan, and the relationship of the Kurdish people vis-à-vis the new regime and the future of Kurdistan.

"After the fall of the Shah everything was out of control in the country. It was a bad situation. There were no police, no structure; everybody was armed. With no administrative system in place, he invited me to help his party write regulations to govern in the free areas of Kurdistan, areas not under control by the new regime. 'We need experienced people to serve our people,' Dr. Ghassemlou said to me. 'We need a law to govern Kurdish society.'

"He asked me to find two or three lawyers as collaborators to prepare internal policies and regulations. He told me I could stay some days there; I accepted his request. He was pleased with the document we worked out and invited us to stay on with him."

Over the course of the next several years, Ayoubzadeh conducted classes for the peshmerga and for those with some education, and wrote political articles in both Kurdish and Persian for the party's journal and radio. "Ghassemlou too gave courses to the educated members of the PDKI regarding democracy and the future of which he had written," he reported, "with the idea that these cadres were then to teach others."[14]

Not only Kurds, but Iranians who fled the regime also found refuge in Kurdistan. They were hosted at the PDKI daftar sometimes for months as they waited for their safe passage across the border to be ready.[15]

☙

One thing the PDKI lacked from the beginning was funds. "The PDKI basically had no money," explained one party member, who worked at Mili Iran, the Iranian National Bank in Mahabad.

By the time the revolution had engulfed Iran and Iranian Kurdistan, the Iranian National Bank had holdings of eleven million dollars. This attractive cache was up for grabs, and any of the revolutionary groups active at that time could come for it.

Since the PDKI had emerged as the major political force in the region, Ghassemlou was alerted about the money. In the summer of 1980, on a Thursday after the bank closed for the day, the vault was emptied. The confiscated funds were taken to the party's political bureau in the mountains, in the Valley of the Democrats. There it awaited Ghassemlou's return from overseeing armed engagements going on in the area between Baneh and Sardasht.

Six or seven months previously, one of Ghassemlou's colleagues remembers him sharing, Tudeh had published in their journal *Mardoum* that the PDKI had received $9 million from NATO. This was regarded as part of a smear campaign against Ghassemlou and the party. In fact, however, party colleagues recalled, the party at that time had only about ninety thousand *toman* [equivalent to about $10,000] in its coffers.

Now the party had more than the alleged $9 million!

Hélène Krulich had proposed that the PDKI open a bureau in Paris "staffed by exiled, well-educated Kurds to look after the external affairs of the party." Her reasoning was clear: "because in 1980 Kurdistan was not well-known to the outside world, it was important to publish a bulletin to rectify this . . . to share news of the positive and negative developments in Kurdistan and Iran."[16] Hélène took charge of the PR and finances, including placing PDKI funds in banks outside Iran.

ॐ

The open hospitality extended by the daftar, and Ghassemlou's acute and continuous appraisal of the shifting political developments in Tehran and Baghdad, were noted by visitors, as Ayoubzadeh's eyewitness account of events in May 1981 attests.[17]

On May 17, 1981, the PDKI prison in Dollatu,[18] near the Iraqi Kurdish border, was bombarded with napalm by Iraqi aircraft. The presumed intent of the bombing was to thwart negotiations the PDKI was then holding with the Iranian government. The Iraqis claimed the bombardment had been by mistake; their target, they maintained, had been a congress of the Iraqi Socialist Party, which had headquarters on the Iraqi border close to the PDKI prison.[19]

Some days later, Iranian president Abolhassan Banisadr sent two representatives to see what had happened. The counterclaim of the Islamic regime was that the PDKI, and Ghassemlou, had agreed to the bombardment.

Banisadr's emissaries filmed and took photos of the site, then asked to see the wounded and spent four or five hours alone with them.

Their review done, they went to Ghassemlou.

Ghassemlou greeted them as they entered: "I am surprised you are still alive," he told them, "because according to Islamic propaganda, all Kurds are cannibals." Everyone laughed.

There followed an exchange between Ghassemlou and the Iranian envoys about Iran and Kurdistan. Toward the end of the conversation, Ghassemlou expressed concern for President Banisadr's political situation: "I'm not sure," he told them as they were leaving, "that you can get back to your president in time. I believe he will not be president for much longer."

Everyone there was surprised. Not everyone, it seemed, was aware of the tension developing between Banisadr and Khomeini over human-rights abuses and many other issues.[20]

"When you arrive at Sardasht," Ghassemlou went on, "if you hear on the radio that Banisadr is alive and in office, then all is fine. If not, you can come back and I can help you go wherever you wish.

"If you arrive in Tehran alive, I will be glad. But if you have problems, you can always come back and I can help."[21]

Ghassemlou's observation was prescient. In fact, Banisadr's days in office were numbered: the very next month, on June 21, he would be impeached. He managed to go into hiding a few days before his impeachment and then, in disguise as women, he and Massoud Rajavi fled to Paris.

☙

Between 1980 and 1983, Hélène recalls, the PDKI had begun laying groundwork for developments the region had never seen before: compulsory school attendance for all children—girls as well as boys—to be conducted not in Persian, but in Kurdish; manuals for the first two years of primary education, to be implemented, in Kurdish; and radio and press communication now being conducted in Kurdish.[22]

In 1982 Hélène returned, once again, to Kurdistan as the PDKI began a new retreat: "I saw with my own eyes," she said, "how they had abandoned the valley and moved to another." Little by little, the peshmerga, cadres, and civilians who worked for and had joined the PDKI began to settle in the Kurdish territory on the Iraqi side of the border, where they have remained since 1984.[23]

When the retreat began, Ghassemlou informed his French friends that he needed doctors and medical equipment. In Paris, his friend Kendal Nezan, president of the Kurdish Institute, mobilized humanitarian aid, and three groups of doctors got ready to travel into Kurdistan: Aide Médicale Internationale (AMI), Médecins du Monde (MdM), and Médecins Sans Frontières (MSF). During the years of war, these Western doctors were direct witnesses to the harsh realities facing the Kurdish people.

Hélène witnessed the work of these medical NGOs as they vaccinated children, treated illness, performed surgeries on civilians and wounded military alike, broadcast educational programs on hygiene and child-rearing. She was especially impressed with the work of Dr. Frederic Tissot, a French physician with AMI, who had "turned a long-abandoned police headquarters in ruins into a well-run hospital."[24]

The first group of medical volunteers came through Turkey in January of 1981. After fifteen days of trekking through northern Iran, they arrived at the Valley of the Democrats, south of Piranshar. Dr. Fréderic Tissot was in charge; soon afterward, Dr. Florence Veber, also from AMI, arrived. For months, they stayed to help to create the first hospital in Oshnavieh. But the doctors and nurses encountered countless problems. The first who attempted to enter Iranian Kurdistan via Turkey were unsuccessful; they were detained by the Turks and incarcerated for eight months. So because their only access at that time was through Turkey, the MSF stopped sending volunteers. Given the war with Tehran, medical staff would need to reroute their entry through Baghdad.

Michel Bonnot, a third AMI doctor, remembered traveling clandestinely carrying medicines. He had crossed the border with the help of a guide who eluded the Turkish patrols. For fifteen days they had traveled on foot toward the daftar. Theirs was not an easy task. The Turkish police detained one MSF team. One of the women doctors was found with anti-Turkish political propaganda, arrested, and handed over to civil jurisdiction. This constituted a serious situation: because Turkey had been under a military regime since 1981, she was sent to face a military tribunal.

Another AMI doctor was also detained en route back to Paris through Turkey. But the organization sent two representatives to Turkey who met with the civil judge. They were able to convince him to declare that he was competent to judge the case, rather than remanding the doctor to the military. The doctor was freed in two weeks. But this group had no way of informing

Florence Veber and Frédéric Tissot, who were returning to Europe from Kurdistan through Turkey during those days.[25]

When Ghassemlou became aware of this fragile situation, he asked for permission to allow the French doctors to leave via Baghdad. This confidential route had been reserved for his personal movements; with this directive, he revealed his logistical relations with the Iraqi regime.

"The Turks knew that the French doctors were crossing their territory, so we decided to recruit doctors from Germany," recounted Bonnot. "The Germans traveled in the guise of tourists going fishing. Inside the fishing rods they carried notes for the PDKI peshmerga and were able to pass as trout fishermen."

Ghassemlou welcomed the first doctors who arrived and asked if they were from the MdM and the MSF. They replied that they were from AMI.

"How wonderful! With this free-flowing system, I am sure that I'll always have French doctors," he answered laughing.

"This was the type of relationship we had with him and with the Kurds," said Florence Veber, remembering those times. "He always spoke jokingly and with a touch of provocation."[26]

Ghassemlou received Tissot with warmth. The doctor found Ghassemlou to be "very sure of himself, of his battle, the political battle, and the support of the Kurdish people."[27]

If it is true that the winds of war were blowing, these times were certainly better than those to come. Between 1981 and 1982, the Kurds controlled a significant portion of Iranian Kurdistan. And the military and political situations were propitious to them. They had set up an administration—and the doctors perceived an enthusiasm in the PDKI that the Kurds all recognized in themselves.

"There was a marvelous atmosphere in the daftar," Tissot reported. "We ate well. Everything was clean. They were all happy. Rahman surprised us with his knowledge of French literature, his reflections on Kurdish, Persian, and Turkish politics, and also his thoughts on French politics."[28]

Other visitors, like journalist Chris Kutschera, recounted similar impressions. The daftar was composed of several stone huts bordering a river. Among them, a little house of two rooms was assigned to Ghassemlou, who proudly announced, "It's the first time that I have ever owned a house!"[29] Near the daftar were two camps where the peshmerga lived, charged with the protection of the general headquarters. All told there were about three hundred people in residence. What was most difficult, Ghassemlou said, was "making bread for all those people."[30]

During a trip to the city of Baneh, Tissot realized that Ghassemlou "seemed to be holding the destiny of the Kurdish people within his being. Each time we stopped at the daftar the peshmerga received him as the person who represented the hopes of the Kurdish people. He was a man of a keen intelligence with a great capacity for concentration. Everything rested upon him and people felt, deep down, that only he could resolve things. He recognized this fact, but he was not capable of setting up an organization that could continue without him. Even though he admitted it needed to be done, Ghassemlou said there were not enough cadres."

This situation worked against the internal unity of the party, within which there were serious differences. These differences centered on negotiations with the central power and relations with the Komala leftists and their military strategy.

"They reproached me, saying that they felt that democracy came before anything else for me," Ghassemlou told journalist Christian Dubois of the French weekly *L'Express* in 1983.[31] "My friends thought this was an excuse for not taking action, especially in times of war, but I believe it was just the opposite."

Ghassemlou's absolute commitment to democracy was noted by all political actors—Kurdish, Iranian, and European alike—who were close to him. Iranian Kurdish activist Nouri Dehkordi[32] remembered that Ghassemlou had taught party activists many things. "But the most valuable," he said, "was internal party democracy, and fighting—along with long-term political realism."[33] Known in his party as "the teacher of democracy," Ghassemlou made clear to party cadres how daily activities could be managed "in a democratic way."[34] "He believed deeply in democracy," noted his party colleague Abdullah Hassanzadeh; "and he tried with all his capabilities to consolidate democracy both within the party and in society. And if at times the PDKI suffered some loss because of the development of democracy, he would say: This is the cost of democracy, and if one would have democracy, one must pay its cost."[35]

At the daftar a guide explained to the journalist from *L'Express*, "The democracy of the party is a form of fighting the common anarchy that exists among the Kurds. They all see themselves as warriors, but they need our military schools to coordinate their actions and learn the strategy to use against the 130,000 to 150,000 Iranian soldiers that are being thrown against us."[36]

The daftar, observed one visitor, was "a military camp and a school for revolution where young militants confront their opinions on Marx, Lenin, Mao, Guevara." This reflected the diversity of political tendencies among its members and the capacity of the party to encourage open debate to prepare them for future governance. At the same time, the political differences among the different Kurdish political parties revealed a divided Kurdish nationalist movement.[37]

Outside the discussions of theory, the "school for revolution" was always in session, in ways both practical and progressive—and sometimes surprising. In every way, Ghassemlou was above all an educator of his people. Bonnot remembered, for example, that he did not want to cut trees to make fires. The Kurdish forests, he said, were extremely valuable.

"One day we saw the footprints of a bear and her cub. Ghassemlou told them, 'The first person who touches that bear . . .' I don't recall what threat he made, but no one dared kill the animal."[38]

Ghassemlou was forward-looking in his views on gender equality as he was in his concerns for both democratic capacity and environmental sustainability. Equality between women and men was then, and remains today, a critical issue in Iran and the Middle East. Ghassemlou supported the rights of women as a principle to implement both within the party and in the Kurdish community at large; in his view, this constituted an important standard for both human rights and a democratic order.[39]

In a speech on International Women's Day a decade later, Ghassemlou would spell out very clearly his view of women's role in Kurdish society and politics.

"The fact of the matter is that ours is an underdeveloped country. However, women are the most underdeveloped segment in Kurdish society. They are not responsible for this state of underdevelopment; unfortunately, centuries-old customs in Kurdish society have prevented women from participating in the struggle as well as in the [political] affairs and actions in our country to a sufficient extent. When we say that women constitute half of [the population of] society, we have stated a fact. At the same time, we have to admit that not only is our society backward, but that those, including most of our own comrades, who claim that women should be free have not fully embraced the idea that women should participate in all aspects of the struggle [for the liberation of the Kurdish people] as well as to be included in all spheres of Kurdish society.

"When we address [women's] rights, we [at the same time] address the problems facing women; and it is because such problems exist. Similarly, when we address the Kurdish issue, and we demand that the Kurdish issue must be resolved, it means that the Kurdish nation should have the right to self-determination. This is also the case with respect to the question of women. In fact, women must have the right to determine their own destiny; if they don't take their destiny into their own hands, their rights will not be obtained by anyone else.

"I am not saying that during the Shah's regime women were free, but the fact of the matter is that since the Islamic Republic has taken power, we have seen a reversal of the participation of women in most places of society. Now they have been consigned to the confines of the kitchen and are in fact in a state of imprisonment 'behind the black curtain,' under the black chador. If contemporary Iran is a huge prison for the whole population of Iran and the oppressed nations, it is, by the same token, a huge prison for all women.

"Therefore, the struggle for the liberation of women, the struggle of women to obtain their rights, is in no way separate from the struggle of our nation for democracy and autonomy. Wherever democracy has advanced and [oppressed] nations have obtained their rights, women have obtained greater degrees of freedom. These three forms of struggle are similar. Yet, I must add as a historical remark that the struggle for the rights of women is going to take longer than the struggle for autonomy.

"In the movement [toward freedom] women should have a special place in both political and party activities," he added. "Our party believes in equality between women and men. But to accept rights and to *implement* them—[on this level] there is a substantial gap in the community. This gap needs to be bridged. To the degree that women are active in political and social activities, we believe, to that degree is a society modern; and to the degree that women are active and participate in nationalist movements, to that degree are such movements democratic. And the chances of *winning* are [also] greater if women participate."[40]

Ghassemlou, Tissot observed, communicated a constructively positive attitude. He did this to the point that the Kurds surrounding him "assumed his habit of having serene discussions—a trait that I did not find present in many of the Iraqi Kurds."

Ghassemlou preached tolerance, and genuinely practiced it. He treated with respect the different groups he had given refuge to, including the Mujahedin, even despite their attitude of superiority toward the Kurds.[41]

His open-mindedness is borne out in a humorous anecdote reported by Iranian political activist Mehdi Khanbaba Tehrani about Ghassemlou's encounter with an Iranian opposition organization whose ideology was Marxist-Leninist:

"A member of Cherik-e Fedai [IFPG, the Iranian People's Feda'iyan Guerrillas] had contacted PDKI for help printing an announcement for them, because they had no equipment to do so." Hélène identifies this IFPG member as Soheyla, Ghassemlou's niece, and notes ironically that her request for one hundred sheets of paper amounted to a request for materials with which to slander the PDKI and Ghassemlou.[42]

"Ghassemlou said to her: 'Why do you say that PDKI is not democratic? Can one be more democratic than this? In this very announcement you have attacked and profaned us, and we have printed it for you with our equipment and at our expense! You live in a region that is controlled by us, and we've got a house for you to use as a garrison, and we also provide security for you. Where can you find [anything] more democratic?'"[43]

He coexisted easily with political forces at the more extreme end of the spectrum, including Komala, the Organization of Revolutionary Toilers of Iranian Kurdistan, which preached Maoism and regarded the PDKI and its leader Ghassemlou as bourgeois. For Komala, ideological struggle against the forces representing capitalism was more crucial than fighting the newly established Islamic Republic.[44] For Ghassemlou, PDKI was a party leading a liberation movement in Iranian Kurdistan—hardly a party that could be called "bourgeois."[45] Despite these differences, Ghassemlou allowed Komala to move freely in the zones dominated by the PDKI. The PDKI permitted them to administer their own camps and, as Ghassemlou described it, gave them the room "to make the mistake of imposing a land reform from outside. They don't fight. They are intellectuals from Tehran."[46]

Komala was an organization typical of middle-class urban cadres, with very few roots in the population and scanty experience. For them, the most fundamental principles underpinning action were their Marxist-Leninist beliefs, steeped in Maoism.[47] Given the party's Marxist ideology, Komala regarded themselves as representatives of the proletariat, and the PDKI as exemplifying the bourgeois in Kurdish society. Komala's leadership used every opportunity "to expose the bourgeoisie," inflaming the tension with the PDKI.[48] Identity as Kurds was secondary. In 1983 Komala, together with two small Iranian leftist groups (one a splinter from the Mujahedin), joined to form the Communist Party of Iran.[49]

Ghassemlou maintained the same attitude of tolerance toward his old comrades of the Tudeh, who in early 1982 had ended their artificial honeymoon with Islamic fundamentalism in an unfortunate way.[50]

During the period when the Tudeh was still fraternizing with Khomeini, Radio Moscow repeatedly denounced the Kurds as "valets of American imperialism." When Tehran turned and vehemently attacked the Communist Party and Tudeh militants were detained and persecuted by the hundreds, Radio Moscow began to regularly salute the "just cause" of the Kurds.

For Ghassemlou, who had been influenced by Marxism-Leninism—and studied it seriously and closely—since his youth, such orthodoxy had lost most of its value. In his own book on Kurdistan published in 1965, he had informed his readers in the introduction that his was an economic and political essay "in light of Marxist-Leninist teachings."[51] Now, twenty years later, he had revised his political views considerably and had espoused democratic socialism.

Democracy, as he analyzed it, was a unitary phenomenon, yet could be said to have three fundamental aspects: social democracy or social justice; economic democracy, the equitable distribution of resources and the means of livelihood; and political democracy, a voice in governance and broad access to power. In his view, both Eastern Soviet socialist states and Western capitalist states were imperfect systems; he criticized each for their lack of one or more of these essential components.[52] For Ghassemlou, therefore, "democratic socialism" was the missing link: a third model and PDKI's highest goal,[53] incorporating democracy fully, an appropriate balancing of the components in mutual dialectical relationship.

In his writing, he eventually took issue with the theoretical and ideological assumptions and premises of Marxism. While he remained committed to social justice, Ghassemlou had all along been at odds with Marxism for its exclusive focus on the working class and its inability to recognize nationality and gender as legitimate political categories alongside social class. Dogmatic Marxists had the habit of reducing oppression of stateless nations and minorities, and also oppression of women, to symptoms of capitalism, in the dream that once socialism was established, nationality and gender would cease to be politically or socially significant. As a Kurdish intellectual and political actor, Ghassemlou knew early on that there were a plurality of legitimate struggles for human emancipation. He would naturally come to be at odds not only with Marxism, but with all totalitarian ideologies that denied individual freedom. The fact that he had lived in Prague and had witnessed firsthand the flaws of the Soviet model of socialism would only reinforce his belief in liberty and democracy.

The struggle of the Kurdish people could also be said to represent the right of a people to its own cultural integrity and self-determination; and in Ghassemlou's vision, this must go hand in hand with the struggle for sociopolitical reform. In 1984, in A Short Treatise on Socialism, he would write that the PDKI was not Marxist, Marxist-Leninist, or Communist, and not a working-class party. So why would the PDKI speak about socialism? Ghassemlou's response was that the PDKI was "a progressive political party in the sense that it seeks to solve social problems in parallel to the struggle in pursuit . . . of the rights of our nation. In setting this goal, we have not only considered the experience of other nations in the world [in general], but also the past experience of the Kurdish nation in particular."[54]

Continuing his analysis, Ghassemlou would note: "What experience do we have in mind? The lesson to be learned from the political history of the Kurdish nation is as follows: the organization seeking the leadership of the Kurdish movement, if it were to be entirely nationalist—that is to say, if it attended solely to the cause of nationalism—would end up in a situation where social problems remain unresolved; which, in turn, would make the attainment of national rights futile. In any case, since social problems would linger, an alternative party would emerge that places a premium on the need for solving these matters and, in the process, would attract a large segment of the toilers of Kurdistan to itself."[55]

Ghassemlou saw this dynamic and its consequences clearly in the experience of the Kurdish struggle in Iraq: "For instance, in Iraqi Kurdistan two strong movements emerged after the June 14, 1958 revolution. First, the Democratic Party of Kurdistan—which focused on national issues; to reach its goal it was ready to cooperate with the most reactionary groups and classes in the society of Iraqi Kurdistan, use any method in the struggle, and establish ties with anyone. Second, the Iraqi Communist Party—focused on social issues to attract the toilers of Kurdistan to itself. However, in the end it became clear that neither of those parties succeeded."

Equally clear was the take-away lesson: A Kurdish national movement must address cultural and sociopolitical issues to mobilize the populace at large and succeed in building a future society that was just and inclusive.[56]

Even if national rights were attained, they would be without value in the absence of considerations of social justice. The three pillars of Ghassemlou's political philosophy in the commitment to liberation of the Kurdish nation, as crystalized in A Short Treatise on Socialism, were individual liberty, social justice, and gender equality. He was ahead of his time, not only locally in respect to Kurdish politics but from a global perspective, in acknowledging a plurality of legitimate struggles[57] from a vantage point that was increasingly pragmatic and flexible.

"He explained that almost two thirds of his cadres had been formed by the Tudeh, and that the ideological change in them had been slow,"

Bonnot recalled. "He understood that Communism was not for the Kurdish peasant. Rather he thought that social and political change had to happen slowly."

Dr. Bernard Granjon, who would return to Kurdistan after Ghassemlou's death, remembered how the Trotskyist sister of one of the volunteer nurses one day told Ghassemlou that the PDKI was a "bourgeois" party. Instead of answering with his typical humor, he said seriously and with nostalgia, "You remind me of my youth. I used to believe in all you are saying. But I don't believe it anymore."[58]

His aim, Ghassemlou told Granjon, was "Democracy, just democracy": "I think that it is possible to go from a dictatorship to a democratic regime without having to pass through an intermediate dictatorship [of the proletariat]. . . . Admittedly, it takes longer to explain than to give orders but ultimately it works out well from the point of view both of morale and of efficiency. . . ."

"We are twenty-five million and no one knows about our existence or our struggle," Ghassemlou told him. How can one export one's cause when one is not involved in a conflict between East and West, when one refuses political assassinations, hostage-taking and hijackings?"[59]

His increasingly flexible thinking could be misread at times, even by friends. "There was an ideological void in him," Granjon said later. "He told us that one day some journalists asked him, 'You always speak of democracy. But what does it mean? Are you talking about the people's democracy, or the bourgeois democracy?'"

Ghassemlou replied, "Democracy. Period."

"That doesn't mean anything. Do you agree with class struggle?" the journalists insisted.

"Who spoke about class struggle?" Ghassemlou asked them. "It was Marx. But where?"

"In *Das Kapital*," they answered.

"Are you sure?" Ghassemlou replied. "If you wish, we may continue this dialogue in the evening. But please find in which part of *Das Kapital* class struggle appears."

In the evening, the journalists told him that they had searched in vain—that they could find no mention of the struggle of socioeconomic classes in *Das Kapital*.

"So, where does it speak about class struggle in *Das Kapital*?" they hesitantly inquired.

"Marx never spoke in *Das Kapital* about class struggle. He spoke about it in an article written at the end of his life. And if you are truly Marxists, you cannot speak about class struggle," Ghassemlou said.

Ghassemlou understood Marxism to be a theory about capitalism in its formative phase, but understood also that capitalism had evolved. About this he said, "Marx and Engel's books, like any other, are susceptible to debate. For a Muslim, the Qur'an is inarguable, but social science is not a verse of the Qur'an and it can be questioned. . . . For instance, Marx in *Das Kapital* talks about capitalism, and his research on this issue is unique. However, the capitalism he refers to is what existed a hundred and fifty years ago. Since then, capitalism has undergone changes. Undoubtedly, if Marx were to write about capitalism today it would be different. . . . Hence, many of the claims in *Das Kapital* do not correspond to contemporary reality."[60]

"We are a democratic party," he went on, "in that we do not subscribe to a single ideology; our members espouse different ideologies, but all of them have come together under the banner of our party because they have endorsed the political program of this party."[61]

In line with this awareness, he criticized the views of those who were not ready to endorse the democratic socialist model; for instance, those influenced by Tudeh and other Iranian leftist groups. His criticism, voiced in *A Short Treatise on Socialism*, was intended primarily for internal debate; it also served to distinguish PDKI from other Kurdish and Iranian opposition groups, including Komala. "On the one hand," he wrote, "adherence to [the concept of] proletarian dictatorship by a democratic-nationalist party like ours is meaningless. On the other hand, even from a Marxist perspective it [the dictatorship of the proletariat] should not be considered an unchangeable and incontrovertible matter."[62]

Indeed so it would prove: even in its most intransigent form—Soviet Communism—the Marxist perspective would undergo inevitable modification, as Ghassemlou recognized very early. For Ghassemlou, therefore, increasingly and up to the end of his life, the crux of the matter would always remain summed up in one word: *democracy*.

Speaking with the BBC a month before his assassination, Ghassemlou would restate his position clearly, vis-à-vis both Iran and the Soviet situation. "At the present time, I believe that the main issue of the leftist Marxist groups in Iran is the issue of democracy.

"The Marxist Left lost a very valuable opportunity after the revolution. They followed Khomeini, because they believed Khomeini's regime was anti-imperialist. But even at that time, we said—and wrote—that a regime that is willing to limit freedom and oppress its own people could not be a democratic, anti-imperialist regime.

"That is past now. The crisis of the leftist Marxist forces in Iran has its roots in history, and one of these roots is misconception of the reality in Iran. . . . Instead of paying attention to the facts and reality on the ground, they [the Marxist groups] tried to apply theories by the book. They did not even have the original sources of Marx's and Engel's texts; what they had was more second- and third-hand, written mostly by the Tudeh and spread throughout Iran. . . .

"Now . . . there is another parameter fueling the crisis within the leftist parties in Iran, and that is the current situation in the Soviet Union. The Soviet Union, as the largest socialist entity, is being democratized very fast— [as evidenced in] the policies of glasnost and perestroika. Yes, Gorbachev has initiated these policies; but this process is a historical necessity, and Gorbachev's part is that he felt his historic role at the right time.

"The Marxist organizations have only two choices: either to be brave and confess and accept that they have been mistaken [that their policies have been wrong] and start the process of democratization from square one, from the ground up—democratize internal party relations, accept pluralism, and stop pursuing dictatorship. Or not—and remain as before, unchanged.

"I believe, in the end, that few will remain without adjustments, and some will be brave enough to accept these democratic transformations. Unfortunately, I have to predict that there will be more splits and divisions within these organizations in the future. I hope that after this wave of divisions the process of unity begins within and between pro-democracy groups, including those who believe that socialism will not exist without democracy.

"We are not a Marxist party, it's true; what we want as our agenda, our long-term goal, is democratic socialism. This [shift in direction] developed a long time ago, around five years ago. And the reason? To establish clear distinctions between PDKI and those groups who were walking toward totalitarian dictatorship."[63]

Ghassemlou was clear-minded about these distinctions. He knew equally well the threat to life and liberty presented by Soviet expansionism and the dangers that a fundamentalist regime presented to its own populace. During those days, the Kurds closely followed events in Afghanistan—a country with a long border along Iran that had been invaded by the Soviet army. In a conversation with his physician friend Bonnot, Ghassemlou declared that the Afghan guerrillas were authentic fanatics.

Bonnot was shocked and reproached Ghassemlou for this statement; the West was then actively debating the need to support insurgent groups in the struggle against Soviet incursions. Ghassemlou, from brutal personal experience, could see both sources of danger and the need to tread a narrow path between them. "I condemn the Soviet invasion of Afghanistan," he said; then paused, and added, "But I cannot say it too loudly."[64]

Ghassemlou was perhaps ahead of his time in his recognition of the perils that according legitimacy to and normalizing relations with fundamentalist insurgencies, at the expense of supporting global human rights, would pose to the international community. In a meeting at the U.S. embassy in Baghdad reported back by cable to the U.S. State Department, Ghassemlou voiced his perplexity that "the president of the united states has received 'a ragtag bunch of backward afghan fundamentalists' and persists in trying to bolster 'nonviable nicaraguan groups,' while not affording attention to 'true democratic groups' who are fighting for 'universally recognized human rights.'"[65]

His prescience was remarkable.

&

In 1982 Dr. Michael Bonnot participated in a PDKI political session, held in a place that was kept secret until the last moment for security reasons. "It was a semi-subterranean place, a big building. They were afraid of being bombed by helicopters as they screened old film documentaries about the North Vietnamese resistance against the Americans. It was decidedly retro, kitsch. Ghassemlou did not believe in these politics any longer, but he had to go along with it. When he spoke he was firm, but not radical. It's true that he personalized the PDKI, and why not? At the beginning, the PDKI was a Marxist-Leninist party,[66] and he knew that this political philosophy would not work in Kurdistan. The final thesis he introduced was that of democratic socialism. There are no 'working classes' in Kurdistan."

In 1981, the medical-aid doctors accompanied Ghassemlou into the city of Baneh, near the Kurdish-Iranian front line. They were impressed by his qualities as a leader. "He was a dignified, serene leader who went to the front with his commanders," said Dr. Fréderic Tissot. "Some people repeatedly cautioned him that he needed to be careful."[67]

There was considerable concern for his security. Ghassemlou recounted to Fréderic Tissot an incident that once happened during skirmishes near where he was staying. Ghassemlou came running out of his house, gun in hand. Outside, there were some women. One of them approached him and in a dramatic gesture ripped off her outer garments and pleaded, "You cannot go; you are our last stronghold!"

Bonnot was part of the third team of French doctors, the first that arrived via Baghdad. "The political police [Iraqi intelligence operatives] picked us up and took us to a hotel. Three days later, they put us in a car with smoked windows. We couldn't see anything. They took us to the border, to no-man's-land, where Ghassemlou's peshmerga met us. There the mood changed immediately. After twelve days of marching, we arrived at the hospital.

"We stopped at the daftar. It was buried in a snowbound valley where you couldn't see anything. The cabins were hidden in the mountain. All the offices were buried, and it was terribly, terribly cold. We had to leave our mules with the medical supplies because there was so much snow we could not pass.

"Little by little, I got to know Ghassemlou. He had a reception room filled with books from La Pléiade [the famous French collection of world literature]; it was impressive. His library was filled with foreign literature. He spoke seven languages. He held an impressive knowledge of culture. He had the only shower and did not lend it out freely. We would make a fire on the roof to heat water for showering."

Sadegh Sharafkandi[68]—an analytic chemist by training[69] and the number-two man in the party—and Ghassemlou were a team. Sharafkandi, known as "Said," was in charge of the peshmerga. "He was a dry man. Ghassemlou was the politician, the strategist, and the diplomat. But the firmness, the party's organization, lay with Said," Bonnot recalled.[70] "When the Kurdish front disintegrated under constant pressure from the government troops, I preferred that Said keep me informed because Ghassemlou always tried to calm me down. Said was direct; Ghassemlou had the political gifts and clout."

There were differences between Ghassemlou and Sharafkandi, who was to succeed him in party leadership following Ghassemlou's assassination. AMI physician Florence Veber thought that between them existed a "mutual friendship and respect. But there were also deep differences that surfaced at some point."[71]

Ghassemlou's military policies were sometimes criticized; some critics held him responsible for the deaths of some Kurdish military leaders in combat. But according to Kawe Bahrami, a former military commander, although

Ghassemlou was a political leader, he did have a very insightful understanding of war and military strategy.[72] In fact Ghassemlou once said "it is good to strike at the enemy, but not at any cost; peshmerga should try to avoid casualties." In the view of Colonel Simko Aliyar, an officer in the Kurdish peshmerga, such accusations of direct responsibility were unfounded. Neither Ghassemlou nor any other political leader would give orders for specific military operations; it was the commanders who had both the responsibility and the authority to plan, launch, and execute such actions. Moreover, military confrontations with the regime were generally not "pre-planned," but responded to developments on the ground; Ghassemlou would be informed only after the fact.[73] In any military conflict, casualties are, sadly but inescapably, a given.

But "even those who separated from the party felt that there was only him," reflected his friend Fréderic Tissot. "He knew that his was a historic destiny."

"Though he had no aptitude or inclination to be a dictator," Tissot said, "it's true that at times he could adopt authoritarian attitudes. In discussions with the politburo and the commanders, I often saw him acting quite authoritarian. Nevertheless, I never saw him lose his temper . . . Well, yes, sometimes, because the toilets were dirty or a glass was dirty. Then he would say, 'This is not a place for savages.'"[74]

Ghassemlou's predilection for discipline in group and individual action seemed intimately linked with his sense of what was necessary for his people's uplift. "One of the things he criticized in the PUK was that there were no showers or WCs in their camps," remembered Mohamed Hassanpour, Ghassemlou's close assistant for many years. "When we moved on to a different site, even if it was just for one night, Kak Doctor would have WCs or latrines built. During the negotiations between the Iraqi government and the Kurds in 1982, I went with Kak Doctor to see Talabani, who showed us the great progress they had made: they had bathrooms. And Kak Doctor said, 'Now you are in a village, but when you go to the mountains you must continue doing the same.'"[75]

Ghassemlou used to eat with his men in the daftar dining hall. "He ate simply, like them," said Bonnot. "He was a very down-to-earth and humane person. He spoke to his men with conviction. He did not need to issue orders. He had about twelve thousand peshmerga who were utterly fascinated with their leader. They were mainly workers from the countryside."

"At the beginning," remembered Sharafkandi, "we did not have a work schedule. But bit by bit he imposed a schedule, and that way he found time to read, especially at lunchtime and during the evening after dinner. He asked that he be interrupted only if there was an emergency. He also rested on Fridays and holidays.

"When Dr. Ghassemlou would tell me that he was tired or sick, it was because he wanted to read. He had an electric generator that allowed him to work until very late. He slept little. Reading was a calming activity for him and he read extremely fast. He loved classical music, Beethoven and Mozart— and Kurdish and Persian music, too."[76]

Every time he returned to Kurdistan, Bonnot had the habit of bringing the best wine with him. When welcoming his friend, the first thing Ghassemlou would ask with a smile was, "What have you brought?"

This was an absolute ritual. That day at an insignificant location in the mountains, at an altitude of more than two thousand meters, a Kurdish leader and a French doctor sipped the best French wine.

Notes

1. By February 1981, 10,000 Iranian Kurds had died either in battle or in Khalkhali's summary mass executions. David McDowall, *A Modern History of the Kurds* (London, New York: I. B. Tauris, 2004), 262.
2. Chris Kutschera, *Le défi kurde ou le rêve fou de l'indépendance* [The Kurdish defiance, or the mad dream of independence] (Paris: Bayard Éditions, 1997), 197.
3. Hasan Ayoubzadeh, phone interview with the author, March 22, 2015. Ayoubzadeh, who worked for three years as a deputy prosecuting attorney in a number of cities of Kurdistan, joined the PDKI in 1979 after Khomeini launched his attack against the Kurds. He created an elementary commission to teach basic law and inform PDKI peshmerga on PDKI discipline and party ground rules. He was a member of the editorial board of the party publication and the PDKI radio until the end of 1988, when he left the party.
4. Hélène Krulich-Ghassemlou, *Love Against All Reason: A European Woman Involved in the Kurdish Fight for Freedom in Iran* (Vienna: Lit Verlag, 2017), 197.
5. Ibid., 208.
6. Ibid., 199.
7. Hélène Krulich-Ghassemlou, personal communication to the author, August 27, 2017.
8. Hélène Krulich, interview with Gabriel Fernández and the author, Paris, 1990.
9. Krulich-Ghassemlou, *Love Against All Reason*, 207.
10. Ibid., 205.
11. Ibid., 213.
12. Hélène Krulich, *Une Européenne au pays des Kurdes* (Paris: Éditions Karthala, 2011), 223. Kutschera reported, "By spring 1982, PDKI had opened more than 500 schools in the liberated areas; a Kurdish alphabet was published in an edition of 50,000 copies [for distribution]. Judges were named, village councils were elected to lighten the administrative

burden . . . and allow peasants to manage their own affairs. These were to become the base of the future autonomous administration.

"The military budget, estimated at 1.5 million *tomans* per year, was financed by dona-tions from [PDKI] members and by the war treasure taken at the beginning [of the militant movement during the outset of the Iranian revolution]." Kutschera, *Le défi kurde*, 196–97.

13. Hasan Ayoubzadeh, interview with the author, March 22, 2015. Ghassemlou's book was written and published while he was living and teaching in Prague; Abdul Rahman Ghas-semlou, *Kurdistan and the Kurds* (Prague: Publishing House of the Czechoslovak Academy of Sciences, 1965).

14. Hasan Ayoubzadeh, interview with the author, March 22, 2015.

15. Krulich, *Une Européene*, 224–25.

16. Krulich-Ghassemlou, *Love Against All Reason*, 230.

17. Hasan Ayoubzadeh, interview with the author, March 22, 2015.

18. *Dollatu* means "Valley of Berries."

19. At the time of the bombing, a member of the PDKI central committee reported, the prison housed hundreds of inmates, including captured pasdaran, soldiers, and other Ira-nian military personnel, as well as Kurdish peshmerga and civilians charged with commit-ting crimes. Commentary on the bombing featured prominently in Kurdish newspapers: "As the result of the bombardment 42 people were dead—among them six peshmerga lost their lives—and fifty [more] were injured," one published report stated. "The PDKI central committee condemns this inhumane act of the Iraqi regime, and on behalf of the PDKI and of the Kurdish people in Iran, they are calling on all humanitarian organizations . . . to condemn this cruel act of the Iraqi regime." Reports cited from *Kurdistan*, May 13, 1981 (number 75), 2, 3, 11; translation Beyan Farshi.

The Iranian regime, reported Kurdish media, blamed the PDKI for the bombing by the Iraqi regime and held the PDKI responsible for the death of the Dollatu prison inmates. The PDKI responded to the regime's claims with a strong public statement: "In this brutal act, six of our best peshmerga were killed, plus the prison inmates; the killing of the prisoners is the act of the Islamic Republic of Iran alone. We, as PDKI, respect human rights and have never been involved in such acts of cruelty. . . .

"The Kurdish people in Iran will not rest until peace and freedom are established. We will never cease our struggle for achieving peace and democracy in Iran."

All statements are as reported in *Kurdistan*, May 13, 1981 (number 75), 2, 3, 11; translation Beyan Farshi.

20. Chief among the issues that brought Banisadr into confrontation with the Ayatollah were his conviction of the threat posed to Iran's security by what he regarded as ministerial incompetence; opposition to the continuing captivity of hostages from the American embassy; concern with the need for military reorganization; and alarm at a deteriorat-ing economy. For a summary see *Encyclopædia Britannica*, http://www.britannica.com/biography/Abolhasan-Bani-Sadr.

21. Hasan Ayoubzadeh, interview with the author, March 22, 2015.

22. Krulich-Ghassemlou, *Love Against All Reason*, 207.

23. Until 1982–1983 much of the countryside remained in Kurdish hands, though most of the towns were at least loosely in the grasp of the regime and subject to repeated rebellions. McDowall, *A Modern History of the Kurds*, 262.

24. Krulich-Ghassemlou, *Love Against All Reason*, 207.

25. Michel Bonnot, interview with the author, Paris, 1991. Further statements from Bonnot are from this interview.

26. Florence Veber, interview with the author, Paris, 1991. Further statements from Veber are from this interview.

27. Fréderic Tissot, interview with the author, Paris, 1991. Further statements from Tissot are from this interview.

28. Ibid.

29. Kutschera, *Le défi kurde*, 198.

30. Ibid.

31. Christian Dubois, "Kurdes: guerre à Khomeiny" [Kurds: war with Khomeini], *L'Express*, July 29, 1983, 68.

32. Dehkordi would be assassinated, together with Sadegh Sharafkandi and two colleagues, on September 17, 1992, in Berlin's Mykonos Restaurant one in a long series of political murders carried out by Iran's Islamist regime.

33. Publications and presentations of Ghassemlou, collected by Kawe Bahrami in a series entitled *The Waterfall of Truth*, Volume 2 (2006), 248; cited by Ali Monazzami, "Ghassemlou's ideas of Democracy and Iranian-Kurdish relations in contemporary Iran," thesis in satisfaction of Master's in Peace and Conflict Transformation, Centre for Peace Studies, Faculty of Social Sciences, University of Tromsø (Tromsø, Norway: Spring 2011), 36; http://munin.uit.no/bitstream/handle/10037/3496/thesis.pdf?sequence=2.

34. Monazzami, "Ghassemlou's ideas of Democracy," 36.

35. Abdullah Hassanzadeh, as cited by Kawe Bahrami, *Ghassemlou, Modern Leader and Democratic Revolutionary*, 231.

36. Dubois, "Kurdes: guerre à Khomeiny," 68.

37. Kutschera, *Le défi kurde*, 198.

38. Michel Bonnot, interview with the author, Paris, 1991.

39. Monazzami, "Ghassemlou's ideas of Democracy," 50, citing Iranian political sociologist Hossein Bashiriyeh, *Democracy for All*, trans. Hussain Mohammadzadeh from Persian to Kurdish (n.p., n.d.).

40. Abdul Rahman Ghassemlou, sound recording of a speech given March 8, 1989, https://www.youtube.com/watch?v=V4akovj8rhE; see also https://www.youtube.com/watch?v=fjvW8Xey0qE. Translation Esmail Ibrahimi. Along with the growing participation of women as peshmerga in military operations across Kurdish regions—especially against ISIL and in Syria—the issue of women's position and gender equality are currently receiving increasing recognition and attention in Kurdish media. See, for example, Zakarya Khezeryan, "Ghassemlou the Feminist?," The Kurdistan Tribune, July 12, 2014, http://kurdistantribune.com/2014/ghassemlou-feminist/.

41. Krulich-Ghassemlou, *Love Against All Reason*, 216.

42. Ibid., 218.

43. Monazzami, "Ghassemlou's ideas of Democracy," 46, citing Bahrami, *Ghassemlou, Modern Leader and Democratic Revolutionary*, 102.

Khanbaba Tehrani has been described as a good friend of Ghassemlou and an active opposition figure in Iranian politics over the past sixty years. Prior to the Iranian revolution, as a Communist, he ran a Persian radio program in Beijing, China. He now lives in Germany and maintains a website at http://www.khanbaba-tehrani.com (accessed March 20, 2015).

44. Komala's position toward the PDKI was exemplified in a 1982 leaflet entitled "The Neces-sity of Timely and Firm Measures against the Democratic Party," which stated: "Whether the Democratic Party [PDKI] or the regime of the Islamic Republic rules Kurdistan, essen-tially it's the same. Both are the oppressors of society and the protectors of the capitalist system and of the oppression of society by means of capital." The booklet further added that "even if we concede territories to the Islamic Republic, if we deliver a jaw-breaking response to the crimes of the Democratic Party, then we can face off the regime having preserved our forces." Document and translation Sharif Behruz.

Among other differences, PDKI and Komala were in opposition on the principle of negotiation with the regime; their differences grew once they went underground and found refuge in the liberated zones. Kutschera, Le défi kurde, 203.

In 1984 an internecine war between the two Kurdish parties began after a land dis-pute and the killing of a PDKI commander by Komala. Hard-headed elements, especially among the military corps of both parties, ignited the clashes and prolonged what amounted to a civil war. For more on Komala see McDowall, A Modern History of the Kurds, 265–66, and Martin van Bruinessen, "Major Kurdish Organizations in Iran," Middle East Reports, No. 141 (July/August 1986).

45. Monazzami, "Ghassemlou's ideas of Democracy," 48, citing Bahrami, The Waterfall of Truth, Vol. 1, 44.

46. Dubois, "Kurdes: guerre à Khomeiny," 69.

47. Komala would later renounce Maoism "as inappropriate to Kurdish conditions in Iran." Nader Entessar, Kurdish Politics in the Middle East (London: Lexington Books, 2010), 50.

48. Writing in the mid-1980s, in a survey of key parties and movements among Iranian Kurds, Martin van Bruinessen noted of Komala: "In the last years of the shah's regime, the Komala had played a role in organizing peasant resistance against landlords in the Marivan area. Immediately after the revolution, the Komala found much support among young, educated urban people attracted by its radicalism: the Komala calls itself Marxist-Leninist, and was more uncompromising than the KDPI in its attitude towards the central authorities, land-lords and tribal chieftains and also towards the Tudeh Party and the Soviet Union." Mar-tin van Bruinessen, "Major Kurdish Organizations in Iran," MERIP Reports 141, Vol. 16 (July/August 1986)."

49. Ibid. See also McDowall, A Modern History of the Kurds, 275. This action was led by Abdullah Mohtadi, one of Komala's founders.

50. In February 1982, armed with a list of party members from the CIA and information from the British labeling Tudeh as "Soviet agents," the Iranian regime arrested and imprisoned party leaders on charges of espionage. This was the first in a wave of arrests that saw over five thou-sand party members, "cadres and supporters" arrested, and the party outlawed. U.S. concern "that a post-Khomeini Iran might move to the left" was the grounds for CIA involvement.

Further depredations were in store for the unfortunate Tudeh. In the summer of 1989, the Islamic Republic summarily "tried and sentenced to death thousands of polit-ical prisoners. The real number of executed prisoners is still unknown, but human rights organisations such as Amnesty International put the figure at more than five thousand prisoners from various political parties and organisations." Iran Chamber Society, "History of the Tudeh Party of Iran," http://www.iranchamber.com/history/tudeh/tudeh_party03. php#sthash.kJvhjTRh.dpuf. For more on the Tudeh and U.S. perceptions during the early Cold War period see "The Tudeh Party: Vehicle of Communism in Iran," CIA report July 18, 1949, http://www.foia.cia.gov/sites/default/files/document_conversions/89801/ DOC_0000258385.pdf.

51. Abdul Rahman Ghassemlou, *Kurdistan and the Kurds* (Prague: Publishing House of the Czechoslovak Academy of Sciences, 1965).

52. Monazzami, "Ghassemlou's ideas of Democracy," 30, citing Bahrami, *The Waterfall of Truth*, Vol. 1, 37.

53. Monazzami, "Ghassemlou's ideas of Democracy," 30.

54. Abdul Rahman Ghassemlou, *Kurtabas* [A short treatise on socialism] [in Kurdish] (Sweden: Ktebi Erzan publications, reprinted 2003), 7; translation Salah Piroty.

55. Ibid., 8.

56. Ibid.

57. Ghassemlou acknowledged this legitimacy long before the "post-Marxist" intellectual movement (see http://www.sok.bz/web/media/video/Postmarxismus.pdf), although as a leader of the Kurds, he had prioritized specifically the liberation of the Kurdish people.

58. Bernard Granjon, interview with the author, Paris, 1991. Further statements from Granjon, except where indicated, are from this interview.

59. Bernard Granjon, then vice-president of Médecins du Monde, "A French Doctor Looks Back," in *A. R. Ghassemlou, Man of Peace and Dialogue* (Paris: PDKI publications, 1989), 87.

60. Ghassemlou, *A Short Treatise on Socialism*, 80–81; translation Salah Piroty.

61. Ibid., 80.

62. Ibid., 38–39; translation Salah Piroty.

63. Abdul Rahman Ghassemlou, interview by Enayat Fani, June 1989; translation Beyan Farshi and Esmail Ebrahimi. An extended version of the interview was broadcast on BBC Persian TV in July 2014. See YouTube, "Abdul-Rahman Ghassemlou, BBC Persian," posted July 16, 2014, https://www.youtube.com/watch?v=SGsfvkcMn8U (accessed February 20, 2017).

64. Michel Bonnot, interview with the author, Paris, 1991.

65. According to a cable released by WikiLeaks, Ghassemlou's remarks occurred in a conversation with the political chief of the U.S. embassy in Baghdad. WikiLeaks, "View of Iranian Kurdish Leader Qassemlu," Embassy Baghdad, February 16, 1988, Reference ID 88BAGHDAD855; see https://wikileaks.org/plusd/cables/88BAGHDAD855_a.html.

66. This is how Bonnot, speaking from his experience with the party and his acquaintance with Ghassemlou's background, characterized the party. From within the party, PDKI members do not see the party this way.

From its inception, PDKI's focus was Kurdish nationalism, with a concern at the same time for economic justice and sociopolitical reform. The party developed strategic alignments at times with the Soviets; and so close was its relationship with Tudeh that by the early 1950s it had become virtually an arm of Tudeh. However, while it is true that its preeminent leader, Ghassemlou, was classically educated in Marxist thought and maintained ties with the European left, PDKI as a party was not truly Marxist. What is interesting here is that the party was often *seen* as Marxist not only by its enemies, but also by its friends, as well as by those who knew and worked with the party and its leader. Ghassemlou established the ideological distinctiveness and political independence of PDKI in relation to the Tudeh and other forces. This was one of the reasons why Tudeh engaged in vicious propaganda against him.

PDKI sees itself as a progressive left-centrist political party with a broad base and support from religionists, conservatives, Marxists, atheists, and liberals alike for its nationalist agenda.

67. Fréderic Tissot, interview with the author, Paris, 1991.
68. Dr. Sadegh Sharafkandi's political activism with PDKI dated back to 1973, when he was busy pursuing his doctorate in Paris," reported PDKI politburo colleague Salam Azizi. "He got to know Dr. A. R. Ghassemlou and his party, the PDKI, while in Paris. Following his return to Iran, Dr. Sharafkandi became ARG's liaison with certain activists inside Iran.
   "In 1979, he was appointed to a consulting position with the central committee and in that same year, he was elected a member of the PDKI central committee at the Fourth Congress. In the summer of 1980, he returned to Kurdistan full-time and was elected a member of the politburo in the plenum, a high position he held after each congress until his murder in 1992. In 1986, he was elected ARG's deputy secretary-general and became secretary-general following ARG's death in 1989." Salam Azizi, *Seferi be Geranewe* [Going abroad without returning] [in Kurdish] (Iraqi Kurdistan: PDKI publishing, 1999), 30–31; translation Sharif Behruz. Salam Azizi, for years a PDKI politburo member and a comrade of Sharafkandi, died in Koya, Iraqi Kurdistan, in 1999; PDKI member Sharif Behruz, personal communication, July 23, 2014.
69. Sharafkandi held a PhD in analytic chemistry from the University of Paris.
70. "Dr. Said" was Sadegh Sharafkandi's alias.
71. Florence Veber, interview with the author, Paris, 1991.
72. Private conversation between Kawe Bahrami and a Kurdish scholar who for security reasons does not want to be named, 2014.
73. Colonel Simko Aliyar, interview with PDKI member Salah Piroty, April 7, 2017. In 1979 Colonel Aliyar founded a military school in a village near Sarderabad, where he trained nearly three hundred PDKI peshmerga. Between 1979 and 1982, Ghassemlou consulted him on military matters. Colonel Aliyar now lives in Sweden.
74. Fréderic Tissot, interview with the author, Paris, 1991.
75. Mohamed Hassanpour, interview with the author, Iraqi Kurdistan, July 2009.
76. Sadegh Sharafkandi, interview with Bernard Granjon, PDKI headquarters on the Iraqi border with Iranian Kurdistan, 1991.

· 2 ·

THE FRENCH CONNECTION

❧

One day Ghassemlou confided to Bonnot his concern that the Iraqi Communist Party (ICP) had captured some French nationals as hostages. He was totally opposed to terrorism and kidnapping. Soon after, Bonnot saw some Kurds leaving Ghassemlou's house. "They were not very nice. They did not even say hello. This was not common among the PDKI. These Kurds were from the ICP. Ghassemlou had invited them to tell them he disapproved of their methods."[1]

Dr. Bonnot often walked by the ICP headquarters, knowing that the hostages were there. Without waiting for his guide he approached that spot one day. "The Communists looked at me as if I was mad and asked who I was.

"'French,' I answered. I turned around and pointed to the peshmerga and said, 'Democrat. Ghassemlou.' And they let us pass. After that, we began to bring mail to the hostages."

France had more than one reason to be upset by the kidnapping of French citizens in Iraq. While the United States provided limited support to Iraq during the Iran-Iraq war, Paris was betting on the regime in Baghdad. In 1981 when the Israeli air force bombed the nuclear plant of Osirak south of Baghdad, they destroyed a project that had been built with French capital and technicians. As a result of the close French-Iraqi bond, nearly seven thousand French technicians worked in Iraq. It was two French engineers that the Communists had kidnapped near Kirkuk.

This was a delicate moment for international relations. In Paris, Anis al-Naqqash, a Lebanese militant who had been influenced by the Iranian revolution, had tried to assassinate the former Iranian prime minister, Shapour Bakhtiar. He was not successful, but two people died in the attempt.[2]

Ghassemlou told Bonnot that he knew that the Iranian Islamic regime wanted to "buy" the two French hostages from the ICP group. As an exchange, they had even offered weapons.

"Why do you tell me this?" Bonnot inquired.

Ghassemlou just smiled.

"Later, when I arrived in Paris," Bonnot recalled, "I did not know what to do. I was working for an NGO that was neutral by definition." But he made his mind up and called the Ministry of Foreign Affairs: "I think I have been asked to give you a message."

Paris immediately began negotiations through Parviz, a secret representative of the PDKI in Paris. After two days of meetings there, Parviz traveled to Kurdistan. Ghassemlou's party served as the intermediary between the kidnappers and the French—and was able to free the hostages.

Nonetheless, it was not easy to get them out of there. The engineers had to stay for a while in Iraqi Kurdistan, and in their impatience, they accused the PDKI of being their new jailers.

Tissot tried to calm them, telling them, "You're free."

But they did not believe it. One of the doctors recalled that once the engineers were finally liberated, one of them kept in contact with the daftar, but his company did not even thank the PDKI.

"Ghassemlou rescued our hostages," Bonnot declared. "The French authorities recognized this fact. I think that after that, the PDKI was allowed to open an office in Paris[3] and bring twenty men wounded in war to be treated at the French hospitals. AMI was the go-between."

French Socialist Alain Chenal attested that Ghassemlou traded his own weapons to free the hostages and later, in a similar situation, repeated such an exchange—and this time paid with money. For this reason, between 1981 and 1982, the French state "realized they could negotiate through Ghassemlou."[4]

The bond established between Ghassemlou and the French was so solid that it served as a guarantee for the French Socialist Party to later recognize the National Council of the Iranian Resistance, which was formed by the PDKI, by-then-former Iranian president Banisadr,[5] Mujahedin-e Khalq leader Massoud Rajavi, and other political notables in exile.

"When Ghassemlou left the council, we took some distance because the council became an instrument for manipulation, for the glorification of Rajavi. This council functioned as a cult," said Chenal, who later concluded that the French had made a mistake by supporting Banisadr when the revolution triumphed. "Practically speaking, Banisadr and his people were Jacobins without mercy," Chenal said emphatically.

Chenal and Lionel Jospin, secretary-general of the French Socialist Party [PS, Parti Socialiste] and future prime minister, were the only French politicians—and possibly the only European politicians—who had officially visited

Tehran in 1980. There they had confirmed that Banisadr and his team were only playing with the future of the American hostages and were interested in their own political gain. While presenting a humanist front on the surface to the French, they were attacking the Kurds with merciless violence.

The two French politicians had let the Iranians know that they supported the revolution, but were troubled by the Kurdish question. The Kurdish problem was what convinced them of how poorly the Iranian revolution was going.

"At the beginning, we had very little information about the Kurds," said Chenal. "Ghassemlou was a person full of life, warm and brilliant. We immediately established good relations with him. Jospin was very impressed with him. Even when he became the secretary-general of PS, Jospin continued meeting with Ghassemlou. Though he did not always receive all those he had met when he oversaw Third World matters within the party, he made an exception with Ghassemlou. He had a particular interest in him, and a feeling of respect and friendship. He always asked me about him. He was extremely impressed by him."

Chenal was a witness to the way Ghassemlou created a path for relations between the PDKI and PS. "I can say I imposed those relations with the party. Since the eighties, we've had formal relations with the PDKI and Talabani's party, the Patriotic Union of Kurdistan, PUK.[6] We formally invited him [Ghassemlou] to all of our congressional sessions. We were the first European Socialists to do this; then the Swedes did. The same has not happened with the Turkish Kurds because the situation there is more complex. Ghassemlou seduced us, he convinced us. He always acknowledged the support he received from the French Socialist Party."

Ghassemlou asked them to help him contact other socialist parties. "He had support from the French, Austrian, and Swedish parties," said Chenal. "In Istanbul, Talabani asked me to put him in contact with the Spanish PSOE [Partido Socialista Obrero Español], and I introduced him to Elena Flores. So in the International Socialist Congress in Sweden, they were all there: Talabani, Barzani, and Ghassemlou. And they introduced themselves as a bloc." Even the Lebanese Druze leader Walid Jumblatt, of Kurdish origin, was with them, and at the Congress he raised the issue of the Kurdish question.

The PS, Chenal said, gave material support to the PDKI through the June 21 Association[7] and provided scholarships for some Kurdish students. "But Ghassemlou never asked me for weapons, or radio supplies. He must have had other sources."

"Nevertheless," remembered AMI physician Florence Veber, "regardless of all this, he was never able to have a representation of any standing in France."[8]

After the liberation of the French hostages, Ghassemlou traveled to France and was received officially in Paris at the Quai d'Orsay by the secretary-general of the Ministry of Foreign Affairs. "Unfortunately," reported Kendal Nezan, "I believe this was the highest level of reception he ever had with the French Socialist government. On the other hand, he was received by the first secretary of the PS, Lionel Jospin, and they put him in contact with other socialist parties in Europe."[9]

In 1985, five years into the Iran-Iraq war, over a period of several months the PUK kidnapped dozens of foreign technicians.

"The kidnapping," explained Jalal Talabani in the Kurdish mountains, "is a way of showing the countries whose companies are in Kurdistan that the Iraqi government is not sovereign [here]. Those that profit from the exploitation of Kurdish oil are the Arab, foreign, and Iraqi regimes. The people don't receive anything. Whoever defends the people must find arms and ammunition, for we receive no support from outside. These companies are obliged to pay us something. If they don't do it, we kidnap their personnel."[10]

The PUK kidnapping was ongoing. "We've already freed twenty-five hostages," Talabani added. "We're still holding one South Korean. But we are hoping to get some others [hostages]."

In 1988, as reported by a cable from the U.S. embassy in Baghdad, Ghassemlou made an appeal for American "moral and political support"; the PDKI, he stated, "has always had a policy of strongly objecting to terrorism and hostage-taking."[11] The cable added that Ghassemlou acknowledged having recently met the Italian ambassador and promised to help free three Italians held by Talabani's PUK. In the past, he said, he had been able to influence Talabani to release hostages, and he was confident that he would get them freed. "Qassemlu," the embassy reported, "betrayed a trace of annoyance that other groups' willingness to resort to terrorism had gained them greater attention than that given the PDKI,[12] even though the PDKI, he asserted, [was] a 'much more firmly and widely based organization.'"[13]

The refusal to resort to acts of terror would remain, for Ghassemlou, a lifelong commitment. It was a commitment he had affirmed in a letter to Javier Pérez de Cuéllar, Secretary-General of the United Nations, in August 1988, outlining the need for an end to the Iranian regime's war on the Kurds as an indispensable prerequisite to a lasting peace between Iran and Iraq: "With 43 years of political activity," he wrote, "our party has always been against arbitrary killing, the taking of hostages, airplane hijacking, and in sum all those actions that threaten the life of civilians and of defenseless people."[14]

Addressing an audience later that year in Madrid, at the Institute of Political Studies with Latin America and Africa (IEPALA), in October 1988, Ghassemlou would publicly confirm this commitment: "As a democratic organization, the Kurdish Democratic Party of Iran has always opposed all acts of terrorism, be they airplane hijacking, setting bombs, or kidnapping hostages," he said. "In summary, we do not support anything that could threaten the life and security of populations. To renounce our principles and thus lose our image as a responsible, democratic, and humanist political party in return for fleeting publicity is both vain and useless."[15]

Ghassemlou lamented that "the Soviets always tend to see the PDKI as supported by the Americans and the Americans always suspect the Soviets,"[16] while in fact the PDKI had no friends. "Our only friends," he said, "are the mountains."

Notes

1. Michel Bonnot, interview with the author, Paris, 1991. Further statements from Bonnot are from this interview.
2. Shapour Bakhtiar would be assassinated in Paris by two Iranian agents who had infiltrated his staff during the summer of 1991; see IHRDC, *No Safe Haven*, 4.7 Shapour Bakhtiar, in https://iranhrdc.org/no-safe-haven-irans-global-assassination-campaign/ (accessed January 18, 2019).
3. Kawe Madani noted that the Paris office was opened in 1981. Kawe Madani, interview with the author, February 26, 2016.
4. Alain Chenal, interview with the author, Paris, 1991. Chenal, of the French Socialist Party, specialized in concerns and developments in the Third World. Further statements from Chenal are from this interview.
5. Abolhassan Banisadr, the first president of the Islamic Republic of Iran, from February 1980 to June 1981, was in office during the American embassy hostage crisis.
6. The Patriotic Union of Kurdistan was founded by Jalal Talabani in June 1975, after the collapse of the Iraqi Kurdish rebellion of 1974–1975. The PUK is one of the two principal parties in Iraqi Kurdistan; the other is Barzani's KDP.
7. Humanitarian association created by French First Lady Danielle Mitterrand. In 1986 L'association du 21 juin and Cause commune, established by Mme. Mitterrand in 1982 and 1983 respectively, merged as the Fondation Danielle Mitterrand-France Libertés. Focused on the defense of human rights, the organization's chief concerns have included

political and cultural self-determination, access to and control of indigenous natural resources such as water, and food security. See "UN panel pressures French rights group over Tibet," World Tibet Network News, January 18, 2002, posted by Canada Tibet Committee, http://www.tibet.ca/en/library/wtn/archive/old?y=2002&m=1&p=18_6; and Reuters, "Human Rights Group Criticised by China," World Tibet Network News, Canada Tibet Committee, http://www.tibet.ca/en/library/wtn/archive/old?y=2002&m=1&p=18_2 (accessed September 30, 3025).

8. Florence Veber, interview with the author, Paris, 1991.

9. Kendal Nezan, presentation given during international symposium entitled "Hommage à Abdul Rahman Ghassemlou," Paris, July 17, 2009.

10. Jalal Talabani, interview with the author, PDKI general headquarters in Kurdistan on the Iraq-Iran border, 1985.

11. WikiLeaks, "View of Iranian Kurdish Leader Qassemlu. "In his appeal for American 'moral and political support,'" the cable read, Ghassemlou "stressed that he was not calling for money or arms. 'Of course one always likes more,'" the cable quoted him as saying, "'but we have plenty.'" Over the years, he told them, the PDKI had "been able to capture ample arms" from Iranian forces. Ibid.

12. Ghassemlou's October 6, 1988 statement at the Institute of Political Studies with Latin America and Africa (IEPALA) in Madrid was reported in *Actualités du Kurdistan*, no. 34 (Paris: PDKI publication), September–October 1988.

13. WikiLeaks, "View of Iranian Kurdish Leader Qassemlu."

14. Abdul Rahman Ghassemlou, letter to the Secretary-General of the United Nations, August 3, 1988, in *Kurdistan* journal, Volume 140; translation from Farsi, Salah Piroty.

15. *Actualités du Kurdistan*, no. 34, September–October 1988.

16. WikiLeaks, "View of Iranian Kurdish Leader Qassemlu."

· 3 ·

IRANIAN OFFENSIVE

જ

In the mountains of Kurdistan, the doctors continued their work. The war was prowling, like a wary cat. Wounded PDKI peshmerga, captured pasdaran, and soldiers of the Iranian army injured in battle were all arriving at the Kurds' new hospital.

"I remember in the autumn in 1982, the PDKI gave up their hold on the front line. Along the route from Piranshar to Sardasht, we built a second hospital. We did everything, and the day we finished, the front collapsed. The wounded began to arrive. It was terrible," recalled Bonnot. "They [the Iranian forces] had fired upon civilians and there were many wounded. We even lost that hospital. The peshmerga were trying to hold the head of the valley. I saw the pasdaran attack; there were around four hundred. The peshmerga had three cannons, and moved them from place to place so that the pasdaran thought there were more."[1]

Suddenly trucks loaded with peshmerga began to arrive. There were many, and the troops were highly disciplined. Bonnot did not know who they were.

"Who are they? They're not democrats [PDKI]," said Bonnot.

Abdullah Ghaderi-Azar explained it to him: Jalal Talabani had sent two thousand men to support the PDKI.

Since for Bonnot the Iranian peshmerga were the "democrats," the Iraqi Kurds—the PUK, Jalal Talabani's people—were the *Jalali*, and the pasdaran were the *pasdar*.

The Jalali, Bonnot observed, had a different way of fighting. They stayed together, while the PDKI fighters would disperse. So when a bomb fell, the PUK would suffer many more casualties.

Even more casualties were suffered by the pasdaran. By the reckoning of French journalist Christian Dubois, who visited the daftar in 1983, one peshmerga would fall in the fighting for every ten pasdaran. "The peshmerga worship freedom, not violence. . . . They save lives; they do not take more risks than necessary. They don't want too many arms from the enemy, nor want to take prisoners. They want to assure their retreat. Of all the guerrillas, the Kurds are the least violent."[2]

"There will be no more gendarmes of the Shah or Khomeini to commit torture or murder," Ghassemlou told his peshmerga. "You will learn to speak and write in Kurdish. We will build hospitals, schools, and houses in our lands in Kurdistan. To realize this essential objective of the PDKI, our number-one motto is the reestablishment of democracy in Iran. One day, Khomeini will die and that will be the end. We will have won. For now, we fight, and between fifteen and twenty pasdar die for every one of our peshmerga."[3]

"The peshmerga are always alone," wrote Dubois. "They advance or retreat one by one. You can never kill two peshmerga together. A Kurdish proverb says, 'If there are too many combatants, there will be many dead among them.'"[4]

Observers noted differences in leadership between the Kurdish forces. "For a long time, we were treating Talabani's men," Bonnot explained. "When he [Talabani] came to the hospital, he was not affectionate with them. In contrast, Ghassemlou would hold their hands; he knew their names, he knew about their lives. He spoke to them about their village and their family. Ghassemlou had such an incredible human quality that he would listen to each and every one of the peshmerga and their stories."

Ghassemlou's devotion to his peshmerga went hand in hand with a fairness that left no room for favoritism. His concern for his people and loyal party cadres was not negotiable, even when the safety of his own family was concerned.

"Ghassemlou's brother, Dr. Hussein, was detained by the Islamic regime," recalled Ghassemlou's colleague Hasan Ayoubzadeh. "After several months, the regime proposed an exchange of prisoners for Dr. Hussein. A member of the political bureau agreed.

"When Ghassemlou was informed, he was very angry. He said, 'I have many relatives; if we do this exchange they will arrest all of my relatives. You can tell the government that they can kill my brother. He is innocent, he's not related to the party—but I will not exchange a relative for government prisoners. I will only exchange peshmerga for pasdaran.'

"I was astonished. He told me, 'My family . . . is my family. Yet I am responsible for the peshmerga, not for my family. I don't accept this dirty proposal.'"[5]

Besides the difference in leadership, Bonnot also found significant differences between the guerrilla groups headed by Talabani and Ghassemlou. The "democrats," the PDKI, were miserably outfitted compared with the Jalali. "They were extremely poor," said Bonnot. "They wore sneakers and kept bread and cheese inside their shirts. They froze out in the field. They had clothes made of nylon. In contrast, Talabani's men wore cotton clothes. In the hospital, the Jalali had Coke and cookies; the democrats only had bread and goat cheese."

"Talabani's PUK had a big income from people's donations, more than the PDKI," reported PDKI member Mohamed Hassanpour. When negotiations between Iraq and the PUK failed, and Talabani and his people had to retreat to the mountains, "Kak Doctor asked Mam Jalal—Talabani—how much money the PUK had, to continue the resistance.

"'Two or three months' worth,' Mam Jalal said.

"'This is untenable in the present context,' Ghassemlou answered; 'a party cannot do this; you have to consider prospects for the future.'

"'This is our income,' Talabani said, 'but we don't know how much our expenses are.'

"Kak Doctor told Talabani to send someone from his accounting [staff] to the PDKI, and there they were taught how to do their accounting. Four months later Ghassemlou asked Mam Jalal, 'So now how much do you have?'

"Talabani answered, 'We have enough for a hundred years in the mountains.'"[6]

ঔ

Those were days of anguish in the hospital. The men arrived exhausted from the front line. Dr. Bonnot remembered how one day a rider arrived at the hospital.

"He was an old man on a white horse, and asked for our hospitality. He took care of his horse; then he went to wash himself and dressed in splendid clothes. He had a Chinese hunting rifle. That night, he rode away on his horse and galloped toward the front line. The next day I found him among the dead. That is Kurdistan."

In Kurdistan, Ghassemlou also had to address matters of the heart among peshmerga and European volunteers. There was the case of a German nurse who fell in love with a peshmerga and did not want to go back to her country without him. When Ghassemlou found her depressed one night, he called the peshmerga and told him, "Is it true that you dared to look the nurse face to face, directly into her eyes?" The peshmerga answered, "Yes."

"Good . . . you either get married or go to the front line," Ghassemlou replied.

The peshmerga chose to go to the front line and the nurse returned—alone and sad—to Germany.

Odile's was another case: a nurse who fell in love with a peshmerga named Suleiman. They strolled around the mountain and dared to touch each other's hair in public. Odile traveled to Paris but returned to Kurdistan because Suleiman asked her to do so. Ghassemlou imposed a one-month period of reflection. Suleiman went to the front line, returned, and then married Odile.

Ghassemlou himself showed easy charm, humor, and humanity in his relations with women in the field. His humor, often laced with a decided flirtatiousness, is clearly portrayed in an anecdote related by his colleague Ayoubzadeh.[7]

The encounter occurred during the war between the peshmerga and pasdaran in 1983, on the road to Sardasht. Ghassemlou, driving by in a Land Rover, passed Ayoubzadeh on the road. "He was with a guest, a woman," Ayoubzadeh said—possibly an Iranian journalist.

Ghassemlou's driver stopped by Ayoubzadeh to talk. By way of introducing Ayoubzadeh to the woman, Ghassemlou told her: "This is our minister of justice. He has proposed a provision to our judicial commission for approval. His proposed rule is an extreme one, and I'm afraid if the judicial commission approves his proposal, then he could send me to jail."

Astonished, the woman asked, "How?"

"He has a law about kissing women," said Ghassemlou: "when a man kisses a woman he will be jailed for six months. So how many years must I be in jail?"

To which Ayoubzadeh responded, "Dr. Ghassemlou, when a woman accepts, there is no law against him."

ॐ

Dr. Florence Veber traveled in the third group of medical-aid workers who attempted to enter Kurdistan. She left France on November 1, 1981, and arrived at the daftar via Baghdad, where the "black cars of the Iraqi police" were waiting for her.

"For three days," she reported, "they locked us up in a house. But it was a golden prison. We drank whisky and ate pistachios. They took us to Kirkuk, where the Kurds picked us up, and we crossed the mountain with the smugglers."[8]

As were the others, Veber was fascinated with Ghassemlou. "We were many, and we laughed a lot . . . but his presence intimidated us. His charisma and authority were evident."

Veber saw that until 1983, the enthusiasm among the Kurds was maintained; there was a tangible feeling of liberty. The PDKI had become solid. On a military level, the PDKI was organized and was putting an administrative structure in place within the region. "We discussed law, civil courts, health, and schools," said Veber. "There was an inspired combination of ideas, and we felt everything was possible."

Upon their arrival in the mountains, the medical team did not know what to do. Kurdistan was a new experience for them. The surgeons who had been there for a while had recently left for a Kurdish surgical hospital in Ghalwe, near Mahabad. The new team began to work with Sharafkandi broadcasting a radio program on health. Then they moved on to set up the first dispensary in Hangewe, in the Piranshar plains.

"We were with one or two peshmerga," Veber remembered. "In the villages, every door was left open. We felt the party was well integrated with the people."

Ghassemlou followed their movements closely; he encouraged them by radio. For security reasons he scarcely left the daftar, yet he never lost his good humor and appreciation of lightheartedness. One day as he was returning to the daftar, he told Veber, he was with a friend who got out of the car at the first PDKI checkpoint. The peshmerga guarding the entrance stopped him and asked, "What have you come to do here?"

"I've come to assassinate Ghassemlou," his friend answered, joking.

The guard tensed up. He lifted his Kalashnikov, and relaxed only when Ghassemlou got out of the car to reassure him that there was no cause for alarm.

Ghassemlou traveled with the doctors to the city of Baneh during the winter of 1982. They wanted to set up a health dispensary. They were riding in three cars and drove up to within four hundred meters of the Iranian garrison. The Iranians fired upon them. At that moment, Ghassemlou told a joke.

"Everyone except for Frédéric [Tissot] and me was aware of the shooting," Veber said later. "When we arrived at a small hill, we all got out of the car. We asked what was happening, and discovered that the Iranians had fired against us. All the men in the car had to get out to pee because they'd been so scared."

They arrived at a village near the front line. People received Ghassemlou with tremendous emotion but were shy to speak with him. He settled into a house and began to receive people by rank. "A certain distance was kept, but there was still a warmth in these meetings."

Then Ghassemlou went to the mosque to give a speech. "They asked me to cover my head," said Veber. "We laughed. We were on his side. He loved that situation. He was with the French, with whom he had a certain familiarity—knowing that for us this situation was out of the ordinary. At the same time, he was totally integrated with those with whom he spoke. The peshmerga were fascinated. They knew he was the leader, but not everyone had seen him before. There was no television, so his face was not well-known."

The doctors set up a health dispensary and a surgical hospital, and set to work. Florence Veber returned to Paris. Fréderic Tissot stayed on. When Veber came back in 1983, she found the national situation had changed.

"There was no more sense of human contact within the country. There were no more wonderful evenings spent with people. So many changes! People were distant from one another, and there was so much weariness!" The sense of euphoria so palpable at her earlier arrival in 1981 had, by the end of 1982, begun to wane. "We had many problems. The hospital had been bombed, so we had to evacuate it and build another near Iraq. This one was also attacked.

"Abdullah—Abdullah was the director of the hospital—would return by car at night to rescue the medical materials. One night his car slid off the road, but thankfully no one was injured."

A journalist asked Ghassemlou why he did not write a book. Ghassemlou laughed. "I have to tell everyone that I'm sick so I can read for a few hours! Right now I am reading a book about Kazantzakis in Czech. I promised my wife I would do this! In between the editorials for the radio, the political decisions, and visits to various front lines, I have no time for anything else."[9]

∾

Truly speaking, 1983 was a dreadful year. According to Sheikh Ezzedin, the government offensive that year was one of the worst. Military divisions in Kurdistan were reinforced while pasdaran and members of the Basij were being sent to the area in an effort "to encircle liberated areas, cut our links with the outside world and open the road to the Iraqi frontier for their own use."[10]

At the end of July, the Iranian army launched an offensive west of the city of Mahabad. Iranian forces, reinforced by the Revolutionary Guards, occupied the King Summit, 2597 meters in elevation. One unit of Iraqi artillery set up at its high point had been threatening the neighboring Iranian villages.

This summit commanded a clear view of the Haj Omran barracks in Iraqi territory; six kilometers from the front line, the barracks were the main objective of the Iranian offensive. Two hundred square kilometers of mountainous terrain, traversed on the Iraqi side by the Piranshar-Rawanduz road, was the corridor through which the Iranian forces advanced.

Iranian parliamentary president Hojatoleslam Hashemi Rafsanjani publicly stated that the offensive was intended as a threat to the northern Iraqi oil fields. Given the French support to Iraq, paid for in part by Iraqi oil, the Iranian leader declared the added goal of compromising the French economy.[11]

The final objective of the offensive, he noted, was "to show the world—which pretends that we don't control Kurdistan—that we have the possibility of making war in that difficult and mountainous region and remaining in control of the situation."[12]

By the end of 1983, most territory formerly held by the Kurds was once more in the hands of Iranian forces. And by July of 1984—in a forced evacuation of their last territorial areas under their control—their headquarters, hospitals, and radio stations, and a wrenching abandonment of their schools and village councils—the PDKI was compelled to retreat more deeply across the border into Iraqi Kurdistan.[13]

Notes

1. Michel Bonnot, interview with the author, Paris, 1991. Further statements that follow from Bonnot are from this interview.
2. Christian Dubois, "Kurdes: guerre à Khomeiny" [Kurds: war with Khomeini], *L'Express*, July 29, 1983, 67.
3. Ibid., 67–68.
4. Ibid., 68.
5. Hasan Ayoubzadeh, interview with the author, March 22, 2015.
6. Mohammed Hassanpour, interview with the author, Koya, 20
7. Hasan Ayoubzadeh, interview with the author, March 22, 2015.
8. Florence Veber, interview with the author, Paris, 1991. Further statements from Veber are from this interview.
9. Dubois, "Kurdes: guerre à Khomeiny," 68. Ghassemlou did, however, manage to write *A Short Treatise on Socialism* and *Forty Years of Struggle* during those years.
10. Fred Halliday, "Interview with Shaik Izzedin Husseini: A Dictatorship under the Name of Islam," *Middle East Reports*, No. 113 (March–April 1983), 9.
11. *L'Aurore*, Paris, July 25, 1983.
12. Ibid.
13. McDowall, *A Modern History of the Kurds*, 274–75.

· 4 ·

JOURNEY TO THE MOUNTAINS

෨

In 1985, it was extremely risky to reach Abdul Rahman Ghassemlou in his daftar. Each time someone made the journey, it became more arduous to get there. Nonetheless, the doctors went on with their work. From time to time, a journalist would actually make it to the PDKI general headquarters.

The daftar was situated in a fifteen-kilometer strip of no-man's-land along the Iraq-Iran border. The territory itself was unforgiving. In the seventies, three hundred families had been living there, in an area under the protection of General Barzani. When the Treaty of Algiers was signed in 1975 between Iran and Iraq, the Iraqi government destroyed all the villages along the border. The Iraqi army burned every dwelling, blocked up the water wells, and forced the people to migrate. To prevent Kurdish resistance from taking hold, the area became a forbidden zone. Whoever was found in this area suffered dire consequences. If the captured person knew how to read and write, he was condemned to death; if he was illiterate, he would be thrown into prison.

It was in this zone that the PDKI settled in 1984. It was now controlled by Iraqi Kurdish guerrillas led by Jalal Talabani; other groups that opposed Iran's Islamic regime had also settled here.

"All the Iranian leaders of the opposition came to our general headquarters, including Ghassemlou," remembered Talabani. "We received them in Yakhsamar. The Tudeh, the Mujahedin-e Khalq, Komala, the Feda'iyan, all came. Within a few days, each group had organized their space. It was not Iraq who helped them. We did. We gave them peshmerga units, and we trained them."[1]

A team from the French TV agency Gamma traveled to Kurdistan in June 1985 via Baghdad. There were two women—a French audio woman and myself, a Venezuelan journalist—and a cameraman, also French.

The running account I kept, day by day, in my journal, forms this narrative of events and encounters. "We arrived in Baghdad at night," I wrote the first evening. "Abdullah Ghaderi-Azar, representative of the PDKI, was waiting for us with an Iraqi official. The luggage and equipment were checked, but they kept our passports. A white air-conditioned jeep was waiting for us."

The air was humid and heavy, and the only visible traces of the war were the barricades for antiair defense. Saddam Hussein's portrait was posted everywhere.

The neighborhood where we spent the night in Baghdad reminded me of Venezuelan seaside towns in the fifties. There was a garden with palm trees, a building with white walls and a square entrance, a flat roof, and protective bars across the large windows. Inside the house was a long table in front of a television set. There was scant furniture. I could feel this was a transient place of passage.

For breakfast, we had yoghurt, bread, and tea. Then we left in the jeep. Once on the road, we saw a train of military vehicles pass by. We left behind us the monument in honor of the martyrs. Traveling along the banks of the meandering Euphrates River, we left the city.

The sky was a strange leaden color. The heat was so stifling that the sky seemed to press down on the earth. The landscape we crossed was arid and harsh. Men with long robes and turbans, and women dressed in black, like crows, stood out upon this bleak land as they crossed the highway. The branches of the palms disappeared under their coat of gray dust. The landscape never changed. It was heavy and spoke of utter poverty.

The change in terrain came with the mountains, when a mustard-colored terrain of thistle, and women wearing colorful dresses, suddenly appeared. The men wore black-and-white or red-and-white turbans, wide pants, and vests, with cloth sashes around their waist. The women wore long multicolored scarves and skirts. It was as if life had once again entered the landscape with the array of colors. Everywhere there were checkpoints, military bases, tanks, armed men, and the continuing presence of soldiers. The war of the Kurds with Iran was in its fifth year.

We arrived at Kirkuk before noon. They took us to a military center to get a *laissez-passer*. We waited for two hours and then left for the stark mountains. After several hours of travel over up-and-down terrain, we found ourselves following a beautiful blue green river. We crossed a very low bridge and arrived at Kareza, the last village before entering the no-man's-land. Herds of sheep moved across the hills; women were washing their clothes in the river while children played and splashed near the banks.

A jeep with several peshmerga was waiting for us. We were escorted along a dirt road into the valley. The mountains became steeper, sharper and craggier, with more greenery. One hour later, these men left us. We had entered the zone controlled by the PDKI.

A wooden barrier was lifted, and suddenly we were in the daftar. We went up a narrow path. At the end, there were three small houses: two faced each other and the third was higher up the path by itself. That was the house of the secretary-general.

The guesthouse sat in front of a hill and had two empty but carpeted rooms and a veranda exposed to the wind. The shower was outdoors, at the end of an extremely narrow path. To the right, below, was the WC: a hole in the ground swarming with flies, with a foul smell.

Ghassemlou had a visitor, so we had to wait. At 5:00 p.m., as we were sipping a cup of tea, a young man appeared and said to us in very formal English, "Dr. Ghassemlou is waiting for you. Please follow me."

Ghassemlou welcomed us wearing traditional Kurdish clothes. We sat under a thatched roof at a table with two benches. We spoke for a while and then we all had dinner.

Dinner was served by Ghassemlou's assistant. It was steamed rice cooked with a crispy base, called *benker*, chicken in tomato and onion sauce, roasted lamb, fresh chives, bread, watermelon, water and wine. And after the meal, we all sipped several cups of smoky tea.

The evening was dark, and by the time we finished it was almost midnight. The electric generator was turned off, and the daftar was enveloped in darkness. Before we went back to our quarters to sleep, Ghassemlou showed us his house. It had two rooms joined by a corridor.

"This is my only privilege. I have hot water," he smiled as he showed us his bathroom with a touch of pride.

It had a toilet—another hole in the ground—a shower, a small sink with a mirror, and a shelf for his toothbrush and shaving brush.

One of the two rooms was his library and office. It had two high tables built by the daftar carpenter, and two maps on the wall: one of Kurdistan and one of Iran. On his bookshelf, there were photos of his daughters and grandchildren.

His other room was small. Ghassemlou slept on a light single mattress in a corner against the wall. Several large pillows served as a headrest.

To one side were a television set and a video player. Along the front wall, a curtain hid the closet and Ghassemlou's few clothes.

The daftar was sheltered by jagged mountains and protected by antiair defense mounted up in the hills. Peshmerga, with turbans and Kalashnikov rifles, watched the surrounding mountains with vigilance.

At night, we could hear their footsteps intermingled with the buzz of the crickets and the barking of a hyena pack. During the day, the sounds of war came to us like an echo from the other side of the hills. This was a land of stones, rocks, walnut trees, and grass scorched by the sun.

A few kilometers away from the daftar was Gawrade, a miserable village where the peshmerga rested. *Gawra* means "big village," yet there is also a belief that *Gawrade* derives from the word *gaour*,[2] which means "fire worshiper"—a memento of Zoroastrian ancestry among the Kurdish people.

Sadegh Sharafkandi, known as Kak Said, who was responsible for radio broadcasting, accompanied us to the hill where the station was located. To climb that hill under the sun, in that heat, was a physical feat of immense determination.

The radio station was organized in three departments: public opinion, military, and Ghassemlou's comments and editorials. It allowed the PDKI to communicate not only within the region, but also with the outside world.

Each region had its own set of codes for confidential communication. Twenty local sections of the PDKI sent coded messages signed off by the political person in charge, with two destinations: the general population and the political bureau of the party.

This radio station was essential to the Kurdish effort. Every day at five in the afternoon, the country virtually closed up shop when Radio Kurdistan began to broadcast. In the hands of the Kurds, the radio had become a powerful weapon. The government in Tehran tried to interfere with the broadcast, but the Kurds swiftly modified the frequency and avoided their interference. Over the course of the war, the radio was relocated several times.

The antiair defense, composed of Katyusha rocket launchers, SA-3 SAM (surface-to-air missiles), and BKC machine guns, protected the installations. The peshmerga took turns guarding these mountain summits, from which they controlled the entire horizon. They also maintained a refuge for people and equipment. To bring this equipment up into the mountains had not been easy. It all had to be transported on men's shoulders or by mules.

From a camouflaged room, the radio broadcast *The Voice of Kurdistan*. The party's flag decorated the wall. The news began with the Kurdish national hymn, followed by a passage from a Mahler symphony. It gave information about the combats, the victories, the casualties. In the mountains, this radio was the only connection the men had with the outside. It had become both a moral and a tactical support.

The PDKI political bureau, or politburo, was composed of seven people, and the party's central committee of twenty-five. Ghassemlou's emphasis on democracy was exemplified in the structure of party leadership. "The PDKI forbids personality cults," Ghassemlou explained, "because this nation has paid very dearly with the death of its leader. What is important is the party, and not an individual figure."

That is why there were no photos of Ghassemlou. But there were photos of Qazi Mohammad, founder of the PDKI and president of the onetime Democratic Republic of Kurdistan.

The daftar was actually a small village, with its school, bakery, resident families, and a hospital under construction—under the auspices of Aide Médicale Internationale and Médecins du Monde. There, in the PDKI political and military school, the party trained all its peshmerga to use weapons, taught them to read and write, and gave them courses in politics. There were also courses on Kurdish sociology, taught by Dr. Hussein Khaliqi, the school director.

An hour away by jeep was the PDKI's prison, an open-air compound that served as a detention center. Getting out of the jeep at the end of the rutted road, you then had to walk for about another thirty minutes, along a narrow trail flanking a mountain. It did not seem like a prison camp, but a small isolated settlement.

In 1983, the Kurds had captured two thousand Iranian officers and soldiers. All of them were freed without a trial, except for a known torturer who was responsible for many murders and ended up being condemned by a court of three professional judges. Ghassemlou's colleague Hasan Ayoubzadeh, known as Goran, served as one member of this panel of judges.

The majority of prisoners the PDKI released were executed by Khomeini's forces. To make propaganda about the Kurds' supposed cruelty, the Iranian authorities would attribute the soldiers' death to the Kurds. The soldiers' grieving families believed that their loved ones had already attained Allah's promised paradise.[3]

That day of our visit, June 22, 1985, there were forty-five prisoners: ten pasdaran; six jash—Kurds who had been Iranian collaborators; fifteen men of the leftist organization Komala; soldiers of the Iranian army; and peshmerga being disciplined for misdemeanors.

The prison was a typically Kurdish square compound comprised of several houses; it had low roofs, mud walls, and one entrance. All the structures had interior courtyards. Peshmerga kept guard on the rooftops. Truly speaking, the PDKI did not have the capability of looking after the prisoners. The imprisoned men all prepared their own food and took care of their dwellings. The inmate Iranian soldiers were very young, as were the pasdaran. They watched all the visitors with curiosity. With their shaved heads, they looked helpless and somewhat forlorn.

They were all well treated. But within the Iranian regime, to be made a prisoner was considered a dishonor. For this reason, when prisoners were freed, some preferred to become part of the PDKI. They were afraid to return home disgraced.

Outside the enclosure, there was another kind of prisoner: the Basij—boys between eight and fifteen years old that Tehran was sending off to war.

"I don't want to return, because they will send me again to the front line," explained one of the boys. The only prisoners who tried to leave, and many times managed to escape, were the jash, Kurds who had collaborated with Tehran.

Very early on Sunday, June 23, back in the daftar, Ghassemlou was waiting for us. By his side was Commander Abdul-Rahman, who was to accompany us into Iranian territory. Abdul-Rahman was a silent man. His appearance was somehow childlike. Ghassemlou gave us a note to hand to the head of the Baneh region in Iran.

We walked with him and the commander to a clearing where about sixty peshmerga were waiting for Ghassemlou. With his hands clasped behind his back, Ghassemlou spoke to his gathered men. He spoke softly. They all listened very attentively in silence. His words evoked love and respect in them, visible on their faces. We said good-bye with a firm handshake.

We left in two jeeps followed by one with armed peshmerga. Another jeep escorted us. We crossed the mountains of no-man's-land, swallowing dust along the way and suffocating from the heat. At noon, we arrived at a small hamlet with ten houses and there had lunch under the shade of a tree.

The Kurds spread a long piece of plastic over the ground as a tablecloth. They passed out the dishes and one spoon for each person. The cup for water and the one for liquid yoghurt were shared by all. With so few cups and utensils, the hygiene norms imposed by Ghassemlou in the daftar could hardly be maintained here.

We had to wait for hours. The Iranian translator, Parshang, explained that we had to wait to enter Iranian territory until the mules arrived and the sun went down. The heat was still extremely heavy.

Toward five in the afternoon, the mules appeared. The tinkling of their bells announced their arrival. The peshmerga supervised by Kak Abdul-Rahman loaded the mules with ammunition. Though the mules seemed fragile, they were capable of carrying up to a hundred and twenty kilos apiece.

We were mounted on enormous padded saddles with rounded corners that kept us seated very high, with our legs stretched out in front of us. It was a particularly uncomfortable position. There were six mules. Four of them carried us and our equipment. The other two carried only ammunition.

We set out along a tree-shaded path that ran along the bank of a stream. The shade and water were so refreshing! The peshmerga spoke and laughed among themselves. Some women watched from the top of a water tank as we left. Forming a long column, we began to climb our first mountain ridge. The mules were wearing harnesses, without a bit; they picked their way along the narrow stony track of the zigzagging trail.

We approached the top of a hill that hid the radiance of the sun. The peshmerga who was leading my mule was singing something that sounded like a lament, while other voices joined him in response. The mountain was rocky and arid. It was clear why this zone was called *germian*, the hot land.

We were on our way to *zozan*, the cold land of Kurdistan. The ultimate destination was not the summit of the mountain. There was always a new mountain ridge to ascend and a new height that concealed another view of the sun.

The landscape changed slowly. More trees appeared. Foliage began to emerge on the river's banks. The caravan stopped several times to have a drink and fill our water bottles.

Two hours had passed in this lilting rhythm, and night had not yet fallen. Suddenly, something astonishing came into view below: hundreds of loaded mules and hundreds of men were making their way toward a cluster of white tents next to the river. It was the Miravah bazaar, the meeting point of the smugglers from Iran and Iraq. It looked like something from the Thousand and One Nights.

The smugglers brought their goods to this bazaar, which was controlled by the peshmerga of the Patriotic Union of Kurdistan. This gathering assured the continuity of commerce within Kurdistan and between both countries during the war. It was a hidden hub of activity.

Hundreds of tents displayed their goods under the light of gas lanterns, lit as the shadows began to lengthen across the late afternoon. Seated on rugs, men played cards, drank tea, and smoked while negotiating with buyers. Rice, tea, whisky, videos, and oil arrived from Iraq, and from Iran came pistachios, soap, carpets, and samovars. All the men in this makeshift bazaar were conspicuously armed.

We sat around a wooden table to eat. We were served *kebab* covered with flies. I remember we drank Pepsi Cola; in Iran, we would have been drinking Coca Cola instead.

There was suddenly a big fuss. Men were laughing and speaking loudly. Suddenly I was very nervous. There was a peshmerga in front of me eating and laughing with a mortar pointing at me. Through signs, I asked him if he could point it away from me and he laughed.

We spent three hours in this bazaar. Then Kak Abdul-Rahman announced we would be leaving soon. The information was confusing, and we felt suddenly quite uneasy. We wanted to know exactly when we were leaving.

"Soon," Kak Abdul-Rahman answered in English.

The whole journey was like that. We never knew where we were going, nor when we would arrive.

The answer was always the same.

When?

"Soon."

Where?

"Behind that mountain."

We had to learn to allow the Kurds to lead us and accept that their timing had nothing to do with any predetermined schedule and everything to do with security and danger, flexibility, the exigencies of the present moment.

The men in our escort group became agitated. The night was dark. Kak Abdul-Rahman approached us and pointed to the mules. When we left, there were no longer six mules and sixty peshmerga traveling with us. Now there were about two hundred men and fifty mules.

We set out in columns under the moonlight. Orders came and went; men marched, flanking the river toward the mountain. Flashlights were turned on only for fleeting moments. The whole column seemed like a traveling fair, slowly drawing away from its resting place.

Our column was the last one to depart. I was at the end and this, too, made me nervous. I could not see any peshmerga protecting me from behind. The trail became even narrower. Below, on my right, I could hear the rumble of the river. The peshmerga holding my mule's reins would flick on his flashlight from time to time to show the way.

All of a sudden I heard voices on my left, and turned in the saddle. Several peshmerga were protecting the flank I'd thought was unguarded. Then I understood why Ghassemlou always repeated that the mountains were the only friends the Kurds had. The Kurds and the mountains were one and the same; they understand one another.

After some hours, the wind began to blow. It was cold, and we were still climbing. The landscape began to change: there were fewer trees as we left the river behind us. What never changed was the ever-present chain of mountains. The mules zigzagged as they climbed the trail, lit by the sporadic flashlight beams. The animals' respiration was labored as the slope became steeper, but the peshmerga kept walking without any difficulty. The mules were climbing with increasing effort, and the men had to urge them on: "*Hajawara!* Go, move!"

We arrived at an immense plateau in the heights of the mountains. For me, it was a surprise to find the area full of people: again there were hundreds of peshmerga and smugglers whose mules were covered with white cloths that seemed to illuminate the depth of night. There wasn't a single light, only the pale radiance of the moon. In the distance, we could see the flickering lights of the city of Baneh, across the border in Iran.

The noise was overwhelming; it was a cacophony of sound. On this plateau, controlled by the PDKI peshmerga, the smugglers paid a transit tax in the very midst of the firing line between Iraq and Iran.[4]

The night sanctioned our transit as long as everyone and everything remained in darkness. We crossed the plateau amid the shouting and dust. For the first time, I could feel the proximity of the danger of war. Passersby had to cross rapidly because this plateau was visible from the military bases of both countries. One flicker of light, the glow or spark of a lit cigarette, could draw gunfire.

Our journey now had become a nightmare. We had been traveling for more than five hours. We were exhausted, and it was very cold. We arrived at a plain that bordered a winding river, dotted with scrub and small trees. It was 2:30 a.m. and now the peshmerga divided into groups.

We were taken to Kak Abdul-Rahman's group. The warmth of a campfire and the whispering of peshmerga were comforting. As I fell asleep, I felt the commander covering me with a blanket.

We slept for less than three hours. At 5:00 a.m., the fragrance of hot tea woke us up as dawn was rising. An ashen color in the sky was giving way to the first rays of sun. We women went to the river first. It was our only WC. Afterward the warmth of the fire and the hot tea reinvigorated us.

At 6:30 a.m. we were once again on our way. There were no longer two hundred men; now it was simply the initial battalion of sixty men. We were still in Iraq; we had not yet crossed the border. We continued trekking for several hours under the sun and became covered in dust.

Suddenly Kak Abdul-Rahman pointed. It was the border, marked by the Choman River.

Fording the shallow river was a joyous experience. The splashing of horses and mules crossing the current evoked the joy of childhood's games. The peshmerga, with their pants rolled up and their shoes in their hands, moved along throwing water at each other. Others were crossing balanced on the rumps of the mules, carrying their companions' guns. Everyone began to laugh. Finally, we had passed into Iranian Kurdistan.

The Kurdish military heads for the Baneh region were waiting for us near the frontier in a neighboring village. We journalists were going to spend the next ten days with them. A crowd of noisy, curious children met us and ran alongside. An array of chickens scrambled around while women leaned out of their doorways.

The village was small and dirty. Standards of hygiene were only found in towns controlled by the PDKI. Among these villages lost in the mountains, everything was tossed outside. People cooked and ate surrounded by detritus, while the domestic animals scavenged everywhere.

We slept for a while in a room filled with flies, our heads and faces covered with the cloth from our turbans to protect ourselves from buzzing insects. The men took the cameraman to the river so he could wash himself. This time we, the women, were not allowed to go to the river. We insisted, and a young Kurdish woman accompanied us to a place where the water rushing down from the mountain was channeled into a tank. Parshang, the Iranian translator, dove in, stripped to her bra and underwear. The Frenchwoman and I washed ourselves naked. Water was never so appreciated.

The young Kurdish woman stared at us with curiosity and utter surprise. This situation would repeat itself throughout the trip. Our relationship with our body, as Westerners, is vastly different from Kurdish tradition. On the one hand, the Frenchwoman and I felt shy when we were relieving ourselves. Suddenly we would find ourselves surrounded by women and children who would laugh as they watched us. On the other hand, the Kurdish women were shy about being naked. They never took their clothes off to bathe. Instead, they only washed their hands, arms, and faces.

One day as a young woman was watching us wash ourselves, naked, she abruptly began taking off some of her many layers of clothes. She walked into the water, but remained modest, covered in the remaining layers.

Kurdish women, we see, wear wide pants under a color-patterned skirt. They usually tuck this skirt inside their pants so they won't soil it. They wear a colored vest over laced shirts with a round neck. All these layers of clothes hide the curves of the hips as well as any insinuation of breasts. In general, women do not cover their heads in Kurdistan. We only saw women with their heads covered in a town that was mainly Shi'ite.

Women work extremely hard in Kurdistan. Rising at dawn, they prepare the bread, fetch water from the river—which is sometimes very far—till the fields, and take care of the children. They prepare large blocks of dung to dry into cakes to feed the fire in winter, when the houses may be buried several meters under snow. When they are mourning, they cut their hair.

But things were beginning to shift in the Kurdish world. Now among the PDKI peshmerga there were women with Kalashnikovs on their shoulders.

Men, it seems in the villages we visit, typically go to war or spend their days sitting, drinking tea and talking. They always carry a cup for their tea, sweetened with pieces of white sugar knocked from a large lump with a metal hammer.

In the villages where we stop, women do not share the men's space. They watch in silence as the peshmerga go by and they offer their houses with a smile or a whispered word.

Hospitality is an ancient custom. A Kurd never asks a guest who he is, where he is going, where he comes from, or how long he is going to stay. The man or woman of the house always offer the best they have.

We dined with Commander Ibrahim, a bearded man with green eyes who was dressed like a Latin American guerrilla, and with Kak Ghafour,[5] the political leader of the region. Ghafour served us whisky in tin cups so the religious leader who was there would not realize we were drinking alcohol. That night we slept on the rooftops, under the stars.

We all woke up at 6:00 the next morning for breakfast with tea, bread, and yoghurt. Then the caravan moved on again: on mules to another bazaar controlled by the PDKI, situated below a hilltop Iranian base.

Suddenly, at our backs, there was an explosion. It was a mortar, launched into the village we had just left behind. In response, artillery shells exploded against the hill where the Iranian military base was positioned. Both groups were exchanging threats. But Kak Ghafour explained that there was no danger as long as one remained out of range at the far side of the bazaar. We could clearly see pasdaran pacing along the crest of a hill keeping watch.

There were certain rules of behavior between the Islamic forces and the Kurds. The Islamists controlled the cities and roads during the day. When night arrived, they would hole up in their bases; then it was the peshmerga who occupied the roads, and sometimes even entered the cities. At the crack of dawn, we would hear fighting between the local authorities and the peshmerga who were retreating from the cities.

Before we left the bazaar that morning, in a jeep, Kak Ghafour received a bag filled with pieces of paper. They were written messages. There has been a custom of the Kurdish resistance since the times of the Democratic Republic of Kurdistan: the Kurds write their messages in minuscule letters, then double and redouble the paper until it becomes a small packet covered with tape. This way they can swallow it if need be. All messages, from political bureau communiqués to love letters, use this same courier method.

Kak Ghafour took the bag and stowed it in the jeep. On the road, he stopped at two villages to drop off correspondence. One hour later we arrived at the end of the road.

We continued on foot along a trail on the mountainside. We ran into four men on horses. Kak Ghafour spoke with them, and the men dismounted. The horses were given to us, the Western women. Parshang was riding a mule. Kak Ghafour bought some *shuti*, watermelon; he cut it up and distributed the pieces, which we ate as we rode.

We ran into the peshmerga who a few days before had taken the reins of my mule. Finding faces I recognized in these lost mountains, I thought to myself, gave me a feeling of familiarity.

We never slept in the same village twice, and we were always on the move. We arrived at another village, and again messages were exchanged. Our caravan learned that other peshmerga were near. We continued on foot through a tobacco field where women and elderly men were working. We passed a hidden village, near a river called Chomani Alani Sardasht. We continued by jeep to a vantage point from which we could see the city of Baneh and also the Iranian military bases. Peshmerga awaited us in a village nearby.

There we slept in the house of the family of one of the peshmerga, who had an indoor bathroom. Nearby was a river, where the women were able to wash their clothes. At night, the peshmerga met around a campfire and danced to the rhythm of voices and one man's clapping. The children danced with Kalashnikovs clutched in their arms; the women wailed and clapped.

Kak Ghafour signaled us, and we followed him into a house where the radio technician was speaking with Ghassemlou. Hundreds of kilometers away, Ghassemlou was concerned about our security and safety.

We woke at 5:00 a.m., with time only to brush our teeth. Astride our scrawny horses, we left the village in a hurry. It was cold. The sun had not yet risen; the faces of the peshmerga were grave. We were going to film a land-mine setup. Kak Abdul-Rahman was an explosives expert; the previous night, under the protection of darkness, he had left a mine in the military road that joined Baneh with Sardasht.

Two hours later, we arrived at a tiny, poverty-stricken hamlet, dangerously close to three Iranian bases. Our pied-à-terre was an old woman's house. She was very nervous with our presence there because she considered it highly risky. A green vegetable garden, covered with dew, surrounded her house. The morning sunlight filtered through the window, illuminating dust motes dancing in the room. We were served a meager breakfast of yoghurt, bread, and tea.

Suddenly we heard gunfire. The pasdaran and peshmerga that had occupied a small village during the night were fighting five kilometers away. The pasdaran had attacked at dawn, and the skirmish lasted several hours. Then Iranian reinforcements arrived, three thousand soldiers. The peshmerga who brought the news was talking about the death of fifty pasdaran, one civilian Kurd, and two peshmerga. The Iranians were attacking the village with mortar fire.

The hours passed, and anxiety began to overwhelm us all. Kak Ghafour approached and informed us that we would not be able to film the explosion of the land mine because the objective of their attack, a military truck, had not passed and they were not expecting another one.

We left for High Soyuk, where many Iranian Kurdish families fleeing the Iraqi air-force bombing offensive had found refuge. In Baneh, the attacks would result, by the end of the conflict, in the death of two hundred civilians and leave hundreds wounded. Both Iraq and Iran took advantage of the war to decimate the Kurdish population on each side of the border.

We passed through the village surrounded by curious children. They all wanted to be photographed. "Pictures, pictures!" they called.

We had dinner in one of the houses under gas lamps. There was an underlying mood of conspiracy in the room. The commander, Ibrahim, was constantly looking around, speaking in whispers with Kak Mansur, another peshmerga. When we asked what was happening, he explained to us that there were jash in Kurdistan and that the attack planned for the following day could fail if there were any leaks. The element of surprise was essential. Only the commander and the high command knew what time and where the attack would be. That night I slept fitfully at best.

The next morning, hopeful to witness scenes we could film, we left at 10:00 a.m. in groups of ten. We arrived at still another village and settled ourselves into a granary with the commander and one of the local leaders. The mail arrived. Kak Ibrahim opened the small pieces of paper that brought news about the war, and also a series of papers with photos. Ibrahim read them all with intent concentration.

These, he explained, were reports of activities of jash in the region. The PDKI had a somewhat rudimentary intelligence system. Their agents were in the villages, the cities, and the mountains, and also had infiltrated the government apparatus. Periodically, they sent military information and reports on Kurdish collaborators.

We left on foot around 4:30 that afternoon. It was hot, and the ridge we were climbing seemed never-ending. At the top was another group of peshmerga. They were preparing themselves for an operation against a control post that guarded the approach to three military bases on the Baneh road. They laughed while covering themselves with branches for camouflage. They were even taking photos. I was taken aback at this festive atmosphere before the attack.

We sat on the hillside to wait. When the gunfire began, I could not see anything. I could only hear the shooting. Suddenly, a hundred meters to my left, there was a muffled explosion and then a thick white cloud. This was a shot from a mortar. Kak Mansur signaled that it was best to leave. Keeping down, we moved away, crouching low, among small, sparse trees.

At the top of another rise, we found four peshmerga waiting in a sheltered area. I began to feel more secure. The shooting and mortar explosions continued. I was already recognizing the difference between the Kalashnikovs' fire and the mortar detonations. Suddenly we heard a loud whistling shot.

"They're firing the Duschkas [antiaircraft equipment]," said one of the peshmerga. "The pasdaran in the bases are afraid, and they're shooting with everything they have. Are you afraid?"

I lied. "No."

"If a bomb falls nearby, throw yourself on the ground and cover your head with your hands," said Kak Mansur. "No point in trying to run."

I felt the danger, very close. From the bases, the military were firing with mortars against the mountain. To me the shooting seemed to be random, and these shots could land anywhere. We moved downhill, into a ploughed field. It was difficult to walk fast. By contrast, the peshmerga walked calmly, picking vegetables.

As we trekked up and down the lines of never-ending slopes, the mortars were falling. All I wanted to do was to get out of there, but there came a point where I had no more strength to climb one more rise. I found a large rock and leaned against it with my back to its solidity, seeking protection.

Then I saw a peshmerga on horseback coming down the hill. I felt enormous relief: if I could get my hands on a horse, I could go on. I waved at him to come to me, and asked him to give me his horse. He gestured that his horse was not easy to ride. Urgent, I insisted. He got off the horse, and I climbed on and galloped my way up the hill, eager to move away from the bombing.

I reached an area that was calm; I could breathe again, and simply sat there on the horse and waited. The peshmerga who had given me his horse appeared, mounted on another horse. We dismounted and sat peacefully waiting. Suddenly another peshmerga arrived and informed us that the Kurdish combatants had gathered. The attack had been victorious and had lasted less than an hour. There were eight Iranian dead and no Kurdish casualties.

We remounted our horses and cantered toward the meeting point. On the vast, open plateau, their guns lying on the ground or hanging from trees, the peshmerga were dancing in circles, singing and shouting against the majestic Kurdish mountains and an orange sky as the sun began to set.

We arrived at a village that night, where we slept. The following day, we headed to Tajaban, a base that the peshmerga had taken fifteen days before. There we found the remnants of a violent combat. Empty cartridges, remains of Soviet and American grenades, and Czech and Russian bullets were strewn about. Belts and boots were scattered around; a bloody cap with bullet holes lay there forlorn; a burned-out Toyota jeep sat mounted with a Duschka. All were clear signs of destruction.

But we had not succeeded in filming scenes of combat. We asked our guides to allow us to get near the front line, but we needed Ghassemlou's permission. We spoke with him over the radio.

The cameraman was insistent: we had no images of the recent combat. "He needs to get closer," I explained to Ghassemlou.

"It's too dangerous," he responded. "I cannot allow you to risk your lives." But we persisted.

"All right," answered Ghassemlou. "But I will not allow you to get closer than five hundred meters."

When the communication ended, Kak Mansur explained that the situation was particularly critical. About twenty thousand Iranian soldiers had arrived in the region, and the peshmerga had to change their plans. The government's policy was to harass them in order to exhaust them.

We rested in the village. We women went to a nearby river to bathe and spent some time soaking in the sun as the river washed over us. When we returned, we were scolded like children for having taken so long. There was a lot of movement. Three hundred peshmerga had occupied the surrounding villages, waiting for an attack from the pasdaran. We had to leave hastily on muleback, accompanied by a few peshmerga.

After two days' travel, we arrived at night at a village and spoke with Ghassemlou again by radio.

"You must leave immediately," he said. "The situation is very dangerous. Plans have changed. The government offensive is imminent. You have to leave tomorrow."

Kak Ibrahim announced we were to return to the daftar with a battalion of peshmerga that was marching south. This battalion had suffered a surprise attack the night before, and there were four dead and four wounded.

There was great sadness in Kak Ibrahim's eyes. A heavy silence fell while we sipped our tea. The radio was always on. The men were waiting to hear news from Radio Kurdistan.

I recognized the PDKI hymn and the selection from the Mahler symphony. The voice of the broadcaster emerged with strength. Suddenly, Parshang screamed and began to cry. We did not understand what had happened. Kak Mansur told us in his broken English that Kak Abdul-Rahman, the silent commander with a childlike look, had died in a night attack by Komala leftists. For the first time, I felt deeply the harshness and random cruelty of war.

On our way back, we climbed high mountains to a hidden, isolated village. There Hassan Shiwasali, the commander of the battalion that had suffered losses the night before, was waiting.

Commander Shiwasali, Ghassemlou had told us, shy with women, was a brusque and heavy man who was preeminently a warrior respected for his courage and military prowess.

This was his description of what happened that night:

"We were returning from the south after three days of marching and were attacked by some jash, but we disarmed them. It was three in the morning. We were exhausted. I had three sentinels in the hills. We were sleeping when the enemy began to shoot. We grabbed our weapons to defend ourselves, leaving our shoes and belts behind. I fought for half an hour and tried to recover my shoes. But the attack—this time it was government troops—was getting more and more aggressive.

"I ordered the vanguard to resist so that the rest of the division could retreat. Commander Aliyar was wounded in the groin during the first attack.[6] He could not walk. I went to look for my horse in the midst of the shooting, and while I was untying the reins they opened fire on us. My horse fell, mortally wounded. In his agony, he softly bit my arm. It was the last gesture of tenderness of that animal who has been my companion in this long war."[7]

Sixteen peshmerga were left to cover those who were retreating. As dawn was breaking, the Iranian artillery hit with full strength. Those who stayed had to resist four more attacks. The numbers in this battle were totally disproportionate: seventy-three peshmerga were facing two thousand soldiers from Tehran.

PUK peshmerga had confronted the Iraqi army a few days before. Both Iranian and Iraqi governments, which were accustomed to creating division among Kurdish groups, did not appreciate the good relations between Ghassemlou and Talabani. Each was allied with the other's primary enemy; while they maintained their friendship, they remained independent in conducting their respective battles.[8]

We all returned to Iraqi territory, back toward Ghassemlou's daftar. When we arrived at the border, the Iraqi soldiers would not let us go through. We were left stranded there for many hours. It was a way of harassing the PDKI because of its close ties with Talabani's PUK.

We were carrying four wounded men who needed medical assistance. We waited under the scorching midday sun. The few trees around us were dotted amidst a dried-up field of thistle. We unwound our *aghabanus* (turbans) and laid them out in strips on the ground so we could lie down and try to sleep. There was no water or food. We were covered in dust and did not know when we could cross.

Before sunset, two jeeps from the PDKI appeared. We journalists and the wounded were allowed to pass. The commander and Shiwasali's division had to sleep there that entire night. Later, en route, we stopped at a PDKI field hospital to leave the wounded. The following day we arrived at the daftar.

Ghassemlou received us. He announced that the PUK had handed over an Italian hostage to the PDKI, and his liberation was in the works. The Italian hostage was a worker with close ties to the Communist party in his country. He had just found out that he was being freed. In his relief, he could not stop talking.

A few days later a group of Germans arrived: a parliamentarian from the Green Party, a journalist, and a Persian who lived in that country. French journalists had also arrived to cover the story. They were received, as all visitors were, with a banquet. Everyone talked late into the evening. That night, in the middle of the mountains, with gunfire sounding in the distance, the daftar became a cosmopolitan meeting place.

No one in the daftar paid attention when there were bursts of gunfire and artillery shells. The only sound that truly created fear in our hearts was the sound of airplanes flying overhead. It was only a few months earlier that the Iranian air force had bombed the daftar itself.

One morning Ghassemlou, at work on a communiqué, stopped writing; the peshmerga froze and looked up at the sky. It was a false alarm: the sound overhead was just Iraqi planes returning to their bases. Every time they flew past, there was an explosive concussion—the sonic boom caused by the breaking of the sound barrier. The crash reverberated for a long time through the natural stillness of the mountains.[9]

Notes

1. Jalal Talabani, interview with the author, PDKI headquarters on the Iraqi border with Iranian Kurdistan, 1985.
2. *Gaour* or *giaour*, in Turkish a pejorative term for non-Muslims, seems to have been derived from Persian *gaur*, a variant of *gabr* "fire-worshiper," referring to practitioners of the Zoroastrian religion. See *Online Etymology Dictionary*, http://www.etymonline.com/index.php?allowed_in_frame=0&search=giaour&searchmode=none.
3. Christian Dubois, "Kurdes: guerre à Khomeiny" [Kurds: war with Khomeini], *L'Express*, July 29, 1983, 66.
4. Smuggling was a lively business and widely attested. A cable from the U.S. embassy in Baghdad stated that Ghassemlou was reluctant to discuss his financial sources while claiming that "every family in Kurdistan makes voluntary contributions, but in the course of conversation it became clear that both the PDKI and the PUK sustain themselves in large part through taxing the smugglers. Qassemlu said he only charges 'three percent duty' on goods passing from Iraq into Iran, as opposed to 'as much as twenty percent' levied by talabani [*sic*]." WikiLeaks, "View of Iranian Kurdish Leader Qassemlu," Embassy Baghdad, February 16, 1988, Reference ID 88BAGHDAD855; see https://wikileaks.org/plusd/cables/88BAGHDAD855_a.html.

5. In August 1994, Ghafour Hamzaye was murdered at the front door of his residence in Baghdad by unknown assassin, shot at close range. At that time, Mr. Hamzaye was serving as PDKI's representative in Baghdad. Personal communication from PDKI member Salah Piroty, January 30, 2017.

6. "Commander Aliyar in this case was Major Karim Aliyar, who like many officers had joined PDKI at the time of the revolution in 1979, served as general commander of PDKI's peshmerga forces. He was the brother of Colonel Simko Aliyar, who supported the PDKI with training and military advice. Personal communication from Salah Piroty, January 30, 2017.

7. Hassan Shiwasali, interview with the author, Iranian Kurdistan, 1985.

8. The PDKI maintained tactical relations with Iraq, and the PUK with Iran.

9. In a letter to the author two years later, Ghassemlou wrote that on August 16, 1987, the daftar was intensively and savagely bombarded by heavy artillery. The bombing lasted from 1:00 until 4:00 in the morning. All the hills and mountains around were burned.

· 5 ·

POLITICS, RELIGION, AND LAND REFORM

കൈ

There were two Sunni clerics at the daftar, Ahmad Darvishi and Khalid Azizi. They were both mullahs who had embraced the nationalist Kurdish party with all the consequences this political stance implied. For many years, they had rebelled against the oppression of the Kurds.

Both were born near Urmia in northern Iran, the land of Ghassemlou's clan. When they were children, they had been sent far away to complete their clerical studies.

"When we were studying, there were no public schools that served the human culture, the Kurds, or Kurdistan," said Darvishi, who was fifty-two years old. "Neither the government nor the feudal lords had any interest in having the Kurds study. Whenever we received a letter, we had to go from village to village to find someone who knew how to read.[1]

"Our ancestors," he continued, "tell us that a humanist person from Reza Shah's time came to Azerbaijan and told the feudal lord named Nuri Beg to build schools, and they would send him teachers. Nuri Beg answered, 'It's not right for the Kurds to be literate, because then they will obey neither you nor us. An illiterate person is like a dead person, and that is why they can be controlled. If a person is instructed, the person becomes alive, and will not obey when he thinks something is not right. As long as the Kurds remain illiterate, the government and we will be more able to use them.'"

Ghassemlou, as acting interpreter, was translating from Kurdish to French as the mullahs spoke.

"If the government envoy had really been convinced about what he was offering the Kurds, he would have not listened to the landowner," Darvishi reflected. If there had been an official decree back then, he believed, the feudal lord would have had to comply. "But the government too was interested in keeping the Kurds illiterate. They agreed not to build schools and this way both could continue to exploit the Kurds."

The result was extended misery and the continued cultural and educational isolation of the Kurdish people, who were among the most underdeveloped in all of Iran.

It was in the city of Tehran and its suburbs that the Shah's Persia concentrated its riches and luxury. The city was an enormous island surrounded by misery. Tehran was the symbol of a pharaonic growth. This sprawling city, the dynastic capital of Persia since the end of the eighteenth century, was a city made of clay, encircled by walls. The first automobile arrived only in 1910. The car belonged to the monarch Ahmad Shah, and he could not drive it fast because his servants had to follow him on foot. These mullahs in the remote mountains, Kurdish nationalists who alternated between their prayers and their rifles, looked upon him as a profligate.

When the revolution triumphed in 1979, within Tehran was concentrated half of the country's industry, the bulk of its public bureaucracy, a fourth of its working force, the great majority of doctors, dentists, and attorneys, 70 percent of the publishers in the nation, and a quarter of the movie industry. One out of eight of the almost forty million inhabitants of the country lived in or around the city. The capital monopolized the nation's health, education, information, and political and economic resources and power.[2]

Backwardness, hunger, malnutrition, and illiteracy were so vast that they infected and virtually disfigured the rest of the country, upon which fell the greed of the centralist state. The greed was such that for centuries peasants had constructed their houses in the most inaccessible places to avoid the incursion of despotic tax collectors.

At the height of Reza Pahlavi Shah's reign, 21,000 villages still existed in Iran with fewer than fifty inhabitants. Only thirty-nine out of every hundred children in the countryside went to school. Scarcely 40 percent of the Iranian population had completed their primary education. Of the 820,000 newspaper issues printed daily in the country, only 20,000 copies were read outside of the capital.

Though Iranian Kurdistan has rich lands and a long tradition of agriculture, the fertile fields of its mountain-sheltered river valleys had been developed to provide local subsistence, not to bring wealth and profit to the Kurds themselves. During the 1980s, the war with Tehran had impoverished the population even further. There was a scarcity of seed and fertilizer, and for the majority of the poor, fuel was unobtainable.

After 1981, farmers had been forced to return to the old system of planting, sowing, and reaping without the aid of any modern machinery. The result was a 50-percent drop in productivity. This led the people to scrounge for many necessities of life in the cities' black markets, occupied by Khomeini's forces.[3]

Ghassemlou's French medical teams were firsthand witnesses to the region's impoverishment and decimation. In 1983, three members of Aide Médicale Internationale described the reality of Kurdish life: "We have observed that the Kurds eat mostly rice and potatoes. They have meat once a week. During our time in the country, we suffered onslaughts of fleas and mosquitoes, and we had to be watchful for snakes. We lived in houses of adobe dried in the sun, and we were only able to shower once a week."[4]

After several months in Iranian Kurdistan, the three relief workers sent by AMI were evacuated as Tehran's army advanced toward the area. Foreign doctors had become one of the targets for the government forces.

Dr. Fyot, a French physician from Dijon, reported: "It's evident that the real problem [for the regime] is created by our testimony. Our presence is even a problem for them because we are doctors and we heal. In that sense, we are perhaps the last witnesses of human rights."[5]

Aide Médicale Internationale, which between March 1981 and November 1982 had sent thirty-five doctors, nurses, and anesthesiologists to the Kurdish region, stated publicly: "The sanitary conditions there are those of an underdeveloped country. There are hygiene problems, child mortality, parasites, and lack of medications. These conditions are worsened by the state of war imposed by Tehran and its aftermath of military and civil wounded, its particular traumas and the economic embargo that limits movement between Kurdistan and the rest of Iran—including, unfortunately, the hospitals."[6]

"Under the Shah there was an agricultural reform that weakened the feudal lords, but it did not make them disappear completely," said Darvishi, describing his own impressions of events during the Shah's so-called White Revolution. "SAVAK worked in close collaboration with the landlords; there was an alliance between the landowners and the central government. The landowners robbed the people and helped the government." The perception Mullah Ahmad Darvishi was voicing was one certainly shared by many Kurds in the rural areas. While collaboration with the regime was widespread among many large landholders, it was not universally the case; the situation on the ground was often a bit more complicated. The outcome, however, was to vitiate the possibility of any genuine revolution.

A true revolution, as a passage of power from one social class to another, implies a certain degree of violent upheaval: no class will let go of what it holds without a fight. But the Shah's "revolution," while weakening some large landowners as competitors to the royal power, had not jeopardized either the holdings of royalty or the profits of foreign investors.

"In Kurdistan and other areas of Iran where there were minorities," explained Ghassemlou, "the agrarian reform moved slowly so as not to trouble the Kurdish tribal heads. The government knew that if their lands were touched, they would not only incite the chiefs to rebel with tribal support, but would provoke a national uprising. So the agrarian reform came much later to Kurdistan."[7]

The Islamic revolution, too, did not change the situation for the great masses of farmers. Disputes over land reform were exacerbated after the fall of the Shah as government officials armed some landlords—for example, in Urmia and Mahabad—to enable them to regain their lands.[8] Many Kurdish observers read this as deliberate intent on the part of the Islamist regime to generate chaos and disruption in Kurdistan.[9] So much unrest was stirred up that the PDKI intervened, seeking to maintain unity.

"After the Islamic revolution," Ghassemlou recounted six years after Khomeini's ascent to power, "the feudal Kurdish chiefs of the north and south and some from the center returned to regain their lands. The PDKI supported the farmers to prevent their being stripped of their land. We even had strong-arm confrontations. We fought against the landowners. In the center and north, the sons and grandsons of these tribal chiefs became jash, and wielded a powerful influence that still exists. Today the large properties of the landowners have eliminated the last owners of peasant origin."[10]

The PDKI presented a project of reform more radical than the Shah's, and more authentic and thoroughgoing than that of the Islamist "revolutionary" regime. Administratively, Ghassemlou explained, "we divided Kurdistan into three sections [or regions], and wherever there were large properties we broke them up and portioned them out among the farmers."

Along with their efforts to reform land ownership, it was the PDKI who achieved a radical change in the political situation of Kurdistan as well.

"This is the first time," said Ghassemlou, "that the Kurdish movement is not led by a tribal chief, which is why it always ended up failing in the past.

It was always very easy to eliminate the movement. All you had to do was kill the leader."

Truly, this was the first time in Kurdish history that a political move-ment existed with its own dynamic, culture, and ideology. "A movement," said Ghassemlou, "needs to be more advanced than the central power, which is medieval. It has to be a modern party, with its own military organization, radio, newspaper, and culture. The Iranian regime may be stronger militarily, but culturally speaking they are medieval and reactionary, while the PDKI is a democratic and layperson's party. That is why we have won the sympathy of all Iranians.

"Many ask that we change the name of the party to 'Democratic Party of Iran.' We have won support in Kurdistan, and I don't understand why the same reasons that the Kurdish people support this party wouldn't also move the Persians or Baluchis."

❧

The Shah had been deified in 1965 when the Majlis gave him the title of *aryamehr*, "Light of the Aryans." That year, Reza Pahlavi had summoned the whole world to Persepolis to celebrate twenty-five centuries of unbroken royalty. During an ostentatious celebration that lasted for days, hundreds of invited guests had paid homage to him.[11]

For the general populace, for mullahs like Darvishi and Azizi, these royal festivities were offensive: they incensed their revolutionary conscience.

Darvishi, who had directed his energies against the imperial regime, described the story of his militancy: "Before I joined the revolution, we were searching for a force that would protect and organize our struggle against the government. The anti-feudal political struggle and the one against the government have existed for the last thirty years, but the armed struggle has existed for sixty years. When I saw the regime that was subjecting my people, and the feudal lords who were stepping on the rights of these suffering people, I felt obliged to prepare and organize the people. I wanted to organize, and then confront the government and the feudal lords; we had to unite against these two inhumane elements."

His sentiment of rebellion was both deep and lifelong. He was quite young when the Democratic Republic of Kurdistan was declared, so he was not able to play an active role in it. It was evident that he regretted that. "When I turned fifteen and felt the repression, we knew we had to rebel," he added. "We joined the party and continued with our struggle. Recognized as mullahs by our robes, we began informing people of our political struggle."

The mullahs became underground activists, agitators of conscience. They were popular clergy, progressive men who were fed by what people gave them.

"In Kurdistan," Darvishi said, "there was only destruction, only military establishments. There were no schools, no health centers, and no universities. There was nothing that served the people. The Kurds were a people deprived of all rights during the Shah's time. Now, with this regime, it is even worse. There is a military base every few kilometers to cut the relations between the peshmerga and the people. But even if they establish more bases, they will never achieve their goal, because the peshmerga come from the people, and the people are the peshmerga.

"The Shah's regime was not able to deter the Kurds from their struggle, and neither will Khomeini's government be able to crush the people. The Kurds will never give up until they attain their rights."

Azizi, who was a few years older than Darvishi, had become affiliated with the PDKI as a boy. He was born into a poor family of farmers. When the Shah began his agrarian reform, Azizi was named director of a village cooperative, where he worked for ten years. He used his job to put forth information to help farmers.

In 1979, with the revolutionary triumph, he and his two sons took up arms and joined the Kurdish struggle. In 1980, he and other mullahs joined the PDKI. Since they were learned people, they collaborated with the party's juridical section. Azizi then joined the party's political bureau and was responsible for political and religious information in Naghadeh and Piranshar.

"I've come to the daftar to rest," he said.[12]

Ghassemlou asked him if his duties as a nationalist were like his religious duties.

"The nationality that does not have a religion is not a good nationality," he answered.

"Why are you in the PDKI?"

"We consider this party to be a lay party but not against religion. We were looking for a party that would lead us toward our goals. I'm proud of belonging to this party. The PDKI's goal is the well-being of the people."

"Modernity—does it accord with religious tradition, or are they contradictory?" Ghassemlou asked him.

"If we want to follow the real religion of Islam, we have to adapt to the present. The Qur'an is against neither progress nor development. The PDKI is a nationalist party, drawing people of all religious sorts. The majority of Kurds are Sunni Muslims, but there are also those of other beliefs. Politics must follow its own path, and so must religion."

The PDKI supports separation between the state and religion, a remarkable position in the Middle East given the cultural context, as well as the fact that the majority of PDKI members are Muslims: one fourth are Shi'ites and the rest are Sunni.

"In the Qur'an it is said that we are all the same," Azizi went on. "What the government is doing against the Baha'is is a monstrosity. Khomeini is wrong in oppressing them.[13]

"There are two kinds of sins—those that are minor and those that are major. The minor ones are dissolved with good actions. The major sins are of two types: sins against people, and sins against God. Not even humankind can forgive any of these. God decides. But God does not forgive what is done against people.

"Islam as a religion," Azizi added, "is not against progress."

"But there are mullahs who are against any modernization. They support Khomeini's regime that is preventing progress." With a straight face, but a twinkle in his eye, Ghassemlou spurred him on.

"The mullah is respected if he does not lose his way. He must always be with the people and never abandon them," Azizi responded.

This conviction that the mullahs should share the people's condition—a conviction shared by both Sunnis and Shi'ites—is something that the Shah had dismissed. He had also ignored something as basic as the fact that religion fully permeated Iranian life, as it had in Christian Europe during the Middle Ages.

And this was perplexing, because while the Shah was fascinated with modern technology, he was also a truly religious man.

The Shah, who was also a sad man, avowed that God had given him the task of governing, and as a child had offered him visions. As an adult, he had religious dreams.[14]

The Shah had survived two murder attempts, and he declared that it was a miracle that had saved him. "My reign has saved the country, and it has done so because God was on my side," he asserted.[15] Yet he seemed to scorn the mullahs who had so much influence in Iranian society.

A week after the Shah's wedding with Soraya Esfandiari, his second wife, in 1951, a devout Muslim shouting *Allah akbar!* shot and killed the Shah's prime minister, Ali Razmara, in a mosque.

This was a serious message. Even more serious was that the Shah could not find one mullah to officiate at the funeral. The Iranians hated Razmara, whom Prince Abdorreza, the Shah's younger brother, called "a snake in the grass."[16]

Abdul Rahman Ghassemlou was not a religious man. He had never been one, even though he'd grown up in a Muslim nation. His mother, an Assyrian Christian, used to take him secretly to Bible classes. As a boy, Ghassemlou had gone to the Qur'an school, as did all boys of his age. His intellectual interest in religious phenomena had deepened with the years. He had studied the sacred books of Islam and had read the writings of the ayatollahs who held power in Tehran.

Now, after the revolution, he would criticize with irony the words of a jingle that the radio and television broadcast: "My God, my God, until the Mahdi arrives, Khomeini protects us." Shi'ite fundamentalists repeated this with fervor.

"This is a contradiction," he argued. "If Khomeini is going to be alive until the arrival of the Mahdi, the Twelfth Imam, this means that life will be terrible while Khomeini is alive—because the Mahdi is supposed to come when catastrophic things happen on earth."[17]

Ghassemlou would explain the historical politico-religious developments in the region between Persians and Kurds as follows: "One fourth of Kurds are Shi'ites. At the beginning, when they were ruled by the Sassanids, the Kurds resisted the Arabs for a very long time. When the Safavids took control of the Persian Empire, they [the Safavids] realized they were powerful enough to contest the Ottoman Empire. This was the only way to defend the Shi'ites and thus become the protectors of Shi'ites against the Ottomans, who were defenders of the Sunnis. Thus was born the Shi'a fundamentalism. Khomeini's fundamentalism has its origins in the Safavid Empire.

"There are differences among the Shi'ites," Ghassemlou explained. "The Safavid Shi'ites condemn Khomeini's fundamentalism. The Shi'ites call themselves *Ja'fari* after Ja'far al-Sadiq, the Sixth Imam. But the Ja'fari Shi'ites are not fundamentalists; they are a moderate Shi'ite group. For example, Shariatmadari, an ayatollah in Tabriz, is a Ja'fari."

Ghassemlou would make fun of the meticulousness with which the Shi'ite Islamists appropriated facts and words from the past. "My generation is the first to know when they were born. Not even my father, who came from an educated family, knew the year he was born. When the Shi'ites write about the month of Muharram, or the ninth or tenth day (Ashura), or when the battle of Karbala took place, they talk about all the things that happened, precisely, moment by moment; they talk about what was said, the words Hussein and his companions spoke. You'd think they had cassette recorders, to know when each one was born and when he died . . ."

Ghassemlou was aware of the importance that the one hundred thousand and more Shi'ite mullahs played in Iran's life. "Unfortunately," he would say, laughing, "Khomeini has several hundred-year-old kinsmen. Idleness and religion benefit the body."[18]

For Sheikh Ezzedin, the new constitution was a Shi'i one in which the Sunnis had no place. "They are not forcing individuals to convert but they are trying to prepare a situation in which all Iranians convert to Shi'ism. In the areas of Kurdistan under their control, they are changing the teachers in the schools, bringing in members of the Revolutionary Guard as what we call *pasdar muallem*—Guard teachers. At the same time, they have given responsibility for religious affairs in Kurdistan to Shi'i clergy and have opened a school for Shi'i clergy in Urmia."[19]

In 1988, Aide Médicale International inaugurated another hospital in the Kurdish mountains. Ghassemlou wanted to name it after a doctor from the organization who had died of natural causes while working in Kurdistan. But finally it was given the Kurdish name *Azadi*, which means "freedom."

French physician Bernard Granjon believed that Ghassemlou's request for the humanitarian medical organizations to build hospitals in Kurdistan was, whether consciously or not, more political than medical. At the outset of the hostilities with the regime, the Kurds had access to Iraqi hospitals, and they also had access to a hospital in Iran. "So at the beginning, we did not think that the construction of another hospital was a top priority. We felt that the most valuable thing was to have first-aid staff that could treat the wounded who sometimes took fifteen days to get to the hospitals. So for two years, this is what we did. In 1986, we were able to build a hospital that was now much needed because the relations between the Kurds and Iraqis were becoming tense. In the Iraqi hospitals, the Iraqis were taken care of first and the Kurds were not.

"The Kurds took care of the military and administrative aspects, and the doctors took care of the medical problems. This was true until 1990, when we thought there would be future problems, so we began the education of doctors, surgeons, anesthesiologists, nurses, etcetera," added Granjon.[20]

Things got worse for Ghassemlou with the years. "He was fulfilled with the contact with people," said AMI physician Florence Veber.[21] "He needed that relationship. But he did not have it in Iraq. He suffered the lack of this, and he could only find it in his contact with the peshmerga. In 1981, many people surrounded him. In 1988, when I saw him again in the Iraqi mountains, the situation was hard and austere. Many of his friends had disappeared.

"He used to say that after Khomeini's death, things could be mended. Perhaps it was due to the solitude and the weariness he had developed that he was not aware that he was walking into a trap in Vienna. He was burdened by his separation from the people, by his life in an Iraqi daftar, and by the closed world of men."

Notes

1. Ahmad Darvishi, interview with the author, PDKI general headquarters in Kurdistan on the Iran-Iraq border, 1985. Further statements from Darvishi are from this interview.
2. Robert Graham, *Iran, the Illusion of Power* (New York and Oxon: Routledge, 2011), 25.
3. Ahmad Rafat, "Kurdistan: I rebelli de la montagna" [Kurdistan: The mountain rebels], *Dialogo Nord-Sud* magazine, Rome, June 8, 1983.
4. Testimony from French surgeon Michel-Ives Grauwin, anesthesiologist Didier Goullar, and nurse Marie-Hélène Charlet as recounted in *La Voix du Nord*, Pas-de-Calais, July 10, 1983.
5. *Le Bien Public*, Dijon, July 1, 1983.
6. Aide Médicale Internationale, *Bulletin*, number 3, Paris, 1983, on its activities in 1982.
7. Abdul Rahman Ghassemlou, interview with the author, PDKI headquarters on the Iraq-Iran border, 1985. Except where otherwise cited, further statements from Ghassemlou in this chapter are from this interview.
8. Abdullah Hassanzadeh, *Niw Sede Xebat* [Half a century of struggle: A retrospect of struggle and activity of the Democratic Party of Iranian Kurdistan] [in Kurdish], Vol. 1 (Gawrade: Press Commission of the Kurdistan Democratic Party of Iran, August 1995), 153–54; translation Salah Piroty.
9. "This issue [of land ownership and redistribution] galvanized opposing stands from both sides. On one hand government officials, in particular the gendarmerie and the revolutionary committees, would egg on landlords to regain their land by distributing weapons to them. Their purpose, in fact, was to create chaos in Kurdistan. On the other

hand, some small organizations—in an effort to show they were 'revolutionary' but without thinking of the consequences—pushed the peasants to confront the landlords and to plow up the lands [to assert their right to till the lands they had taken over]." Ibid., 152–56.

10. Abdul Rahman Ghassemlou, interview with the author, PDKI headquarters, 1985.

11. At the celebration of the Shah's apotheosis, the world became solicitous. This was a unique moment in Iranian history. On October 13, 1965, in the Pasargadae plains where the first Persian capital was founded, His Imperial Majesty Mohammad Reza Shah Pahlavi Aryamehr said: "To you, Cyrus, great king, king of kings, Achaemenid king, on behalf of myself, the *Shahanshah* of Iran, and on behalf of my people, hail!"

    Heads of state, prime ministers, kings, princes, and dignitaries from all the corners and continents of the world were present at this unusual ceremony which sought to link the son of an illiterate sub-officer with a sovereign who, two thousand five hundred years before, had reigned over an empire that spanned Asia Minor and stretched from the Nile River to India.

    That day, under a merciless sun, the whole world rendered homage to this new Persian demigod. Present were King Constantine of Greece, Emperor Haile Selassie of Ethiopia, Marshal Tito of Yugoslavia, Princess Anne and Prince Philip of England, Soviet President Nikolai Podgorny, and Arab, Chinese, European, American, and African leaders.

    The Shah received homage after homage. He was *doctor honoris causa* of twenty-one universities and received thirty-one consecrations abroad. He was convinced that monarchy was the only possible way of governing Iran. He told Italian journalist Oriana Fallaci that his rulership "would last longer than your regimes." Oriana Fallaci, "The Shah of Iran: An Interview with Mohammad Reza Pahlavi," *The New Republic*, December 1, 1973 in https://newrepublic.com/article/92745/shah-iran-mohammad-reza-pahlevi-oriana-fallaci. As in the Oriental tales of old, the Shah dazzled his guests with delicacies and fresh flowers flown in from Paris and Holland; light-and-sound shows; and military parades of thousands of men dressed as Cyrus the Great's soldiers. It is believed that this celebration cost $300 million. It was the most expensive party in the history of humanity.

12. Khalid Azizi, interview with the author, PDKI general headquarters in Kurdistan on the Iran-Iraq border, 1985. Further statements from Azizi are from this interview.

13. Baha'i, a religion founded in the mid-nineteenth century by Bahá'u'lláh, a Persian prophet who proclaimed the need for and the inevitability of human unity, promotes spiritual development and the principles of universal peace. Baha'i has followers around the world. More than one hundred Baha'is were murdered by Islamist elements during the two years after the revolution's triumph. Many of them were accused of being spies and executed.

14. Oriana Fallaci, "The Shah of Iran: An Interview with Mohammad Reza Pahlavi."

15. Ibid.

16. Mohamed Heikal, *Iran: The Untold Story* (New York: Pantheon Books, 1982), 55.

17. Abdul Rahman Ghassemlou, interview with Jonathan Randal, Paris, 1986. Except where otherwise indicated, further statements from Ghassemlou are from this interview.

18. Christian Dubois, "Kurdes: guerre à Khomeiny" [Kurds: war with Khomeini], *L'Express*, July 29, 1983, 68.
19. Fred Halliday, "Interview with Shaik Izzedin Husseini: A Dictatorship under the Name of Islam," *Middle East Reports*, No. 113 (March–April 1983), 9.
20. Bernard Granjon, interview with the author, Paris, 1991.
21. Florence Veber, interview with the author, Paris, 1991.

Abdul Rahman Ghassemlou at the PDKI headquarters in Iraqi Kurdistan, 1985. © Carol Prunhuber

Abdul Rahman Ghassemlou at the entrance of the PDKI headquarters with his peshmerga, 1985. © Carol Prunhuber

Peshmerga with antiaircraft defense weapon, PDKI headquarters, 1985. © Carol Prunhuber

PDKI Commander Ibrahim in Iranian Kurdistan, 1985. © Carol Prunhuber

PDKI peshmerga celebrating victory over an Iranian military objective, 1985. © Carol Prunhuber

The author with PDKI peshmerga in Iranian Kurdistan, 1985. © Carol Prunhuber

Children in a village in the region of Baneh, 1985. © Carol Prunhuber

PDKI peshmerga resting after attack on Iranian military objective, 1985. © Carol Prunhuber

Abdullah Ghaderi-Azar with Abdul Rahman Ghassemlou, Madrid, 1986. © Carol Prunhuber

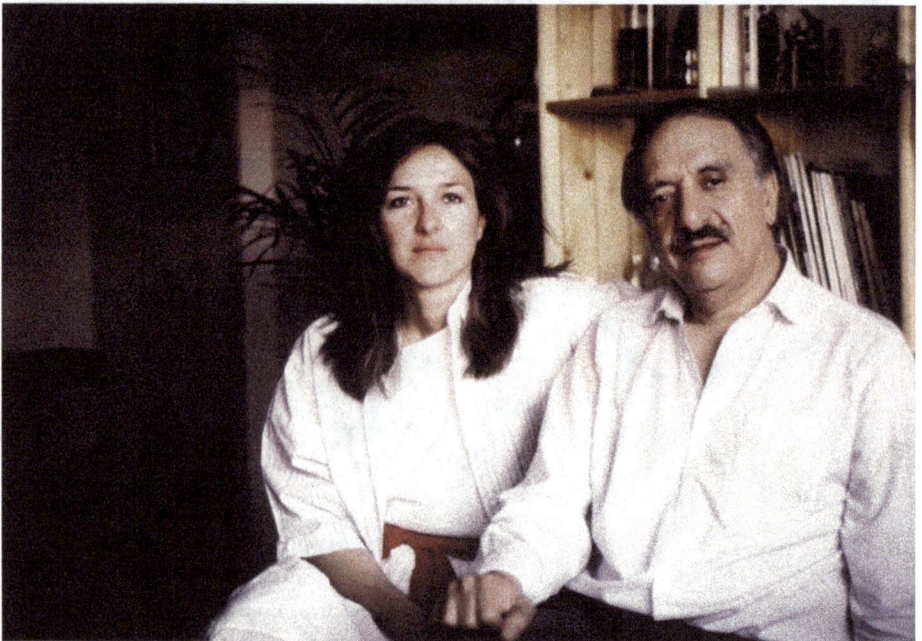

The author with Abdul Rahman Ghassemlou, Madrid, 1986. Photo courtesy Carol Prunhuber

PART IV

RAHMAN THE KURD

· 1 ·

SONS OF SIMKO

❧

Abdul Rahman Ghassemlou was born on December 22, 1930, in the city of Urmia[1] in Iranian Kurdistan. This is according to Ghassemlou's uncle, who insisted his nephew was born during winter. His mother always claimed that he was born in the summertime.

The season may have been questionable, but at least Ghassemlou knew what year he was born. His generation was the first to register even the year of birth. "My father," he said, "was probably born around 1867 and was approximately sixty-three years old when I was born. He died at the age of eighty-four.[2] My father claimed that he was legally married to nine women, but my mother would say there were sixteen.[3] If I'm correct, my mother was his third wife. She was Assyrian and converted to Islam."[4]

His mother's name was Naneh.[5] She took the name of Fatima when she married and became a Muslim.

"We were seven brothers and I was the youngest," Ghassemlou recalled. Truly speaking, it was a large family, even by Kurdish standards. Ghassemlou's colleague Q. M.[6] remembered: "I knew his older brother, who was a radiologist; his nieces; and his brother Hassan. I went once or twice to the Ghassemlou Valley.[7] It was an immense valley with several springs, and the air was fresh. There were many tobacco and fruit fields. The lands had been divided since the Shah's time. One part was in the hands of the Ghassemlou family. Ghassemlou's father had been a great feudal lord, but Ghassemlou did not own lands. Even his older brother's home was a small country house.

"The Ghassemlous were well-known and respected," Q. M. went on. "They had been involved in local and national politics for a century, when the elder Ghassemlou held the seat of advisor to the shah [at that time, Mozaffar ad-Din Shah Qajar] during the nineteenth century.[8] Persia was a different country then, and there was no 'Kurdish problem,' even though the Kurds were victims of the centralist despotism.

"The last time I saw Rahman was several years ago at a family wedding," Q. M. recalled. "He was happy, as always. We talked and danced. He always told stories to make people laugh."

In the late 1890s the shah named Ghassemlou's father head of the royal stables for his son, Crown Prince Mohammad Ali. Known as Woussouq Agha or Mohammed Khan, Ghassemlou's father was a rich Sunni landowner among the Shikak, one of the principal tribes of the region. In Iranian Kurdistan, among the more than sixty tribes, the Shikak live northwest of Urmia. Woussouq-e Divan owned the entire Ghassemlou Valley, a few kilometers from Urmia near Iran's northwest border with Turkey.

Most prominent during the early twentieth century as a chief of the Shikak was Ismael Agha, known as Simko.[9] A warrior in his youth, Simko was seasoned in raids against the settlements of the plains and valleys, a population that included Kurds unaffiliated with tribal structures as well as Azeri, Armenian, and Assyrian communities. From a purely practical point of view in a region with no structure for tax collection, the raids he carried out were an administrative necessity to maintain his military forces. His conduct, in practice common to other tribes at the time, has been described as an "effective way of raising revenue to pay for the upkeep of tribal solidarity."[10] By their reputation, the Shikak were not indiscriminate looters; Jafar Agha, Simko's older brother, was said to have taken from the rich and then given a share of the takings to the poor.[11]

When the armies of the Russian czar had come into Iran at the opening of the twentieth century, they had expelled the Ottomans and lent support to the indigenous Assyrians, who were predominantly Nestorian Christians, in committing atrocities against the Kurdish population. The Azeri Turks, too, suffered depredations. With the breakout of World War I, the Russian presence in Kurdistan was strengthened from the north, and Christians from southern Turkey and Armenia found refuge in the region around Urmia and Oshnavieh, where the Russian presence would protect them. In 1917, with the Bolshevik Revolution raging at home, Russia withdrew its troops and with them its protection. The ongoing influx of Armenian refugees, however, with access to arms left behind by the czar's troops, strengthened the Assyrian position, and with it the existing tension in the region.[12] In 1918 Simko, apparently at the instigation of the governor of Tabriz, invited the Assyrian leader and patriarch Mar Shimun for negotiations, and treacherously murdered him.[13]

In the aftermath of World War I and the defeat of the Ottoman Empire, Kurdistan was swept by a wave of nationalism. Enthusiasm was sparked by news of Wilson's "Fourteen Points," among them the right of national self-determination, and rumors of British plans for a "Kurdish buffer state" in the Middle East.[14] Simko, now established as a local leader, allied with Kurdish nationalists to push back against the Iranian central government with the goal of gaining autonomy and self-determination for the Kurds. He was murdered in 1930 by emissaries from Reza Shah with whom he was to negotiate a peace treaty. The same fate befell his brother.

Woussouq-e Divan had been a friend of Simko's; both had supported the Kurdish nationalist movement. But against the reconfigurations on the world stage that followed the Great War, the Kurds, along with other minorities, posed a problem for Reza Shah's project of establishing "one nation with one language and one identity"[15] through systematic consolidation of power in a centralized state.

Toward solidifying this unitary national identity, Reza Shah initiated strategies that ranged from administrative structure and infrastructure—constructing the Trans-Iranian Railway, establishing a central bureaucracy, funneling foreign trade through Tehran, and restructuring provincial administration[16]—to specifically targeted deconstruction of ethnicity: outlawing traditional ethnic dress, forbidding non-Persian publications, even designating a committee to "purge Persian of Arabic words." As the most powerful blow to ethnicity, the shah put an end to schools operating in minority languages, instituting a statewide educational system featuring instruction only in Farsi as the official language.[17]

From the point of view of the shah's nationalizing project, notes political theorist Abbas Vali, "Tribalism was the main source of political instability and the main threat to the authority of the state in Kurdistan."[18] Tribalism posed a threat to the politics of territorial centralism throughout Iran[19]—not only Kurdish tribal structure, but that of stronger tribes in the south and southwest, like the Bakhtiari and Qashqai. While oppression of ethnic minorities was conducted predominantly as cultural warfare,[20] the Kurds' military and political organization also constituted a force that the shah sought to curtail.[21]

The assault on tribalism was far more than an attempt to rein in the obvious threat from tribal leaders' fighting forces, raiding parties, or capacity for armed resistance. It is not clear, on the face of it, how Kurdish ethnicity *per se* would have posed "immediate danger to Pahlavi absolutism," as Abbas Vali points out.[22] And further, as noted by Kurdish observers, by the mid-1940s tribalism was becoming less relevant in Iranian Kurdish politics with the increasing modernization of society on all levels, both Iranian and Kurdish.

The question can be asked, then: What was it in the tribal presence that Reza Shah found so threatening?

The stakes were ideological: the shah's project of a narrowly Persian Aryanization. Reza Shah's agenda for reconstruction of a new national identity based on an ultranationalist ideology not only set out to deny the distinctiveness of Iran's multiple cultures and ethnicities, but more drastically even sought to replace those cultures' own self-narratives, both written and oral, with a substitute narrative that endowed the entire populace of Iran with "a common 'Aryan ancestry.'"[23]

Herein lay the threat. From the point of view of Reza Shah's dominant ethnicity—the culture with the self-ascribed right to define the state as its own—the presence and coherence of other national cultures appeared intrinsically separatist. "First and foremost," writes Azeri-Canadian sociologist Alireza Asgharzadeh, the very existence of tribal societies "meant different languages that these supposedly 'tribal' communities spoke, which were not the same as the language that Reza Khan spoke—Farsi." The presence of such differences, to Reza Shah, was inherently subversive, for they gave the lie to the image of a unified Iran he wished to project. Importantly, these differences carried the potential for divergent political action. "The nomadic, transitory lifestyle of these communities," notes Asgharzadeh, "served to effectively resist, among other things, the attempted amputation of their language, culture, and history. And this posed a major challenge to Reza Khan's Persianization politics." Resistance to the will of the state, in the shah's view, could only be construed as criminal. "So," Asgharzadeh concludes, "he became determined to annihilate this unique lifestyle by all means possible."[24]

The shah's campaign was draconian and came with long-lasting consequences, some of them unanticipated. "The way they settled the tribes was the way of execution and annihilation, not education and reform," writes historian Homa Katouzian. And ironically, he adds, "it is precisely this approach that has sapped the strength of the Iranian society and weakened the hope of national unity."[25]

As the essential step in forging a Persianized unity, state-sponsored primary education—an unparalleled "ideological instrument" to institute and spread the Shah's programs more broadly—was established throughout Iran. In the case of Kurdistan and other non-Persian communities, left deliberately underdeveloped, "education" was about suppressing multiculturalism in all its forms by imposing a uniform and indivisible Persian identity on all Iranians.

Alireza Asgharzadeh, writing as a scholar-observer, also speaks to the impact of this program from personal experience. "I completed my primary and secondary education in a schooling system where I was not allowed to read, write, and even speak my own mother tongue," he writes. "The education system in Iran promoted and enforced a superficial sense of nationalism based on Persian language and identity. The richly multicultural, multiethnic, and multilingual character of Iranian society was explicitly denied. . . . In essence, monoculturalism and monolingualism became the official doctrine of nation-building processes in the country.

"As a result, the Iranian education system itself came to function as a huge engine for linguicide, deculturation, and assimilation,"[26] Asgharzadeh sums up. "The non-Persian communities were thus forced to witness the eradication of their native culture, language, history, and heritage on a daily basis."[27]

This mandate of a national unity of language and modernity of dress was deeply oppressive for the Kurds. The writing of Kurdish—for language is the deepest lifeblood of a culture—was forbidden by decree in 1935.[28] In the forging of a unitary Persian and modernized nationalism, traditional ethnic costume was banned as well: The face of the new national identity, "to mark its break with the ethnic and primordial past," would be three-piece suits and ties and bowler hats.[29] The ban on ethnic attire and the insistence on European dress struck a second blow at a most visible form of Kurdish pride and self-definition.

So it was that after Simko's assassination, the central government launched a period of massive repression in Kurdish-populated areas of Iran. The Kurds, with the systematic ban on their language, were no longer to write or teach their history. But from generation to generation they have transmitted the details of Reza Shah's rage against everything that symbolized Kurdish identity.

Ghassemlou did not witness those events because they were before his time, or beyond his horizon of awareness as a very young child. He'd heard about them, however, and used to recount the story of the gendarme who berated a Sufi holy man who refused to change his Kurdish clothes for Western ones. "They were on the Oshnavieh Bridge. Furious, the gendarme slashed the Sufi's pants. The Sufi was humiliated and retaliated by killing the gendarme. The Sufi was imprisoned and awaited his death," said Ghassemlou. "But my father had so much influence, he was able to save the Sufi's life."[30]

His father had significant influence in young Ghassemlou's nationalist education, as did his maternal grandfather. The grandfather used to regale his young grandson with entertaining anecdotes about the ways women should be treated.

When Reza Shah was dethroned in September of 1941, Ghassemlou was ten years old. "At that age, I was already interested in politics. However, in my home there usually was no talk of politics," Ghassemlou said, "even though my father was a notable—though he was affiliated with no single party. We also never spoke about smuggling, which is a regular commercial activity in that part of the world. The fabrics people wore, for example, came from Iraq. They were brought by very thin and nice women who suddenly became very fat from wearing so many smuggled clothes around their bodies."

Ghassemlou's father knew how to read and write—an exceptional skill during that era. He insisted that his children—at least, his sons—receive an education. His daughters, however, were not included in this wish.

The family house was in the center of Urmia, a place of beauty: lush with groves, fruitful orchards and vineyards, watered by a crystal-clear river. As a newcomer there, Hélène Krulich found the city a merging place for a vibrant spectrum of nationalities and religions living side by side: "Kurds, Azerbaijanis, Armenians, Assyrians, Turkmen, Russians; Muslims, Christians, Jews, Zoroastrians,"[31] she wrote. "They had coexisted for centuries, their activities were intermingled, complementing one another, their children went to the same schools, they visited each other—and all loved their town."[32]

To get to school, young Ghassemlou had a thirty-minute walk. "I remember that when I was five years old, one winter it snowed so much that when I left home, all I could see was a narrow canyon of road before me. There was so much snow piled to the sides that it formed large white walls. I could not see anything and was afraid."

During Reza Shah's regime, while schools were government-run, education was still a costly investment. Even though tuition was free, books and uniforms and supplies were not, and time in school essentially took a child out of the family workforce. The investment was especially relevant for farming families; it was the task of children to tend the sheep, in a land where animal husbandry was the backbone of Kurdish economic life.

After six years of elementary school, his father began to demand of his youngest son that he become the best. As *Abdul Rahman*, "Servant of the Most Merciful," the boy had to live up to his name.

Ghassemlou was bright and studious. By the time he was a teenager, he could already speak several languages: Farsi in school, Turkish Azeri in the streets, Arabic in the Qur'an school, and Assyrian in the Christian house of worship where his mother took him to learn surreptitiously about her own traditional religion. In his home, he spoke Sorani, one of the Kurdish dialects spoken in Iranian Kurdistan and most of northeastern Iraq. Later on he would also learn French, Russian, Czech, and English. He would also become familiar with German and Slovenian.

The remote mountain fastnesses of Kurdistan would not remain untouched by larger geopolitical realities. In 1941, as World War II expanded into the Middle East, young Ghassemlou witnessed the arrival of the Soviet troops that would occupy the northwestern part of Kurdistan. "My first impression came in the town of Balalish, ten kilometers along the road in the Ghassemlou Valley that leads to Urmia. The Soviet troops were all in the valley. I think it was August twenty-fifth. The allies were arriving; the British were coming from the south, and the Soviets from the north. I went with a friend to Balalish, where the Soviets had already stationed their tanks.

"During World War I, the Russian occupation had been bloody, and the memory of those horrors provoked fear and mistrust among the Kurds. That is why the Kurdish people were all getting ready to flee to Iraq.

"But this time, the Soviet soldiers were smiling. They gave us chocolate and distributed pamphlets in Farsi, Azeri, and Kurdish that read: 'Do not fear. We are friends.' It was the first time that I saw something actually written in Kurdish. The pamphlets fell from the airplanes overhead."[33]

❧

The presence of foreign forces there was not surprising. Given its wealth and strategic position, Iran had always been a target for foreign powers. In 1907, Great Britain and Russia had signed a treaty that divided the country into three sectors: in the north, a large area under Russian influence; a smaller area in the south under British influence; and between them a neutral zone that included Tehran. One year later, Iran's value as a nation on the international level took an upward turn when the British extracted oil from their area of influence.

In 1941, as the Allies' battle against Nazi Germany ratcheted up, Iranian territory became a conduit for the United States and the Western bloc to supply weapons to their Soviet ally. The deployment of Allied forces there also served to protect the oil fields from the rapacity of the Nazi armies. Reza Shah, who in his own project to unify Iran under an "Aryan" Persian identity had sympathy toward Nazi Germany and its racist ideology, had established a strategic bridge between German and Japanese forces. The Allies moved to neutralize German influence by removing Reza Shah from power and replacing him with his son, Reza Pahlavi.[34] Retreating before the Soviet incursion, the Iranian army fell back toward the south, and its weapons and munitions fell into the hands of the Kurds.

Twenty-eight thousand English-speaking soldiers—the majority dedicated to furnishing weapons to the Russian front—now occupied the country.[35] The foreigners installed their own advisors in departments of government. They controlled the economy, the army, the police, even the Office of Transportation.

In the region around the city of Mahabad, in the uncontested area between the British forces in the south and the Russians in the north that would prevail for the duration of the war,[36] the Kurds were essentially left to their own devices to direct their own affairs.[37] American intelligence officer Archie Roosevelt, Jr., visiting Mahabad during his 1946 tenure in Tehran, would note: "It was in the large area between the British and Soviet forces, in the vacuum left by the fleeing Iranians, that the Kurds were able to regain their autonomy."[38]

As in earlier moments of its long history, once again Iran had become the focus for the clash of great powers. Within its boundaries, Iran embraces immense diversity: the most arid deserts, mountains with perpetual snows, vast plains, and the endless coasts of the Persian Gulf and Caspian Sea. For thousands of years, it has stretched out along the caravan route that joins Europe and the Mediterranean with the East. Alexander the Great passed through this territory pursuing the Achaemenid king Darius III, as did Genghis Khan's Mongols, Tamerlane's Turks, and seventh-century Arab armies. These later military campaigns brought Islam to the country. Yet so deeply rooted was Iranian civilization—the Kurds, especially, offered fierce resistance to the Arab invasion and Islamization—that the conquerors did not make Iran an Arab country, or even an exclusively Islamic one. Military activity did ultimately unite religious belief within and across its borders, but did not level its ethnic diversity. Persians, Kurds, Azeris, and Arabs have continued to coexist as distinct cultures.

The caravan route sought after by the European Crusaders was the trail that Marco Polo followed on his way to China. It was not an easy road, but a challenging journey filled with danger. Mid-nineteenth-century Iran, with its vast expanse, had little in the way of infrastructure; for a traveler there was a journey of fifty-two days, seven hundred jolting miles on donkey back, from Bushehr on the Persian Gulf to Tehran.[39]

The European powers of the day—England, France, and Russia—did not hesitate to launch themselves in the region. In 1798, the English gained the first concession to trade with Persian tobacco. Over half a century later, Jamaluddin Al Afghani, traveler and intellectual, found Great Britain and Russia fighting like two vultures for "the dead body of Persia."[40]

In 1886 the Belgians constructed the first railroad there: ten miles of track between Tehran and Rey, to appease the monarch. In 1911 a second railroad, financed by the Bank of Russia, laid down eighty-eight miles of track to link Tabriz, the city of tapestries and carpets, with Jolfa, along the Armenian border. In 1925 Reza Shah constructed a railroad that joined Bandar-e-Shapur, on the Persian Gulf, with Gorgan on the Caspian Sea. Nine hundred miles of railroads now cut across the enormous territory from north to south. This iron trail that crossed deserts and mountain chains and joined two seas would be the route the Allies would use during World War II to supply the Soviet Union.

Tehran itself, still a relative *parvenu* in promotion to the seat of government, remained unmarked by grandeur or any outward sign of the supremacy it would assume. Even into the early twentieth century, notes one Iranian writer, "Tehran was really an overgrown version of the remote, disease-ridden village it had been in the eighteenth century, when the first Qajar shah decided to make it his dynasty's capital." By the 1930s, despite its massive growth, the city was still for the most part "a sprawling mud-brick town of mazy, crooked streets too narrow for any traffic but wagon, mules and camels."[41]

The power and presence of the foreign empires in Persia was such that upon arriving in Tehran, a city composed of simple adobe buildings without the historic splendor of a Shiraz or Isfahan,[42] travelers would mistake the British embassy for the imperial palace.

మ

At its outset in 1941, the Soviet occupation of northern Iran was flexible and careful. Fearing a Kurdish alliance with agents of the Axis based in Turkey, the Soviets established relationships with prominent Kurds, seeking to make inroads and gain influence with the goal of expanding Soviet ideology. Courting both tribal leaders and notable members of the traditional urban educated class—among them Mahabad's well-respected judge Qazi Mohammad—the Russians permitted the return of tribal chiefs who had been driven into exile in Iraq by Reza Shah.[43] In the zero-sum struggle to recoup their earlier hegemony, returning chieftains and aghas jockeyed to slot themselves into niches within the larger Iranian political structure that would bolster their reclaimed authority.[44]

Amidst growing urbanization and the emerging nationalist and social ferment among young, educated urban Kurds, the tribal chiefs remained dynamic players. "The chiefs were still a fact of life," notes historian David McDowall, "with their own political agenda to be played within the tribe, within the wider context of town and countryside and between the external powers, Tehran, the Soviet Union and the British."[45] Internecine and intertribal rivalries, compounded by continually shifting tribal alliances with the Iranian state, wreaked a havoc among the Kurds nearly equal to that inflicted by Tehran's deliberate oppression. "It was inevitable," then, one historian has noted, "that in the Soviet zone, or more particularly on its fringes, Kurdish leaders weighed up carefully the balance of benefit between the Soviet administration and Tehran."[46]

Beyond support for the Allied front, Soviet concerns in Iran were to buffer its own long border with Kurdistan and to safeguard access to Iranian oil. For the Kurds—tribal chiefs and emerging nationalist leaders alike—Allied intervention seemed the opportunity to press for Kurdish autonomy. Initial overtures to the British fell on deaf ears; mindful of stirring Arab resentment and inflaming Arab nationalist aspirations, Britain could not afford to show support for the Kurds.[47]

The Soviets were not so hampered. While early on they were "evidently unprepared for active work among the Kurds," reported military attaché and eyewitness Archie Roosevelt, the Soviets came to realize "the potentialities of the situation. The year 1944 saw Azerbaijan and Kurdistan filled with Soviet political officers and other agents, mostly Moslems from Soviet Azerbaijan."[48] As competition heated up between tribal leaders returning to reclaim their former hegemony among the towns of the valleys and plains and once more levying a tax of passage in the zones they controlled, the Soviets moved to put an end to the reigning chaos, especially in the region of Urmia.[49]

ॐ

Toward the end of 1941, perhaps to preempt rumored British plans to meet with Kurdish principals, Soviet authorities invited thirty distinguished

Kurdish leaders to visit the Azeri Soviet city of Baku. Among those attending, representing Mahabad, was Qazi Mohammad—himself a judge, and member of a prestigious family of religious judges.[50] The Kurdish leaders asked of the Soviets that the Kurds be allowed to keep the weapons they had taken before and after the war. The Soviet response was ambiguous. No concrete assurances were made, but the meeting, with its intimation of Soviet support, may have swelled the momentum of the movement for Kurdish nationalism.[51]

Ghassemlou remembered particularly well that first visit to the city of Baku because his father was part of the Kurdish delegation. "He returned with a hunting rifle, a bag of sweets for me, and a lot of sugar, which was then very scarce. 'Father, you said you were going to the USSR to recover Kurdish rights, and you only come back with a gun and sweets,' I rebuked him. My father looked at me and said: 'That—recovering Kurdish rights—will also happen.'"[52]

Given the relative freedom from Iranian and Western political interference in Mahabad generated by wartime conditions and the Soviet presence, in September 1942 a small group of young educated urban nationalists created the first Kurdish political organization, Komalay Jiyanaway Kurdistan (Society for the Revival of Kurdistan).[53] Their objectives were strictly nationalistic, with a clear orientation toward social reform together with claims for the recognition of Kurdish identity, and their new party "marked the advent of modern nationalist thought and practice in Iranian Kurdistan."[54] Only Kurds were allowed as members, whether they were Shi'ite, Sunni, or Assyrian Christian.

Komalay Jiyanaway Kurdistan, popularly known as Komala, grew so fast in the cities and the countryside that it had to organize itself and establish a political program. Initially set up covertly in underground cells, the party reached out across Iran's borders to Kurds in Turkey, Iraq, and Soviet areas.[55] Close to home in the region around Mahabad, it even attracted interest among the aghas who, despite its reformist leanings, saw it as the standard-bearer for independence from Tehran. "This did not imply solid support," however, McDowall has cautioned; "The chiefs were notorious for their mercurial politics."[56] In any case, burgeoning membership soon made the party an open secret; in the broad daylight of widespread public recognition, its clandestine cell structure simply dissolved. It needed protective coloration, a safe venue in which to meet openly without drawing suspicious attention. And this the Soviets—concerned by now to contain and channel the "independently minded" Komala—were delighted to provide.[57]

In April 1945, Komala publicly "came out" in an event under the aegis of the Kurdistan–Soviet Cultural Relations Society,[58] an association founded by Soviet propaganda organizations.[59] The Soviets moved to consolidate their influence on Komala in its new setting by cultivating Qazi Mohammad and promoting him as party leader.[60] By this time the Soviet Union, bargaining with the Iranian government for a coveted oil concession, was pressuring Tehran by actively encouraging the formation of autonomist movements among the Azeris and the Kurds.[61] Thus encouraged, Komala sought independence, with its ultimate goal the formation of a Kurdish state encompassing all areas of Kurdistan.[62]

Komala's life would be short but significant. "It did not collapse or disintegrate," notes Abbas Vali, but at the height of its preeminence would, through further Soviet involvement, be preempted and enfolded into the PDKI in August 1945.[63]

As Komala strengthened its public presence and its nationalist rhetoric attracted broader popular acceptance in the region, the party found it must confront the realities of how authority was structured in what was still a very traditional society. "Popular religion, primordial loyalties and local tradition," it turned out, "remained indispensable to political legitimacy in the unfolding nationalist political process."[64] Komala had begun as a movement among urban progressives; but now, in the process of expansion and gathering widespread mass support, its leadership realized that it needed to abandon its "parochial organizational structure"[65] and pursue political legitimacy through linkages with the traditional holders of power in agrarian Kurdistan.

By 1944 Komala had accordingly established relations with sectors of these traditional forces of Kurdish society—aghas, landowners, tribal chiefs, merchants, and religious leaders. These longstanding holders of political and economic power, uneasily mindful of Komala's growing popularity among the masses in the towns and cities, now "declared their commitment to the nationalist project and refrained from overt collaboration with the Iranian and military authorities."[66]

"The collaboration with the traditional forces," in Abbas Vali's analysis, "was the price paid for the development of the nationalist movement" which laid the groundwork for promoting Qazi Mohammad's leadership and the transformation of the party into the PDKI that would follow on August 16, 1945.[67]

While the new party and an autonomist movement received Soviet support, it seems clear now that Soviet intentions did not, in fact, extend to the establishment of an independent, self-standing Kurdish state. The Soviets were backing the formation of an Azeri republic in the region as they positioned themselves during the outset of the Cold War, and their intention for the Kurds was to fold them into that enterprise.

In late September 1945, summoned by the Soviet consul in Tabriz to a second meeting in Baku—this time with Mir Jafar Bagherov, president of the Azerbaijan Soviet Socialist Republic—Qazi Mohammad and his colleagues were told that Komala was "the creation and instrument of British imperialism" and were urged to dissolve Komala in favor of their newly established "democratic party."[68]

The outcome of this meeting was interpreted by some as the proposal of a fully autonomous Kurdish state with the support and backing of the Soviets.[69] As Abbas Vali has pointed out, however, what President Bagherov most likely proposed was development of the PDKI as a vehicle for administering Kurdistan "as an integral part of the Azeri autonomous state in Iran."[70]

This may not have been what members of the delegation were willing to hear or receive. Vali notes that in the absence of records of the negotiations in Baku, "existing accounts of these negotiations, for the most part, . . . tend to give unreliable if not implausible explanations."[71] He cites diplomat William Eagleton's report of an account offered by members of the Kurdish delegation ("presumably the tribal chiefs," Vali adds) which had Bagherov urging patience to the Kurds' request for help setting up a parallel Kurdish state: "Although the creation of a united Kurdish state was a general policy objective to which the Soviet Union was committed," Bagherov is said to have responded, "at present priority should be given to the Azeri case, and in the meantime, the Kurds should try to realize their aspirations in the juridico-political framework of the autonomous Azeri state in Iran."[72] A united and self-standing Kurdistan, Bagherov may have pointed out, must await "the triumph of popular forces" across the Kurdish heartland—in Turkey and Iraq, not unilaterally Iran.[73] The Kurdish delegation, Eagleton's informant went on to assert, had rebuffed Bagherov's counsel and remained adamant in their goal of a state of their own.[74]

Whatever the details of the conversations in Baku, their effect on events was clearly energizing. Back in Mahabad from this heady encounter, Qazi Mohammad convened a gathering of Kurdish leadership and in an eight-point declaration publicly announced the formation and program of the Kurdistan Democratic Party, the core of what would become the PDKI.[75] The response was enthusiastic; a manifesto signed by 105 prominent Kurds was immediately drawn up declaring the desire of the Kurdish people "to take advantage of the liberation of the world from Fascism and to share in the promises of the Atlantic Charter."[76]

The eight points of the declaration, reiterated as the party's aims in the manifesto, called for the recognition and use of the Kurdish language in administration and education; for local elections and local oversight of both "state and social matters"; for the appointment or employment of local persons in state offices within the region; and for a single set of laws for "both peasants and notables."[77] The document declared the party's commitment to striving toward "unity and complete fraternity . . . in their struggle" with the Azerbaijani, Assyrian, Armenian, and other peoples of Azerbaijan,[78] and to bettering "the moral and economic state of the Kurdish people" through improvements in resource development, agriculture, commercial economy, public health and hygiene, and education. "We desire," declared the manifesto, "that the people living in Iran be able to strive freely for the happiness and progress of their country."[79]

The manifesto demanded that Tehran, under and within Iran's existing constitutional provisions, allow Kurdistan administrative self-governance with its own provincial council, and proclaimed the newly formed Kurdistan Democratic Party "the party which will be able to secure its national independence within the borders of Persia."[80] Whatever the disparate initial concepts of what "nationalism" or "independence" entailed for the Kurds, at this moment in time it appears that all the actors had in mind a federal system of republics within Iran, along the lines of the Soviet model. Komala was formally dissolved, and all its members were incorporated into the new party.[81]

The new party brought together in a tentative alliance "traditionalist" leadership with the influence of growing educated or intellectual elites in urban settings.[82] Tribal support, however, was unreliable. It was reinforcements from an unexpected quarter at this critical transition that bolstered the party and Qazi Mohammad's leadership: the arrival of Mulla Mustafa Barzani in October 1945, fleeing persecution from Iraq, with about one thousand fighting men. The Soviets brokered the arrangement, instructing the Barzanis to place themselves under Qazi Mohammad's direction and ordering the Iranian Kurds to accommodate the refugee Barzanis.[83]

From the outset, tribal chiefs remained "wary" of the new party for its links with the Soviets.[84] The end of World War II heralded significant geopolitical shifts; there can be no doubt that the Soviet promotion of the Azerbaijan People's Republic now aimed to draw the region into line with broader policies that embodied a growing hegemonic intention. By summer 1945, the Soviets were, in the observation of attaché Archie Roosevelt, clearly "considering a new and ambitious plan—the attachment of northwestern Iran to the Soviet Union."[85]

But though midwifed by Soviet maneuvers, the fledgling party—and the newfound polity that it would bring into brief existence—quickly expanded beyond all bounds of what the Soviets had apparently intended. Within a very few months, the Soviet response to the announcement of the Kurdistan Republic would plainly demonstrate that as far as the Soviets were concerned, the party "was never intended as a party representing popular nationalist demand for an autonomous Kurdish government based in Mahabad."[86] Soviet and Azeri opposition to the Kurdish drive for autonomy, notes Abbas Vali, was apparently "the official stance agreed upon" sometime between the September visit of the Kurdish delegation and the November establishment of the Azeri Democratic Republic.[87]

The Kurds would see this for themselves soon enough at the November 12, 1945 opening of the Azerbaijan National Assembly in Tabriz.[88] Qazi Moham-mad had sent five members of the PDKI as delegates to participate. But they were not only poorly received but "discovered they had joined the Assembly 'not as representatives of a separate Kurdistan, but merely as deputies from specific constituencies, like all others'. They soon became aware that under the new dispensations Kurdistan was to have merely a town council inferior to the provincial council of Azerbaijan. The Kurds proclaimed their dissatisfaction in Mahabad."[89] In reaction, PDKI leadership would experience a division between moderate elements (Qazi Mohammad among them) willing to accept the proposal of integration with Azeri governance and more radical elements who in defiance would declare an autonomous Kurdish republic. Over the next month, amid ensuing maneuvers, decisions, and events, and with significant popular support, the radicals would apparently take the day.

Ultimately, neither the party nor the republic would be a Soviet puppet, but would maintain a commitment to self-determination, cultural integrity, and human rights within a constitutional framework. While mistrusted by tribal leaders for its Soviet connections and its proposals for social reform, the party would always maintain broader appeal among the people. From its birth, the PDKI—from its inception as PDK through its transition as PDK (Iran)—has remained the only large Iranian Kurdish political organization. It has had its ups and downs, owing to its mostly clandestine existence under the duress of various regimes. Born as a nationalist progressive and secular party, the PDKI would soon enough find itself forced to take up arms to defend Kurdistan.

∾

As eager as it was to shake off Iranian oppression, the young Kurdistan Democratic Party would before long find itself embroiled in political struggles with its Azeri counterpart. When Iranian Azerbaijan inaugurated the Azerbaijan National Assembly in November 1945, it became clear, from the earliest parliamentary sessions, that no recognition would be extended to Kurdistan as a politically sovereign entity.[90] No sooner had Qazi Mohammad declared the desire for an autonomous Kurdish state than he was summarily advised by Tabriz that he could form a government in Mahabad only under the "guidance" of the Democratic Party of Azerbaijan.[91]

On December 10, 1945, a month after the inauguration of the Azerbaijan National Assembly, the Iranian Azeris, with the support of the Soviets, took military and civil power in the province of Azerbaijan[92] and proclaimed their full autonomy. They were led by Jafar Pishevari,[93] who headed Firqah-i Dimukrat, the Azerbaijan Democratic Party. The eastern half of Iranian Azerbaijan was now under the rule of the newly constituted Azerbaijan People's Government.

The Kurds by now needed little encouragement to quickly follow suit: just a week later on December 17, despite the misgivings of the party moderates and in defiance of both Soviet and Azeri opposition,[94] Kurdish autonomy was declared in Mahabad, formalizing the independence which had existed *de facto* for some time.[95] The nationalist direction of the party, perhaps to the surprise of Qazi Mohammad and the moderates, was acclaimed by the populace: crowds of people came out in support, and the new Kurdish flag was raised on the roof of an Iranian government building, the Department of Justice.[96]

The unexpected vigor of the people's approval, amounting to a democratic mandate, may have convinced Qazi Mohammad that the Soviets and Azeris, served with a *fait accompli*, would accept a Kurdish republic.[97] On January 22, 1946, a large crowd gathered in Chwar Chira, Mahabad's central square. The streets of the city were lined with the colors of the Kurdish flag—red, white, and green. Along with Kurdish tribal leaders, members of the PDKI were present, dressed in Western clothes with turbans on their heads. Qazi Mohammad stepped onto the platform, and in a speech of less than fifteen minutes, he affirmed the identity of the Kurdish people—its right to self-determination and to occupy its own lands. He proclaimed the Kurdistan Republic,[98] and publicly thanked the USSR for their material and moral support.

ॐ

The Kurdish declaration of autonomy would create tremendous tension[99] between the young republics, which were already in continuous friction over border regions claimed by them both.[100] In Kurdistan's dealings with its sibling Azeri republic, as in its relationship with the central Iranian state, critical Soviet intervention would again come into play: "It was only the Soviet support he [Qazi Mohammad] enjoyed," notes historian David McDowall, "which persuaded the Azarbaijanis to tolerate a Kurdish administration independent of Tabriz."[101]

In truth the acceptance by the Soviets of the Kurdish Republic was calculated to allow them to continue to influence the PDKI leadership to "agree to the Azeri plan, that they [the Kurds] should become part of the Azeri Republic."[102] The Soviets convinced the Kurds, in February 1946, that they would support and defend them by providing them "small firearms and ammunition."[103]

In April 1946, urged and even pressured[104] by the Soviets to resolve Kurdish/Azeri differences so as to present a united front to Tehran, Qazi Mohammad negotiated a treaty between Mahabad and Tabriz providing for "mutual military assistance" and for "negotiations with Tehran to be in 'the joint interest' of the two administrations."[105] In its details and language, however, this agreement essentially marginalized the Kurds in submission to the Azeri government. Taking the lead and co-opting representation of the Kurds in negotiations for autonomy with Tehran, Pishevari commenced parleys with the central regime on April 28.

The Soviet maneuvers had rendered the Kurds a "bargaining chip in the political haggling" with the Iranian government. The treaty, with no mention of Kurdish demands for autonomy, defined them as "the Kurds living in Azerbaijan" and essentially stripped them of their national identity.[106]

This talk of treaties and mutual assistance, however, as far as Iran was concerned, "smacked of complete independence" from the central state.[107] It raised an alarm in Tehran which, together with the edgy ambiguity always at play in Kurdistan's self-definition—was Kurdistan an autonomous region, or an independent nation?—would be sure to have consequences.[108]

Notwithstanding its link-up with the USSR, the Kurdish nationalist movement as exemplified by the PDKI was taking on an unambiguously democratic flavor. The party's program reflected genuine widespread aspirations among the Kurdish people and naturally attracted broad-based support. In an interview with Agence France Presse, Qazi Mohammad evoked the history of the Kurdish people as marked again and again by the struggle for freedom—a project unsuccessful even after the 1919 Treaty of Versailles, which had affirmed the creation of a Kurdish state. "If today we are requesting, with much insistence, the partial autonomy of our country," he said, "the fault is due to the central government, which has done nothing for our rehabilitation. We are anxious to enter the path of progress. We aim to imitate neither the Americans nor the Soviets, but we refuse to live as beasts of burden to the 'civilized' countries."[109]

"Never did Qazi Mohammad express more clearly, publicly, his ideological affinity," comments journalist Chris Kutschera of Qazi's statement. "This independence of spirit, this willingness to not be inducted by anyone explains perhaps why Qazi Mohammad was rejected by the West, which saw in him a 'road companion' [fellow traveler] of the Soviets."[110]

Even while Qazi Mohammad accepted Soviet tutelage, he was firm in his nationalist goals. "Ideologically," his cousin Rahim Qazi said of him, "Qazi Mohammad was neither Marxist nor socialist nor liberal. He was the intelligent leader of a national liberation movement; he was a nationalist leader with an open mind, *esprit*."[111] In an interview published in the local Mahabad semiweekly *Kurdistan* in January 1946, Qazi was asked: "In Tehran, they say that you have sent some people to Baku [in Soviet Azerbaijan]. . . . Is it true that you formed a Communist Party?" Qazi replied: "These stories are fabricated by the military authorities and are not true. . . . The formation of a Communist Party is a lie. Here in Kurdistan, and according to the constitution of Iran, people have full freedom of their opinions. We have an open party, which is the Kurdistan Democratic Party."[112] Regarding the republic's support from the Soviets, he was very straightforward: "The Kurds are compelled to accept help from anyone who will give it," he summed up, "but will not accept domination by anyone."[113]

Nevertheless, not only from its very inception but throughout its short existence, the Democratic Republic of Kurdistan depended on Soviet support; only with the backing of the Red Army did it have a chance.[114]

According to agreements with Tehran, however, the Soviet troops were due to leave Iran by six months following the war's end.[115] The Soviets managed to delay this draw-down for months while they pressed Tehran for an oil concession in the northern provinces. In anticipation of the USSR's pull-out, however, Tehran began to mass its military for more vigorous action. Because Russian withdrawal would leave the Kurds vulnerable to Iranian forces, the Kurds' continuing need for Soviet assistance would soon show itself to be a core problem of the People's Democratic Republic of Kurdistan.[116]

Yet the fact remains that even without the appearance of a Kurdish alignment with the Soviets, the West would not have offered support to the young republic. Qazi Mohammad had reached out to Britain and the United States to no avail; British and American administrations maintained their existing alliance with Iran. A CIA report of 1948 confirmed Qazi's efforts to glean U.S. and British support and his turn to the USSR in the absence of a response from the West: "Although Kurdish nationalists have shown, through their many appeals to international bodies, that they feel outside support to be necessary," the report noted, "the USSR alone has taken an active interest in the Kurds, and then only after long neglect."[117]

Ultimately, regardless of either the appearance or the reality of Mahabad's relationship with the USSR, the Kurds were isolated, denied an alliance with or support from the West. And ultimately the Soviets, too, would drop their support.

∽

As a boy of fourteen, somewhere on the sidelines of these unfolding events and developing his own personal fascination with the Soviets, Ghassemlou was then a student in school. "I read a great deal," he recalled; "newspapers, books, and even papers I would find in the streets. While others took a nap, I used the time to read."[118]

The Russian presence was pervasive, even in the schoolroom. Ghassemlou cited the example of an encounter with a teacher of literature and Persian who was very unpleasant: "He used to call us stupid idiots." The teacher assigned the class an essay and the only one that met his approval was an anti-Soviet example. "He used to tell us that the Bolsheviks picked up kids and put them in a hole," said Ghassemlou. "When they were so hungry that they begged for food in the name of Allah, the children would not get any. But if they asked for food in Stalin's name, they would be fed."

Ghassemlou received an award for one of the essays he wrote. He had submitted his paper to the school principal, who also taught classes at the school.

The prize for his essay was a book. As he recalled it, it was "a book on Lenin written by a Westerner, called *The Greatest Revolutionary of All Times*."[119]

The young student never understood why they gave him this book. The fact is, however, that it had an enormous influence upon him and awakened his curiosity for all things Soviet. This was his first intellectual contact with the Soviet revolution, though not with the Russians themselves. Among visitors to the Ghassemlou home were many distinguished Soviet officials based in the north of Iran. Kharkharov was one who came by often.

Kharkharov, the Soviet political commissioner for Urmia, was an expert on the northern Kurds, especially on the Shikak tribe. Kharkharov was of Kurdish background himself and used to often visit the home of old Ghassemlou.[120] There he would have meals and play chess. He also brought young Abdul Rahman books, in Farsi and Azeri, about the Soviet Union. Contact with the Russian satisfied Ghassemlou's curiosity.

Though the PDKI had a style of internal organization similar to that of Communist parties in other developing areas it had no doctrinaire political direction. In any case in those times, Hélène Krulich has noted in her recent memoir, "fighters for liberty considered Communism as a synonym for democracy."[121] A youth section was created, and while this was subject to the discipline of the party's central committee, it maintained its own identity. Its militant fervor soon outstripped that of the mother organization.

Before long, the PDKI began to set up youth sections in cities across Kurdistan. By early 1946, Ghassemlou had become a member of the youth section in Urmia and headed the local group there. He kept his political involvement a secret until his brother found out. "It was spring. My older brother and I shared a bedroom. He found my member badge for the PDKI youth section and threatened to tell my father if I did not obey him. When I refused, he reported me."

When his father found out, he gave young Ghassemlou one piece of advice: "Since you have made the choice," he told his son, "all I can say is that you must do well whatever you decide to do and never stray from the path you have chosen."[122]

❧

Mohammed Woussouq-e Divan traveled to Mahabad for the public announcement of the republic, but did not bring young Abdul Rahman with him. This was something Ghassemlou always regretted.

Jalil Gadani, who would be a member of the future leadership of the PDKI, was then thirteen years old. He remembered, "For the first time, we had some liberty. We occupied the government garrison and divided the weapons among everyone. I was a schoolboy, but since I was a curious child and my father a Kurdish patriot, I followed these events very closely.

"One year later, we clandestinely created a section in school to learn Kurdish; in Reza Shah's time, it was forbidden to teach our language. My Kurdish teacher invited us to attend patriotic ceremonies. I remember that before the fall of the Iranian government in Mahabad, I went to the public baths with my mother. A policeman named Mamadali came toward her and tore her dress off. I asked her why he had done this, and she explained that the Kurds were not allowed to wear their traditional dress. It was forbidden."[123]

For the present, though, Mahabad was thriving, and under the rule of the PDKI and Qazi Mohammad, observers found the Kurdistan Republic to be "a going concern."[124] Qazi himself drew admiration from Western visitors as he did from many among his own people, impressive as "a man of deep convictions, backed with a rare courage and self-sacrifice . . . tempered with broad-mindedness and moderation."[125]

Thanks to his father, Ghassemlou met Qazi Mohammad. Young Ghassemlou was already an enthusiastic Kurdish nationalist and had resolved to work in Urmia with the representatives of the republic. But there was one man with whom Ghassemlou did not get along, and he decided to write and complain about him to President Qazi Mohammad. According to Ghassemlou, the president was impressed by his letter and remarked to the director of his school that boys like him made him feel optimistic about Kurdish youth.

The Democratic Republic of Kurdistan existed in a state of liberty unknown until then in the region. Archie Roosevelt, visiting the city from Tehran in his capacity as American military attaché, confirmed this. He was surprised by the atmosphere in Mahabad, in great contrast to the rigidity of neighboring Soviet Communist Azerbaijan.[126] "By the conclusion of my visit," he would later write, "I was convinced that Qazi Mohammad had managed, with Soviet help, to set up a virtually independent Kurdish republic. Although he looked on the Soviet Union as his best friend, the Soviets were not visibly interfering in the internal affairs of Kurdistan."[127]

Freedom of expression and the absence of political persecution were reflected in many publications, among them the journal *Kurdistan*. Although the press glorified Soviet leaders, it did not promote Communist propaganda.

Unlike the oppressive diktats of Tabriz, Mahabad undertook no doctrinaire "revolutionary decrees": no bank nationalizations, no forcible land reform or redistribution. People could come and go as they pleased, listen freely to foreign radio broadcasts.[128] The Kurdish language was declared official and was used in schools and in public administration. Women participated for the first time in sociopolitical life through the newly formed women's section of the party. The economy also grew, through commerce with the USSR and regular tax collection and donations to the party by tribal leaders. Trade was flourishing with contraband products from Iraq.

But the alignment with the Soviet Union would soon prove a liability. With the rising fear of Communism as the Cold War took shape in the postwar world, the republic would find itself closed off from longer-term protective alliances with the West.[129] Despite Kurdish overtures to the U.S. and Britain, the West continued to see the Azerbaijan and Kurdish enclaves as Soviet satellites—or, at the very least, as tempting openings to Soviet expansionism.[130] Contemporary pronouncements in the Western press painted the Kurds as rebels, insurgents, and unwitting tools of the Soviets. "There is little chance that any strong backing for an independent Kurdistan will be found in the United Nations," reported *Foreign Affairs* in the summer of 1946. "If it should be established, it would offer no promise of internal stability or permanence. . . . [T]he Kurdish movement . . . is the most dangerous of all the troubles which now beset the Middle East—because of the support which it has from Soviet Russia. . . . Grievances, ammunition and a fighting people— this is the explosive combination with which the Soviet Union is playing the hoary tsarist game of expansion."[131] From the Western powers, there would be no support to the fledgling republics; when the time came, the West would side with its established ally, Iran. In fact, it can be said that the fate of the young republics became a casualty of the opening volleys of the Cold War.[132]

It was only after Iran's petition to the United Nations and repeated demands on the part of the Western powers[133] that the Soviets, on March 26, 1946, announced a promise to withdraw within six weeks. They continued to stall until Tehran agreed "to form a joint Soviet-Iranian oil company, subject to ratification by the Majlis,"[134] but finally withdrew in May 1946.[135] Materiel and assistance allegedly promised to the Kurds in the form of planes, tanks, heavy weapons, and military training never materialized.[136]

Without Soviet backing, Mahabad's only recourse was a plea for support from the tribes—"a formidable but divided force consisting principally of the Barzanis,"[137] but also including the myriad smaller Kurdish tribal groups in the region. But with anti-Soviet sentiment strong among tribal leaders, Qazi Mohammad's appeals to rally support met with no success and his autonomist government found itself virtually without defenders.[138]

Recognizing full well that the Kurdish and Azerbaijani republics would never survive Soviet withdrawal, Soviet advisors now urged both the splinter republics to negotiate a settlement with Tehran.[139] To protect itself and its gains, Tabriz moved quickly to an agreement in June 1946 by which all Azerbaijan, including Kurdish areas, "formally reverted to Iranian sovereignty." By the terms of the agreement with Tehran, Azeri government ministers managed to transmute their status into that of provincial administrators, keeping their power and position. The immediate outcome was that the Azerbaijanis "legalized their position and avoided Iranian reprisals, but left Mahabad isolated as a rebel enclave *within* the province of Azarbaijan, in disregard of their agreement with the Kurdish Republic."[140]

❧

Events were moving quickly now. In August, Qazi Mohammad traveled to Tehran to negotiate with Iranian prime minister Ahmad Qavam, widely regarded as a political moderate, to establish Kurdistan too as an autonomous province. The Kurds hoped for success. But with hindsight it seems clear that Qavam, who would dupe the Soviets by finding a way to renege on the oil concession agreement, had now also duped both the Azeris and the Kurds. As a CIA report would see the situation in 1948, "Prime Minister Qavam hastened the disintegration of the Kurdish state by promising the Kurds favorable treatment if they cooperated with his efforts to re-establish the central government's authority."[141] Qavam's talks with the Kurds almost certainly were meant to buy time, a strategy well used in Persian politics both past and future, while readying the Iranian army to strike Mahabad and Tabriz.

The same 1948 CIA report, speaking from the point of view of U.S. objectives in the Middle East, goes on to describe the Kurds and "the Kurdish question," "manipulated by the Soviet agitation," as "a disruptive force which will continue to threaten, sporadically, the delicate balance of the present Near East state system." In retrospect, aspects of the CIA's analysis would be remarkably clear-sighted about the formidable challenge posed to the Kurds by the centralist regimes they would continue to face. "There is no real prospect for a settlement of the Kurdish grievances," the CIA would report. "The governments of the parent states are doing very little to improve the conditions which are the subject of Kurdish complaints, and although they may be impelled to promise the Kurds reforms, there is no indication that they will actually carry them out."[142] From the perspective of U.S. interests in the region, the Kurdish autonomist movement "would not only serve the Soviet's propaganda before the world but a Kurdish revolt could threaten to destabilize not only weak states like Iran and Iraq but the whole Middle East region."[143]

In Mahabad itself, the always "uneasy alliance" between urban nationalists and tribal forces rapidly fell to pieces: "It was inevitable," says historian David McDowall, "that the tribes should begin to abandon Mahabad from the moment the Tabriz-Tehran deal was broadcast."[144] Tribal chiefs, never wholeheartedly on the side of the Kurdish movement, were always ready to act opportunistically to preserve their privileges.

In the fall of 1946, following Soviet withdrawal and further buildup of Iranian armed forces, Shah Mohammad Reza Pahlavi, with support from the United States and Great Britain, announced plans to organize elections throughout the country. To guarantee that the elections would run smoothly, the Shah further announced, he would send troops to the rebellious northwest provinces; and Qavam, in his capacity as prime minister, authorized the movement of troops into Kurdistan and Azerbaijan.[145]

Many tribal chieftains, who since the end of the summer had already "completely deserted [the Mahabad enterprise] or negotiated their own private settlement,"[146] could see which way the political winds were blowing and were clear where their interests lay.[147] Within a week of Qavam's announcement, the tribes were actively aiding government forces in the "recapture" of Kurdistan and Azerbaijan.[148]

On December 10, 1946, the Azeri resistance collapsed. While Azeri nationalist leaders, Pishevari among them, took refuge in the USSR, the imperial army entered Azerbaijan and retook Tabriz without any opposition.

Those days in December 1946, Ghassemlou said later, profoundly affected him: "The confrontation between the Iranian army and the Azeris and Soviets lasted several days. It was very cold, and our house filled up with refugees.[149] People thought that no one would dare attack my father's house. The PDKI asked me to take a message to Kharkharov. I felt very important. I was a messenger until Tabriz fell."

On December 13, Sadr Qazi, negotiating on behalf of his brother Qazi Mohammad, advised the Iranian commander that Mahabad was prepared to receive the Iranian forces peacefully. The commander agreed to enter, with the stipulation that the Barzanis evacuate the area. On December 15, the Iranian army occupied Mahabad without any difficulty; and on December 17, a year to the day from the republic's inauguration, the formal surrender of the city and the republic swiftly followed.[150]

❧

Iraqi Kurdish leader Mulla Mustafa Barzani, driven out of Iraq, had been in Mahabad since October 1945 with a thousand of his men from the Barzani tribe.[151] In the face of the Iranian offensive, Barzani refused to surrender and decided to retreat to the USSR. On December 16 Barzani urged Qazi Moham-mad to flee with him to the Iraqi border, but the president and his collabora-tors resolved to stay in Kurdistan.[152] Qazi Mohammad raised no objections to others' fleeing, but quietly confirmed his commitment to remaining with the people "whom he had sworn to protect."[153] Resistance was clearly futile and never contemplated.[154]

The next day Qazi Mohammad and his collaborators were seized. Within months they would be tried by a military tribunal and condemned to death. Barzani and his men, for their part, made it across the border to Iraq. In his epic retreat, Barzani fought his way through Iraq, relentlessly pursued by Ira-nian forces, and then continued his flight, crossing through Turkey and dou-bling back across northern Iran into the USSR. Battling all the way, he and 493 men covered 220 miles across the Zagros Mountains.[155]

Ghassemlou remembered well the resistance of General Barzani: "Barzani was the only one who resisted. When he was retreating with his men, they passed near our home. I discovered this because I was listening to the radio. Sud-denly there was interference, and over the radio I heard officers from the Iranian army talking among themselves. They knew Barzani was somewhere nearby. So I sent a message to Barzani. I felt great admiration for him, as did my father."

Qazi Mohammad, his brother Sadr Qazi—then minister of war—and his cousin Seif Qazi were hanged "in secrecy and with maximum security" at dawn on March 31, 1947, in the Chwar Chira square. Their demise was witnessed only by those who executed them; but householders in the neighborhood of the square recalled hearing "the sound of troubled voices" in the darkness of the early hours.[156] For a full day, to serve as an object lesson, their bodies were left hanging, forlorn and ignominious, in the public square.[157]

"I will never forget those times," said Jalil Gadani. "The fall of the repub-lic hit me hard. I could not understand why those leaders had been executed.

I saw their bodies hanging in that same square where they had declared the republic. It was a public [display of their] execution. The Kurdish people gathered around the square and demanded that the bodies be given back to them. We [the Kurds] would never forget Qazi Mohammad's legacy."[158]

Ghassemlou himself was in his final year of boarding school, in Tehran, when Mahabad fell. He later shared his experience with Hélène. "For Abdol Rahman," Hélène writes, looking back, "the events only confirmed the validity of Marx's and Lenin's ideas." The upshot, she adds, was a conviction that expressed itself in action: in defiance of "the strict regulations of the boarding school" Ghassemlou, "as a member of the Communist Youth Organization, engaged himself in the resistance movement against the Pahlavi regime."[159]

The egregious executions of the young republic's leaders strongly impacted the populace, and within the year clandestine resistance had begun.

و

The Democratic Republic of Kurdistan had fallen. "Within a few days," reported journalist Chris Kutschera, "all traces of the existence of the Kurdish Republic of Mahabad were wiped out: those who participated in the movement hurried to 'disappear' compromising documents—photos, newspapers, flags—while the [Iranian] government prohibited the teaching of Kurdish, and soldiers burned Kurdish books in Mahabad's squares."[160] The people were persecuted and repressed. Killings began to mount in every city of Kurdistan. "Every night the army would kill fifty or sixty democrats," Ghassemlou said. "My father became furious."

His father's anger at times lent him a startling fearlessness. There was, for instance, his encounter with General Zanganeh. The general, Ghassemlou recounted, "was a Kurdish man from Kermanshah who was a friend of my father. He had fought against the democrats in Urmia. One night a petty officer came to our house. We did not like soldiers; we considered them an occupying force. My father, who was in his seventies at this time, asked him what he wanted.

"'My general, Zanganeh, has sent me, and you are to come with me immediately,' he said.

"'I will not go,' my father answered firmly. 'If Zanganeh needs me, he can come to my house.'

"'The general will be angry,' answered the petty officer, taken aback.

"'I have the balls . . . ,' my father swore. 'If Zanganeh wants, he can come and take my dollars.'[161]

"The petty officer finally left in total silence. Soon afterward an officer my father knew came and said, 'The petty officer told me that you insulted the general.'

"'Tell me what he told you,' my father responded. It turned out that the soldier had assumed his swearing was an insult. '[No, it's just that] I'm an old man and I don't want to go,' my father explained.

"The officer showed him a letter written in Kurdish and asked that he read it. It was a letter from Sheikh Ahmed Barzani to the general announcing the following: four Kurdish officers who had given themselves to the military authorities with the guarantee that they would receive amnesty had been executed. Barzani said it was not his fault but their fault because they did not belong to the Barzani tribe.

"I did not like that comment," said Ghassemlou. "It was very tribal.

"The letter also mentioned," Ghassemlou added, "that [Sheikh Ahmed] Barzani had captured the son of a prominent Iranian general, and he was willing to free him."

Ghassemlou's apprehensions about narrow tribal allegiances, as exemplified by Barzani's comment, would continue to loom large. He was clear-sighted about the dangers of such attitudes in the struggle for Kurdish nationalism. From the beginning, the Democratic Republic of Kurdistan was weakened by the division among the Kurds and their lack of unity. There were tensions between the tribal chiefs and the urban Kurds and within the Kurdish leadership itself. The Barzanis, for instance, had been "by no means universally welcomed," notes historian David McDowall. "The very fact that they provided the Republic with its most credible fighting force disturbed the world of tribal politics."[162] There was also the heavy weight laid on the local economy by the presence of the Barzanis. "The Kurdish tribesmen depended largely on their tobacco crop for their livelihood," noted Archie Roosevelt, "and now that their market in the rest of Iran was cut off they suffered considerable hardship. In certain areas food supplies already strained had to be shared with the destitute Barzanis, who had long outworn their welcome."[163]

In the same way that many among the tribal chieftains had countenanced the republic's alliance by necessity with the Soviet Union, now in the face of economic distress, the end of Soviet support, and the shifting balance of power, many decided to strike a deal with Tehran. Many of the tribal chiefs harbored misgivings about the venture, some because they saw the republic as a puppet state of the Soviet Union, others because they did not wish to burn their boats with Tehran.[164]

The tribes had rallied behind the republic as long as it offered economic and military advantages. A central dilemma of Kurdish nationalism, however, as Archie Roosevelt witnessed, was that while its leadership and its membership were recruited predominantly from among the urban and educated population, "its military strength has always had to come from the tribes and their chiefs," with a longstanding culture of resistance to government control. To Archie Roosevelt, in his visit to Mahabad, it appeared tribal leaders "felt as restive under Qazi Mohammad as they had under the Central Government."[165] Adding to this their mistrust of the Soviets and Qazi's reliance on the increasingly unreliable Soviet connections, and their sense of the shifting balance of power, the tribes would abandon Qazi and throw their support to the Iranian army.[166]

In Roosevelt's view as a sympathetic Western witness, "The principal immediate reason for the collapse of the republic was the failure of Soviet support to materialize."[167] Blame lay clearly in his estimation with the Soviets, who had manipulated "a young and strong nationalist party which might have united a majority of educated Kurds," supported it only "for their own purposes and then let it be destroyed."[168]

Ghassemlou outlined the trajectory of the ephemeral Democratic Republic of Kurdistan in very similar terms: "The Soviets allowed the fall of Mahabad. But it is also true that Mahabad did nothing to save itself. It was only later that I realized Stalin was a bastard."[169]

৵

Despite being the largest stateless nation with an ancient history dating back thousands of years, Kurdistan is yet to exist as a sovereign entity. In Iran, the Kurds are the third largest ethnic group, after Persians and Azeri Turks, among the seven ethnic groups that comprise the country. Yet centralism and systematic oppression have condemned their territory to the status of the most backward region.

Nevertheless, the territory the Kurds occupy is extensive. Their land, sprawling across what is now Iran, Iraq, Turkey, and Syria, and with enclaves in the former Soviet Union, is approximately five hundred thousand square kilometers, about the size of Spain.[170]

Sumerian textual evidence supports the Kurds' assertion of ancient origin.[171] They are Indo-European, like the Persians. In his *Anabasis* ("The March

Up-Country," recounting the desperate trek of Greek mercenaries fighting their way northward from Persia to the Black Sea), the historian Xenophon called them *Karduchoi*, and described them as descendants of the Guti and Lulubiti:[172] "They were a people . . . dwelling up on the hills, addicted to war, and not subject to the king; so much so that once, when a royal army one hundred and twenty thousand strong had invaded them, not a man came back, owing to the intricacies of the country."[173] So it is not strange that they have maintained, at least orally, memories of notable cultural connections that look back to the Medes as well as Zoroastrians.[174] Their poetry, dedicated to love and war, is well-known.

The Kurds had their opportunity when the Ottoman Empire fell after World War I. Having been dominated by Turks and Persians, the Kurds were now incorporated by the Allies—the Russian and British empires, France, the United States, and Italy—into the oil-rich province of Mosul and given an autonomous regime. This was established following World War I in the Treaty of Sèvres in 1920.

The Middle East at that time was quite different from what the map shows today. Nation-states we know today as Syria, Lebanon, Iraq, and Jordan did not exist as political entities. They were carved out by the economic and geopolitical interests of London and other colonial powers.

The promises of Sèvres vanished in 1923 after the victory of Mustafa Kemal Atatürk in Turkey. In the Treaty of Lausanne, recognizing the boundaries of Turkey as the final settlement of World War I, the European powers decided to ignore their commitments and divide the Kurds and their homeland among the states of the region. The Kurdish response was the opening broadside in a cycle of rebellions that began in Turkey and later spread to Iraq and Iran.

In 1905, the first Kurdish rebel insurgency erupted. In the 1930s, another uprising followed. In 1946, the Kurds founded the Democratic Republic of Kurdistan. In the 1970s, the guerrilla movement was reborn, and in 1979, under the leadership of Abdul Rahman Ghassemlou, the PDKI became a party of the masses with an army of several thousand peshmerga that offered a serious military challenge to the government of Tehran from their mountain strongholds.

Everywhere in their territory across the Middle East, Kurds have faced repression. In Turkey, during World War I, some nationalist Turkish leaders had come to perceive the Kurds as subversive, capable of siding with the Russians in the war. They sought to eliminate this political threat with massive

Kurdish deportation. In the years 1916 and 1917, hundreds of thousands of Kurds were forcibly displaced from their ancestral lands. A great number of those who were deported during this period perished in the process.

When, following Turkey's 1919–1922 war for independence, Atatürk proclaimed the Republic of Turkey in 1923, the Kurds at first had trusted him, given his stated progressive goals and reputation. While fixed on modernizing his country, however, Atatürk also pursued a policy of "Turkification": he crushed successive Kurdish uprisings, continued the massive displacement of the Kurdish population, and imposed martial law in Turkish Kurdistan.[175] As of 1924 all political and religious organizations, schools, and publications in Kurdish were prohibited in Turkey.

Following Atatürk's death in 1938 and the end of the era of one-party rule in 1945, Turkey's decades of economic and social unrest, political polarization, strikes, and street violence were punctuated by military coups in 1960, 1971, and 1980. Against this chaotic background, 1978 saw the formation of the PKK, Partiya Karkerên Kurdistanê, the Kurdish Workers Party. By 1984 PKK had become a guerrilla organization which mounted an insurgency on behalf of Kurds' cultural and political rights. Ongoing conflict between PKK and the Turkish government has seen the death of forty thousand people and displaced hundreds of thousands of refugees.[176]

Throughout the twentieth century, wholesale razing of Kurdish villages in Turkey and forcible dislocation of populations continued, even into the 1990s.[177] Executions of Kurds became commonplace; even children have not been spared.[178] Kurds have filled the prisons simply because they are Kurdish. As recently as 1991, Turkish law established a prison sentence of six months for speaking Kurdish. "The Turkish state," writes Turkish journalist Uzay Bulut, "which has not built a school for Kurds, has, however, built hundreds of jails in which to incarcerate them when they demand national or human rights."[179]

Essentially, in Turkey the Kurds officially do not exist. With their designation as "Mountain Turks," it is argued that "Kurdish is not a 'real' language."[180] "For decades," Bulut sums up, "that was Turkey's official policy: There are no Kurds—so there is no problem."[181]

This reality persists even into the twenty-first century. As a result of pressure from the European Union, strictures eased somewhat in 2002, and again in 2003, when the political role of the military was trimmed back by the then-moderate Islamic government of Turkish prime minister Recep Tayyip Erdoğan. Despite further openings for Kurdish language and culture in education and media broadcasting since 2008, repression against the Kurds, both cultural and political, still prevails. In fact, during the massive regional destabilizations of 2014–2015 generated by the aggressions of the self-described Islamic State, Turkey's governmental repression and conflict with both the PKK and more moderate Kurdish political voices have intensified.[182]

Between 2013 and 2015, hopes were raised that the enduring Kurdish-Turkish conflict might be heading toward a permanent resolution. These hopes were dashed in the summer of 2015 when a group from the PKK's youth wing known as the Patriotic Revolutionary Youth Movement barricaded themselves in a dozen cities and declared the cities autonomous.[183] The crackdown this prompted on the part of the Turkish government, in the words of one United Nations report, reduced thirty Kurdish towns and city centers to "vast parking lots" and "moonscapes."[184]

Across the border in Syria, right up to the eve of the civil war that broke out in 2011, one million Kurds have had no cultural rights or benefits.[185] Kurds in Syria have been displaced, their employment restricted; many have been deprived of their citizenship and denied public services. Relative to the Kurds of neighboring countries, the Kurds of Syria have always been the forgotten ones. Damascus has never acknowledged their presence. Some Kurds in Syria have lived as citizens so long as they have accepted their assumed Arab identities. Some have been regarded as *Ejnebi*, "foreigners," treated as such and with limited rights. The rest, *Maktoumeen*, "the invisible ones," have not been not allowed to register themselves or own property or send their children to school.[186]

In August 1962, in order to ensure Arab control of the province of Jazira, the Syrian government led a targeted census there. Of all ethnicities surveyed, only the Kurds had to prove they had been residents in Syria prior to 1945. Unable to do so, 120,000 Kurds "were stripped of their citizenship as were their descendants and the descendants of the progeny of male non-citizens even when the mother was an attested citizen of Syria."[187]

Syria's Arab Socialist Ba'ath Party[188] perpetuated the repression of the Kurds after it came to power there in 1963. In 1965, the government created an "Arab belt" one hundred and eighty miles long and ten miles wide along its border with Turkey, with the goal of separating Syrian Kurds from those in Turkey, expropriating Kurdish lands and handing them over to Syrian Arabs.

Thousands of Kurds were forcibly relocated to Syria's southern desert region. The use of the Kurdish language was banned; Kurdish private schools and books written in Kurdish were forbidden, and children were not allowed to be registered with Kurdish names.

Syria's policies of Arabization and compulsory relocation of Kurdish populations have further complicated the situation for the Kurds' pursuit of autonomy. "The Kurdish areas in Syria," notes a recent report, "do not constitute a contiguous Kurdish region, making the development of a Kurdish autonomy more difficult. The Kurds in Syria remain spread between three unconnected Kurdish enclaves (Afrin, Ayn al-Arab or Kobane and al-Jazeera), located in the governorates of Aleppo and Hasakah, which are surrounded by Arab and Turkmen-inhabited areas. There are also Christians living in these areas."[189]

When the Arab Spring reached the borders of Syria in 2011, the Kurds were cautious about joining it en masse. A year later, when Bashar al-Assad withdrew his forces from the Kurdish areas to focus on quashing the rebel forces of the Free Syrian Army, Kurds took control of their territories. Following the democratic confederalism model of Abdullah Öcalan, whose revolutionary intellectual leadership was strongly inspired and shaped by the writings of social theorist Murray Bookchin, Syrian Kurds set up local administrations.[190]

In 2014, jihadi groups declared a holy war on the Kurds. ISIS attacked the border city of Kobani and vowed to take the other Kurdish cities one by one. When Kurds put up a stiff resistance, the U.S. Obama Administration moved to support them. The Kurdish fighting spirit coupled with American air support proved to be an irresistible force. Over four years, ISIS has been driven underground. Today, under the name of the Syrian Democratic Forces, the Kurds and their Arab allies control one third of Syria, the region east of the Euphrates.

ISIS at this writing may be subdued and out of the media limelight, but no one—least of all the Kurds—thinks Syria and the Middle East have seen the last of it. With the Trump Administration's abrupt and impulsive decision to withdraw American troops from Syria, Turkey has vowed to fill the vacuum. No one, certainly no Kurdish observer, holds the illusion that Turkey's intention there is to fight the remnants of ISIS. "Everyone knows," Kurdish political activist Kani Xulam says, "their intent is to take on the Kurds, the one-time American allies, who defeated the Islamic State."[191]

In ex-Soviet territory, Kurds continue to reside in the republics of Azerbaijan, Turkmenistan, Armenia, Georgia, Kyrgyzstan, and other areas of the former USSR. Until the 1950s, repressive measures against the Kurds routinely took place there as well. Once the Soviet Union fell, Armenians and Azeris stripped the Kurds of any cultural privileges they had gained. During the 1988–1994 war between Armenia and Azerbaijan over Nagorno-Karabakh,[192] the Kurds were caught in the crossfire; Kurdish areas were destroyed and, while precise numbers are contested, it is clear that thousands of Kurds were deported by separatist Armenian forces to central Azerbaijan and Krasnodar.[193]

Even in Iraq, where in the twentieth century they have achieved some degree of political or at least administrative autonomy, the Kurds have faced repression. When General Abd al-Karim Qasim[194] overthrew Iraq's Hashemite monarchy in 1958 and established a republic, he promised political and cultural rights to the Kurdish people and invited Mustafa Barzani to return to the country. In 1961, under Barzani's leadership, the Iraqi Kurds took up an armed struggle for their autonomy. The Soviets supported them until 1971, when in an about-face the USSR turned to backing the government of Baghdad. Barzani looked for support from the Shah and the Americans. After the Algiers Accord in 1975 between Saddam Hussein and the Shah, the Iraq-Iran border was closed, driving a wall through the Kurdish heartland.

Though the border was never completely impervious to the clandestine movement of people or goods, its closure limited trade and effectively paralyzed anything resembling "normal life." Maintaining social and economic relationships became a dangerous game; travelers setting out to visit family members along the border did so in jeopardy of losing their lives simply for being in the "wrong place."

Throughout their territory in space as throughout their history in time, the story of the Kurds has been one of persecution and even genocide from local regimes and failed promise from the world powers. It remains to be seen how the fate of Kurdistan and its people will play out amidst the constantly shifting realignments the Middle East now witnesses in the early years of the twenty-first century.

Notes

1. Hélène Krulich, *Une Européenne au pays des Kurdes* (Paris: Éditions Karthala, 2011), 21. During the Pahlavi dynasty the city was called Rezaieh. The city is situated administratively in the Iranian province of West Azerbaijan.

2. According to Hélène Krulich, Ghassemlou's father was born in 1875; Krulich, *Une Européenne*, 22. The elder Ghassemlou lived a long and healthy life; Hélène recalled

that Abdul Rahman was out of the country, in Europe, when his father passed away at nearly one hundred years of age. Hélène Krulich-Ghassemlou, *Love Against All Reason: A European Woman Involved in the Kurdish Fight for Freedom in Iran* (Vienna: Lit Verlag, 2017), 62.

3. "Woussouq-e Divan [a royal title given to Ghassemlou's father by the Qajar shah, Mozaffar al-Din Shah] had many wives. According to him, he had nine; according to Khanum Naneh, there were twenty-five, but only three [of his wives] gave him descendants." Krulich-Ghassemlou, *Love Against All Reason*, 15. *Woussouq-e Divan* means "deserving the trust of the king," Ibid., 16, n4.

4. Abdul Rahman Ghassemlou, interview with Jonathan Randal, Paris, 1986. Except where otherwise noted, further statements from Ghassemlou in this chapter are from this interview.

5. Krulich, *Une Européenne*, 21.

6. Q. M., interview with the author, 1991. Q. M., a Kurdish Iranian politician who resides in Europe, agreed to speak with the condition that his identity not be revealed for fear of consequences from Tehran. Further statements from Q. M. in this chapter are from this interview.

7. Ghassemlou's father owned seven villages and the Valley of Ghassemlou. When the administration adopted the practice of assigning and recording last names, he took the name of the valley as his own. Krulich, *Une Européenne*, 22.

8. Mozaffar ad-Din Shah Qajar (March 23, 1853–January 3, 1907), the fifth Qajar ruler of Persia, reigned from 1896 to 1907.

9. For the Iranian Kurds Simko was an admired and beloved nationalist hero, but by repute also a ruthless man—not only in battle—who had no compunction about killing innocent people. The fact is, however, that we know very little about Simko from firsthand documentation, and it is likely that much of what has been written about him reproduces propaganda presented in the form of anecdotes. Given the raids he had carried out against cities like Mahabad, there has been some posthumous demonization of him even among the Kurds themselves.

Recent Kurdish studies have shown, based on analysis of what remains from his leadership—a journal published in Kurdish, letters he wrote to the British government—that he was a nationalist, but had to rely on tribal structures. "The social structure, political organization and leadership of Semko's movement were predominantly tribal," writes Kurdish political theorist professor Abbas Vali. "However, there is a body of evidence, cited by both opponents and proponents of Kurdish nationalism, which suggests that the tribal leadership—and in particular Semko himself—entertained the nationalist idea of a united and independent Kurdistan." Abbas Vali, *Kurds and the State in Iran: The Making of Kurdish Identity* (London, New York: I. B. Tauris, 2011), 13, https://www.academia.edu/7221780/Kurds_and_the_State_in_%C4%B0ran-Abbas_Vali (accessed November 13, 2017).

For an extensive discussion of Simko, see Martin van Bruinessen, "A Kurdish Warlord on the Turkish-Persian Frontier in the Early Twentieth Century: Isma`il Agha Simko," in Touraj Atabaki (ed.), *Iran and the First World War: Battleground of the Great Powers* (London: I. B. Tauris, 2006), 69–93; accessed as a single document at Academia, https://www.academia.edu/3555229/ (October 25, 2015). Also see John Bulloch and Harvey Morris, *No Friends but the Mountains: The Tragic History of the Kurds* (New York: Oxford University Press, 1992), 198–200.

10. Vali, *Kurds and the State in Iran*, 13. Such a practice had also been common enough in Medieval Europe before the formation of centralized states.

11. Van Bruinessen, "A Kurdish Warlord on the Turkish-Persian Frontier," 14–15.

12. Ibid., 2.

13. During the unraveling of the Ottoman Empire toward the close of the nineteenth century, it had been British missionaries who had come to the defense of the region's Assyrian Christians. Like the British, the Russians in their turn would champion the Assyrians against the Kurds. It was only some months following Russian withdrawal that Simko would strike back against the Assyrians, who had taken control of Urmia during riots in February of 1918. "Famine and mutual depredations, in which the departing Russians had no small share," van Bruinessen writes, "led to increased bitterness between Christians and Muslims. It was especially the Azaris and the 'non-tribal' Kurds that suffered, for the Christians were better armed. The Iranian government was incapable of restoring order." This was the moment that the governor of Tabriz approached Simko to ask for his intervention. Van Bruinessen, "A Kurdish Warlord on the Turkish-Persian Frontier," 17. "In many respects," van Bruinessen points out, "[Simko's] career exemplifies the relations between Kurdish tribes and the states in whose peripheries they exist." Ibid., 2.

Van Bruinessen locates the roots of Kurdish nationalism in the early 1800s, in reaction to Iranian centralization and dismantling of the Ottoman emirates in Kurdistan. Following an unsuccessful revolt in 1880, Kurdish nationalism surged between the world wars, in the aftermath of the Allies' breakup of the Ottoman Empire. Ibid., 11–13.

For Mar Shimun see *Zinda* magazine, http://www.zindamagazine.com/html/archives/2004/3.15.04/; and Ashor Giwargis, "The Patriarch Mar Binyamin Shimmun: A Martyr of the Assyrian Nation & the Church of the East," originally published in *An-Nahar* [in Arabic], March 14, 2004, http://marshimun.com/mar-benyamin-shimun/(accessed May 14, 2014).

14. Van Bruinessen, "A Kurdish Warlord on the Turkish-Persian Frontier," 13.

15. Alireza Asgharzadeh, *Iran and the Challenge of Diversity: Islamic Fundamentalism, Aryanist Racism, and Democratic Struggles* (New York and Hampshire, England: Palgrave Macmillan, 2007), x.

16. This included abolishing two provinces, Kurdistan and Arabistan, and splitting the province of Azerbaijan into two, one of them largely populated by Kurds. Ervand Abrahamian, "Communism and Communalism in Iran: The Tudah and the Firqah-i Dimukrat," *International Journal of Middle East Studies* 1(4), 1970, 291–316; text referenced is page 296.

17. Ibid., 296.

18. Vali, *Kurds and the State in Iran*, 16.

19. Ibid., 1–2.

20. Ibid., 15, 18.

21. Ibid., 15, 16.

22. Ibid.

23. Asgharzadeh, *Iran and the Challenge of Diversity*, 87.

24. Ibid., 88.
25. Homa Katouzian, *Musaddiq and the Struggle for Power in Iran* (London: I. B. Tauris. 2003), 28, cited in Asgharzadeh, *Iran and the Challenge of Diversity*, 89.
26. Ibid., preface, x.
27. Ibid., 87.
28. Vali, *Kurds and the State in Iran*, 18.
29. Ibid.
30. Abdul Rahman Ghassemlou, interview with Jonathan Randal, Paris, 1986.
31. Krulich-Ghassemlou, *Love Against All Reason*, 56.
32. Ibid.
33. Abdul Rahman Ghassemlou, interview with Jonathan Randal, Paris, 1986. Speaking later with journalist Chris Kutschera, Ghassemlou added that he had gone with a friend to see the Russians, on his own initiative, without telling anyone: "It was the first time I saw tanks. We observed from afar, and then we found courage. . . .

    "When we returned home, my father interrogated me. Reassured by our story, he had our baggage unpacked"—the clothes, food, and valuables the family had packed to take with them as they fled. "These first contacts were followed by many others," Kutschera added, "and Mohammed Ghassemlou would be one of the Kurdish 'notables' to be invited to Baku" to meet with the Soviets regarding support for Kurdish nationalism. Chris Kutschera, *Le défi kurde ou le rêve fou de l'indépendance* [The Kurdish defiance, or the mad dream of independence] (Paris: Bayard Éditions, 1997), 159.
34. Oddly, notes Alireza Asgharzadeh, "there was no public protest against the dethroning of Reza Khan, a fact that testified to the extreme shallowness and unpopularity of the Pahlavi regime." Asgharzadeh, *Iran and the Challenge of Diversity*, 94. Young Mohammad Reza Shah Pahlavi, not yet twenty-two years of age, took the throne on September 16, 1941, following the forced abdication of his father in the wake of the Allied invasion in August. See Iran Chamber Society, http://www.iranchamber.com/history/mohammad_rezashah/mohammad_rezashah.php (accessed July 1, 2014); see also Martin van Bruinessen, "A Kurdish State," in Susan Meiselas, *Kurdistan: In the Shadow of History*, Second Edition (Chicago and London: University of Chicago Press, 2008), 176. To create some sort of legitimacy given the fact of his peasant origin, Reza Shah had taken for his dynastic title the name of the language of pre-Islamic Persia, Pahlavi. See Mohamed Heikal, *Iran: The Untold Story* (New York: Pantheon Books, 1982), 31. Though placed on his father's throne by Western fiat, the son soon enough would show himself devoted to "his father's dream of a Fars-centered, aggressive nationalism"—and just as soon to be challenged by autonomist demands from ethnic minorities, chief among them those of the Kurds and Azeris. Asgharzadeh, *Iran and the Challenge of Diversity*, 94.
35. In response to Britain's call for aid in funneling supplies to Russia through the "Persian Corridor," the U.S. set up the Persian Gulf Service Command, 30,000 troops strong, to "serve in the Corridor in a technical capacity and to see to it that the necessary war materials were delivered to Russia." Ahed George Samaan, "The policy of containment and the Middle East, 1946–1958," *Dissertations and Theses*, Paper 967 (Portland, OR: Portland State University, 1972), 15.

36. Van Bruinessen, "A Kurdish State," in Meiselas, *Kurdistan*, 176.

37. Archibald B. Roosevelt, Jr., *For Lust of Knowing: Memoirs of an Intelligence Officer* (Boston: Little, Brown and Company, 1988), 253. "Archie" Roosevelt, Jr. (February 18, 1918–May 31, 1990) was the grandson of former U.S. President Theodore Roosevelt. His father, Archibald Bulloch Roosevelt (April 10, 1894–October 13, 1979), Theodore Roosevelt's fifth child, served in the U.S. Army with distinction during both world wars. An uncle, Kermit Roosevelt, would play a critical role as the CIA director of the 1953 Iranian coup. See Irwin Molotsky, "Kermit Roosevelt, Leader of C.I.A. Coup in Iran, Dies at 84," *New York Times*, June 11, 2000, http://www.nytimes.com/2000/06/11/us/kermit-roosevelt-leader-of-cia-coup-in-iran-dies-at-84.html (accessed June 24, 2014).

38. Archibald B. Roosevelt, Jr., "The Kurdish Republic of Mahabad," *Middle East Journal*, no. 1 (July 1947), 247–69. For a comprehensive account of the formation and dissolution of the Republic of Mahabad, see also Chris Kutschera, *Le mouvement national kurde* (Paris: Flammarion, 1979), 154–83.

39. The traveler, in this case, was Joseph Arthur, Comte de Gobineau, a French writer and social thinker and a contemporary of Alexis de Tocqueville, posted in Tehran during France's Second Empire. His theories of racial determinism would influence later developments of racist thinking in western Europe.

40. Heikal, *Iran*, 28.

41. Sattareh Farman Farmaian with Dona Munker, *Daughter of Persia: A Woman's Journey from Her Father's Harem Through the Islamic Revolution* (New York: Three Rivers Press, 1993), 52–53.

42. It was only in 1786 that Tehran had been elevated to the status of Persia's administrative capital by Agha Mohammad Khan (1742–1797), founder of the Qajar dynasty. See *Encyclopædia Britannica*, http://www.britannica.com/EBchecked/topic/585619/Tehran (accessed May 15, 2014)

43. Roosevelt, "The Kurdish Republic of Mahabad," 248.

44. David McDowall, *A Modern History of the Kurds* (London, New York: I. B. Tauris, 2004), 235.

45. Ibid.

46. Ibid.

47. Roosevelt, "The Kurdish Republic of Mahabad," 250.

48. Ibid., 251.

49. Ibid. For an extensive discussion of the Soviet concern to maintain order and stability in the region, see also Vali, *Kurds and the State in Iran*.

50. McDowall, *A Modern History of the Kurds*, 235.

51. Roosevelt, *For Lust of Knowing*, 254.

52. Abdul Rahman Ghassemlou, interview with Jonathan Randal, Paris, 1986.

53. Vali, *Kurds and the State in Iran*, 19–20; Roosevelt, "The Kurdish Republic of Mahabad," 250; Roosevelt, *For Lust of Knowing*, 254.

54. Vali, *Kurds and the State in Iran*, 20.

55. McDowall, *A Modern History of the Kurds*, 238.

56. Ibid., 239.

57. Ibid., 240.

58. Ibid.

59. Roosevelt, *For Lust of Knowing*, 267.

60. McDowall, *A Modern History of the Kurds*, 240. At Qazi Mohammad's initial approach to Komala "discreetly offering his adherence," party leaders had declined his inclusion in the party. Given his powerful personal presence and the natural deference he commanded, they feared he would inevitably dominate the party and vitiate its essential "democratic character." "When at Soviet insistence the Komala finally did admit him," Archie Roosevelt wrote, "there came about precisely the result they feared—one-man rule of the party," and a tighter alignment with Soviet policy. Roosevelt, "The Kurdish Republic of Mahabad," 253, here speaking from his own observations and from interviews with leaders in Kurdistan.

61. McDowall, *A Modern History of the Kurds*, 239.

62. Vali, *Kurds and the State in Iran*, 43. "Komalay Jiyanaway Kurdistan was a political association with a nationalist programme which defined its objectives, above all the creation of a national state in a united Kurdistan." In this context, "united Kurdistan" can be taken to mean a reunification of all areas of Kurdistan.

63. Vali, *Kurds and the State in Iran*, 25.

64. Ibid., 45.

65. Ibid., 47.

66. Ibid., 46.

67. Ibid., 47. The PDKI would soon, as Ghassemlou would write, attain "considerable popularity" and "gain the support of large sections of the peasantry, town working people, petty bourgeoisie, middle landowners and the patriotic tribes." Ghassemlou's statement is cited by Borhanedin A. Yassin, "Vision or reality? The Kurds in the policy of the Great Powers, 1941–1947" (doctoral dissertation), in Lund Studies in International History, 32 (Lund, Sweden: Lund University Publications, 1995), http://lup.lub.lu.se/record/1472832, 40 (accessed July 13, 2014)

68. McDowall, *A Modern History of the Kurds*, 240; see also Vali, *Kurds and the State in Iran*, 51–52.

69. Roosevelt, *For Lust of Knowing*, 267.

70. Vali, *Kurds and the State in Iran*, 52. See also Yassin, "Vision or reality?"

71. Vali, *Kurds and the State in Iran*, 50.

72. Ibid., 51. "Autonomous Azeri state" in this context, as viewed by the Soviet sponsors, likely meant some form of federal arrangement, like that of other Soviet "republics" within the single polity of the Soviet Union as a federal state.

73. Yassin, "Vision or reality," 121.

74. Ibid., 51–52, in Eagleton, *The Kurdish Republic of 1946*, 44.

75. Yassin, "Vision or reality," 120.

76. Roosevelt, "The Kurdish Republic of Mahabad," 254.

77. Yassin, "Vision or reality," 119.

78. Ibid.

79. Ibid., 120.

80. McDowall, *A Modern History of the Kurds*, 240.

81. Ibid.

82. Yassin, "Vision or reality," 118.

83. Roosevelt, "The Kurdish Republic of Mahabad," 255–56.

84. Ibid., 255.

85. Ibid., 253.

86. Vali, *Kurds and the State in Iran*, 52.

87. Ibid.

88. William Eagleton, Jr., *The Kurdish Republic of 1946* (London: Oxford University Press, 1963), 60.

89. Ibid.

90. Roosevelt, *For Lust of Knowing*, 268.

91. McDowall, *A Modern History of the Kurds*, 242.

92. Ali Akbar Derakhshani, an Iranian general, has provided an account of the Tabriz takeover as viewed by a commander of Iranian forces: "The Red Army posts were stationed around us [the Iranian Army's main garrison in Tabriz]. We were concerned that in case of an attack by the *fedaian* [Azeri paratroopers] and our consequent returning fire at them, Red Army personnel might be hit. I discussed the matter with the commander of the Red Army in a message and demanded that the Soviet troops move away from their posts. In reply, the commander wrote: 'The onus is on your side to be careful, to make sure that nothing happens—because if one of our soldiers get killed, or even injured, we will hit Tabriz with our tanks.'" Ali Akbar Derakhshani, *Khaterat-e Sartip Ali Akbar Derakhshani* [The memoirs of General Ali Akbar Derakhshani] [in Farsi] (Bethesda, MD: Iran books Inc., 1994), 37; translation Sharif Behruz.

93. A founding member of the Tudeh, Iran's Communist party, Pishevari had become both a journalist and a Communist activist during the 1920s. It was in August 1945 that Pishevari, "under Soviet instruction," had arranged to replace Tudeh with the newly constituted Azerbaijan Democratic Party. Roosevelt, *For Lust of Knowing*, 225.

94. Vali, *Kurds and the State in Iran*, 54.

95. Roosevelt, "The Kurdish Republic of Mahabad," 257.

96. Eagleton, *The Kurdish Republic of 1946*, 61.

97. Ibid., 60–61; Vali, *Kurds and the State in Iran*, 56. As it transpired, Qazi Mohammad's reckoning was correct, at least in the short term; Soviet and Azeri acceptance was reluctant at best. The Kurds' refusal of subordination to the Azeris was reported to Tehran on February 4, 1946, by the British Consul General in Kermanshah. Four days later, on February 8, the British Consul General in Tabriz advised Tehran that while Pishevari still hoped to subsume the Kurds under Azeri administration, Qazi Mohammad remained insistent on Kurdish autonomy. "He is unlikely to have done so," the Consul added, "unless confident of the Russian support." Vali, *Kurds and the State in Iran*, 56.

98. Officially designated the Kurdistan Republic, the fledgling democracy came to be commonly but inaccurately known outside of Kurdistan as the Republic of Mahabad.

99. Abdullah Hassanzadeh, personal communication to the author, Paris, 2008; see also Roosevelt, "The Kurdish Republic of Mahabad," 258–60. About the causes of the growing friction between the Kurdish and Azerbaijani states, a declassified CIA report from 1948 has this to say: "Of increasingly greater importance, however, was Kurdish disillusionment over Soviet methods and unfulfilled promises and the impression made by US firmness

against the USSR's expansionism." Central Intelligence Agency document ORE 71–48, *The Kurdish Minority Problem*, published December 8, 1948, 10, http://www.foia.cia.gov/ sites/default/files/document_conversions/89801/DOC_0000258376.pdf (accessed June 10, 2016). This declassified document provides a clear picture of early Cold War views on the Kurds in the international context, funneled through the perspective of the U.S. Central Intelligence Agency.

100. Roosevelt, "The Kurdish Republic of Mahabad," 258.
101. McDowall, *A Modern History of the Kurds*, 242.
102. Vali, *Kurds and the State in Iran*, 57.
103. Ibid., 59.
104. Ibid., 57.
105. McDowall, *A Modern History of the Kurds*, 242–43.
106. Vali, *Kurds and the State in Iran*, 59–60.
107. McDowall, *A Modern History of the Kurds*, 242–43.
108. Ibid., 246.
109. Interview with Qazi Mohammad, cited by Kutschera, *Le mouvement national kurde*, 176–77.
110. Ibid.
111. Ibid. Qazi Mohammad's cousin Rahim Qazi lived in Baku; his brother was Seif Qazi, who served during Qazi Mohammad's administration as minister of war.
112. Interview with Qazi Mohammad, from Kurdish publication *Kurdistan*, January 13, 1946, in Meiselas, *Kurdistan*, 182; translation Amir Hassanpour.
113. Roosevelt, *For Lust of Knowing*, 278.
114. Roosevelt, "The Kurdish Republic of Mahabad," 268.
115. This provision was stipulated in the January 1942 treaty between Iran, Britain, and the Soviet Union by which Iran agreed to provide "nonmilitary assistance to the war effort" and the Allies agreed to respect Iranian political and territorial integrity. Glenn E. Curtis and Eric Hooglund, eds., *Iran: A Country Study*, Fifth Edition, First Printing (Washington, DC: U.S. Government Printing Office, Federal Research Division, Library of Congress, 2008), 30; see http://lcweb2.loc.gov/frd/cs/pdf/CS_Iran.pdf (accessed July 17, 2014). Allied promises of non-interventionism were reinforced by the November 1943 Tehran Conference when, by the "Declaration of the Three Powers Regarding Iran," the U.S., Britain, and the Soviet Union declared their shared "desire for the maintenance of the independence, sovereignty, and territorial integrity of Iran." U.S. Department of State, Office of the Historian, Milestones 1937–1945, http://history.state.gov/milestones/1937-1945/tehran-conf (accessed July 20, 2014).
116. Archie Roosevelt would identify this clearly as a key point in "The Kurdish Republic of Mahabad," his eyewitness report and analysis of 1947.
117. CIA document ORE 71–48, *The Kurdish Minority Problem*, 13.
118. Abdul Rahman Ghassemlou, interview with Jonathan Randal, Paris, 1986.
119. Hélène's recollection was a little different; she recalled his telling her that it was a book by Lenin himself, *On the Right of Nations to Self-Determination*. Krulich, *Une Européenne*, 25.

120. Ghassemlou's memories of this time are seconded by Archie Roosevelt's observations of Soviet officers and agents in the region. "The work in Kurdistan centered around the Soviet Consulate in Rezaieh, attached to which was at least one of the Soviet Union's 100,000 Kurds, known as 'Captain Jafarov,' who wandered freely among the tribesmen and villagers in Kurdish dress. Soviet activity in Mahabad dates from the time two of these agents, known as 'Abdullahov' and 'Hajiov,' appeared, ostensibly to buy horses for the Red Army." Roosevelt, "The Kurdish Republic of Mahabad," 251.

121. Krulich-Ghassemlou, Love Against All Reason, 20.

122. Krulich, Une Européenne, 19.

123. Jalil Gadani, interview with the author, Paris, 1991. Further statements from Gadani in this chapter are from this interview.

124. Roosevelt, "The Kurdish Republic of Mahabad," 261.

125. Ibid., 262.

126. Ibid., 264; see also Eagleton, The Kurdish Republic of 1946, 102.

127. Roosevelt, For Lust of Knowing, 282.

128. Kutschera, Le mouvement national kurde, 178; see also Eagleton, The Kurdish Republic of 1946, 102.

129. McDowall, A Modern History of the Kurds, 243.

130. William Linn Westermann, "Kurdish Independence," Foreign Affairs, July 1946, quoted in Meiselas, Kurdistan, 183.

131. Ibid.

132. Elton L. Daniel, The History of Iran (Westport, CT: Greenwood Press, Second Edition, 2012), 146. Roosevelt himself characterized it as "the first scene of the first act of the Cold War"; Roosevelt, For Lust of Knowing, 224.

133. Daniel, The History of Iran, 146–47.

134. McDowall, A Modern History of the Kurds, 243. Ultimately, the Majlis would reject ratification and Iranian oil production would be nationalized under Mossadegh's government. "The fact that the Majles was bound not to consider concessions while foreign troops were present was a powerful inducement for the Soviets to remove their forces." Daniel, The History of Iran, 147.

135. Tadeusz Swietochowski, "Islam and the Growth of National Identity in Soviet Azerbaijan," Chapter 3 in Edward Allworth, ed., Muslim Communities Reemerge: Historical Perspectives on Nationality, Politics and Opposition in the Former Soviet Union and Yugoslavia, Central Asia Book Series (Durham, NC: Duke University Press, 1994), 55.

136. Roosevelt, "The Kurdish Republic of Mahabad," 260.

137. Ibid., 265.

138. Ibid.

139. Van Bruinessen, "A Kurdish State," 176.

140. McDowall, A Modern History of the Kurds, 243; see also Roosevelt, "The Kurdish Republic of Mahabad," 258–59. Roosevelt summed up, "Whereas the Azerbaijani Democrats had legalized the positions they had seized, Qazi Mohammad's government now had no legal basis at all. The Kurds had progressed from the condition of a minority in the Iranian state to that of a minority in an Azerbaijani Turkish state"; Roosevelt, "The Kurdish Republic

of Mahabad," 259. Soon enough, however, the Azeri republic itself would fall to Iran, and its leaders would flee to the Soviet Union.

141. CIA document ORE 71–48, *The Kurdish Minority Problem*, 10.

142. Ibid., 2.

143. Ibid.

144. McDowall, *A Modern History of the Kurds*, 243–44; see also Daniel, *The History of Iran*, 147.

145. McDowall, *A Modern History of the Kurds*, 245.

146. Van Bruinessen, "A Kurdish State," 176.

147. McDowall, *A Modern History of the Kurds*, 245.

148. Ibid.

149. Unlike the situation in Mahabad, where real democracy prevailed and the government maintained significant popularity in the city, the regime in Azerbaijan had shared many similarities with that of the Soviet Union and was therefore resented. At the fall of Azerbaijan, "peasants, workers, and shop-keepers massacred the Democrats at the first indication of their collapse. This spontaneous reaction clearly indicated the hatred felt by the people for the regime." Roosevelt, "The Kurdish Republic of Mahabad," 267. While the leadership escaped to the USSR, those who had supported the government were forced to flee with their families. Roosevelt, *For Lust of Knowing*, 241.

150. Kutschera, *Le mouvement national kurde*, 181.

151. McDowall, *A Modern History of the Kurds*, 290–93.

152. Eagleton, *The Kurdish Republic of 1946*, 115.

153. Ibid., 112.

154. Ibid., 112–13.

155. Jonathan Randal, *After Such Knowledge, What Forgiveness* (New York: Farrar, Strauss and Giroux, 1997), 133; McDowall, *A Modern History of the Kurds*, 246. For more on Barzani's epic retreat see Eagleton, *The Kurdish Republic of 1946*, 119–29.

156. Ibid., 122.

157. Kutschera, *Le mouvement national kurde*, 182.

158. Jalil Gadani, interview with the author, Paris, 1991.

159. Krulich-Ghassemlou, *Love Against All Reason*, 21.

160. Kutschera, *Le mouvement national kurde*, 182.

161. "Dollars": Ghassemlou told Jonathan Randal that his father would often use this expression, which, like "the family jewels" in vernacular English, was a slang term for "testicles."

162. McDowall, *A Modern History of the Kurds*, 242; for a detailed discussion, see 242–45.

163. Roosevelt, "The Kurdish Republic of Mahabad," 265.

164. McDowall, *A Modern History of the Kurds*, 242.

165. Roosevelt, "The Kurdish Republic of Mahabad," 268.

166. Ibid.

167. Ibid. Mustafa Barzani echoed this sentiment when he told a journalist: "The Kurds were not defeated by the Iranian army. . . . Rather, it was the Soviet Union which was beaten by the United States and Great Britain." Mustafa Barzani, interview with Chris Kutschera, Bokan, Iraq, December 11, 1946, cited in Kutschera, *Le mouvement national kurde*, 182.

168. Roosevelt, "The Kurdish Republic of Mahabad," 268.

169. Abdul Rahman Ghassemlou, interview with Jonathan Randal, Paris, 1986.

170. Kurdistan has been described as "an arc of mountain chains enclosing a series of interior basins, astride the international borders of Iran, Syria, Iraq and Turkey." Its mountainous north includes the Pontic, Taurus, and Zagros ranges. "In the west, the mountains become rolling hills down to the Mesopotamian Plain; to the east lies the Iranian Plateau; and to the north the mountains become the highlands of Armenia and Anatolia." Maria T. O'Shea, *Trapped Between the Map and Reality* (New York and London: Routledge, 2004), 23.

171. G. S. Reynolds, "A Reflection on Two Qur'ānic Words (Iblīs and Jūdī), with Attention to the Theories of A. Mingana," *Journal of the American Oriental Society*, Vol. 124, No. 4 (October–December 2004), 675–89, especially 683, 684, 687; F. Hennerbichler, "The Origin of Kurds," *Advances in Anthropology*, 2.2 (2012), 64–79; see https://www.research-gate.net/publication/265947486_The_Origin_of_Kurds (accessed November 2, 2014).

172. See Basile Nikitine, *Les Kurdes* (Paris: Éditions d'aujourd'hui, 1956), 8, n2.

173. *Anabasis*, Book III, Chapter V, Project Gutenberg eBook #1170, produced by John Bickers and David Widger, trans. H. G. Dakyns; released August 13, 2008, updated January 15, 2013, http://www.gutenberg.org/files/1170/1170-h/1170-h.htm (accessed April 25, 2014).

174. O'Shea, *Trapped Between the Map and Reality*, 23.

175. Report of Amnesty International, AI Index: EUR/44/65/88 (November 1988), "Briefing on the Turkey Campaign: Human Rights Denied," http://ob.nubati.net/en/campaign.php (accessed November 29, 2014).

176. Michael Gasper, "The Making of the Modern Middle East," in *The Middle East*, ed. Ellen Lust (Thousand Oaks, California: CQ Press, 2014), 44.

177. "At least three million Kurds were displaced and left homeless" during that decade, reports journalist Uzay Bulut, "with 3,438 Kurdish villages destroyed and burned down by Turkish soldiers. Even a Turkish parliamentary commission concluded that in the 1990s, more than 3,000 villages and farm settlements were burned, razed and emptied of their inhabitants, and some 378,000 people displaced." Uzay Bulut, "Turkey and the Kurds," Gatestone Institute: International Policy Council, November 28, 2014, http://www.gate-stoneinstitute.org/4903/turkey-and-the-kurds (accessed May 2, 2015).

178. Between 1988 and 2014, at least 580 Kurdish children and minor teens were killed by forces of the Turkish state, largely for their part in demonstrations. These figures are reported by the Diyarbakir branch of the Human Rights Association (IHD), as detailed by Uzay Bulut, "Turkey and the Kurds."

179. Bulut, "Turkey and the Kurds."

180. Ibid.

181. And this denial "was accompanied by state terrorism, carried out in massacres, extrajudicial killings, enforced disappearances, unlawful arrests and, of course, torture." Ibid.

182. At this writing, emerging developments are reported daily in the international press by such news outlets as Al-Jazeera, *The Guardian*, and Al-Monitor. See, for example, reports in Al-Monitor's Turkey Pulse: "The leader of Turkey's main pro-Kurdish political party has warned that the country is on the verge of civil war between state forces and militant Kurdish separatists. The remarks made by Selahattin Demirtas, co-chairman of the Peoples' Democratic Party, followed scenes of violence and firebombing in Turkey last week, with

hundreds of reported attacks by nationalist mobs on offices belonging to Demirtas's party, known by the Turkish abbreviation HDP, as well as on ordinary Kurds." Metin Gurcan, "As both sides rattle sabers, is Turkey on verge of civil war?," December 14, 2015, trans. Timur Göksel, http://www.al-monitor.com/pulse/en/originals/2015/12/turkey-clashes-between-pkk-and-security-forces-civil-war.html# (accessed December 15, 2015).

183. Laura Pitel, "Turkey in crisis: The Kurdish teenagers fighting—and dying—in urban clashes with security forces," *The Independent*, January 18, 2019, https://www.independent.co.uk/news/world/middle-east/turkey-in-crisis-the-kurdish-teenagers-fighting-and-dying-in-urban-clashes-with-security-forces-a6820201.html (accessed January 20, 2019).

184. Office of the United Nations High Commissioner for Human Rights, "Report on the human rights situation in South-East Turkey, July 2015 to December 2016," February 2017, http://www.ohchr.org/Documents/Countries/TR/OHCHR_South-East_TurkeyReport_10March2017.pdf (accessed January 15, 2019).

185. "Kurds make up between 7% and 10% of Syria's population, with most living in the cities of Damascus and Aleppo, and in three non-contiguous areas around Kobane, the north-western town of Afrin, and the north-eastern city of Qamishli." BBC News, *Who Are the Kurds?*, October 21, 2014, http://www.bbc.com/news/world-middle-east-29702440 (accessed November 29, 2014).

186. Maureen Lynch and Perveen Ali, "Buried Alive: Stateless Kurds in Syria," Refugees International, January 2006, https://www.refworld.org/docid/47a6eba80.html; "Syria, The Silenced Kurds," Human Right Watch/Middle East, October 1996, Vol. 8, No. 4 (E) in https://www.hrw.org/sites/default/files/reports/SYRIA96.pdf (accessed January 20, 2019).

187. McDowall, *A Modern History of the Kurds*, 474. For discussion of the census and its aftermath, see also Jordi Tejel, *Syria's Kurds: History, Politics and Society* (London: Routledge, 2009), 51–52; for an account of the Syrian and Iraqi military campaigns, see I. C. Vanly, "The Kurds in Syria and Lebanon," Chapter 8 in *The Kurds: A Contemporary Overview*, ed. P. G. Kreyenbroek and S. Sperl (London: Routledge, 1992), 151–52.

188. Ba'ath, the Arab Socialist Ba'ath Party, was founded in 1947 by Michel Aflaq and Salah-al-Din al-Bitar, two Syrian university students. *Ba'ath* means "resurrection" or "renaissance"; the party's principles included adherence to socialism, political liberty, and pan-Arab unity. Its objectives included unification of all Arab countries into a single state and countering Western hegemony in the Middle East. The party still rules in Syria.

189. Wladimir van Wilgenburg, *Kurdish Strategy Towards Ethnically-Mixed Areas in the Syrian Conflict*, Jamestown Foundation, Terrorism Monitor Volume 11 Issue 23, December 13, 2013; available at UNHCR, the UN Refugee Agency's Refworld page, http://www.refworld.org/docid/52aef0e34.html (accessed November 29, 2014).

190. Sophia Hussein, "Murray Bookchin and the Ocalan connection: the *New York Times* profiles the students of PKK Rojava," *Verso* About Books, Authors Blog, December 2, 2015, https://www.versobooks.com/blogs/2368-murray-bookchin-and-the-ocalan-connection-the-new-york-times-profiles-the-students-of-pkk-rojava (accessed January 20, 2019); Claudia Gallo interview, "Debbie Bookchin: Kurds are practicing the most democratic form of government there is on the planet," *Verso* About Books, Authors Blog, May 18, 2016, https://www.versobooks.com/

blogs/2644-debbie-bookchin-kurds-are-practicing-the-most-democratic-form-of-govern-
ment-there-is-on-the-planet (accessed January 20, 2019).

191. Kani Xulam, a political activist based in Washington, D.C., is the director of the American Kurdish Information Network (AKIN), accessed at http://kurdistan.org/ (January 20,
2019).

192. Alexey Zverev, "Ethnic Conflicts in the Caucasus 1988–1994," Chapter 1 in *Contested
Borders in the Caucasus*, Bruno Coppieters, ed. (Brussels: VUB [Vrije Universiteit Brussels]
Press, 1996); see http://poli.vub.ac.be/publi/ContBorders/eng/ch0102.htm (accessed July
22, 2014).

193. McDowall, *A Modern History of the Kurds*, 493.

194. Abd al-Karim Qasim, nationalist Iraqi military officer who took power in 1958, ruled as
prime minister until his overthrow by a Ba'athist coup and his execution in 1963.

· 2 ·

RIFTS AND RIVALRIES

෯

As the year 1947 dawned, all that was left of the Democratic Republic of Kurdistan was a richly heroic national legacy and a small political force, the PDKI, which Ghassemlou would define in 1988 as "the avant-garde party" of Iranian Kurdistan, its mission "the fulfillment of the national and democratic demands of the Kurdish people."[1]

The party born in 1945 would not be the same organization in 1989, when the Iranians would assassinate its secretary-general in Vienna. By then, the PDKI would have lived through the repressions of successive regimes, and crises born out of the ambitions of some of its own members.

In the wake of the collapse of the Kurdistan Republic, the party had gone underground; during this passage, in its shift to the left as a clandestine opposition party, a close alliance with the Communist party Tudeh was forged. After the shock of Qazi Muhammad's death and the implosion of its experiment in autonomy, the party was in chaos. Its leaders found themselves in prison or in hiding, or abandoned the party or the country and went into exile. Tudeh seized the momentum and recruited both new Kurdish members and more seasoned cadres from the PDKI. As PDKI tentatively reinitiated activity in Kurdistan under Tudeh's auspices in the early 1950s, the party became, essentially, a *de facto* chapter of Tudeh.[2]

By 1959, following a decade of persecution that would further decimate its membership, most of its remaining leadership had escaped to Iraq, then on to Eastern Europe in the early 1960s when the political climate in Baghdad deteriorated.

By 1979, at the onset of the Iranian revolution, the party had begun rebuilding as leaders returned from exile or were released from prison in the heady early days of revolutionary upheaval. Its strengthened political and military organization was reinforced by Kurdish army officers who joined its ranks, and the party soon established itself as the Kurdish political vehicle "most firmly rooted in the population, especially in the area that had comprised the Mahabad Republic."[3]

Ghassemlou's efforts would lay the groundwork for the party's renaissance and growing strength. As will be seen, however, the party's reconstruction would be accompanied by significant costs: growing brittleness in relations with Tudeh and with the Iraqi Kurdish KDP, and schisms within PDKI itself.

On his return from Europe in the early 1950s, Ghassemlou had reentered Kurdish political life as Tudeh's Kurdistan chief and had himself became a Tudeh member. This political link would be disrupted within a few short years as the PDKI reorganized. Ghassemlou would be instrumental in reestablishing the ideological and organizational independence of PDKI and weaning it away from its dependence on Tudeh; the separation would be formalized in 1955. For this breach, Tudeh would embark on a campaign against Ghassemlou that would last for decades.

Party dynamics were to be strained as well by relations with KDP, Mulla Mustafa Barzani's Kurdish party in Iraq. Within the PDKI itself, developments during the 1950s and 1960s reflected complex contending interests among the Kurdish community at large. Initially, in alignment with the cross-border struggle for Kurdish rights, the remnants of the party in Iran had lent allegiance, material support, and hundreds of PDKI militants to Barzani in his war with Baghdad, which began in September 1961. Relations with Barzani would, however, develop a disruptive edge.

In 1964, the party suffered a kind of internal coup led by Abdullah Ishaghi, a contender for leadership, and other elements within the PDKI who opposed Ghassemlou. They belonged to the extreme self-styled "nationalist" wing which had little faith that the "Kurdish question" could be resolved within the borders of Iran and which sought a tighter alignment with Barzani's KDP in Iraq.[4] Ishaghi, a prominent member of the PDKI also known as Ahmad Tawfiq, was much influenced by Barzani and his more conservative form of leadership.[5]

By the time Ishaghi convened the PDKI's questionable Second Congress in Iraqi Kurdistan near the Iranian border in 1964, Hélène Krulich recalls, he was making active moves to exclude Ghassemlou from party leadership because of Ghassemlou's "strong personality and high level of education" which was not matched by either Ishaghi or other members who opposed him. Ghassemlou's liberation from a SAVAK prison seven years before, in 1957, provided the pretext for accusing him of treason.[6] Surely, Ishaghi suggested,

Ghassemlou must have revealed the names of party members to the SAVAK in exchange for his freedom.

Hélène Krulich shared an interesting version of Ghassemlou's earlier arrest and release from detention, this from Ghassemlou's half-brother Ahmad Agha. He said that Abdul Rahman had been arrested by Colonel Zibaïe, a cruel and corrupt man who used to extort gifts and money from prisoners' families in exchange for good treatment for the detainees and even to buy their freedom. The colonel visited Ahmad Agha at his home in Tehran and asked for 5000 toman, a very large sum in the 1950s, but "not exorbitant considering the importance of the movement."[7] Ahmad agreed on the condition that the colonel bring Ghassemlou to his home; he would pay only on seeing Abdul Rahman released. Zibaïe accepted. Once freed, Abdul Rahman left the house immediately, and it would be many years before Ahmad Agha had any news from him.

In any case, the congress Ishaghi went on to organize was an illegitimate one that violated both the program and the independent status of the party. Neither the assembly itself nor the way it was conducted was appropriate. The majority of the delegates were elected in such a way that they represented only the direction of those leading the coup. Many leftist party members who should have participated, including Ghassemlou, were not allowed to do so, and were even excluded by use of force; Barzani himself lent his assistance in preventing their attendance.[8] Some resolutions adopted then were typical of harsh police methods the party would take up during that era.

In retrospect, a number of observers see the focus of the intraparty conflict as the issue of allegiance to Mustafa Barzani. In the view of Abdullah Hassanzadeh, party member and chronicler of the Kurdish movement, factional infighting in PDKI had begun once the leadership moved its headquarters to Iraq during the height of persecution in Iran, following the 1958 Ba'athist revolution that took down Iraq's ruling Hashemite dynasty.[9] In the schism between Ghassemlou and Ishaghi, Hassanzadeh acknowledges a left/right dimension, but identifies the primary question as PDKI's independent standing and its relationship with Barzani: where Ghassemlou "was a resolute advocate of the political and organizational independence of PDKI," in Hassanzadeh's view, Ishaghi "had turned PDKI into an appendage of [Iraqi] KDP and was in practice under the leadership of KDP and later of Barzani."[10] During the tenure of Ishaghi's leadership, for instance, the only publication the party produced was entitled *Disan Barzani*, "The Return of Barzani." Looking back on this period, Hassanzadeh also points out the pressure Ishaghi and Barzani exerted on the Iraqi government to have Ghassemlou expelled from Iraq.[11]

Until 1966 the PDKI's aid to the Iraqi Kurds made, in Ghassemlou's estimation, "a major contribution to the survival of the movement led by Mustafa Barzani."[12] But as Barzani developed an alliance with the Shah, who sought to weaken the Iraqi regime by offering material aid to the Iraqi Kurds, younger PDKI party cadres backed away, repelled and distrustful.[13] "In early 1967," Ghassemlou reported, "several Iranian KDP [PDKI] leaders and militants concluded that they could no longer support the policy of co-operation between Barzani and the Tehran government; they left Iraq and returned to Iran."[14]

They were right to distrust the Shah. To Ghassemlou it seemed clear: the Shah's aid was not only meant to weaken the Iraqi regime—a regime he never forgave for the overthrow of the Hashemite monarchy—but also intended as a "means to secure some direct influence within the Kurdish national movement." "This idea," Ghassemlou wrote, "was to make Barzani's movement dependent upon the aid and to increase that aid as the movement grew, so that eventually the Kurdish movement's very survival would depend upon it."[15]

In March 1967 party cadres and militants who had returned to Iranian Kurdistan formed a new revolutionary committee, led by nationalist PDKI members and ex-members of the Tudeh like Ghassemlou—then living in Paris—to conduct a limited armed resistance against the Shah's regime.[16] This resistance was mounted in direct contradiction to Barzani's explicit command[17] to "do nothing to provoke the Tehran government into carrying out its threat to cut off all Barzani's aid."[18]

The revolutionary committee, which included militants opposed to Ishaghi's collaboration with the Iraqi Kurdish leader, naturally drew Barzani's fire. In May, Barzani issued an ultimatum to PDKI party militants who, in the course of conducting insurgency, were operating back and forth across the Iran-Iraq border: "You either stay in Baghdad and stop all your [political and military] activities or you return to Iranian Kurdistan and burn all [your] bridges with us."[19] Essentially expelled by Mustafa Barzani from Iraqi Kurdistan, the party cadres sought refuge in Iranian Kurdistan.

To the Shah's advisors, the influx of PDKI refugees was alarming. In the spring of 1968, the Shah's armed forces launched an attack on the PDKI; party members had no option but to resort to weapons to defend themselves.[20] This confrontation initiated an armed rebellion that lasted eighteen months and became drenched in blood. During this drawn-out confrontation, Ghassemlou reported, "more than 40 Iranian KDP militants were either killed or arrested and turned over to the Iranian authorities by Barzani's men."[21]

Ghassemlou, it has been said, had warned during the 1960s that conditions were not favorable for a successful armed struggle, and had written as much to PDKI leaders. While no record of such correspondence has come to light, Hassanzadeh cites a finding in a report by the party's third central committee of a lack of preparation for armed struggle at that time. He had himself heard from party leaders who considered such a struggle ill-advised. A year before the outbreak of hostilities, in the spring of 1967, Hassanzadeh had received a letter from Mela Aware (Mela Ahmad Shalmashi), one of the leaders who would later lose their lives in the uprising. "As you know," Aware wrote, "talking about an armed struggle has been going on for a while. Armed struggle without organization, armed struggle without guns and ammunition, armed struggle without rear-front and . . . I am asking you in any way possible to not let this idea spread out and to settle among people."[22]

The reasons for failure of the PDKI-led revolt were many. The party lacked adequate organization and logistical support. The discipline to carry out an organized armed rebellion was not yet developed. The movement did not possess the structure of a revolutionary party. It had no clear program of action delineating a political direction that would win widespread ongoing popular support. There were tactical and strategic errors arising from political and military inexperience. The movement was limited to a single region, and this allowed the enemy to concentrate its forces. The rebels were not able to liberate a zone from which to direct their struggle. They waited for external aid that never arrived. Ultimately, the conditions for a successful rebellion were nonexistent in Iranian Kurdistan, and the movement found itself tremendously isolated. The insurgents' reputation as heroes, however, would live on, fueling distrust for Barzani among Iranian Kurds and lending cachet to the PDKI's popularity by the eve of the Iranian revolution.[23]

In 1969, excluded in disgrace from the PDKI's Second Conference,[24] Ishaghi resigned from party leadership. His resignation was accepted a year later. Cadres who had left the party rejoined it and formed a new leadership. Regardless of the many uncertainties, the new leadership organized its Third Conference[25] in June 1971 and adopted a new program, promoting improvement of workers' conditions and the free handover of land to farmers. The party also adopted a new slogan: "Organization is our best weapon." It was following this conference that the party changed its official designation to PDK (Iran).

However, the party still lacked cadres who were adequately prepared for political work. Aware of this shortcoming, and under their circumstances during the reign of the Shah, the only option they saw was armed struggle. The PDKI espoused the philosophy of guerrilla warfare which was so in vogue in those days. Yet this was no more than a political statement, because the party was intrinsically weak. And it would remain so until the revolution of 1979.

In the aftermath of Ishaghi's bid for power, the PDKI suffered its next major schism following the Iranian revolution in the spring of 1980 and its Fourth Congress, which took place in Mahabad. The reason for this division: the clash between the nationalists and the pro-Communists, in which Tudeh was actively implicated.

"There were members[26] of the party who were pro-Tudeh, pro-Soviet, and they wanted to ally themselves with the government of the Islamic Republic because it was anti-imperialist," explained party leader Sadegh Sharafkandi. "The other Kurdish democratic demands were not significant for them. We were against this political posture. Seven members of the leadership abandoned the party, along with some cadres."[27]

Among those who left was Ghani Bulurian. Bulurian—whose long-standing commitment to Kurdish nationalism was attested by his involvement with the Kurdish Republic at Mahabad and twenty-one years of imprisonment by the SAVAK, from his arrest in 1958 to his release in December 1979—was a member of the party's central committee. Abandoning the party in rejection of Ghassemlou's leadership methods, the direction he was taking the party, and his "departure from [Fourth] Congress resolutions," Bulurian and the group denounced Ghassemlou, alleging he had arrangements with the Iraqi regime in Baghdad for support in the form of arms. In fact, Iraq's support was solely logistical, providing the means for movement and shelter which would later be important not only for Ghassemlou but for other PDKI activities, including safe travel for medical volunteers from Europe.

In the initial leadership meeting following the return of many of the party's leaders from Iraq, Bulurian had launched a campaign for his own election as party secretary-general. This proposal was put forth by his colleague Mohammed Amin Seraji on the claim—promoted by his supporters, known as the "Band of Seven"—that with his election to office, the PDKI would garner support from the Soviet Union.[28] Tudeh, in the interest of subsuming the party within its own organization, had instructed the allies it had cultivated within the party[29] to propagate this message. Bulurian's group also advanced the argument that "the struggle against imperialism" should be given priority over PDKI's demands for democracy for Iran and autonomy for Kurdistan; like many others, they regarded the Islamic Republic as "anti-imperialist." To his supporters, Bulurian, after his many years in prison, was clearly a candidate of merit.

Ghassemlou was elected secretary-general with an overwhelming majority. Bulurian, a member of the party's politburo, then proposed himself for appointment as "party president." By the PDKI's charter, however, no such position existed within the party, and his proposal was rejected summarily, without being passed on to the central committee.[30] It was following this failure and the realization that Ghassemlou would pursue independent policies that the "Band of Seven" left the party and joined Tudeh.

Inside Tudeh, Bulurian soon placed himself in a position of leadership, becoming a member of Tudeh's politburo. Hard on the heels of these developments, Tudeh and Bulurian's faction initiated a smear campaign, arguing that Ghassemlou aimed to team up with Iraq against the revolutionary regime in Tehran. In the view of PDKI chronicler Abdullah Hassanzadeh, the objective was to take over the leadership of PDKI and make it subservient to Tudeh, and in that way to force PDKI to support the Islamist regime in Tehran and renounce its calls for democracy and autonomy in favor of "anti-imperialism."[31]

Aziz Mameli, who in 1979 had served as Ghassemlou's assistant in Mahabad, felt that Bulurian's loss to the party was particularly detrimental, that it left the party without any alternative to what he regarded as Ghassemlou's single-handed direction. This one-man rule, in Mameli's view, "was his [Ghassemlou's] weakness."[32]

Ghassemlou would sustain a degree of similar criticism from other friends in the party, but the impact—the extent of damage—of Bulurian's exit from the party may be overstated. Both the lead-up and the aftermath to that departure may have seemed especially challenging because of another set of forces to be factored in: the level of influence that Tudeh—and to some extent the regime—had in this campaign against PDKI and Ghassemlou. Once the Tudeh sympathizers, described by Hassanzadeh as "infiltrators," left the party, PDKI was able to achieve internal coherence. This small band of Tudeh sympathizers, all of whom had been given an assignment to break the political independence of PDKI and who went on to join Tudeh, had created turmoil. Countering their maneuvers consumed tremendous time and energy for PDKI leadership and political cadres. Despite all their proclamations of "anti-imperialism" as the cornerstone of their campaign prior to leaving the party, Hassanzadeh writes, the group later issued a statement conceding that disruption indeed had been their mission all along—to dismantle PDKI polit-ically from within.[33]

In this campaign Tudeh, whether knowingly or not, had to some degree served as an instrument of the Islamist regime. In the early days following the revolution, the new regime had given Tudeh a free hand in conducting political activities; the intent was to use Tudeh to infiltrate opposition or trou-blesome parties, including PDKI. There were even agents of the regime posing as Tudeh supporters, who embarked on an anti-PDKI and anti-Ghassemlou campaign that would damage the party's unity and public standing.[34]

Disruption would recur two years later in 1982, in a further schism at the time of the party's Fifth Congress. This new disunion, like the last, high-lighted a divergence between nationalist and pro-Communist outlooks. The division, said Sadegh Sharafkandi, was preceded by shady maneuvers. The pro-Communist contingent arrived for the Fifth Congress at Mahabad with armed guards to put pressure upon the party and its leadership. But only authorized members of the central committee were allowed into the congress. Having failed in their takeover attempt, the pro-Communists left the party.

Those who left the party criticized Sharafkandi as well as Ghassemlou. "He was too hard," said Ghassemlou's former assistant Aziz Mameli. "Dr. Said [Sharafkandi] wanted to get rid of all those who maintained their intellectual independence. He wanted people who were in the service of Ghassemlou and himself."

It needs to be noted that other witnesses have seen it otherwise, remark-ing on Sharafkandi's integrity, which more than once showed itself in clashes with Ghassemlou on specific matters. Privately, Ghassemlou is said to have confided to a colleague: "With Sharafkandi, I have disputes, but he is a devoted and reliable man."[35] Had Ghassemlou not respected intellectual inde-pendence, had he feared potential rivalry, he might well have marginalized Sharafkandi; instead, he took great pains to pass on his legacy, to cultivate Sharafkandi's strengths as the successor to party leadership. In this it seems clear that Ghassemlou's concern was not for loyalty per se, but for competence and clarity.

It was also part and parcel of Ghassemlou's concern for party institu-tionalization and structure. Under his tutelage, PDKI was at that time the only Kurdish party with backup leadership, with a deputy secretary-general. Charismatic as he was, Ghassemlou was a transitional figure in the politics of the region: intent on forging a structure that would avoid the pitfalls of cha-risma and avert the classic endgame his people had witnessed again and again.

Iran's policy, Ghassemlou would note more than once, was perennial: "Kill the leader and the movement will collapse." In the struggle for autonomy and democracy, it was imperative that Iranian assassination attempts not destroy this movement.

Sharafkandi, in his own right strongminded and straightforward, has sometimes been described as blunt and obdurate. In party matters, he could certainly be firm on the rules of engagement. At crucial times and in critical matters, it is easy to imagine him closing ranks with Ghassemlou, and in his insistence on clear points of order, he could certainly be perceived as hard.

"Ghassemlou," Mameli said, "did not do anything to fix this."[36] As departures from the party continued, Mameli himself would be lost to the party. "I left in 1982," he said; "I ended my activities with the party."[37]

At the Fifth Congress in 1982, prior to his departure, Mameli spoke up about his concerns: "We have a lack of democracy. This is the problem: one person decides—the secretary-general. His presence is essential for the people and the party, but we need to make sure that the central committee proceeds with full powers and that decisions be collective.

"Tomorrow," Mameli warned the congress, "it will be too late." Ghassemlou, he said later, was angry.

Looking back on these events in the light of a further, and devastating, party schism in 1988, Mameli reflected, "Those people who would be part of the split-up [in 1988] did not listen [in 1982], because they were in power then. When they left, I told them: The time when you needed to react was in 1982."

ॐ

In 1984 the party, which was now celebrating its Sixth Congress, would once again live through quite a turbulent internal storm.

Within the party there remained cadres still soaked in Stalinist ideas. Ghassemlou put forward his position—his stand for democratic socialism—and declared that if it was not accepted, he would step down as secretary-general. And this, he pointed out, would leave the direction of the party in the hands of those who supported a hard stance.[38] There followed further division of the party, with the triumph of the more moderate members.

Q. M., then a respected leader within the party, reproached Ghassemlou: You do not give people enough time, he told him, to develop their thoughts on appropriate directions for the party. Ghassemlou had, after all, lived in

Czechoslovakia in Stalin's time, and had also lived in the democratic milieu of France. A lifetime of experience had brought him to the conclusion that democracy was the best system, and the best solution for Kurdistan. But since Kurds had joined the party with all their divergent political tendencies intact, Q. M. saw Ghassemlou's adherence to his point of view as a trigger to rupture of the party.

"First we needed to inform the people that we did not have to impose a specific direction,"[39] explained Q. M. Once a wealthy man in Kurdistan, he had now been living in exile for years and supporting his family by working as a taxi driver in a European city.

"The party represented all of the Kurdish people. Ghassemlou was much more forward thinking than the other leaders. But if he was speaking to the people, it would have been better for him not to move so fast and leave them behind.

"The party had become divided, and this weakened it at a time when it was still in a process of development. The cadres who had been trained for many years then left the party. Ghassemlou imposed his own personal ideology. He wanted to impose his ideology even to the point of threatening to step down from a leadership position if his direction was not followed."

Q. M. did not agree with Ghassemlou's leadership methods; still, he stayed in the party. He would not accept any responsibility on the central committee, however, and ultimately, he ended up leaving the PDKI.

"There were enormous costs," he said, "but I do not want to discuss this. I felt Ghassemlou had surrounded himself with young people who did not know much and could not contradict him. I always agreed with the idea of Kurdish independence. I did not agree with creating electoral lists, because in this way, Ghassemlou's group would be elected, and his opinion would automatically be imposed.

"Ghassemlou's thoughts and opinion were important to everyone. When Ghassemlou selected my name [for a position on the central committee], it was certain that I would be chosen. I did not agree with this method."

Little by little, Q.M. said, all the key roles in the central committee were left in the hands of young members under the age of twenty-five. Q. M. did not hide his admiration for the leader regardless of their differences; nevertheless, he thought that Ghassemlou "avoided surrounding himself with people who were more seasoned." Reflecting later, Q. M. said, "It was easier for me to say no [to disagree with Ghassemlou] than it was for a young man. Young people were not able to confront Ghassemlou. It is true, [however]," he added, "that Ghassemlou did keep Sadegh Sharafkandi, who was very talented."

Within a few short years, it would be such disaffections over questions of party structure and electoral procedures that would come to a head.

❧

The schisms of 1980–1982 had highlighted the disaffections of pro-Tudeh, pro-Soviet critics, who denounced the PDKI as a bourgeois organization that had strayed from the Soviet Union and reproached Ghassemlou for his alleged reactionary stance. The final schism in 1988 would revolve instead around the issue of leadership style, strategy, and active engagement with the rank and file of party members. Sharafkandi, for instance, a member of the party's central committee since 1979 and now serving on the politburo, was noted for the strength of his insistence on maintaining discipline. Even in the face of opposition within the party, Sadegh Sharafkandi was intransigent—"frank, resolute, and short-tempered,"[40] as one party member has described him. His preferred method was to make decisions quickly with a strictly majoritarian democratic vote: whoever lost would have to accept the will of the majority.

But some of Ghassemlou's friends criticized these leadership methods, and Ghassemlou's as well. Jalil Gadani, also a member of PDKI's politburo, maintained that Ghassemlou did not allow a debate in party decisions. He felt that resolutions were not thoroughly discussed, and opinions of others were not taken into consideration.

But "between Jalil and Rahman," said Dr. Fréderic Tissot of Aide Médicale Internationale, "the difference was more about form than content. I believe their goals were the same. I told Jalil that given the circumstances of the war, it was impossible to act as he was advising. Perhaps Ghassemlou's actions were not very democratic, but in the midst of the war . . ."[41]

In the midst of the war, with the almost constant demand for critical decision and action, Ghassemlou felt imperative the need for close teamwork among core party leadership. He put forth a "fixed list"—a proposed slate of candidates to be adopted as a single package, a team he could trust. "Jalil," said Tissot, "said that Ghassemlou arranged election[s] so that he would gain the votes. Ghassemlou did not have the right to make fixed lists of candidates. They really were arguing about the electoral method. Jalil wanted resolutions to be voted on unanimously, but this would have paralyzed them [the party]."[42]

In the face of party dynamics that led up to the Eighth Congress of January 18–22, 1988, such a fixed list of candidates was in fact developed, to shield party leadership from the ambitions of party dissident Hassan Restegar.

Restegar, whom Ghassemlou criticized for undisciplined conduct, had as head of the party's social commission commanded allegiances from too many people working under him at party headquarters. Restegar had created a faction around himself, not so much on political issues as for personal gain. Ghassemlou and Sharafkandi saw him as a threat to the party's objectives, cohesion, and discipline. Perceptions of him, even among his supporters, were that he was very cunning, but extremely lazy. During one party congress, Ghassemlou was remembered as having said that he could not tolerate Restegar's conduct anymore—that he enjoyed his company, but could no longer work with him.[43]

Dr. Hossein Khalighi, who joined the PDKI in 1979, expands on these events in his multivolume memoir, *Jan u Jiyan*.[44] He cites, first, a personal conflict between Ghassemlou and Restegar, and second, Ghassemlou's desire for committed cadres and peshmerga to carry on a strong armed struggle with the regime. Those who either were labeled as "lazy" or, as Khalighi suggests, had a dissenting opinion in party matters ended up in the party's social commission, which was headed by Restegar. This commission, set up soon after the revolution when the party took on control of areas in Kurdistan, oversaw the party dealings with issues of social impact—land distribution and complaints regarding land and road construction—and social concerns like polygamy, traditions relating to marriage, and other social structures.[45] With the commission's swelling ranks, Restegar had created a base for himself, and it was his membership in the politburo, Khalighi suggests, that enabled him to do so.

From Restegar's point of view, the engagement in the social commission that he offered cadres dismissed by other committees—the politico-military committee, for instance—served "to prevent them from either leaving the party or taking refuge abroad."[46]

From the viewpoint of Ghassemlou and Sharafkandi, however, party members involved in the social commission were either incompetent or evading difficult tasks, such as returning to the front line or carrying out risky political and military responsibilities.

Restegar saw the social commission as a place for dissidents within the party. This appears to have troubled Ghassemlou. The response Ghassemlou ultimately arrived at, in preparation for the Eighth Congress, was the concept of presenting a fixed list of candidates to exclude Restegar, along with Restegar's allies Hashem Karimi and Nabi Ghaderi, then members of the party's central committee.

The fixed list, as understood within the party, was essentially a complete slate or roster of candidates presented as a bloc for approval. By PDKI's charter, periodic regional meetings designated as conferences functioned essentially as electoral primaries in which delegates were nominated by broad party membership to attend the party congress. Nominations were open: any member could nominate any other member—or even themselves—to be placed on the list of candidates. Such slates were said to be "open lists."

The party congress, attended by about 150 delegates, would in turn elect the party central committee, a leadership body of about twenty-one members. And the central committee, in its turn, would then elect from among its ranks the politburo and the office of secretary-general.

In the midst of this intricate, multilayered party process, a curious detail is noted by Hélène Krulich: the extraordinary fact that Ghassemlou himself "never obtained a majority of votes from the congress delegates."[47] But because it was the central committee—not the congress as a whole—that chose the secretary-general, Ghassemlou always carried the election for that office.

Going into the Eighth Congress, however, there was dissension among the central committee, split as it was between essentially two factions. Ghassemlou, for the sake of party strength and unity, wanted a homogeneous leading team, a team he trusted and could work with. It was not possible for the party to work, he said, while the central committee had divided points of view. It was for this reason that he put forth his own list of candidates for the central committee with the proposal that it be voted as a unitary bloc by the congress. The list was fixed, but not exclusionary; the option remained open for other nominations and for the congress to choose and vote on other lists or individuals.

In Khalighi's view, while dissension had now taken the form of a power struggle, the struggle was clearly justified as a matter of safeguarding the party's internal democratic process. In the evolution of Kurdish politics from a focus on charisma, personality, and traditional power brokers such as sheikhs and aghas to modern organizations based on principles of internal democracy, "the mechanisms of democracy" needed to be institutionalized within the party.[48]

Throughout the maneuvers of Restegar and his claque leading up to the Eighth Congress, the aim was, Khalighi writes, to set a bilateral agreement by "a majority of the elected members of the central committee" on selection of the secretary-general and politburo membership, and to prevent Sharafkandi's election to both the politburo and the central committee. The goal, ultimately: "to gain control of the internal policies of the party and its external relations."[49]

There was one problem with this scenario, Khalighi notes: their faction lacked real leadership capacity.[50] Without Ghassemlou and his natural leadership, as even Restegar's faction had to acknowledge, "the formation of the central committee and the running of the party at that juncture would not have been a viable option." Resentful though they were of Ghassemlou, the Restegar faction recognized that he was indispensable to the party; they had no alternative candidate to put forth for the post of secretary-general.

Consequently, Khalighi continues, during the debates of the congress the Restegar faction—Hossein Madani, Fatah Kawyan, Nabi Ghader, and Hassan Restegar himself—"all glorified Dr. Ghassemlou beyond limits." Their strategy aimed to enlist Ghassemlou's popularity as a boost to their own, preempting his supporters—in particular, sidelining Sharafkandi—"and take center stage" for themselves in the elections and in the party, maintaining personal power and privilege.[51]

The Restegar camp, in the view of observers, might well have been happy to remain in the party had they been able to garner status and privilege through an alliance with Ghassemlou. Without these, it was not worth their while to stay within the party, and these disaffections were the real motivation for their leaving.

These intrigues formed the backdrop for the heated debates during the Eighth Congress. The faction reckoned without the strength of the working relationship between Ghassemlou and his deputy Sharafkandi. In the face of dissension in the social commission, which in his view threatened to undermine the party, degrade discipline, and demoralize the PDKI's ranks, Ghassemlou issued an ultimatum: if the fixed slate of candidates did not get the necessary votes, "In that case," he announced, "I will not run for the central committee. I promise, as a cadre, that whoever will be elected as secretary-general and [to the] politburo, I will do my utmost to collaborate with them."[52]

"Considering the level of competence and popularity of Dr. Ghassemlou," writes Khalighi, "this ultimatum shocked the delegates." No matter how they urged him, Ghassemlou was insistent: "If things develop in this manner," he said, he would refuse to run for office.

"Out of necessity," Khalighi sums up, "the delegates voted a second time. And this time, the fixed list was accepted. . . ."[53] Ghassemlou's support for a group of candidates that he could work with productively "had tipped the balance."[54]

To all this, Mameli too was a witness. And about Ghassemlou at this juncture, Mameli said: "He should have then foreseen what happened afterwards—
that is, the division [of the party]."

Mameli had shared his concerns with Hélène: "No one can influence
Ghassemlou," he said to her. "I have great respect and esteem for him, but he
has to accept the reality. Certain reforms needed to begin with him.

"He monopolized all the power: he was secretary-general of the party,
he was responsible for communications, he was president of the party organization, he was chief and commander-in-chief of the PDKI peshmerga. It's
impossible to hold all these posts."

In point of fact, Ghassemlou did not hold all the strings of power and
decision making; these operational functions were actually delegated to others within the party. It was Sharafkandi, not Ghassemlou, who was responsible
for communications, both radio and publications. True, too, that while Ghassemlou was commander-in-chief of peshmerga, his colleague Mustafa Hijri,
the current secretary-general of the PDKI, was for many years head of the
politico-military committee, and was in essence the central figure for those
functions.

In his book on the history of decline and divisions within the PDKI
that encompasses the losses of two prominent leaders and three splits within
the party, Hijri, a longtime confidant of both Ghassemlou and Sharafkandi,
details the high degree of trust in Ghassemlou's leadership up to the Eighth
Congress even among the prominent leaders of the 1987 split. "In voicing
their opposition in the congress, these comrades objected to the fixed list, but
their loyalty to the party was evident, and even their approval and commen-
dation of Ghassemlou was to a degree that was never expressed or thought of
by the supporters of the fixed list.

"If it had been predicted that such an initiative [the exclusion of Restegar
from the pre-agreed leadership team] would lead to the split of a group of
cadres and peshmerga, I believe both Dr. Ghassemlou and all those who supported the fixed list method would have agreed to Hasan Restegar's inclusion
in the list to avoid such a huge blow to the party,"[55] he adds.

Party leadership, even given Ghassemlou's preeminence, was neither
unilateral nor monolithic. Khalighi and others have attested to disagreements between Ghassemlou and Sharafkandi so severe that colleagues in
the party were aware of them; there were periods when, outside of party
leadership meetings, they would not communicate directly with each other
for a time.[56] Nevertheless, colleagues recall, when the split in 1988 was

finally anticipated, Sharafkandi called the radio staff for a meeting, telling
them how important it was to remain loyal to Ghassemlou. "He is not just
the leader of this party," Sharafkandi told them; "he is the leader of the
Kurdish people."[57]

So clear was Ghassemlou's vision, so strong was his presence, that despite
all his efforts to transform the politics of a movement from charismatic leadership to democratic discourse, the fear Mameli voiced to Hélène still held no
resolution: "If something happens to him, who can follow?"

෮

Those who lost in the electoral process did not give in, however, and many
abandoned the PDKI[58] to establish a separate group, the Kurdistan Democratic Party of Iran–Revolutionary Leadership (PDKI–RL).[59]

This final rupture was highly traumatic. In Q. M.'s view, the secessionists left because they wanted to keep their leadership positions: "They only
decided to leave when they lost their positions in the political bureau. Their
attitude was petty. When you commit to the cause of the people, you don't
backtrack for money or a position. I don't respect them."[60] Hijri essentially
concurs: "We can say the split occurred because of the interest and egoism of
a small group, above them all Hasan Restegar."[61]

For Ghassemlou, the breakage was painful. "This divisiveness deeply
affected Ghassemlou," Sharafkandi would later acknowledge. The dissident
group was formed by former military personnel for whom Ghassemlou had
a particular fondness. "He had no fear politically, but he felt much sadness
that they left and publicly slandered him." Ghassemlou "was indignant,"
adds Iraqi Kurdish intellectual Ezzedin Mustafa Rasul, "that some of those
within the party that he had helped rise within the ranks then opposed
him."[62]

The cleavage in the party was traumatic for others as it was for Ghassemlou. Hasan Ayoubzadeh, who had by this time been with Ghassemlou and the
party for years, explained why he felt he had to leave the PDKI a year after the
party division: "First, the party was split up, but I had friends on both sides.
The party wanted to fight against those who had left; there was an armed
confrontation. It was a catastrophe. Between one side and the other, there
was no difference.

"'Don't leave,' Ghassemlou said to me, 'I need you.'

"'I cannot bear this situation,' I told him.

"Ghassemlou was not satisfied. He was very sad. He decided to send me [as an intermediary] to the group that had split off. 'I'm ready to reunite, to come together,' he told me, 'and have a party congress in six months, and hold elections for the congress and representatives.'

"He sent me there with a letter. I stayed two days with them. I gave the letter to Fatah Kavian,[63] one of their politburo, and waited for [Jalil] Gadani to come back.

"But Restegar, their deputy secretary, told me, 'Sorry, it is too late.'

"They did not accept the invitation to come back and reunite. They had received support from the Mujahedin, PUK, Komala, and Ezzedin to help them separate from the party.

"I came back to Ghassemlou. When I arrived, he asked me, 'Are you a lion, or a fox? Have you obtained something good, or not?'

"'Sorry,' I told him; 'It is too late.'

"He was very sad. The cup of coffee he held his hand was trembling, and his lips were taut.

"Then he got angry. 'Why did they do this? Look at what they have done! This is the work of jash. Between here and Baghdad there are a quarter of a million jash; they fight for Saddam. If one day they decide they want to capture the PDKI, they can accomplish that in two days . . . Why do the Kurds have such terrible behavior?'

"I was speechless. What could I say?

"He fell silent. He had a cigarette in his hand, and I left him.

"This was the worst and saddest day for me."[64]

"Even those opinions that circulated around that the PDKI–RL before their declaration of separation had established contacts with the Mujahedin and with their blessings, enticement, and support had made their final decision to separate, came to be true. This incident was a perfect opportunity for the Mujahedin,"[65] writes Hijri in his memoir about the decline and divisions within the party.

"They [the Mujahedin] needed another Kurdish alliance to relink themselves with Kurdistan, and if that ally happened to be against the PDKI and Dr. Ghassemlou, that was even better."[66]

☙

For Ghassemlou, this day was clearly harrowing. He had held fast through so much in his life, for the sake of his people. It may be a measure of how much the party split wounded him—that he could stay cool through out-and-out warfare; maintain diplomatic firmness face-to-face with Ayatollah Khomeini; rally peshmerga and civilian refugees alike, and take command in moments of terror; but faced with what could only have felt like failure and betrayal within his own party, the experience was one of devastation.

Like a poker player, Ghassemlou used to hide his emotions the way any politician does. He was never fearful in the political arena. Even in the worst moments, he had always maintained his composure. He lost it only on the rarest occasions—for example, when his headquarters was being bombed. But he would immediately regain his self-control. "During the times when we had to run for the shelters," said Sharafkandi, "he would always send the others first. He was always the last one to seek shelter."

❧

The final time Ghassemlou saw his father was in 1957. "He did not agree with what I was doing," Ghassemlou said later. "He did not like that I was living underground. He also did not like my leftist radicalism and Communism. My father was a religious man. But he told me, 'When a man has a conviction, and he begins something, he must do it to the end.' Eight days later, he died."

Ghassemlou had a fatalistic attitude toward death. On one occasion, he shared with Kurdish film director Yilmaz Güney and his wife Fatosh that all he had were some antiaircraft artillery and a few weapons—and these were not enough to wage a war. They both laughed at the fact that he was waging a war with so little. Yilmaz was very surprised.

After her husband's death from cancer, Fatosh saw Ghassemlou often. "He always told me that I had to keep on living," she shared. "He told me that once, in the mountains, a woman came to see him who had twice lost a husband. She had several children. She was dressed in black and was crying. He told her to stop weeping and to remarry, that life continued.

"Ghassemlou also told me that you do not find happiness; you have to create it. If you don't create it, you will never find it."[67]

In the worst moments, Ghassemlou "was stronger than all of us," said Sharafkandi. "When a close friend from the central committee or any other leader was killed, I or another companion would write a communiqué. But if Ghassemlou saw that it was too painful, he would immediately rewrite it and say to us, 'When a friend falls in battle, what you have to do is not cry, but do something so that his struggle continues.'"

Notes

1. *Actualités du Kurdistan*, no. 34 (Paris: PDKI publication), September–October 1988.

2. PDKI member Sharif Behruz, personal communication with the author, November 2015. Since its inception during the Second World War as a pro-Soviet and populist leftist party and its dramatic expansion following the War, Tudeh had become the object of repression from the monarchy and with the blessing of the U.S.; it remained largely clandestine. Tehran had signed an agreement with the United States in 1947 providing for U.S. military aid and assistance with military training, and the West was nervous about Tudeh's popularity and the Soviet sphere of influence in Iran. An abortive assassination attempt on the Shah in February 1949, for which the Tudeh was blamed, resulted in a crackdown: Tudeh was banned, and its leaders were arrested or fled into exile abroad. See Iran Chamber Society, http://www.iranchamber.com/history/tudeh/tudeh_party02.php#sthash.W33dScja.dpuf (accessed January 28, 2018).

3. Martin Van Bruinessen, "Major Kurdish Organizations in Iran," *Middle East Reports*, No. 141 (July/August 1986).

4. Sharif Behruz, personal communication with the author, September 2014. What Ishaghi and his allies did not understand at that time was "the international and regional obstacles" to their aspirations. Ghassemlou, in contrast, aside from believing in the right of Kurds to self-determination was "much more pragmatic, and given his experience in international relations, to him freedom and democracy were paramount to the resolution of the Kurdish issue inside Iran; furthermore he believed that resolving the Kurdish quagmire outside the existing international borders was quite complex and somewhat impossible. . . . His approach to the national issue was different from those advocated by traditional nationalists such as Ishaghi, as it is still today." Ibid.

5. Edmund Ghareeb, *The Kurdish Question in Iraq* (Syracuse, NY: Syracuse University Press, 1981), 13.

6. Hélène Krulich-Ghassemlou, *Love Against All Reason: A European Woman Involved in the Kurdish Fight for Freedom in Iran* (Vienna: Lit Verlag, 2017), 178.

7. Ibid., 165–66.

8. "Mulla Mustafa helped prevent the attendance of undesirable delegates, just as he chased off his own troublesome leftists." David McDowall, *A Modern History of the Kurds* (London, New York: I. B. Tauris, 2004), 253. But as would be seen, this alliance between Barzani and Ishaghi would not last.

9. Abdullah Hassanzadeh, *Niw Sede Xebat* [Half a century of struggle: A retrospect of struggle and activity of the Democratic Party of Iranian Kurdistan] [in Kurdish], Vol. 1 (Gawrade: Press Commission of the Kurdistan Democratic Party of Iran, August 1995), 27–34; translation Salah Piroty. Hassanzadeh makes the further observation that conflict between Barzani and Jalal Talabani within KDP, the Iraqi Kurdish party, had a negative impact on PDKI as well.

10. Ibid., 28.

11. Ibid. Hassanzadeh goes on to describe Ishaghi's authoritarian style, similar to that of his mentor Barzani.

12. A. R. Ghassemlou, "Kurdistan in Iran," in *A People Without a Country: The Kurds and Kurdistan*, ed. Gerard Chaliand (New York: Olive Branch Press, 1993), 111.

13. Van Bruinessen, "Major Kurdish Organizations in Iran."

14. Ghassemlou, "Kurdistan in Iran," 112.

15. Ibid.

16. McDowall, *A Modern History of the Kurds*, 253; Ghareeb, *The Kurdish Question*, 13.

17. Van Bruinessen, "Major Kurdish Organizations in Iran."

18. Ghassemlou, "Kurdistan in Iran," 112.

19. Chris Kutschera, *Le défi kurde ou le rêve fou de l'indépendance* [The Kurdish defiance, or the mad dream of independence] (Paris: Bayard Éditions, 1997), 153.

20. Hassanzadeh, Half a Century of Struggle, Vol. 1, 45–47; translation Salah Piroty.

21. Ghassemlou, "Kurdistan in Iran," 112. Ghassemlou told reporter Jonathan Randal that over a fifteen-year period, from 1960 to 1975, Barzani had killed, imprisoned, or handed over to the Tehran regime over forty PDKI militants. Abdul Rahman Ghassemlou, interview with Jonathan Randal, Paris, 1986. See also McDowall, *A Modern History of the Kurds*, 253; Kutschera, *Le defi kurde*, 153; Van Bruinessen, "Major Kurdish Organizations in Iran"; and Hussami, *My Memoirs* [in Kurdish], Vol. 3 (Stockholm: 1988), 38, 56, 64, 66, 71. According to Hussami, his friend Anwar Dilsoz, "apparently a confidant of Barzani's KDP . . . had complained about the resistance movement in Iraqi Kurdistan being totally manipulated by Iran": "Stories are told of fierce clashes between Iran's gendarme forces and the Kurdish insurgents around Khane city [Piranshar], where the Kurdistan fighters cross to the other side of the border into Iraq's Balakan region to take refuge. Ahmad Haji Barzani [a tribal commander in Barzani's KDP] and his men, along with Barzani's fighters and accompanied by a group of gendarmes, surrounded them [the Iranian Kurdish insurgents] in the village of Alane. They killed one and arrested three others and handed them over to the Ajams [Iranian gendarmerie]. All three were hanged in the city of Piranshar. Anwar further told me," Hussami wrote, that "Mulla Mustafa has fully entangled himself with the Shah against the resistance movement in Iranian Kurdistan." Translation Sharif Behruz, who noted the accuracy of Hussami's memoirs, based as they were on "the correspondence he has had with notable PDKI leaders of the time who were involved with the 1967–1968 armed struggle." Sharif Behruz, personal communication to the author, September 1, 2013.

22. Hassanzadeh, *Half a Century of Struggle*, Vol. 1, 46; translation Salah Piroty.

23. Van Bruinessen, "Major Kurdish Organizations in Iran."

24. Kutschera, *Le defi kurde*, 153.

25. The meeting was designated as a conference because a quorum could not be made to convene a congress. But it was treated as a congress, and the Fourth Congress followed in 1979. Hassanzadeh, *Half a Century of Struggle*, Vol. 1, 67; comment from Sharif Behruz.

26. In the last days of spring 1980 a 30-page statement in the name of supporters of the Fourth Congress was released and signed by Ghani Bulurian, Rahim Saifi Qazi, Fawzieh Qazi, Faruq Keokhosrawi, Ahmad Azizi, Nawid Moeini, Ahmed Azizi and Hemin the poet, who was honorary member of the Central Committee. Abdullah Hassanzadeh, *Half a Century of Struggle*, Vol. 1, 238; translation Sharif Behruz.

27. Sadegh Sharafkandi, interview with Bernard Granjon, Kurdistan, 1991. Statements that follow from Sharafkandi are from this interview. Writing of this schism a few years later, Martin van Bruinessen would comment, "Only small numbers followed them. Qasimlu, the party's undisputed leader, is a man of great abilities who enjoys wide popularity." Van Bruinessen, "Major Kurdish Organizations in Iran."

28. See Hassanzadeh, *Half a Century of Struggle*, Vol. 1, 230; translation Sharif Behruz.

29. Ibid.

30. Ibid., 231.

31. Ibid., 232–33. Bulurian would go on to become Tudeh's representative in Soviet Eastern Europe.

32. Aziz Mameli, interview with the author, Paris, July 2015. Statements from Mameli throughout this chapter are taken from this interview. Mameli, an attorney, joined Ghassemlou in 1979, became his chief of staff and legal advisor, and took on responsibility for communications and international relations. He served as the PDKI representative in Europe, based in Paris, between 1980 and 1982. Never a member of Tudeh, he never agreed with their politics, and he supported Ghassemlou in his posture toward Tudeh adherents within the PDKI. In his view, Tudeh had betrayed the democratic movement in Iran after the 1979 revolution and stabbed the Kurdish movement as well. Mameli was sidelined by the powerful Tudeh camp within the party and would himself leave the party in 1982.

33. Hassanzadeh, *Half a Century of Struggle*, Vol. 1, 232–33.

34. Sharif Behruz, personal communication to the author, citing conversations with veteran PDKI members detailing memories from that period, December 2, 2015.

35. The party colleague who shared this confidence asked not to be named.

36. Aziz Mameli, interview with the author, Paris, July 2015.

37. Ibid.

38. Regarding his proposal of democratic socialism, Ghassemlou had prepared a brief and circulated it among the ranks of party members. There was a widespread opposition, and the Tudeh-linked leftists within the party were hard at work against it. The rejection of Ghassemlou's democratic socialist doctrine and his subsequent departure would have left the party in the hands of those who opposed democratization or modernization of socialism and who opposed the party's further embrace of democracy. "In general, it was his diehard opponents who were agitated by Ghassemlou's popularity within the party. The party's split four years later in 1988 had its roots in these frictions." Sharif Behruz, summarizing conversations with longtime party members, personal communication, May 14, 2014.

39. Q. M., interview with the author, 1991. For reasons of security, Q.M. asked that his identity and location remain confidential.

40. Sharif Behruz, personal communication with the author, September 23, 2015. Interestingly, following Sharafkandi's succession to the post of secretary-general, some party members noted that his leadership style became much more like Ghassemlou's, softening and aimed at convincing people by putting forth arguments. During the challenging years of guerilla war, Ghassemlou and his deputy played two different roles; peshmerga have shared that without Dr. Said's leadership, it would have been difficult to maintain discipline. Ibid.

41. Fréderic Tissot, interview with the author, Paris, 1991. Statements that follow from Tissot are from this interview. Ironically, Jalil Gadani himself was included on the list, and was

elected; as chronicled by Hassanzadeh, it was later that he and others began criticizing the electoral procedure, joined with Restegar, and left the party.

42. Ibid.

43. Dr. Hossein Khalighi corroborates Ghassemlou's stating publicly that he could not work with Restegar. See Hossein Khalighi, *Jan u Jiyan* [Life and suffering] [in Kurdish], Vol. 3 (Stockholm: n.p., 2002), 311–24. Translation by a Kurdish scholar who for security reasons does not wish to be named.

44. Ibid., 311–24; and Vol. 4, 173–82, translation Esmail Ebrahimi and Beyan Farshi. Khalighi holds a degree in philosophy and taught sociology at the University of Tabriz for many years before joining PDKI in 1979. He is the author of a two-volume work entitled *Komalnasy Kurdawar*, "The sociology of Kurdish society."

45. Party structure included a number of commissions, each addressing specific functional concerns under the oversight of individual politburo members. Under the wartime conditions that came to prevail when the all-out struggle with the regime erupted in earnest, the social commission was unable to function; it became inactive and was merged with the finance commission. PDKI member Salah Piroty, personal communication, April 14, 2017.

46. Khalighi, *Life and Suffering*, Vol. 3, 312, and Vol. 4 (2005), 173–82; translation Esmail Ebrahimi and Beyan Farshi.

47. Krulich-Ghassemlou, *Love Against All Reason*, 223.

48. Khalighi, *Life and Suffering*, Vol. 4, 179–82.

49. Ibid.

50. Ibid., 183.

51. Ibid., 186.

52. Khalighi, *Life and Suffering*, Vol. 3, 322.

53. Ibid.

54. Ibid., 186.

55. Mustafa Hijri, *Nisko u Dabiran* [Resilience in the face of decline and division] [in Kurdish] (Kurdistan: Sardam Publishing, 2015), 92. Translation Chiman Moradi and Esmail Ebrahimi.

56. Along with Sharafkandi and Hijri, Hossein Khalighi makes note of Hassan Sharafi, a member of the politburo, and other key figures with important responsibilities. While Sharafkandi and Hijri were loyal to Ghassemlou, Sharafi is said to have flip-flopped on many issues. Hassanzadeh too, the party's chronicler, was a significant actor in PDKI. Khalighi regards him as unreliable and opportunistic; his refusal to run for a position on the central committee in the Eighth Congress, Khalighi says, was due to his belief that the Restegar faction would prevail. As a consequence of this reluctance, Hijri was appointed as deputy secretary-general by Sharafkandi. See Khalighi, *Life and Suffering*, Vol. 3, 311–24, and Vol. 4, 173–82.

57. A former cadre of the radio staff shared this anecdote many years later with a Kurdish scholar; personal communication to the author.

58. This group, which included fifteen executive members of the party, accused Ghassemlou of leading the PDKI astray with the change of direction from socialism to social democracy. Led by Jalal Gadani, they formed the Kurdistan Democratic Party of Iran–Revolutionary

Leadership (PDKI–RL); McDowall, *A Modern History of the Kurds*, 276. After Ghassem-lou's murder the PDKI–RL declared, "Dr. Qasimlu became a tragic victim of his own polit-ical mistakes and compromising stance toward the reactionary terrorists who govern the Islamic Republic. . . . We hope that Dr. Qasimlu's death would teach a lesson to those who sanctioned the policy of compromise over armed struggle at the VIIIth Congress." Ibid., 277.

59. Nader Entessar, "Los kurdos en Irán," in *Estos son los Kurdos: Análisis de una nación*, ed. Manuel Férez Gil (México: Editorial Porrúa, 2014), 120; author's translation. "However," Entessar adds, this party was "never able to become a large popular organization, and even-tually weakened as a functional entity." Ibid.

60. Q. M.'s view about the motives among the secessionists was echoed by Ghassemlou's former colleague Hasan Ayoubzadeh, though his recollections of the composition of the splinter group differed. "Some people had lived [in exile] in Iraq; before coming to Iran, they had been with other parties—Tudeh, Komala. They brought these ideas to our party. They had a different behavior, a different level of education.

"There was a group of politicians with different ideas who did not like Ghassemlou. What they were after was power and privileges. They would not speak about this in front of him; there was a lot of back-stabbing [speaking behind his back]. Ghassemlou was open to discussion, but in a political discussion with him, these others could not back up their positions knowledgeably." Hasan Ayoubzadeh, interview with the author, March 22, 2015.

61. Hijri, *Resilience in the Face of Decline and Division*, 90.

62. Ezzedin Mustafa Rasul, interview with the author, Koya Sanjak, Iraqi Kurdistan, July 2009.

63. Fatah Kavian, formerly with PDKI's central committee, left the PDKI in 1988 to become a member of the breakaway Democratic Party of Iranian Kurdistan–Revolutionary Lead-ership (PDKI–RL); there he served in the politburo. Hassan Restegar, previously with PDKI's politburo, became deputy secretary and later secretary of the PDKI–RL.

64. Hasan Ayoubzadeh, interview with the author, March 22, 2015.

65. Hijri, *Resilience in the Face of Decline and Division*, 81.

66. Ibid., 82.

67. Fatosh Güney, interview with the author, Paris, 1991.

· 3 ·

A REVOLUTIONARY VISION

❧

For Ghassemlou, the PDKI was a party he believed could shape a viable future, a party whose mission was to fulfill "the national and democratic demands of the Kurdish people."[1] The vision he developed for it was both transformative and, he insisted, achievable, even in the face of a formidably reactionary regime. In speaking of the party's forward-looking stance, Ghassemlou would write: "Imam Khomeini is a live portrayal of religion fallen into the hands of the enemies of the people and transformed into a terrible weapon to divide the people using the concept of 'divide and reign.' In this case, religion becomes a factor of regression and an obstacle to progress." Ironically, he would note, "It is this same religion which in the hands of the forces of progress caused the historical leap forward that led to the fall of the Shah. In the latter case, it was an example of progress."[2]

It was not the forces of progress that were operative now. "The arrival of Khomeini to power produced the union of state and religion," Ghassemlou wrote. "If we analyze the reactionary and bloody practices of the regime in the name of Islam, we tend to think that it was because of religion that this tyrannical government stayed in power. Khomeini played with this phenomenon, trying to convince the population that the attacks against his regime were a direct attack against Islam. With this goal set, he spared no efforts in manipulating the naïve Shi'ite religious masses in order to turn them into allies of his repressive apparatus."[3]

Khomeini, a consummate master of zero-sum power politics, had deployed religious rhetoric to define the terms of the game. To Ghassemlou, the dangers of a conversation constrained by those terms were clear. "By falling into the trap of challenging religion," he warned, "we [the Kurds] are playing into Khomeini's game. The PDKI should have a clear position toward religion. . . . The combatants for democracy in Iran and autonomy in Kurdistan should beware of falling into this snare of the regime."[4]

As a party and as a movement, the PDKI's appeal was to a different set of principles: "It is the nationalistic feeling," Ghassemlou said, "that predominates among the Kurds, rather than the religious feeling. It's true enough," he continued, "that the majority of the Kurdish population belongs to the Sunni denomination, which fully opposes the fanatical Shi'ism of the central government. . . . [But] the PDKI is a political lay organization that works for the fulfillment of the national and democratic demands of the Kurdish people rather than for religious ideas. The PDKI recruits its militants among the people of Kurdistan based on their acceptance of the party's principles and the party's program, not upon ethnic or religious criteria. Religious belief does not constitute a condition of belonging or not belonging to the PDKI."

However, Ghassemlou was quick to clarify, "The definition of a lay organization applied to the PDKI does not mean that it is an anti-religious party. The PDKI is the avant-garde party of the people of Kurdistan of Iran. In its activities, it follows scientific ideas and the theory of evolution. It considers religion to be a personal matter, and therefore introduces into its party platform the principle of separation between state and religion. The party respects freedom of creed and the right of difference."[5]

Ghassemlou's vision for Kurdistan diverged equally, on the other hand, from a doctrinaire Marxist perspective; his preeminent concern was democracy. For years to come under Ghassemlou's influence, the PDKI would maintain the decision to abandon concepts such as proletarian dictatorship, and to establish democratic socialism as the party's official political direction. About this Ghassemlou said, "In our current phase, the struggle for national rights is essential. [In] the next phase, after we attain autonomy—meaning national rights—class struggle will become more obvious. However, what is essential for us . . . is the struggle for democracy . . . [which] shall never be eclipsed by the fight for national rights or by class struggle. . . . [T]his is a fundamental reason for establishing the Democratic Party. As long as the Democratic Party survives, democracy is its goal and purpose."[6]

From a lifetime of sharpening, honing, and refining his understanding, Ghassemlou summed up his political stance in an interview a month prior to his death.[7] "Before autonomy," he told interviewer Enayat Fani, "we ask for democracy. It is not because democracy is primary, the real point, and autonomy is something secondary. No. It's that without a progressive democracy in Iran, we believe, there is no guarantee for autonomy.

"Right now," he explained, "our weapons are the only chance for survival, but we all know that one cannot depend on weapons forever. There should be other options, and we believe that democracy is the best alternative for these conflicts. Democracy is the only solution.

"Our understanding of democracy is very simple. Democracy in our view means pluralism: freedom for all, freedom of speech, freedom of thought, and freedom of religion, freedom of national languages, freedom of culture, freedom of political parties, and rule of the people by the people. We believe that no dictatorship can enable the nationalities[8] in Iran to meet these goals: there is no difference between a shah's dictatorship, an Islamic dictatorship, or a proletarian dictatorship. We believe that Iran needs a democratic system of government that will consider our history and culture. By preserving democratic values, and respecting the values stated in the [Universal] Declaration of Human Rights and the declaration of the United Nations, we can take our country forward.

"Even in Kurdistan, where I can assure you that the majority of people support our party, we don't consider ourselves as the sole decision maker, or owner, of Kurdistan. The Kurdish people are to decide if it will be our party that will govern the autonomous [region], or if it will be another organization. We believe that once the war is over, all the groups and organizations should put their agenda and programs before the Iranian people, and Iranians should be able to choose freely and elect what they want.

"So what we believe in is a deep democracy, a democracy that will respect the rights of all, respect the rights of the oppositions—for we believe that no democracy can exist without respecting the rights of the opposition." The democracy he envisioned was authentic, thoroughgoing, self-sustaining and structurally sustainable. "For that reason," he went on, "we are against all organizations that try to establish dictatorship in any form in Iran; and further, we are not willing to cooperate with the monarchists, as we believe that our history has demonstrated that monarchy has been despotic.

"In the history of Iran, all the power has always been centralized [in Tehran]; so when we ask for autonomy, autonomy means decentralization. We do not want all the powers to be in one place, to amass in Tehran. We want the power to be distributed [shared] among the Iranian people, all the Iranian nationalities, and even all the provinces. In this era, in the last years of the twentieth century—in fact, in all of the developed countries—power is being decentralized. Powers are not accumulated in the center, in the hands of a sole person, not centralized. Therefore, we are against any and every group that is trying to establish dictatorship in Iran under different names or forms.

"The question of such groups' success or failure is a different issue. I think in the future in Iran, after the Islamic Republic, even if a dictatorship succeeds, it would be a long-lasting regime, and unfortunately I could say that it could drive the situation in our country toward civil war. Therefore, first of all, all our demands, for [both] democracy and autonomy, are posited within the country of Iran.

"We regard ourselves as Iranians, and wouldn't permit any group to consider themselves more Iranian than we are. However, within our common family, our common country, Iran, we want our rights respected, and not to be considered as second-class citizens. We want us all to be equal constitutionally, in rights before the law.

"For these reasons," Ghassemlou concluded, "we think that our demands, of both types—our demands with respect to democracy, and our demands related to national rights—should also be granted to other suppressed nationalities in Iran just as for Kurds. All of these demands are possible to attain within the framework of the country, and that's the reason that 'democracy for Iran' is our primary goal."

☙

To Ghassemlou, democracy was clearly the way forward. Democracy made demands on a movement and the individuals who carried it: clarity, attention, self-education, discipline. Democracy was the counter to a lifetime of witnessing the excesses of every *ism*—Soviet totalitarianism, the absolutism of the Shah's imperial monarchy, the state terror of SAVAK, and now the institutionalized fanaticism under Khomeini. The fruit of this witness was an almost instinctual recognition that means cannot justify ends—that goals take shape in ways that mirror precisely the means deployed to reach them.

Ghassemlou's vision, in consequence, held no place for terrorism or its justification in any form. Both his firsthand experience and his critical thought allowed him to see it, recognize it, and name it in all its forms. His analysis of terrorism and its workings was as cogent as his understanding of democratic principles and practice. He saw clearly how the label "terrorist" was weaponized to vilify groups struggling for recognition of individual and collective rights. And he saw just as clearly the nature and extent of the state terrorism that defined the terms of the conversation.

In 1988, he addressed this issue in the PDKI journal *Kurdistan*, in an article entitled "Terrorism: Another Point of View."[9]

"Terrorism," he wrote, "is an attack on life, on the individual liberty of defenseless innocents, who are not responsible in the disputes which pit terrorists against their adversaries.

"In Western countries, the only acts of terrorism recognized are those that take the form of explosives in public places, hostage-taking and plane hijacking, actions that threaten civilians.

"But in the Western concept of terrorism, promoted largely by the media, there is a tendency to forget that there are other aspects to the phenomenon of terrorism. . . . It is dishonest to limit the notion of terrorism to the act of setting explosives or taking hostages.

"Let us leave aside the matter of the liquidation of adversaries by different countries' secret services, a commonplace practice . . . often tolerated or inspired by political power.

"Let us ask ourselves the question that provokes so much controversy: Who is a terrorist?

"A government which in the name of national security terrorizes its own population? . . . A national liberation movement that opts for terrorism in the name of liberty and independence? . . . A state that occupies another country, and imposes its power by terrorizing the population? . . .

"Who, finally, is a terrorist?" This question can be answered only within the context of a definition of terrorism itself. Reading down the list of possible candidates, Ghassemlou asks, "Is it the Kurds, who, weapons in hand, are waging an unequal combat to save their national identity? Or is it Khomeini's regime, which for the last seven years has destroyed cities and villages in Iranian Kurdistan and massacred the civilian population? Or the government of Ankara, which, not content with directing a savage repression against the Kurds in Turkey, is now bombarding Kurdish civilians in Iraq? . . .

"If terrorism means an attack against liberty, an attack on innocent and defenseless human beings, then anyone who commits a terrorist act must be considered a terrorist—be that an individual, an organization, or a state.

"It is this definition which must serve as a starting point, and not the point of view of Western countries who are happy to 'expose' the effects of terrorism without taking into consideration the causes and researching the root."

Having reexamined the concept of terrorism itself, Ghassemlou next reframed the conversation about its nature and how to address it. "If the legitimate claims of people are realized and injustices wiped out, terrorist acts will be unanimously condemned, because it is by legitimate political claims that the terrorists justify their own actions," he wrote.

"The West tends to confuse national liberation movements, revolutionary violence, and terrorism. It seems that terrorism is convenient for many governments—so much so that if it did not exist, it would have to be created.

"There are abundant examples: South Africa, Israel, Chile, Iran—these need terrorism to justify their own terrorist policies, paradoxically baptized 'anti-terrorist.'

"For them, the terrorists are all the blacks who demand the abolition of apartheid, all the Palestinians who fight for their right to a country, all the Chileans who battle the dictatorship, and all the Iranians who reject the despotism of the Ayatollah.

"PDKI, the Democratic Party of Iranian Kurdistan, has for the last seven years been forced to resort to an armed struggle against the regime of Ayatollah Khomeini, but has never resorted to terrorism. On the contrary, we have contributed to the liberation of many hostages, including seven French nationals. . . .

"We refuse terrorism by principle, because we consider that it is an attack against liberty and human dignity. Not only that, but also because on a political level if it attains certain objectives, it hurts the long-term prestige of the movement, it denaturalizes it and tears it apart from within. . . .

"The media in the West have fallen into the trap of the terrorists. While terrorist actions are on the front pages of the newspapers, a democratic movement that fights for freedom and human rights is ignored and forgotten.

"The 'Islamic jihad' that represents a small group of individuals is celebrated around the world, but the cause of 20 million Kurds is barely known among political circles.

"Does this enormous disparity not encourage democratic and antiterrorist movements to resort to this form of action in order to be heard?"

Ghassemlou went on to make clear the vulnerability of Western democracies to terrorist manipulation by means of political rivalries. A principal example he cited was Khomeini's pressure in the U.S. elections of 1980 or the Hezbollah blackmail exercised through the kidnapping of Western citizens in Lebanon in 1985 and 1986. Terrorist regimes like that of Khomeini, he pointed out, want to destabilize democracies and export to the West the conflicts that ravage their own countries. The Western defensive reflex, he said—to retreat into imposing limitations on the practice of democracy and the exercise of civil liberties—is to play into the game of the terrorists.

"Under these conditions," he wrote, "how can you end terrorism? There needs to be awareness that terrorism will not be extirpated from one day to another, that the efforts must be systematic and coordinated long-term.

"You have to attack not only the effects but also, and especially, the causes of terrorism."

And, he added, you have to be very careful even in addressing the effects or outward tactics of terrorism. "You are not helping hostages when there is a lot of publicity around them—which is what the terrorists want, which makes a government, and an entire country, the 'hostage of hostages.'"

He took some time to detail concerns about hostages and how to deal with hostage taking. Among the means, negotiation should not be excluded; but the question is, with whom to negotiate. It is important to negotiate not with those who are being manipulated in the situation, but to identify the real terrorists—who are not the ones placing the bomb and taking the hostages. "Why negotiate with Hezbollah," he asked, "when we know they are being directed by Tehran?

"To negotiate," in short, "you must have a true interlocutor." And, he implied, you must identify the leverage you hold. In the case of dealing specifically with the state terrorism of Iran, he pointed out, "Ayatollah Khomeini needs money to continue his war against Iraq, and Iran's income has been affected by the fall of oil prices, and the economy is in a catastrophic situation."

Even when leverage is identified, the barriers to exerting it must be recognized and addressed. "There exist other groups manipulated by governments, which is why the fight against the countries that feed and support terrorism—and at the head of them all is the Iranian regime—is as necessary as internal mobilization. . . .

"During the 444 days of detention of the American hostages in Tehran many European countries continued to have good relations with the Ayatollah's regime, even profiting by the American absence to carve out parts of the Iranian market."

He went on to underline the hypocrisy of European countries like West Germany or England in continuing to do business with the Iranians even while French hostages were taken in Lebanon by orders of the Ayatollah. Western "business as usual" was supporting a regime that maintained what he described clearly as "terrorism as a state doctrine."

Yes, it was logical, Ghassemlou said, to condemn Arab terrorists who endanger the lives of innocent people in the big cities of Europe. "But at the same time," he said, "you must condemn the Israeli bombings of Palestinian camps in Lebanon." It was "normal," too, "to deplore the attack on a synagogue in Istanbul," which compounded the death of twenty-four people with the undermining of religious freedom. "But why haven't we condemned the raid launched by Turkey against Kurdish populations in northern Iraq?" he asked, which left several hundred dead. Western governments' unanimous condemnation of terrorist attacks on European soil was a development he saw as "encouraging." "But it was disappointing to see them hesitate," he added, "in sanctioning the racist regime of South Africa.

"It is time to end this discrimination, which is based on the unspoken idea that on our planet, there are people regarded as second-class citizens, people whose lives don't have the same value as those of citizens of the developed countries.

"So in the fight against terrorism, we can only count on the solidarity of people of the Third World.

"To support morally and politically the movements that fight for their liberty without resorting to terrorism," he concluded, "is also a way of fighting terrorism."

Notes

1. *Kurdistan d'Iran* (Paris: PDKI publication), 1986.
2. Ibid.
3. Ibid.
4. Ibid.
5. Ibid.
6. Abdul Rahman Ghassemlou, *Kwrtabas la sar sozialism* [A short treatise on socialism] [in Kurdish] (Sweden: Ktebi Erzan publications, ed. Salah Sheshe, 2003), 64; translation Salah Piroty.
7. Abdul Rahman Ghassemlou, interview with Enayat Fani, June 1989; broadcast on BBC Persian, July 2014, https://www.youtube.com/watch?v=SGsfvkcMn8U (accessed February 2, 2016]. The extended statement by Ghassemlou that follows is from this interview.
8. In this statement Ghassemlou used terms that distinguish between *mardom-e Iran*, "people of Iran" or "the Iranian people," and *khlalgh-e Iran*, "people" in the sense of "a people," "the peoples of Iran," "Iran's nationalities" or historical cultural populations. This term was commonly used in PDKI literature; *Khalgh-e Kurd*, for example, designates "the Kurdish nation," not "Kurdish persons or individuals." *Khalgh*, as an alternative term for "nationalities" with a sense between *melat* and *ghawm*, was used by the PDKI and other leftist organizations during the revolution to avoid uproar among those who would be disturbed by the word *nation*. It is still used in that sense by the party.
9. Abdul Rahman Ghassemlou, "Terrorism: Another Point of View," originally published in the journal *Kurdistan*, 162 [in Farsi] (Gawrade: Iranian Kurdistan Democratic Party Publishing Commission, n.d.). French translation published in *Kurdistan d'Iran*, "Le Terrorisme: Un autre point de vue," no. 20, Décembre 1986–Janvier 1987; translation by the author.

PART V

THE INVESTIGATION AND
THE AFTERMATH

· 1 ·

AFTER THE CRIME

❧

Vienna. Thursday, July 13, 1989. While the assassination of Abdul Rahman Ghassemlou, Abdullah Ghaderi-Azar, and Fadil Rasul was taking place in cold blood, Susanne Rockenschaub was with some friends. She had gone to the theater to see the musical *Les Miserables*. That afternoon, her husband Rasul had left the house without mentioning where he was going.

At the end of the show, Susanne returned to her home at Wasagasse. It was 10:30 p.m. She slowly climbed the stairs to the first floor. When she arrived at the door of her apartment, she found herself surrounded by a formidable group of policemen armed with machine guns.

The police were accompanied by Rasul's two brothers. When she unlocked her apartment door, the police entered with her. They searched the rooms thoroughly and had many questions. She could not understand at all what was happening, not even after one of the policemen informed her that three Arabs had been murdered.

The phone rang at 11:00 p.m. Susanne answered, but the police motioned her not to speak about their presence in her home. The wife of a journalist friend was calling to tell her that Rasul had been assassinated. Susanne's first thought, in the instant of hearing the news, was that the murderers had been Iraqi.

Thirty minutes later, the phone rang again. It was the former Iranian president, Banisadr, calling from Paris. The agents were watching her carefully while she spoke with him, trying to grasp some clue. About this conversation, Banisadr recalled,[1] "They told me that something had happened with Rasul. I called his house and his wife answered, but she did not know what was happening."

Banisadr had received reliable information that Tehran was organizing a political assassination. "Even though I did not know against whom, I had informed Rasul about this soon after, and suggested that he pass this information on to the Iranian opposition."

At 1:30 in the morning, the police brought Susanne to the police station. It was there they informed her that her husband had been murdered.

In this tragedy, where three Kurds lost their lives, Rasul remains the most controversial character. For the former Algerian president, Ahmed Ben Bella, Rasul was "a pure being, who had the quality of reflection." Banisadr considered him a friend and "a brilliant intellectual." H., close advisor to Banisadr, considered Rasul "a man of integrity, solid, and a victim of his own naïveté."[2]

Susanne would take Rasul's body to be buried in Iraqi Kurdistan. Rasul was convinced, she believed, that Abdul Rahman Ghassemlou was the man capable of bringing the Kurds together. "That is why he agreed to be an intermediary [between Ghassemlou and the Iranian government]," she confided one winter night, almost two years after the crime, in a Chinese restaurant near her home.[3]

Fatah, the PDKI's representative in Vienna, shared Susanne's opinion. "Rasul wanted to be the intermediary between the Kurds and Tehran," he said.[4] Not all observers have seen Rasul's motivation as being so clear-cut. French journalist Marc Kravetz cautioned, "Rasul's role was ambiguous. I think he was less brilliant than Susanne has said."[5]

The members of the small Kurdish community in Vienna and their friends around the world have debated copiously about the crime and the role that Rasul played in it. In general, they do not like him. None believe that he wanted to lead Ghassemlou and Ghaderi-Azar to their death. But in a certain way, his name is associated with the shadow of treason and the crime. "He only wanted money," scoffed a woman from the Kurdish community in a derogatory way.

Talabani, the Iraqi Kurdish leader, thought that the young man had created a deluded personal agenda: he was trying to prove that he could mediate between the Kurds and the governments that oppressed them. He longed to play an important role in resolving the entire Kurdish question.[6]

In this desire to be a player in crafting a settlement, he seemed moved by ambitions similar to those fueling his work editing Al Hiwar, "Dialogue," an Islamic journal in Arabic founded by Banisadr. Rasul "used to explain that his main aims were to initiate an international Islamic reform dialogue from Vienna," a recent study points out; his vision of himself was "as an international Islamic Kurdish reformer, initiator and mediator." A reformer, however, whose achievement fell far short of the broad recognition he longed for, and whose hopes could be easily played upon.[7]

"That is why he encouraged Ghassemlou to travel to Vienna," Talabani said. "He was an opportunist. Banisadr and Ben Bella do not know him well. I've known him since he was a kid. He was in our ranks since high school, along with his older brother. He was a member of the students' organization and our party. When we formed the Iraqi Komala party, he joined us. Later on, he went to the Iraqi Communist Party, to the revolutionary wing. Afterward, he became a Maoist and finally an Islamist, a fundamentalist. He had good relations with Banisadr and Ben Bella because of the Islamic fundamentalism."[8]

All who knew him confirmed Fadil Rasul's complex political and ideological journey. He was a Kurdish militant in Iraq; he turned toward Maoism and later became an exile. An admirer of Mao Zedong, he went to China in 1978 and returned there to visit again in 1983 and 1986, when he had converted to Islam. This series of shifts in outlook and direction could certainly be read by observers as marking some fundamental instability of character—and like the young man's ambitious self-regard, could also mark him as a weak link, an entry point for infiltration, and an invitation to manipulation.[9]

Talabani certainly felt antipathy toward him. "Rasul," he insisted, "was moved by his vanity. He always sought to attract attention. He was constantly with the girls. He was thrown out of the student organization because he went after the girls. In our countries, you know how that works. To even kiss a girl there is a crime."

Azad painted a similar picture of Rasul. "He was frivolous. He liked women and he had a lover. Her name was Renata."[10] Under Islamic law, Renata could have been considered Rasul's second wife. She was Austrian and had been a friend of Susanne's for many years. They were both feminists who participated in leftist student movements. Even though they both shared Rasul's bed and his religious faith, it seemed Susanne never accepted her husband's relationship with Renata. But still Susanne did not break with him.

"Of course, Rasul wasn't as dumb as some people said," sarcastically commented one of the women of the Kurdish community at an interview. "He was so eloquent that he convinced two Austrian women to marry him and become Muslims."

Renata taught German. They say she helped Rasul prepare a book about the Kurdish situation; it was a thesis about the role the Soviet Union played in the Kurdish question.

The book's subject matter had been the focus of a three-way public debate between Rasul, a university professor of political science, and an Iranian. Charlotte, Azad's wife, attended the debate. She was surprised at how badly

Rasul spoke German: "He spoke poorly, pronounced poorly, and his discourse had no structure."[11]

When the murder was committed, *Al Hiwar*, Banisadr's magazine of reflections on Islam, presented Rasul as a martyr. But it did not mention the participation of Iranians in the crime. This infuriated the Kurds, who never forgave this publication for having printed an apologia for the Islamic revolution. This same magazine had defended Khomeini's position toward the Islamic constitution and published, among other things, translations of articles by officials of the Tehran regime.[12] While it is clear that Rasul wasn't a man who was made for politics, he had dedicated a great deal of his life to this activity.

Rasul had arrived in Vienna some time after his elder brother, Fuad, who as the first representative of Talabani's PUK in Austria was well regarded as a political moderate and a "person of integrity." A second brother, from Iraqi Kurdistan, was a member of the security detail for Ghassemlou's first set of negotiations with the Iranians in December 1988–January 1989,[13] and Talabani had in fact used Rasul's home for one round of those talks.

Talabani acknowledged the past usefulness of Rasul's services as a political mediator. "He was my intermediary with the Iranians; Rasul mediated between Banisadr and myself in 1982."

To be fair, the young man had something more than sex appeal. He had good contacts and a certain ability to work with people that others could not fail to recognize.

Why did the Iranians choose him for their meeting with Abdul Rahman Ghassemlou? Was it because of his experience? Certainly not. Their reasons for selecting Rasul for this important task were most likely his naïveté and proven vanity.

It is clear that Rasul was not a person who *knew* people, not someone with subtle discernment of character and motivation. During the month of January, when he had brought the Iranian negotiators to his house, his wife had found them disagreeable. Rasul insisted that they were refined and cultivated people.

In the aftermath of the murder Talabani would say he was convinced that what the Iranians wanted to do all along was to kill Ghassemlou. Given his own prior role as a mediator or facilitator, it is not clear at what point he reached this conviction.[14] But in Rasul, he believed, the regime had found the ideal front man for their plan. "I believe they chose him," Talabani later summed up, "because the Iranians knew the weaknesses he had."

In an intricate web of connections, Tehran drew on every available contact to choreograph the outcome: connections between Islamic scholars in

Iran with Rasul and his magazine in Vienna, ties—these will be detailed—between Hashemi Rafsanjani and Jalal Talabani. Undoubtedly there were others, profiles and dossiers compiled, secret service and security networks.[15]

For many of Ghassemlou's compatriots, the nature of Rasul's involvement, especially, would remain an open question: Was he a player, or was he being played by the Iranians? Throughout his intercession with the Iranians it seemed that Rasul never became aware that he was being used to bring Ghassemlou into a position of vulnerability. His motive seemed to be pivotal as a point of leverage: the desire to be part of the historical event of bringing about a peace accord between the Kurds and the Iranian regime.

One odd piece of information that would come to light in the police investigation was the timing of an upscale real-estate transaction.

On July 15, 1989, an attestation reported to the police by a notary's office revealed that in December—just prior to the first set of Iranian negotiations with Ghassemlou—Fadil Rasul had purchased a condominium in downtown Vienna on behalf of Ahmed Ben Bella. Ben Bella, it was noted, was "former Minister President of Algeria," and was "responsible for the agreement." The cost of the purchase in Austrian schillings was ÖS 1,450.000, a substantial sum. "And what kind of relationship Dr. Rasul [had] to Ben Bella," the report concluded, "could not be ascertained."[16]

The questions this transaction would raise: Where did Rasul—or Ben Bella—acquire the funds for such a purchase? Was there the implication of a payoff of some kind—financial promises by the Iranians for engagement in luring Ghassemlou to a death-trap? Did the Iranians pay for the apartment? Was this line of inquiry pursued further? If not, was this matter deliberately buried? Or was the timing of the purchase a matter of the purest coincidence?

Queries that remain open and unresolved, awaiting further investigation, include another anomalous detail: the fact that Ghassemlou had no security at the negotiations. Would not Rasul, as the organizer of the meetings, have been responsible for making security arrangements? Was he, in this omission, an inadvertent victim of his own naïveté?

Notes

1. Abolhassan Banisadr, interview with the author, Versailles, 1991. Further statements from Banisadr are from this interview.

2. "H," interview with the author, Paris, 1991. For security reasons, H. prefers not to be identified.
3. Susanne Rockenschaub-Rasul, interview with Gabriel Fernández, Vienna, February 1991.
4. Fatah, interviews with Gabriel Fernández, Vienna, 1990–91.
5. Marc Kravetz, interview with the author, Paris, 1991.
6. Jalal Talabani, interview with the author, Paris, 1991. Unless otherwise noted, statements that follow from Talabani in this chapter are from this interview.
7. Ferdinand Hennerbichler, "Assassination of Abdul Rahman Ghassemlou (1930–1989): New Assessment," in *Wiener Jahrbuch für Kurdische Studien 2013, Schwerpunkt: Transnationalität und kurdische Diaspora in Österreich, Jahrgang 1/2013* (Vienna: Österreichische Gesellschaft zur Förderung der Kurdologie / Europäisches Zentrum für kurdische Studien, 2013), 300.
8. Jalal Talabani, interview with the author, Paris, 1991.
9. Hennerbichler, "Assassination of Abdul Rahman Ghassemlou," 300.
10. Azad, interview with Gabriel Fernández, Vienna, 1990.
11. Charlotte, interviews with Gabriel Fernández, Vienna, 1990–91. The book, *Kulturelle Dialog und Gewalt* [Cultural dialogue and power], was published by Junius Editorial with Susanne's collaboration and a prologue by Ahmed Ben Bella. Its focus was the politics of the great powers, the struggle for the liberty of Kurdistan, and Soviet politics in the Middle East.
12. Written in Arabic, *Al Hiwar* had the following address: P.F. 33, 1092 Wien, and it maintained a checking account (Konto Nr601485303) with the Zentralsparkasse-Wien und Kommerzialbank. The Kurds asserted that it was financed by the Iranians.

Fadil Rasul was born in Sulaimaniya, Iraq, in 1948, to a nationalist Kurdish family. There he finished high school. In 1963, at age 15, he was detained and tortured for his political activities. In 1968–1969, he was secretary of the Union of Students of Iraqi Kurdistan. Along with his studies of law and political science at the University of Baghdad, he began practicing journalism. At the beginning of the 1970s, he created with other militants of the Kurdish cause—Chahabi Sheikh Nouri among them—the Association of the Workers of Iraqi Kurdistan. When he finished school in 1978, he was still politically active, but clandestinely. In 1978, because of the internal struggles of the PUK and KDP, he abandoned Iraqi Kurdistan and moved to Beirut, which was then a vital political center in the Middle East. There he worked for some time at the Center for Palestinian Studies.

In 1980 he moved to Vienna, where he finished his doctorate in political science. At the same time, he maintained contacts with a number of Kurdish organizations without being a member of any one of them. He developed relations with various intellectuals of the Arab and Iranian world.

Abolhassan Banisadr founded *Al Hiwar* in 1986 to facilitate the interchange of ideas and reflection about the Muslim world. The magazine gained importance among Muslim intellectuals owing to its high quality. Rasul was its chief editor. He was a researcher at the University of Vienna and also collaborated with the Kurdish Institute of Paris. He had published a number of articles and two books in German, including *Iraq-Iran Urzachen und Dimensiones eines Konfliktes* (Berlin: International, 1987). *Bulletin de liaison et d'information de l'Institut Kurde de Paris*, July–August 1989.

13. Hennerbichler, "Assassination of Abdul Rahman Ghassemlou," 300. However, Hennerbichler notes, following the 2003 takedown of Saddam Hussein's regime, files came to light revealing that this brother "had worked as an agent for the toppled regime." Confronted with the evidence, he claimed "to have done so in order to protect Kurds from persecution." He was imprisoned under threat of execution but ultimately pardoned by Talabani following Talabani's election as president of Iraq; Ibid.

14. Talabani himself would later find himself "accused of having initiated Abdul Rahman Ghassemlou into disaster and being ultimately responsible for his death in Vienna"; Ibid., 298. When a Lebanese newspaper published such an accusation, however, Talabani would sue for libel and win the court case in Beirut. Jalal Talabani, verbal communication to Ferdinand Hennerbichler, 2012, reported in Hennerbichler, "Assassination of Abdul Rahman Ghassemlou," 289 n29.

15. Ibid., 301.

16. "Inquiry of Information Notes from July 15, 1989 (Dr. Rassoul-Ben Bela—Apartment Purchase)," Federal Police Headquarters, number I-Pos 400/IIIa/15/89 res regarding "Assassination Attempt in Vienna 3, Linke Bahngasse 5/12," Vienna, July 17, 1989, unpublished document. See Appendix, "Austrian Police Reports," for copies of the English translation of the original German sworn statements.

· 2 ·

STUNNED

࿈

The news of the murder stunned people around the world. Fatosh Güney, widow of the Kurdish film director Yilmaz Güney and personal friend of Ghassemlou, found out the next morning, July 14. That day was a national French holiday. France was celebrating the bicentenary of the Revolution and its proclamation of human rights.

"I was invited to the Élysée Palace and the parade," she recalled.[1] "Kendal Nezan called and informed me. I did not attend any of the events that day. I did not want to believe it. I could hear people singing and dancing in the streets and I would keep seeing his body filled with bullets. That was a terrible day."

Q. M. heard the news early in the morning while listening to Radio Israel. Dr. Bernard Kouchner found out through French radio and television. Jonathan Randal heard the news through London's BBC. And from the offices of the Spanish newspaper *El Pais*, the journalist Rafael Fraguas confirmed the news to me.

Ben Bella recalled, "That night, we had gone to a concert with my wife and children. It was held in an old palace. We returned at about one in the morning. Susanne called my wife and told her that Anwar [Fadil Rasul] had died. We immediately went to see her. She needed to be with someone. We knew that Anwar had been going to see the Kurds and the Iranians. It was the day of Eid al-Adha, the Festival of Sacrifice.[2] Immediately we knew it had been the Iranians. It felt as though the sky fell upon us."[3]

"Anwar" was the name Ben Bella used for Fadil Rasul, a man for whom he felt great affection. "I would do anything for Anwar," he confessed.

"In Kurdistan," remembered Sadegh Sharafkandi, "when we found out that Ghassemlou had been killed, we were paralyzed. I could not move. Then Mamosta [Abdullah Hassanzadeh] said: 'Have you forgotten what he used to say? When a friend dies, we should not cry. We have to work, so his work will continue.'"[4]

A peshmerga commander remembered Sharafkandi's message to the peshmerga after the assassination: "Dr. Ghassemlou is no more," said Dr. Said, "but the party is intact and the struggle continues." This timely message, he felt, had saved the peshmerga from demoralization.

Months after Ghassemlou's death, Sharafkandi continued to speak of his legacy. "Despite the great loss of our beloved leader, Dr. Ghassemlou," he said in a public address in 1990, "still, the party has endured. This year, the party showed not only that it stayed on course but also that it has more sense of responsibility in spite of the blow it suffered. The flag that Dr. Ghassemlou held up, now everyone has committed themselves to be responsible for holding it." What this meant, he added, is that "the spirit of continuity of struggle has been established."[5]

Bernard Granjon, a physician with MdM, returned to Kurdistan two months after the assassination. "The people were traumatized," he shared later.[6] "Several people committed suicide. There was a state of desperation. People played cassette tapes with praises about Ghassemlou that repeated, 'You will always be with us.' They all thanked me for what I had done for the burial. In truth, I had not done much. But because I loved him, I was given credit. Even Said [Sharafkandi] and his people were in a state of utter confusion. Still today, when Said speaks about him, his eyes fill with tears.

"The leaders decided that the best example of loyalty was to continue his battle. You saw his photo everywhere, something that never happened when he was alive. All the artists celebrated him. It was like a painful rebirth following his violent death.

"His death also gave the Kurds a symbol; he turned into a kind of 'De Gaulle Kurd.' I think he would have liked to have died while in action with his two favorite weapons: negotiation and dialogue. He had grown afraid that eventually power would dominate him. His project, which some saw as utopian, was not. He insisted that it was not necessary to go through the stage of proletarian dictatorship to achieve democracy. When I spoke with a young man in Kurdistan after Rahman's death and asked what Dr. Ghassemlou meant to him, the young man answered simply, 'He is democracy.'

"Ghassemlou liked to play with ideas, with people—and perhaps in that last meeting, he also played with his life. Said quoted a phrase that Rahman used to repeat when speaking about the martyrs: 'If a man is a revolutionary, his death will also be a revolutionary act.'"

Remembering that day, Florence Veber recalled some words Ghassemlou had spoken to her in the mountains: "I would like to die in Kurdistan." She added, "Rahman was afraid of dying in Europe."[7]

❧

The night of July 13, 1989, Hélène was asleep in her small Parisian apartment when the phone rang. She woke up, startled, thinking it was already daylight and she was waiting for the morning sun to warm her body.

"Hello . . ." she answered, still half asleep.

She did not understand what the person calling was saying.

Then there was a pause. Recalling that moment later, she said, "And then I knew. A terrible sense of catastrophe fell over me."

"Nasrin Janum," the caller said, "Forgive me, I can't . . ." Hélène felt paralyzed, like someone who has been condemned to death. She could not speak.

"Kak Doctor has died," said her caller.

They were both silent for an interminable instant.

"That's it . . . That's it . . ." he repeated over and over again.

She forced herself to hang up and take a few steps to put her thoughts in order. But she could not. "It's the end," she told herself. "The circle has been closed."

Then she thought this might be a very bad joke. How many anonymous calls had she received before? "Yes, yes, it must be," she thought. "I'm going to call the party."

But it was too early to do so; and she knew that this time it was true, that it wasn't a joke. She knew that it had been faithful Fatah who had called her from Vienna. She had recognized his voice; it was just that she didn't want to accept the reality.

Ghassemlou had said goodbye to her in Paris on July 11, Tuesday. He had called her that day and the next, Wednesday. But that day, Thursday, July 13, her phone had remained silent.[8]

"Abdul Rahman went to meet with the wolves," she said later. "He told me the day before he traveled to Vienna. He was convinced that Rafsanjani and the Iranian government would not dare to harm him. He was certain that the government needed an agreement with him and the Kurds. They needed this compromise to assuage global public opinion. They needed it to stay in power."[9]

Indeed, the circle had closed. The circle Hélène was thinking of that night had begun in Prague one night in 1951, when she was singing in the university chorus in a celebration to honor a professor . . . She had met Rahman that night. She was turning eighteen; he was twenty-one. That night the chorus was singing in praise of Stalin and the proletarian revolution of 1917—an event in which they both believed with religious fervor.

Since she was the only one who spoke English, the chorus director had sent her to host the four foreign young men who were sitting at one of the tables. She thought there were two Czech nationals (one of them had a Slovak accent), a Syrian, and an Iraqi.

But suddenly she discovered that they all spoke the language and had no need of her. They began to flirt, which irritated her. She left them, but the director insisted she return. She did, and had a delightful evening. The four young men made her laugh; they told her about their problems in the Middle East and their political struggles.

When it was time to go, all four offered to take her home. Hélène was a beautiful girl: slender, five foot six, with jet black hair and very light blue eyes.

"Why should all four of us go?" asked the Slovak. "One will be enough." He accompanied her home and said good-bye to her at her doorstep. Two months later, she ran into him by chance—and she found out that he wasn't Slovak, but an Iranian Kurd. His name was Abdul Rahman Ghassemlou.

Shortly after the crime, an American woman wrote Hélène from the United States, asking her to tell the story of her life with Ghassemlou in a magazine article. Hélène refused. The woman insisted. Hélène overcame her resistance and summarized in one thousand words her relationship with her husband of almost forty years. Hélène's story ended like this: "July 11, 1989, was the last time I said good-bye to him."

Hélène did not actually know how many times they had said good-bye. She only remembered that ever since she'd met him, her life had been a whirlwind and she had lived in thirty-three different homes. In Tehran alone, between 1954 and 1956, she moved eleven times.

"It was not a horrible life, no," she reminisced, sipping a cup of tea in a café in Vienna. "I do not regret having lived that way. But it was not a stroll."[10]

They shared many things, from the small domestic details to the discussions about political strategy. But he was often an absent husband, far away on secret missions, crossing borders with false passports, living in a clandestine way, risking life and freedom.

She never demanded anything, she said. She acquiesced to living in the midst of that whirlwind. She thought it was a mistake, now, that she gave herself fully to him—only to discover one day that she could not change anything.

Notes

1. Fatosh Güney, interview with the author, Paris, 1991.
2. Eid al-Adha is an annual religious festival celebrated by Muslims all over the world. It commemorates the willingness of the patriarch Ibrahim to sacrifice his son to God. Once Ibrahim demonstrated his willingness to follow God's commands, God took mercy upon him and told Ibrahim to sacrifice a ram placed before him, rather than his son.
3. Ahmed Ben Bella, interview with Gabriel Fernández and the author, Hammam Bou-Hadjar, Algeria, 1991. Further statements from Ben Bella in this chapter are taken from this interview.
4. Sadegh Sharafkandi, interview with Bernard Granjon, PDKI general headquarters in Kurdistan, 1991.
5. Oration at the PDKI Cemetery of Martyrs, Qandil mountains, Iraqi Kurdistan, July 15, 1989; translation Salah Piroty.
6. Bernard Granjon, interview with the author, Paris, 1991.
7. Florence Veber, interview with the author, Paris, 1991.
8. Hélène Krulich-Ghassemlou, *Love Against All Reason: A European Woman Involved in the Kurdish Fight for Freedom in Iran* (Vienna: Lit Verlag, 2017), 238.
9. Hélène Krulich, interview with Gabriel Fernández and the author, Paris, 1990. Except where noted, statements that follow from Hélène are taken from this interview.
10. Hélène Krulich, interview with Gabriel Fernández, Vienna, 1991.

· 3 ·

BEN BELLA ACCUSES

❧

The day after the murder, Susanne was interrogated by the police. The police chief, Oswald Kessler, treated her with great consideration, for she was the daughter of a well-known member of the Socialist Party. He informed her that it had not been the Iraqis, but the Iranians, who were the perpetrators of the crime.

She knew that the Iranians had not wanted either Talabani or Ben Bella to participate in the negotiation. But no one, apparently, had informed Ben Bella of this. Susanne communicated this to him, and the old Algerian fox, seasoned from so many battles, concluded that if he had been informed beforehand, he would have known that what was being prepared was an assassination.

"The police saw me at Susanne's house," Ben Bella said later,[1] "and I told them what I knew. They said they wanted to see me again at their office. I know the police very well. Susanne naïvely thought that they were good guys. But I felt something was going on. The head of the police is an asp, a snake. He was trying to trick her."

Interrogating Ben Bella, the police tried a deception: according to a recording they had, they told him, Ghassemlou had asked that he, Ben Bella, be present for the negotiations and the Iranians had refused. The police asked Ben Bella if he had been at the scene of the crime. He denied this. They asked if he spoke Persian.

"It was a trap to see if I had been present, even silently, in which case I would be an important witness. Then I said, 'Show me the recording.' They looked at each other and told me it did not exist. I exploded and said to them, 'You are accomplices of the Iranians. You hid the facts and did not detain them, because they bought arms from you. I will be president of Algeria, and I swear that you will hear from me, you and your government. This affair will not stay buried. Anwar was my brother, and you will pay for this.'"

In light of this reaction they decided to end the interrogation, but Ben Bella was righteously indignant.

"Continue," he said. "You are a policeman, a *flic*,[2] that is what you are. I have seen many flics in my life. You are but a small flic."

Later, Ben Bella met with Susanne and told her, "He's an asp. He is not our friend in this affair. He is a pathetic policeman from a banana republic called Austria that sells arms, that sells everything—even their honor."

Ben Bella severed his relations with Iran. He wrote an article against the Iranian government, denouncing them. "A revolution that does this is finished. It's something very dirty. That same day, I wrote against the Iranians. At that time, no one was sure who the murderers were. They were searching other trails. I was sure it was them. They organized it very well. It was an almost perfect murder.

"That day I hated Iran and its revolution. I wrote an article in *Al Bedir*. I wrote in a monthly newspaper. I knew from before that the revolution had erred in its direction, but the situation with Anwar was . . ." He shook his head.

Ben Bella believed that with the negotiations, the Iranians were hoping to achieve an advantageous agreement for Tehran. In case this did not happen, he said, "Ghassemlou had to be killed. I think that they prepared everything in case he would not concede. They were in constant contact with Tehran, and the order to murder him came from there.

"I believe that the Iranian embassy in Vienna was involved. Perhaps they did not know the details, but they were accomplices. You have to know the revolution. They act under the reality of power; the pasdaran are the power. Ghassemlou's demands were not radical. He thought that after Khomeini's death, the circumstances were favorable for a negotiation.

"Sahrarudi was a man close to Rafsanjani. He [Rafsanjani] knew about the plan; it could not have happened without his knowing it. Rafsanjani gave the green light. They thought they would decapitate the Kurdish movement and the opposition."

French journalist Marc Kravetz, reporting as the crime investigation unfolded, said much the same. Sahrarudi, as Rafsanjani's man, was in his estimation the strategist of the assassination operation.[3] But pointing beyond Sahrarudi, Kravetz too could see, "there is no doubt where the assassins came from"[4]—Rafsanjani.

For Rafsanjani, said Kravetz, decapitating the Kurdish movement necessarily meant removing its irreplaceable leader, Ghassemlou.[5] It was his leadership, more than that of any other, that set direction for the Kurdish cause in Iran. "Ghassemlou was a man of an entirely different stature and standing from Jalal Talabani," Ben Bella said. "He had this as an image: he was a good and honest man. He was an important man."

In light of Ghassemlou's preeminence and careful judgment, "I was surprised that Ghassemlou would negotiate with such uncultivated people," commented Abolhassan Banisadr.[6] "They had no weight. But Susanne told me that Ghassemlou was *à bout de souffle* [exhausted], and that he wanted a solution.

"I asked her why Rasul had not asked me about the Iranians. But Rasul was under a lot of pressure from both sides. If he'd said anything, he could have been accused of betrayal [of the confidentiality of the negotiations]. I'm sure it's Rafsanjani who gave the order. It was the Ministry of Foreign Affairs that organized all this, and the ministry was in Rafsanjani's hands.

"From Iran, we were informed that among the pasdaran, there was talk about the murder before it happened. One had asked, 'Why Rasul?' The director of information, or [Commander Mohsen] Rezae, head of the pasdaran, answered that Rasul was a *munafiq*[7] [a hypocrite] and that he worked with the opposition against Rafsanjani—which means me and Montazeri [among others]."

Ben Bella never returned to Austria. Every time he'd traveled there before, it was Anwar who was waiting for him at the airport. He could not bear his absence. Now, he said, it was Susanne who came to Algeria to visit them.

કૢ

Hélène arrived in Vienna on Sunday, July 16, in a state of disarray. Despite the luminosity that enveloped the city that morning, her meeting with the Kurds waiting for her at the airport was heartbreaking. No one understood how Ghassemlou could have made the error of entering the trap that had been laid for him.

In Paris, the funeral was prepared for that Tuesday. But on Monday, administrative hurdles to getting the bodies to Paris had ground everything to a halt. By Tuesday, even by four in the afternoon, nothing had been accomplished.

In Vienna, faced with so many obstacles to the release of the bodies, Hélène was assailed by a terrible doubt: "Perhaps it's not really them." So she decided to go to the morgue and see the bodies.

"Abdullah was unrecognizable. I knew it was him [only] because of the mole on his face," she said.[8]

Abdul Rahman was disfigured, but not unrecognizable. His body lay on a trolley, naked, with his head on a pillow. As they had done with Abdullah, the forensic physicians had opened Ghassemlou up to examine his organs. A seam sewn up with a thick thread ran down his body from trachea to pubis.

They had washed the body, and his dark hair was all disheveled. He had cotton in his nostrils and in his left ear. His earlobes, completely white, stood out against large bruises: one on his left eye, near where the bullet which presumably killed him had entered; another on the right side of the neck where one of the three bullets had exited his body.

The four wounds—three entering and one exiting his body—had been sewn up: at his left temple, his forehead, the left superior maxillary, and the right side of his neck. The suture along his forehead lifted his eyebrows, which gave his face a strange expression. His generous mouth was halfway open and seemed to reflect a profound pain, which he could not have felt, since the shots had killed him instantly. Two of the projectiles had lodged inside his skull.[9]

The French medical organization AMI had sent two staff to Vienna to help with the formal procedures. The French embassy also intervened to help with the process of getting the bodies out of Vienna. On Wednesday, July 19, and no one knows how, the bodies of Ghassemlou and Ghaderi-Azar were embalmed and sent to Paris.

In the French capital, Fatosh prepared the hall at the Kurdish Institute, where the vigil was to be held. "There were three tables where we were to put the two coffins," she said. "I asked for a sheet, but they did not have one. We only had the one we had used for Yilmaz's funeral, but it did not fit. I had to cut it, and I sewed it the whole night. The next day it was like reliving Yilmaz's funeral. The same struggle, the same people, the cemetery . . ."[10]

"We did not know where we would be able to bury them," remembered Dr. Michel Bonnot. "We had to fight to bury them in Paris. We finally found them a resting place in Père Lachaise."[11]

Notes

1. Ahmed Ben Bella, interview with Gabriel Fernández and the author, Hammam Bou-Hadjar, Algeria, 1991.
2. Pejorative term, in French slang, for the police.

3. Marc Kravetz, "Téhéran-Vienne: Récit d'un crime," *Libération*, August 7, 1989.

4. Marc Kravetz, interview with the author, Paris, 1991.

5. Kravetz, "Récit d'un crime."

6. Abolhassan Banisadr, interview with the author, Versailles, 1991.

7. In Islam, a hypocrite, *munāfiq*, is denounced in the Qur'an as a Muslim in appearance only, one who harbors indifference toward the faith and even works to undermine the community of believers. Hypocrisy itself is termed *nifāq*; https://www.al-islam.org/hypocrites-a-commentary-of-surah-al-munafiqun-jafar-subhani/hypocrisy.

8. Hélène Krulich, interview with Gabriel Fernández, Vienna, 1991.

9. See Appendix, "Austrian Police Reports," for the report of the autopsy.

10. The funeral was conducted on Thursday, July 20, 1989. Fatosh Güney, interview with the author, Paris, 1991.

11. Michel Bonnot, interview with the author, Paris, 1991.

· 4 ·

TWO POLICE REPORTS

❧

The day the coffins left Vienna for Paris, Hélène and the Kurds were still in the dark about much of the crime. They had no doubt the murderers were Iranians. They knew Ghassemlou and Ghaderi-Azar had attended a negotiation, which very few knew about until after the crime. Even the party didn't know. The crime was a massive unknown, a blank wall, and unending doubt weighed upon them. For Ghassemlou's widow, as for the Kurdish leaders of the PDKI, a long, laborious, and complex investigation began that ran parallel to that of the police.

A police report reconstructed the facts of the crime in this way:[1]

The positions of the victims as indicated by the witness, Sahrarudi, did not coincide with the findings of the physical evidence—the placement and specific features of the wounds and the trajectory of the projectiles.

According to the positions of the projectiles and the wounds of the victims, it was determined that there were two gunmen.

Two weapons were involved, both pistols: a Beretta and a Llama. Each was fired eight times. Silencers were used at short range, a fact confirmed by the biological remains found on the Llama.

When Ghassemlou was hit, he was probably positioned between a table and the sofa, with his back to the window. He was first hit twice in the left temple with the Beretta. The gunman, therefore, firing at such short range, was also between the sofa and the table.

With these two shots, Ghassemlou fell to the floor, slumped in a half-seated position with his back against the sofa. Then the gunman with the Llama approached him and put the weapon to his forehead. While evidence suggests that Ghassemlou's death came quickly at the start of the action, we can't say with precision the sequence in which Ghassemlou fell in relation to the other two victims.[2]

Ghaderi-Azar was between Ghassemlou and Rasul, Ghassemlou to his left and Rasul to his right, in front of the sofa. He was shot from behind, from the left, with the Llama. The gunman could have been standing by the armchair, to the left of and behind Ghaderi-Azar.

Ghaderi-Azar apparently got up and fell as he turned around; at this moment, the gunman with the Beretta was also probably firing at him. He fell after Rasul had fallen, because Ghaderi-Azar was lying at the feet of the table, his body partly covering Rasul's. A final shot, to his forehead, was fired with the Llama.[3]

Rasul's body lay in a position almost parallel to Ghaderi-Azar's. He was shot with the Llama from the left, two or three times. He fell to the floor. The shot to his neck and perhaps one of the shots to the head were fired, most probably with the Beretta, after he had fallen.

Sahrarudi was wounded by a single bullet. It penetrated his left arm, traveled through the left side of his back, up his neck into his mouth, and then was lost. Sahrarudi apparently offered his left side to the gunman, probably with his left arm extended. His position in the crime scene cannot be reconstructed.

Sahrarudi's version, that the gunmen fired from the doorway across the room, does not coincide with the chemical analysis of the bullet traces on the clothing of the victims; judging from these, the shots were fired at short range. Another telling feature is the use of silencers, which assure only short-range shooting precision. The positions of the projectiles show clearly that they were not fired from the area close to the door.

Afterward, in the photos handed over to the attorneys by the police, Ghassemlou's body appears seated on the floor, his back resting against the sofa. What Ghassemlou's friend Azad thought he'd seen when he and his friends arrived at the apartment that fateful night was Abdullah lying on his back in the middle of the room and a third man lying face down near the door; but the photos show something different.

A later report summarized the data succinctly as the reconstruction of the facts:

Two gunmen fired two guns with silencers.
The gunmen were in two different positions.
They fired at short range.
No gunman was close to the door.
The findings of the report contradict Sahrarudi's version of events.

In conclusion:

Dr. Abdul Rahman Ghassemlou was killed by three shots, undoubtedly from two gunmen.

The shots were instantly fatal.

The bullets from two of the shots were found in his skull, which allowed the weapons to be identified: the shot in the left temple was fired by a Beretta, the one in the forehead, with a Llama. This was a shot fired directly to the forehead.

The sequence of the shots fatal to Ghassemlou was also established: Dr. Ghassemlou was killed by the first two shots to the head on the left side, one from the Beretta. And a final shot was fired to his forehead with the Llama.

Notes

1. See Appendix, "Austrian Police Reports," for copies of the police reports, ballistics reports, and autopsy reports in English translation.
2. The fact that Ghassemlou apparently had no time to react or engage in any kind of defensive maneuvers strongly suggests that he was the first one targeted and killed.
3. Ghaderi-Azar's wounds included one to the back of his head, two wounds to his torso, one to his temple, one to the throat, one to the shoulder, and one to the index finger of his right hand. His injuries suggest that he tried to fight back against his attackers. IHRDC, *No Safe Haven*, 4.4. Dr. Abdol-Rahman Ghassemlou, in https://iranhrdc.org/no-safe-haven-irans-global-assassination-campaign/. Given the ballistics report associating four bullets with Ghaderi-Azar's multiple wounds, and the sheer number of wounds, active resistance on his part seems very likely. See Appendix, "Austrian Police Reports," for autopsy and ballistics reports.

· 5 ·

WINTER IN VIENNA

ॐ

The figure of a dictator contributes to
the establishment of a regime. When
that dictator dies the establishment
begins to wobble, and falls.
—Abdul Rahman Ghassemlou

Abdul Rahman Ghassemlou's murder was the culmination of a long hunt
for the Kurdish leader by the Islamic Republic. Evidence suggests that the
regime was stalking him for years, certainly watching him from very close
range, and likely looking for the right opportunity to eliminate him. According to Khanbaba Tehrani, former Tudeh member and leader of the National
Democratic Front, Rafsanjani's and Khomeini's big concern was how to over-
come the opposition groups—meaning the political parties—in Iran. They
knew that they would be forced to agree with a diplomatic solution. "That's
why they formed a group," Tehrani said in a 2013 interview, "'The Room of
Thoughts,' where they made a list of opposition leaders, and at the top of the
list were Dr. Ghassemlou and Massoud Rajavi." Sahrarudi was chosen to per-
petrate Ghassemlou's murder.[1]

During the three years leading up to Ghassemlou's death, from October
1986 to July 1989—right up to the very month of the assassination—Sahrarudi himself was reported to be living in a remote mountain village only a few
kilometers from the PDKI daftar.[2]

After years of outright warfare had failed to eliminate Ghassemlou in the
mountains, it took some time for the Iranians to prepare another trap. This
new plan attempted to close in on Ghassemlou in Vienna; it was initiated
through the first set of negotiations during the winter of 1988–89 and culminated with his death in the summer of 1989. In this patient but deadly pursuit
of Ghassemlou, Fadil Rasul, knowingly or unknowingly, became an instrument of the Iranians. This became clear afterward.

In the summer of 1986, Jalal Talabani passed by Ghassemlou's daftar in Iraqi Kurdistan. Talabani's own PUK daftar was nearby. Being Iraqi, Talabani was receiving aid from Tehran; being Iranian, Ghassemlou was supported by Baghdad. This is the law of opposites that has enlivened the life of the Kurds for many years and which Talabani summarized as follows: "We Kurds have the right to benefit from the conflicts that exist between the states that divide and dominate us—as long as we maintain our independence and we do not fight against the Kurds of the other areas."[3]

Talabani was on his way to Tehran, and he asked Ghassemlou if he had any message he wanted to send.[4]

"If they are willing to negotiate, so are we," Ghassemlou answered.

A few days later in Tehran, Hashemi Rafsanjani asked Talabani about Ghassemlou.

"How is he? Do you see him? Is it true that he has been wounded?" In Tehran, they thought Ghassemlou had been wounded during a bombing of his daftar.

"Of course I see him," responded Talabani. "We are neighbors. I just saw him, and he is doing well. He is always laughing."

"What is his attitude?" asked Rafsanjani.

"About what?"

"About us."

"He's ready for a peaceful political solution," responded Talabani.

"Very interesting," murmured Rafsanjani without any further comment.

Toward the end of 1986, Agha Mohammadi, deputy from Hamadan[5] and Rafsanjani's assistant, told Talabani that they wanted to negotiate with Abdul Rahman Ghassemlou. Commander Mohsen Rezae, head of the pasdaran, also conveyed that they wanted to negotiate, but under the condition that the PDKI's peshmerga collaborate in the war against Iraq.

This was not possible. "When I returned to the PDKI's daftar," Talabani said later, "Dr. Ghassemlou told me that they could not participate in our fight against Iraq. But if the Iranians were sincere, he was ready to negotiate. They could send a delegation to my daftar and they could meet there." Talabani sent Ghassemlou's response to the Iranians.

In April of 1987, the Iranians said they were ready to negotiate. Then a decisive battle supervened, and Talabani's forces took control of a large zone in Iraq. "The Iranians were there and were convinced that Ghassemlou was not a tool in the hands of the Iraqis," Talabani later explained. "Toward the end of 1987 when I returned from Kurdistan to Tehran to travel abroad, they told me once more that they were willing to see him outside the country."

Ghassemlou had suggested Paris as a place for the meeting. Had it taken place there, Sharafkandi would say in hindsight, the French authorities would have been informed, for they were friends of the PDKI and would have kept the meeting secret. But the Iranians responded that their relations with France were bad and proposed Berlin instead.

Ghassemlou refused to go to Germany. "We had no friends there," Talabani explained, "and we could not assure his protection."

The Iranians next proposed Switzerland and Ghassemlou ruled this out as well. He consulted with Talabani, who advised Ghassemlou that the PUK had a good organization in Vienna and that the Iranians did too. "And we [PUK] also had weapons there," Talabani said later, "as did the PDKI."

The process of negotiation had begun. It was the first time the Islamic Republic announced itself ready to send representatives to meet abroad with a Kurdish leader—one who was then still leading an insurgency against the Islamist regime from the mountains. The situation was so unusual that Ghassemlou cautiously reminded himself of the warning his father used to repeat: "If you see a Persian, kill him, or run—because if you do not, he will betray and kill you."

ঽ

At the end of summer 1988, Ghassemlou traveled to Europe for about three months, staying on into October; among places he visited were Paris, Madrid, and Barcelona. His intention, as far as the party understood, was to meet with European political parties and government officials. He did in fact carry out this project. In Madrid, where I was living at the time, he called me and asked if I could set up a visit and meetings with press and Spanish officials. In a lobbying effort to inform and garner support, he sought an opening to air Kurds' concerns with the press and politicians. He told me, too, that he wanted to bring in Talabani, who was then in Europe and downhearted over his own frustrated attempts to gain a hearing for the Kurds in Europe.

The time, as it turned out, was auspicious: the end of the Iran-Iraq war was now sparking interest in the Kurdish situation, and I was able to organize a conference with IEPALA, the Institute of Solidarity with Latin America and Africa. In addition to Talabani, who was invited at Ghassemlou's request, Kendal Nezan, of the Kurdish Institute of Paris, attended the conference. Talabani, always very concerned with his own security, requested and was assigned bodyguards from the Spanish government during his stay.

The Ministry of the Interior phoned me, to see if Ghassemlou wanted bodyguards as well. Ghassemlou, mindful of PUK's questionable practice of kidnapping foreign visitors and workers in Iraqi Kurdistan, responded, "He who is afraid wants bodyguards. Since we (PDKI) do not do this kind of thing, we are not afraid." He refused the suggestion.[6]

Government protection, Ghassemlou said later, was something that Talabani invariably asked for. Ghassemlou, in contrast, did not agree with this practice: how could he know, he asked, if such security forces has not been infiltrated or coopted? He preferred, he said, to travel anonymously in the company of trustworthy friends.[7]

In any case, Ghassemlou was very happy with this visit, especially with the contacts he'd made in Spain with the Ministry of Foreign Affairs and with the media. He'd been heartened as well by a visit to Catalonia with Kendal Nezan. Nezan had previously met Jordi Pujol, president of the Generalitat de Catalunya, in 1985–1986, and took the opportunity to reach out to him. Talabani and Ghassemlou were very well received by Pujol and top officials of the regional government. In Pujol's sharing of his imprisonment during Franco's dictatorship and the struggles that followed for Catalans to achieve their own freedom and autonomy, there was certainly a sense of solidarity.[8]

A TV interview was arranged for Ghassemlou, Talabani, and Nezan. The journalist, looking for an angle to highlight the interview, led off with a provocative comment to Ghassemlou: "So, three Kurds have come to declare independence."

Ghassemlou moved quickly to defuse the potentially inflammatory statement: "No," he said, "I did not come with them. I just ran into these two other Kurds at the entrance." He laughed; the journalist was disarmed.[9]

There were opportunities enough for fireworks over provocative statements. At the conference at IEPALA, Ghassemlou spoke on the situation of the Kurds in Iran, Iraq, and Turkey. Kendal Nezan recalled Talabani making a virulent attack on the Turkish government, which unsurprisingly provoked a flurry of articles in Turkey.[10] To Talabani, even negative press notice could be useful: "It's better to have the media speak about you than not at all," he remarked to Ghassemlou.[11]

Back in Kurdistan, the party received reports of events in Madrid, and featured Ghassemlou's conference talk in the party's published bulletin. Ghassemlou's intention to meet with European political parties and government officials was known and understood. What the party did not know, however, was that during this European trip, Ghassemlou had accepted the invitation to a meeting with representatives of the Iranian regime.[12]

෨

The first round of negotiations that winter of 1988–1989, Talabani would later report, was "under our control and mediation. We fixed everything: the location, the vehicles, everything. I went to Vienna and told the minister of the interior that I needed bodyguards. He gave me a car, and Austrian police-men were armed to protect me.[13] We found three apartments. We never met in the same place more than once.

"The first meeting was in the morning. We placed two of our armed men outside the door.[14] I had a gun, and so did Ghassemlou, in a small bag. We did not tell the Iranians where the meetings would be held. We found them accommodations, and that morning, we sent a car to pick them up. They did not know where they were going. We changed houses for every meeting. That way they never knew where the next meeting would be held. Ghassem-lou, Abdullah, and I always arrived before anyone else. All our people were armed." Armed security personnel were Iraqi Kurds.[15]

The negotiations took place in two sessions, December 28–30 of 1988 and January 19–20 of 1989. The negotiators were always two Iranians; one of them was Sahrarudi. For the final round, three Iranians came. The third man was said to be a bodyguard, Amir Buzorguian, who "was in charge of fetching food for the participants but was never allowed out of sight of the meeting place unless he was accompanied by a PUK minder."[16]

Talabani participated in two of the rounds. The first round included three or four meetings. According to Mustafa Hijri, Ghassemlou informed the political bureau that at one meeting, at Fadil Rasul's home in December, Ben Bella was also present.[17] According to Talabani, sometimes the atmo-sphere was very tense. "Sometimes Dr. Ghassemlou was sharp; sometimes he was soft."

During one of the meetings, a meeting which appears as the first on the tapes, Talabani can be heard acknowledging Ghassemlou for having previ-ously facilitated dialogue with Baghdad, though there had been no resolution. "I hope that a day will come," he says, "to return the favor to Dr. Ghassemlou and take him to Tehran; he took me to Baghdad but we did not get any result. But I will take him to Tehran to reach an outcome." Opening the meeting diplomatically, he characterizes it as a mutual approach in good faith: "As far as we are aware," he says, "both sides want to solve the political problems with seriousness and with honesty. We think both sides have a wish for it." Equally diplomatically, he emphasizes the reality of the Kurds' working within the existing geopolitical framework of a sovereign Iranian state: "We must accept that the Islamic Republic is the best country with which we [the Kurds] can have a strategic relation, to collaborate under the flag of united Islamic republics. I think each of these countries must make some appeasement with their Kurds; after that, Kurds can make good progress toward human ideals, Islamic and justice."

Then one of the envoys, probably Sahrarudi, outlines some backstory: that in 1986, in Yakhsamar, Talabani had informed the Iranian authorities of a desire for negotiations and that it had taken a full year of messages back and forth to agree upon a meeting. "Since we were more or less aware of some issues going on within the party," however—the series of intraparty divisions and secessions—"we did not pay much attention" to the overtures for negotiation; "we did not take any initiative because we did not trust." But since a recent message from Talabani asking for a negotiation had prompted discussion and assessment with Iranian authorities, "it was decided to conduct a direct negotiation."[18]

The second envoy audible on recordings of the meeting—probably Mostafawi—adds that at the beginning of the Iranian revolution, before the new central government could stabilize itself, it had been put in a very difficult situation by events in Kurdistan. Speaking allusively, the speaker does not spell out those "events," but says that they generated many problems for the country and "we suffered irreparable damage." If these events in Kurdistan had not taken place, he asserts, Tehran believes that Iraq would not have attacked Iran, Ghassemlou speaks, to set the picture straight: "We have always been in favor of negotiations, from the outset. And we are now, and in the future will be as well, because the Kurdish issue in Iran has no military solution. With all the blame, criticisms, harsh rhetoric and accusations against us, we have never turned away from this principle."

The Kurds, he affirms strongly, are Iranian, and their demands are limited to provisions within the country. "There has been no Kurdish separatist political party in Iran, and that's true now. I am not talking about individuals, but about political parties. If we want to obtain results, we have to accept that our demands limit themselves to within Iran."

His party, he acknowledges, will be accused by both the left and the right for sitting down with the regime. "They are calling us 'negotiation seekers' and we have responded very straightforwardly that indeed we are. We do not see any problem with this, and principally fight for negotiations. Our perspective is that the issue of Kurdistan has no military solution."

Not missing a beat, Ghassemlou further makes it clear that war was imposed on the Kurds twice by the regime: on August 19, 1979, and in the spring of 1980.

Ghassemlou agrees to keep the negotiations secret until there is an outcome. During the weeks that he and the regime have been messaging back and forth, however, twenty-four members of the party who had been in prison for many years had been executed, and it was possible that the number might be higher. Therefore, he adds, there will be no ceasefire until an agreement has been reached.

The question that becomes clear here, looking back, is whether any agreement can be realistically hoped for. Eyewitnesses to the sessions, members of Talabani's contingent who were providing security, recall the Iranians repeatedly stating that they represent only one fraction of Tehran leadership ready for compromise. They cannot "give any guarantee" that any proposal from Vienna will find acceptance with Tehran, given the internal differences that exist within the Islamic regime.[19]

Nevertheless, this is the opening that has presented itself, and Ghassemlou does not mean to let it go unused. Finally the agreement is reached to include two items on the agenda for further negotiation: first, legalization of the PDKI as a party with the right to work and even continue to push for autonomy, to produce publications, to have a legal public presence. Second, actual discussion of the question of autonomy for Kurdistan.

With the agreement on this agenda, the meetings concluded. Negotiations had not been successful in substance, but at least there was the beginning of an agreement on the frame for dialogue.

࿓

Ghassemlou had not informed the party that he would be meeting with the Iranians. He had been close-lipped. The only hint of his activities came in a letter to Hélène at the beginning of 1979: "I wish you a Happy New Year," he wrote her at the end of December. "Unfortunately, it is impossible for me to return to Paris now. I am leading some very important negotiations here with representatives of the Iranian regime. Of course, these negotiations must be kept absolutely secret," he went on. "No one except you should know anything about them. Kak Abdollah[20] is with me, but he should not know that I have told you about them. After the first days of discussions, I am moderately optimistic, but they continue and for this reason I must stay here until the end of this week. I will have three days for myself. I may travel to Prague."[21]

Two days later, on January 1, he also spoke about these meetings by phone with Austrian journalist and former diplomat Ferdinand Hennerbichler, then stationed in Nicosia.[22] He spoke with the understanding that what he shared would not be made public so as "not to jeopardize" the negotiations. Ghassemlou had hoped, Hennerbichler reported, for direct connection with Rafsanjani, since the Iranian had played a crucial role in bringing the Iran-Iraq war to an end.

Hennerbichler's own reading, after the fact, was that Rafsanjani during this period had "presented himself as a cautious diplomat and repeatedly signalled some interest in a rapprochement with the Western world," while simultaneously insisting on "the reestablishment of Iran as a strong regional power." Suggestions of openness to rapprochement included Rafsanjani's advocacy for "privatization of state-held industries, liberalized trade and a free market economy."[23] Hennerbichler's impression was that Ghassemlou was convinced that dealing directly with Rafsanjani could "make a difference and personally support the beginning of promising talks." But with this contact denied him, Ghassemlou had to accept going the indirect route of discussion with delegates.[24]

In his interview with Hennerbichler, Ghassemlou outlined his analysis that the Islamic government was weak, the morale of the pasdaran was low, and it was therefore the right time to negotiate.[25] If "the Islamic Republic was able to change its policy about war, which was the most important problem of the country," he reasoned, "why could the Islamic Republic not be able to change its policy concerning the Kurds?"[26] He was convinced this was possible.

Searching for support to his firm belief that Rafsanjani wanted to resolve the Kurdish issue, he said, "I am a very modest man, but a few days ago I found an article I wrote more than four years ago in Le Monde, and there is a sentence saying that in the future Rafsanjani will open the door to uproad [a road upward], it means to Western countries, to open the way for cooperation with Western countries from one side, and from the other side within the country he is obliged, he is forced to have some kind of liberalization."[27] Rafsanjani, he added, "is the strong man of the regime, and he is controlling some parts of Pasdaran and army. He is controlling mass media, because, as you know, his brother is the chief of radio and television. He is very close to Khomeini himself. . . . I think Rafsanjani is a very pragmatic man. So, everything is possible with him."[28]

Once again, seeking signs that he was on the right path, Ghassemlou had convinced himself that international opinion vis-à-vis the Kurds was shifting. The fact that he was received by top government officials in his visits to European countries was a sign. He also considered of utmost significance the resolution in December 1988 by the Council of the Socialist International on the Kurdish problem—the first such recognition accorded by an international organization. "It means," said Ghassemlou, "that really there is a change in the position of the international community towards the Kurdish question. And it now is our aim and our goal to profit from this new situation in order to push more and more the Kurdish question."[29]

Ever optimistic, Ghassemlou returned to the party's mountain headquarters, with cassette recordings of the negotiations, and reported back to party leadership. His enthusiasm may have been strengthened by Ben Bella's and Talabani's participation in one of the sessions, at Rasul's home and perhaps organized by Rasul,[30] a presence that may have seemed a confirmation that the Iranians were taking the negotiations seriously. The party political bureau, however, expressed its disagreement with the meetings and with the fact that neither they nor the central committee had been informed. Hijri strongly expressed his upset that Ghassemlou himself, the single most important person in the party, would take the risk of meeting with envoys of the regime that was even then waging a war against the Kurds. Not only had Ghassemlou met with low-ranking officials, Hijri added; he did not even know the real names of the men he had met with. As far as Hijri was concerned, Ghassemlou should have sent party representatives, not attended himself. Hijri was further appalled that Ghassemlou had taken no security precautions, when he'd had any number of options: there were many loyal party members in Vienna who "would sacrifice their lives" for him.[31]

Ghassemlou explained that the Iranians had insisted that the meetings be held with specific envoys and that they be kept secret from the many within the regime who were opposed and would derail them. While Ben Bella had been present at one of the sessions, Ghassemlou reported, the Iranians also stipulated that Talabani or Ben Bella would not be present in future meetings.[32] Ghassemlou was not concerned about his security, he said, because Talabani had posted armed guards outside the meeting room. The stipulation that Talabani and Ben Bella would be excluded from future meetings might have raised a red flag, but Ghassemlou was convinced that the regime's representatives were serious in wanting to end the conflict with the Kurds, and he did not want to miss this opportunity.[33]

Ghassemlou told the politburo he agreed with a suggestion from the Iranians that the next meetings take place in Kurdistan.[34] "It's not worth it to go to Europe," he said. "We can continue the talks at the border."

This too the politburo opposed because there was no way to guarantee either security or confidentiality for the negotiations. Still, the consensus was that seeking a peaceful solution was the right course of action. And so, after having listened to the taped conversations and having discussed the subject for hours, the political bureau reached the conclusion that negotiations would continue but without Ghassemlou as the front-line negotiator. Rather, a delegation would be chosen from among PDKI members and leaders to treat with the Iranians, and Ghassemlou would be brought in to confirm the decisions only after the details had been finalized.[35]

Sadegh Sharafkandi, then a member of the politburo, later shed light on details of party leadership's concerns. "In the first place," he explained,[36] "the emissaries that came were not at the same level as Dr. Ghassemlou, protocol-wise. There was a government employee and a pasdar. They were not political leaders. The secretary-general of the PDKI would not speak again with people of this level.

"In the second place," he added, "it was useless to explain once more what autonomy is. We had already put forward many declarations and publications about it, and the Iranian government knew what autonomy was. The essential thing was whether they accepted it—and for them to officially declare to agree with the principle of autonomy. We were ready to halt the armed struggle and negotiate the content for autonomy. The process could last one or two years, but the war would end, and the irreversible principle of autonomy would be maintained. We felt we could arrive at a definite agreement through [such] negotiations."

In follow-up meetings with the central committee March 9–14, Hijri reports that the recommendations to pursue negotiations, with Ghassemlou to join the talks only at their conclusion, received party approval. It was agreed that the political bureau send a representative to Vienna to establish contact with emissaries from the Islamic government to continue the dialogue. Ghassemlou traveled abroad at the end of April. During the last plenum before his trip, Ghassemlou shared with party leadership his confidence that the democratic party's struggle would continue. He was convinced the party was strong. In words that would prove hauntingly premonitory, he added: "Even if one, two, or three of its most effective leadership members become martyrs or for other reasons leave the party, the party still will strive."[37]

The political bureau waited to receive a communication from the Iranian authorities on the next steps. Ghassemlou would be informed and a meeting would be set up with party members. But they would have no more news about the negotiations until that fateful July 13.

⅋

According to Talabani, when he returned to Tehran, the internal political situation had changed. The Iranians admitted the existence of two positions in opposition within the regime: whether to dialogue with the Kurds—or not. Khomeini's health was declining, and the fight for the succession had intensified. Those who wanted to dialogue were harassed. They asserted that the hard-liners were against the negotiation. And this, Talabani averred later, he knew to be true.

For Mustafa Hijri, however this "admission" of internecine Islamist jockeying was a game—the perennial Iranian parading of its factionalism in a gambit to deceive its opponents. And from the very beginning, the insistence on secrecy was itself another tool wielded in the Iranian arsenal of manipulation, disorientation, and maneuvering.

One day, for example, the Iranian government informed Talabani that his people had talked too much and therefore they were halting the negotiations. Talabani said later that he'd written Ghassemlou to share his thoughts. Talabani was convinced that the Iranians did not really want to concede anything.[38]

"In truth," Talabani concluded now after the assassination, "they did not want an agreement or a solution. But I never imagined they wanted to murder him."

Indeed, a negotiated agreement was not in their plan. "Since Iran had other intentions, they knew they could not do anything with the way Talabani had organized the first three meetings," says Abdullah Hassanzadeh, former long-time member of PDKI leadership and a good friend of Talabani's. "The Iranians leaked information about the meetings and then blamed the PUK so they could leave them out of the negotiations. They could not have Ben Bella there, either, because they did not want to antagonize the Arab countries."[39]

In continual shifts and feints generating confusion as a means to pry open points of vulnerability, the Iranians resorted to acting "with openly expressed frustration and even with phony protests criticizing secrecy links when they realized the tight security measures provided by PUK men at the beginning. There was virtually no space for preparations to kill Ghassemlou as long as Jalal Talabani and his men were present."[40] Ben Bella himself, in retrospect, expressed much the same thought: "After the first round [of discussions], they said Talabani had talked about the meetings," he later said; for Ben Bella this was a way of justifying the decision that neither Talabani nor he, Ben Bella, should be at the next round.[41]

Ghassemlou himself, perhaps harboring some uncertainty in the face of this jockeying, at times sounded out colleagues. "Dr. Ghassemlou asked me what I thought if the Islamic Republic was willing to resume the negotiations: should we negotiate?" recalls Ghassemlou's collaborator Abdullah Hassanzadeh. "I told him that if the conditions that we had demanded were accepted, then yes, we should negotiate. [Our conditions were,] first, that it be a formal negotiation between the party and the government; second, that negotiations be based on the Kurdish demands; third, that a third party should supervise the negotiations."[42]

Ghassemlou was still anxious to seal an agreement with Tehran before Iran and Iraq made a final deal and reached an understanding. "Afterward," he said to Talabani, "we will have nothing. We will not be able to attain anything; there will be no concession from either side."

"He pushed me," admitted Talabani, "to negotiate with Iraq by mediating between Baghdad and us. His political analysis was correct. If Iran and Iraq reached an agreement, there would be nothing for the Kurds. I think it was because of this eventuality that Dr. Ghassemlou was in a hurry." PDKI leader Mustafa Hijri too saw this as a critical concern for Ghassemlou: the window of opportunity might be brief, and closing—little time left to "consider the possibility that the ceasefire would give the regime more strength and freedom to focus on fighting the peshmerga forces, and that would make the [continued] resistance more difficult and more dangerous."[43]

This was not the only reason. Hassan Shiwasali, former military head of the PDKI, who opposed the negotiations with Iran, recounts a conversation he'd had with Ghassemlou on May 20, 1989:[44] "Ghassemlou explained why he wanted to meet with the Iranians. He first explained that the situation of the Islamic Republic was different [now] because of the damage the war with Iraq had done to the country. The Western world had backed Saddam Hussein and Iran was isolated internationally. The Islamic Republic had lost the war, and it was in a vulnerable position.[45] As Ghassemlou saw it, the mullahs knew the PDKI and Komala were ending their confrontation and a coalition of anti-Islamic forces was building. He was convinced that the Islamic Republic believed that solving its problems with Kurdistan would eliminate a significant obstacle in their desire to expand to other countries in the Middle East.

"But there was a more pressing issue. Ghassemlou was feeling the strain of his relations with Baghdad. The PDKI had accepted the relationship because they needed a way in and out of Kurdistan, and Iraq had offered this channel without any conditions. Ghassemlou explained that he constantly reminded the Iraqis, 'Nevertheless, as I travel from Kurdistan to Baghdad, I do so with discomfort and a burning conscience. Many Iraqi Kurds who are not aware of the relations we have with the Iraqi government consider we are [aligned] with the Ba'athists,' he said.

"He knew that many Kurds in Iraq had died due to the Anfal Operation which was displacing Kurds from their homes—Kurds who then disappeared. He was distressed by the chemical bombings of Halabja, Balisan, and other places.[46] 'In the beginning' [Ghassemlou told Shiwasali], 'we considered our relationship with the Iraqi government as inappropriate [but necessary], but now it is extremely inappropriate and shameful. We cannot surrender to either Iran or Iraq. The best way is to end our relationship with the government of Iraq. And the wisest thing is to negotiate [with the Iranian regime]. . . . If we can legally return to our country and openly go about our political affairs, if we can preserve our independence and attempt to establish democracy in the country, then we can achieve a peaceful situation and continue our struggle honorably. That would be the time when we can tell the Ba'athists that we are done. I hope there will come a day when we will be able to, once and for all, proudly give our last message to the Ba'ath, which is: Good-bye.'"[47]

Ghassemlou's analysis of the political realities of Iranian leadership in the wake of Khomeini's death and the Iran-Iraq war convinced him that the time was ripe for negotiations. In addition, the consequences of recent episodes of militant resistance had looked increasingly bleak; the summer of 1988 had seen the dire fate of an abortive show of militancy by the Mujahedin, which collapsed in the face of regime forces when the spontaneous uprising of the population they hoped for had not materialized.[48]

Ghassemlou shared his thinking in an interview early in the summer of 1989:[49]

"Now that Khomeini is gone, I don't think that Khomeini's death will be the fall of the Islamic regime. The regime still has some resources. It will take time before the crises gain momentum, stronger than before, and the power struggle within the leadership will be more obvious. It is natural that right after the death of Khomeini, the akhunds [clerics] show some unity, and I believe it is fabricated and temporary. The conflicts are more serious than they can cover up for long. Especially the problems of the country [keshvar, the country as a whole]. And the crises [that exist] are [severe] to a degree that will force the leaders to take positions and actions that will create conflicts of interest within these groups that exist within the regime.

"Therefore, Khomeini's regime won't fall with Khomeini's death; however, the fact [of his passing] helps the process of deep changes in our country, and I am sure that this process has already started. In other words, Khomeini's death in fact is the beginning of the end of the Islamic Republic."

❧

But Ghassemlou was alone in this thinking. Though the party had approved the idea of pursuing a diplomatic resolution, his people did not truly have faith in the negotiations. And so, in July 1989, he traveled to Vienna without informing his comrades. He told only his ex-wife, a few French friends, Rasul, and Abdullah; and, through a hint from Rasul, Ben Bella also knew the secret.

Two years later, in a Paris hotel room, Jalal Talabani recalled these circumstances surrounding the murder of his friend. "Ghassemlou should have realized why the Iranians cut us [the PUK] out of the negotiations: it was because they had prepared everything, and with us involved, they could not do it. They could not kill two Kurdish leaders at one time.

"I don't understand how Ghassemlou was fooled by Rasul, because I never saw him [Ghassemlou] again. He wrote me some letters where he complained that some of my people had talked, and I accepted that he was right. He was upset. 'You know very well that the Kurds cannot keep a secret,' I told him.

"I'm surprised that he was deceived so easily," Talabani confessed, "[and that he agreed to the meeting] with no bodyguards. As a consequence, Dr. Ghassemlou was left with the responsibility of taking care of himself. He also made technical errors. Why did he meet in the same place twice? How was it that he agreed to go to that place without bodyguards? No one can understand this."

Nonetheless, Ghassemlou was convinced that the Kurds had made a small step forward in the December and January negotiations: there was an agreement of principle to review autonomy status for Kurdistan.[50]

In the first meetings, the Kurds had expressed their hopes while still abiding by the motto that the party had adopted earlier: "Democracy for Iran! Autonomy for Kurdistan!" Such a motto was not common in the Third World, but it was not strange at all to those who knew the party. The PDKI was an unusual organization with its push for democracy instead of a Communist-style government so popular among revolutionary movements at that time.

As with many minorities around the world, the Iranian Kurds demanded recognition of their identity, respect for their language, and the right to teach Kurdish along with Persian in their schools. As well, they wanted to place regional law enforcement in the hands of the peshmerga, their own police force.

The PDKI at that time represented the majority of the Iranian Kurdish population. It was a party of materially impoverished people denied their cultural and political rights and living in a world of shifting alliances. As a party, the PDKI demanded democracy in a country that had always lived under a dictatorship, and claimed autonomy for one of the most underdeveloped regions in all of Iran.

"What is important for us," Ghassemlou said in his June 1989 interview, "is what the majority of Iranian people want. Iranians want peace, freedom and democracy, safety and comfort. And those who will be able to offer such an agenda and win the Iranians' trust in their ability to practice this agenda, such a group will be the winner in the future of Iran. I believe that no one group alone is able to gain the ultimate power in Iran, no single group is able to establish dictatorship again, and if any group should be able to gain such power, that will result in civil war.

"We the PDKI believe that we are able to weaken the regime; we can strike them and even, to a degree, we can ease the path of destruction and fall of the regime. However, alone, we cannot be the only alternative.

"For this reason we are looking for allies in other parts of Iran. We want to create an alliance, a wide and democratic coalition. A front that would bring all the democrats and republicans together, to work together—so the next time, after the Islamic Republic, no more dictatorship . . . will gain power in Iran."[51]

Throughout the half-century of its existence, the party has been perhaps the only Third World revolutionary movement that, even while it has resorted to an armed struggle, has also rejected all terrorist methods that were so in vogue during the seventies and eighties. "[Ghassemlou] insisted," summed up journalist Marc Kravetz, "that not even under the most difficult situations should the Kurds sacrifice their general goals in combat to the needs of the moment. No end justifies the means."[52]

"We have several drawbacks," Ghassemlou used to repeat. "In line with our principles, we do not hijack airplanes, we do not take hostages, nor do we put bombs in cities. We do not do this even in Iran, despite the fact that if one does not commit these types of actions, no one even speaks about you. Neither do we fight directly against the United States to induce the socialist countries to support us, nor fight against the Soviet Union to garner support from the United States.

"Above all, we are Kurds. We have the misfortune of being Kurds. There is no government interested in helping us. For example, the Palestinians and the Eritreans can always count on the support of some governments. We, on the other hand, are trapped by our geopolitical situation."[53]

To the French minister for humanitarian aid, Bernard Kouchner, Ghassemlou was "the only democrat among the guerrillas that I have met. Rahman was the only guerrilla leader who never oppressed or assassinated anyone."[54]

Ghassemlou, in Kravetz's estimation, "fully assumed his military responsibilities. His condemnation of terrorism was a question of principle, and it was part of the pedagogy of his cause. A moral choice but also a political choice. 'Today I lead a movement of fighters, but we also have a responsibility vis-à-vis the future. What will we do tomorrow with men to whom we give such [terrorist] orders? What type of society can we build with them and how will they lead a normal life? If we behave like our adversaries, we are not worth more than they are and our discourse would become lies.'"[55]

આ

Two years later, in the warm silence of the hot springs near Oran at the resort called Hammam Bou-Hadjar, Ahmed Ben Bella remembered the circumstances of the second round of negotiations:[56]

"Anwar [Rasul] told me that it was possible there might be a meeting [of Iran] with the Kurds. He told me that Ghassemlou wanted to see me. We met at Anwar's house and spoke about the meeting with the Iranians. Ghassemlou was exultant. It seemed fine. His demands were not extraordinary. I told myself, 'This time the negotiations will be successful.' Ghassemlou was only asking for autonomy. It was so little."[57]

Even though he asked for "so little," the assassination came to pass. Looking back, Ben Bella said: "I asked myself questions. Was it because he was [aligned] with Montazeri? So was I. The [Iranian] ambassador in Vienna was in contact with Rasul, and [Rasul] told me he [the ambassador] agreed with Montazeri. He seemed to be someone who was open. I don't know if he really was, or if he spoke with the leadership in Tehran . . .

"The Montazeri affair[58] and the magazine [the article in *Al Hiwar* that had presented Rasul as a martyr] bothered the Iranians," Ben Bella explained. "Montazeri had many problems with them, with Rafsanjani, etcetera. His view of Islam was contrary to that of the Shi'a."

Ben Bella had been advised, he said, that his own involvement might be solicited for the second round of meetings, "Anwar asked me about the possibility of participating in the meetings. They asked the Iranians for me to assist. I knew he had seen the Iranians but did not know when. I said yes, and I waited."

As is clear now, nothing would come of this possibility. In the end, Ben Bella said, "an intermediary was necessary. The negotiations could not be held in a place where they would leave any trace. Rasul was a wonderful solution. He would find them a place without leaving any trace, and so that he would not speak, they had to kill him."

და

Rasul and Ben Bella had worked together for a long time on the publication of the Arabic-language magazine *Al Hiwar*. "That magazine happened owing to my collaboration," Ben Bella said, "but the work fell on Anwar. I gave him letters to pass on to different thinkers, and Anwar traveled to Egypt, visited the Lebanese. . . . All the great Arab Islamic thinkers have written for the magazine. Anwar and I were great spiritual friends."

Ben Bella and Ghassemlou had met in Paris a few years before. They were living out their respective exiles. Ben Bella had sympathizers, but he lacked a strong political organization in his country. On the other hand, Ghassemlou, admired by many Kurdish activists and intellectuals, from his vantage point in the mountains led an army of thousands of peshmerga who held the government of Tehran in check.

Ghassemlou had also begun to look for external support and had collaborated in forming an opposition alliance against Khomeinism, called the Council of Resistance. His partners were the exiled former Iranian president Abolhassan Banisadr, with Massoud Rajavi, leader of the Mujahedin, and with other Iranian politicians.

In 1981, in Paris, former Iranian president Abolhassan Banisadr and his son-in-law Massoud Rajavi, leader of the Mujahedin-e Khalq, who had fled Iran together, formed with other politicians of the opposition the Council of National Resistance. Ghassemlou was a party to it, representing the PDKI. In June 1983, Mustafa Hijri, member of the political bureau of the PDKI, declared that the intention of the party was "to create a relationship between the Kurds' struggle and that of other regions of Iran. Within Kurdistan, the PDKI does not need any help from any other Iranian force. What we expect from the Mujahedin is that they extend the fight to other regions, in order to alleviate the burden of the government forces' attacks on us."[59]

Nonetheless, with so many Iranian opposition parties headquartered in Iraqi Kurdistan at the sufferance of the Ba'athist regime, soon the Council of National Resistance found itself a tool of Massoud Rajavi, whose political organization gave up control, more and more, to Saddam Hussein. On March 31, 1984, it was announced in Paris that Banisadr had decided to abandon the Council of Resistance. Father-in-law and son-in-law broke off their political relations.

In January 1983, Rajavi met in Paris with Tariq Aziz, Iraqi minister of foreign affairs, who declared: "I would be very happy to see my dear friend [Rajavi] as the next president of Iran." The Council of Resistance had previously declared its intention that Banisadr be the president of a provisional government.

In *Actualités du Kurdistan*, Ghassemlou explained that the experience of 1979 had showed that it was not enough to change a regime. "The people then wanted the regime to fall, but there wasn't a coherent and structured political alternative. What organizations could contribute to this united opposition front? The opposition was poor. On one hand, you had the monarchists; on the other, the Council of National Resistance, an organization led by Rajavi, totally dependent on Saddam Hussein and on the money and the resources that the American CIA gave it. Finally, you had groups with different ideologies upon whom the Kurds counted, trusting that with them they could, potentially, bring down the regime and replace it with a republic worthy of that name, independent and democratic."[60]

For the PDKI, the monarchists, with whom they were tied only by their common opposition toward the regime, had to be excluded. "The people of Iran demand the creation of a democratic republican system," the party affirmed. "They want an independent and non-aligned Iran in which the national rights of the oppressed people, democratic freedoms, and economic and social demands are assured." And all of this was in contradiction with the concepts of the Iranian monarchy, based on "dictatorship and foreign dependence. That is why the people of Iran overthrew it on February 1, 1979. The position adopted by the Mujahedin and their annoying tendency of imposing their hegemony have favored the drifting apart of the democratic and independent forces that participated in the Council. In other words, they have been an obstacle for the realization of the goals set by the Council itself. For these reasons, even if some independent personalities apparently remain in the Council, it's the Mujahedin of Rajavi who are pulling the strings."[61]

Asked if it was possible to collaborate with the Mujahedin, Ghassemlou answered: "Because of their politics, they have denaturalized the ambitions of the Council of Resistance and closed all the doors for the future collaboration of the democratic and progressive organizations of the country, to the point that the Iranian population is asking itself what changes could the Mujahedin bring if they came to power. That organization has only one goal: replace Khomeini with Rajavi, and the pasdaran with the Mujahedin.

"What can democracy offer an organization whose internal rules oppose democratic liberties?" asked Ghassemlou. "The Mujahedin cannot be an alternative to the current power. Like the monarchists, the Mujahedin will never play a leading role in the realization of the essential and legitimate demands of the Iranian people."[62]

In December 1988, six months before his assassination, Ghassemlou had said in Vienna, "Collaboration with the Mujahedin is impossible for many reasons. In the first place, there is no democratic practice in their organization, and in the second place, they are hostile to any difference of opinion and, therefore, to any opposition."[63]

Nevertheless, the PDKI proposed the creation of an opposition front that included all the forces of the Left in an independent organization, realistic, creative, political, with its own personality. "Despite the difficulties that we see, the constitution of a democratic, anti-imperialist front that overthrows the regime of the ayatollahs and replaces it with a popular democratic system is a historical necessity."[64]

Ben Bella said later that he'd shared with Ghassemlou his own similar concerns about alliance with Rajavi. "I didn't like it at all. I told him that he should not trust Rajavi and that he should not compromise the Kurdish minority, because his problem was important and complicated. The Kurds are in [divided up across] five countries! It's terrible!

"Sometimes minorities despair. They make mistakes and delay the course of history. The leaders have to be top quality and not make mistakes. The [Iraqi] Kurdish leaders have made many mistakes. Not so Ghassemlou."

Ben Bella would have seemed an ideal intermediary for the negotiations and Ghassemlou would have accepted him with pleasure. But the Iranians preferred Rasul, and when the latter proposed, with commendable modesty, that someone important, with noteworthy status—for example, former president Ben Bella—preside over the conversations, they said no.[65]

In his naïveté, Rasul accepted this dictate from his Islamist friends. This single decision constituted a grave error; but an even greater error was that he did not tell anyone. This error was to cost him his life. Surely Rasul had in mind that Talabani's people had been accused by the Iranians of being indiscreet; being discreet, therefore, was of prime importance. So Rasul—with the single exception, apparently, of his hint to Ben Bella—kept the entire operation under maximum security.

The Iranians had demanded complete secrecy, citing as a reason the internal division within the regime vis-à-vis negotiations with the Kurds. This rationale was stated by Sahrarudi in the tapes recorded in Vienna during the negotiations. "We agreed that these meetings should be kept totally secret because there are enemies who do not want these problems to be resolved. . . . Even within the Iranian government, there are people who do not want these meetings to take place; within the executive [branch], it is not possible to speak openly about this problem."[66]

Banisadr said that Rasul told him seriously that he would come to Paris to meet him. "But before he came, he mentioned that he had a meeting—though he did not say anything to me about the meeting in Vienna."

❧

That day in July 1989, less than two hours before the first meeting between the Iranians and Ghassemlou, Ben Bella found Rasul restless, tense, crispé.

Ghassemlou, on the other hand, he found "calm, happy, and exultant." "I knew they were going to see the Iranians," Ben Bella said. "When they left me, they went to their meeting."

Ben Bella, the old lion, was soon to turn seventy-three. That day at noon he did not know, he told me, while they shared their thoughts and sipped tea or coffee, that the Iranians had vetoed him as a negotiator. Ben Bella knew and was known to the principals involved. Not only did Ben Bella know

Ghassemlou; he was also a friend of Rasul's. He'd had personal interactions with and would have recognized at least one of the presumptive assassins. He was aware that Sahrarudi was known in Vienna, and involved in negotiations for the sale of weapons between Austria and Iran. Even after the assassination, Ben Bella would be fed information from many directions: the day after the murder, Talabani himself would call him from Tehran to say, "I just left Rafsanjani—he said that he had nothing to do with the murder."[67] He knew too much; he was too well connected; his presence in the meetings could not be risked. The Iranians had laid their plans well: the preparations, the setting, the first day's sense of progress that may have disarmed the sense of danger, that drew their target in to a fixed location with no protection, no security measures.

Reviewing the murderous plot two years later, Ben Bella found the pain of his young friend's death still fresh in his heart. "They asked Anwar to find the location so they would not leave a trace. They had calculated very well. So he asked a woman, Renata, with whom he had a relationship, for help; she had been in Cairo. He asked Renata for her house, and that way they left no trace. I think they had already decided to kill him with the others."

૭

Abdul Rahman Ghassemlou was correct when he argued about the Islamic regime's weakness; there was good reason to think it prepared to negotiate. At the end of 1988, Iranian politics were marked by internal strife between factions in the Islamic regime.

In December of 1987, Khomeini had passed on his political testament to the Iranian leaders in a televised ceremony. They all supposed he was seriously ill, and by then, national life revolved around Khomeini's poor health. Post-Khomeinism had begun, and it was ushered in by an intensification of repression. When the old man died, all the political sectors were preparing to seize power in Iran.

A few weeks prior, Ayatollah Seyyed Tabatabai Qomi, one of the five Shi'ite clerics who held the title of *ayatollah al-uzma* or Grand Ayatollah, had denounced the regime as non-Islamic and condemned the continuation of the war with Iraq as a sin. He accused the regime of holding mass executions of innocent people and treating prisoners in an inhuman way, of confiscating private property and violating civil liberties.

The Grand Ayatollah was confined to house arrest.

Three months before, in September 1987, the government had executed Mehdi Hashemi. He was accused of having "launched a war against Islam," and of being "corrupt," the most heinous crime in Islamic law. Hashemi was the brother of Ayatollah Hossein Ali Montazeri's son-in-law. He had been a prominent Islamic militant, condemned to life imprisonment under the Shah for having killed a conservative cleric who had publicly insulted Montazeri. He was freed during the revolution in 1979. He was president of the World Islamic Movement, which, under the control of the pasdaran, had the mission of supporting Islamic liberation movements abroad.

Hashemi persisted in radical militant actions. He kidnapped a Syrian diplomat and four Afghan diplomats traveling by train to the Soviet Union, and introduced military advisors in Afghanistan to help the anti-Soviet guerrilla movement there. These actions had encumbered the diplomatic goals of Iranian president Seyyid Ali Khamenei and Rafsanjani.[68]

The imminent changes and bloody confrontations between the principal Iranian leaders led Westerners to believe that there now existed a "liberal" group in Iran, in opposition to another that was conservative and hard-line. In truth what separated one from the other were differences over the need for ameliorating relations with the Western world, a certain easing of the political life, and a liberalization of the economy.

Rafsanjani, minister of foreign affairs Ali Akbar Velayati, and Ayatollah Ali Montazeri were in favor of change, even while the latter maintained an orthodox position toward foreign policy. Khomeini, however, remained opposed to any opening toward the West.

The situation got even more complicated in 1988 with a wave of executions. The majority of the victims were leftist militants who had been in prison, and also some clerics. Many of them were followers of Montazeri, who had condemned the ongoing internal repression.

The number of executions is unknown,[69] but reports released by the United Nations oscillated between several hundred and five thousand, according to intelligence from the Mujahedin and the Tudeh. Amnesty International received reliable reports of about three hundred executions, but estimated that there may have been thousands. According to one report, eight hundred and fifty prisoners had been executed and their bodies transported in secret to the cemetery of Behesht Zahra to be buried in a common grave. Another story said that six hundred had been found dead after a mass execution following an explosion and fire in the Evin prison near Tehran. Thirty-six clerics were executed during the month of November alone.[70]

According to Karim Lahidji, president of the League of Defense for Human Rights in Iran, between September and November 1988 the regime executed more than three thousand political prisoners who were serving their prison terms. They were people who had been sent to summary trials—trials that lasted three minutes, without respect for the judicial process—and were condemned to prison.[71]

This was not the first time thousands of political dissidents had been executed by the Islamic Republic of Iran. "However," IHRDC reported, "the 1988 massacre stands out for the systematic way in which it was planned and carried out, the short time period in which it took place, throughout the country, the arbitrary method used to determine victims, the sheer number of victims, and the fact that the regime took extensive measures to keep the executions secret and continues to deny that they took place."[72]

The situation was so serious that Montazeri wrote, on October 14, 1988: "People have complained to me that family members who were serving small sentences for political offenses had been executed without any explanation. This is not the way Islamic justice should be acting. . . . If the authorities continue ignoring public opinion, the people will turn against us in armed opposition."[73]

On November 1, Montazeri wrote to the prime minister: "The present shortage of supplies, discrimination, social injustice, low salaries, depressed sectors of society, and exorbitant prices are a natural consequence of your government. We are not going to resolve anything by torturing, imprisoning, and executing our opponents. It is clear that this repressive political maneuvering has distanced the people from the authorities. What the arbitrary detentions and torture of people have provoked is our isolation from the international community. Islam is based on principles of forgiveness and compassion, but we still need to learn this from the noble legacy of the Prophet."[74]

Around mid-November, in a veiled reference to Montazeri, Khomeini denounced those who "through slogans and deceptive propaganda increase the people's expectations from the regime." The government decreed an amnesty, but even so there were still more than one thousand leftist detainees in the prisons. "The people of the world think that in Iran, our only task is to kill people,"[75] wrote Montazeri on February 12, 1989.

But Khomeini still did not back down. To ratify his position, two days later, he issued a *fatwa* condemning the British Indian author Salman Rushdie and the publishers of *The Satanic Verses*. In his edict, he exhorted all Muslims to "execute them quickly where they find them."[76]

Rafsanjani, for his part, declared that he was not afraid to clash with the West in order to confront a "global blasphemy."

On February 22, Khomeini gave a talk that, according to the London-based magazine *Middle East International*, was the clearest expression of the "schism between the two groups fighting for power in Iran."

"While I'm alive," said Khomeini, "I will not allow the government to fall into the hands of the liberals. . . . I will not deviate from the principle of being with neither the East nor the West."

Once Iran decided to end the war with Iraq in July 1988, division now appeared to manifest openly between two rival factions. Despite the regime's continuing and unremitting terrorist actions, many Westerners and Iranian academics came to posit a distinction between "radical" and "pragmatist" groups, conflating factional power struggles and infighting with ideological conflicts within the echelons of the Islamist state. Among those labeled "radicals" were the minister of the interior, Ali Akbar Mohtashami; the hojatoleslam Mohammad Reyshahri; the attorney general, Mohammad Moussavi Joenia; and Ahmed Khomeini, son of the Imam. Among the supposed "pragmatists" were Rafsanjani, Montazeri, and the minister of foreign affairs, Ali Akbar Velayati. Western perceptions, labeling elements as "liberals" or "pragmatics," did not and do not truly define the rival factions. Despite differences over tactics and perhaps socioeconomic issues, differences do not extend to ideological issues or goals; all groups are Islamist and support a theocratic regime.

In April 1989, there was another attack against Montazeri. He had renounced his appointment as Khomeini's designated successor in March, and very soon thereafter, his followers clashed with Khomeini's in Najafabad, Montazeri's birth town in the western part of the country. The skirmish left several dead.

As always when his position was threatened, on April 21 Rafsanjani presented himself once again as a radical denouncing the discovery of a "nest of spies" established by the United States during the last ten years. The *Middle East International* wrote that Rafsanjani's strategy had always been to "hit when he was about to lose control of the situation to his enemies, overcoming them by situating himself as the champion of their cause."

"One of the most interesting biographies to do," journalist Marc Kravetz told me, "would be that of Rafsanjani—to write about how this man has risen, step by step, walking over the dead bodies of all those that could have hindered his career. For example, the fact that he left five minutes before the explosion in 1980 that caused the death of the main Islamic leaders and dozens of members of parliament. He was way below the top of the political hierarchy and suddenly, he gets to the top. He is the only successor for Beheshti. A kind of Richelieu, [a kind] of Mazarin.

"I will always remember the image of Rafsanjani the day after Khomeini's funeral at the University of Tehran. Everyone was crying, and he was calm. He's cold-blooded, he kills without personal motives. He senses where the next blow should be dealt. Killing Ghassemlou was a great success because he knew no one could replace him."[77]

The murder, said Kravetz, was convenient for Rafsanjani, who wanted a solution for Iranian Kurdistan, but who "had never shown any particular esteem toward Abdul Rahman Ghassemlou and the PDKI. The final result was a decapitated PDKI that was deprived of a man who was irreplaceable.

"In truth, the two theories [about the maneuverings behind Ghassemlou's assassination]—one, a struggle within the regime, or two, a deliberate decision of the Iranian government—these two theories have the same end result and served Rafsanjani's cause.

"Perhaps Mohammad Reyshahri [the minister of intelligence] is the only guilty one. . . . But Reyshahri is not an unknown leader of a clandestine group. He is the minister of a government. Iran's responsibility has been compromised unless Rafsanjani publicly states that his minister will be arrested for murder and high treason."[78]

૭

In Iran, the economic situation was grim. According to Ghassemlou, the Iran-Iraq war had cost between US$300 billion and $500 billion. Merely to repair the oil terminal of Khark would cost $500 million and eighteen months of labor.

But the worst thing for the regime was the disclosure in the Lebanese weekly *Al-Shiraa* of the details of a visit to Tehran in May 1986 by Robert McFarlane, former American national security advisor (1983–1985). He was involved in negotiations for the clandestine sale of weapons to the Iranian regime. The followers of Mehdi Hashemi were suspected of having leaked the information that would be known around the world as Irangate or Iran–Contra.

Following Hashemi's detention, Montazeri traveled to Tehran. He met with Khomeini and intervened in Hashemi's favor. After this and his criticism of the regime's heavy hand toward opposition, Montazeri's influence began to decline.

Despite his involvement in the Irangate affair, Rafsanjani skillfully gained influence. He was reelected in May as vice president of the Iranian parliament. Then in June, the Imam himself named him commander-in-chief of the armed forces, a role that until then had been held by President Khamenei. In this way he extended his power base: he was now in charge of the war effort. He was the coordinator of the army, the pasdaran, the police force, and the Basij (Popular Mobilization Army).[79] Montazeri's efforts to halt Rafsanjani's climb to the heights of power were useless.

"The Iranian regime is a conglomerate of elements," explained Kendal Nezan, director of the Kurdish Institute of Paris. "The radical faction always wanted to eliminate the main personalities of the opposition who had an audience within and especially outside of the country. Mohtashami, who was in charge of the Ministry of the Interior, had sworn that he would eliminate all of the 'corrupts' who had spilled Muslim blood, those who had fought against the Islamic Republic."[80]

Given this panorama, Ghassemlou was convinced that Rafsanjani was ripe for negotiation. "Iran is prostrated," he declared in Madrid in October 1988, two months before his first conversations with Iranian emissaries in Vienna. There were more than one million dead and wounded, Iraqi and Iranian alike; hundreds of schools and hospitals had been destroyed; millions of people had been thrown out of their homes and off their land. The young people refused to go to war.

"On the one hand, the isolation of the Islamic Republic in the international arena is due to its terrorist practices, its disdain for human rights and diplomatic rules. The difficulty in getting weapons should be added to the internal factors provoked by the conflicts among the supreme authorities of the Republic and the panic of the leadership class," Ghassemlou declared. "The pressure of the great powers of the Gulf—and particularly that of the Americans—has made the fragile power of the ayatollahs more vulnerable every day. The Iranian government, led by Khomeini, has understood that prolonging the war threatened the existence of the Islamic regime. It was to save this power that the religious men were forced to accept the ceasefire."[81]

ॐ

The war between Iran and Iraq had ended, but Ghassemlou did not exclude the possibility that history could repeat itself, that Tehran and Baghdad would reach an agreement to crush the national Kurdish movement. And this, he told the party leadership, would be a black day.[82] "This is the worst-case alternative," he said. "In this context, the Kurds really have only one solution: to unite and defend themselves by any means possible. Let me make myself very clear: there will be no capitulation this time. The uprising of the Kurdish people will continue to happen in the cities and countryside, and we will use every form of resistance. Today in Kurdistan a well-organized movement exists with a revolutionary leadership at its helm.

"There will be no enduring peace in the region as long as the Kurdish question is not resolved," he prophesied. "More than five hundred kilometers of the border that separates Iran from Iraq run through Kurdistan, a region controlled in part by the national Kurdish movement.

"The Kurds must act to internationalize the Kurdish problem. It is truly sad that the Kurdish question has attracted the attention of the international public opinion only after the Kurds were victims of the chemical bombings in Iraq."[83]

Notes

1. Khanbaba Mehdi Tehrani, interview with VOA, posted July 15, 2013 at http://khanba-ba-tehrani.com/; translation Beyan Farshi and Ebrahimi (accessed January 14, 2015; the web domain is no longer active).
2. Hasan Ayoubzadeh, phone interview with the author, March 22, 2015.
3. Jalal Talabani, interview with the author, PDKI general headquarters in Kurdistan at the Iran-Iraq border, 1985.
4. Jalal Talabani, interview with the author, Paris, 1991. Except where indicated, further statements from Talabani are from this interview.
5. Midwestern region of Iran.
6. A colleague, Rahim Qaderi, remembered this well; Rahim Qaderi, personal communication to the author, December 5, 2017.
7. Abdul Rahman Ghassemlou, in conversation with the author, Madrid, October 1988.
8. Kendal Nezan, personal communication to the author, January 18, 2018.
9. Rahim Qaderi, personal communication to the author, December 5, 2017.
10. Kendal Nezan, personal communication to the author, January 18, 2018.
11. Ibid.
12. Mustafa Hijri, *Nisko u Dabiran* [Resilience in the face of decline and division] [in Kurdish] (Kurdistan: Sardam Publishing, 2015), 288, n969. Translation Chiman Moradi and Esmail Ebrahimi.
13. Jalal Talabani, interview with the author, Paris, 1991.

There are alternative reports about the arrangements for the meetings themselves and for the security. In a personal communication to the author (July 17, 2016), Mustafa Hijri reported that a first meeting that included Talabani and Ben Bella was held at Fadil Rasul's apartment. Concerning communications with the Austrian authorities and security for the sessions, Hennerbichler adds: "According to available information Austrian authorities in Vienna were not informed formally and officially, they were never asked for any permission, but they knew about the meetings through their own channels. They also had information that some seven Iraqi Kurds (belonging to PUK), armed with pistols, protected the participants in Vienna. Official Austria therefore tacitly tolerated the meetings. It was implicitly accorded that the participants would provide for the necessary security by themselves. At the same time the arrangement should ensure Austria would not be blamed in case anything should go wrong." Ferdinand Hennerbichler, "Assassination of Abdul Rahman Ghassemlou (1930–1989): New Assessment," in *Wiener Jahrbuch für Kurdische Studien 2013, Schwerpunkt: Transnationalität und kurdische Diaspora in Österreich, Jahrgang 1/2013* (Vienna: Österreichische Gesellschaft zur Förderung der Kurdologie / Europäisches Zentrum für kurdische Studien, 2013), 299.

14. From interviews with Talabani, Hennerbichler details security arrangements: "Talabani had one man in the street, another at the entrance, a third at the elevator and several within the apartment but outside the living room where the talks were happening." Hennerbichler, "Assassination of Abdul Rahman Ghassemlou," 299.

15. Ibid.

16. John Bulloch and Harvey Morris, *No Friends but the Mountains: The Tragic History of the Kurds* (New York: Oxford University Press, 1992), 192.

17. Mustafa Hijri, personal communication with the author, July 17, 2016, further clarified July 18. "What Dr. Ghassemlou told us in the politburo was that Mam Jalal [Talabani] and Ben Bella took part in only one meeting in the winter of 1988, which in fact was the last meeting before Dr. Ghassemlou returned from Vienna to Kurdistan and briefed the politburo," Hijri said. More accurately, the time could be described as the winter of 1988/89, because the final meeting in that series occurred in January 1989. "Dr. Ghassemlou only mentioned one meeting with the representatives of the [Iranian] regime in which Mam Jalal and Ben Bella had been present, not two [meetings]. The meeting was held in Fadil Rasul's home." The question of whether Talabani was present at a single session or during two sessions seemingly could be resolved by the tapes, but only if the tapes can be trusted to be accurate and unmanipulated. Translation by a Kurdish scholar who for security reasons does not wish to be named.

18. The source of much of the dialogue is from a briefly available audio uploaded to YouTube, "Regarding the first round of negotiations of the Iranian Islamic Regime with Dr. Ghassemlou, with the participation of Jalal Talabani, December 28, 1988," uploaded February 25, 2019, https://youtu.be/zrSTPi8XyB4 (accessed February 26, 2010). It is worth noting that no source for the upload was named and that the date claimed for the audio as "spring 1988" was inaccurate. While the recent emergence of such evidence seems invaluable, the upload was removed and is no longer accessible. Translation of the material was provided by a PDKI member.

19. Hennerbichler, "Assassination of Abdul Rahman Ghassemlou," 299.

20. Abdullah Ghaderi-Azar, Ghassemlou's young colleague.

21. Hélène Krulich-Ghassemlou, *Love Against All Reason: A European Woman Involved in the Kurdish Fight for Freedom in Iran* (Vienna: Lit Verlag), 236.
22. Hennerbichler, "Assassination of Abdul Rahman Ghassemlou," 297.
23. Ibid., 297.
24. Ibid.
25. Ibid., 303.
26. Ibid., 305.
27. Ibid., 306.
28. Ibid., 307.
29. Ibid., 308.
30. Mustafa Hijri, personal communication with the author, July 17, 2016; translation by a Kurdish scholar who for security reasons asks not to be named.
31. Hijri, *Resilience in the Face of Decline and Division*, 10–11; translation Chiman Moradi and Esmail Ebrahimi.
32. Mustafa Hijri, personal communication with the author, July 18, 2016. Also see Hijri, *Resilience in the Face of Decline and Division*, 20.
33. Hijri, *Resilience in the Face of Decline and Division*, 12.
34. Sadegh Sharafkandi, interview with Dr. Bernard Granjon, PDKI headquarters in Iraqi Kurdistan, 1991.
35. Hijri, *Resilience in the Face of Decline and Division*, 20.
36. Sadegh Sharafkandi, interview with Dr. Bernard Granjon, PDKI headquarters, 1991.
37. Sadegh Sharafkandi, speaking a year later in recognition of the anniversary of Ghassemlou's death, July 15, 1990, at the Cemetery of Martyrs in Kurdistan's Qandil mountains.
38. Jalal Talabani, interview with the author, Paris, 1991.
39. Abdullah Hassanzadeh, interview with the author, Koya Sanjak, Iraqi Kurdistan, July 2009. Hassanzadeh's friendship with Talabani was attested by Hélène Krulich; personal communication, July 2015.
40. Hennerbichler, "Assassination of Abdul Rahman Ghassemlou," 299.
41. Ahmed Ben Bella, interview with Gabriel Fernández and the author, Hammam Bou-Hadjar, Algeria, 1991.
42. Abdullah Hassanzadeh, interview with the author, Koya Sanjak, Iraqi Kurdistan, July 2009.
43. Hijri, *Resilience in the Face of Decline and Division*, 16; translation Chiman Moradi and Esmail Ebrahimi.
44. Hassan [Ibrahimi] Shiwasali, statement July 17, 2011, http://arkiv.peshmergekan. eu/Deng/kak_mela_hassan/mela_hasam_qasmlu_danishtn_20110717_.mp3?fbclid= IwAR0YulYSIfzDIWHSD9iYZdXMFmP0WdafW50w_FUnH-te6zjeeSof5m8hfG0; translation Salah Piroty (accessed December 12, 2018). Shiwasali, military commander in the Sardasht region, was formerly a member of the PDKI leadership and is currently an honorary member of the PDKI central committee.
45. Hijri, too, speculates on Ghassemlou's thinking, citing his own witness of "the situation of the regime itself, weakened by the destruction of many cities and towns, and the resettling of thousands of internally displaced Iranians who had lost everything. The rising demands of Iranians for freedom, jobs, income, and all the rights that during the war—with the

regime facing a foreign enemy like Saddam Hussein—they wouldn't ask for. But now, as the war ended, it came time to demand these rights, and in this context the Kurdish nation and PDKI would have a better chance in seeking its goals." Hijri, *Resilience in the Face of Decline and Division*, 16.

46. Video footage generated by Britain's ITN, Independent Television News, suggests just how close to home some of these "other places" were. The description for one entry in the ITN archive, tagged "Yaksamar: IRAN/IRAQ WAR: CHEMICAL WEAPONS," February 19, 1988, Story ref A5190288022, reads: "Camerawoman Hero Talabani, 19.2.88 who's just returned from Northern Iraq, says she has new TX evidence that Iraqi troops are using chemical weapons against Kurdish guerrillas there. She filmed a mustard gas attack on the village of Yaksamar." ITN Source, http://www.itnsource.com/en/shotlist/ITN/1988/02/19/AS190288022/.

47. Hassan Shiwasali, statement July 17, 2011.

48. "Two great mistakes had given the regime motivation and helped them to stand up again. First was the mistake by the Mujahidin (MKO) that after the ceasefire between Iran and Iraq, they gathered a large force and under the support of Iraqi tanks, started an operation called Forugh-e Javidan (Eternal Light). . . . [T]heir plan was to march full speed toward Kermanshah city and then, nonstop, toward Tehran, to overthrow the regime and take power. But after a short distance, they were stopped by the Iranian forces and defeated very badly and lost all their forces." Hijri, *Resilience in the Face of Decline and Division*, 19–20.

49. Abdul Rahman Ghassemlou, interview with Enayat Fani, June 1989; broadcast on BBC Persian, July 2014, https://www.youtube.com/watch?v=SGsfvkcMn8U (accessed February 2, 2016); translation Beyan Farshi and Esmail Ebrahimi. The extended statement by Ghassemlou that follows is from this interview.

50. For the first time in the history of PDKI negotiations with Tehran, the Iranian emissaries had not, in principle, refused the demands of autonomy for Iranian Kurdistan. They had accepted, as agenda items, reunification of the Kurdish region, recognition of the Kurdish language as the official language together with Persian/Farsi in Kurdistan, the right to use Kurdish in the schools, legalization of the PDKI, and the right to freely publish Kurdish journals, wrote Marc Kravetz in *Libération* on August 7, 1989 ("Téhéran-Vienne: Récit d'un crime"). It was also reported by *The Independent* of London (July 25, 1989) that the previous negotiations had resulted in an agreement of principle to legalize the PDKI, and to begin development projects in Kurdistan.

51. Abdul Rahman Ghassemlou, interview with Enayat Fani, June 1989.

52. Kravetz, "Épilogue," in Hélène Krulich, *Une Européenne au pays des Kurdes* (Paris: Éditions Karthala, 2011), 270.

53. Abdul Rahman Ghassemlou, interview with the author, PDKI general headquarters in Kurdistan, 1985.

54. Bernard Kouchner, interview with the author, Paris, 1991.

55. Kravetz, "Épilogue," in Krulich, *Une Européenne*, 271.

56. Ahmed Ben Bella, interview with Gabriel Fernández and the author, Hammam Bou-Hadjar, Algeria, 1991. In this interview Ben Bella did not mention he had been present in the first set of meetings.

57. Ibid.

58. Montazeri, initially designated successor to Khomeini, fell out with the Imam in 1989 over human-rights abuses and government corruption.

   Looking back, Ben Bella's statement characterizing the Iranian reaction raises questions. It seems strange that the same article that, given its omission of the Iranians' participation in the crime, deeply offended the Kurds as "an apologia for the Islamic revolution" should have "bothered" the regime.

59. *Actualités du Kurdistan*, no. 34 (Paris: PDKI publication), September–October 1988.
60. Ibid.
61. Ibid.
62. Ibid.
63. Ibid.
64. Ibid.
65. According to journalists John Bulloch and Harvey Morris, who do not cite their source, "both the Iranians and Ben Bella accepted the proposal, and on the eve of the July talks Qassemlou, Rassoul and the Algerian met in Vienna to discuss the arrangements. Because of the Iranian demand that the encounter should be kept totally secret . . . [t]he Kurds even bowed to the Iranian's demand that Ben Bella should not be allowed to attend the talks in person." Bulloch and Harvey, *No Friends but the Mountains*, 193. We have no way of knowing that Ghassemlou and Rasul accepted this demand. In the 1991 interview the author and Fernández had with Ben Bella, the Algerian stated he was not aware the Iranians had vetoed him.
66. Tape recording alleged to be of the final meeting between Ghassemlou and the Iranian delegation in Vienna, July 13, 1989, as quoted in Chris Kutschera, "Kurdistan d'Iran: Ghassemlou et le guet-apens de Vienne," *Le Monde*, January 1, 1998. Hélène Krulich shared the transcripts of the full set of tapes with Gabriel Fernández and the author in 1990 in Paris.
67. Ahmed Ben Bella, interview with Gabriel Fernández and the author, Hammam Bou-Hadjar, Algeria, 1991.
68. Radical Iranian cleric Mehdi Hashemi was charged with counterrevolutionary activities and executed in September 1987. "The real reason for the arrest, however, was that Hashemi and his supporters had come to know about [U.S. negotiator Robert] McFarlane's secret visit to Tehran and had attempted to sabotage the negotiations. . . . [After the publication of the news] Rafsanjani was forced to disclose the story of secret arms-for-hostages deals." Baqer Moin, *Khomeini: Life of the Ayatollah* (New York: Thomas Dunne Books, 2000), 264.

   It had come to light that in 1986 Robert McFarlane, former national security advisor to Ronald Reagan, had visited Iran to conduct negotiations for the clandestine sale of weapons to the Iranian regime in the affair later known as the Iran–Contra affair, or Irangate.
69. According to IHRDC, thousands were tortured and executed during the course of a few months. "The victims included prisoners who had served their sentences, but had refused to recant their political beliefs, prisoners who were serving sentences of imprisonment, people who had been detained for lengthy periods but had not been convicted, and former prisoners who were rearrested. Many had been arrested when they were teenagers for commission of low-level offenses such as distribution of pamphlets." IHRDC, *Deadly Fatwa:*

Iran's 1988 Prison Massacre (New Haven, CT: September 2009). See https://iranhrdc.org/deadly-fatwa-irans-1988-prison-massacre/ (accessed July 24, 2017).

70. *The Independent*, London, December 9, 1988.
71. Karim Lahidji, presentation at international symposium "Hommage à Abdul Rahman Ghassemlou," Paris, July 17, 2009.
72. IHRDC, Iran Human Rights Documentation Center, *Deadly Fatwa: Iran's 1988 Prison Massacre* (New Haven, CT: May 2008).
73. Gerhard Konzelman, *La espada de Ala: El avance de los chiitas* [The sword of Allah: The ascent of the Shi'ites] (Madrid: Editorial Planeta, 1990).
74. Ibid.
75. Robin Wright, *The Last Great Revolution: Turmoil and Transformation in Iran* (New York: Alfred Knopf, 2000), 20.
76. Moin, *Khomeini*, 283.
77. Marc Kravetz, interview with the author, Paris, 1991.
78. Kravetz, "Récit d'un crime."
79. Basij is a volunteer-based paramilitary force created on Khomeini's order, consisting of young boys or old men who could not serve in the regular military forces. They became famous during the Iran-Iraq war as "human-wave assault" against Iraqi artillery and tanks. Many young Basijis were sacrificed on the minefields to clear the way for the Iranian army.
80. Kendal Nezan, interview with the author, Paris, 1991.
81. Abdul Rahman Ghassemlou, speaking at the Instituto de Solidaridad con América Latina y África, in Madrid, October 6, 1988; reported in the PDKI Paris Office bulletin *Actualities du Kurdistan*, no. 34, *September–*October 1988.
82. Ebrahim Salehrad Lajani, PDKI central committee member, remembered Ghassemlou's strong warning of the "black day." Personal communication to the author through a Kurdish scholar who for security reasons asks not to be named.
83. Ibid.

· 6 ·

THE ASSASSINS

જે

Let us imagine the scene of the murder:

Three Kurds and two Iranians are sitting in a small living room. A sofa, some armchairs, and some dining-room chairs are arranged in a circle around a low table. Behind the sofa is a window. Stage front is the door through which you have entered the living room. One door. One window.

The Kurds and Iranians negotiate for two hours. The crime leaves many unanswered questions. For example: Which of the Iranians was the first to interrupt the dialogue and take out his weapon? Sahrarudi, with the Beretta? Mostafawi, with the Llama? Where were the weapons? Hidden beforehand somewhere in the apartment? In the bathroom, the kitchen, waiting for someone to retrieve them? Perhaps under the armchairs in the living room? Or that day did the Iranians come already armed, carrying weapons to number 5 Linke Bahngasse? Was it difficult to walk in without attracting attention while carrying two or three pistols, one nearly the size and shape of a submachine gun? Did they have direct access to the apartment, or was it necessary that their friend Rasul open the door to his lover's home?

Where was Buzorguian, the bodyguard? Did he leave the apartment to fetch the weapons?

Buzorguian had arrived in Vienna a month before the negotiations and met publicly with Rasul and his brother Fawzi. An Iranian visiting a European capital for an extended period and with links to the embassy of his country does not travel unnoticed by a host country's secret-service agencies.

While Susanne found him vulgar, Rasul's older brother thought he had refined taste for a bodyguard. He remembered Buzorguian as "an intelligent and courteous man. He knew the city well, including the tramway lines and the Oriental restaurants."[1] They went out together and spoke about politics in general terms, of life in Iran and the changes that would come about with

Rafsanjani as president. Buzorguian did not hide the fact that he had traveled to Austria on behalf of his government and he complained that life here
was very expensive. He stayed at the Post, a nearby hotel, for seven hundred
schillings a night, until Fawzi took him to Hotel Donauwalzer, which was two
hundred schillings less. When Sahrarudi and Mostafawi arrived in Vienna, he
stayed with them at the Hotel Stiegel-Braue.

It does seem strange that a man like this, who relished a good meal, would
go to a McDonald's, as he stated to the police. And go to such lengths to get
there: in Vienna, that establishment is far from Linke Bahngasse, at the far
end of the Vordere Zollamtsstrasse bus station.

But none of Buzorguian's statements were consistent. His justification to
the police about the way he had spent his time was hardly credible. He did not
explain why he, as a bodyguard, was absent so long from his appointed venue.
Nor did he talk about how he was going to justify to his Tehran bosses that
in his absence his protégé had been wounded. He never spoke of this. Whom
had he called on the phone[2] when he left the bleeding Sahrarudi for a few
minutes? He never revealed this either.

"The erratic use of his time that he invents," wrote journalist Marc Kravetz
just weeks after the crime, "does not fit in with the discipline of a bodyguard.
His presence with a wounded Sahrarudi, in front of the building when the
police arrived, would indicate instead that he never left the perimeter of the
building. Not to mention adding the absolutely incoherent phone call that
he made to an in-law of Fadil Rasul's brother a few minutes before joining his
boss, all covered in blood, when the only available phone was the one in the
apartment where the three Kurds had just been murdered.

"Therefore, we must conclude that Amir Buzorguian did not report everything he knew."[3]

&

About Sahrarudi, it's possible that the Viennese police had more knowledge. He was a commander in the Revolutionary Guards, the pasdaran, and a
trusted agent of Rafsanjani and of Ali Khamenei, the outgoing president. He
specialized in matters of intelligence.[4]

Though he arrived in Vienna with a diplomatic passport signed by the
minister of foreign affairs, Ali Akbar Velayati, Sahrarudi did not announce
himself to the local authorities. Still, the Austrians already knew him as a
weapons buyer. In 1984, with the alias Rahimi, he had traveled to Athens as

an official representative of his country to participate in the business of buying and selling weapons.

A specialist in Kurdish affairs, Sahrarudi worked with the foreign security service of the pasdaran and was in charge of activities along Iran's eastern border. He had contacts with various Kurdish opposition movements in Iraq. The most important was with the PUK of Jalal Talabani, whom he regularly saw in Tehran.

Talabani, for his part, did not deny the connection. When asked in an interview with *Kayhan* about the relationship begun in 1987 between his PUK and the Islamic Republic, Talabani had told the press: "We, as PUK, are not hiding our cooperative relationship with Iran, as we believe that this relationship does not imply any weak point, but is in the best interests of the Kurds and their revolution. Besides, this political and military relationship is necessary, as well as very advantageous to Kurdish interests."[5]

Sahrarudi "was important among the pasdaran," Talabani told me. "He was quiet, cold, calm; a tall man." In Talabani's estimation, Sahrarudi was "always in favor of resolving the Kurdish question in a peaceful way. He was never with the SAVAK. A young and enthusiastic supporter of Khomeini, he worked with the Imam before the revolution. He always gave the impression of being a good man. He represented Rafsanjani."[6]

Sahrarudi's self-presentation could be quite professional. After the first set of negotiations in December 1988 and January 1989, Ghassemlou found Sahrarudi "agreeable,"[7] while he thought Mostafawi was "discourteous." Ghassemlou's assistant Abdullah did not differentiate between them, and he expressed his hostility toward them both.

Ben Bella disagreed with Talabani's estimation of Sahrarudi, and made his impressions clear in an interview with me and a colleague in Algeria on May 16, 1991. "He [Sahrarudi] was a pasdar," he said. "One day he came in the name of the Iranian leaders, and asked me to help him find a solution to the Kurdish problem. This was a year prior to the assassination. I saw him for two or three hours at Anwar's house. He spoke in Arabic; so Anwar translated.

"He sent me regards from the Iranian leadership—Montazeri, Khamenei, Rafsanjani. Khomeini was still alive. I told Sahrarudi that the Kurdish problem was an open wound in the Islamic revolution, in the Muslim world. The problem exists in several countries. 'If you find a democratic solution,' I told him, 'you will prove that the Islamic revolution can find democratic solutions. You are isolated': I said hard things like this to him about the Islamic revolution. 'There is too much blood running. It does not mean that blood must not run; but economize.'"[8]

Sahrarudi was of middle height, strong, and between thirty-five and forty years old, Ben Bella told us. "He was very calm."

"Intelligent?" we asked.

Yes, affirmed the Algerian.

"A political cadre?"

"He's a *tueur*, an assassin, someone who is used to killing. He is very balanced, calm, even cold. But not with me, with whom he was very open. He's a pasdar. He's used to shooting.

"While I spoke he took notes," Ben Bella said, then added: "I never saw him again."

"You must not forget," explained the former Algerian president, "that the Iranians practice the *taqiyya*, concealment. Given their long history, they practice a double language to save themselves. This is permitted to them."[9]

The full measure of this concealment—and of the long and deliberate tracking of Ghassemlou, with the aim of his entrapment—has emerged only recently. According to Ghassemlou's colleague Hasan Ayoubzadeh, during the three years leading up to Ghassemlou's death, from October 1986 to July 1989—and in fact right up to the very month of his assassination—Sahrarudi was living very near the PDKI daftar, in the village of Yakhsamar.[10]

In October of 1986, Ayoubzadeh stated, Talabani had gone to Tehran, with a delegation of five members of the PUK central committee, and signed an agreement with the Quds intelligence service. The agreement was for the PUK and Quds to establish headquarters in Kermanshah and Yakhsamar, respectively. The chief Iranian representative to be stationed there was Mohammad Jafari Sahrarudi. He operated under a number of aliases; in Kurdistan, he went by the name of Rahimi.

Ayoubzadeh's testimony has been corroborated by statements from Iraqi Kurdish political leader Mustafa Nawshirwan on the establishment of relations between the Iranians and Talabani's PUK. After Talabani's trip to Tehran and agreement with Quds, and Iran's decision to conduct official cooperation with the PUK, he wrote, it was soon thereafter that the PUK opened its office in Kermanshah, in Iranian Kurdistan, while the Iranian office opened in Yakhsamar, in Iraqi Kurdistan.

The Revolutionary Guards were now conveniently located in Yakhsamar, with the headquarters of the intelligence service in Ramazan; and Sahrarudi was in charge.[11]

For three years, then, Sahrarudi was operating from a village about five to ten kilometers—not more than three to six miles—from Gawrade, where Ghassemlou's daftar was located.

The truth, it now seems clear, is that Sahrarudi, in his role as envoy in the meetings in Vienna, had never been on a sincere diplomatic mission to resolve the Kurdish issue; his pretense of seeking dialogue was for the sole purpose of fulfilling his role in the assassination of their leader Ghassemlou.

৵

About Mostafawi, the police knew much less. Like Sahrarudi, he had come into Austria with a diplomatic passport. He was an officer of the Iranian security machinery, a trusted man of Mohammad Reyshahri, the minister of intelligence and one of the hawks of the regime. He was responsible for the secret service in western Iran, which is to say, Kurdistan. He was married to a Kurdish woman from the Barzani family.

Mostafawi was the first of the putative killers to escape Vienna after the assassination. Some witnesses said they saw him on the street near the wounded Sahrarudi. Afterward he was recognized by a taxi driver, whom he asked to take him to the airport.

Once on their way, Mostafawi changed his mind and gave the driver the address of the Iranian embassy on Jean Jauresgasse. Talabani attested that weeks later, Mostafawi was moving freely through the streets of Tehran.

Among the theories that were considered, one suggested that Mostafawi had fled the scene on a Suzuki motorcycle. Perhaps he was in a rush; because at some point in the investigation the police found the rearview mirror from a Suzuki motorcycle that had been purchased by Sahrarudi on January 10, 1989. The seller was traced by the police thanks to the bill of sale found in a garbage bin, and recognized Sahrarudi among five photos he was shown. The police then took him to the hospital and showed him the pasdaran chief. The seller identified him with certainty. All this unfolded on Monday, July 17, 1989.

৵

On a freezing afternoon in February 1991, Hélène Krulich slowly left her room in a Viennese apartment. She had a fever. A cold had kept her in bed. Vienna's streets were covered with snow and the cold wind left passersby numb.

Hélène had organized a press conference for the following day. There was concern that she would not be able to be present because of her health.

Nevertheless, she had to attend; because that day, surrounded by attorneys and personages from France, Germany, and other countries who had come to Vienna for this event, she was going to announce, after the failure of all the legal proceedings, that she had decided to take the Austrian state to court. There was no way she could prosecute a minister, the government, or the president. Austria's curious legislation meant that she had to prosecute the state itself.

In her suit against the Republic of Austria, which she filed after months of preparation on August 2, 1991, she accused the government of refraining from investigating diligently the assassination of Dr. Ghassemlou, and allowing the assassins to leave Austria safely. She alleged that the Austrian government had willfully barred the police authorities from investigating the case because of pressure from the Islamic Republic of Iran and illegal arms deals between the state-owned Austrian enterprise Vöest and the Iranian government during the Iran-Iraq war. She claimed damages for the funeral expenses of her husband.[12]

Now, on this February morning in a small room in the Landtmann Café in Vienna, Hélène sat at a table and began to go through her papers. There were legal documents, statements in German, translations to Farsi and English, and reports in French. One of them was dated December 4, 1989, and came from the Direzione Centrale della Polizia Criminale del Ministero dell'Interno d'Italia. In French, it informed the Viennese Interpol (in response to request number 1.263 297/1-II/10k-1 of August 23, 1989) about the origin and characteristics of two weapons implicated in the murder:

> Beretta Pistol mod. 70, cal 7.65 mm with the fabrication number erased by abrasion . . . was manufactured in the establishment Pietro Beretta S.P.A. founded in Gardone Val Trompia, Brescia, in 1980, and was destined for export. That is why it has the inscription *disassembly* under the button that allows the gun to be disassembled. Weapons destined for the Italian market carry the word *montaggio*.

> 20 Pistolet Mitrailleur Beretta mod. 12/5, cal. 9 mm parabellum with fabrication number F . . . 31. It has not been possible to establish the addressee of this firearm. [There is attached a seven-page list of weapons whose fabrication numbers begin with the letter F and finish with the number 31.]

The other weapon in the assassination, the Llama, was the regulation firearm used by the Spanish police until 1982. It was made in Guernica, in the

Basque country, by a company called Gabilondo. It was, and is, one of their best.

Spain is one of the main producers of handguns in the world. Latin America buys them, among other markets. Spain produces the Llama, the Star, and the Astra Unceta, which has ample ammunition capacity: fifteen rounds.

The Llama uses potent ammunition of the parabellum type, which may explain how, when a bullet bounced, it wounded Sahrarudi. It is also used with silencers, and is the weapon of choice for terrorists throughout the world and for professional assassins.

According to official information from the Spanish police, in the last years the Basque region had been involved in the sale of firearms to Iran.

Notes

1. Marc Kravetz, "Téhéran-Vienne: Récit d'un crime," *Libération*, August 7, 1989.
2. "At 19.30, Rasul's brother-in-law received a phone call from Buzorguian telling him that a tragedy had happened and that Rasul was dead." *Bulletin de liaison et d'information*, Institut Kurde de Paris, July–August 1979.
3. Kravetz, "Récit d'un crime."
4. For more recent developments for Sahrarudi see Vahid Sepehri, "Iran: New Commander Takes Over Revolutionary Guards," Radio Free Europe, September 4, 2007, http://www.rferl.org/content/article/1078520.html (accessed July 29, 2017).
5. Regarding the Kurdish movement in Iran, Talabani went on to say, "In accord with our agreement with the Iranian authorities, we are not intervening with Iran's problem [with the Iranian Kurds]. But as for us—the Kurds in Iraq—we will decide our destiny after the fall of the Iraqi regime." Jalal Talabani, interview with *Kayhan*, Tehran, December 3, 1987, issue 13193.
6. Jalal Talabani, interview with the author, Paris, 1991.
7. National Democratic Front leader Khanbaba Mehdi Tehrani, describing the Iranians' arrangements for meeting with Ghassemlou, told VOA in 2013 that Ghassemlou had rejected the idea of discussions with a Revolutionary Guard officer and specified that he wanted to meet with diplomats. The plan, therefore, was to introduce Sahrarudi as a diplomat. Khanbaba Mehdi Tehrani, interview with VOA, posted July 15, 2013, http://khanbaba-tehrani.com/ (accessed April 19, 2015). It is not clear that this piece of the plan was in fact carried out, or that Ghassemlou would not have recognized Sahrarudi's identity or status as a member of Iran's elite security force.
8. Ahmed Ben Bella, interview with Gabriel Fernández and the author, Hammam Bou-Hadjar, Algeria, 1991.
9. Based on the verse in the Qur'an that says: "Even though you hide what you carry in your heart, Allah knows it." "Shiism constructed the doctrine of *taqiya* (precaution), which it

considers fundamental and according to which it is the duty of the believer to hide his real religion when he is under the rule of the nonbeliever (this includes the Sunnis). In sum, they have the moral permission to lie when it's for the good of the Shiite community." Marc Kravetz, *Irano Nox* (Paris: Éditions Grasset, 1982). For further discussion of taqiya as a tactic employed by Ayatollah Khomeini, see Amir Taheri, *The Spirit of Allah: Khomeini and the Islamic Revolution* (Bethesda, MD: Adler & Adler, 1986), 230.

10. Hasan Ayoubzadeh, interview with the author, March 22, 2015.

11. Mustafa Nawshirwan, *Xulanewe le naw Bazne da* [Going around in circles: The inside story of events in Iraqi Kurdistan 1984–1988] [in Sorani Kurdish] (Berlin: no publication data available), 102–06; translation Beyan Farshi. Nawshirwan was a founding member of the PUK and deputy secretary of the PUK between 1976 and 2006. In 2009 he left PUK and established Gorran, "Movement for Change," which became the official opposition to the two dominant Kurdish parties in Iraq, KDP and PUK. In regional parliamentary elections in Erbil in 2013, Gorran took second place as a political force in Kurdistan after Barzani's KDP. *Iraq-Business News*, http://www.iraq-businessnews.com/2013/10/20/all-change-on-iraqi-kurdish-political-scene/ (accessed March 25, 2015)

12. IHRDC, Iran Human Rights Documentation Center, *No Safe Haven: Iran's Global Assassination Campaign* (New Haven, CT: May 2008), 29.

· 7 ·

THE CONVERSATION

෨

If a man was a revolutionary in his life,
his death will be a revolutionary act.
—Abdul Rahman Ghassemlou

Apart from the Iranians who are still at large, taped cassettes are the only witnesses of what the Iranians and Kurds said to each other that fateful Thursday
in July 1989.

It's probable that the tapes that appeared in Abdul Rahman Ghassemlou's
briefcase were manipulated, and are not the ones that actually recorded the
conversations that day. Someone may have prepared them as part of the assassins' plot to confuse the inevitable investigation. In any case the conversation
they contain has been transcribed from spoken Farsi dialogue into German,
French, Spanish, and now English. In addition, the audio quality at times is
quite poor, with marked interruptions, entire breaks in the dialogue, and the
grammatical idiosyncrasies of spoken language.

This conversation has been transcribed as accurately as possible given the
limitations of the original evidence, and may appear inexact and awkward in
places. But speculations aside, and the witnesses having disappeared, the cassettes are an essential piece of evidence to shed light on what happened that
day in the living room at Linke Bahngasse 5.[1]

The tape begins with Sahrarudi: "Peace be with you," he says. "We
agreed that these contacts should remain completely secret" because
there are those within the regime that "do not want these problems to be
solved." Even within the executive, he says, "it is not possible to speak
openly about this problem."[2] Iranian society, he continues, is not willing
to accept the problems that Kurdish autonomy would bring. He argues that
Iran is worried about the war with Iraq. The recent ceasefire had required
great courage from the Islamic authorities. Khomeini himself, he says, had
admitted that for him to make peace with Baghdad was like drinking a glass

of poison. "We don't want your autonomy to get stuck like a thorn in our throats," argues Sahrarudi.

He gives a long discourse on the subject of the economy and concludes by repeating the Shi'ite slogan popular since the beginning of the revolution: Islam opposes both capitalism and socialism because Islam has its own way of conducting its political affairs.

"'Autonomy can be compared to an economic system," he says.

"We don't agree with that," interrupts Ghassemlou.

"Well, some call it autonomy, others say *vilayet* [province], etcetera,"[3] says Sahrarudi. "But the truth is that enemies like NATO could *use* this autonomy [politically]. This could lead to separatism! It's something that we need to discuss and it's something that we would not do here. This does not concern the PDKI. This is the answer: the only goal of our meeting is to clarify the relationship between the PDKI and the Islamic Republic."

↬

The moment they took out their weapons, Ghassemlou would have had no time to react.

Ghassemlou was a decisive man, a man of action. When he was a boy, he would quickly take up a stick and position himself against his older brothers.

He had remarkably good aim when he was a boy, he told Hélène. She thought he was exaggerating until one day, as they were taking a walk with some friends in Urmia's fields, a snake crossed their path. Rearing up and ready to strike, the snake stood as tall as a human being, Hélène insisted.

Ghassemlou, standing to the side of the path, became aware of the situation.

He carefully approached and aimed with a stone. "One of us is doomed," Hélène told herself, convinced that he would miss the shot and that the snake, known in the region for the virulence of its venom, would kill them both. But Ghassemlou's stone hit its target. That snake was killed with a single shot.[4]

A man of action, yes; but Ghassemlou was neither a cowboy nor a gunman. Bernard Kouchner, French minister and physician, remembered Ghassemlou in Kurdistan wearing a turban and with a gun at his waist. "He looked like an operetta peshmerga,"[5] Kouchner used to say. What could a peshmerga like him do at fifty-eight years of age, unarmed and caught by surprise? Or a former peshmerga like Abdullah, now dedicated to the political work in Europe, and for two days suffering from painful stomach spasms? Did Ghassemlou have time to size up the situation, to calculate a move and then try to maneuver it?

In 1957, detained in Tehran by the SAVAK and accused of being a spy, Ghassemlou had endured the secret police interrogations for two weeks and was able to mislead one of his interrogators by repeating a contrived story. The officer was convinced and asked Ghassemlou to collaborate with him; again Ghassemlou deceived his captors by agreeing to do so. In this way he gained his freedom and escaped to Kurdistan.

"He was very smart," said Jalal Talabani.[6] "The general who was interrogating him, Teymur Bakhtiar, would repeat, 'You're a smart man. We must cooperate,' and 'I am in favor of the Kurds.' Bakhtiar was organizing a coup d'état against the Shah and was looking for support.

"Ghassemlou took advantage of this and said to him: 'I'm happy that a Kurdish general is so brilliant. Kurdish intellectuals should cooperate with you.'

"Then Bakhtiar released him and Ghassemlou escaped. If he had not done so, he would have been imprisoned for at least ten years."[7] The clandestine party, too, had owed a great debt to Ghassemlou's quick-wittedness that day.

But here and now, in that apartment in Vienna in 1989, how would he have been able to mislead his interlocutors? What misdirection could he have offered his murderers if he had already told them what they wanted to know?

৵

"What is important is that we cannot accept your point of view," Ghassemlou is heard clearly saying in the last part of the second tape. "You say that the main thing to resolve is not the question of the autonomy of Kurdistan, but the question of the relations between the PDKI and the Islamic Republic. That is your opinion, not ours. The reason why we have come here today is to obtain from you, representatives of the central government, an agreement on the principle of autonomy." And autonomy, he makes clear, means decentralization of power.

Two years later in Vienna, reading the transcription of the tapes translated from Farsi into German and English, Hélène said about this passage: "This was his death sentence."

Ghassemlou attempts to convince the emissaries from Tehran that an autonomous Kurdistan would be a peaceful and feasible solution in a democratic Iran. He reiterates that his party does not want anything else.[8] But Sahrarudi and Mostafawi are uncompromising.

"Ours is a cruel relationship, a relationship of war," Sahrarudi reminds him. "What the PDKI says is that it wants to continue being that way and discuss autonomy. This is clearly unacceptable. You must know that in Islam, we do not have autonomy."

Ghassemlou, Ghaderi-Azar, and Rasul would have been listening attentively to these words and realizing that they were far from reaching any real understanding.

"Let us not kid ourselves," Sahrarudi says. "We are at war. The PDKI is illegal. You cannot work legally and come to the parliament to explain anything. You say, 'Accept autonomy and we will work legally.' All our problems lie there. Autonomy is something that has not been accepted. Therefore, this is not a solution."

He has clearly summarized Tehran's position. The Kurdish party has to accept the central government's position without insisting upon talking about autonomy for Kurdistan. "Perhaps we will discuss it one day, in two or three years."

❧

From Tehran's point of view, the important thing was that the party adopt a submissive attitude toward the central power of the Islamic Republic.

What else could the PDKI expect from the fundamentalist clerics? After all, the PDKI was a Kurdish party that was born as genuinely nationalistic and secular, with aspirations to further the rights of the Kurds within Iran, and which eventually opted for democratic and socialist positions. This was a party whose head hobnobbed with the leaders of the international socialist countries. It was a party whose members were mainly Sunni, but was not in itself religious, though it recognized the need for consideration toward the religious sensibility of the people from which it drew its support. Above all a secular party, it had a large following among a population which was traditionally religious but for whom the cause of Kurdish nationalism superseded religion as the focus of its program and activities.

While he was respectful of religion, and well-read in the scriptures, Ghassemlou was not a religious man. No one remembers seeing him with the *tasbih* beads, the Muslim rosary, slipping through his fingers.

The PDKI was a clandestine organization that counted the majority of the Kurdish population among its members. But that population was under suppression from more than one hundred thousand army troops and pasdaran.

For years now, this collective resistance had been headquartered in the mountains, safe beyond the border. Its leader, Abdul Rahman Ghassemlou, was an intellectual nearing his sixties who now, in this room in Vienna, was trying to negotiate with the Iranians the beginnings of an agreement toward autonomy.

Ghassemlou could rely on his powers of persuasion, but he could be a hard man when circumstances demanded it. Within his party, he was known for these qualities. Fifty cadres had recently left the ranks of the party, accusing him of being authoritarian. Above all else, he was unbendable in his resistance to the Islamist regime, as he had been with the Shah. He would not yield. Sahrarudi and Mostafawi had persecuted him for years and knew this.

His passion was politics. "My political life occupies the first place in my life," Ghassemlou wrote. But he was also a sensitive man who dreamed of writing literature, perhaps his autobiography. He loved and needed his country, and he talked about this in his correspondence. "I want to stay and spend my life in Kurdistan."[9]

At the same time, he was feeling tired, and he paid for his dedication to the Kurdish cause with long periods of solitude and loneliness. In the winter of 1985, he wrote: "It's fifteen degrees below zero. To get to the daftar, I had to walk for two hours in the snow. The house is in bad shape, but the shower worked. After several months of absence, I felt happy to be among my companions once again."[10]

In the mountains he found refuge in music and reading, when he had the time. These were his only luxuries, and at times he would say he was not feeling well, so he could find time for himself. "If it were up to me, I would like to retire," he admitted one day. For him this was a difficult confession.

Did his interlocutors know this? Were they aware of the enormous longing this man had? This man who had been educated in Europe, who had spent years away from all family love, art, the pleasures of modern life, and lighthearted conversations, immersed in silence and exposed to a dire ongoing danger?

It's possible. Perhaps the regime thought about this, and concluded that he was ready to negotiate under conditions that would leave him vulnerable. All they needed, all they had been angling for, was a single moment: that single moment of utmost secrecy with the slightest loosening of security.

"With respect to autonomy"—the voice on the tapes is Sahrarudi's—"we have not received a positive answer from Tehran. But they say that the PDKI could function legally and this would be the object of a political discussion. It would have to be taken to the parliament. This will take time. But it is impossible to decide anything here."

Mostafawi then intervenes: "We've had the goodwill to come and sit here with you. In exchange, you should show the same goodwill when the relations are more open and the time comes to be in contact with higher powers."

He pauses for a moment. There is a silence and he begins with a religious invocation.

"*Bismillah al-Rahman al-Rahim* . . . Politics is the art of the possible, not of the impossible . . ."

Rahman interrupts, laughing. The art of the possible: it was a saying that he often used. Then the voices on the tape are jumbled.

"You said," Mostafawi continues, addressing Ghassemlou, "that if autonomy was given to the Kurds, nine hundred kilometers of the Iran-Iraq border would be well protected. You said the Islamic Republic would win the trust of the Kurds on the border with this act. I have no doubt about this, but the contrary [the possibility of a completely different outcome, that the Kurds would come to constitute a threat] is also true."

Mostafawi is speaking of the crux of the problem: the danger of a chain reaction within the Kurdish universe. The Kurds are not an isolated or insignificant ethnicity within Iran. They are an essential piece of the puzzle that impacts the four principal countries where they live. Any alteration in the status quo could be an element that could disrupt the balance of power and usher in a new regional order where the Kurds become a significant geopolitical power in their own right. In the four capitals, the belief prevailed that if one part of the Kurdish world were to achieve autonomy, a contagion would break out that would overrun the borders.

"And if Iraq did the same?" Mostafawi inquires. "We are not alone in knowing this. The enemies of the revolution on the other side—Iraq and Turkey—also know this. Every coin has its reverse side, its positive and negative."

❦

There is autonomy, there is independence, and there is secession. For the region's governments—Tehran, Baghdad, Damascus, Ankara—these are a recurrent specter. They ignore them, if possible. When they appear, troops are sent. There is never even the pretense of a dialogue.

In Turkey, from 1984 until the arrest in 1999 of Abdullah Öcalan, leader of the insurgent Kurdistan Workers Party (PKK), thousands of Kurdish villages were destroyed and more than three million Kurds were deported from their home region by the Turkish army. It is estimated that about thirty-five thousand people were killed during those fifteen years of conflict between the PKK and government forces.[11] In Iraq, the Ba'athist regime razed four thousand villages and towns in the 1980s and then herded the people from the mountains down to the plains along the Euphrates River. The intention was to eradicate the Kurds, forcing them away from their mountains, from their identity. In 1988 Saddam Hussein did not hesitate to send his air force over the small town of Halabja and bombard it with chemical weapons. Five thousand Kurds died from the choking gases.

Shah Mohammad Reza Pahlavi obliterated the Democratic Republic of Kurdistan with blood and fire in Iranian Kurdistan in 1946; and he continued to repress the Kurds until the monarchy's demise in 1979.

The Kurds thought the fall of the Shah was a blessing, but the Islamic regime had not been any more generous with them. In 1980, a few months before he escaped Iran by dressing as a woman, President Abolhassan Banisadr had ordered the army, "You will not take off your boots until you have crushed the Kurds."[12]

It is completely certain that neither Sahrarudi nor Mostafawi believed in Ghassemlou's promise of adherence to the Republic of Iran. The Islamic regime, like the Shah's, was convinced that what the Kurds wanted was simply—independence. And it is also true that these authoritarian regimes could not even tolerate opposition among their own Persian nationals. The urge to hegemonic domination has spawned unending regional wars and conflicts.

In fact, the fear Iran's leaders held about the Kurdish demands had multiplied at the outset of the revolution. The secret service had given the Iranian regime information that Iraq was planning a war. In Iraq's plans, asserted Banisadr, the PDKI would be launched against the Iranian forces and receive all the military and financial aid they needed.

A correspondent for *Le Monde*, Eric Rouleau, visited President Banisadr and spoke to him of the Kurds' desire to obtain autonomy for their region. Banisadr, who maintained his presidency despite growing opposition from the mullahs themselves and gave consideration to the opinions of European journalist friends, later justified his position in this way: "I told Rouleau that I named him as representative of the Iranian government to let the PDKI know that, if they were willing to distance themselves from the Iraqis, we could reach an agreement. Rouleau went to Kurdistan. He met with the Komala and the PDKI, and then went to Baghdad and wrote, in effect, that those organizations were under Iraqi control. He called me and told me they were not as independent in their decisions as they said they were."

Ghassemlou reacted with great irritation to the article written by the French journalist, who was close to Banisadr. He wrote to the newspaper refuting the information given by their correspondent and contended that the journalist had distorted his words.

According to information the Tehran government held, the Americans were pushing Saddam Hussein against the Islamic Republic. Banisadr recalled asking Talabani why the Kurds were playing into the game of the great powers. "Talabani told me I was right," Banisadr said. "The supposed agreement of the Kurdish nationalists with Baghdad against Iran," he concluded, "could mean nothing other than a desire for independence.

"We had a signed document between Komala, the PDKI, and the Feda'iyan in which they agreed to divide among themselves the plunder from the division of Iran following the defeat," he asserted. "There was a conspiracy of twenty-two officers who were going to divide the weapons. Those officers were arrested. Half of the weapons were for the PDKI, and as for the rest—two parts were for Komala and one for the Feda'iyan. This proves that they [the Kurds] were not as innocent as they say. They were under Iraqi pressure, and they did not want just autonomy."

"All of this is false," countered Hélène. "This would excuse Banisadr and his behavior toward the Kurds. The relations between the PDKI and Iraq were status quo [that is, essentially unaltered from what they had been for some time]. In 1979 and 1980, Rahman decided to ask for permission to go through Baghdad to Europe. Baghdad agreed."[13]

This authorization included certain conditions, but Rahman never explained to his wife what they were.

"If you want to work and survive in Kurdistan, you must find a way of coming in and out of the country," concluded Hélène. But the PDKI, she insisted, never collaborated with Baghdad. More importantly, in private Rahman criticized Saddam Hussein. This was confirmed when after 2003 the release of Iraqi intelligence archives showed no documents or evidence that implicated the PDKI in any such collaboration.[14]

There are many testimonials to Ghassemlou's abhorrence of Hussein's politics. French politician Alain Chenal reported, "In private Ghassemlou would tell me about the horrors of the Iraqi regime, but he was obliged to be discreet. He also had relations with the office of Claude Cheysson [French minister of foreign affairs] and his assistants, who had connections with Iraq."[15]

Jalal Talabani denied any submission to Baghdad on Ghassemlou's part. "Dr. Ghassemlou had relations with Iraq since 1971. Since then, he had returned to Iraq, where he worked as an economics expert. He never severed these relations, but he never used them against Iran.

"When the Iran-Iraq war began," continued Talabani, "the Iraqi government invited Dr. Ghassemlou [to Iraq], asking him to form a Kurdish state. They offered him everything: money and weapons. Even the budget for the future Kurdish government was to be paid by the Iraqis, who would completely recognize it. They wanted to divide Iran. Dr. Ghassemlou's response was that he wanted democracy and autonomy within Iran."[16]

Talabani's account of Ghassemlou's relationship with the Iraqi regime is especially meaningful. In 1983 Ghassemlou had mediated during negotiations between Talabani and Saddam Hussein. "When we went together for the first time to Baghdad and entered Hussein's office, he warmly embraced Dr. Ghassemlou," Talabani reported. "The latter said to me, 'Jalal, now that I have brought you to see your president, it's your turn to take me to see my president in Tehran.' He said things to Saddam that others dared not utter. He was very smart. He knew how to express himself but he never conceded [a single point] to the Iraqis regarding the Kurdish problem."

The Iraqi regime's invitation to Ghassemlou was recently corroborated by Khanbaba Mehdi Tehrani, a long-time active opposition figure in Iranian politics. Speaking in an interview with Voice of America, Tehrani said: "During the Iran-Iraq war, Saddam Hussein asked to have a meeting with Dr. Ghassemlou, and in that meeting he suggested Dr. Ghassemlou announce Kurdistan's independence.

"From Saddam's point of view, Iran was in an extremely bad political and economic situation. Iran was under enormous pressure; Iran was isolated, both politically and economically, and had no relation to the outside world—not to the Arab world, not to the Western world, nor to the U.S. and Canada. Having Iran's weak political situation in mind, Saddam was ready to support Dr. Ghassemlou in finding allies to recognize an independent Kurdistan—just to weaken Iran's situation further, which would have been to Saddam's benefit.

"However, Dr. Ghassemlou's response was to think about the offer and to ask his party members' opinions.

"Two months later, in a follow-up meeting, Dr. Ghassemlou told Saddam: 'Kurdistan relies upon Iran economically; in Kurdistan we do not have a strong economic base. If we make such a decision, the Kurdish people will be put under pressure, and we will lose our people's trust and support.'"[17]

"Kak Doctor had to have a relationship with the dictatorial regime of Saddam Hussein," remembered Ghassemlou's assistant Mohamed Hassan-pour.[18] "We were treated with respect; there was no humiliation. Today there is not the same respect. We have lost the shade that protected us. He represented discipline and respect.

"In 1983, during the negotiations between the PUK and Saddam Hussein, we traveled to Talabani's to pick him up and accompany him to the meetings. When we arrived, there were people from the PUK leadership waiting for us.

"But Hero Khanum, Talabani's wife, asked Kak Doctor, 'What guarantee do I have that my husband will return?'

"Ghassemlou replied, 'I am the guarantee.'"[19]

According to Ezzedin Mustafa Rasul, when the PDKI had to leave Iran for Iraqi Kurdistan, Ghassemlou "was forced to establish relations with Saddam Hussein. But when he sat down with Saddam he was very clear and said to him, 'We have a common enemy, and you want to overthrow him. We [the Kurds] want to find a space to live in. If one day I leave this alliance, don't tell me I have abandoned the fight."[20]

∼

"When the Islamic revolution triumphed ten years ago"—the voice as the tape continues is Mostafawi's—"it had to confront a problematic situation: the Kurdish problem. Yesterday, Dr. Fadil Rasul said the success the Republic of Mahabad enjoyed was due to the oppression it faced from the central power and the Shah's politics. I accept this. Nevertheless, I've not read anywhere that it was just autonomy that was being requested on that occasion." Ten years of war in the region and problems with the United States "have not allowed us to take care of it [the Kurdish question]," Mostafawi admitted, but now they, the Iranian regime, were going to do it. Tehran was going to study the Kurdish problem, and when they arrived at a conclusion, this would be incorporated into their military position.

"Then the knot of the Kurdish problem will be untied," Mostafawi announced. "When the military politics address it, then they will be able to propose limits, and give their opinion."

In summary, they were saying, the approaches to the Kurdish problem would ultimately rest upon the chiefs of staff, the military position.

"Allow me to respond," said Ghassemlou. "It is possible that in the beginning, the Islamic Republic's leaders did not take national [Kurdish] matters into consideration. They did not realize that this problem even existed. The six months during which I discussed this with many of them convinced me that this was the case. But today, even you admit that the problem exists, and this [admission] seems positive to me. Where there is a national problem, the national rights [of the minorities] are at stake."

Ghassemlou then began to explain the three possible solutions to the "national problem": "One is independence, which is the ultimate [solution]; you struggle for separation to create an independent state. . . . Two is that federalism exists. . . . Three is autonomy. If independence represents the ultimate solution, then autonomy is the minimum. Nothing less than autonomy exists.

"It's important for us to know if the Islamic Republic really wants to resolve the [Kurdish] national problem or not," he continued. "If they do, do they want a federation for Iran? Or do they want to tell all their minorities, 'Separate. Have your independence'? Or is it the model for autonomy? We have proposed the minimum. We reject the ultimate possibility, and we say so openly.

"Since it is logical," he went on, "we would approve federalism if the rest of the minorities want it. We would accept a federal union, a central government and all those things that belong to autonomy. It is the federal central government's duty to be responsible for the main affairs: defense, monetary, and long-term planning." In conclusion, he stated that the Islamic form of government was "more or less federal."

Speaking to Mostafawi, Ghassemlou said, "As you can see, I want to discuss this directly with you. If you do not accept autonomy, which is the minimum, that means you do not have the intention of negotiating the national problem. The solution of national rights has only three forms. Any other form does not exist in this world, and we cannot create a new one."

Ghassemlou did not raise his voice. He hardly ever did. It must have been clear to the Iranians that he was not going to give in.

"We have not come here to discuss our relations with the Islamic Republic," he repeated. "If our relations have deteriorated, it's for tangible reasons.

But the essential point continues to be national rights, which for us are included in autonomy.

"The war with Iraq was a reality that lasted for many years," he admitted. "But this Kurdish national question should be put on the table. Do it. We will wait.

"And if, while we wait, we continue our combat or not, this depends upon our decision to find a means of not fighting . . .

"That is another problem. Anyway, you cannot expect the PDKI to be on your side. Even if we did not exist, nothing would change with whoever comes after us."

"Meanwhile, you said it was possible to find a way to stop the conflict . . ." responded Mostafawi.

"We will discuss that later . . ."

Here the tape recording is interrupted by confusing voices. Then Ghassemlou continues.

"You speak of economy. You know that I'm an economist by profession. If you ask me . . . I will give you my opinion. After all, Iran is my country, be it an Islamic Republic or . . .

"I've had much experience in the socialist countries, in the Western countries, and in those of the Third World. This is my specialty. Our problem is different. In our country, we are a people at war; there are losses on both sides and many victims . . . This is not the time to delay the solution. It's time to solve it and make decisions."

He reminded them that they had also highlighted how important this problem was for the Islamic Republic and that Iraq, and Turkey as well, could profit from it.

"Get ahead of them. There are more advantages on the Iranian side from a historical, linguistic, and cultural point of view. The Kurds have Iranian roots; all the Kurds are interested in Iran. Use this. The Shah, with his repulsive politics—you as well as we were sick of them—wanted to take advantage of these [facts]. Why don't you profit from this occasion? You, the Islamic Republic, can move faster than Iraq and Turkey. I don't see any obstacle . . .

"We, as Iranians and Kurds, would like to see the Islamic Republic be the first. Believe me, you will not regret it. First, this would be a historic event, and as such would benefit the Islamic Republic one hundred percent. Second, it's incorrect to say that the national question is a new problem, because we have been waging war against each other for the last ten years."

He also spoke of the Kurds' repression at the hands of the Turks, who had deported massive numbers of Kurds to the central Ankara region, with the idea that they would be assimilated into the Turkish population.

"So they would stop being Kurds! Today there are almost sixty villages on the outskirts of Ankara that are completely Kurds! They arrived from different places and created their villages. More important, though, when Mustafa Kemal began his politics of assimilation, there were about three million Kurds in Turkey. Today, there are between twelve and fifteen million. Some parliamentarians are Kurds, because the Kurds of Ankara and Istanbul gave them their votes.

"What I want to say," continued Ghassemlou, "is that the problem cannot be resolved through half-solutions. Today the Turkish government is [still] very worried about the Kurdish problem. This is after sixty-three years! Since nineteen twenty-five!

"Why should we in Iran repeat similar experiences? Let's have a better experience. Let's find a solution that will not harm anyone in Iran. I repeat: neither its independence, nor its freedom, nor the unity of its land, nor its territory . . ."

The recording ends here. The section of tape that follows is blank.

In the final tape, you can hear Ghassemlou's voice trying to convince them that separatism is not in anyone's mind.

"Do not pay attention to irresponsible words. You represent the Islamic Republic. The Republic of Mahabad existed scarcely eleven months. Read what Qazi Mohammad said, read the PDKI's program, read their newspaper *Kurdistan*. Qazi Mohammad insisted that we were Iranians . . . We, in Iran, have never had the intention of separating in our tradition. Not even Komala and the Feda'iyan asked for separation when they were much stronger.

"Separatism does not have roots in our country. Only some newcomers say: 'We have fought for ten years for autonomy and what have we achieved? It's best that we fight for independence!' We hear these arguments. We receive letters from people who are ten thousand kilometers away from the battleground. However, we have consistently demanded only autonomy . . . Whoever asked [us] that question—be it the Swedish prime minister, or Willy Brandt, or Pierre Mauroy, or *Le Monde*—I have always spoken in those terms."

It's possible that Ghassemlou was trying to show them that he was an interlocutor with the great men of Europe, while the Iranian regime was totally isolated from the international community.

"Accept the principle of autonomy and allow me to explain it on television and the radio. When I wanted to do it, you did not give me the necessary airtime. Therefore, give me the time now so I can explain it all, and you can be sure that from our standpoint, the problem will quickly be resolved."

Notes

1. Copies of the full set of transcripts were provided to Gabriel Fernández and the author by Hélène Krulich in Paris, in 1990. Except where otherwise noted, this is the primary source quoted throughout this chapter. An additional source, transcript excerpts in English translation provided in Ferdinand Hennerbichler's analysis, are based on an account by journalist Chris Kutschera, in French. Ferdinand Hennerbichler, "Assassination of Abdul Rahman Ghassemlou (1930–1989): New Assessment," in *Wiener Jahrbuch für Kurdische Studien 2013, Schwerpunkt: Transnationalität und kurdische Diaspora in Österreich, Jahrgang 1/2013* (Vienna: Österreichische Gesellschaft zur Förderung der Kurdologie / Europäisches Zentrum für kurdische Studien, 2013), 311–14. Some also appeared briefly uploaded to YouTube as "The first round of negotiations of the Iranian Islamic Regime with Dr. Ghassemlou with the participation of Jalal Talabani," in 1988, posted February 25, 2019, https://youtu.be/zrSTPi8XyB4 (accessed February 26, 2019); translation Hasan Ayoubzadeh.
2. Hennerbichler, "Assassination of Abdul Rahman Ghassemlou," 311.
3. Hennerbichler's access to Kutschera's material clarifies *vilayet* and fleshes out context: "Now to autonomy. . . . His Holiness Ali ruled from the headquarters of the Caliphate, but there were other areas that were called 'Vilayets' (provinces), and the 'valis' (governorates) that were much larger than those of autonomy (areas)." Ibid., 312.
4. Hélène Krulich-Ghassemlou, *Love Against All Reason: A European Woman Involved in the Kurdish Fight for Freedom in Iran* (Vienna: Lit Verlag, 2017), 67.
5. Bernard Kouchner, interview with the author, Paris, 1991.
6. Jalal Talabani, interview with the author, Paris, 1991. Further statements by Talabani in this chapter are from this interview.

   Teymur Bakhtiar, head of the SAVAK between 1957 and 1961, maintained contact with the Israelis and the CIA until 1961, when he was dismissed from his post. He was murdered by members of the SAVAK in Iraq in 1970.
7. Ibid.
8. "For us there are four key points," Ghassemlou can be heard saying: "autonomy, which means decentralization of power. The second key point for us is the Kurdish language: Kurdish should become the official language of the Kurdish region. The third problem is the delimitation of the autonomous region. For that we must take into account the geographic, economic, and above all the will of the people where Kurds live. The fourth point is essential for the Kurdish population—that security within the Kurdish region must be ensured by the Kurds." See "The first round of negotiations of the Iranian Islamic Regime with Dr. Ghassemlou with the participation of Jalal Talabani," 1988; translation Hasan Ayoubzadeh.
9. Abdul Rahman Ghassemlou, letter to the author, 1985.

10. Abdul Rahman Ghassemlou, separate letter to the author, 1985.

11. Comité international pour la libération des députés kurdes emprisonnés en Turquie, *Quelle Turquie pour quelle Europe?*. Dossier published with the collaboration of the Institut Kurde de Paris and the Fondation France-Libertés (Paris: December 1995).

12. Abolhassan Banisadr, interview with the author, Versailles, 1991. Further statements from Banisadr are from this interview.

13. Hélène Krulich, interview with Gabriel Fernández and the author, Paris, 1990.

14. Mahmoud Othman, Kurdish independent member of the Iraqi parliament, in a speech to the PDKI headquarters in 2003, noted that while the PDKI had to establish relations with the Iraqi regime given their geopolitical situation, these were never used to the detriment of the Iraqi Kurds. The PDKI bore the disadvantages of this relationship but never allowed Iraqi Kurds to be hurt. For Othman this was something that the PDKI should be proud of. After the fall of the Iraqi regime many documents were confiscated from the Iraqi *Estexbarat*, intelligence services. No negative information about the PDKI, only positive points, he said, were extracted from these documents, demonstrating the honesty of the party and its leadership. See Dr. Mahmoud Othman says the PDKI should be proud of itself. https://www.youtube.com/watch?v=5lZXwqDPiFQ, posted August 19, 2011 (accessed September 10, 2015). Translation Salah Piroty.

15. Since Valery Giscard D'Estaing's time as president of France (1974–1981), the French have played their cards in the region in favor of Iraq. Their investments there were important. Paris constructed the nuclear reactor at Osirak, which the Israelis destroyed in 1981. During the Gulf War, beginning in 1991, a decidedly pro-Iraqi sector of François Mitterrand's government defended Iraq's position.

16. Jalal Talabani, interview with the author, Paris, 1991.

17. VOA interview, posted July 15, 2013, accessed at Tehrani's website, http://www.khanba-ba-tehrani.com/; translation Beyan Farshi. Active in Iranian opposition politics for over sixty years, Tehrani, as a Communist, produced a Persian radio program in Beijing, China, before the Iranian revolution; he now resides in Germany. His testimony is included in the Harvard Iranian Oral History Project, tape 05: "Former member of Tudeh, student leader in Europe, member of Radio Peking Persian Service staff, and leader of the National Democratic Front," http://ted.lib.harvard.edu/ted/deliver/~iohp/Tehrani,+Mehdi+Khan-baba.05 (accessed March 4, 2015).

18. Mohamed Hassanpour, PDKI member, interview with the author, Koya Sanjak, Iraqi Kurdistan, 2009.

19. Ibid.

20. Ezzedin Mustafa Rasul, interview with the author, Koya Sanjak, Iraqi Kurdistan, 2009.

· 8 ·

CREAKING ON THE FLOOR

❧

"In conclusion," said Ghassemlou, "we have two demands to make: democracy and autonomy. You came here to speak with us. In a simple friendship it would be different, but in politics it works this way: when you want to get something from us, you must also give us something back.

"We are not in a position to accept the minimum possible from you and then you receive the maximum from us. We must try to do what benefits our country. It's because of this that I also insist that you accept the principle of autonomy. You must have realized that I'm far from saying anything out of pure courtesy or irresponsibility. I'm very aware of what I am saying. I, Abdul Rahman Ghassemlou, know that I cannot accept less than autonomy, less than the principle of autonomy."

"Is it for *Kurdanamosi*, the Kurdish way of honor?" inquires an unidentified voice in Farsi. With this reduction of Ghassemlou's insistence on autonomy to no more than a means to save face, it is clear that the Iranians are mocking the PDKI, its leader, and the legitimacy of the Kurds' needs and demands.

"No," responds Ghassemlou, maintaining equanimity and authority in the face of this sneer. "I'm a university professor. This has nothing to do with my honor in being a Kurd. What we want from you is this at the minimum. Believe me, we want a minimum agreement that we can accept, and the maximum that the Islamic Republic can offer us.

"All the other problems can be resolved. We have all the necessary time. But I cannot return and say: 'For now, they limit themselves to *examining* the question of autonomy'! It cannot be like it was in the socialist countries where they never said no. Instead, they said they would examine the case, and this [situation] might last for years. Therefore, be kind and do not 'examine' anything now."

There is laughter and then Mostafawi responds:

"For the reasons that you have given yourself, allow me to ask you this question: Don't you think . . . that you are not in any position either to concede or to withdraw the word *autonomy*? Apart from what the others [Kurds] who are fighting for this slogan may think. You said that a peshmerga said that he would marry [i.e., go on with his life] once he obtained autonomy. Don't you think the same is true for the Islamic Republic?"

"We do agree. I do not see any difference of opinion here. When will the representatives of the Islamic Republic be convinced that autonomy will harm neither the unity of the country nor its independence and integrity? What are they afraid of?

"I repeat that I want the leaders of the Islamic Republic to understand that if we wanted something other than autonomy, we would say so. In our world, it is not a sin to demand independence. There are smaller nations than us—of two hundred thousand, three hundred thousand, one or two million— that reclaim independence. We do not want it. After much analysis, after having imagined ourselves in the same position as you, and having considered the situation in Iran, the Middle East, and the world overall, we have returned to our slogan [of democracy for Iran, autonomy for Kurdistan]. If any of our Kurdish friends do not like it, it's their problem that they want something else. We represent the Iranian Kurds . . . At least, under the present conditions, and to demand independence supposes a long term . . ."

Then Ghassemlou appeals to the religious sentiment of the Islamists. "I have not found in any part of the Qur'an anything against autonomy," he says. "Since I know Arabic, I read religious books. And I have heard what the leaders in Qom—religious and nonreligious—have said. If you read, in any sura of the Qur'an, that autonomy is unacceptable under any circumstances— anyway, you will not read anything about this anywhere.

"But we have not come here to insist that all of our demands be accepted immediately. We are not dreamers. We are not irrational. The only thing we want is to forge the way. We have fought against you for the last ten years. Imam Khomeini had courage. Why wouldn't his heirs have it also? This needs *some* courage; it doesn't need too much. It doesn't require as much as the Imam's, because this is not a case that can affect others. This is an internal problem in a country that is looking to resolve its internal problems.

"It's obvious that once you accept autonomy for Kurdistan, others will come to demand the same thing. You will create laws that will resolve the problems of centrifugal force [the problem of other minorities' wanting to separate]. Do not forget that at the other end [of Iran] live the Baluchis and the Azeris, who live in the Soviet Union as well. There are the Arabs in Iraq and the Turkmen in the USSR . . . All the nationalities that live in Iran have their counterpart [ethnic kin] on the other side of the border. There are also the Kurds in Turkey and Iraq. Someday this epidemic will turn against our country if we do not deal with it now and find a solution."

After his long discourse, Ghassemlou ended, "I have nothing more to add. If anyone would like to ask anything . . ."

There's a confusion of voices, then Rasul saying something unclear about the timekeeping.

"Tomorrow afternoon we can discuss everything you want," responds Ghassemlou.

Someone asks for more time and someone else adds that it does not matter. Rasul suggests that they could prolong the conversation until late in the evening.

Ghassemlou jokes, "You're inviting us to dinner?"

"I'm alone," Rasul answers. "If you all agree, when we finish, we can go someplace? . . ."

"Good, it's clear. We will bring bread and cheese and then we will eat here."

A voice in Farsi: "If all you need is bread and cheese . . ."

Then they all start speaking at the same time. You can hear Ghassemlou's voice recounting an anecdote: "Do not be like the Komala . . . The Komala people entered a tent and an old lady brought them bread and cheese . . ."

Once again the tape is interrupted. The voices are superimposed over each other. In the moment before the murder, you can only hear Fadil Rasul, who is interrupted twice by a voice in Farsi. Except for Mostafawi's voice, there are no sounds that denote the presence of other people.

Rasul is speaking in a style as if addressing a group of friends who have distanced themselves from one another. He refers to Ghassemlou and Ghaderi-Azar as "brothers." His words are the opening to a long discourse that precedes the crime. Whoever listens to these tapes, and knows that their deaths are imminent, feels like a helpless spectator watching a tragedy about to unfold.

"I understand, and with your permission, I need to add that you are asking for our brothers from the PDKI to, first, clarify their position toward the Islamic Republic . . . The brothers say that, without autonomy, without a statement about the possibility of autonomy, there can be no agreement with the Islamic Republic. What we all now accept is that it could take years before autonomy becomes a reality, or before you arrive at a solution for autonomy. In Iraq itself . . ."

Rasul cannot stop referring to his own country, Iraq. Since Iraq had become a republic, he reminds them, there had been no solutions to many of its problems. "Some have worsened, like the Kurdish problem." And he goes on to narrate the history of the Kurdish combat headed by Mustafa Barzani.

There is another interruption in the tape, and whoever is listening feels tempted to wonder if the tape has been tampered with, or if Ghassemlou may have stopped it so he wouldn't have to listen later to a historical explanation that he knew very well.

"You say [you], the brothers, treat the subject democratically"; Rasul now addresses the Kurds. "This is a good starting point . . . Now there are two issues: either you continue waging war until you obtain autonomy, or you try to find a common outlook to continue the negotiations without either of the sides compromising their own [goals] . . . If the war in Kurdistan continues another two or three years, we should consider whether the possibilities for a peaceful agreement would be better, or worsened . . ."

Another interruption in the tape.

". . . Then it will depend on the balance of forces," Rasul's voice continues. "The opportunity, the occasion that you have today—please use it. Negotiate until you find a solution to your differences. If you cannot resolve them, how are you going to coexist?"

"We accept that proposal," Ghassemlou said.

These were his last words.

❧

Now there are voices all speaking at the same time. "I'm not speaking only about these conversations . . ."

Rasul's voice: "To know what we are going to do . . ."

If the tapes are an authentic witness to this drama, we must register a pause of five seconds during which all you hear are light footsteps on the creaking floor. Not a voice is heard, nor a scream of terror. There are no questions. No calls for help. Nothing.

Are the three Kurds still alive while the tape records this silence?

Five seconds later the shooting begins. The ballistics experts will find sixteen spent cartridges in the apartment and fifteen bullets—six of these bullets in two of the the three bodies—but from the tape, you only hear a few shots fired. And these are muffled. This may due to the silencers the perpetrators placed on their guns.

The experts who examine the tapes will admit there is a possibility that the sounds of gunfire you hear may not be the actual gunfire. What are they, then?

If the tape had continued to record, what was actually happening during the crime itself? How did the police find it in Ghassemlou's briefcase? Who put it there? Why would the Iranians not have taken any real evidence with them?

There is another incomprehensible fact: during the gunfire, you can hear unrecognizable voices in the background. The voices continue for a long time. It seems to be a discussion in Farsi, interrupted by laughter, after which someone else arrives who speaks with the others in German.

æ

Hélène listened to the tapes one hundred times. She studied the translation to German and she found experts who helped her arrive at definite conclusions. In November of 1990, she knew that not everything was clear-cut regarding these tapes.[1]

There was a definite possibility that fraud had been committed and the tapes that appeared at the crime scene were not the originals. The tapes recorded on Thursday, July 13, 1989, could have been switched with others that were prepared beforehand.

It would have been the last thing the murderers did. While one was putting away the weapons, another left with the tapes recorded that afternoon and placed the falsified ones in Ghassemlou's briefcase. That's where the police say they found them.

The goal would be to give, during the police and judicial investigations later, the impression that everything had happened in a straightforward way. This would mean eliminating any compromising sections of the conversation: shouts, threats, bribes, blackmail . . .

The negotiators had come into the country with official diplomatic passports signed by the Iranian minister for foreign affairs, Ali Akbar Velayati. They had not presented themselves to the local authorities upon their arrival. Would it not have been more convenient for the Iranians if the police had not found *any* audiotapes? If virtually no one knew about the negotiations or the identity of the Iranians, why reveal or confirm after the crime that official envoys of the government of the Islamic Republic had been there at all?

To throw doubt on the authenticity of the tapes, it could be said, contributes to a conspiracy theory that puts Austria in a bad light. But the fact is that the thorough analysis done by specialized technicians outside of Austria clearly showed signs of the tapes having been tampered with.

This study was ordered by Hélène Krulich some time after the murder, and she did not hesitate to point out its findings: "Two places exist in the third tape which have probably been altered and there is a third place where there is no doubt that the tape was cut and pasted back together."

The report of the Austrian investigators did not mention these facts. So "it is natural," Hélène said, "that we don't have a serious analysis." More recently, she explained, "The tapes gave me reasons to suspect them, especially the last one—I had it 'cleaned' but it was so opaque that the result was null."[2]

Hélène's objections are reasonable. If the tapes were altered—and it seems they were—more questions are raised about the murder plot. For example: if the assassins had been individuals outside of the negotiations, as the Iranians have alleged, how did they have hours of conversations in their hands, recorded the day before, to create such a deception as this?

The voices of the main characters in the conversation are authentic. The long conversation that appears in the tapes could only have been held the day before, on Wednesday, July 12. Ghassemlou's remark, "Tomorrow afternoon we can discuss everything you want," points toward this likelihood. Had conversations recorded during the previous rounds of negotiations, in December and January, been spliced into the tape, it would have been evident, and evidence of a clumsy fraud attempt.

There exists a third possibility, about which there was widespread speculation at the time: that the manipulation was done after the crime was *discovered*, when the tapes were in the hands of the police and the Austrian judges.

Let's consider again. After the crime the authorities in Tehran informed the world about the assassination, and declared that the objective of the negotiations had been to agree to give Abdul Rahman Ghassemlou safe conduct to return to Iran. The story put out by Tehran was that Sahrarudi "had met with Ghassemlou on two previous occasions, and Iranian state television announced that the third fateful meeting . . . took place at the KDPI's request to discuss an amnesty program for the peshmerga who had fought against the government forces."[3]

None of this appears at all on the tapes. If someone had spoken about this, it has been erased. Nevertheless, it's possible that the decision to kill Ghassemlou, which meant killing the other two Kurds present, had been taken when Ghassemlou refused to accept such a deal: when he said no, Ghassemlou could have hastened his own end.

Was any such passage erased by an official, by request of the Austrian authorities, to hide evidence that could affect Tehran? Or as part of a submissive Austrian response to strong pressure from Iran, a country with whom they had a lucrative business, not all of it clean? Is this possible?

In theory, the answer is yes. But it is difficult to give a clear judgment. There is no proof that this is the way events actually played out. And what is more: this would open the door to the terrible suspicion that the Iranian assassins could have counted on criminal complicity within the police or judicial apparatus of a democratic country in Western Europe.

Two facts, at least, are clear. The first is that Ghassemlou himself was meticulous and careful never to rerecord on tapes that had been previously used. So if the tapes were truly Ghassemlou's, recorded on July 13 and somehow packed back into his briefcase before his murder took place, there is no logical explanation for the interruptions the experts say they found in the tapes. And the second is that the tapes bear signs of tampering at the very least, and even of outright substitution of content. What even now is not clear is at what point this was done, for what specific purpose, and by whom.

Notes

1. Hélène Krulich, interview with Gabriel Fernández and the author, Paris, 1990. Except where specified, further comments from Hélène Krulich throughout this chapter are from this interview.
2. Hélène Krulich, personal communication to the author, April 26, 2016.
3. Nader Entessar, *Kurdish Politics in the Middle East* (London: Lexington Books, 2010, 47, n87.

· 9 ·

COBRA II

~

The night of the crime, Oswald Kessler, Staatspolizei[1] chief of operational forces, arrived at number 5 Linke Bahngasse. This crime clearly fell within his jurisdiction as chief of the EBT (Einsatzgruppe zur Bekämpfung des Terrorismus), the special unit within the Staatspolizei focused on counterintelligence, organized crime, and counterterrorism. He studied the crime scene and the position of the bodies, entrusted specific tasks to his men, and sent officers out around the city to the small Kurdish neighborhoods in Vienna. He spent all night working on the crime.

Kessler was a man with the necessary reflexes to come up with clear conclusions about the scene in which he had found three bodies mowed down by multiple volleys of gunfire.

At 8:00 in the morning the following day, Friday, July 14, he informed the minister of the interior, Franz Löschnak, to whom he was answerable, that a political crime planned from abroad had taken place once more in Vienna.[2] Three Iranians, he told Löschnak, had assassinated three Kurds.

That same Friday afternoon, Kessler would confide this conclusion to Susanne Rockenschaub-Rasul. Two days later, on Sunday, July 16, he would repeat without hesitation to Fatah, Mostafa, and Azad—leaders in the Kurdish community—the same opinion he had given the minister: "It is obvious what has happened here. Three Kurds have been assassinated by three Iranians who were present."[3]

He told the Kurds that it was a political murder and he couldn't do anything. Nonetheless, despite the fact that it all seemed very clear, the obligatory discretion inherent to all law enforcement led him to moderate his expressions.

In retrospect, there was clearly more to his reticence than this. Weeks later he would tell the attorneys who represented the relatives of the victims that his English was very poor and the conclusion he'd voiced to the Kurds— that the crime was political—was all a misunderstanding. A strange apology, seeing that he had undoubtedly spoken not in English, but in German, "which everyone around understood perfectly," points out Austrian journalist Sissy Danninger.[4]

At the same time, the Kurds and their friends began to run into obstacles—elusive responses from the police officers and from officials of the ministries of the interior, justice, and foreign affairs.

Without a doubt, the official response to the murder was about politics, dictated from the highest levels of political power, because Austrian officials have responded since then with evasive answers to any question regarding the crime. They constantly repeat: "We have a democratic country and an independent judiciary." This seems to be only partly true when interests of the state are at risk, as this case demonstrates.

A year and a half after the crime, in November–December 1990, Oswald Kessler would rise to the highest position in Austria's security police force. From chief of operational forces, an already powerful office, he had now been designated chief of the Staatspolizei.

In comprehensible English, though with an imperfect pronunciation due perhaps to the speed with which he was speaking, Kessler would explain vehemently to Hélène Krulich and interviewer Gabriel Fernández that Austria was a very complicated country with regard to its security organizations.[5]

In fact, Vienna is a capital that shelters a host of international organizations where, among other things, the complex matters of nuclear disarmament and the prices and quotas of oil are decided. And owing to its neutrality, negotiated at the end of World War II, and its geographical position as a country between the two Europes, Austria was a paradise for spies during the four-decade Cold War.

Even though Kessler did not say it, a history of this type of activity going unpunished has been the norm in the former capital of the Austro-Hungarian Empire.

We deduce this from the words of a former chief of police who is now retired. He wanted to write a book that would expose this fact: that the great majority of important political crimes committed in Austria have never been resolved.

"The political morality," he said, "has fallen in a shocking way in Austria during the last ten years."[6] Understandably he asked that he not be named. This world is made up of ordinary people, not heroes. While willing to express his concerns, his natural desire was to preserve the hope of living in peace for the remainder of his life.

Kessler seemed to be trying to convince Hélène and journalist Gabriel Fernández that Austria lacked a good intelligence service. He had fought a long battle to organize one, which provoked attacks upon him from all sides.

The thinking he expressed ran along these lines: Is it realistically even possible to have information about the various mafias—Italian, Turkish, and Yugoslavian—that operate in the country? How could we possibly know the details of the activities of the Palestinian agents and the Israeli Mossad, the spies from the West German Stasi, the Spanish Basque ETA terrorists, and the Irish Republican Army?

His concern was logical. At the same time, it was interesting that in his enumeration, he did not mention the activities of the extreme right groups, the neo-Nazi organizations that are active and very present in Austria.

꙳

Up to this point, the person in the public spotlight who was fighting to get the murder of the three Kurds resolved was Peter Pilz, Green Party spokesperson in parliament. His battle, though courageous, had so far been without results. Pilz had his own opinion regarding the reasons the murders had not been solved. Long-standing Austrian tradition, he said, encouraged the police not to worry about extreme-right terrorist organizations.

"The police are totally blind. There has never been enough information about the extreme right, about the main Nazi groups or about the international extreme-right groups like the Turkish Grey Wolves. At times, I suppose that there are groups within the Staatspolizei itself that have close personal ties with extreme-right groups outside of Austria," Deputy Pilz said in an interview in 1991.[7]

In the fifties and sixties, the Austrian police were fundamentally very anti-Communist. This should not come as a surprise; so were all the European police. In the seventies, the police began to concentrate on the Green movement, feminism, the pacifists, and the leftist union workers.

"All these groups, especially the Green, were watched in a strict way by the secret police," Pilz declared in perfect English. "When we have meetings anywhere, you can be sure there is always someone present from the secret police."

Kessler would have shared such concerns and views. How can you control, Kessler seemed to want to say, the thousands of illegal immigrants that have established themselves permanently in Austria? In 1989 alone, 21,882 people—double the number from the previous year, the majority of them from Eastern Europe—had requested political asylum in Austria. In the first three months of 1990 alone, five thousand had requested it; almost all were from Romania. They arrived by the hundreds every day during the month of February, fleeing from the revolution that ended the regime and the life of Nicolas Ceauşescu.

Therefore, in March of 1990 the Austrian government decided to reduce the influx of immigrants by imposing restrictions upon entry into the country from Hungary. Hungary and Austria, the remnants of a former empire, had become the passageway through which great numbers of people escaped from the Eastern zone, and even from East Germany.

The new arrivals were required by Austrian customs authority to have sufficient funds to cover living expenses for a specified period of time or a visa indicating passage to another country. Parliament approved strict measures that allowed for the deportation of illegal immigrants, greater power for the border police, and control of potential refugees who flew in. Since January 1990, the authorities had demanded a limited three-month visa for incoming Turks.

Among the Viennese—especially the elderly formal ladies with their picturesque hats who fill the trams and read their newspapers in the cafés—you could hear many complaints about the increase in crime that was without precedent.

Pilz disagreed with Kessler. "The Austrian secret police are very well informed," he said, "about the people who think differently from the government. Foreigners are strictly watched. If you cross the Austrian border, your personal file is incorporated into the police computers, and these computers are linked to the computers of Germany and the European Community. So there is a control net over the foreigners."

❧

Austria, with seven million people and an area of over eighty-three thousand square kilometers, is a country invaded by an unending flow of tourists from the entire world. Very few cities can boast the wealth of architecture and art that Vienna has, or the attraction of Salzburg for music lovers. All over the world, people think of Vienna as the city of the *belle époque*, immortalized by Strauss waltzes.

Imperial Vienna was a magnificent city. It was here that Sigmund Freud gave birth to psychoanalysis. Ernst Mach's and Ludwig Boltzmann's philosophies of science were born here, as were Ludwig Wittgenstein's analytic philosophy, Alexander Zemlinsky's and Arnold Schönberg's atonal and dodecaphonic music, Adolph Loos's functional architecture, and Victor Adler's Marxism.

In Vienna, where anti-Semitism was always fierce, Theodore Herzl's Zionism was born, advocating in 1896 the creation of a national Jewish state. In March of 1938, Adolph Hitler entered the city without encountering any resistance and proclaimed the *Anschluss*, the annexation of the country to the New Germany. Vienna began to darken. Its magnificent cafés, theaters, and bookstores began to close as its intelligentsia emigrated.

Modern Vienna has long left behind the miseries of the postwar aftermath. Vienna is a clean city, orderly, solemnly majestic. Snowy in winter, luminous in spring, the capital of the former empire has erased all the dark evidence of its Nazi past and the Soviet invasion.

Only its open anti-Semitism—which explains in part the election of former Nazi officer Kurt Waldheim to the presidency in 1986—continues to appear like a stain on a beautiful face.

And foreigners are considered, by a great part of the population, as second-class citizens, especially if they are from the Third World.

❧

The Kurds know this well because they have personally suffered this persecution in their own skin. In February 1991, Thomas Prader, attorney and advisor to the Green Party, denounced the fact that a Kurd was being prosecuted for a murder he had nothing to do with, simply because he was a Kurd.

"The Kurds in Austria are second-class citizens," Prader said. The Staatspolizei knew that the Grey Wolves had planned the murder of eight Kurds exiled in Austria, he revealed, and had not warned the victims, despite the fact that some of these potential victims were by this time Austrian citizens.[8]

These are the daily dramas of a city that are ignored by the constant river of visitors. How many of these unconcerned visitors know that an army of refugees has arrived from faraway Palestine or the mountains of Kurdistan? These refugees may be trying to lay down roots in this magnificent Central European city. Yet they know that there is no assurance for them in returning home and no future or fulfillment for them in remaining here.

One hundred and eighty-eight million people, the majority of them tourists, crossed the Austrian border the year Ghassemlou and his companions were murdered. Statistics registered that at least eighty million visitors stayed overnight in Austria that year.

Among those millions of tourists, there were three Iranian assassins and three Kurdish victims: tiny ripples in a vast, moving sea. At least, it seems that was what Kessler wanted to communicate that afternoon in 1991 at the Ministry of the Interior.

The Austrians are not surprised by drama; they don't even seem to care. It's not that a special racism exists in Austria, said attorney Manfred Weidinger, defender of the Ghassemlou cause. Weidinger understood that the behavior of the population corresponds to something like "a way of avoiding problems. It's like one Austrian has said: 'There are no Austrian victims; therefore, let us stay away and avoid any problems.'"[9]

Naturally Kessler knew all this very well. While he did not give the impression of being a cultivated man, there is no doubt that he was an ambitious man— or even an opportunist, according to his critics from the Green Party. He was linked to the Trevi Group, an elite group of high officials formed by the European ministries of interior and justice. This group was particularly concerned about terrorism and threats to the security of prosperous Europe that might come from a Third World periphery: North Africa, the Middle East, the Persian Gulf, traffickers serving some of the drug cartels (Colombians and Thais chief among them).

Unlike the majority of his fellow citizens, Kessler also knew very well the guts of the capital; he knew the sordid corners of political power, the insides of the police stations, the underworld, the misery of the immigrants, the subterranean world of crime, and the sewers of this society that appeared so educated in its cafés.

Kessler did not ignore at all—and by then no one could ignore—that the secret service agencies of Austria and Iran had collaborated upon more than one occasion.

❧

The chief of the Staatspolizei spent part of his time holed up in a bunker that the government had constructed inside the Modena Palace.

At Herrengasse 7, in the heart of old Vienna, a few steps from the incomparable Michaelerplatz, is the Bundesministerium für Inneres, the Ministry of the Interior. The entryway to the Innenministerium is through a large gate, which debouches onto a cobbled path. Then begins a long trajectory through silent corridors interrupted by hermetic doors which can only be opened by an officer of the place, courteous but cold. Then there is an elevator and a door that opens with a coded number. All told, there are twelve such doors until you reach an office with an enormous conference table. The place is a fortress.

How illuminating that Austrian authorities chose this place to install their office for police affairs. And down on the corner is the city's central café, where the revolutionary Leon Trotsky, a fugitive from Stalin's purges, used to debate in Russian with his comrades.

Leon Trotsky would be stabbed to death in Mexico with a mountaineer's ice axe by Ramon Mercader, a self-avowed supporter actually sent by Stalin to assassinate him. And half a century later, when you travel to Vienna to reconstruct the political assassination of three Kurds, you find a parallel scenario: murderers sent, in this case, from Tehran, with the ostensible purpose of negotiating a peace agreement.

It is a strange parallel. Trotsky had been sentenced to death in absentia by Stalin, three years before his execution. Ghassemlou had been condemned ten years before, also in absentia, by Imam Khomeini.

It is no less interesting to note that next to the Ministry of the Interior, at number 9, in the old palace of Mollar-Clary, mere meters away from the valuable files that hold the personal, political, and criminal history of hundreds of thousands of Austrians and foreigners, innocently stands the Landesmuseum Niederösterreichisches. Among its holdings of magnificent sculpture and paintings are masterworks by Albrecht Dürer. Art and death go hand-in-hand in the beautiful streets of old Vienna.

ॐ

It's not that Oswald Kessler was in hiding in this palace. On the contrary, Kessler was well-known for his courage. His reputation was built in the eighties, when he confronted a group of terrorists who had barricaded themselves into the Vienna airport.

Kessler had entered law enforcement in 1975; he was soon an officer in Vienna's police department. He moved on to the Staatspolizei. In 1987 he organized the Einsatzgruppe zur Bekämpfung des Terrorismus, EBT, the antiterrorist group popularly known as Group II or Cobra II.

His career culminated when he was asked to come before the Innenministerium, in November–December 1990, for his appointment as head of the secret police. He was then only thirty-six years old and the *neuer Mann für die Staatspolizei* characterized by the *Kurier* as the "*Polizei-Yuppie.*"

But Kessler could not share more than he had already divulged. He knew too much, perhaps even too much for his own good. His certainty of the political nature of the assassination, certainty that the Iranians had murdered the Kurds to weaken the leadership of their resistance movement, had almost surely put him at political risk in the Austrian halls of power. He had risen very high and must be reasonably convinced that if he did reveal more, it would not be of use to the cause of this hardworking and peaceful Kurdish community in Vienna or the elegant and firm Czech widow, who fought on to no avail for the investigation to move ahead with hopefully some official result.

But what else does this lady want? he seemed to be thinking. The German translation of the recorded conversations between the three Kurds and the Iranians in Farsi, which conclude abruptly with gunfire and the sound of light footsteps, had taken the official police translator months of work. This translation was defective, and at Hélène Krulich's insistence, it had taken a second translator another four months to produce a transcript in Farsi with a German translation. The cost had mounted to an additional hundred and twenty thousand schillings (about $12,000).

Today it seems clear that the maneuvering of the Austrian government showed their lack of interest in getting the case solved. From the outset, they had held up the investigation through the breach of normal procedures, through the premature release of Sahrarudi that short-circuited any thorough interrogation. And now, they vitiated the investigation by not allowing Oswald Kessler to conduct it. Three foreigners had been killed in Vienna; it was an organized crime, it was terrorist activity, and Kessler should have remained at the helm of the investigation. How reasonable was it, then, that Mayor Helmut Zilk ordered the case transferred to the Bundespolizeidirektion Wien, the Federal Police Directorate of Vienna? Was this decision one that came from the upper echelons? Who made it? What can be said about Zilk or those he answered to? At this distance we can do little more than speculate. But what we do know is that though Zilk had been a member of Austria's governing Socialist Party, it would be discovered after his death that he had a shady past with the Czechoslovak secret police.[10]

We cannot know if Kessler had been directed to pull back from the investigation. But to the importuning of the Kurds, Kessler was specific: the crime investigation of the murder of the three Kurds was at this point in the hands of the local police. He was not responsible.

Nonetheless, according to Austrian legal norms, it was, and is, the Staatspolizei—and therefore the experienced and knowledgeable policeman with trim white hair and chiseled features—that has the duty to investigate the big crimes like bank thefts, drug traffic, and kidnapping.

☙

It was a rainy day and Kessler was speaking in the Café Landtmann: "If it's a political crime," he conceded to Hélène and interviewer Gabriel Fernández, "the Staatspolizei should be in charge."[11]

Kessler could not say so publicly—then, or later[12]—but it was a given by now that indeed this crime was political. Kessler was where he was because of his efficiency and because of a scandal that had ended with his predecessor, Anton Schulz. The scandal had dragged on for a while and touched a large portion of the Austrian political class, which baptized it the *Noricum Prozess.*

It is revealing that Noricum, the arms division of the vast nationalized steel conglomerate Vöest-Alpine,[13] was involved with the far-reaching corruption of high-level Austrian officials who participated irresponsibly in the sale of enormous shipments of nationally manufactured weapons to Iran and Iraq during the combatants' 1980–1988 war. "It was a time," Hélène Krulich points out, "when foreign governments were keen on renewing relations with Iran severed after the hostage crisis."[14] And a time when Oswald Kessler had been "transferred to another post and his original police report . . . modified to conform with the requirements of the time."[15]

The politicians not only violated the obligatory neutrality of Austria. They also hid the facts, they lied, and, though they will never admit it, it was this commercial exchange of weapons with the Islamic Republic that determined this additional outcome: that the authorities of this democratic nation in Western Europe would cover up a state murder and thus become by omission the accomplices to a terrorist act. A parliamentary investigation in 1990 would conclude that the illegal arms trade to Iraq "had made Austria vulnerable for blackmailing by Iran."[16] And in this vulnerability would lie repercussions for the investigation of Ghassemlou's assassination.

On January 26, 1988, the former general director of the company Noricum, Herr Peter Unterweger, admitted at a press conference that his company had sold weapons in the value of four million schillings (about $400,000) to Iran between 1984 and 1986. He admitted to having done so, disregarding Austria's legal obligations since 1955 as a neutral state, one obliged not to sell weapons to nations at war.

The activities of Noricum were not clear. One year earlier, the press had disclosed that the company had been regularly selling military equipment to Libya since 1986. And this during times when Libya was being singled out by the Western countries as one of the most active centers of international terrorism.

In the last decades, the Austrians, despite their neutrality in the heart of Europe and their democratic system, had been shaken by infamous political scandals. As a consequence of one of these, the Lütgendorf scandal,[17] in 1977 the minister of defense was forced to step down over illegal military arms deals and the parliament had amended Austrian law regulating imports, exports and transits of military arms and equipment.[18]

In 1979 Vöest-Alpine decided to produce cannon in their main subsidiary company, Noricum. Socialist chancellor Bruno Kreisky, under whose sphere of influence fell state-run industries, agreed. Since a 1955 Austrian state treaty with the Allies prohibited cannons in Austria with a range of more than thirty kilometers, the conclusion was inescapable that the howitzers that came out of the Noricum plant would be exported.

In 1980–1981, Iraq bought two hundred cannon which arrived by way of Jordan. In 1984, Iran also ordered two hundred cannon that were officially billed to Libya. The contract was negotiated by an Iranian arms dealer, Mohammed Reza Hadji Dai, who in July 1985 complained to Herbert Amry, Austrian ambassador in Athens, that he had not received his commission for the sale. Iran had organized a straw company, named Fasami, to avoid paying for the weapons. Amry in turn informed Austria's Ministry of Foreign Affairs. It is not certain his suspicions or his final communiqué ever reached the minister's desk; he died mysteriously shortly thereafter, his remains were quickly cremated, and any trail of evidence came to a dead end.[19] A few days prior Amry had warned his diplomat colleague Ferdinand Hennerbichler to be careful because their lives were in danger.[20]

The minister of foreign affairs, Leopold Gratz, had given instructions to important government officials not to check the destination certificates of the weapons. In August 1985, the magazine *Basta* investigated the death of Amry, sparked by the suspicion that he could have been poisoned. The entire affair, a train of events that would come to include numerous deaths by "heart attack" or murder of individuals involved in the sale of a "super cannon," proven cover-ups, false statements, and forgeries of documents and files by state officials and politicians, would be known as the Noricum scandal.

Rumors spread, and in an emergency meeting, chancellor Fred Sinowatz and minister of the interior Karl Blecha agreed that the minister of nationalized industries, Ferdinand Lacina, should "examine" the case. Nevertheless, nothing was done. The affair seemed to be finished.

But in November 1985, Intertrading, another Vöest-Alpine subsidiary, went bankrupt from its operations in the oil market, which had demanded enormous subsidies on the part of the Austrian taxpayers. The head of Intertrading was dismissed from his post. He countered by threatening to publish details of the cannon exports. But he changed his mind after receiving a large sum of money from Noricum.[21]

In January 1986, American government officials demanded that the export of cannon to Libya stop immediately, in view of tense relations with the Libyan leader Colonel Muammar al-Gaddafi. In February, Sinowatz, Blecha, and Gratz officially declared to a parliamentary committee on foreign affairs that there had been no arms exports to Iran. But in March 1986, the Austrian police were informed by the Japanese embassy that Fasami was in fact an Iranian straw company.

In June 1986, Sinowatz and Gratz resigned following Kurt Waldheim's election as president. The new chancellor, Franz Vranitzky, was advised by his personal secretary of the exports to Iran. In 1987 and 1988, Karl Blecha, minister of the interior in a Socialist-Conservative coalition (SPÖ-ÖVP),[22] contributed to falsifying and destroying important documents pertaining to the cannon exports and in particular to the final telex from Herbert Amry, the late Austrian ambassador in Greece.

In September 1989, the Austrian parliament created a committee of inquiry and the scandal went public. The committee was to determine who knew about the arms shipments, and who had given the approval to continue with them. It was up to the committee not only to determine how much the politicians knew, but also to decide to what extent the politicians were deceived by the company's executives.

The trial against eighteen Noricum executives for violating Austria's neutrality began in Linz on April 4, 1990. The judicial inquiry to determine Blecha's, Gratz's, and Sinowitz's participation had begun on July 7, 1989;[23] and in September, the tribunal in charge of the case began its preliminary investigations into the role played by the Socialist minister of finance, Ferdinand Lacina.

The scandal and its attendant investigation brought to light that all the sales by Noricum to Argentina, Brazil, Bulgaria, Jordan, Poland, and Thailand had been ways to provide Iran and Iraq with weapons.

The whole affair could have been avoided had Gratz examined the certificates of destination.

As it would be with the investigation surrounding Ghassemlou's murder, the "excessive disinformation" surrounding the scandal was attributable to the action of Austrians.[24] The upshot would be political losses of credibility and the undermining of both domestic and international trust in Austrian rule of law and democratic systems.[25]

And a further upshot, in 1989: the Iranian Islamist regime could rightly calculate that "potential diplomatic consequences and complications following the assassination of Ghassemlou would be handled more easily with Austria than with any other country."[26] And at hand living in Austria was a liaison ideal in his naïveté. The choice was made, the invitation extended: Vienna would be the venue.

Notes

1. Staatspolizei: StaPo, "State police," the domestic security and intelligence service of the Ministry of the Interior; a forerunner of the Austrian Federal Agency for State Protection and Counterterrorism, responsible for national security, including the investigation of organized crime and crimes of an extremely serious nature.
2. "Once more": The previous instance had taken place on December 27, 1985, when, at Vienna International Airport, terrorists launched an attack on passengers queuing to fly to Tel Aviv. A simultaneous attack was carried out at Rome International Airport. The PLO, initially blamed for the incidents, denied responsibility; Yasser Arafat denounced the action. Authorship of the strike was later claimed by the organization Abu Nidal, allegedly in reprisal for Israeli bombing of PLO headquarters. The incident was widely reported in the international press that same day; see online archives of *The Miami News*, "Terrorists kill 13 at El Al offices," AP wire, December 27, 1985, and *The Pittsburgh Press*, "Terrorists raid 2 Europe airports," AP wire, December 27, 1985, both at http://news.google.com/newspapers (accessed December 12, 2017).
3. Oswald Kessler, interview with Gabriel Fernández, Vienna, 1990. Further statements from Kessler are from this interview.
4. Sissy Danninger, personal communication to the author, February 16, 2019.
5. Ibid.
6. "X," interview with Gabriel Fernández, Vienna, 1990.
7. Peter Pilz, interview with Gabriel Fernández, Vienna, 1991. Further statements from Pilz are from this interview.
8. Attorney Thomas Prader, interview with Gabriel Fernández, Vienna, 1991.
9. Attorney Manfred Weidinger, interview with Gabriel Fernández, Vienna, 1991.
10. Hasan Ayoubzadeh, personal communication to the author, May 3, 2015.

11. As reported by Gabriel Fernández and Hélène Krulich, both present for the discussion with Oswald Kessler, Vienna, 1990.

12. At the time of Ghassemlou's assassination, Dr. Oswald Kessler headed the EBT, the task force for combatting terrorism (Einsatzgruppe zur Bekämpfung von Terrorismus). "To the best of my knowledge," Austrian journalist Sissy Danninger informed me, Kessler was "withdrawn from this front soon afterwards because he insisted on his conviction that the Iranians had murdered the Kurds to weaken their leadership. From 1990 to 1995 he was the head of the Staatspolizei before being transferred to a department of the Ministry of the Interior dealing with information technology—the support unit for the central population register. In this function he is hidden from public perception. His title *Ministerialrat* [ministerial or departmental counsel] also says his career did not advance in the common way. At his age, with a university degree in law and after such a long period of service he should have reached a higher rank. According to the regulations for officials in Austria he will not even be allowed to speak freely after his retirement, which is to be expected within a few years." Sissy Danninger, personal communication, February 21, 2012.

13. VÖEST (Vereinigte Österreichische Eisen und Stahlwerke, United Austrian Iron and Steelworks), nationalized in 1946 during postwar reconstruction, was merged in the 1970s with Österreichisch-Alpine Montangesellschaft and related companies; the conglomerate entity took the name VOEST-ALPINE AG. Restructured in 1988, it underwent subdivisions in 1993, followed by privatization between 1995 and 2003. See http://www.voestalpine.com/group/en/group/history/.

14. Hélène Krulich-Ghassemlou, *Love Against All Reason: A European Woman Involved in the Kurdish Fight for Freedom in Iran* (Vienna: Lit Verlag), 2018, 240.

15. Ibid.

16. Ferdinand Hennerbichler, "Assassination of Abdul Rahman Ghassemlou (1930–1989): New Assessment," in *Wiener Jahrbuch für Kurdische Studien 2013, Schwerpunkt: Transnationalität und kurdische Diaspora in Österreich, Jahrgang 1/2013* (Vienna: Österreichische Gesellschaft zur Förderung der Kurdologie / Europäisches Zentrum für kurdische Studien, 2013), 319.

17. "Kreisky's aristocratic minister, arms deals and a mysterious death," *Nachrichten*, Octobe 15, 2014. In https://www.nachrichten.at/nachrichten/politik/innenpolitik/Kreiskys-adeliger-Minister-Waffengeschaefte-und-ein-raetselhafter-Tod;art385,1520790

18. Austrian journalist Sissy Danninger, personal communication to the author, February 14, 2019.

19. "Herbert Amry: The mysterious death of the ambassador," *Die Presse*, December 6, 2015, https://diepresse.com/home/zeitgeschichte/4753694/Herbert-Amry_Der-mysterioese-Tod-des-Botschafters.

20. Ibid.

21. Louis Allen, *Political Scandals and Causes Célèbres since 1945: An International Reference Compendium* (Essex, United Kingdom: Longman Group, UK Limited, 1990).

22. SPÖ-ÖVP: Sozialdemokratische Partei Österreichs (Social Democtatic Party of Austria) and Österreichische Volkspartei (Austrian People's Party).

23. Armin Thumher, "Wenn Spatzen Kanonen exportieren" [When sparrows export cannons], *Die Zeit*, April 9, 1993, https://www.zeit.de/1993/15/wenn-spatzen-kanonen-exportieren/komplettansicht; Hans Werner Scheidl, "20 Jahre 'Noricum': Waffen, Spione, Tote

und Millionen" [20 years "Noricum": weapons, spies, the dead, and millions], *Die Presse*, February 4, 2010, https://diepresse.com/home/politik/556091/20-Jahre-Noricum_Waffen-Spione-Tote-und-Millionen (accessed February 24, 2019).

24. Hennerbichler, "Assassination of Abdul Rahman Ghassemlou," 319.
25. Ibid.
26. Ibid., 318.

AN UNFINISHED STORY

❧

> It is never too late for justice.
> —Hélène Krulich-Ghassemlou

One rainy morning in February 1991, at the Café Landtmann, Hélène Krulich stood up in front of a group of convened journalists. She announced that she had initiated a legal proceeding against the national state of Austria for the crime against Ghassemlou.[1] It was Hélène, not the PDKI—a party illegal in Iran, with no official recognition anywhere in the world, and with no lawful standing—who must bring the suit. "Only Hélène," at Sharafkandi's urging, "could collaborate with the investigators and demand justice."[2]

She was surrounded by attorneys, Kurdish leaders, Austrian politicians, and some persons of eminence who had come from other countries. Sadegh Sharafkandi, Ghassemlou's successor in the PDKI, excused his absence in a letter. "Unfortunately, the Austrian authorities in the embassy of Paris have not allowed me to be present in Vienna," he wrote.

After speaking about Ghassemlou's murder, she added, "The same people who supposedly came to negotiate a political solution to the Kurdish question in Iran were, in reality, terrorists sent by the Iranian regime. . . . For us and for all the Kurdish people, the question of why Austrian justice is silent in the face of this crime is still pending."

The media and public opinion in Austria continued to demand that the legal authorities and the government resolve the crime and bring the Iranian suspects to justice. "The Green Party accused the government of 'collapsing in the face of terrorism' and the daily newspaper *Der Standard* charged that 'the authorities did everything to facilitate the departure of witnesses and suspects to avoid light being shed [on the case].' In response to a Foreign Ministry official's protest that Iran had threatened reprisals if its nationals were taken into custody, the daily newspaper *Arbeiter Zeitung* commented: 'This kowtowing to Iran will protect Austria for a while from the mullahs' wrath. But it's an invitation saying, "Austria's pretty; come here to kill." ' "[3]

Characterizations of Iranian "swinishness" in the murders from Austrian officials like former foreign secretary Alois Mock, or condemnation of the "evil, brutal and prepared crime" by parliamentary president Heinz Fischer,[4] seemed empty rhetoric; there was no forward movement in the investigation. For Austrian journalist Sissy Danninger, "Those responsible unfortunately did not show anything even close to civil courage. Their priorities were economic interests in Iran, reasons of state, and thus inevitable cowardice. In this attitude Austria showed lasting consistency."[5]

Consistency in bowing to "reasons of state" was so rampant and so well-known as to be criticized publicly by an experienced law-enforcement officer in an interview with the weekly *Profil*. "Political directives to let the murderer run and escape also existed in the case of Ghassemlou and two other Kurds in Vienna," Vienna's former chief of police Max Edelbacher, now retired, said to journalists. He cited "many other cases" where police were "instructed by politicians not to interfere," and "criticized the long-standing tradition of the right to issue political directives to security forces."[6]

In the face of this stalemate, October 1989, an international conference on the Kurds was held in Paris and a special resolution was passed asking the Austrian authorities to clarify the circumstances leading to the crime.

The investigation, meanwhile, remained at an impasse. Even though the autopsies had been done quickly, the forensic and ballistic reports were not completed until November. It was on November 28, 1989, that the Austrian judiciary finally issued three international warrants of arrest for the three Iranian emissaries. The Iranian embassy, where Buzorguian had found refuge, had been under surveillance by the Viennese police since July. "In November at last the guards were reduced—and thanks to Buzorguian's disappearance immediately after, none of the suspects were available in this country anymore."[7]

The crime continued to remain unpunished. The investigation inevitably was bogged down. The witnesses had disappeared.

ॐ

Buzorguian is believed to have left Austria by air on November 30, 1989.[8] "Mostafawi was sent to Sulaimaniya after 1989, to kill more people, more opposition leaders," said Ezzedin Mustafa Rasul, Fadil Rasul's uncle and

Ghassemlou's longtime friend. About Mostafawi and Buzorguian, he summed up, "We have no more news of their whereabouts today."[9]

Sahrarudi, back in Iran, was "celebrated and then promoted."[10] From his hospital bed in Tehran, where he lay recuperating from his injury, he gave a televised interview in which he "denounced the killers as terrorists and vowed to cooperate with the Vienna police until they were apprehended."[11] It's worth noting that Rafsanjani would say something similar when asked about the murder at a press conference in Tehran, as noted by the journalists who detailed Kurdish history in No Friends but the Mountains,[12] and reiterate such assertions years later in an interview with PBS Frontline in 2007.[13] There is every indication that Rafsanjani, Sahrarudi, and other Iranian officials and terrorists had coordinated scripts for public consumption.

Promoted to the rank of brigadier general in the Revolutionary Guards, Sahrarudi became the head of the Quds Force's Intelligence Directory. In 1996, Sahrarudi, now a "senior member of the intelligence branch of the Islamic Republic Revolutionary Guards Corps," would travel to Talabani's headquarters in Sulaimaniya, Iraq, "to inaugurate a Shi'ite mosque built with Iranian government funds."[14]

The Kurds went on with their lives, fighting in the mountains or in exile.

‡

In autumn of 1992, the Austrian high court ruled that "there had been no deficiencies in the proceedings, because the respective and relevant facts had not been clear to the authorities in time, the judge said."[15] The court dismissed the case without hearing evidence, ruling that Ms. Krulich had failed to make a *prima facie* case and that it lacked jurisdiction to hear a case against the Islamic Republic of Iran. This decision was confirmed by the Oberlandesgericht Wien, the appellate court of Vienna, and the suit was dismissed on September 15, 1992.[16]

Hélène had succeeded at least in forcing the issuing of an international warrant against the three criminals and the Iranian minister of justice. She had taken legal action against the responsible ministers; her attorney Manfred Weidinger had drawn up the indictment, but as nonpolitical in nature.

The Austrian Supreme Court not only rejected the lawsuit but demanded that she pay the costs. When she received the verdict she wrote back to the Court refusing to cover the costs of "justice sided with state terrorism" and added if that they insisted on being paid she was ready to go to debtor's prison.

She never received an answer.[17]

Meanwhile, according to *Time* magazine, Wolfgang Schallenberg, secretary-general of the Austrian Foreign Ministry, denied there was any pressure from Tehran to release the suspects. "The police made their determination according to the information available to them at the time," he said. Such statements were in contradiction to former Iranian president Abolhassan Banisadr's forceful, repeated assertions from his exile in Paris that Tehran had threatened Austria "with the publication of details [regarding Austria's illegal arms sales] should it prosecute the Iranian perpetrator-emissaries in Vienna."[18]

"But," the *Time* report continued, "another top-level Vienna bureaucrat privately pointed out what may be a more compelling reason for Austria's laxity: 'No country wants to prosecute a terrorist case. It's a threat to your government, to your stability, to your penal system. A convicted terrorist faces a life sentence, which means in Austria at least fifteen years. That means for fifteen years you are at risk.'"[19]

❧

Hélène Krulich, dedicated to the end to pushing the investigation forward, went on living in a small apartment in Paris. Susanne Rockenschaub continued practicing medicine in Vienna. She traveled to Iraq with Fadil Rasul's body and had him laid to rest in Kurdish earth while she stood by the grave embracing her husband's mother.

In the Kurdish communities of Vienna, Paris, and other capitals of Western Europe, the memory of Abdul Rahman Ghassemlou and Abdullah Ghaderi-Azar remained an open wound. The tears welled up in the eyes of many when asked about the details of those tragic days of July 1989.

After Mahmoud Ahmadinejad's unsurprising election as president of Iran in the summer of 2005, Austrian parliamentarian Peter Pilz requested that the dossier on Ghassemlou's murder be reopened, and asked for a parliamentary inquiry. The request was denied.

According to Pilz's statements to *Der Standard*,[20] Ahmadinejad[21] and Iranian former president Hashemi Rafsanjani were alleged to have participated in the planning of the assassination of the Kurdish leader. The case was left without any definitive legal resolution for reasons of state and the suspicions were never proved.

❧

Neither have the suspicions been laid to rest, however. Decades after the assassination, allegations and evidence continue to emerge.

In 2005, former Iranian president Abolhassan Banisadr brought forth a confession by a member of the alleged assassination team. The confession was made through an Iranian journalist, who in turn shared this declaration with Banisadr. Banisadr brought this information to the attention of Austrian parliamentarian Peter Pilz that same year.

The confession itself came from one Nasser Taghepour,[22] who reported that he had headed one of the commando teams that was ordered to assassinate Abdul Rahman Ghassemlou and his two companions. After the assassination, feeling himself in danger, he decided to entrust his confession to a friend to ensure that if he did disappear, the truth would be known. Taghepour's friend, in turn, passed this testimony to his brother, the Iranian journalist who revealed it to Banisadr. The journalist escaped Iran, and now lives in exile in Paris.

As reported by Banisadr, this was Taghepour's testimony:

There was a meeting in Tehran in 1988 at the offices of Rafsanjani, president of the Islamic Republic of Iran. The presidential office ordered the Sepah-i Quds, the branch of the Revolutionary Guards in charge of missions outside of Iran, to prepare teams to eliminate Ghassemlou.

"We were two teams," Taghepour told his friend, as reported by the friend's journalist brother. The person in charge of the mission was Haj Ghafour Darjazi, a member of the Sepah-i Quds. This was the real name of the "bodyguard" known as Buzorguian: "He organized this terror mission."

The operation would be executed in two phases, Taghepour told his friend. During the first phase, Iran would propose a meeting to Ghassemlou to negotiate a solution. Once he agreed to this process and took the bait, the second phase would begin. "A few months later, he accepted, so we decided to negotiate in Vienna."

The first team included Nasser Taghepour and another member of the Sepah-i Quds known as Asgari. The first negotiations took place December 28 and 30, 1988; a further round of negotiations would be slated for July 1989.

The Iranian embassy in Vienna was responsible for acquiring the weapons for the operation. Haj Ghafour was in charge of choosing the meeting site. Taghepour and Asgari traveled to Vienna in July, a week before the murder, via the Arab Emirates, with European passports.

Taghepour and his teammate Asgari visited the chosen location to get to know the layout and the logistics. The Iranian emissaries negotiating with

Ghassemlou were charged with prolonging the talks as much as possible to give the assassins time to get into position.

On July 13, 1989, Taghepour told his friend, the team entered the building. At the apartment, Mostafawi opened the door to the assassins. Ghassemlou had no time to react; according to Taghepour, neither did his two companion Kurds.

The room was not well lit. Sahrarudi, a commander of the Sepah-i Quds present at the negotiations, was wounded.

Taghepour and Asgari left the premises. Sahrarudi was taken to the hospital. Haj Ghafour was detained, but twenty-four hours later he was freed, thanks to the intervention of the Iranian embassy.

Taghepour repeated that there were two assassination teams: if the first team had not succeeded, the second one would have moved into action. The second team, Taghepour said, was headed by Mahmoud Ahmadinejad; he was also responsible for picking up the weapons from the Iranian embassy and passing them to Taghepour and Asgari.

The two men who served on the first team, Taghepour and Asgari, were later murdered. Asgari's assassination took place at the military facility where he worked; he was shot by the military officer in charge.

Taghepour was sent on a mission. He had the intuition that his life was in danger. Before he left, he told his friend: "If I don't come back from this mission, it means I have been eliminated. This mission they have ordered me to do is not a mission but a trip to death. If I do not come back, please publish what I am telling you."[23]

He never returned.

The journalist, brother of the friend to whom Taghepour had entrusted his confession, was in hiding in France when he agreed to a phone interview with a writer from the Austrian magazine Profil. About Taghepour, the journalist—known as "Witness D"—told Profil's interviewer, "The Pasdaran also participated in 'development projects': out of a kind of populism. In light of his qualifications, he [Taghepour] was extremely surprised that he would be deployed for such a development project. And he was clearly afraid. A short while later, what he was afraid of in fact occurred. He was found drowned in the south of Iran—after having gone diving in the Karun River, it was said."[24]

Peter Pilz met with the Iranian journalist at Banisadr's home. On the strength of the testimony he heard, Pilz requested a parliamentary inquiry, and asked that the case be reopened.

According to Banisadr, this is what ensued:

"The Austrian Ministry of the Interior got in contact with me to ask me if the journalist would testify officially. I spoke with him and he agreed. The ministry staff were supposed to come, and did not.

"They called again and said there was a problem with the French authorities; they said they would come the next week to hear the journalist.

"They did not come. I asked the French, because the Austrians were saying that it was the French who were not authorizing them to come. The French told me it was Austria that did not want to come and hear the journalist.

"Recently an Austrian journalist interviewed me. Given the economic relations of Austria with Iran, Vienna does not want the case to be reopened. In a certain way, Austria is responsible, because the murder happened there—and they, the Austrian authorities, released the witnesses."[25]

&

Determined to bring this matter to light and to some form of justice, Peter Pilz redoubled his efforts. In a press conference June 18, 2009, Pilz, now Green Party security spokesperson, once again accused Ahmadinejad of participation in the assassination, with what he considered further corroborating evidence that had recently emerged. He said a German weapons dealer serving a prison sentence in Trieste—a second witness known only as "S"—had made a deposition to Italian prosecutor Francesco Mandoi "and three Austrian officials in the Trieste prison in April 2006" that he had "cooperated with the Iranian secret service (presumably, the VEVAK) from 1989 to 1993" in trafficking illegal arms deliveries.[26]

"Witness S" attested that an Austrian business partner had introduced him to a "Mr. Borhan," an Iranian secret-service agent, who requested his help supplying weapons "to the Bosnians, the brothers of the Iranian Muslims." The meeting was concluded to their mutual satisfaction with an agreement to deliver the necessary armaments. Then, almost as if an afterthought, "Borhan" had added another request:

"As we were leaving," S reported, "he asked if I would be prepared to supply a friend of his, who likewise was a member of the secret services, with 5–10 pieces of light weaponry on short notice.

"I assured him that this was no problem."[27]

A second meeting was arranged for S with two "influential and important" colleagues of Borhan at the Hotel Hilton in Vienna. "On this occasion,"

S said, "I assured him that I was able to supply the light weapons about which they had asked within 8 days of the order."

A third meeting, this time to deliver the weapons, took place at the Iranian embassy at the beginning of July 1989 "with three Iranians," S said: "Borhan, a certain 'Mohamed' [sic: Mahmoud Ahmadinejad] who later became president [of Iran], and a certain Sahidi." S stated that Sahidi and "Mohamed" were "particularly interested, even thrilled or enthralled by the weapons." S also claimed to have a photocopy of Sahidi's diplomatic passport.[28]

Pilz found the arms-trafficker's testimony creditable and alerted the press to the allegations he would raise. About Ahmadinejad, "Pilz said, 'I have no doubt he was involved,'" the *Austrian Times* reported, "adding that Ahmadinejad may have pulled the trigger on one of the guns used to kill the men. Pilz claimed there had been two Iranian teams involved in the assassinations—a negotiations team and an execution team."[29]

According to the information Pilz had received through Abolhassan Banisadr, Pilz revealed further that "Ahmadinejad had been responsible for gathering and preparing the weapons used and had been a member of the commando. . . . Pilz said he had passed on documents about the case, translated into German, to the Ministry of the Interior and the state prosecutor's office."[30]

Evidence continues to come forward. Even more recently, the involvement of the Iranian embassy in protecting and "disappearing" the suspected members of the assassination team has received collateral confirmation. A former Iranian diplomat posted to Geneva and New York, Darwish Ranjbar, stated in an interview with VOA in 2013 that one of Ghassemlou's killers was in fact concealed for some time in the embassy.

While on a mission connected with the International Atomic Energy Agency in September 1989, Ranjbar said, he had spent two weeks in Vienna. There he would go to the Iranian embassy for lunch. On the second day there, he said, he noticed the cook taking food downstairs, and asked who the food was for. The cook, apparently surprised that the diplomat was not informed, told him it was for one of Ghassemlou's killers who was sheltered in the embassy.[31]

There the matter rests, uneasily. After flurries in the press, there has been no further government or investigative action and no official pronouncement. Austrian journalist Sissy Danninger, who has kept concern alive for the case, has attested to the official silence on the matter. "Nothing has ever happened as far as I know," she responded when I recently contacted her. "The story is sleeping (or rather has completely disappeared quite soon after some media coverage long ago) in the Orcus"—the underworld—"of history."[32] And from the Austrian government has come no word at all.

࿔

In the Avenue Circulaire, in the thirty-fourth division of the Père Lachaise cemetery in Paris, there is a simple tomb with an inscription that reads:

Dr. Abdul Rahman
Ghassemlou
Dirigeant Kurde
Né le 22 Décembre 1930
à Urmia (Kurdistan d'Iran)
Assassiné le 13 Juillet 1989
à Vienne (Autriche)
Mort pour la liberté
du peuple Kurde
Mort pour le Kurdistan

Next to it is another tombstone, similar in form and color, for Abdullah Ghaderi-Azar, murdered in Vienna on the same day. For Ghassemlou, the tombstone reads, "Died for the freedom of the Kurdish people. Died for Kurdistan."

Ghassemlou's resting place today remains a site of pilgrimage and remembrance for many, the simple stone often garlanded with flowers. "I go every year to the cemetery," says Ghassemlou's early assistant at Mahabad, Aziz Mameli. "I have only respect for him; he's a martyr."[33]

With Ghassemlou's death, the national Iranian Kurdish movement had been decapitated once more through the preferred method of the Islamic Republic: the physical elimination of its leadership.

࿔

The assassinations would continue. According to a report published in May 2008 by IHRDC, the Iran Human Rights Documentation Center: "Since 1979, high-level officials within the Islamic Republic of Iran, particularly those within the Revolutionary Guards and the Ministry of Intelligence, have been linked to at least 162 extrajudicial killings of the regime's political opponents around the globe. These attacks have been carried out on the authority of the Supreme Leader of the Islamic Republic and have been planned and coordinated at the highest levels of the clerical establishment. The Iranian government has made extensive use of its own intelligence facilities as well as terrorist proxies, such as the Lebanese Hezbollah organization, to mount attacks on foreign soil in contravention of national and international law."[34]

The murder of political leaders of opposition to the Iranian revolution had begun soon after its triumph.[35] On December 7, 1979, Prince Shahriar Mustafa Shafigh was the first to fall; the Shah's nephew, he was murdered in Paris.

The French capital was a favorite for the scenario of hired assassins. On February 7, 1984, General Gholam Ali Oveissi, former military governor of Tehran, and his brother Gholam Hosseini Oveissi were murdered in Paris. The culprits had a name: they were the pro-Khomeini group Islamic Jihad and the Iranian Revolutionary Organization for Liberation and Reform.

In August and December 1985, several Iranian former officers close to Bakhtiar, among them Behruz Chaverdi, were assassinated in Istanbul. On October 2, 1987, Mohammad Ali Tavakoli-Nabavi and his youngest son, Nuredin, were found, their skulls riddled with bullets, in their London home. Authorship of this assassination was claimed by the Revolutionary Guards of the Islamic Republic, the pasdaran.

On May 19, 1987, Hamid Reza Chitgar, researcher for the Pasteur Institute in Strasbourg, an Iranian extreme-leftist activist, disappeared; on July 12, he was found murdered in Vienna.

In 1989, in addition to Ghassemlou's, the assassinations that most stood out were those of Gholam Qeshavar and Sadiq Tamangar, leaders of Komala, the first in Cyprus and the second in Iraq. There was also the death of Efat Ghazi, the daughter of Qazi Mohammad, in Sweden, when she opened a package bomb addressed to her husband.

On April 24, 1990, agents of the Islamic Republic hunted down Kazam Rajavi, brother of Mujahedin-e Khalq leader Massoud Rajavi, in Switzerland. In the German-speaking countries, television stations broadcast a long report naming former Iranian president Rafsanjani as the one who had inspired the crime.

On October 23 of that same year, Cyrus Elahi, a leader in the pro-monarchy organization Flag of Iranian Liberty, was shot in the head in Paris.

On April 18, 1991, Abdul Rahman Boroumand, industrialist and leader of the National Resistance Movement founded by Bakhtiar, was stabbed in Paris.

Shapour Bakhtiar had escaped alive on July 18, 1980, from an attack in which a policeman and a neighbor died. The head of the commando, the

Lebanese intellectual Anis Naccache, was arrested and condemned to life imprisonment. In 1990, to facilitate relations between France and Iran, French president François Mitterrand pardoned him. One year later, on August 1991, Bakhtiar was stabbed to death, together with his secretary, in his home in the outskirts of Paris.

Violence incited by Imam Khomeini was visited on two men linked with the writer Salman Rushdie: on July 3, 1991, Ettore Capriolo, Italian translator of *The Satanic Verses*, was attacked by a man who called himself a representative of the Iranian embassy; ten days later, on July 13, 1991, Mitoshi Igarashi, the Japanese translator, was stabbed in Tokyo.

On September 17, 1992, Sadegh Sharafkandi, secretary-general of the PDKI after Ghassemlou's assassination, was shot to death in Berlin together with Fatah Abdulli, representative of the PDKI in Europe; murdered with them were Homayoum Ardalan, representative of the PDKI in Germany, and Nouri Dehkordi, an Iranian political activist.[36]

According to Karim Lahidji,[37] president of the League of Defense of Human Rights in Iran, many Iranian political dissidents were assassinated in Vienna, Paris, Switzerland, Cyprus, and Turkey. In the majority of these political murders—the trial for Sharafkandi's assassins was an exception—those that ordered them had total immunity in Iran, and those that executed them often had diplomatic passports. "I was present," explained Lahidji, "in the trial for the murder of Bakhtiar and his assistant in Paris. The criminals were allowed to leave the country where they committed the murder and returned to their bosses.

"This happened not only in Austria," he continued. "In France the alleged murderers were returned to Iran. France did not respond to Switzerland's demand for extradition despite the fact that there exists an agreement between the two states. Switzerland went to the UN Security Council, to no avail. This was during Baladur's government, with Charles Pasqua as minister of the interior, and they were already talking about 'reasons of state.'

"And what are reasons of state? Political and economic interests. Business. This is the politics of the majority of the states of the European Union. This primacy of political and economic interests, under a state of law in a Western democracy, has encouraged the autocrats, despots, tyrants in committing the most atrocious crimes without a minimum sanction or a serious investigation."[38]

A more recent political assassination of an Iranian dissident, outside the territory of Iran and Iraq, that can be linked directly to the Islamic Republic was that of Dr. Reza Mazlouman, deputy leader of the Flag of Freedom organization, who was murdered, also in Paris, in May 1996.

The assassination of the four Kurds—Sharafkandi, Abdulli, Ardalan, and Dehkordi—in 1992 led to a trial that lasted almost four years and ended in the conviction of four assassins, in 1997: one Iranian and three Lebanese who had been members of Hezbollah. The court also issued an international arrest warrant for the Iranian intelligence minister Hojatoleslam Ali Fallahian,[39] accused of having ordered the assassination. The verdict also implicated Iran's Supreme Leader Ali Khamenei and former president Hashemi Rafsanjani.[40]

The verdict on the Iranian leadership resulted in the immediate withdrawal of nearly every European Union ambassador from Tehran for several weeks. Germany went further by imposing trade restrictions on Iran. Ultimately these sanctions may have had beneficial outcomes. In the view of Iranian-American scholar Ray Takeyh, "Given the value of European commercial trade and diplomatic ties, Iran abandoned the practice of targeting exiles abroad, and closed one of the darker chapters in its terrorism portfolio."[41] One Kurdish scholar adds dissenting nuance: "My interpretation is different: essentially, following Sharafkandi, no significant Kurdish or Iranian leader remained to assassinate. Rajavi is one, but no one knows where he is and he has never been in Europe. Also, Iran stopped assassinating PDKI leaders after the decision to halt the armed struggle. The day PDKI resumes armed struggle, which might happen again, Iran will start assassinating PDKI members and, if possible, PDKI leaders abroad."[42]

❧

While the Iranian regime may appear to have "closed one chapter" of its "terrorism portfolio" in the late 1990s, its terrorist activity and connections were to continue into the twenty-first century—and in fact to expand beyond the initial aim of eliminating domestic opposition leaders at home and in exile. Five years after Ghassemlou's assassination, in events half a world away, on July 18, 1994, terrorists would bomb a Jewish community center in Buenos Aires, the Argentina Israelite Mutual Association (AMIA), leaving eighty-five people killed and hundreds more wounded. Argentine federal prosecutor Alberto Nisman would accuse Iran of organizing the attack and Hezbollah of carrying it out.[43]

Only much later, in November 2007, would six individuals accused of involvement be included in Interpol's "Red Notice" list—among them, high-ranking members of the Iranian regime.[44]

In 2013, prosecutor Nisman would further accuse Iran of pervasive ongoing infiltrations since the 1980s throughout South America—not only in Argentina, but in Brazil, Paraguay, Uruguay, Chile, Colombia, Guyana, Trinidad and Tobago, and Surinam—to launch terrorist attacks in the region. New evidence would emerge to link Iranian government involvement with the 1994 AMIA terrorist bombing, and further reports would point out two of the suspects—Mohsen Rezai and Ali Akbar Velayati—as candidates in Iran's presidential elections.[45] That spring, in May, former Iranian diplomat Darwish Ranjbar would declare in an interview with Voice of America that it was during Velayati's 1981–1997 term as Iran's foreign minister that 170 Iranian dissidents were assassinated abroad, and that Velayati himself was involved.[46]

Published that same year, the U.S. Country Report on Terrorism 2012, designating Iran as a State Sponsor of Terrorism since 1984, would reveal that the Islamic Republic had stepped up its terrorist-related activity. Two years later, the follow-up U.S. Country Report on Terrorism 2014 would detail further expansion.[47]

In fact Iran's active and shady presence in Latin America was not paranoia on Nisman's part. It was real. It came about through the close ties that developed between Iran's president Mahmoud Ahmadinejad and Venezuela's president Hugo Chávez. Even beyond developing bilateral commercial and military relations, they became close political allies who formed an "axis of unity" against U.S. "imperialism."[48] Chávez opened the door for Iran to establish friendly relations and alliances with other regional leaders in Brazil, Bolivia, Ecuador, and Argentina.

But Iran's presence in Latin America was not only for trade and business. American intelligence reported that agents from Iran's Revolutionary Guards and Hezbollah were granted safe haven in Venezuela and allowed to use the country "as a base for a drug-trafficking and money-laundering network." Further, Ahmadinejad, according to "a former senior official in Chávez's government" who was allegedly present at a meeting between Ahmadinejad and Chávez, asked the Venezuelan leader to intercede with the Argentine president for "access to Argentine nuclear technology."[49]

Argentine federal prosecutor Alberto Nisman would be shot to death on January 18, 2015, the day prior to his planned testimony before Argentina's congress on allegations that Argentine president Cristina Fernandez Kirchner, foreign minister Hector Timmerman, and others had worked with Iran to cover up the Islamic Republic's role in the 1994 terrorist attack on AMIA.

As reported in *Time* magazine, Nisman's "mysterious death" would be "under investigation and now considered a murder."[50]

❧

Abdul Rahman Ghassemlou knew the history of such assassinations very well—and would hardly have been surprised by the string of executions that would follow his own—and, although there has been speculation on whether some third party had promised him security, no one can understand why he moved toward his death in such a naïve way.

His attitude reminds one of Julius Caesar's, who went to the senate on that fateful day even though his wife begged him not to because she had dreamed of his death. Neither did Caesar listen to the admonitions of the soothsayer, who warned him of danger during the ides of March.

Ghassemlou did have a foreboding of his end. For years he had thought of writing his autobiography. However, the pressure of work and the internal problems of the party never allowed him to do it. There was only one attempt at crystallizing his life in a book: the biographical interview conducted by American journalist Jonathan Randal, following many hours of conversation with him.

A year before he died, Ghassemlou told me that if he had ever written his autobiography, it would have begun like this: "On many occasions, Kurdish leaders in Iran have been assassinated due to treason by Persian authorities. It happened with Jafar Agha and later with Simko, one of our most important contemporary leaders. While Simko's blood ran through the streets, in a house nearby a boy was being born. That boy would be me."

"Did it really happen like this?" I asked in amazement.

"No," he answered. "Simko was murdered in June 1930, the same year I was born, but not on the same day. Do you realize how strong that beginning is? One Kurdish leader dies and at the same time another is being born."

Notes

1. Hélène Krulich's press conference was attended by journalist Gabriel Fernández, from whose report the statements in this chapter are taken. In 1992, the Austrian high court would reject Krulich's lawsuit. Hélène Krulich-Ghassemlou, *Love Against All Reason: A European Woman Involved in the Kurdish Fight for Freedom in Iran* (Vienna: Lit Verlag, 2017), 242.

2. Ibid., 241.

3. Jonathan Randal, "The Hostage Drama; Austria Said to 'Kowtow' to Iran in Murder Case; Reprisal Feared in Kurdish Leader's Death," *Washington Post*, August 2, 1989.

4. Ferdinand Hennerbichler, "Assassination of Abdul Rahman Ghassemlou (1930–1989): New Assessment," in *Wiener Jahrbuch für Kurdische Studien 2013, Schwerpunkt: Transnationalität und kurdische Diaspora in Österreich, Jahrgang 1/2013* (Vienna: Österreichische Gesellschaft zur Förderung der Kurdologie / Europäisches Zentrum für kurdische Studien, 2013), 316.

5. Sissy Danninger, "Dr. Ghassemlou, Twenty Years after the Assassination in Vienna," presentation at international symposium "Hommage à Abdul Rahman Ghassemlou," Paris, July 17, 2009.

6. Hennerbichler, "Assassination of Abdul Rahman Ghassemlou," 316.

7. Ibid.

8. IHRDC, *No Safe Haven*, 27.

9. Ezzedin Mustafa Rasul, interview with the author, Koya Sanjak, Iraqi Kurdistan, July 2009.

10. Ibid.

11. Nader Entessar, *Kurdish Politics in the Middle East* (London: Lexington Books, 2010, 47, n87.

12. John Bulloch and Harvey Morris, *No Friends but the Mountains: The Tragic History of the Kurds* (New York: Oxford University Press, 1992), 194: "At a press conference in Tehran, later that year, we asked Rafsanjani what information he could give towards identifying the killers. All the resources of the state, he told us, had been committed to resolving the case." The observation about Rafsanjani, and the links to the press conference in Tehran and a further interview on PBS, are provided by a Kurdish scholar who for security reasons asks not to be named.

13. "Showdown with Iran: Interview Mohammad Jafari," PBS *Frontline*, Aug. 2, 2007, http://www.pbs.org/wgbh/pages/frontline/showdown/interviews/jafari.html.

14. Kenneth R. Timmerman, "A Wasted Opportunity to Help Iranian Kurds," *Washington Times*, July 31, 1996. Sahrarudi's career has continued on an ascending trajectory as "a key element in the regime's machinery to export terrorism and fundamentalism. . . . Especially after the occupation of Iraq by American forces—he organized and led assassination squads and bombings in Iraq, stoking sectarian conflict." He fought with the Badr Brigade of the Supreme Council of the Islamic Revolution in Iraq (SCIRI) in Iraq.

In 2007, Sahrarudi became commander of Iran's Revolutionary Guards (IRGC); Vahid Sepheri, "Iran: New Commander Takes Over Revolutionary Guards," Radio Free Europe/Radio Liberty, September 4, 2007, http://www.rferl.org/content/article/1078520.html. As head of the IRGC and member of the Supreme National Security Council, he was in charge of issues in Iraq. He continued "terrorist efforts in Iraq" as advisor and chief of staff to Majlis speaker IRGC Brigadier General Ali Larijani.

Despite an active arrest warrant in force since 1989, Sahrarudi as recently as October 2013 accompanied Ali Larijani, chairman of the Parliament of Iran, to a meeting of the Inter-Parliamentary Union in Geneva, traveling under the name of Mohammed Ali Jafari; see ICANA, Iran Consultative Assembly News Agency, http://www.icana.ir/Fa/NewsReportPicture/238607.

On December 27, 2014, Iran sent a delegation to Erbil, the administrative capital of the Kurdistan Regional Government in Iraq, which included Sahrarudi. For many this was seen as a warning "to remind the Kurds that the tide of friendship could turn" as Iranian-backed Shi'ite militias supported the Kurds and Iraqis against ISIS. Iranian Kurds were incensed that Barzani and members of his administration in Iraq's Kurdistan Regional Government were seen shaking hands with Ghassemlou's alleged murderer. For this visit to Erbil in 2014, see Jassem Al Salami, "Iran Sent an Assassin to Intimidate the Kurds," posted on War Is Boring, https://medium.com/war-is-boring/iran-sent-an-assassin-to-intimidate-the-kurds-b9910697e2ef).

As late as 2013, the report emerged of a very interesting incident in 2007 during which Sahrarudi, lending support to Iranian-backed militia activity in Iraq as the head of the IRGC, had become a target of pursuit by American forces, but was never captured; Dexter Filkins, "Shadow Commander," *The New Yorker*, September 30, 2013. "[American commanding general] McChrystal received reports that General Mohammed Ali Jafari [Sahrarudi], the head of Iran's Revolutionary Guard, might be in a convoy heading toward the Iraqi border. . . .

"McChrystal's men tracked the convoy as it drove a hundred miles into Iraq, to the Kurdish city of Erbil, and stopped at a nondescript building, which had a small sign that read 'Consulate.' No one knew that such a consulate existed, but the fact that it did meant that the men inside were operating under diplomatic cover. The Americans moved in anyway, and took five Iranians into custody. All were carrying diplomatic passports, and all, according to McChrystal, were Quds Force members. Neither [Qassem] Suleimani nor Jafari [Sahrarudi] was there; they had evidently broken off from the convoy at the last minute and taken refuge in a safe house controlled by the Kurdish leader Masoud Barzani." Ibid.; see http://www.newyorker.com/magazine/2013/09/30/the-shadow-commander.

15. IHRDC, *No Safe Haven*, 29.
16. Ibid.
17. Hélène Krulich-Ghassemlou, *Love Against All Reason*, 241–42.
18. Hennerbichler, "Assassination of Abdul Rahman Ghassemlou," 391.
19. Thomas Sancton, Nomi Morris, Elaine Shannon, and Kenneth R. Timmerman, "The Tehran Connection," *Time* magazine, March 21, 1994, http://www.time.com/time/magazine/article/0,9171,980361,00.html#ixzz2QBiQeiPu (accessed April 2, 2013).
20. William J. Kole, "Ahmadinejad suspected of involvement in 1989 attack in Vienna," Associated Press, July 2, 2005; see also "Austria Seeks to Interview Journalist over Ahmadinejad Murder Accusations," Agence France Presse, July 5, 2005.
21. In 1980, Ahmadinejad was named district governor in Maku, West Azerbaijan. One of his tasks was to squelch the Kurdish rebellion and drive the peshmerga out of the district. After 1986 he was reported to be an officer of the Revolutionary Guards at the Ramazan headquarters in Kermanshah in Iranian Kurdistan. He joined the Revolutionary Guard's Quds Force, the elite group trained to carry out commando-style attacks outside of Iran.
22. As reported by an article in the Austrian weekly *Profil* based upon testimony given by an Iranian exile designated as "Witness D": Sibylle Hamann and Martin Staudinger, "Iran: Der Mörder und der Präsident," [Iran: The assassin and the president], *Profil*, September 7, 2005, http://www.profil.at/home/iran-der-moerder-praesident-116605 (accessed December 30, 2015).

23. Abolhassan Banisadr, interview with the author, Versailles, July 15, 2009. The rest of the narrative is as reported by John Rosenthal, "Accomplice to an Assassination?," blog article on the conservative website FrumForum, July 5, 2009, http://www.frumforum.com/accomplice-to-an-assassination/ (accessed August 20, 2015; the link is no longer available).

24. Ibid., as interviewed by Georg Hoffmann-Ostenhof, "Supplement: An Interview with 'witness D." The interview was cited in full on Rosenthal's 2009 blog; if it was issued in print in *Profil*, the issue in which it may have appeared has not been located.

25. Abolhassan Banisadr, interview with the author, Versailles, July 15, 2009.

26. Rosenthal, "Accomplice to an Assassination?," FrumForum, July 5, 2009; see also "Ahmadinejad a suspect?" *Wiener Zeitung*, June 18, 2009, in https://www.wienerzeitung.at/weltpolitik/234901_Ahmadinejad-tatverdaechtig.html (accessed March 2, 2019). If these years saw Iran supplying weapons to Bosnians, where the civil war began in 1992, it suggests Iran was supplying arms to Bosnian Islamists even before the outbreak of civil war; this pointed out by a Kurdish scholar who for security reasons asks not to be named. On Iran's relations with Bosnian Islamists, see "Iran in the Balkans: A History and a Forecast," *World Affairs*, January/February 2013, http://www.worldaffairsjournal.org/article/iran-balkans-history-and-forecast.

27. Rosenthal, "Accomplice to an Assassination?"

28. The story of "witness S" is as reported by John Rosenthal in his blog piece "Accomplice to an Assassination?," July 5, 2009, on the FrumForum site.

29. "Dr. Ghassemlou: Twenty years of silence is enough," *EKurd Daily*, July 11, 2009, https://ekurd.net/mismas/articles/misc2009/7/irankurdistan487.htm (accessed August 10, 2009).

30. As reported in the *Austrian Times*, June 18, 2009. See also IHRDC, *No Safe Haven*.

    In a recent memoir published twenty years after the assassination, Reza Kahlili, a former Iranian Revolutionary Guard who later became a CIA agent, also names the Iranian regime as responsible for Ghassemlou's murder. In a communication to his handler in Iran, the agent had written: "Through Akbar, a Guard in our unit, I learned that the Foreign Ministry has assigned members of the Revolutionary Guard's Special Forces to Iranian Consulates and Embassies. These are not political assignments; it is a diplomatic cover for their operations. Their task is to take control of all intelligence activities overseas, including assassinations, abductions, and the transfer of arms and explosives." Reza Kahlili, *A Time to Betray: The Astonishing Double Life of a CIA Agent inside the Revolutionary Guards of Iran* (New York: Threshold Editions, 2010), 164. Reza Kahlili (a pseudonym) worked undercover as a CIA agent for several years in the 1980s and 1990s; see ""A Time to Betray" by Reza Kahlili, http://atimetobetray.com/about/, https://www.youtube.com/user/ATimeToBetray (accessed October 23, 2014). "Did you know that our government [Iran] had our agents contact Ghassemlou, the Kurdistan Democratic Party leader, in Vienna for a meeting to offer peace? Then our agents killed him and his aides." Kahlili, *A Time to Betray*, 300–01. Sensational though Kahlili's dramatic confession and suspenseful memoir may be, his statements and the details he provides have the ring of truth.

31. Darwish Ranjbar, interview with VOA, May 31, 2013, posted at http://www.youtube.com/watch?v=AfdiPSK5mL8 (accessed September 20, 2014); translation Salah Piroty.

32. Sissy Danninger, personal communication to the author, December 29, 2015.

33. Aziz Mameli, interview with the author, Paris, July 21, 2015.

34. IRHDC, *No Safe Haven*, 3. Agents of the Islamic Republic have assassinated opposition figures in the Philippines, Indonesia, Japan, India, and Pakistan in Asia; in Dubai, Iraq, and Turkey in the Middle East; in Cyprus, France, Italy, Switzerland, Germany, Austria, Norway, Sweden, and Great Britain in Western Europe; and across the Atlantic in the United States. For a list of those assassinated outside of Iran, see Appendix 1 of the report: IRHDC, *No Safe Haven*, Chronological list of those killed during the Islamic Republic of Iran's global assassination campaign, 67–76.

    Former undercover CIA agent Reza Kahlili independently noted that "Europeans [especially France, England, and Germany] raised no objection to Iranian agents murdering the opposition . . . inside their countries." Kahlili, *A Time to Betray*, 225, 227.

35. "According to a Beirut-based source well connected with Iran, and cited by Robert Fisk in *The Independent*, there was a standing order, dating back to the mid-1980s, by the Islamic Revolutionary Guards Corps' intelligence committee 'to neutralize all armed opposition to the regime wherever it was.'" Dilip Hiro, *The Iranian Labyrinth* (New York: Nation Books, 2005), 265.

36. As all revolutions have done, the Iranian disposed of many people, within the country as well as overseas. Political assassination has been the norm of the regime since 1980. Apart from Bakhtiar, many other figures have fallen to the bullets of assassins sent by the Iranian government. "They have murdered several colonels, Massoud Rajavi's brother, and someone from Komala," said former Iranian president Banisadr. "After my trip to the United States [in 1991], the Iranians decided to kill me. In regard to Ghassemlou, in Iran we say that if you cut the head off the Kurdish movement, it falls. It's a tribal organization. Essentially the murders are done by the inside and to eliminate all opposition, even overseas." Abolhassan Banisadr, interview with the author, Versailles, 1991.

    Iran, Kawe Bahrami told a Kurdish scholar, is wrong to believe that these assassinations as such have weakened the PDKI. In his view, it was the decision to leave the Qandil mountains and later to halt armed struggle that dealt the major blow to the party. Leaving Qandil and resettling in camps in Iraqi Kurdistan, where Iran could assassinate hundreds of PDKI cadres, was a strategic mistake. Iran also attacked the bases in Koya in 1996. It was only following the appearance of US airpower that Iran withdrew its forces. Personal communication from the Kurdish scholar, who for personal safety asks not to be named.

    For further discussion of other political assassinations in and by Iran, see IHRDC's report published 2008, *No Safe Haven*; Lord Eric Avebury, *Iran: State of Terror* (London: Parliamentary Human Rights Group, 1996); and *Iran: Fatal Writ, An Account of Murders and Cover-ups* (London: British Committee of Iran Freedom, 2000).

37. Karim Lahidji, presentation given at international symposium "Hommage à Abdul Rahman Ghassemlou," Paris, July 17, 2009.

38. Ibid.

39. IHRDC reported: "Ali Fallahian, head of Iran's Ministry of Intelligence under the government of Hashemi Rafsanjani, boasted in a televised interview in August 1992 that his organization had been able to 'strike a blow' at many of the opposition groups outside Iran's borders."

    In the interview, broadcast by Iranian television (IRIB) on August 30, 1992, Fallahian was "remarkably frank": "Overall, no opposition groups can be found in this nation at present. They have been forced to flee. . . . We are currently following them and are constantly watching them outside of this nation. We have infiltrated their central organizations and are informed of their activities. We have been able, thanks to God, to keep their activities under our constant control. . . .

"As you know, one of these active opposition groups is the Kurdish Democratic Party [of Iran], which through two organs, the main group and the auxiliary department, operates in Kurdistan. . . . We have been able to strike decisive blows at their cadres."

"At present," noted IHRDC in 2008, Ali Fallahian "is the subject of no less than three international arrest warrants. Since November 2007 he has been the subject of an Interpol Red Notice, making him one of the world's highest-profile fugitives from justice. Nonetheless, Fallahian currently serves on the Council of Experts responsible for selecting Iran's Supreme Leader and remains an influential figure in Iranian politics as a security advisor to Ayatollah Khamenei, Ayatollah Khomeini's successor as Supreme Leader.

"Fallahian was personally congratulated by Ayatollah Seyyid Ali Khamenei for his 'great achievements in combating and uprooting the enemies of Islam, inside and outside the country.'" IRHDC, *No Safe Haven*, 11.

40. Roya Hakakian, "The End of the Dispensable Iranian," *New York Times*, April 10, 2007.

41. Ray Takeyh, *Hidden Iran: Paradox and Power in the Islamic Republic* (New York: Times Books, 2006), 225.

42. Personal communication to the author by a Kurdish scholar who for securing reasons asks not to be named, May 20, 2017. Despite the apparent hiatus in assassinations outside of Iran, recent reports suggest they have resumed, with a recent assassination in the Netherlands of Iranian Kurds. See "Iranian opposition leader confirmed shot dead in The Hague," Dutch News.nl, November 9, 2017, https://www.dutchnews.nl/news/archives/2017/11/iranian-opposition-leader-confirmed-shot-dead-in-the-hague/; Rahim Hamid, "Quds Force Assassinates Iranian Dissident in Europe," News Analysis, Clarion Project, November 14, 2017, https://clarionproject.org/quds-force-assassinates-iranian-dissident-europe/; and Fred Stratton, Chief Security Officer, "Iran: The Prime Suspect in a Dissident's Death," Stratfor WorldView, November 17, 2017, https://worldview.stratfor.com/article/iran-prime-suspect-dissidents-death (all accessed December 7, 2017).

43. "The attack followed a nearly identical one two years earlier, in which a truck bomb exploded outside the Israeli Embassy in Buenos Aires, killing twenty-nine people and wounding two hundred and forty-two. A wing of Hezbollah claimed responsibility, and many American officials believed that the Iranian regime had approved and helped carry out the attack. In the AMIA bombing, too, they suspected that Iran and Hezbollah, which often act together, were the main culprits." Dexter Filkins, "Death of a Prosecutor," *The New Yorker*, July 20, 2015, http://www.newyorker.com/magazine/2015/07/20/death-of-a-prosecutor (accessed December 19, 2015).

Filkins goes on to say, "Still, many American officials believe that Iran was involved in the bombing. Hezbollah would never carry out such an operation without Iran's approval, they said. 'The assumption was that the Iranians were involved, because the attack was carried out by a unit that they created,' Robert Baer, a former American intelligence official who tracked links between Hezbollah and Iran, said. 'Mugniyah never did anything without the green light of the Supreme Leader.'" Ibid. On Khamenei's relation with this terrorist, see "Ayatollah Sayyed Ali Khamenei: Mughniyeh's blood would double resistance," http://sayyidali.com/viewpoints/ayatollah-sayyed-ali-khamenei-mughniyehs-blood-would-double-resistance.html (accessed March 14, 2016).

44. "INTERPOL Executive Committee takes decision on AMIA Red Notice dispute," INTERPOL, March 15, 2007, http://www.interpol.int/News-and-media/News/2007/PR005 (accessed December 19, 2015).

45. "AMIA bomb suspects run for Iran presidency," *The Jerusalem Post*, May 23, 2013, http://www.jpost.com/Iranian-Threat/News/Two-AMIA-bombing-suspects-running-for-Iran-president-314128 (accessed February 10, 2015).

46. Darwish Ranjbar, interview with VOA, May 31, 2013, http://www.youtube.com/watch?v=AfdiPSK5mL8 (accessed September 20, 2014); translation Salah Piroty.

47. U.S. Department of State, Bureau of Counterterrorism, *Country Reports on Terrorism 2014*, Chapter 3: State Sponsors of Terrorism Overview, Iran, http://www.state.gov/j/ct/rls/crt/2014/239410.htm (accessed December 19, 2015).

48. Parisa Hafezi, "Iran, Venezuela in 'axis of unity' against the U.S.," Reuters, U.S. edition, July 2, 2007, http://www.reuters.com/article/us-iran-venezuela-idUSDAH23660020070702 (accessed December 22, 2015).

49. Dexter Filkins, "Death of a Prosecutor."

50. Noah Ryman, "Prosecutor Found Dead Had Drafted Arrest Warrant for Argentine President," Milestones, *Time*, February 3, 2015, 26, http://time.com/3694273/alberto-nisman-argentina-kirchner-arrest-warrant/ (accessed September 20, 2015). See also Simon Romero, "Draft of Arrest Request for Argentine President Found at Dead Prosecutor's Home," *New York Times*, February 3, 2015, http://www.nytimes.com/2015/02/04/world/americas/argentina-prosecutor-alberto-nisman-arrest-warrant-cristina-de-kirchner.html?module=Notification&version=BreakingNews&region=FixedTop&action=Click&contentCollection=BreakingNews&contentID=29492236&pgtype=article&_r=0 (accessed December 20, 2015).

EPILOGUE

THE CLOSING OF THE CIRCLE

SIMKO

&

When someone writes my biography,
he must say that I was born when Simko
was murdered.

—Abdul Rahman Ghassemlou

That clear afternoon in the month of June, Simko was accompanied by ten armed men as he approached the city of Oshnavieh, where emissaries of Reza Shah waited to negotiate with him. Over and over again, he would remember the old Kurdish saying: "The only Persian you can trust is a dead Persian."

The sun was falling over the stones along the narrow and dusty path in the mountains on which the riders passed. The horses, nervous, pricked their ears and stretched their necks, measuring each step.

Suddenly, Simko's black stallion stumbled and some stones loosened and tumbled downhill. They disturbed the silence of the men, the concert of insects, and the echo of the horse's hooves. Simko tightened the reins, sharpened his ear, and listened to the stones as they tumbled into the river. The rider at the front of the column turned to his chief and Simko gave him the hint of a smile.

Simko was of medium height and rather thin. The virile moustache of the Kurds that he wore hid perfect teeth and a shy smile. But in the set of his mouth you could read, once more, the old refrain that his father used to repeat every time he told the feats of the Shikak tribe to which he belonged.

Sitting on rugs and leaning on large cushions, Ismael Agha (Simko) and his brother, Jafar Agha, had attentively listened many times, and with a feeling of pride, to the ways their ancestors had confronted Turks and Persians, sabers in hand. They heard stories of their ancestors' coming down from the Cherik Mountains to plunder the villages of the valleys and plains.

Jafar Agha had followed in the footsteps of his ancestors by becoming a hero for the poor. When he stripped some rich man, he would distribute some of the booty among the poor.

In Jafar Agha's lands, the Persian government had no authority. But this chief, beloved, respected, and feared, committed the tragic error of forgetting the old refrain. Without malice he agreed to visit the governor of Azerbaijan, who had solemnly on the Qur'an sworn safe passage for him. In 1905, Jafar was murdered by a bullet to his heart as he mounted the stairs toward the governor's office.

And now, on this afternoon in 1930, Simko, the leader of the Shikak, was on his way to Oshnavieh to negotiate with the emissaries of Reza Shah. The Shah, who had seized power five years before, saw in Simko a symbol of the growing feeling of Kurdish nationalism. This man represented a danger to his policies of centralization and assimilation of minorities in Iran.

On horseback in the mountains, Simko and his men spotted the road that led to the city of Oshnavieh, populated by Kurdish friends. Tension was etched in the men's faces. They seemed to be waking up after a long torpor. Each one adjusted the rifle strapped over his shoulder, as if to ensure that the weapon was still there.

Simko was restless in the saddle. He raised himself up, supported on his stirrups, and looked toward the city that now appeared before his eyes. With a single movement of the head, he ordered one of the men to gallop forward, toward Oshnavieh, moving ahead of the group.

Simko and his men continued along the road, inhaling the dust stirred up by the hooves of the horses. He recalled the old refrain like a litany: "The only Persian you can trust is a dead Persian." And then brushed this thought away.

He became suddenly aware that his mouth was dry, with a slight metallic taste of fear. He took hold of his water bottle, drank a sip, and spit it on the road; with the second mouthful he not only calmed his thirst, but all his feelings of doubt. He knew he was risking his life. But now he said to himself that he was in an advantageous position and risk was his only ally.

At sunset they arrived at the gates of Oshnavieh. An explosion of color reverberated on the mountainside. The city was enveloped in a burst of flame as if on fire. Simko felt that fire banishing all the shadows from his body. Emotion was coursing through him. The moment of truth was here. After all those years of struggle, today was going to culminate in a great victory of peace.

His horse became agitated, restless to charge toward his destiny. Simko tightened the reins and halted the march. The forward scout was headed back at a full gallop. The Shah's emissaries were waiting for him in the governor's residence. The news was comforting: there were only a small number of soldiers protecting the house.

Simko entered Oshnavieh with the night. A breeze stroked their tired bodies, mingling the odor of the horses' sweat with that of the riders. The city was calm. You could hear only the nervous pacing of the horses, the creaking of leather, and the tapping of rifles across the men's chests. The inhabitants had withdrawn into their homes. Life's eternal rounds, the bustle of day and the solace of night, cycled on unabated.

When he reached the central square, Simko perceived a brightly lit house. Inside he could see women coming and going. But his attention was drawn immediately to the torches at the far end of the square that announced the governor's residence.

They advanced, scanning the doorways of the houses, the roofs and the streets, alert for any signs of the enemy. Serene and filled with confidence, Simko was approaching his destiny.

About ten soldiers surrounded the residence. The governor was waiting at the door, flanked by two unarmed men. Simko dismounted, gave the reins to one of his men, and approached the doorway surrounded by his Kurds, rifles in hand. The governor stretched out his hand with a measured cordiality and introduced the other two, emissaries of the Shah. Seven Kurds stayed outside, and two unarmed men accompanied him inside.

Six men sat on the rugs in the living room and after having tea served, they began to discuss the situation of the Kurds in Iran. Simko was attentive and listened to the main emissary. He then explained his own demands. Simko noticed that the emissary's voice began to waver and that he was often wetting his lips. The gas lamps that hung on the walls cast a whitish light over the faces.

One of the emissaries got up to stretch his legs and remained standing. No one spoke. You could only hear the tinkle of the spoons on the teacups, interrupted by the main emissary clearing his throat. Simko became absorbed in his own thoughts, as though he was trying to escape that sensation of uncertainty building in the pit of his stomach. He lifted his eyes toward the emissary and found a gun pointing straight at him.

Time stood still. A heavy silence fell over the entire room while Simko, remembering once more the old Kurdish refrain, realized that the Kurds had lost once again.

He had no time to get up. A bullet had already pierced his forehead.

One of his men fell by Simko's side. The emissary standing up had shot him in the neck. But the other Kurd, Simko's loyal assistant and the silent companion of the last few years, threw himself like a wounded beast at the assassins, who fired every bullet they had left into his young body.

Outside, the bodies of Simko's men were also falling.

While the echo of soldiers' boots reverberated, Kurdish blood ran through the streets of the city. In the house that had drawn one of Simko's final glances, a woman heard through the red mist of her labor the first cry of her newborn son. It was a Kurdish boy.

"He will be named Abdul Rahman, which means 'Servant of the Most Merciful,'" said the father with solemnity, already weeping for Simko's death—Simko, who embodied the staunch pride and independent fervor of being a Kurd.

ACKNOWLEDGMENTS

The years since an earlier edition of this biography, *The Passion and Death of Rahman the Kurd*, have witnessed massive geopolitical shifts across the world the Kurds inhabit. Recent years have seen, too, the emergence of significant new information bearing on the death of Abdul Rahman Ghassemlou and his life as a leader in the context of his times. This revised edition, much expanded, incorporates the contributions of so many who have offered their valuable time, memories, insights, and perspectives with such generosity.

I would like to thank the valuable support given by Hélène Krulich-Ghassemlou for the realization of this book, her personal encouragement, and her time with the interviews given in Paris and Vienna—and for taking the time to answer my never-ending questions, to review and offer her knowledge and insight for this updated edition. I also want to thank the Kurdish community in Vienna for their collaboration, as well as the many people who contributed with interviews, suggestions, and documentation which made this book possible.

My heartfelt thanks to the American journalist Jonathan Randal, who generously offered me the transcript of hours of conversation he had with Ghassemlou. It is thanks to those notes that I was able to reconstruct situations and dialogues without which the writing of this book would not have been possible. My thanks, too, for his constant support throughout the years.

This edition draws on interviews with many people, to whom I offer thanks. The following people were interviewed: Abdul Rahman Ghassemlou (Kurdistan, 1985; Paris, 1986; Madrid, 1987–88); Iraqi Kurdish leader Jalal Talabani (Kurdistan, 1985; Paris, 1991); former Iranian president Abolhassan Banisadr (Paris); former Algerian president Ahmed Ben Bella (Algeria); French minister and physician Bernard Kouchner (Paris); French Socialist politician Alain Chenal (Paris); Kendal Nezan, president of the Kurdish Institute of Paris; Peter Pilz, Austrian parliamentarian and leader of the Green Party (Vienna); Oswald Kessler, head of the Austrian Staatspolizei (Vienna); Iranian politician Naser Pakdaman (Vienna); Susanne Rockenschaub-Rasul (Vienna); French physicians Fréderic Tissot, Michel Bonnot, and Florence Veber (Paris); Kurdish politician Jalil Gadani; Iraqi politician Ibrahim Auyyar (Paris); Iraqi Kurdish intellectual and professor Ezzedin Mustafa Rasul; PDKI military commanders Hassan Shiwasali, Kawe Bahrami, Babasheikh Nasseri, and Colonel Iraj Ghaderi; Kurdish officer Hamid Gohary; French journalists Chris Kutschera and his wife Edith; Sunni clerics Ahmad Darvishi and Khalid Azizi; Austrian attorneys Manfred Weidinger and Thomas Prader; Iranian Kurds Abdullah Hassanzadeh, Hasan Ayoubzadeh, Jafar Hamedi, Ebrahim Salehrad Lajani, Aziz Mameli, Mohamed Hassanpour, Kawe Madani, Rahim Behruz, Rahim Kaderi, Merad, Azad, Abdullah, and others who spoke without wishing to be named; Fatosh Güney, widow of Turkey's Kurdish film director Yilmaz Güney; and French intellectuals Gérard Chaliand, Juliette Minces, and Joyce Blau.

Sadegh Sharafkandi, Ghassemlou's successor as secretary-general of PDKI, the Kurdistan Democratic Party of Iran, was interviewed for the book by Dr. Bernard Granjon, in the summer of 1991, in Kurdistan.

French journalist Marc Kravetz, writing for the daily *Libération*, who detailed the most complete investigation of the crime a few days after it happened and who knows the Kurdish world extremely well, offered me a valuable perspective.

Some of the Iranian and Kurdish interviewees who were close to Ghassemlou asked that their names not be mentioned for security reasons. In some cases, I have quoted them with pseudonyms. Others have simply not been quoted directly.

At a later stage, as challenging as the initial phase of writing the manuscript, thanks are due to my brother Roger Prunhuber for his support and to my mother Luisa Prunhuber for her enthusiastic faith, from beginning to end, in the work; to Edgar Nunes for his invaluable support with the photographic material; to Beyan Farshi and Esmail Ebrahimi for their ongoing willingness to translate documents and video material from German, Kurdish, and Farsi; to Sadegh Vaziri, who provided valuable material via correspondence; to Austrian journalist Sissy Danninger for her review and keen attention to the detail and nuance of events in Austria; and to Hasan Ayoubzadeh for making available reports from the Austrian police and his readiness to search for documents pertinent to the investigation.

A special thank-you to Salah Piroty for his enthusiasm for this book, for his readiness to be called upon, for his constant support in fact-checking and research, for his precise revision and useful suggestions, for conducting collateral interviews, and for translation of important documents from Kurdish and Farsi.

I also want to especially thank Sharif Behruz for his ongoing support, his impeccable review and accurate fact-checking, the timely interviews he supplied for me, and his review and translation of publications in Kurdish and Farsi. Sharif always makes himself available and has helped in innumerable ways to move this project forward.

My profound gratitude to Ellen Porter for her perseverance and willingness to launch into the translation of the earlier Spanish edition of this book. Her deft mastery and love for the written word come through in her editing.

To my long-term editor, Cynthia Briggs, for her spectacular dedication and meticulous, skillful, and thorough approach to this project—even into the wee hours of the night—through the various permutations of this book. I am indebted to her for all the time she has generously given and her support of the Kurds through this endeavor.

To Dr. Farideh Koohi-Kamali of Peter Lang Publishing for her interest and enthusiasm in taking this project forward in such a swift and supportive manner.

To all those who read the manuscript and offered valuable comments.

And very special thanks to my colleague Gabriel Fernández, Spanish journalist, for his invaluable collaboration throughout the process of writing the book and especially for the reconstruction and investigation of Ghassemlou's murder in Vienna. Gabriel passed away, victim of cancer, without having seen this impassioned investigation published, but surely he will celebrate with us, wherever his vantage point—possibly even in the company of Abdul Rahman Ghassemlou—that these pages finally made it to a printer. The publication of this journalistic endeavor is the best way I have to honor them both.

To all the people committed to Abdul Rahman Ghassemlou's memory, and to the Kurdish cause, my deepest gratitude.

GLOSSARY

aghas. Well-to-do and influential landowners.

AMI. Aide Médical Internationale, French humanitarian aid organization.

arabanu. Turban.

ayatollah. A high religious position in Shi'ite hierarchy. Literally, "miraculous sign of God."

Azeri. Member of an ethnic and linguistically Turkic group in the Republic of Azerbaijan and northwestern Iran.

bazaar. The marketplace; a political, economic, and social force in Iran. As an institution, it played an important role in the Islamic revolution.

chador. Traditional garment that covers a woman's body from head to foot. Considered modest and decent.

daftar. General headquarters; designation for the PDKI command center of the Kurds; literally, "bureau."

DGSE. Direction Générale de la Sécurité Extérieure, the French intelligence agency for foreign security.

Katyusha. Antiaircraft rocket launcher.

fatwa. Religious edict.

Feda'iyan. "Freedom fighters"; extreme left Kurdish party.

flic. Derogatory term for police in French argot.

hojatoleslam or *hojjat al-Islam.* Member of Shi'ite religious hierarchy; literally, "authority on Islam" or "proof of Islam."

ICP. Iraqi Communist Party.

imam. For Shi'ites the figure of the religious leader or imam is a descendant of Ali, Muhammad's son-in-law, chosen by God to be the perfect example and to lead humanity in all aspects of life. The hidden truth of the Qur'an's revelation can only be known through the imam, who strengthens the bond between God and man. Only the imam is infallible.

jash. Literally, "donkey"; derogatory term for those Kurds who collaborate with the Islamic regime.

jihad. Literally, "to strive" or "to struggle," a religious duty of Muslims. In the West the term is generally understood as holy war on behalf of Islam.

Kak. Common expression in Sorani, Kurdish dialect spoken mainly in Iraqi Kurdistan and western Iran; an honorific which can mean "sir" or "older brother."

Kalashnikov. Russian submachine gun.

KDP. Kurdistan Democratic Party of Iraq (Barzani's party).

Komala. Kurdish minority Marxist-Leninist group.

Mahabad. Iranian Kurdish city, political center of Kurdish nationalism.

Mahdi. The Twelfth Imam for Shi'ite "Twelvers"; "The Guided One." The promised redeemer, descendant of the Prophet Muhammad, who will return to establish a perfect Islamic society on earth, a reign of justice and peace.

Majlis. "Assembly"; term used for the Iranian parliament.

MdM. Médecins du Monde, "Doctors of the World," French humanitarian aid organization.

MSF. Médecins sans Frontières, "Doctors Without Borders," international humanitarian aid organization, now based in Geneva.

mullah. Islamic cleric or preacher.

mostazafin. Literally, "deprived" or "oppressed." Iranian subproletariat that supports the mullahs.

Mujahedin-e Khalq. The People's Mujahedin of Iran; an Islamic Marxist group.

NIOC. National Iranian Oil Company.

PDKI. Kurdistan Democratic Party of Iran (Ghassemlou); originally PDK, then transitionally PDK (Iran), and finally PDKI, its current designation.

PLO. Palestine Liberation Organization.

PS. Parti Socialiste; French Socialist Party.

PSOE. Partido Socialista Obrero Español; Spanish Socialist Worker's Party.

pasdaran. Iranian Revolutionary Guards (Guardians of the Revolution); military organization of the Islamic Republic of Iran, separate from and parallel to the Iranian army. Created in 1979 by Ayatollah Khomeini as a loyal military force.

PUK. Patriotic Union of Kurdistan; Talabani's party in Iraq.

peshmerga. Literally, "he who walks in front of death"; originally, Kurdish guerrilla; now also Kurdish organized military force.

Qom. Sacred city south of Tehran; a religious center for Shi'ites.

Rezaieh. Name for the city of Urmia in northwestern Iranian Kurdistan during the Pahlavi dynasty (1925–1979).

SAVAK. Organization of Intelligence and National Security; the secret police, domestic security and intelligence service established by the Shah of Iran in 1957 with help from the United States.

SAVAMA. Political police of the Islamic regime; successor to the SAVAK.

Sepáh-i Quds. The Quds Force, a specialized unit of elite members of the Revolutionary Guards, charged with operations outside Iran.

Shi'ite. Member of the Muslim branch distinct from the Sunnis. Shi'ites disregard the first three caliphs who succeeded Muhammad and recognize only the fourth caliph, Imam Ali, the Prophet's son-in-law, and his successors as the legitimate heirs. Shi'ites number approximately fifty million and live mainly in Iraq and Iran. The term comes from *shiat Ali*, "the party of Ali."

Staatspolizei. Austrian national security police force that specializes in counterterrorism and counterintelligence.

Sunni. Member of the branch of Islam that accepts the first four caliphs as rightful successors of Muhammad. Worldwide, Sunnis are in the majority in Islam. The term refers to the *sunnah*, the words, actions, and examples of the Prophet.

Supreme Leader. Literally, "leadership authority," a position created by Khomeini and included in the constitution of the Islamic Republic of Iran, in accordance with the concept of *velayat-e-faqih*, Guardianship of the [Islamic] Jurist. It is the highest political and religious authority in Iran, a role above that of president, to which all branches of government are ultimately answerable.

sura. Chapter or section of the Qur'an.

taqiyya. Literally, "precaution"; moral permission to lie or dissemble when it is for the well-being of the Shi'ite community.

tasbih. Muslim rosary.

Tehran. Capital of modern Iran and of nineteenth-century Persia.

Tudeh. Iranian Communist Party which stayed close to and aligned with the USSR and followed its directives.

tueur. Assassin.

Turkmen. Turkish-speaking cultural or tribal group living in Turkmenistan, historical region of Central Asia that extends from the Caspian Sea to the Mongolian desert, with significant minority populations in Iran, Iraq, and Syria.

ulama. Literally, community of religious scholars or "learned men." Persons of Islamic knowledge; Muslim legal scholars. Those who possess the quality of *'ilm*, "learning."

Urmia. City in northwestern Iranian Kurdistan.

velayat-e-faqih. "Guardianship of the Islamic Jurist." A concept in Shi'ite Islam which gives the *faqih* (the Islamic jurist) guardianship over those in need of it. The idea of absolute velayat-e-faqih was advanced by Ayatollah Khomeini and became the basis for the Islamic constitution of Iran. According to Khomeini, those most knowledgeable about Islamic law (*shari'a*) should guide and rule society. In Iran, the guardianship of the faqih is in the hands of the clerics through the Supreme Leader, the Council of Guardians, and the Assembly of Experts. The Supreme Leader has power over the military forces and judicial powers and has the right to intervene in all the affairs of state. He is the "model for emulation."

DRAMATIS PERSONAE

Publications in English and other European languages have seen great variability in the spelling of Kurdish, Iranian, Turkish, and Arabic names over the years, owing to historical and cultural fashions, personal choices, and trends in popular international media usage. Rather than redact all forms of given names to a consistently single format—under which *Muhammad*, *Mohamed*, *Mohammed*, and *Mohammad* might all be written as *Muhammad*—my decision has been, wherever possible, to honor individual preferences and the names by which individuals have been popularly known in their own times.

People Affiliated with Abdul Rahman Ghassemlou and the PDKI

Abdulli, Fatah. Representative of the PDKI in Europe since 1989. Assassinated in Berlin on September 17, 1992, by agents of the Iranian government.

Ayoubzadeh, Hasan. Iranian Kurdish lawyer joined the PDKI in 1979. He created a commission to teach basic law and inform peshmerga on PDKI discipline and party ground rules. He was a member of the editorial board of the party magazine and the PDKI radio until the end of 1988, when he left the party.

Bahrami, Kawe. Former PDKI military commander; currently a member of PDKI's board and now commander of the peshmerga force.

Gadani, Jalil. Member of the political bureau of the PDK (Iran), later the PDKI, until the end of the 1980s.

Ghaderi, Iraj. Kurdish general in the Iranian army under Reza Pahlavi's regime; he was among the Kurdish military that took over the Mahabad garrison in 1979.

Ghaderi-Azar, Abdullah. Representative of the PDKI in Europe. Assassinated in Vienna on July 13, 1989, by emissaries of the Iranian government.

Ghassemlou, Abdul Rahman. Secretary-general of the PDKI, Kurdistan Democratic Party of Iran. Murdered in Vienna on July 13, 1989, by emissaries of the Iranian government. Called "Kak Doctor" by the Kurds and known by his initials, ARG, to some friends.

Gohary, Hamid. Kurdish officer in the Iranian army and recruitment officer at the Mahabad garrison. He joined the PDKI after the 1979 revolution; ideological divergence from the party's direction would eventually exclude him from core party leadership. Currently living in Sweden, he has written extensively on post-revolutionary developments for Kurds in Iran.

Güney, Fatosh. Widow of the Kurdish film director from Turkey, Yilmaz Güney.

Hamedi, Jafar. Former member of the PDKI central committee and head of the party's secretariat office.

Hassanpour, Mohamed. Member of the PDKI and a close associate of Ghassemlou's. He and his wife Samira Qaderi were killed by an Iranian missile attack on PDKI headquarters in Koya in 2018.

Hassanzadeh, Abdullah. Member of the PDKI political bureau; Ghassemlou's friend and close collaborator; assumed the office of secretary-general after Sharafkandi was murdered. In 2006 he left the PDKI to join the KDP–I, a group that split in 2004 during the formation of the Kurdistan Democratic Party (Iran).

Krulich, Hélène. Ghassemlou's widow. After his death, she began a determined campaign to resolve the murder.

Mameli, Aziz. Iranian Kurdish attorney; became Ghassemlou's chief of staff in 1979 and legal advisor. He also oversaw communications and international relations, then became PDKI representative in Europe (Paris, 1980–82). He left the PDKI in 1982.

Nasseri, Babasheikh. PDKI peshmerga commander.

Nezan, Kendal. Following an active career as a physicist, has served as president of the Kurdish Institute of Paris since 1983.

Rasul, Ezzedin Mustafa. Iraqi Kurdish intellectual and professor; Fadil Rasul's uncle, and longtime friend of Ghassemlou.

Sharafkandi, Sadegh. Ghassemlou's successor as secretary-general of the Kurdistan Democratic Party of Iran (PDKI); known by the pseudonym "Dr. Said." With Fatah Abdulli, assassinated in Berlin on September 17, 1992, by agents of the Iranian government.

Shiwasali, Hassan (Ibrahimi). Commander of one of the PDKI peshmerga forces and former member of the PDKI leadership; currently an honorary member of the PDKI central committee.

Vaziri, Sadegh. Tudeh Party official who, serving as a representative of Kurdistan in a Tudeh ad hoc committee charged with reorganizing the structures of the PDKI, recommended Ghassemlou in 1952 to manage Tudeh and PDKI militant activities in Kurdistan.

Other Relevant Figures

Ben Bella, Ahmed. Leader of the Algerian nationalist revolutionary movement; knew Ghassemlou and, like Ghassemlou, spent years in exile. President of Algeria from 1962 to 1965, when he was overthrown by a military coup. He died in Algiers in April 2012.

Hussein, Saddam. Leader of the Ba'ath Party and dictator of Iraq. Defeated by American troops and allies during the 2003 invasion of Iraq. Because of the repression and slaughter he directed against the Kurds, among other actions, in 2006 he was judged for crimes against humanity by the special tribunal established by the interim Iraqi government. Executed on December 30, 2006.

Members and Friends of the Kurdish Community in Austria

Anwar. Name by which Ahmed Ben Bella addressed Fadil Rasul.

Azad. Pseudonym of a member of the Kurdish community in Vienna; member of the PDKI.

Charlotte. Pseudonym of a member of the Kurdish community in Vienna; Azad's wife.

Faistauer, Renata. Austrian woman; Fadil Rasul's lover. It was at her apartment that the murder of Ghassemlou and his Kurdish companions took place.

Fatah. Pseudonym of a member of the Kurdish community in Vienna; representative of the PDKI in Austria.

Hildegaard. Pseudonym of a member of the Kurdish community in Vienna; Mustafa's wife.

Mustafa. Pseudonym of a member of the Kurdish community in Vienna; PDKI member.

Rasul, Fadil. Iraqi Kurd intellectual. Murdered with Ghassemlou in Vienna on July 13, 1989, by emissaries of the Iranian government.

Rockenschaub-Rasul, Susanne. Austrian physician; Fadil Rasul's widow.

Iranians Allegedly Involved in the Murder

Ahmadinejad, Mahmoud. Sixth president of Iran, from 2005 to 2013. Named by Austrian Green Party parliamentary spokesperson Peter Pilz as involved in the planning and perhaps even the execution of Ghassemlou's murder. Despite evidence that has surfaced, the case has never been resolved and the suspicions never proved.

Buzorguian, Amir Mansur. Alias of Haj Ghafour Darjazi; Mohammed Jafar Sahrarudi's "bodyguard" and agent of the Iranian secret police. Arrested and freed after the crime; never heard of again.

Magaby, Mohamed. Iranian citizen allegedly involved in the murder; his role in the murder remains unclear. He left Austria protected by the Austrian police a few days after the assassination.

Mostafawi, Hadji, alias **Adjavi or Layevardi.** Official representative of the Islamic Republic of Iran in the negotiations with Ghassemlou in Vienna. He disappeared after the crime without leaving any trace. He was known to have worked for Iranian minister of information Mohammed Reyshahri, a prominent hawk of the regime.

Rafsanjani, Akbar Hashemi. Speaker of the Iranian parliament from 1980 to 1989, and president of Iran from 1989 to 1997. After 1997, he headed the Expediency Discernment Council, an unelected assembly which resolves differences between the Majlis (parliament) and the Council of Guardians. The latter advises the Supreme Leader and has veto power over the Iranian parliament. He died January 8, 2017.

Reyshahri. Hojatoleslam Sheikh Mohammed Mohammadi Nik, known as Reyshahri ("of the city of Rey"); the first minister of intelligence of the Islamic Republic of Iran, in 1984. A hard-liner of the regime, he was widely known as "the scary ayatollah."

Rezae, Mohsen. Commander in chief of the Guardians of the Revolution, the IRGC or pasdaran, from 1981 to 1997.

Sahrarudi, Mohamed Jafari, alias **Rahimi.** Diplomatic envoy for the Islamic Republic to negotiate with Ghassemlou in Vienna in 1989; wounded during the crime. Agent for Iranian intelligence and commander of the Ramazan garrison in Iranian Kurdistan and intermediary in the buying of arms for Iran. Following Ghassemlou's assassination, promoted to head of the Quds Force's Intelligence Directory. After the 2003 Iraq occupation, as head of the IRGC and member of Iran's Supreme National Security Council, he was in charge of issues concerning Iraq: organizing, leading assassination squads and bombings, and "stoking sectarian conflict." Despite an arrest warrant issued for him by Austrian authorities in December 1989, he continued as advisor and chief of staff to Majlis speaker IRGC Brigadier General Ali Larijani and accompanied him to meetings abroad.

Iranians of the Islamic Republic

Banisadr, Abolhassan. President of Iran in 1980. Deposed from office in 1981 because of his opposition to the executions of political dissidents and Khomeini's authoritarianism, he escaped to France, where he has since been living in exile.

Bazargan, Mehdi. First prime minister of the government designated by Khomeini after the revolution in 1979. He opposed the power of the clerics and renounced his post after realizing that he could not carry out the democratic changes he had envisioned.

Beheshti, Mohammed. Important political and religious leader (ayatollah) in revolutionary Iran. President of the Islamic Republic Party and chief justice of the Islamic Republic's supreme court. He died in a terrorist attack in June 1981 with more than seventy members of the party, when a bomb was planted—allegedly by the Mujahedin-e Khalq—during a party conference.

Fallahian, Ali. As head of Iran's Ministry of Intelligence under Hashemi Rafsanjani, pursued policy of assassination of members of opposition groups. Served on the Council of Experts; influential figure in Iranian politics as a security advisor to Khamenei, Khomeini's successor as Supreme Leader. Currently the subject of no less than three international arrest warrants.

Foruhar, Dariush. Minister of the Islamic government sent to negotiate in Kurdistan in 1979. His attempts to reach a peaceful settlement with the Kurds earned him the Kurds' respect. In 1998, at age seventy, he and his wife, aged fifty-four, were brutally murdered in their home. The murder, which was believed to be politically motivated since both were outspoken critics of the regime, was never resolved. It is believed that the Iranian Ministry of Intelligence ordered the assassination.

Hashemi, Mehdi. President of the World Islamic Movement, he was charged with counterrevolutionary activities and executed in September 1987. He and his supporters learned of the visit of former U.S. national security advisor Robert McFarlane to Iran and allegedly tried to sabotage the negotiations of the arms-for-hostages deal known as Irangate.

Khalkhali, Sadegh. Head of the revolutionary tribunals from 1979 to 1989, he was known as "the anger of God." Dismissed from his post after Khomeini's death.

Khamenei, Seyyid Ali. Iranian president from 1981 to 1989. Chosen as Khomeini's spiritual successor in 1989; has since then held the post of Supreme Leader of Iran.

Khomeini, Ruhollah Musavi. Iranian Shi'ite religious leader who led the opposition to the Shah. Presided over the Islamic Republic, founded in 1979, as Supreme Leader. Died in June of 1989.

Mohtashami, Ali Akbar. Served as Iran's ambassador to Syria in the mid-1980s; is believed to have played an important role in the creation of the Lebanese radical Shi'a organization Hezbollah. He later became Iran's minister of the interior.

Montazeri, Hussein Ali. Grand Ayatollah; disciple of Khomeini in Qom and one of the ideologues of the Islamic Republic. Designated successor to Khomeini, he fell out with Khomeini in 1989 over human-rights abuses and government corruption. In 1997 he was put under house arrest for criticizing the authority of the new Supreme Leader, Khamenei. This house arrest ended in 2003.

Shariatmadari, Kazem. Ayatollah from Tabriz, he played a role in the Iranian revolution. He opposed the absolute power of the Supreme Leader which Khomeini imposed in Iran's new constitution. In 1982 he was accused of involvement in an attempted coup d'état against the Islamic Republic. He was put under house arrest, where he remained until his death in 1985.

Taleghani, Mahmoud. Ayatollah; head of the Revolutionary Council during the Islamic revolution; spiritual leader of Tehran. Khomeini's rival, he died in 1979.

Velayati, Ali Akbar. Iran's minister of foreign affairs from 1981 to 1987.

Other Iranians and Iraqis

Auyyar, Ibrahim. Member of the Communist Party of Iraq.

Bakhtiar, Shapour. The Shah of Iran's last prime minister, during a few weeks, in 1979. He sought exile in Paris, where he was brutally murdered in 1991 by agents of the Iranian government.

Diba, Farah. Mohammed Reza Pahlavi's third wife.

Mossadegh, Mohammed. Nationalist from an aristocratic background, as Iran's prime minister he nationalized oil at the beginning of the 1950s. Overthrown in 1953 by a coup d'état organized by the CIA and the British secret service.

Pahlavi, Mohammed Reza. Shah of Persia bought to the throne in 1941 by the Allies; his regime reinforced by the U.S.-British coup of 1953, he was dethroned in 1979 by the Islamic revolution.

Pahlavi, Reza Shah. Founder of the Pahlavi dynasty; father of the last Shah of Iran. Deposed by the Allies in 1941 for his ties with Nazi Germany.

Rajavi, Massoud. Leader of the People's Mujahedin of Iran, Islamic radical opposition group to the Islamic Republic.

Razmara, Haj Ali. Prime minister of Iran under the Shah; assassinated in the 1950s.

Iraqi and Iranian Kurds

Barzani, Masoud. Son of Mustafa Barzani, political heir of the Kurdistan Democratic Party of Iraq (KDP).

Barzani, Mustafa. Leader of the Kurdistan Democratic Party of Iraq; one of the most important Kurdish leaders of the twentieth century. He died in exile the United States in 1979.

Bulurian, Ghani. Member of the PDKI politburo. He and the "Band of Seven" sought to strengthen ties with the Communist party Tudeh. After losing the election for secretary-general to Ghassemlou, who instead wanted independence from Tudeh, he left the party in 1980.

Hosseini, Ezzedin. Sunni cleric of Iranian Kurdistan, known as Sheikh Ezzedin; popular leader of the Left. He called for autonomy for Kurdistan, and a constitution guaranteeing rights of religious minorities in Iran.

Ishaghi, Abdullah (known as Ahmad Tawfiq). A leading member of the PDKI who opposed Ghassemlou and was excluded from party leadership in 1969.

Mohammad, Qazi. Founder of the Kurdistan Democratic Party and president of the Republic of Mahabad in 1946; deposed by the Iranian central government and condemned to death in 1947.

Q. M. Pseudonym, for security reasons, of Iranian Kurdish political leader who resides in Europe.

Simko. Born Ismail Agha Shikak; Iranian Kurdish leader of the Abdui clan of the Shikak tribal confederacy, assassinated by emissaries of Reza Shah in 1930.

Talabani, Jalal. Iraqi Kurdish leader; president of Iraq from 2005 to 2014. Secretary-general of Patriotic Union of Kurdistan (PUK) in Iraq since 1975. Known as Mam Jalal; he died October 3, 2017.

French Figures and Institutions

Bonnot, Michel. Physician with the French humanitarian organization Aide Médicale Internationale, he worked in Kurdistan during Ghassemlou's time.

Chaliand, Gérard. French specialist in international and strategic relations, he has developed theories focused on asymmetric conflicts (terrorism, guerrilla warfare). Author of a number of books on armed conflict, diaspora, and strategy.

Chenal, Alain. French politician, member of the French Socialist Party; specialist in Third World issues.

Granjon, Bernard. French physician. Cofounder of the humanitarian organization Médecins du Monde, he has worked in Kurdistan for many years.

Jospin, Lionel. Secretary-general of the French Socialist Party since 1981; French prime minister from 1997 to 2002.

Kouchner, Bernard. French minister for foreign affairs since June 2007; previously secretary of state and minister for humanitarian aid, as well as minister of health. Served as special envoy of the UN in Kosovo and cofounder of Médecins sans Frontières and Médecins du Monde.

Tissot, Fréderic. French physician with Aide Médicale Internationale; worked in Kurdistan. French consul in Erbil, capital of Iraq's Autonomous Region of Kurdistan, from 2008 to 2012.

Veber, Florence. French physician for Aide Médicale Internationale; worked in Kurdistan.

Foreign Journalists and Writers

Heikal, Mohamed. Influential Egyptian journalist, close to Egyptian president Gamal Abdel Nasser. For years he directed *Al Haram*, a newspaper in Cairo. Author of books on the Middle East.

Kravetz, Marc. Journalist for the French daily *Libération*. Author of several books on the Middle East.

Kutschera, Chris. French journalist specializing in the Middle East and the Kurds. Author of several books on the Kurds. He died July 31, 2017.

Randal, Jonathan. American journalist. Former correspondent for the *Washington Post* in Paris, he covered the Middle East as well and has authored several books.

Austrian Figures and Institutions

Danek, Michael. Austrian judge in charge of the murder investigation after Judge Seda abandoned it.

Foregger, Egmont. Austrian minister of justice from 1987 to 1990.

Kessler, Oswald. Head of the Staatspolizei, Austrian national security police specializing in counterintelligence and counterterrorism. Since 2003, chief of the Support Unit ZMR (Central Register and Residence or Registry Information Service) responsible for e-Government and e-Identity.

Löschnak, Franz. Austrian minister of the interior from 1989 to 1995.

Mock, Alois. Austrian vice-chancellor in charge of foreign affairs from 1987 to 1989.

Pilz, Peter. Austrian parliamentary member and leading spokesperson for the Austrian Green Party; remains active in parliament today.

Prader, Thomas. Austrian attorney and advisor to the Green Party.

Seda, Peter. Austrian judge in charge at the beginning of the investigation of the murder.

Vranitzky, Franz. Austrian federal chancellor from 1986 to 1997.

Weidinger, Manfred. Austrian attorney in charge of Ghassemlou's case, representing his widow.

TIMELINE

Abdul Rahman Ghassemlou and the PDKI

1930
Abdul Rahman Ghassemlou is born in Iranian Kurdistan, in the city of Urmia, on December 22.

1941
Soviet authorities invite thirty Kurdish leaders to visit the Azeri Soviet city of Baku; the delegation includes Ghassemlou's father.

1945
The Iranian PDK, Democratic Party of Iranian Kurdistan, is founded in Mahabad on August 16, with Qazi Mohammad as its leader. The newly designated PDK is initiated to replace Komalay Jiyanaway Kurdistan (the Society for Revival of Kurdistan), founded three years earlier by a group of young educated urban nationalists. The new party is established for the purpose of creating a modern, well-organized, and popular political party with an explicit commitment to democracy, liberty, social justice, and gender equality. While neither Communist nor formally affiliated with the USSR, the young party is sheltered by a cultural organization put in place by the Soviets.

1946
In January, despite Soviet plans to integrate them into the USSR-supported Azeri Republic, Iranian Kurds establish the independent Democratic Republic of Kurdistan, popularly known as the Mahabad Republic. PDK leader Qazi Mohammad becomes president of the fledgling republic.

The PDK begins creating youth sections in several Kurdish cities; Ghassemlou, at age sixteen, is responsible for the branch in Urmia.

The Democratic Republic of Kurdistan falls in December.

1947
Ghassemlou completes high school in Tehran and travels to Europe, passing through Turkey; he stays in Paris to study French.

1949
Ghassemlou wins a scholarship to Prague and enters the School of Advanced Political and Economic Studies; he is elected president of the school's student union.

1950–1951
Ghassemlou participates in the International Congress of Students in Prague and then in Berlin. He meets his future wife, Hélène Krulich.

1952
Ghassemlou marries Hélène Krulich. While Hélène remains in Prague, Ghassemlou returns to Iran, where he begins his clandestine life as a PDK activist during the dictatorship of Shah Reza Pahlavi, working closely with Tudeh, the Communist party among the Iranian Kurds.

1953
Ghassemlou's daughter Mina is born in Prague. Ghassemlou is named head of the party in the region of Mahabad. Following the British-and-CIA-engineered coup against nationalist prime minister Mossadegh, Ghassemlou goes underground for two years.

Hélène, with their daughter Mina, arrives in Tehran.

1954
Ghassemlou, Hélène, and their daughter Mina leave Tehran for Rezaieh (Urmia), where Ghassemlou's parents live.

1955

The Ghassemlous' second daughter, Hiva, is born in Tehran. The PDK breaks away from the Tudeh, the Iranian Communist party. Ghassemlou attends the First Conference of the PDK in the Qalate Resh mountains near the city of Piranshar.

1956

Ghassemlou is detained and tortured by the SAVAK. He is released after promising collaboration, and then escapes.

1957

Hélène and their daughters return to Prague. Ghassemlou, evading capture by the SAVAK, returns separately to Prague and joins them there.

1958

In October, Iraqi Kurdish leader Mustafa Barzani stops in Prague and invites Ghassemlou to return to Iraq with him.

1959

Ghassemlou moves to Iraq with Hélène, while their daughters remain in Prague.

1960–1962

In the wake of shifting political realignments in Iraq and between leadership factions among the Kurds themselves, Ghassemlou returns with Hélène to Prague to teach in the School of Economics and begins his doctorate in economics and political science, which he completes in 1962. He begins to lecture in political economy at the University of Prague and writes the book *Kurdistan and the Kurds*.

1964

PDK suffers an internal coup led by Abdullah Ishaghi, prominent member of the party. Ishaghi convenes the PDK Second Congress in Iraqi Kurdistan with support from Mulla Mustafa Barzani in preventing the attendance of leftist members such as Ghassemlou. At the congress, Ishaghi moves to exclude Ghassemlou from party leadership and accuses him of treason, citing Ghassemlou's liberation from SAVAK in 1956. Ishaghi's alliance with Barzani will not last; Barzani, promised support against Baghdad, aligns with the Shah to curtail PDK influence. By 1969, Ishaghi, after exclusion from the party's Second Conference, will resign from party leadership.

1967

A new revolutionary committee, led by nationalist PDK cadres and ex-members of Tudeh, returns to Iran and begins a limited armed resistance against the Shah's regime. Their uprising lasts only eighteen months; caught between the Shah and Barzani's forces, they are crushed.

1968

The Soviet Union invades Czechoslovakia. Ghassemlou, living in Prague and witnessing this event firsthand, ends his identification with Communism.

In Iraq, Saddam Hussein participates in a coup and is named deputy to the president, Hassan Al-Bakr, and deputy chairman of the Ba'athist Revolutionary Command Council.

The Shah's armed forces launch an attack on the Iranian PDK. Party members, resorting to arms to defend themselves, begin an armed rebellion that will last eighteen months. Mustafa Barzani hands over to the Shah's forces more than forty PDK party members.

1970

Ghassemlou returns to Iraq by government invitation to work as an advisor to the Ministry of Economic Planning.

1971

At its Third Conference, the party redesignates itself as PDK (Iran), and Ghassemlou is elected secretary-general. He begins modernization of the party and establishes its core political idea based on the slogan "Democracy for Iran, autonomy for Kurdistan."

1973

The PDK (Iran) holds its Third Congress. Ghassemlou is confirmed as the party's secretary-general.

1974

In March, Ghassemlou attends negotiations in Baghdad between the Iraqi government and Barzani's delegation. When negotiations fail, Mustafa Barzani takes up arms against the Iraqi government. Though employed by the Baghdad regime, Ghassemlou refuses to condemn Barzani and is forced to leave Iraq. He returns once again to Prague.

1975

On March 15, Iran and Iraq sign the Algiers Agreement (commonly known as the Algiers Accord), settling long-standing border disputes and depriving the Kurds of external support. Baghdad's military forces attack Kurdistan.

1976–1978

In January 1976, Czechoslovakia does not renew Ghassemlou's residence permit and he is forced to leave the country. He moves to Paris and works as an assistant professor in the School of Oriental Languages at the University of Paris. His family follows several months later. He takes on republishing the long-standing bulletin *Kurdistan*, with Farsi and Kurdish editions. With a group of influential figures, he writes and publishes *Les Kurdes et le Kurdistan: La question nationale Kurde au Proche-Orient* (The Kurds and Kurdistan: The Kurdish national problem in the Middle East).

1978

Ghassemlou pays a visit to Ayatollah Khomeini at his home base in exile in the outskirts of Paris, but is not received. He returns to Iran, traveling first to Tehran and then to Mahabad in Kurdistan. He reorganizes the PDK (Iran), creates secret committees, sets the ideological and practical base of the organization, updates the cadres, and incorporates younger activist members in the party.

1979

January

Faced with mounting pressure from all sectors of Iranian society as well as a continuous desertion within his military forces, the Shah names Shapour Bakhtiar prime minister and then abandons the country.

March
In Mahabad, Ghassemlou announces the political agenda of PDK (Iran) and the demands of the Kurdish people. This first political act launches him in the public light.

April
A government delegation led by the ayatollahs Mahmud Taleghani and Hossein Beheshti, together with Abolhassan Banisadr, meets with the (Iranian) Kurds. Taleghani promises the Kurds a certain degree of autonomy and invites them to participate in the nationwide referendum for the establishment of the Islamic Republic. The majority of the Kurds do not participate in this referendum; subsequently, Khomeini proclaims the Islamic Republic of Iran. Ghassemlou begins a tour of Kurdistan announcing the political agenda of the PDK (Iran).

August–October
With a substantial majority of the local vote, Ghassemlou is elected member of the Assembly of Experts for the Constitution. In the face of Kurdish rebellion, Khomeini designates himself commander-in-chief and declares holy war against the Kurds, whom he crushes in an indiscriminate way. During the first session of the Assembly of Experts, Khomeini condemns Ghassemlou and bans the PDK (Iran).

The party, with Kurdish cities suffering the most brutal assaults from Khomeini's forces, retreats into the mountains to avoid the slaughter of civilians. The party's guerrilla campaign begins. The Kurds take control of a large part of Kurdish territory in west Azerbaijan and Kurdistan, and the regime offers to negotiate. The Iranian army begins its permanent occupation of Kurdistan.

1980
The Kurdish Democratic Party changes its name to PDKI, as it is known today. The party then suffers its first schism after its Fourth Congress in a clash between the Kurdish and the pro-Tudeh Communists who want to ally themselves with the government because of its avowedly anti-imperialist stance.

1981–1982

The Iranian regime launches a fierce military attack against Kurdistan. The PDKI retreats further into the mountains, toward the Iran-Iraq border. PDKI peshmerga establish schools all over Kurdistan, build hospitals, and create their own prisons in the mountains. Ghassemlou initiates the flow of humanitarian aid from the French medical organizations AMI, MdM, and MSF.

1984

The PDKI establishes its general headquarters in Iraqi Kurdistan along the Iranian border. After celebrating its Sixth Congress, the party suffers a new division over differences between pro-Soviet cadres and Ghassemlou's proposed direction of democratic socialism.

1988

The PDKI suffers a further rupture among high-ranking officials during its Eighth Congress, as a carryover of dissension by diehard pro-Soviets as well as a power struggle and irreconcilable differences over negotiations with the Iranian regime. The dissenting group accuses Ghassemlou of leading the PDKI astray from socialism; they form the Kurdistan Democratic Party of Iran–Revolutionary Leadership (PDKI–RL).

Tehran proposes a dialogue with the PDKI. Ghassemlou and Iranian representatives meet in Vienna in December 1988 and January 1989; the meetings are organized by Jalal Talabani.

1989

Ayatollah Khomeini dies. Ghassemlou and members of the PDKI participate in the International Socialist Congress in Sweden. Tehran, through the Iraqi Kurd Fadil Rasul, contacts Ghassemlou to resume negotiations in Vienna.

July 1989

Ghassemlou, Abdullah Ghaderi-Azar, and Fadil Rasul are murdered during the negotiations with representatives of the Iranian government. Representatives of the political bureau of the PDKI announce that Sadegh Sharafkandi has been named the party's secretary-general. Ghassemlou and Ghaderi-Azar are buried in the Parisian cemetery of Père Lachaise.

1991

Ghassemlou's widow, Hélène Krulich, initiates legal proceedings against the Austrian state for allowing the murderers of the Kurds to go unpunished.

1992

Sadegh Sharafkandi, secretary-general of the PDKI, is assassinated in Berlin with PDKI European representatives Fatah Abdulli and Homayoum Ardalan and Iranian political activist Nouri Dehkordi. In Austria, the high court rejects Hélène Krulich's lawsuit; in Berlin, however, the courts will pursue legal action against the Iranian perpetrators of the Mykonos murders.

Mustafa Hijri, Sharafkandi's deputy, becomes party interim secretary-general, pending the convening of the 1995 general congress. As the first PDKI leader to travel to the United States, in April Hijri meets with members of Congress in Washington, D.C., and officials from the UN in New York. In June, invited by the British Labour Party, he meets with members of Parliament.

1993

On March 13, Iranian forces bomb the PDKI general headquarters in the Qandil mountains in Iraqi Kurdistan. The assault, aimed at the party's hospital and the camp of families sheltered there, results in the death of four people. This is the beginning of an all-out war against the PDKI and its bases and the beginning of the Iranian military's incursion deep into Iraqi Kurdistan territory and meddling in the affairs of the region.

A delegation led by Mohammad Jafari Sahrarudi, head of the Revolutionary Guards secret service, and Mohammed Mohammedi, director of Iranian president Rafsanjani's office, demand that Masoud Barzani and his KDP disarm the PDKI, which is forced to move its headquarters. Party headquarters in Iraq are relocated from Qandil to Koya Sanjak due to Iranian military pressure and PDKI intelligence reports of a plan for a major military incursion that would be too costly for all concerned. The PDKI is installed in an ancient fort previously occupied by Saddam's army about sixty-five kilometers from the Iranian border. Pressured by Jalal Talabani's PUK, which wishes to reestablish good relations with Iran, the PDKI is forced to stop its radio broadcasts.

1995
In April, during the PDKI's Tenth Congress, Abdullah Hassanzadeh is elected secretary-general and Mustafa Hijri becomes the deputy secretary-general.

1996
In July, two thousand Iranian pasdaran cross the Iraqi border toward Sulaimaniya, escorted by three hundred PUK peshmerga. Iranian artillery shells the PDKI daftar and the refugee camp nearby. PDKI peshmerga repel the pasdaran, but the homes of peshmerga families and the hospitals set up by the French AMI and MdM are destroyed. Iranian forces continue toward Erbil but Allied air forces compel their retreat, as Masoud Barzani's KDP blocks their return through Haj Omran.

During the International Socialist Twentieth Congress, held in New York, the PDKI is granted the status of observer. (In 2005 PDKI status will be elevated to that of advisor.) Party secretary-general Abdullah Hassanzadeh meets in D.C. with officials from the U.S. State Department and the White House.

1997
A German court convicts four men, former members of Hezbollah, of the 1992 assassination of Sharafkandi and three other Kurds. The court also issues an international arrest warrant for Iranian intelligence minister Hojatoleslam Ali Fallahian, charging him with having ordered the assassination, and also implicates Supreme Leader Ali Khamenei and former president Hashemi Rafsanjani.

2004
Following the 2004 general party congress which leads to the ousting of former secretary-general Abdullah Hassanzadeh, top leadership loyal to him is disenfranchised and dissatisfied with the changes in leadership. The congress returns Mustafa Hijri to the position of secretary-general.

2005

Peter Pilz, Austrian member of parliament and leader of the Green Party, accuses Iranian president Mahmoud Ahmadinejad and former president Hashemi Rafsanjani of involvement in the 1989 murder of the Kurds in Vienna. The case is never reopened and never resolved and the suspicions are never proven.

2006

The PDKI becomes a divided party. Despite two years of continuous talks and consultations, Hassanzadeh's group decide to break ranks with that of Hijri and establishes the Kurdistan Democratic Party (Iran) (KDP–I), weakening the PDKI and countering the legitimacy of the party's 2004 Thirteenth Congress that had brought the swift change in leadership.

Since that time, the opposing factions have normalized relations, and there are bilateral talks to reunite the party.

2008

In Iran, authorities continue to discriminate against and repress the Kurdish population. Human-rights activists, journalists, trade unionists, and students are objects of unrelenting judicial pressure. Amnesty International reports that acts of intimidation and repression have been directed against Kurds on the pretext of "internal security." Cases of improper imprisonment, iniquitous trials, and death sentences continue to occur. In August, the European Union publishes a report on behalf of the Kurds and especially expresses its concern for five Kurds who have been sentenced to death in Iran and await execution.[1]

2009

The twentieth anniversary of Ghassemlou's assassination is honored in many cities around the world. In many areas of Iranian Kurdistan, despite warnings from the Iranian authorities, stores close, and at 10:00 p.m. Kurdish homes turn off their lights to honor their beloved leader. Annual traditions of honoring Ghassemlou's memory will continue among Kurds and PDKI members worldwide. International events held in emblematic venues have included an Hommage à Abdul Rahman Ghassemlou, organized by the Kurdish Institute of Paris and French parliamentarian Sergio Coronado, convened in Paris in a hall of the French Senate.

High-level Iranian involvement in systematic murders of opposition leaders is highlighted when, on June 16, Austrian parliamentarian Peter Pilz once again accuses Ahmadinejad of participation in the assassination of Ghassemlou. He brings forth new evidence from a German weapons dealer serving a prison sentence in Trieste, who has confessed delivering half a dozen light weapons to the Iranian embassy in Vienna in July 1989, during a meeting where Ahmadinejad was alleged to have been present.

2010
July 17
Iranian Kurdish activists receive approval from the Austrian authorities to place a memorial plaque in the building in Vienna where Ghassemlou, Ghaderi-Azar, and Rasul were assassinated.

2011
Hélène Krulich publishes her memoirs, *Une Européenne au pays des Kurdes*. In 2018 she publishes an English version, *Love Against All Reason: A European Woman Involved in the Kurdish Fight for Freedom in Iran*.

2013
October
Despite an international arrest warrant against him as the primary suspect in Ghassemlou's assassination, Mohammad Jafari Sahrarudi, now using the name Mohammad Ali Jafari, travels freely to Europe for six days. In Switzerland, he participates in the Inter-Parliamentary Union in Geneva. Protestors demand his immediate arrest.

2014
March
U.S. Federal Bar Association Law Awards honor German prosecutors of the Mykonos case, in which Sharafkandi and his aides were murdered in Berlin 1992. The award is given in New York City.

December
Mohammad Jafari Sahrarudi accompanies the Iranian regime's official parliamentary delegation to Erbil to meet with Kurdistan Region's president Masoud Barzani and top Kurdish officials. The Iranian delegation, including Sahrarudi, also meets with PUK leadership and visits ailing former Iraqi president Jalal Talabani. Iranian Kurds criticize the lack of sensitivity on the part of Kurdistan Regional Government leadership for hosting the suspected assassin of the preeminent Kurdish leader Abdul Rahman Ghassemlou.

2016
After a two-decade hiatus, the PDKI resumes political activism, sending peshmerga across the border into Iran to encourage civilian resistance. Peshmerga respond with counterforce to Iranian attacks.

2018
Iran bombards Iranian Kurdish political headquarters in Koya, Iraqi Kurdistan, killing sixteen people and wounding forty-five. In protest, merchants and shopkeepers in Iranian Kurdistan conduct a strike.

Note

1. *Liaison and Information Bulletin*, Kurdish Institute of Paris, July 2008.

TIMELINE

Historical Events and Geopolitical Context

Seventh century C.E.

The first confrontation of Kurds with Arab expansion comes in 637 C.E. Arabs conquer Kurdistan, and the Kurds in their majority eventually convert to Sunni Islam.

Over the next several centuries, Kurdistan will become a theater of combat for successive waves of invaders, ranging from Timurid Turks to the Mongol Empire.

Twelfth–thirteenth centuries

Seljuk Turks occupy Kurdistan and annex Kurdish principalities. Around 1150, the sultan Sandjar, the last Seljuk monarch, creates a province out of these lands and called it Kurdistan.

Saladin founds the Ayyubid dynasty (1171–1250) in Egypt, Syria, and Iraq, and assumes leadership of the Muslim world.

In 1231 Mongol raiders invade Kurdish territory.

Sixteenth century

Kurdish lands become a target between the Ottoman Turks and the Safavid Persians. Ottomans establish an alliance with feudal Kurdish lords. Sunni Kurds and Ottomans allied against Shi'ite Safavids.

Sharef Nameh, an epic history in Farsi, is written in 1596, describing the origin of the Kurds.

Seventeenth century

The shah of Persia and the Ottoman sultan sign an agreement which legalizes the first division of Kurdistan between their empires.

Eighteenth–nineteenth century

While other European powers—the British, Dutch, and Portuguese—compete for advantage to the south in the Persian Gulf, Russia occupies and dominates northern Iran, including Tabriz. Russia will continue to interfere aggressively in Iran's internal affairs through the mid-twentieth century.

Twentieth century
1907

Without any consultation with Iran, Great Britain and Russia sign a treaty that divides Iran into three sectors: the north, under Russian influence, a smaller area in the south under British influence, and a neutral central zone that includes Tehran.

1920

The Ottoman Empire collapses at the end of World War I. The Treaty of Sèvres proposes the division of the Ottoman Empire in a manner that would establish an autonomous territory for the Kurds east of Anatolia and the province of Mosul.

1921

Persian military commander Reza Khan, who takes the name of Reza Shah Pahlavi, takes power. Modernization of the Persian realm begins. Soviet involvement remains significant, with increased trade between Persia and the USSR. Baku becomes a center for Soviet trade in the Middle East, and the Red Army assists the founding of a short-lived Persian Socialist Republic in northern Iran.

1923

The signing of the Treaty of Lausanne, the final post–World War I settlement, ignores the terms proposed by the Treaty of Sèvres and partitions Kurdistan among Turkey, Iran, Iraq, and Syria.

1926

Coronation of Reza Pahlavi. The Pahlavi era begins. Mohammad Reza, eldest son of Reza Shah, is proclaimed prince heir of Persia.

1930

Simko, Kurdish tribal and nationalist leader, is murdered by emissaries of the central government of Iran. Reza Shah launches a wave of repression in Kurdistan. Hundreds of tribal leaders are deported and the government confiscates their lands.

1941

During World War II Reza Shah supports Germany. The Allies occupy Iran and depose Reza Shah in favor of his son Mohammad Reza Pahlavi. Throughout the war, the Soviets expand their command in northern Iran by establishing military bases along the southern border of their zone of occupation.

1942

A small group of young educated urban nationalists creates the first Kurdish political organization, Komalay Jiyanaway Kurdistan (Society for the Revival of Kurdistan), popularly known as Komala.

1945

August 16

The Kurdistan Democratic Party (PDK) in Iran is born under the leadership of Qazi Mohammad, incorporating many members from Komala.

October

Kurdish tribal leader Mulla Mustafa Barzani, fleeing persecution from Iraq, arrives in Iranian Kurdistan with one thousand fighting men.

December 10

Iranian Azeris, with the support of the Soviets, take military and civil power in the province of Azerbaijan and proclaim their autonomy with the Democratic Republic of (Persian) Azerbaijan.

December 15

Kurdish government is inaugurated in Mahabad, formalizing the independence which has existed *de facto* for some time.

1946

January

Iranian Kurds establish the independent Democratic Republic of Kurdistan. Qazi Mohammad becomes president of the fledgling republic.

February

The Democratic Republic of Kurdistan depends on Soviet military support for its existence against the central power of Iran. The Soviets convince the Kurds that they will support and defend them by providing them "small firearms and ammunition."

According to agreements with Tehran, Soviet troops are due to leave Iran by six months following the end of World War II. The Soviets delay withdrawal while they press for an oil concession. Anticipating the USSR's pull-out, Tehran begins to mass its military for more vigorous action.

March

Following Iran's petition to the UN and demands by the Western powers, the Soviets announce a promise to withdraw within six weeks. They continue to stall until Tehran agrees "to form a joint Soviet-Iranian oil company, subject to ratification by the Majlis."

April

Pressured by the Soviets to resolve Kurdish/Azeri differences and present a united front to Tehran, Qazi Mohammad negotiates a treaty with the Azeris for "mutual military assistance" and for bargaining with Tehran to be in joint Azeri/Kurdish interests. This agreement essentially marginalizes the Kurds to the Azeri government, which takes the lead and co-opts representation of the Kurds in negotiations for autonomy with Tehran.

May

The Soviets finally withdraw. Materiel and assistance allegedly promised to the Kurds in the form of planes, tanks, heavy weapons, and military training never materializes.

Without Soviet backing, Mahabad pleas for support from the tribes. But with anti-Soviet sentiment strong among tribal leaders, the Kurdish nationalist government finds itself without defenders.

June
The Azeris move quickly to an agreement by which all Azerbaijan, including Kurdish areas, formally reverts to Iranian sovereignty. Azeri government ministers keep power and position as provincial administrators, but the Kurds are left "isolated as a rebel enclave" within the province of Azerbaijan.

August
While in Mahabad, Mustafa Barzani creates the Kurdistan Democratic Party of Iraq, also known as the KDP. The KDP holds its First Congress in Baghdad.

Qazi Mohammad travels to Tehran to negotiate with Iranian prime minister Ahmad Qavam, a political moderate, to establish Kurdistan too as an autonomous province.

September–October
Due to political pressures, Qavam backs away from any alignment with PDKI or other reform elements. The Shah announces plans to organize elections throughout the country and to send troops to the rebellious northwest provinces to ensure order.

The tribes turn against both the Kurdish and Azeri republics and aid their "recapture" by Iranian forces.

Mustafa Barzani, fleeing Iran in the face the Shah's assault against the new Kurdish republic in Mahabad, is pursued into Iraq by the Iranian army. Refusing to surrender, he retreats to the USSR.

December
December 10: Tabriz is taken when Azeri resistance collapses.

December 15: Mahabad is surrendered.

1947
In early spring Qazi Mohammad, his brother Sadr Qazi, and his cousin Seif Qazi are hanged in Chwar Chira, the central square in Mahabad.

1951
Nationalist Mohammad Mossadegh is appointed prime minister of Iran and nationalizes the oil industry, which has been under British control since 1913.

1953
The Shah flees the country while Mossadegh is overthrown by a coup d'état organized by the CIA and the British intelligence services; the Shah then returns to Iran.

1958
In Iraq, a coup against the Hashemite monarchy establishes a republic. Mustafa Barzani is allowed to return.

1961
Iraqi Kurds, led by Mustafa Barzani, rebel against the government of Abd al-Karim Qasim. The Iraqi government crushes the rebellion and a confrontation that will last decades begins between the government of Iraq and the Kurds.

1963
In Iran, the Shah begins his campaign of modernization and Westernization, known as the "White Revolution." The secret police, the SAVAK, intensifies the repression against movements of opposition to the Shah's reforms and to his increasingly authoritarian rule.

In a coup d'état in Iraq, army officers of the Ba'ath Party take power; negotiations between Iraq and Barzani, as the preeminent Kurdish leader, stall over issues of Kurdish autonomy and territorial control of the Kirkuk oilfields.

A further coup in November ousts the Ba'athists and brings Abd al-Salam Arif to power.

When Barzani signs an agreement in a truce offered by the new regime, Barzani's KDP suffers internal division. The dissenting progressive faction, led by leftist intellectuals Jalal Talabani and Ibrahim Ahmad, opposes the conservative, tribal elements among Barzani's support base, and Barzani's apparent tradeoff of the Kurds' aspirations for autonomy in return for funds and arms from Baghdad to secure his leadership position. Ultimately their opposition party, the Patriotic Union of Kurdistan (PUK), will be founded in May 1975.

1963–1965
Ayatollah Ruhollah Khomeini, a leading scholar of Shi'a Islam, decrees protests against the Shah's policies and programs, labeling as "non-Islamic" a bill that would grant women the right to vote. He issues a manifesto denouncing the Shah's violation of the constitution, promotion of moral corruption, and submission to Israel and the United States. Banished to Turkey in 1964, Khomeini is later allowed entry to Iraq, where he will maintain his exile in Najaf. He will remain in Iraq until 1978, when he is forced to leave for France.

1966
The Shah of Iran offers military and financial support to Barzani against the Iraqi regime.

1968
In Iraq, a new coup d'état reinstates the Ba'ath Party to power. Saddam Hussein will become its leader.

1970
Iraqi Kurds sign a peace agreement with the Iraqi government that gives them a certain degree of autonomy.

1972
Iraq signs an agreement of friendship and security for twenty-five years with the USSR.

1974

The Iraqi government refuses to give Barzani's Iraqi KDP control of the province of Kirkuk, the center of oil production. Barzani launches an attack against Iraqi forces; the Iraqi retaliation is crushing.

1975

Tehran and Baghdad sign the Algiers Accord, ending the support Iran has been giving to the KDP of Iraq. This provokes the final collapse of the Kurdish revolt in Iraq.

1978

Clerics oppose the secularizing policies of the Shah, while progressives oppose his autocratic politics. His authoritarianism provokes strikes, riots, and massive demonstrations. In Iran, the government imposes martial law. Khomeini arrives in Paris, from where he continues to foment and lead the uprising.

1979

In Iran, the political situation deteriorates. The Shah and his family are forced to flee. Ayatollah Khomeini returns from his fourteen-year exile and proclaims the Islamic Republic of Iran. He designates himself commander-in-chief of the armed forces and declares "holy war" against the Kurds—who are led in their majority by the PDKI, which has taken control of Kurdistan. Iranian government forces occupy the region once more. Members of the PDKI retreat to the mountains and begin their guerrilla campaign.

Iraqi Kurdish leader Mustafa Barzani dies in a hospital in the United States.

1980

Abolhassan Banisadr is elected first president of the Islamic Republic of Iran. Iraq invades Iran. A war begins that will last eight years.

1981

Banisadr is impeached following his criticism of the government for human-rights abuses and its execution of those who have spoken against the regime. Charged with conspiracy and treason, he flees to France.

1988

Ceasefire between Iran and Iraq. The Iraqi government retaliates against the Kurds for supporting Iran during the war. In March, Saddam Hussein launches Operation Anfal, a genocidal campaign against Iraqi Kurds. A mustard-gas attack on the small town of Halabja kills about five thousand people. One hundred thousand Kurds flee to Turkey.

In Iran, political purges mounted by Khomeini's Islamist regime bring the execution of thousands of political prisoners in Iranian prisons—primarily progressives, dissidents, and leftists, including members of Tudeh (Iran's Communist party), the Feda'iyan, and the People's Mujahedin.

1989

Ayatollah Khomeini dies. Akbar Hashemi Rafsanjani becomes the new president of the Islamic Republic, and Hojatoleslam Seyyid Ali Khamenei becomes Supreme Leader, Khomeini's spiritual successor.

Abdul Rahman Ghassemlou, Abdullah Ghaderi-Azar, and Fadil Rasul are murdered in Vienna by emissaries of Rafsanjani's government.

1991

After the Gulf War—waged by a multinational coalition in response to Saddam Hussein's invasion of Kuwait—Iraqi Kurds, encouraged by the United States, rebel against Saddam Hussein. But without Coalition air support for the Kurds, Iraq crushes the revolt, causing the death of thousands of people. The UN Security Council adopts Resolution 688, demanding an end to repression of the Kurds and creating a no-fly zone in which U.S. and British air forces protect northern Kurdistan within Iraq. This zone, where three million Kurds live, becomes a de facto autonomous region.

1992

Free elections in Iraqi Kurdistan. The KDP of Iraq controls the north, and the PUK, the Patriotic Union of Kurdistan, the south. In Berlin, where the Kurds have been participating in the Socialist International Congress, PDKI secretary-general Sadegh Sharafkandi and three colleagues are murdered by emissaries of Rafsanjani's government.

1994

The two primary political parties of Iraqi Kurdistan, the KDP of Iraq led by Masoud Barzani and the PUK led by Jalal Talabani, begin an internecine battle for control of the autonomous region of Kurdistan.

On July 18, following a bombing of AMIA, the Jewish community center in Buenos Aires, Argentine prosecutor Alberto Nisman accuses Iran of organizing the attack and Hezbollah of carrying it out.

1995

The United States imposes economic sanctions on Iran for its alleged support of terrorism, its drive to obtain nuclear weapons, and its provocation of hostility in the peace process of the Middle East. Iran repudiates the accusations.

1996

Jalal Talabani, seeking to improve his relations with the Iranian regime and to leverage advantage in his confrontation with Barzani's KDP, allows and escorts a pasdaran force into Iraqi Kurdistan to attack PDKI's daftar, the party's refuge in Iraqi territory. PDKI peshmerga fight back, and the pasdaran retreat. Iraqi forces continue toward Erbil, where an Allied air force compels their withdrawal. Barzani's PDK refuses the Iranians passage through Haj Omran.

1997

In Iran cleric Mohammad Khatami, wins the presidential election with 70 percent of the vote, besting the ultraconservative elite in power.

1998

In Iraq, Talabani's PUK and Barzani's KDP sign a peace accord, with U.S. mediation, which ends the four-year fighting between these rival groups.

1999
February

Mass protests erupt in cities across Iranian Kurdistan—in part anti-government and in part in support of Abdullah Öcalan, leader of the Kurdistan Workers' Party (PKK) in Turkey, where he is under death sentence. Severe repression of the protests follows, sparked by the fear of a threatening "transnationalization" of the movement for Kurdish autonomy.

Twenty-first century
2000

Liberals and supporters of Khatami win 170 of the 290 seats in Iran's Majlis (parliamentary) elections. They gain control of the parliament, which has been dominated by conservative forces since the Islamic revolution of 1979. The ultraconservatives obtain only 44 seats. However, a new law prohibits the publication of sixteen liberal newspapers.

At the beginning of the twenty-first century, a number of Kurdish activists, writers, and teachers arrested for their work are sentenced to death. The increase in arrests is likely due to the government's crackdown following the nationwide protests at the increasingly repressive legislation despite the good showing of "moderates" in Iran's presidential elections of "reformist" Khatami.

2003

Iraqi Kurds join U.S. and British forces to defeat Saddam Hussein's regime. Four Kurds are designated by the United States to the newly formed Iraqi Government Council.

In Iran, Amnesty International reports public critique by Sunni members of parliament of the regime's prejudicial treatment of the Sunni Muslim community.

2004

PJAK (Party of Free Life of Kurdistan), an offshoot of the PKK, launches an armed insurgency against the Iranian regime from the Qandil mountains in Iraqi Kurdistan, while building underground support among the Kurds in Iran.

2005
April

Jalal Talabani becomes president of Iraq. In June, Masoud Barzani, son of Mustafa Barzani and leader of the Kurdistan Democratic Party since 1979, becomes president of the Kurdistan Regional Government in Iraq (KRG).

In Iran's elections, Mahmoud Ahmadinejad, ultraconservative mayor of Tehran, bests cleric and former president Akbar Hashemi Rafsanjani. Meanwhile, in Vienna, both Rafsanjani and Ahmadinejad are accused by Austrian parliamentarian Peter Pilz of involvement in Ghassemlou's murder.

2005

Riots and demonstrations erupt again across Kurdistan, protesting the killing of a Kurdish opposition activist, whose body has been dragged through the streets of Mahabad. The turmoil and government repression that follow see uncounted numbers of Kurds killed, injured, and arrested, with Kurdish newspapers shut down and their editorial and reporting staff arrested.

2006

In Iraq, Saddam Hussein is tried for crimes against humanity, among them those against the Kurdish people, for which he is sentenced to death and executed.

2007

In November, six high-ranking members of the Iranian regime are included in Interpol's "Red Notice" list, accused of involvement in the Argentinean bombing of AMIA in 1994.

2008

A referendum in Iraq on the status of Kirkuk planned for the end of 2007 is postponed. Lawmakers have not agreed on details of an arrangement for Kirkuk among Kurds, Turkmen, and Arabs. Kurds want the city to become a part of the Kurdish regional government; Arabs and Turkmen want it under the central government of Iraq.

November
Despite international pleas for his release, Kurdish Iranian political prisoner Ehsan Fattahian, the first of over a dozen on death row, is executed.

2010
January
Kurdish political prisoner Fasih Yasamani, like Fattahian tortured and denied a fair trial, stands firm against a forced confession and is executed in Iran for "enmity against God."

May
The execution of four more Kurdish activists—Ali Heydarian, Farhad Vakili, Shirin Alam Hooli, and a teacher, Farzad Kamangar—is ordered in Iran. The government action, taken without warning or notice to the political prisoners' families, denies them access to their lawyers or a fair trial. The activists are subjected to severe torture to coerce false confessions to membership in the illegal organization Party for a Free Life in Kurdistan (PJAK). Mutual denials by both the prisoners and PJAK leadership of any links between them are disregarded, and all four prisoners are executed in the face of widespread international calls for their fair trial or release.

Authorities refuse to return the bodies of those executed to their families. Amnesty International labels the executions "a blatant attempt to intimidate members of the Kurdish minority."

At least sixteen other Kurdish political prisoners are reported on death row; none of them, according to contemporary reports, receive a fair trial.

In protest, strikes and demonstrations flare up in Iranian Kurdistan, supported by Iranian Kurdish parties.

2011–2012

During the flowering of the "Arab Spring," the Syrian civil war ("the Syrian Uprising") erupts in April 2011 when massive protests against the Assad government are met with violent crackdowns. Syrian president and Ba'ath Party leader Bashar al-Assad's forces retreat from the Jazira in 2012; the Kurdish Democratic Union Party (PYD), affiliated with the Kurdistan Workers' Party in Turkey (PKK), takes control in Syria's northeastern Kurdish areas and now maintains a de facto autonomy. The PYD and the Kurdish National Council (KNC) form the Kurdish Supreme Committee, a governing body which in turn creates Popular Protection Units (YPG) to maintain control in Kurdish inhabited areas in Syria. Syrian Kurds have been fighting ISIS, radical Islamist forces, since the beginning of the civil war.

2013

May

Argentine prosecutor Alberto Nisman accuses Iran of involvement in terrorist attacks in South America since the 1980s. New evidence links the involvement of Iranian government officials such as Mohsen Rezae, secretary of the Expediency Discernment Council since 1997 and conservative presidential candidate in Iran's 2009 elections, and Ali Akbar Velayati, minister of foreign affairs 1981–1997 and conservative presidential candidate in the 2013 elections, to the 1994 AMIA bombing in Buenos Aires.

June

Hassan Rouhani, with close ties to the Green Movement in Iran, is elected president. He has promised the Kurds he would provide services and equal opportunity. Some Kurds had hoped he would improve their lives.

U.S. Country Report on Terrorism 2012, which designates Iran as a State Sponsor of Terrorism since 1984, reveals that the Islamic Republic has increased its terrorist-related activity.

In the lead-up to the presidential elections, massive antigovernment protests break out in Iran.

The plight of the Kurds at last receives some international acknowledgment when Canada becomes the first nation to recognize Iran's 1988 massacre of political prisoners as a "crime against humanity."

November
Execution of Kurdish activists fuels protests in Iran's Kurdistan Province, with security forces arresting protestors. Human Rights Watch reports over 400 executions documented in Iran to date in 2013.

2014
UN *Special Rapporteur* Ahmed Shaheed denounces a worsened state of human-rights violations by Iran's Islamic Republic.

Jihadi groups declare a holy war on the Kurds. ISIS attacks the border city of Kobani and vows to take other Kurdish cities one by one. Kurds resist and the U.S. Obama Administration supports the Kurds.

2015
Argentine prosecutor Alberto Nisman is murdered on January 18, the day prior to his planned testimony before Argentina's congress accusing Argentine president Cristina Fernandez Kirchner, foreign minister Hector Timmerman, and others of collusion to cover up Iran's role in the 1994 attack on AMIA. In the U.S., the media reports that Nisman's "mysterious death" is "under investigation and now considered a murder."

March
In the U.S., April is declared "Genocide Prevention Awareness Month" by both houses of the legislature of the State of Georgia. The resolution references the Kurdish Anfal Genocide and the ongoing genocidal practices of ISIS against the Yezidi Kurdish religious minority.

In Iraq and Syria, throughout 2014–2015 the Kurds are the frontline force in the fight against the self-described Islamic State (known variously as ISIL, ISIS, or Daesh). In a dramatic turnaround from the Kurds' abandonment by the West during the Cold War, the Syrian Kurds are now the main ally of the US-led coalition against ISIS.

December

The U.S. House of Representatives approves legislation to bypass Baghdad and send weapons directly to the Kurds fighting against ISIS in the north.

Massive regional destabilization caused by IS aggression intensifies endemic internal difficulties developing in Iraq's Kurdistan Regional Government. Economic slowdown, a drop in oil revenues, and financial strictures imposed by the central government's budget deal severe blows to the sustainability of autonomous governance.

2017

The increase in human-rights violations since Rouhani's 2013 accession to office include unfair trials and rising numbers of executions. By the end of 2017, 328 Kurds have been executed and 400 imprisoned for political or religious activities; 444 Kurdish cross-border porters have been killed or wounded by the regime's security forces.

2018

ISIS is driven underground by Kurdish forces with American air support. Under the designation of Syrian Democratic Forces, Kurds and their Arab allies control one third of Syria, east of the Euphrates.

2019

The Trump Administration decides to withdraw American troops from Syria. Turkey vows to come in and take on the Kurds.

APPENDIX
Austrian Police Reports

Description of the Crime Scene

Federal police headquarters Wien, July 14, 1989

Security office
Roßauer Lände 5/ Tel.345511
Nr: II – 10.337/ SB/89

Subject   Ghassemlou, Dr. Abdulrahman,
           Ghaderi-Azar, Abdullah,
           Rasoul, Dr. Fadel; Murdered by unknowns

Crime Scene description

Report

In the apartment in Vienne 3, Linke Bahngasse 5/12 the following bodies were found in the room at the rear:

Dr. Abdul Rahman Ghassemlou, born 12.22.1930

This body was called no.1.

The body is located at the back of the room by the window.

The upper body is leaning with the back against the sofa and slightly inclined to the left. The left arm is bent and the forearm is flung onto the floor. The right arm is extended and the hand is resting on the right thigh. The left foot is stretched out and the right is lying bent. The carpet is shoved back by the feet. Dr. Montinger Schuss, the forensic physician, was able to provisionally determine one shot to the forehead, one to the left temple; on the right side of the neck there is found a skin defect.

The corpse was dressed in a white shirt (this was totally soaked in blood) with the collar open to the first button, and further with a dark tie, gray plaid pants, gray socks. Striped underwear [shorts].

On the left hand [wrist] was a gold-colored watch with leather strap. The breast pocket of the shirt was empty. The left trouser pocket was empty; in the right trouser pocket there was cash, and the back trouser pocket was empty.

Abdullah Ghaderi- Azar, born 21.3.1952

This body was called no. 2.

This body is stretched out on the floor with the head lying toward the sofa and the feet stretched diagonally toward the door. The body is on its back on the floor. To the left is body 1 and to the right is body 3. The left arm is bent and the left forearm is lying on the left side of the chest. The right arm is slightly extended away from the body, bent, and the hand is approximately at the level of the right shoulder. The left foot is extended and the lower leg is lying somewhat near the backside of body 3. The right foot is also extended. A leg of the over-turned table is found [lying] under both upper thighs.

The dead man was dressed in a white brown-striped shirt; the first button was open at the top. He also wore a gray-and-brown-striped tie, light-colored trousers with a brown belt, light blue socks, white shoes, and white underwear.

On the left wrist is a gold-colored watch with leather band. In the breast pocket of the shirt a 1,000-schilling banknote and 2 toothpicks were found. Both front trouser pockets and the back-trouser pocket were empty.

The following injuries could be provisionally established. Bullet hole in the shirt, approximately at the level of the third button counted from the top, approximately in the area of the heart. A shot through the neck. Right shoulder side heavily penetrated through with blood.

Dr. Fadel Rasoul, born 11.3.1949

This body was called no. 3.

The body is bent to the side with the right side on the floor and the head stretched in the direction of the door, and the feet toward the window. The right hand, forearm, is under the leg of the overturned table. The left arm is bent, with the upper arm resting on the chest area and the forearm resting on the leg of the overturned table.

Both feet were drawn up and lying somewhat near the left thigh of body 2.

The dead man was wearing a light-colored shirt with 5 buttons counted from the bottom up. Gray trousers and gray belt. Also gray socks, white underwear, and white undershirt.

In the breast pocket of the shirt were found cash and notes [scraps of paper]. In the left trouser pocket was a keychain and in the right trouser pocket S20,80- [schillings] in coins. In the back trouser pocket was a handkerchief.

On the body were ascertained a skin wound in the region of the right side of the neck, a bullet, presumably, in the right forehead region, and another bullet hole in the middle of the chest.

The collected objects found with the bodies were secured and handed over to the department.

Hößel, Bzl.

Police Reports regarding Fadil Rassoul and Ben Bella's Apartment Purchase in Vienna on December 1988

Federal Police Headquarters   Vienna July 17, 1989

Number: I-Pos 400/IIIa/15/89 res
Purpose: Assassination Attempt in Vienna 3,
             Linke Bahngasse 5/12;
Here: Inquiry of Information Notes from July 15, 1989
             (Dr. Rassoul-Ben Bela—Apartment Purchase)

Report

Inquiry of information of Dr. Winfried Kralik's notary's office, Wien 18., Nartinstrasse 81, Tel. number, 48-25-48-0*, revealed that as a matter of [attested] fact in December 1988, Dr. Fadel Rassoul purchased a condominium in Wien1, Bäckerstrasse Nr. 3/9, on behalf of Ben Bela (former Minister President of Algeria), who was responsible for the agreement. This condominium has the register number 57, in the Inner City Land Registry (Share 22 + 23).

   This information was provided by Dr. Lunzer. And what kind of relationship Dr. Rassoul [had] to Ben Bela could not be ascertained.

Bzl.

Federal Police Headquarters Vienna July [. . .], 1989

Number: I Pos 400/IIIa/15/89 res
Purpose: Assassination Attempt in Vienna 3.,
  Linke Bahngasse 5/12;
Here: Note encoder.

Memo

On July 16, 1989 at 09.30, the on-call security agency (Bzl. Grandits) made it known that it had received a note from a woman name Mrs. Fucik regarding Dr. Fadel Rassoul.

Mrs. Fuick was called back and she indicated that she was employed at the notary office of Dr. Winfried Kralik, located at Wien 18, Martinstr. 81. She could recall that on December 1988, a Dr. Fadel Rassoul had purchased a condominium in the amount of öS 1,450.000 [Austrian schillings] for the Algerian Minister President Ahmed Ben Bella. The agreement relevant to this purchase was completed by Dr. Rassoul. Ben Bella has only signed the purchase agreement. Mrs. Fuick (tel number: 42–06–452) believed that this information could possibly be of importance in the course of the investigation of this matter.

Bzl.

Autopsy Reports

On July 14, 1989, about 10:00 a.m., the three bodies of Dr Rasul, Dr Ghassemlou, and Ghaderi-Azar were brought to the central [surgical theater] of AKH and were prepared as cadavers for X-ray of the head and torso.

Directing and carrying out the examination was university instructor Dr Missliwetz [*spelling unclear*] and functioning as assistant was Dr Denk.

First of all, an outer inspection of the bodies, in which the hair was shaved from the head of the corpse of Dr Rasul. Next, the unopened bodies were photographed. An inspection of the shooting hand of the corpse was not conducted.

This morning only the bodies referenced [entered into the record; below] were autopsied. The body of Ghaderi-Azar was autopsied the next morning, July 15, 1989, about 9:00 a.m.

The angles of the shots were marked and photographed.

Dr. Ghassemlou

Conducted by the Court/forensic physician [coroner], the corpse [designated] as Person Number 1, Dr. Ghassemlou, was opened at 13.15 hours on July 14, 1989. In the process it was firmly established that the body exhibited 3 gunshot wounds—2 plug shots [shots in which the bullets remained in the body] and 1 through-shot [a shot that went all the way through and exited the body] [as follows]:

- 1 shot in the left temporal region with injury to/rupture of the left hemisphere of the cerebral cortex and penetration through the medulla oblongata. (Fatal). Vollmantelgeschoss [full metal jacket] caliber 7,65 mm established beyond doubt.
- 1 shot in the forehead with the trajectory of the bullet through the fissure between the Grosshirnhälften [the two cerebral hemispheres, the two hemispheres of the brain] and penetrating [embedding itself in] the skull in the occipital region [back of the skull]. Vollmantelgeschoss [full metal jacket] caliber 7, 65 mm established beyond doubt.

- 1 shot in the area adjacent to the left corner of the mouth, pushing through the oral cavity, [inflicting] injury to the teeth and tongue, and subsequently exiting on the right side of the neck with injury to/rupture of the neck vessels. (This [the injury to the arteries of the neck] would have been fatal, but the shot to the head [already] quickly led to death.)

Immediate cause of death: the shot through the medulla oblongata. Contributing/supporting/additional mechanism: inhalation of blood into the lungs and air embolism.

Conducted by the Court/forensic physician [coroner], the corpse [designated] as Person Number 3, Dr. Rasul, was opened at 18.00 hours. In the process it was firmly established that the body exhibited 5 gunshot wounds:

- 3 shots to the head with entry wounds in the left parietal occipital region [in the region of the crown of the head at the back] and exit wounds in the right temporal region of the crown of the head.
- 1 tangential shot to the right side of the neck.
- 1 shot in the left rear side of the neck, with the exit wound on the front side of the chest.

Immediate cause of death: air embolism (air in the heart from sinuses opened in the brain). Head shots and shot in the left side of the neck— in and of themselves—would have been fatal.

Ballistics Report

From the body of Abdullah Ghaderi-Azar a total of 3 projectiles were removed [by forensics during the autopsy]. Of these, two bullets could be assigned to the Llama pistol and one associated with the Beretta pistol, cal. 7–65 NRM. Another bullet was not in the body, but was discovered when it fell out of the collar while stripping the body [for examination]. This . . . [*text unclear*] also comes from the Llama pistol.

[*The text here is unclear. A literal reading seems to say "This floor also comes from the Llama pistol." It's not clear if what is meant is that this bullet was recovered from the floor after falling out of Abdullah's collar.*]

In the body of Dr. Ghassemlou . . . [*text unclear*] were found two bullets. One of the bullets can be assigned to the Llama pistol and the second to the Beretta pistol (cal. 7–65 mm).

[*Here too the text is unclear. Literally it seems to say "Abdullah frames—were found," which does not seem to reference any objects or positions detailed in the crime-scene report or the autopsies.*]

Summary [*Zusammenfassung*]

In the apartment, a total of 16 cartridges [shells] altogether were found, and 9 projectiles [bullets] established beyond doubt. In addition there were 6 projectiles that were determined [in the bodies] by the Institute for Forensic Medicine upon examination [autopsy]. Of [the total of 16 cartridges], 8 cartridges could be assigned to the Llama pistol and an equal number associated with the Beretta pistol.

The Llama pistol fired 8 bullets [of those found] and the Beretta pistol 7. The aforementioned locked case [*Schlosskasten: the terminology is not clear; it may mean a locked briefcase, perhaps the case in which the recorded tapes were found by the police, or a locked suitcase*] has not [yet] been presented for this report. It will accordingly be analyzed immediately upon receipt and reported separately.

The travel alarm clock [Reisewecker] mentioned in the report was submitted to the BMFI Documentation Center for investigation and analysis [*"BMF" is the acronym for Austria's Federal Ministry of Finance, which is concerned, among other matters, with customs administration and documentation*].

INDEX